THE

BOOK BUYER'S MANUAL:

A

CATALOGUE

OF

Foreign and American Books

IN

EVERY DEPARTMENT OF LITERATURE.

WITH A CLASSIFIED INDEX.

NEW YORK:
G. P. PUTNAM, 10 PARK PLACE.
REMOVED FROM BROADWAY.
1852.

N. B.—To COLLEGES, ACADEMIES, PUBLIC LIBRARIES, BOOKSELLERS, and purchasers in quantities, a suitable and liberal discount will be made from the prices affixed. It is superfluous to mention that there must be of necessity a great fluctuation in prices, produced by a variety of causes. The publisher of the present Catalogue does not pretend that it is either complete or free from errors; but to those who may favor him with orders, he is ready to guarantee that the prices charged shall be, on an average, as low as those of any other house in the trade, for the same editions. If any error or overcharge is pointed out by his correspondents, it shall be cheerfully corrected. And for those who are willing to confide in the experience and good faith of the advertiser, no pains will be spared to merit their confidence.

☞ Particular attention given to orders for College and other Public Libraries.

*** A SUPPLEMENT to this Manual, brought down to the latest moment, will be issued, *gratis*, in July.

CATALOGUE

OF

FOREIGN AND AMERICAN BOOKS;

COMPRISING

USEFUL AND VALUABLE BOOKS IN EVERY CLASS OF LITERATURE, THE FINE ARTS, NATURAL HISTORY, SCIENCES, USEFUL ARTS, &c.

MANY OF WHICH ARE

SPLENDIDLY ILLUSTRATED.

FOR SALE BY

GEORGE P. PUTNAM,

No. 155 BROADWAY, NEW YORK.

*** *As many of the books are imported in small numbers, orders should specify if books not on hand shall be specially imported. They would be received in from* 40 *to* 60 *days.*

Abailard et Heloise. Lettres, traduction nouvelle, par le bibliophile Jacob. 1 vol. in 12mo. broché, 87c. Paris.

——— Lettres, traduites sur les manuscrits de la Bibliotheque Royale, par E. Oddoul—précédées d'un essai historique par M. et Mme. Guizot, et de extraits de MM. Michelet, Pope, &c. Illustrée de 200 belles vignettes, fleurons, &c. 2 vols. grand in 8vo. $5 50. Paris.

Abbot, (C.) Treatise on the Law relative to Merchant Ships and Seamen. In five parts. By Charles Lord Tenterden. 8th edition, by W. Shee. Royal 8vo. cloth, $9 50. Lond. 1848.

Abbott, (Jacob.) Summer in Scotland. 12mo. cloth, $1 00. New York, 1848.

——— History of Mary, Queen of Scots. 18mo. cloth, 62c. New York, 1849.

——— History of Alexander the Great. 18mo. cloth, 62c. New York, 1849.

——— Kings and Queens; or, Life in the Palace. 12mo. cloth, $1 00. New York, 1848.

——— History of Charles I. 18mo. cloth, 62c.

——— " of Hannibal. 18mo. " 62c.

——— " of Julius Cesar. 18mo. " 62c.

——— " of Queen Elizabeth. " " 62c.

A'Becket, (Thomas.) Life and Letters, by Rev. Dr. Giles. 2 vols. 8vo. cloth, $7 00. London.

——— Original Letters, Biographies, &c., in the original Latin. Collected by Rev. Dr. Giles. 8 vols. 8vo. cloth, $30 00. London.

Or, separately, as follows:

Vita S. Thomæ, ab E. Grim et Aliis, &c. 2 vols. 8vo. cloth, $7 25.

Epistolæ S. Thomæ. 2 vols. 8vo. cloth, $7 25.

Gilberti Foliot Epistolæ. 2 vols. 8vo. $7 25.

Herberti de Bosham Opera. 2 vols. 8vo. cloth, $7 25.

Abercrombie, (Dr. J.) On Diseases of the Stomach, &c. 3d edition, foolscap 8vo. cloth, $2 00. London, 1839.

The Same. 8vo. $1 50. Philadelphia.

——— On the Moral Feelings. 7th edition, foolscap 8vo. $1 25. London, 1846.

The Same. 12mo. 50c. New York.

——— On Diseases of the Brain and Spinal Cord. 4th edition, foolscap 8vo. cloth, $2 00. London, 1845.

The Same. 8vo. $2 50. Philadelphia.

——— On the Intellectual Powers. 12th edition, foolscap 8vo. cloth, $2 00. London, 1846.

The Same. 12mo. cloth, 50c. New York.

Aberdeen, (Earl of.) Inquiry into Grecian Architecture. Foolscap, 8vo. cloth, $2 25. London.

Abstract of the Field Exercise, and Evolutions of the Army. 12mo. 87c. London.

Abstract of Infantry Tactics. 12mo. 50c. Boston.

Ackerman. Histories of the Universities of Oxford and Cambridge; Westminster Abbey; and Microcosm, or the Public Buildings of London. Illustrated with 400 Plates, Portraits and Views, colored in imitation of Drawings. 9 vols. elephant 4to. $85. Lond. 1812–16.

Acton, Or Thoughts in the Circle of Life. 12mo. cloth, $1 25. New York, 1848.

Acton, (Th.) Complete Practical Treatise on Venereal Diseases, and their Immediate and Remote Consequences. Including Observations on Certain Affections of the Uterus, attended with Discharges. 1 vol. 8vo. and colored atlas of plates, $9 50. London, 1841.

The Same. Colored, sheep, $3 00. New York

Acton, (Eliza.) Modern Cookery in all its branches, reduced to a System of Easy Practice. Cuts, 2d edition, foolscap 8vo. cloth, $1 25. London, 1845.

Adam, (Alex.) Roman Antiquities; or, an Account of the Manners and Customs of the Romans; Enlarged by the Rev. J. R. Major. Map, 8vo. cloth, $1 75. London, 1835.

——— Roman Antiquities; or, an Account of the Manners and Customs of the Romans. New edition, improved by Dr. Boyd. 100 engravings. 12mo. sheep, $1 75. New York.

Adams, (E.) The Polychromatic Ornaments of Italy. Plates, royal 4to. $9 00. Lond. 1845.

Adams, (Mrs.) Letters; with an Introductory Memoir by her grandson, C. F. Adams. 4th edition, revised and enlarged, with the Letters of J. Q. Adams to his Son, on the Study of the Bible. Portrait. 12mo. cloth, $1 63. Boston, 1848.

——— (Thomas.) Exposition of the Second Epistle General of St. Peter. Imperial 8vo. cloth, $6 00. London, 1842.

——— (W. B.) English Pleasure Carriages; their Origin and History; with Descriptions of New Inventions. Illustrated with numerous plates. 8vo. cloth, $2 50. London, 1837.

Adcock. Engineer's Pocket Book for 1842. $1 00.

The Same, for 1850. $1 75. London, 1848.

Adcock, (H.) Rules and Data for the Steam Engine. 12mo. 75c. London.

Addison, (C G.) History of the Knights Templars. Plates. Post 8vo. cloth. $5 50. London.

——— History of the Temple Church. Post 8vo. cloth, $1 50. London.

———On Contracts, and on Parties to Action ex contractu. 8vo. sheep, $4 00. Philadelphia.

——— (Joseph.) Works; with Notes by Hurd. 6 vols. royal 8vo. $22 50. London, 1811.

——— Works complete; comprising the whole of the Spectator. Portrait. 3 vols. 8vo. sheep, $5 00. New York, 1845.

Adler, (G. J.) Progressive German Reader; adapted to the American edition of Ollendorf's German Grammar; with Notes and Vocabulary. 12mo. $1 New York, 1848.

——— A Dictionary of the German and English Languages, compiled from the Works of Hilport, Flügel, Grieb, Heyse, and others. In two parts. Royal 8vo. half Russia, $5 00. New York, 1849.

Æschyli Tragœdiæ, (Gr. et Lat.) cum Notis Variorum, Scholiis, et Var. Lect. edidit Butler; viz. Agamemnon, Septem Contra Thebas, Choephoræ, Eumenides, Persæ, Fragmenta. 6 vols. 8vo. cloth, $6 00. London, 1811–16.

Æschylus. Tragedies; translated by Rev. R. Potter. With an Essay on Grecian Drama. 18mo. cloth, 50c. New York.

——— Prometheus of. Edited by Pres. Woolsey. 12mo. cloth. 63c. Boston.

——— Agamemnon of. Edited by Prof. Felton. 12mo. cloth, 75c. Boston.

Æschylus et Sophocles, et nostra Fragmenta, ed. Ahrens. Gr. et Lat. Royal 8vo. paper, $3 75. Didot, Paris, 1845.

Æschylus. Seven Tragedies. Literally translated. New edition, 8vo. cloth, $2 25. Oxford.

———Lexicon to. By the Rev. Th. Linwood. 2d edition, 8vo. cloth, $3 75. London, 1847.

Æsop. Fables: a new Version, chiefly from the original Greek; purified, and rendered fit for Young Persons and Families. By Rev. T. James. Illustrated with 100 beautiful woodcuts, from designs by John Tenniel. Post 8vo. cloth, $3 00. London, 1848.

Agassiz and Gould. Principles of Zoology; touching the Structure, Development, Distribution and Natural Arrangement of the Races of Animals, living and extinct. Numerous illustrations. 12mo. cloth, $1 00. Boston, 1848.

Agassiz, (L.) Histoire Naturelle des Poissons d'eau douce de l'Europe Centrale. Royal 8vo. in three parts. Colored plates, folio, $37 50. Neuchatel, 1842

——— Monographie d'Echinodermes Vivans et Fossiles, devant former une histoire naturelle complète de cette classe d'animaux. Text and plates. Four parts, 4to. $25 00. Neuchatel, 1839–42.

——— Monographie des Poissons Fossiles du Vieux Grés Rouge ou Système Dévonieu des iles Britaniques et de Russie. Three parts, 4to. and three parts, colored plates, folio, $25 00. Neuchatel, 1844.

——— Recherches sur les Poissons Fossiles, comprenant une introduction à l'étude de ces animaux; l'anatomie comparée des systemes organiques qui peuvent contribuer à faciliter la determination des espéces Fossiles; une nouvelle classification des Poissons, exprimant leurs rapports avec la série des formations; l'exposition des lois de leur succession et de leur développement durant toutes les métamorphoses du globe terrestre, accompagnée de considérations geologiques genérales; enfin, la description d'environ mille espéces qui n'existent plus et dont on a retabli les caractères d'après les debris qui sont contenus dans les couches de la terre. Ten parts 4to. and four parts, colored plates, folio, $162 00. Neuchatel, 1833–43.

——— Etudes sur Les Glaciers. 8vo. et atlas de 32 planches, folio, $10 00. Neuchatel, 1840.

——— Nouvelles études et expériences sur les Glaciers Actuels, leur structure, leur progression et leur action physique sur le sol. 8vo. and atlas, folio, $16 00. Paris, 1847.

——— Etudes Critiques sur les Molusques Fossiles. Four parts 4to. beautiful plates. $27 00. Neuchatel, 1840.

———Mémoire sur les Moules de Molusques Vivans et Fossiles. 4to. $3. Neuchatel, 1839.

——— Description des Echinodermes Fossiles de la Suisse. Two parts, 4to. fine plates, $6 75. Neuchatel, 1839.

——— Nomenclator Zoologicus, continens Nomina Systematica Generum Animalium tam Viventium quam Fossilium, secundum ordinem alphabeticum disposita, adjectis auctoribus, libris in quibus reperiuntur, anno editionis, etymologia et familiis, ad quis pertinent, in variis classibus. Seven parts, 4to. $20 00. Soleure, 1842–46.

Agincourt. History of Art; by its Monuments, from its Decline in the Fourth Century to its Restoration in the Sixteenth. Translated from the French of Seroux d'Agincourt. With 328 plates, comprising 3,325 subjects. The three volumes of the French work complete in one vol., large folio, $30 00. London, 1848.

*** This is a very elaborate, curious, and valuable work. The price is about one third of the original work, while it is more complete and more convenient.

Agriculture. The Journal of, and Transactions of the Highland Agricultural Society.

Agnel, (H. R.) Chess for Winter Evenings; a Complete Guide to the Game. With illustrations, by R. W. Weir. 12mo. cloth, $1 75. New York.

Aide Memoire à la Usage des Officiers d'Artillerie, avec tableaux et planches. 1 vol. 8vo. $3 00. Paris, 1844.

——— A la Usage des Officiers et sous Officiers de Pontonniers. 1 vol. 12mo. 62c. Paris.

——— to the Military Sciences. Framed from Contributions of Officers of the different services; and edited by a Committee of the corps of Royal Engineers. Parts 1, 2, 3. Imperial 8vo. $13 50. London, 1845–48.

Aiken, (Edmund.) Designs for Villas and other Rural Buildings. 31 plates, 4to. $6 50. London, 1831.

Aikin. Select Works of the British Poets; in a Chronological Series, from Ben Jonson to Scott. With Biographical and Critical Notices. 3 vols. 8vo. cloth, $7 00. Philadelphia.

——— (John.) Letters from a Father to his Son, on various topics relative to Literature and Conduct of Life. 12mo. mor. $2 London, 1838.

——— (Lucy.) Life of Addison. 2 vols. post 8vo. cloth, $1 50. London.

——— Memoirs of the Court of James the First. 2 vols. 8vo. cloth, $7 00. Lond. 1822.

——— Memoirs of the Court of Elizabeth. 2 vols. 8vo. cloth, $7 50. London, 1822.

Aime Martin. Education des Mères de famille, ou de la civilisation du genre humain par les femmes. 3d edition. 1 vol. 12mo. 87c. Paris.

——— Lettres à Sophie sur la Physique, la Chemie et l'Histoire Naturelle; nouvelle edition. 1 vol. 12mo. 87c. Paris.

Ainsworth. Latin Dictionary. Reprinted from the best folio edition; with numerous Additions, Emendations, and Improvements, by the Rev. B. W. Beatson, A.M. Revised and corrected by W. Ellis, Esq. A.M. Imp. 8vo. cloth, $6 50. London, 1843.

Ainsworth's Magazine. A Miscellany of Romance, General Literature, and Art. Illustrated by 200 engravings on steel and wood, by G. Cruikshank. 7 vols. medium 8vo. cloth, $14 50.

——— (W. T.) Travels in the Track of the Ten Thousand Greeks. Post 8vo. cloth, $2 50. London, 1844.

Airy, (G. B.) Explanation of the Solar System. Post 8vo $2 25. London.

——— Mathematical Tracts on Physical Astronomy. 8vo. $4 50. London.

Akenside, (Mark.) Poetical Works. Foolscap 8vo. cloth, $1 37; mor. $2 25; mor. by Hayday, $2 50. Pickering—London, 1835.

——— Pleasures of Imagination. J. Aikin. 12mo. $2 25. London.

Akerman, (J. Y.) Numismatic Manual; or, Guide to the collection of Greek, Roman, and English Coins. Illustrated. 8vo. cloth, $5 50. London, 1840.

——— Coins of the Romans relating to Britain, described and illustrated. 8vo. $2 25. Lond. 1844.

——— Introduction to the Study of Ancient and Modern Coins. Plates. 12mo. cloth, $1 75. London, 1848.

Alban, (Dr. Ernst.) The High Pressure Steam Engine investigated; an exposition of its comparative merits, and an Essay towards an improved system of construction, adapted especially to secure Safety and Economy in its use. Translated from the German, by William Pole. Plates. Parts 1 to 4. 2 vols. $4 50. London, 1847–48.

Alcan. Essai sur l'industrie des matières textiles, comprenant le travail complet du coton, du lin, du chanvre, des laines, du cachemire, de la soie, du caoutchouc. 1 vol. 8vo. avec un Atlas de 36 planches. $7 50. Paris, 1847.

Alderson, (James.) Practical Observations on some of the Diseases of the Stomach and Alimentary Canal. Numerous colored plates. 8vo. cloth, $3 50. London.

——— (M. A.) Essay on the Nature of Steam. 8vo. cloth, $3 00. London.

Aldine British Poets. Fifty-two volumes, foolscap 8vo. cloth, $65 00; calf extra, $105; mor. extra, by Hayday, $130. Pickering—London.

Burns	3 vols.	Dryden	5 vols
Thomson	2 "	Parnell	1 "
Collins	1 "	Swift	3 "
Kirke White	1 "	Young	2 "
Cowper	3 "	Akenside	1 "
Surrey, (Earl of.)	1 "	Butler	2 "
Wyatt, (Sir Thos.)	1 "	Prior	2 "
Beattie	1 "	Falconer	1 "
Pope	3 "	Gray	1 "
Goldsmith	1 "	Spenser	5 "
Milton	3 "	Churchill	3 "
Shakspeare	1 "	Chaucer	6 "

Each volume, cloth, $1 37; calf, $2 37; mor. by Hayday, $2 50; mor. extra gilt, by Hayday, $3 00.

Alexander, (Prof. J. A.) Commentaries on the Earlier Prophecies of Isaiah. Royal 8vo. cloth, $3 00.

——— Commentaries on the Later Prophecies of Isaiah. Royal 8vo. cloth, $2 50. New York

"They are among the most learned and erudite works of the kind."—Christian Advocate and Journal.

"The hand of the thorough scholar is evident throughout."—Protestant Churchman.

——— Progress and Present State of the Manufacture of Crude Iron. 8vo. $1 25, Baltimore.

——— (W. Lindsay.) Anglo-Catholicism not Apostolical. 8vo. cloth, $2 25. Edinburgh, 1843.

——— Connexion of the Old and New Testaments. 8vo. cloth, $3 50. London.

Alger, (Francis.) Elementary Treatise on Mineralogy; comprising an Introduction to the Science, by W. Phillips. Fifth edition from the fourth London edition. By Robert Allan; containing the latest discoveries in American and Foreign Mineralogy. 8vo. cloth, $3 00. Boston, 1844.

Alhambra, (The.) Plans, Elevations, Sections, and Details, by O. Jones. 101 plates, of which 67 are printed in colors, and the remainder elaborate engravings in outline; from drawings taken on the spot in 1834, by the late Jules Goury; and in 1834 and 1837, by Owen Jones. With a complete translation of the Arabic inscriptions, and an Historical Notice of the Kings of Granada, from the conquest of that city to the expulsion of the Moors. 2 vols. Columbia folio, half mor. top edge gilt. $150. London.

Alison, (Archibald.) Essay on the Nature and Principles of Taste. 2 vols. 8vo. cloth, $6 00. London.

The Same, with corrections and improvements by A. Mills. 12mo. cloth, 75c. New-York.

——— History of Europe. Second edition, revised and corrected. 20 vols. post 8vo. cloth, $35 00.

The Same, calf extra, $50 00. London, 1848.

The Same. 10 vols. 8vo. sewed, $7 50. Paris, (Baudry.)

The Same. 4 vols. 8vo. sheep, $5 00. New York, 1847.

——— Atlas to History of Europe, constructed and arranged by Johnston, under the direction of Mr. Alison; with a concise Vocabulary of Military and Naval Terms. 96 maps, oblong 4to. cloth, $15 00. London, 1849.

——— Epitome of the History of Europe; for Schools and Young Persons. 2d edition, post 8vo. cloth, $2 25. London, 1848.

——— Atlas to, containing 11 maps, 4to. cloth, $2 25. London, 1848.

——— History of, abridged by Gould. 8vo. sheep, $1 25. New York.

——— Principles of Population, and their Connection with Human Happiness. 2 vols. 8vo. cloth, $9 00. Edinburgh, 1840.

——— Miscellanies. Portrait. 1 vol. 8vo. cloth, $1 25. Philadelphia

——— The Military Life of the Duke of Marlborough. Maps, 12mo. cloth, $1 50. New York, 1848.

——— (W. P.) Outlines of Pathology and Practice of Medicine. 8vo. $2 25. Philad. 1844.

——— Outlines of Physiology. 8vo. cloth, $3 00. Edinburgh.

——— (S. S.) Observations on Organic Alterations of the Heart, &c. Foolscap 8vo. cloth, 75c. London.

Allen, (M.) On Classification of the Insane. 8vo. $1 75. London, 1837.

——— (R. L.) History and Description of Domestic Animals. 12mo. cloth, 75c. N. York.

——— (Joseph.) Battles of the British Navy. 24 portraits. 2 thick vols. 12mo. cloth. $4 25. London, 1842.

Allom, (Thomas.) France illustrated; exhibiting its Landscape Scenery, Antiquities, Military and Ecclesiastical Architecture; with descriptions, by Rev. G. N. Wright. 3 vols. 4to. cloth, $15 00. London.

Almanac, American, and Repository of Useful Knowledge. 12mo. (Published annually.) $1 00. Boston.

Almanac, British, and Companion. 12mo. cloth. (Published annually.) $1 25.

Altar, (the,) or Meditations in Verse on the Great Christian Sacrifice. 12mo. cloth, $1 50. London, 1849.

Altars, Tabernacles, and Sepulchral Monuments of the Fourteenth and Fifteenth Centuries, existing at Rome; published under the patronage of the celebrated Academy of St. Luke, by MM. Tosi and Becchio; edited by M. Mastraca. 50 large engravings, imp. folio, half morocco, $16 00. London, 1843.

Ambrose, (Isaac.) Works, with a Memoir. 8vo. cloth, $1 50. London.

Ambrosius, (St.) Opera Omnia—Studio et labore monachorum ord. S. Benedicti. 4 vols. royal 8vo. sewed, $8 50. Paris, (J. P. Migné,) 1845.

American Biography. The Library of American Biography, edited by Jared Sparks, assisted by several of the most distinguished American writers. Portraits. First series. 10 volumes. 12mo. $7 50. New York.

Containing, viz.

Vol. 1—Gen. Stark, C. B. Brown, Gen. Montgomery and Ethan Allen.
2—Wilson (the Ornithologist,) Capt. John Smith.
3—General Arnold.
4—General Wayne and Sir Henry Vane.
5—John Elliott, (the Apostle to the Indians.)
6—General Pinckney, W. Ellery, Cotton Mather.
7—Sir W. Phipps, L. M. Davidson, Gen. Putnam.
8—Baron Steuben, Sebastian Cabot, Gen. Eaton.
9—Jonathan Edwards, David Brainerd.
10—Fulton, Gens. Hudson, Warren, and Marquette.

——— Second Series, complete, with a General Index to the whole. Plates. 15 vols. 12mo. cloth, $1 00 per vol. Boston, 1844–47.

Containing, viz.

Vol. 1—La Salle, and Patrick Henry.
2—James Otis, and James Oglethorpe.
3—John Sullivan, Jacob Leisler, Nathaniel Boon, and John Mason.
4—Roger Williams, Timothy Dwight, and Count Pulaski.
5—Count Rumford, Zebulon Montgomery Pike, Samuel Gorton.
6—Ezra Stiles, John Fitch, and Anne Hutchinson.
7—John Ribault, Sebastian Rale, and William Palfrey.
8—Gen. Charles Lee, and Joseph Reed.
9—Leonard Calvert; Samuel Ward, Governor of Rhode Island; Thomas Posey, Major-General and Governor of Indiana.
10—Nathaniel Greene.
11—Commodore Stephen Decatur.
12—Edward Preble, and William Penn.
13—Daniel Boone; Benjamin Lincoln, Major-General in the Army of the Revolution.
14—John Ledyard.
15—William R. Davie; Samuel Kirkland, Missionary to the Indians.

American Farmer's Cyclopædia. 8vo. sheep, $4 00. Philadelphia.

American Historical and Literary Curiosities. Edited by Smith and Watson. 4to. cloth, $6 00. New York.

American in Paris; Or, Heath's Picturesque Annual, for 1843. By M. Jules Janin. Illustrated by 18 engravings, from designs by Lami. Royal 8vo. cloth gilt, $2 50. London, 1843.

American Scenery. A Series of elegant engravings on Steel by Bartlett; with descriptions by N. P. Willis. 2 vols. 4to. $12. London

American (The) Loyalists: or, Biographical Sketches of Adherents to the British Crown in the War of the Revolution. Alphabetically arranged; with an Essay, by Lorenzo Sabine. 8vo. cloth. $2 75. Boston, 1847.

American Journal of Science and Art. Conducted by Profs. Silliman, and B. Silliman, Jr. Published bi-monthly. $5 00 per annum.

Analytical Hebrew and Chaldee Lexicon; consisting of an Alphabetical Arrangement of every Word and Inflection contained in the Old Testament Scriptures, precisely as they occur in the Sacred Text; with the Grammatical Analysis of each word, &c. 4to. cloth, $12 00. (Bagster,) London, 1848.

Anatomical Atlas. By Smith and Horner. Imp'l 8vo. cloth, $5 00. Philadelphia.

Ancient Armor, Chronicle of, from the the Eleventh to Seventeenth Centuries; with descriptions, &c., by J. Hewitt. In case, $3 00.

The Same. Elegantly colored, $5 50. London.

Ancient Baptismal Fonts. Norman, Early English, Decorated English, and Perpendicular English. Drawn by J. Simpson. and engraved by R. Roberts. Forty beautifully engraved plates. Imperial 8vo. $4 50. London.

Ancient Monkish Historians of Britain—Rogeri de Wendover Chronica, sive Flores Historiarum, nunc primum editit H. O. Coxe. F. Nicholai Trireti Annales; ad fidem codicum Manuscriptorum recensuit Thomas Hogg. 6 vols. 8vo. beautifully printed, boards. $24 00. English Historical Society, London, 1841–48.

——— Translated; Containing Bedé's Ecclesiastical History; Chronicles of Richard of Devizes; Works of Gildas and Nenniers; Geoffrey of Monmouth's British History; and Chronicles of the White Rose of York. Translated, with Notes and Indices, by Rev. J. A. Giles. Illustrated with fac-similes of Original MSS. 6 vols. 8vo, $21 00. London, 1841–45.

Andersen, (Hans C.) Shoes of Fortune. 16mo. cloth, 50c. New York.

——— Wonderful Stories. First and Second series. 75c. New York.

Anderson, (Christopher.) The Annals of the English Bible. Portrait. 2 vols. 8vo. cloth, $8 50. [1 v. N. Y.] (Pickering,) London, 1845.

——— (George and Peter.) Guide to the Highlands and Islands of Scotland, including Orkney and Zetland; descriptive of their Scenery, Statistics, Antiquities, and Natural History; with numerous Historical and Traditional Notices; Map, Tables of Distances, Notices of Inns, and other information for Tourists. New edition, cloth, $3 00. Edinburgh.

Andre, (le P.) Œuvres Philosophiques, Recueilles et Annotées, par V. Cousin. 1 vol. 12mo. Paris, 1843.

Andrews, (Bp.) Sermons. 5 vols. 8vo. cloth, $16 00. (Library of Anglo-Catholic Theology.) Oxford, 1842

——— (Bishop.) Preces Privatæ quotidianæ, Græce et Latine. Editio tertia et emendatior. 12mo. cloth, $2 50. Londini, (Pickering,) 1848.

——— (E. A.) First Lessons in Latin. 1 vol. 18mo. 75c. Boston.

Andrews, (E. A.) Latin Reader. 12mo 75c. Boston.

——— Latin Exercises. 12mo. 75c. Boston.

——— and Stoddard's Latin Grammar. 12mo. $1 25. Boston.

——— The Parterre; or, Beauties of Flora. Twelve highly finished colored drawings; with Poetical Illustrations. Folio, $6 00. London, 1842.

Andry. Manual of Diagnosis of Diseases of the Heart. Translated from the French, by S. Kneeland. 12mo. cloth, 75c. Boston.

Angler's Souvenir. By P. Fisher, Esq. Embellished with upwards of sixty beautiful engravings on steel, by Beckwith and Topham, and engraved borders. Foolscap 8vo. gilt, cloth, $2 75. London, 1835.

Angling, (Hand-book of.) Teaching Fly-Fishing, Trolling, Bottom Fishing; with the natural history of River Fish; and the best modes of catching them. 12mo. cloth, $3 00. London, 1847.

Anglo-Catholic Theology—Library of. 8vo. viz:

Andrews. (Bp.) Sermons. Vol. 1-5. $16 00.
——— (Bp.) Pattern of Catechismal Doctrine. $3 00.
Beveridge, (Bp.) Works. 9 vols $29 00.
Bramhall, (Archbishop.) Works. 4 vols. $9 00.
Bull, (Bp.) on Justification. 2 vols. $5 50.
Cosins, (Bp.) Works. 2 vols. $6 00.
Crakenthorpe's Defensio Ecclesiæ Anglicanæ. $4 25.
Gunning on the Pascal, or Lent Fast. 8vo. $2,75.
Hammond's Practical Catechism. $6 00.
Hickes' Two Treatises. 2 vols. $5 50.
Johnson's Works. 2 vols. $6 00.
Laud, (Archbishop.) Works. Vol. I. $2 00.
Marshall's Penitential Discipline. 1 vol. $2 00.
Nicholson, (Bp.) on the Catechism. $2 00.
Overall. (Bp.) Convocation Book. $2 50.
Thorndike's Works. 2 vols. $10 50.
Wilson, (Bp.) Works, by Keeble. Vols. 2 & 3. $6 00.

Annals of Horticulture, and Year-book of Information on Practical Gardening. Cuts, &c. Royal 8vo. $3 00. London, 1846.

Annesley, (J.) Researches into the Causes, Nature, and Treatment of the more Prevalent Diseases of India, and of Warm Climates. 2d edition, 8vo. cloth, $4 00. London.

Annual Scrap Book; A Selection of Paragraphs which have appeared in the Newspapers and Periodicals. 12mo. cloth, 75c. London, 1838.

Annual Register, (Dodsley's,) published yearly. $5 each.

*** Complete sets, from its commencement in 1758, imported to order.

Annuaire de l'etat Militaire de France, pour l'année 1846, publié sur les documents du ministére de la guerre. 1 vol. in 12mo. $1 75. Paris.

Anson, (Lord.) Life of, by Barrow. 8vo. cloth, $4 00. London.

Ansted, (D. F.) The Geologist's Text-book. 12mo. cloth, $1 00. London.

——— Geology; Introductory Description, and Practical Illustrations. 2 vols. 8vo. cloth, $11 00. London, 1845.

——— Ancient World; or, Picturesque Tour through Creation. Plates. 8vo. cloth, $3 00. London, 1848.

The Same. 12mo. cloth, $1 25. Philad. 1847.

Ansted, (D. F.) The Gold Seeker's Manual. 12mo. cloth, $1 00. London, 1849.

The Same. 12mo. 25c. New York, 1849.

Anthon, (Prof.) Latin Lessons. 12mo. sheep, $1 00. New York.

——— Latin Prose Compositions, with a complete course of Exercises. 12mo. sheep, $1 00. New York.

——— Latin Prosody and Metre. 12mo. sheep, $1 00. New York.

——— Latin Versification, and a series of Progressive Exercises. 12mo. sheep, $1 00. New York.

——— Zumpt's Latin Grammar; corrected and enlarged. 12mo. sheep, $1 00. New York.

——— Cæsar's Commentaries on the Gallic War; and the First Book of the Greek Paraphrase, with Notes, &c. Map, Portrait, &c. 12mo. sheep, $1 50. New York.

——— Æneid of Virgil; with Notes, &c. 12mo. sheep, $2 00. New York.

——— Eclogues and Georgics of Virgil; with Notes, &c. 12mo. sheep, $1 50. New York.

——— Select Orations of Cicero; with Notes, &c. 12mo. sheep, $1 25. New York.

——— Sallust's History of the Jugurthine War and of the Conspiracy of Cataline. 12mo. sheep, $1 00. New York.

——— Horace; with Notes, &c. 12mo. sheep, $1 75. New York.

——— First Greek Lessons. 12mo. sheep, $1 00. New York.

——— Greek Prose Composition. 12mo. sheep. $1 00. New York.

——— System of Greek Prosody and Metre. 12mo. sheep, $1 00. New York.

——— Grammar of the Greek Language. 12mo. sheep, $1 00. New York.

——— New Greek Grammar, from the German of Kühner, Matthiæ, &c. 12mo. sheep, $1 00. New York.

——— Homer's Iliad; with Notes, &c. 12mo. sheep, $2 00.

——— Anabasis of Xenophon; with Notes, &c. 12mo. sheep, $1 75. New York.

——— Greek Reader, principally from the German of Jacobs; with Notes. 12mo. sheep, $1 75. New York.

——— Germany and Agricola of Tacitus; with Notes. 12mo. sheep, $1 00. New York.

——— Cicero's de Senectute, de Amicitiæ, &c.; with Notes. 12mo. sheep. New York.

——— Xenophon's Memorabilia of Socrates; from the text of Kühner; with Notes. 12mo. sheep, $1 25. New York.

——— Classical Dictionary. Royal 8vo. sheep, $4 75. New York.

——— Dictionary of Greek and Roman Antiquities. Royal 8vo. sheep, $4 75. New York.

——— School Dictionary of Antiquities. 12mo. $1 25. New York.

——— (C. E.) Pilgrimage to Treves; through the Valley of the Meuse and the Forest of Ardennes, in 1844. 12mo. cloth, 75c. New York.

Antiquarian, (The) Repository; or, Miscellaneous Assemblage of Topography, History, Biography, Customs, and Manners. By Francis Grove and Thomas Astle. Views, Portraits, and Monuments, 4 vols. 4to. $32 00. London, 1807.

Antiquites Mexicaines. Relation des Trois Expeditions de Col. Dupaix pour la Recherche des Antiquités du Pays, notamment celles de Mitla et de Palenque. Avec les Dessins de Castaneda suivie d'un parallele de ces monuments avec ceux de l'Egypt et de l'Inde, par M. Alex. Lenoir, etc., etc.; d'une Dissertation sur l'Origine et sur la Linguistique des Populations Primitives des deux Ameriques, &c. &c. Par M. Warden, &c.; avec un Discours Preliminaire des Travaux et Documents divers de MM. Chateaubriand, Farcy, Galindo, Humboldt, et de St. Priest. 2 vols. folio. [The second vol. containing several hundred plates and maps.] Half bound, red morocco, gilt tops, $150 00.

Apostolic Age. Incidents of the Apostolic Age in Great Britain. 12mo. cloth, $1 75. Pickering, London, 1844.

Appleton, (Pres.) Works of, embracing his Course of Theological Lectures, Addresses, Sermons, &c.; with Memoir. 2 vols. 8vo. cloth, $2 50. Andover, 1837.

Aquinas, (Thomas.) Commentary on the Four Gospels, collected out of the Works of the Fathers; translated from the Catena Aurea. 4 vols. 8vo. cloth, $23 00. Oxford.

Arabian Nights' Entertainments. The Thousand and One Nights; or, the Arabian Nights' Entertainment, Translated and arranged for Family Reading; with Notes, &c., by E. H. Lane. Illustrated with several hundred engravings. 3 vols. post 8vo. cloth, $6 00. London.

The Same. 2 vols. 12mo. cloth, $3 75. New York, 1848.

Arabian Nights. Translated by Forster. With an Historical Introduction, by G. M. Bussey. Neat wood-cuts. Royal 8vo. cloth, $2 75. London, 1842.

Arago. Leçons d'Astronomie professées à l'Observatoire Royal; recueilles par un de ces élèves. 4th edition, avec portrait, et 7 planches. 1 vol. in 12mo. $1 00. Paris, 1845.

Aran, (F. A.) Practical Manual of the Diseases of the Heart and Great Vessels. Translated by W. A. Harris. 12mo. $1 00. Philadelphia, 1843.

Arcet (d'), Payen, Brun, etc. Dictionnaire des Arts et Manufactures, description des procédés de l'industries Française et étrangere. Illustré de plus de 2000 gravures sur bois dans le texte, représentant les machines et appareils employés dans l'industrie. 3 vols. grand in 8vo. Paris, 1846.

Archæological Institute. Proceedings at annual meetings held at Winchester, for the years 1845–46. 2 vols. 8vo. cloth, $12 00. London.

——— **Journal.** Published under the direction of the Central Committee of the Archæological Institute of Great Britain and Ireland. Vols. 1, 2, 3, 4, 8vo. cloth, $14 00. London.

——— **Album;** or Museum of Natural Antiquities; with Illustrations, colored and uncolored, by T. W. Fairholt. 4to. cloth. London, 1845.

Archæologist, (the,) and Journal of Antiquarian Science. Vol. I. 8vo. $1 50. London, 1842

Architect, Builder, and Contractor's Pocket Book of Prices for 1849 ; together with Notitia Architecturica. $2 00. London, 1849.

Architectura Canonica; or, Canons of Church Architecture. 12mo. $1 75. London.

Architecture, (Modern.) A series of Twelve Designs for Modern Cottage and Villa Architecture. Plates colored. Oblong folio, half mor. $6 00. London.

——— Glossary of Terms used in Grecian, Roman, Italian, and Gothic Architecture. New edition, greatly enlarged. Illustrated by over 1500 wood-cuts. 3 vols. 8vo. $15 00. Oxford, 1845–46.

——— Abridged, from the fourth edition of the larger work. 440 cuts. 12mo. cloth, $1 75. Oxford, 1846.

——— **of Birds.** (Library of Entertaining Knowledge.) 12mo. cloth, 75c.; half calf, $1 50. London, 1831.

Argyll, (Duke of.) Presbytery Examined; an Essay, critical and historical, on the Ecclesiastical History of Scotland since the Reformation. Post 8vo. cloth, $2 50. London, 1848.

Ariosto. Orlando Furioso. With Memoirs and Notes, by Ant. Panizzi. 4 vols. 8vo. $12 50. Pickering, London, 1834.

——— The Orlando Furioso; translated into English verse, with notes by W. S. Rose. 8 vols. 8vo. $9 00. London, 1831.

The Same. By John Hoole. 6 vols. 12mo. cloth, $9 00. London.

Arioste. Roland Furieux; traduction nouvelle, par Panckouke et Framely, avec une notice sur l'Arioste, par Abe Latour. 2 vols. in 12mo. $1 75. Paris.

——— L'Orlando Furioso. 2 vols. 12mo cloth, $2 75. London, 1848.

Aristophanes' Plutus, Greek, from the text of Dindorf; with English Notes, Critical and Explanatory, by Cookesley. 8vo. cloth, $1 50. London, 1834.

——— Plutus and the Frogs. Literally translated into English Prose; with copious notes. 8vo. cloth, $2 00. Oxford, Talboys, 1822.

——— Birds; translated from the Greek; with copious notes, by the Rev. H. F. Cary, (translator of Dante.) 8vo. cloth, $1. Lond. 1824.

——— Comedies; translated into familiar blank verse, with Notes, Preliminary Observations of each play, etc., by C. A. Wheelwright. 2 vols. 8vo. cloth, $3 00. Oxford, 1837.

——— Comedies of, translated by T. Mitchell. 2 vols. 8vo. $7 50. scarce. London, 1820.

Aristophanis Comœdiæ, ex Recensione Dindorfii. 2 vols. 12mo. $1 75. Oxonii, 1845.

——— Comœdiæ. Accedunt perditarum Fabularum Frag. ex Recensione G. Dindorfii. 7 vols. 8vo. cloth, $21 00. Oxonii, 1835.

——— Fragmenta, ed. G. Dindorf. Menander et Philemon. ed. Dubner. Gr. et Lat. Royal 8vo. paper, $3 75 ; neat half calf, $5 00. Didot, Paris, 1840.

——— Scholia Græca, ed. G. Dindorf et Dubner. Royal 8vo. paper, $3 75; neat half calf, $5 00. Didot, Paris, 1849.

Aristotle's Poetics. Translated, with Notes, and Two Dissertations on Poetical and Musical Imitation, by Thomas Twining. 2 vols. 8vo. cloth, $3 00. London, 1812.

——— Rhetoric. Literally translated from the Greek, with Notes; to which is added an Analysis of Aristotle's Rhetoric, by Thomas Hobbes, of Malmesbury; and a series of Analytical Questions. Post 8vo. cloth, $1 37. London, 1846.

——— Treatise on Rhetoric; literally translated, with Notes; together with an Analysis of Aristotle's Rhetoric, by Thomas Hobbes, of Malmesbury. 8vo. cloth, $3 00. Oxford, 1833.

Armengaud, (aîné.) Publication Industrielle des Machines, Outils et Appareils les plus perfectionnée et les plus récents, employes dans les differentes branches de l'industrié Française et étrangere. Tomes 1 to 4, in 8vo., accompagnés chacun d'un atlas. Paris, 1845.

Armstrong, (Maj. Gen.) Notices of the War of 1812. 2 vols. 12mo. cloth, $1 50. New York.

——— (R.) An Essay on the Boilers of Steam Engines; their Calculation, Construction, and Management, with a view to the Saving of Fuel. 8vo. cloth, $2 50. London.

——— (Robert.) The Influence of Climate and other agents on the Human Constitution, with reference to the Causes and Prevention of Disease, &c. 8vo. cloth, $2 25. London, 1843.

——— Treatise on Agriculture, with a Dissertation on the Kitchen and Fruit Garden. 18mo. 50c. New York.

Arnauld, (Antoine.) Œuvres Philosophiques; nouvelle edition; Collationnée sur les meilleurs textes et précedée d'une Introduction, par Jules, senior. 1 vol. 12mo. 87c. Paris.

Arnold, (Thomas, D.D.) Sermons, chiefly on the Interpretation of Scripture. 8vo. calf extra, $4 75. London, 1845.

The Same. 12mo. cloth, 75c. New York, 1846.

Arnold, (Thomas, D.D.) History of Rome; including the later Roman Commonwealth. 3 vols. 8vo. cloth, $7 50. New York, 1846.

——— (Thomas.) Miscellaneous Works. Collected and republished. 8vo. cloth, $3 50. London, 1845.

——— Introductory Lectures on Modern History; with the Inaugural Lecture. Third edition. 8vo. cloth, $2 25. London, 1845.

The Same. 12mo. cloth, $1 25. New York.

——— (T. K.) Annales Veterum Regnorum et Populorum, imprimis Romanorum, confecti a Car. Timotheo Zumptio. 12mo. cloth, $1 50. Londini, 1844.

——— Practical Introduction to Greek Accidence. Third edition. 8vo. cloth, $1 50. London, 1844.

——— A First and Second Latin Book and Practical Grammar. Revised and carefully corrected, by J. A. Spencer, A.M. 1 vol. 12mo. neatly bound, 75c. New York, 1847.

——— Latin Prose Composition. A Practical Introduction to Latin Prose Composition. Revised and corrected by J. A. Spencer, A.M. 1 vol. 12mo. neatly bound, $1 00. New York, 1847

Arnold, (T. K.) A First Greek Book; with Easy Exercises and Vocabulary. Revised and corrected by J. A. Spencer, A.M. 12mo. 62½c. New York, 1847.

——— Greek Prose Composition. A Practical Introduction to Greek Prose Composition. Revised and corrected by J. A. Spencer, A.M. 1 vol. 12mo. 75c. New York.

——— A Greek Reading Book; including a Complete Treatise on the Greek Particles. Revised by J. A. Spencer, A.M. 1 vol. 12mo. New York.

——— Cornelius Nepos; with Practical Questions and Answers, and an Imitative Exercise on each chapter. Revised, with Additional Notes, by Professor Johnson, Professor of the Latin Language in the University of the City of New York. One neat volume, 12mo. 62½c.

Arnott, (N.) Elements of Physics; or, Natural Philosophy, General and Medical; written for universal use in non-technical language; and containing new disquisitions and practical suggestions. 8vo. sheep, $2 50. Philadelphia.

——— On Warming and Ventilation. 8vo. cloth, $1 50. London.

Arnould, (A.) Les Jesuites; Histoire, Types, Mœurs, Mysteries. Illustrés de 20 gravures sur acier et 100 gravures sur bois. 2 vols. grand in 8vo. $5 50. Paris, 1845–46.

Arrian on Coursing; translated into English, with Annotations and a Memoir; together with some account of the Canes Venatici of the Ancients. By the Rev. William Dansey. Imp. 8vo. 25 fine lithographs, on India paper, cloth gilt, $3 00. London, 1831.

Art de Verifier les Dates des Faits Historiques, des Inscriptions, des Chroniques et autres Anciens Monuments; ouvrage commence par les Benedictines de la Congregation de St. Maur. En avant Jesus Christ jusqu'a nos jours; avec les tables. 41 vols. in 8vo. $50 00. Paris, 1821.

Art of Rigging; containing an Alphabetical Explanation of Terms and Phrases, and Directions for Operation. New edition, revised and recompiled, by George Biddlecombe. 15 steel engravings. 8vo. cloth, $3 75. London, 1848.

Art Union Historic Gallery of Portraits and Paintings, with Memoirs. 2000 engravings. London.

The Same. 2 vols. half mor. $5 50. London.

——— The Union of British Art. A Series of Fifty India proofs, after designs by Wilkie, Prout, &c. Folio, cloth gilt, $6 50. London.

Artis, (E. T.) Antediluvian Phytology, illustrated by a collection of the Fossil Remains of Plants peculiar to the Coal Formations of Great Britain; including Remarks on the Systems of Count Sternberg, Baron Schlotheim, Professor Martius, and Mons. Brongniart; also Communications from Professor Buckland, and other eminent Geologists. 4to. 25 plates, (pub. at £2 10*s*.) $3 50. London, 1838.

Artist's Married Life; being that of Albert Durer. Translated from the German of Leopold Schefer, by Mrs. J. R. Stodart. 12mo. antique boards. $1 75. London, 1848.

The Same. 12mo. boards, 75c. Boston, 1848.

Artist's Book of Fables; comprising a Series of Original Fables, illustrated by 280 exquisitely beautiful engravings on wood, by Harvey, and other eminent artists; after designs by the late James Northcote, R.A. Post 8vo. cloth, full gilt, $3 00. London, 1845.

Artizan Club. A Treatise on the Steam Engine, in its Application to Mines, Mills, Steam Navigation, and Railways. Edited by J. Bourne. Illustrated by 30 plates and 349 engravings on wood. 3d edition, 4to. cloth, $8 00. London, 1849.

Arundale and Bonomi. Gallery of Antiquities, selected from the British Museum; with Descriptions, by S. Birch. Illustrated with 57 plates, some colored. 4to. cloth, $5 50. London.

Ashwell, (S.) Practical Treatise on Parturition. Plates. 8vo. cloth, $5 00. London, 1834.

——— Practical Treatise on the Diseases peculiar to Women. 3d edition, 8vo. cloth, $6 00. London, 1848.

The Same. Edited by Prof. Goddard, 8vo. $5 00. Philadelphia.

Asiatic Researches; or, Transactions of the Society instituted at Bengal, for inquiring into the History and Antiquities, the Arts, Sciences, and Literature of Asia. 12 vols. 8vo. $30 00. London, 1806.

Asmodeus; or, The Devil on Two Sticks, by Le Sage; a new and greatly improved translation, by Joseph Thomas. Illustrated edition, with 250 spirited and clever wood-cuts, by Tony Johannot, imperial 8vo. extra gilt, cloth, $1 75. London, 1841.

*** This is the large edition, and very superior to the demy octavo publication, both in regard to the cuts and the translation.

Athæneum, (The,) Journal of English and Foreign Literature, Science, and the Arts, (published weekly.) $7 00 per year.

——— (The) A Weekly Journal of Science, Literature, and the Fine Arts, from January, 1832, to January, 1847. 15 vols. 4to. half calf, $25 00.

Atlas of Maps; published by the Society for the Diffusion of Useful Knowledge; consisting of one hundred and sixty maps of countries; forty maps of cities, ancient and modern; six of the stars, and one of the principal rivers; with indexes, &c.; colored. Large 4to., half Russia, $40 00.

The Same. Uncolored. $35 00.

——— Black's General Atlas; comprehending sixty-one maps, from the latest and most authentic sources; engraved on steel; with geographical descriptions, index, &c. Folio, half mor. $13 50.

——— Black's School Atlas of Modern Geography; a series of Twenty-five Maps, by W. Hughes; with Index, &c. 8vo. $2 75. Edinburgh, 1846.

——— Quinn's Historical Atlas. A new edition, with maps on an enlarged scale, by W. Hughes. Oblong folio, half morocco, $6 00.

The Same. Large folio, maps mounted. Half Russia, $10 00.

Atlas. Findlay's, (A. G.) Modern Atlas; forming a complete Compendium of Geography; exhibiting, in thirty maps the Extent, Dimensions, Physical and Political Arrangements of every country in the Known World: and containing the latest discoveries in the Polar Regions, Africa, Polynesia, &c. With an Introduction, explanatory of the construction and use of maps, and a copious Index for reference to the maps, &c. Royal 8vo. half calf, $3 50. London, 1845.

——— Tanner's Universal Atlas, containing maps of the various Empires, Kingdoms, States, and Republics of the World; with a special map of each of the United States, plans of Cities, &c. 4to. 117 maps, plans, and sections, colored, half mor. $12 00. Philad. 1844.

——— The National Atlas of Historical, Commercial, and Political Geography; constructed from the most recent and authentic sources, by A. K. Johnston; accompanied by maps and illustrations of the Physical Geography of the Globe; by Heinrich Berghaus; and an Ethnographic map of Europe, by Gustaf Kornbot. Large folio, half Russia, $40 00. Edinburgh.

——— Physical Atlas; A Series of Maps and Notes, illustrating the geographical distribution of Natural Phenomena, by A. K. Johnston; based on the Physikalschen Atlas of Professor Berghaus; with the co-operation of Sir David Brewster, Professors Forbes and Nichols, Dr. Bone, G. R. Waterhouse, J. S. Russel, and Dr. G. Kornbot, in divisions, viz. Geology, Hydrography, Meteorology, Natural History. Large folio, half Russia, $50 00. Edinburgh.

Any of the divisions can be had separately. A cheaper edition, for the use of schools, is in preparation.

——— Chambers' Atlas for the People; accompanied by a Descriptive Introduction; 33 maps. 4to. cloth, $3 50. Edinburgh.

——— Comprehensive Atlas of Modern Geography; colored. Folio, half mor. $10 50. London.

——— Arrowsmith's Atlas. Fifty-four maps, colored. 4to. $9 00. London.

——— Morse's North American Atlas. 4to. half roan, $2 75. New York.

Audibert. Petit Manuel d'Accouchement Anormal; ou description pratique du forceps indicateur, representant sur les branches sur grand nombre de figures. 8vo. broché, 50c.

Audubon, (J. J.) American Ornithological Biography. 5 vols. royal 8vo. cloth, $27 50. Philadelphia and London, 1831–39.

——— Synopsis of the Birds of North America. 8vo. cloth, $3 75. Edinburgh, 1839.

——— Birds of America; from Drawings made in the United States and their Territories. Illustrated with many hundred colored plates. 7 vols. royal 8vo. $75 00. New York, 1845.

——— Birds of America, etc.; containing 185 plates of Birds, all of the natural size, beautifully colored. 4 vols. elephant folio, $800. London, 1828.

Augustin, (St.) Confessions, revised from a former translation by Dr. Pusey. 8vo. cloth, $2 50. Oxford, 1840.

The Same. 12mo. cloth, 75c. Boston.

Augustin, (St.) Opera omnia; opera et studio monarchorum ord. S. Benedicti; editio Parisina, altera, emendatio et aucta. 22 vols royal 8vo. sewed, $45 00. Paris, Gaume, Bros. 1836.

Austria and the Austrians; with Sketches of the Danube and the Imperial States; portraits of the Emperor and Prince Metternich. 2 vols. post 8vo. $2 50. London, 1837.

Authors of England, by Chorley Sixteen portraits, engraved in high relief, accompanied by Biographical Sketches. 4to. cloth, $3 50. London, 1838.

Autobiography. A Collection of the most amusing lives ever published; comprising the lives of Vidocq, Bellini, Du Barri, Goldoni, Marmontel, Whitfield, Lackington, Hardy, Vaux, Hume, Herbert, Eugene, Wolf Tone, &c. 20 vols. 12mo. cloth, $10 00. London.

——— of a Working Man; by One who has whistled at the Plough. Post 8vo. cloth, $2 00. London, 1848.

Autograph Letters. A Collection of Original Letters; collected by the late William Upcott: with Portraits, &c. 3 vols. 4to. half mor. $50 00.

Autographs of Royal, Noble, Learned, and Remarkable Personages, conspicuous in English History, from the reign of Richard II. to that of Charles II.; with Biographical Memoirs, by J. G. Nicholls. Folio, cloth, $9 00. London

Avrillon. The Year of Affections; or, Affections on the Love of God drawn from the Canticles, for Every Day in the Year. 12mo. cloth, $1 75. London, 1845.

Ayre, (Joseph.) Researches into the Nature and Origin of Dropsies, and the Means for their Cure and Prevention. Third edition. 8vo. cloth, $1 75. London, 1847.

Azais, (P. Hyac.) Cours de Philosophie Générale, ou Exposition simple, fidèle et graduelle de tous les faits de l'ordre physique, psychologique, intellectuel, moral et politique. 8 vols. 8vo. $15 00. Paris, 1824.

——— Des Compensations dans les Destinées Humaines. 5th edition, 1 vol. 12mo. 75c. Paris, 1846.

Babault. Dictionnaire Français et Geographique, contenant, outre tous les mots de la langue Français, des sciences et des arts, la nomenclature de toutes les communes de France et des villes les plus remarquables du monde. 2d edition. 2 vols. grand in 8vo. $9 00. Paris, 1846.

Babbage, (Charles.) The Economy of Machinery and Manufactures. 12mo. cloth, $1 50. London, 1847.

Babes in the Wood. Illustrated with designs by the Marchioness of Waterford; engraved by the best artists. Folio, $6 00.

The Same; colored in imitation of the original drawings. Mor. $12 00.

The Same; proof impressions on India paper, mounted on Bristol board, in portfolio, $15 00. London.

Babington, (C.C.) Manual of British Botany. 2d edition, post 8vo. cloth, $3 00. London, 1847.

Babrii. Fabulæ Æsopæ, cum Fabularum, deperditarum Fragmentis; recensuit et breviter illustravit, G. C. Lewis. 8vo. cloth, $1 75. Oxford, 1846.

Babron. Précis des Pratiques de l'Art Naval en France, en Espagne, et en Angleterre. 1 vol. in 8vo. $1 75. Paris, 1817.

Bachelier, (Jules.) Exposé Critique et Méthodique de l'Hydropathie, ou traitment des Maladies pour l'eau fronde. 8vo. $1 00.

Bachelor Butterfly, The Veritable History of. Humorous Plates. Oblong folio. 75c. London.

Bachelor of the Albany. By the author of Falcon Family. 12mo. cloth, 62c. New York.

Bachoffner. Chemistry as applied to the Fine Arts. 8vo. cloth, $2 00. London, 1837.

Backgammon, its History and Practice. Cuts, 50c. London.

Bacon's (Francis, Lord) Works. A new edition, by Basil Montagu. 17 vols. 8vo. cloth, $44 00. Pickering, London, 1835.

"The most complete edition extant; it contains translations as well as the original of the Latin works; and is illustrated by portraits, views, and fac-similes, with a new life of Bacon, by the editor."

The Same. 3 vols. royal 8vo. cloth, $7 50. Philadelphia.

——— Works; both English and Latin, with an Introductory Essay, and Copious Indexes, complete in 2 large vols. imperial 8vo. cloth, $8 50. London, 1838.

——— Essays and Wisdom of the Ancients. Edited by Basil Montagu. Foolscap 8vo. cloth, $1 25. London, 1845.

——— Essays, Moral, Economical, and Political. 12mo. cloth, 50c. Boston, 1835.

——— Advancement of Learning. Edited by Basil Montagu. Foolscap 8vo. cloth, $1 25. London, 1838.

——— Essays or Counsels, Civil and Moral; and the Two Books of the Proficience and Advancement of Learning, Divine and Human. New edition; with a Memoir and Notes, by W. C. Taylor. Square 18mo. cloth, $1 00. London, 1840.

——— Novum Organum; or, True Suggestions for the interpretation of Nature. Foolscap 8vo. cloth, $1 25. Pickering, London, 1844.

Badham, (C. D.) Treatise on the Esculent Funguses of England; containing an account of their Classical History, Uses, Character, &c. Illustrated. 8vo. cloth, $6 50. London, 1847.

Bagster, (Samuel.) The Management of Bees; with Description of the Ladies' Safety Hive. Forty wood-cuts. 12mo. cloth, $2 50.

——— Polyglot Bible, in Eight Languages of the Old Testament, and Nine Languages of the New. Folio, in sumptuous Turkey mor. $80 00.

——— The English Version. Thirteen maps, chart, &c. Morocco, $6 50.

Bagster. Treasury Bible, interleaved with a Biblical Treasury of Parallel Passages, &c. Mor. extra, $9 00.

——— The English Hexapla; containing the Six Early Translations. 4to. cloth, $12 00; mor. extra, $18 00.

——— The Holy Scriptures. Translated by Miles Coverdale. 4to. $12 00.

The various versions of the Holy Bible, published by Bagster & Sons, imported to order.

Bailey, (P. J.) Festus, a Poem. 12mo. cloth, $1 00. Boston.

Baillie, (M.) Morbid Anatomy of some of the most important parts of the Human Body. 12mo. $1 50. London, 1833.

Bain, (A.) Application of Electric Fluid to Useful Arts. 8vo. cloth, $1 25. London.

——— (W.) Essay on the Variation of the Compass in Ships. 8vo. cloth, $2 00. London.

Baines, (E.) History of Cotton Manufactures in Great Britain. 8vo. cloth, $3 00. London.

Baird, (Rev. Dr.) Protestantism in Italy. 12mo. cloth, $1 00. New York.

Baker, (T.) Railway Engineering; or, Field Work, preparatory to the Construction of Railways; with a General Table for the Calculation of Earthworks of Railways, Canals, &c. With two Auxiliary Tables; also Tunnelling and Investigations of the Formulæ for the super-elevation of the exterior rail in curves. 8vo. cloth. $1 50. London, 1848.

Bakewell, (F. C.) Natural Evidence of a Future Life; derived from the Properties and Actions of Animate and Inanimate Matter. 8vo. cloth, $1 62. London, 1840.

——— (Robert.) Introduction to Geology. 8vo cloth, $6 00. London.

——— Introduction to Mineralogy. 8vo. cloth, $6 00. London.

Balbi, (Adrien.) Atlas Ethnographique du Globe, ou Classification des Peuples anciennes et modernes d'apres leurs langues, avec Introduction. 1 vol. in 8vo. et atlas, $7 50. Paris, 1826.

Ball, (S.) An Account of the Cultivation and Manufacture of Tea in China; with Remarks on the Experiments now making for the Introduction of the Tea-tree into other parts of the World. 8vo. cloth, $4 25. London, 1848.

Ballantine, (James.), Treatise on Painted Glass. Royal 8vo. cloth, $3 25. London.

——— The Tradesman's Book of Ornamental Designs; Adapted for the Cabinet-maker, Iron-founder, Painter, Brass-founder, Silversmith, Wood-carver, &c. &c. 4to. cloth, $6 00. London, 1848.

Balzac, (De.) La Peau de Chagrin; edition princeps, imprimee sur magnifique papier jesus velin, ornee de 100 gravures sur acier, tirees dans le texte, d'apres les dessins de MM. Horace Vernet, Johannot, Boulanger, Fragonard, etc. 1 vol. grand in 8vo. $4 25. Paris.

——— Œuvres completes; édition de luxe, ornée de vignettes par Gavarny, Tony Johannot, etc. 10 vols. in 8vo. demi veau, $35 00. Paris, 1842

Bancroft, (George.) History of the United States, from the Discovery of the American Continent. Portraits, Maps, &c. 3 vols. 8vo. cloth, $6 00; half calf, $8 50; calf extra, $10. Boston, 1847.

Banks and Bankers. Treatise on Banking. Post 8vo. cloth, $3 00. London.

Bannister, (J. T.) Survey of the Holy Land; Geography, History, and Destiny. 8vo. half mor. silk sides, $5 50. London.

Baptistry; or, The Way of Eternal Life; by Rev. J. Williams. Plates. 2 vols. 8vo. cloth, $5 00. Oxford, 1842.

Barante, (De.) Histoire des Ducs de Bourgogne, de la Maison de Valois, 1364–1477: ornée de 110 gravures sur bois, papier de Chine, et de 16 cartes géographiques. 12 vols. in 8vo. demi maroquin, $24 00. Paris, 1837.

Baretti, (Joseph.) Dictionary of the Italian and English, and English and Italian languages; to which is prefixed an Italian and English Grammar, ninth edition; corrected and improved, by C. Thompson. 2 vols. 8vo. cloth, $6 50. London, 1839.

Barlow, (H. B.) A Comparative Account and Delineation of Railway Engine and Carriage Wheels. Engravings. 8vo. cloth, $2 00. London, 1848.

——— (Peter.) Treatise on the Strength of Timber, Cast Iron, and other materials; with an Appendix, on the Power of Locomotive Engines, &c., new edition. 8vo. plates, $4 50. London, 1847.

Barnard, (H.) School Architecture; or, Contributions to the Improvements of Schoolhouses in the United States. 2d edition. 8vo. cloth, $2 00. New York, 1848.

Baron, (John.) Life of Edward Jenner, with Illustrations of his Doctrines, and Selections from his Correspondence. 2 vols. 8vo. cloth, $3 00. London, 1838.

Baronial Halls, Picturesque Edifices, and Ancient Churches of England; from drawings by Hardinge, Cattermole, Prout, Miller, Holland, and other eminent artists; executed under the superintendence of Mr. Hardinge. The Text by S. C. Hall. 3 vols. fol. $34.

Barr. (J.) Anglican Church Architecture. Plates. 12mo. cloth, $1 50. London.

Barreswil et Sobrero. Appendice a tous les Traits d'Analyse Chimique, recueil des observations publiées depuis dix ans sur l'analyse qualitative et quantitative. 8vo. broché, $2 00. Paris, 1843.

Barreti, (Rev. Richard A. F.) Synopsis of Criticisms upon those Passages of the Old Testament, in which Modern Commentators have differed from the authorized version, together with an explanation of various difficulties in the Hebrew and English Texts. Royal 8vo. cloth, vols. 1 and 2, $16 50. London, 1847.

——— Vol. 3, Part I. $4 50. London, 1847.

Barrington, (Archibald.) Manual for Students of British Architecture; with a Table showing the Duration of each Style; and a Glossary. Chart, mounted on canvass, folded, $2 00. London, 1843.

Barrow, (Isaac, D.D.) Theological Works; a new edition, including his Latin works. Portrait. 8 vols. 8vo. $32 00. Oxford, 1830

——— Works, with Life of the Author, by Rev James Hamilton. 3 vols. 8vo. $6 00. London, 1843.

——— (Sir J.) Voyages of Discovery and Research within the Arctic Regions; from 1818 to present time. Portrait and maps. 8vo. cloth, $4 00. London, 1846.

——— (John.) Tour in Austria, Lombardy, the Northern Tyrol, and Bavaria, in 1840. Demy 8vo. cloth, $1 00. London, 1841.

Barry Cornwall, Songs of. 18mo. cloth, gilt, $1 00. London, 1847.

Barthelemy et Mery. Napoleon en Egypte, Waterloo et le Fils de l'Homme, précedes d'une notice litteraire, par Tissot, de l'Academie Française; edition illustre par Horace Vernet et H. Bellange. 1 beau vol. grand in 8vo. ornée de 140 gravures et de 17 vignettes tirees separement sur papier de Chine. $3 00. Paris.

Bartlett, (J. R.) Dictionary of Americanisms. A Glossary of Words and Phrases, colloquially used in the United States. 8vo. cloth, $2 50. New York, 1848.

——— (E.) On the Certainty of Medicine. 8vo. cloth, 63c. Philadelphia, 1848.

——— (W. H.) Walks about Jerusalem. Illustrated. 8vo. half mor. $3 50. London.

——— Forty Days in the Desert, in the Track of the Israelites. Illustrated. 8vo. $3 50. London.

Barton and Castles' British Flora Medica; or, History of the Medicinal Plants of Great Britain. Illustrated with upwards of two hundred colored figures of Plants. 2 vols. 8vo. cloth, $10 00.

Basilius, (St.) Opera omnia quæ exstant, vel quæ ejus nomine circumferuntur [Gr. et Lat.;] opera et studio Juliani Garnier; editio Parisina, altera, emendata et aucta. 6 vols. royal 8vo. sewed, $20 00. Paris, Gaume, Brothers, 1839

Bastiat, (J.) Sophisms of the Protective Policy. Translated by Mrs. D. J. M'Cord; with an Introductory Letter by Dr. Lieber. 12mo. cloth, 75c. New York, 1848.

Bateman, (Dr. T.) Delineations of Cutaneous Diseases, exhibiting the Characteristic Appearance of the principal Genera and Species; comprised in the Classification of the late Dr. Willan. 72 plates, beautifully and accurately colored. 4to. half mor., top edge gilt, $28 00. London, 1844.

Bauer and Hooker's Illustrations of the Genera of Ferns; in which the Characters of each Genus are displayed in the most elaborate manner, in a series of magnified dissections and Figures, highly finished in colors, after the beautiful drawings of Francis Bauer, Esq., Botanical Draughtsman to Her Majesty; with descriptive letter-press, by Sir William Jackson Hooker; complete in one large volume, imperial 8vo. half mor. extra, top edges gilt, $30 00. London, 1838–42.

Baxter, (Richard.) Practical Works; with a Life of the Author, and a Critical Examination of his Writings by the Rev. W. Orme. Portrait. 23 vols. 8vo. $55 00. Lond. 1830.

——— The Works of. With an Introductory Discourse by Rev. R. Philip. 4 vols. imperial 8vo. cloth, $17 50. London, 1838.

Bayard, (H.) Manual Pratique de Médécine légale. 12mo. $1 25. Paris, 1844.

Bayle. Dictionnaire Historique et Critique; nouvelle edition, augmentée de notes, extraits de Chaufepie, Joly, Lamounoie, L. J. Leclerc, etc. etc. 10 vols. in 8vo. demi veau, $44 00. Paris, 1820.

Bayley, (Sir J.) Summary of the Law of Bills of Exchange, &c.; with additions, by F. Bayley. 8vo. $3 00. London, 1830.

Beattie. Poetical Works; with Memoir, by Rev. A. Dyce. 1 vol. 12mo. cloth, $1 37; morocco, $2 75. Pickering, London, 1831.

——— The Castles and Abbeys of England; from the National Records, Early Chronicles, and other standard authorities. Beautifully illustrated. Royal 8vo. cloth, $7 00. London.

Beattie and Collins. Complete Poetical Works; with Memoirs of their Lives, by Thomas Miller. Illustrated with engravings, by S. Williams. 8vo. cloth, $3 50. Lond. 1846.

The Same. Morocco extra, $4 50. Lond. 1846.

Beaumont and Fletcher. Dramatic Works; with an Introduction by G. Darley. Portraits and vignettes. 2 vols. royal 8vo. cloth, $9 00; calf, $12 00. Moxon, London.

——— New Edition, with Notes, and Biographical Memoir, by Rev. A. Dyce. 11 vols. 8vo. cloth. $22. London, 1842–3.

Beausobre and Lenfant. New Version of the Gospel according to St. Matthew. 12mo. cloth, $1 00. London, 1838.

Beauties of the Opera and Ballet. Engraved by Charles Heath; from drawings by the first artists. Each page of the letter-press surrounded by an ornamental border, printed in colors. Imperial 8vo. mor. extra, $8 50.

The Same. French edition. Fancy cloth, $7 00.

Beaven, (James.) Help to Catechising. 12mo. cloth, 75c. London, 1843.

Bechstein, (J. M.) Natural History of Cage Birds, their Management, Habits, Food, Diseases, Treatment, Breeding, and the Methods of catching them. Numerous wood-cuts. 12mo. cloth, gilt edges, $2 00. London, 1841.

Becker, (Prof.) Charicles, or Illustrations of the Private Life of the Ancient Greeks; with Notes and Excursus; translated by Rev. F. Metcalfe. Illustrations. Post 8vo. cloth, $3 50. London, 1845.

——— Gallus; or, Roman Scenes of the Time of Augustus; with Notes and Excursus, illustrative of the Manners and Customs of the Romans. Translated by Rev. F. Metcalfe. Illustrations. Post 8vo. cloth, $3 50. Lond. 1845.

Beckman. History of Inventions, Discoveries, and Origins. Fourth edition, carefully revised and enlarged, by Drs. Francis and Griffith. With Memoir and Portraits. 2 vols. post 8vo. cloth, $1 75. (Bohn's Stand. Lib.) London.

Bede, (Venerable.) Ecclesiastical History and the Anglo-Saxon Chronicle, with Notes, Maps, &c. Edited by Rev. J. A. Giles. 12mo. cloth, $1 25. (Bohn's Ant. Lib.) London.

Bedford, (F.) A Chart of Anglican Church Ornament; wherein are figured the Saints of the English Kalendar, with their appropriate Emblems, the different Styles of Stained Glass, etc., etc.; collected from ancient existing examples. Colored, $1 75. London, 1845.

——— A Chart of Anglican Church Architecture, arranged chronologically, with examples. Fifth edition, beautifully colored, $1 75. London, 1845

Beecher, (Edward, D.D.) Baptism, with reference to its Import and Modes. 12mo. cloth, $1 25. New York, 1848.

Beechey. Botany of Captain Beechey's Voyage; comprising an Account of the Plants collected by Messrs. Lay and Collie, and other officers of the Expedition, during the Voyage to the Pacific and Behring's Straits, performed in Her Majesty's ship Blossom, under the command of Captain F. W. Beechey; by Sir William Jackson Hooker and G. A. W. Arnott, Esq., illustrated by 100 plates, beautifully engraved; complete in ten parts. Done up in one vol. 4to. extra cloth, $30 00. London, 1831–41.

——— Zoology of Capt. Beechey's Voyage; compiled from the Collections and Notes of Captain Beechey, and the scientific gentlemen who accompanied the Expedition,—the Mammalia, by Dr. Richardson; Ornithology, by N. A. Vigors, Esq.; Fishes, by G. T. Lay, Esq., and E. T. Bennett, Esq.; Crustacea, by Richard Owen, Esq.; Reptiles, by John Edward Gray, Esq.; Shells, by W. Sowerby, Esq.; and Geology, by the Rev. Dr. Buckland. Illustrated by 47 plates, containing many hundred figures, beautifully colored by Sowerby. 4to. extra cloth boards, $22 00. London, 1839.

Belcher, (Edward.) Treatise on Nautical Surveying; containing an Outline of the Duties of the Naval Surveyor, &c. Imperial 8vo. cloth, $6 50. London, 1835.

Belinaye, (H. G.) On the Removal of Stone from the Bladder. 8vo. $1 25. London, 1835.

Bell, (Robert.) Lives of the Most Eminent English Poets. 2 vols. foolscap 8vo. London.

——— (Sir Charles.) Anatomy and Philosophy of Expression, as connected with the Fine Arts. Third edition, enlarged. Numerous engravings and wood-cuts. Imperial 8vo. cloth, $6 50. London, 1845.

——— (Thomas.) History of British Quadrupeds; including the Cetacea. Illustrated by nearly 200 wood-cuts. 8vo. cloth, $6 50. London, 1837.

——— (John.) Compositions from Morning and Evening Prayer. A series of thirty-six beautiful outline engravings. 4to. cloth, $5 00. London, 1844.

——— (R.) History of Russia. 3 vols. 12mo. cloth, $5 00. London.

Ben Jonson, the Dramatic Works of. (Moxon's edition.) Royal 8vo. cloth, $4 50; calf extra, $6 00. London.

Bennett, (Prof. J. H.) On Cancerous and Cancroid Growths. Illustrated by 190 engravings on wood. 8vo. cloth, $3 50. Lond 1849.

Bentham, (Jeremy.) Works; edited by Bowring. 11 vols. royal 8vo. $28 00. London.

Bentley, (Richard.) Boyle Lecture Sermons. Edited by Rev. A. Dyce, 8vo. cloth, $4 00. London, 1838.

——— Works; containing Dissertations upon the Epistles of Phalaris, Themistocles, Socrates, Euripides, and the Fables of Æsop; Sermons, Boyle Lecture; Remarks on Free-thinking, &c. Edited, with copious Indices and Notes, by the Rev. Alexander Dyce. 3 vols. 8vo. cloth, $6 50. London, 1836–38.

Benvenuto Cellini. Memoirs, written by Himself. Now first collated with the new Text of Guiseppe Molini, and enlarged. Translated by Thomas Roscoe. With fine portrait. Post 8vo., cloth, 87c. (Bohn's Standard Lib.) London, 1847.

Beranger, (J. P. de.) Œuvres Completes. Nouvelle edition, illustrée. 2 vols. grand in 8vo. $8 00. Paris, 1847.

Berkeley, (George.) Complete Works; with an Account of his Life, and a translation into English of the Latin Essays, by G. A. Wright. 2 vols. 8vo. cloth, $3 50. London, 1843.

Bernal Diaz, Memoirs of. Written by Himself; containing a True and Full Account of the Discovery and Conquest of Mexico and New Spain. Translated by J. L. Lockhart. 2 vols. 8vo. cloth, $3 00. London.

Bernan, (W.) On the History and Art of Warming and Ventilating Rooms and Open Buildings by Open Fires; Hypocausts; German, Dutch, Russian, and Swedish Stoves; Steam; Hot Water; Heated Air; &c. 240 figures of Apparatus. 2 vols. 12mo. cloth, $2 75. London, 1848.

Bernardi. L'Art de Donner des Bals et Soirées, ou le Glacier Royale. 12mo. $1 00. Paris, 1845.

——— (de St. Pierre.) Paul et Virginie. Illustrés par Tony Johannot, &c. 1 vol. grand in 8vo. $7 50. Paris.

——— Œuvres complétes; nouvelle edition, ornés d'un tres-beau portrait. 2 vols. grand in 8vo. $6 50. Paris.

Bernardus, (St.) Opera omnia, ex secundis curis Johan. Mabillon; edition quarta, emendata et aucta. 4 vols. royal 8vo. $13 50. Paris, Gaume, Brothers, 1839.

Berrington, (Joseph.) Literary History of the Middle Ages; comprehending an Account of the State of Learning from the close of the reign of Augustus to its Revival in the Fifteenth century. Post 8vo. cloth, 88c. (Bogue's European Lib.) London.

Berthollet. Art of Dyeing and Bleaching; translated from the French; with Notes and Engravings. By Andrew Ure. 8vo. cloth, $3 50. London, 1841.

Berzelius, (J. J.) The Use of the Blowpipe in Chemistry and Mineralogy. Translated by J. D. Whitney. Post 8vo. cloth, $1 50. Boston, 1845.

Bessemer, (H.) The Resistance of the Atmosphere to Railway Trains, and the means of lessening the same; together with an account of some improvements in Railway Carriage Axles. 4to. paper, two plates, 75c. London, 1847

Betham, (Sir W.) Etruscan Literature and Antiquities. 2 vols. 8vo. cloth, $12 00. London.

Bethune, (G. W.) History of a Penitent. 12mo. cloth, 50c. Philadelphia.

——— British Female Poets; with Biographical and Critical Notices. 12mo. cloth, $2 00; gilt, $2 50; mor. $3 50. Philadelphia.

——— Lays of Love and Faith. 8vo. cloth, $1 50; cloth gilt, $2 00. Philadelphia, 1848.

Bevan, (Edward.) The Honey Bee; its Natural History, Physiology, and Management. Plates. 12mo. cloth, $2 00. London, 1838.

Beveridge, (Bp.) The Church Catechism Explained. 12mo. cloth, $1 00. Oxford, 1843.

——— (Bp.) Thesaurus Theologicæ: or, a Complete System of Divinity summed up in Brief Notes upon Select Places of the Old and New Testaments. 2 vols. 8vo. cloth, $6 00. London, 1848.

——— (Bp.) The Doctrines of the Church of England consonant to Scripture, Reason, and the Fathers; in a Discourse upon the xxxix Articles. 2 vols. 8vo. cloth, $3 50. London, 1846

Bible Geography; or, Some Account of the Countries and Places mentioned in Scripture. 16mo. cloth, 50c. London.

Bible (La Sainte) en Latin et en Français, trad. de la Maitre de Sacy, suivie d'un dictionnaire etymologique, geographique, et Archéologique. Avec 64 vignettes d'apres les dessins de Devéria. 13 vols. grand in 8vo. demi maroquin, $40 00. Paris, 1828–34.

Biblia Sacra. Vulgatæ editionis Sixti V., jussu recognita et Clementis VIII. auctoritate edita. 8vo. half morocco, $3 50. Paris, 1844.

Biblical Inquirer. An Attempt to show that Scripture is its Own Interpreter. 8vo. cloth, $1 50. London, 1846

Bibliotheca Londinensis. The London Catalogue of Books, published from 1814–46. 8vo. cloth. $7 75. London, 1847.

——— A Classified Index to the above; and serving as a Key to it. 8vo. cloth, $4 50. London, 1848.

Bickersteth, (Rev. E.) The Signs of the Times in the East; or, Warning to the West. 12mo. cloth, $1 75. London. 1845.

Biglow, (Dr. J.) Plants of Boston and its Vicinity, with their Genera and Specific Characters, &c. 3d edition, enlarged. 12mo. cloth, $1 50. Boston, 1840.

——— (J.) Treatise on the Materia Medica. 8vo. sheep, $2 00. Boston, 1822.

Bilson, (Thomas, D.D.) The Perpetual Government of Christ's Church; new edition, with Biographical Notice by Rev. R. Eden. 8vo. cloth, $3 50. Oxford, 1842.

Bingham, (Rev. Joseph.) Works; containing the Origines Ecclesiasticæ, or Antiquities of the Christian Church; new and improved edition, carefully revised, with an enlarged Index. 2 large vols, imperial 8vo., handsomely printed, extra cloth, $7 50. London, 1846.

"Bingham is a writer who does equal honor to the English clergy and to the English nation, and whose learning is only equalled by his moderation and impartiality."—Quarterly Review.

Biographia Britannica Literaria; or, Biography of the Literary Characters of Great Britain and Ireland; arranged in chronological order. By J. Wright. 2 vols. 8vo. cloth, $7 50. London.

Biographie Universelle, Ancienne et Moderne, ou histoire, par ordre alphabetique, de la vie publique et privee de tous les hommes, qui se sont fait remarquer pour leurs ecrits, leurs actions, leurs talents, leurs vertus, ou leurs crimes; ouvrage redige par un societe de gens de lettres et de savants; avec le continuation. 81 vols. in 8vo. demi veau, $175 00. Paris.

Biot, (J. B.) Traité Elémentaire d'Astronomie Physique. Troisieme edition, corrigée et augmentée. 4 vols. 8vo. and Atlases. $16 00. Paris, 1844.

Bird, (Golding.) Elements of Natural Philosophy; being an Experimental Introduction to the Study of the Physical Sciences; with 372 illustrations. From the revised and enlarged third London edition. 12mo. cloth, $1 25. Philadelphia, 1848.

Black, (W.) A Practical Treatise on Brewing. 8vo. cloth, $3 25. London, 1844.

Blackmore, (Rev. R. W.) Doctrine of the Russian Church; translated from the Sclavono-Russian Originals. 8vo. cloth, $3 00. Aberdeen, 1845.

Blackwood's Magazine; from its commencement in 1816, to December, 1846. 60 vols. 8vo. half calf, gilt backs, $100 00.

Blaine, (D. P.) Encyclopædia of Rural Sports. Numerous engravings on wood. Thick 8vo. cloth, $15 00. London.

——— Dictionary of Veterinary Art. 8vo. cloth, $6 25. London.

——— Canine Pathology. 8vo. cloth, $2 75. London.

——— Outlines of the Veterinary Art; or, a Treatise on the Anatomy, Physiology, and Curative Treatment of the Diseases of the Horse; and subordinately of those of neat Cattle and Sheep; illustrated by Surgical and Anatomical plates. 8vo. cloth, $5 50.

Blair, (John.) Chronological and Historical Tables; new edition, carefully corrected and brought down to the present time. Imperial 8vo. half mor. $10 50. London.

——— (Robert.) Grave, a Poem; with a Life of the author, by R. H. Cromeke; with twelve plates, from designs by Blake. 4to. $7 50. London, 1813

——— (Rev. Hugh.) Sermons; with a Memoir, by James Finlayson. 8vo. cloth, $2 00. London, 1840.

Blakey, (Robert.) History of the Philosophy of Mind; embracing the Opinions of all writers on Mental Science, from the Earliest Period to the Present Time. 4 vols 8vo. cloth, $16 00. London, 1848.

Blakiston, (Peyton.) Practical Observations on Diseases of the Chest, and of the Principles of Auscultation. 8vo. cloth, $1 75. Philadelphia, 1848.

Blanc, (Louis.) History of Ten Years, 1830–1840. Maps, &c. 2 vols. 8vo. cloth, $3 00. Philadelphia, 1848.

The Same. 2 vols. 8vo. calf, $7 00. London.

——— History of the French Revolution. Vol. I. $1 75. Philadelphia, 1848.

Bland. Experimental Essays on the Principles of Construction in Arches, Piers, Buttresses, &c. Cuts. 8vo. cloth, $2 25. Lond.

Bloomfield, (Robert.) Poems. Illustrated. 12mo. cloth, $2 00. London.

——— (Rev. G. B.) Sermons adapted to Country Congregations. 12mo. cloth, $1 50. London, 1846.

——— (Rev. S. T.) The Greek Testament, with English Notes, Critical, Philological, and Explanatory. Sixth edition. 2 vols. 8vo. cloth, $11 00. London, 1845.

The Same. American edition. 2 vols. 8vo. $5 50. Philadelphia.

Bloxom, (M. H.) Principles of Gothic Ecclesiastical Architecture, with an Explanation of Technical Terms, and a Glossary of Architectural Terms, collected from Building Contracts, and other Sources, prior to the Reformation. Illustrated with 228 wood-cuts, by O. Jewett. Eighth edition, enlarged. 12mo. cloth, $2 00. London, 1846.

Blunt, (C. F.) The Beauty of the Heavens; a Pictorial Display of the Astronomical Phenomena of the Universe, exhibited in 104 Scenes, accompanying and illustrating a Familiar Lecture on Astronomy, from Original Drawings, Paintings, &c. Small 4to. cloth, $6 00. London, 1847.

——— (Rev.) Works of; viz. Histories of our Saviour, of St. Paul and St. Peter; of Abraham, Jacob, and Elisha; and Sermons. 4 vols. 12mo. cloth, $4 00. Philadelphia.

Boase, (H. S.) Treatise on Primary Geology, being an Examination, both Practical and Theoretical, of the Older Formations. 8vo. cloth, $2 00. London, 1834.

Boccaccio's Decameron; or, Ten Days' Entertainment; in English, complete in one vol. 8vo. cloth, gilt, $2 00. London, 1845.

Bœckh. The Public Economy of Athens. Translated by G. C. Lewis. Second Edition, revised and improved. 8vo. cloth, $5 50. London.

Bogue's European Library; a Collection of the Best Works of the Best Authors; at the low price of 88c. per volume; post 8vo. cloth.

The following works have appeared in this series. Each work is complete in itself, and any volume may be purchased separately.

Berrington's Literary History of the Middle Ages. 1 vol.
Bouterwek's History of Spanish Literature. 1 vol.
Carrel and Fox, Hist. of Counter English Revolution. 1 v.

Dumas—Marguerite de Valois. 1 vol.
Duppa and De Quincey—Lives of Michael Angelo and Raffaell. 1 vol.
De Vigny—Cinq Mars. 1 vol.
Galt and Cavendish, Life of Cardinal Wolsey. 1 vol.
Guizot. History of Civilization in Europe. 3 vols.
" History of English Revolutions. 1 vol.
Luther. Table Talk. 1 vol.
Michelet. History of Roman Republics. 1 vol.
Mignet. History of French Revolution. 1 vol.
Michelet. Life of Luther. 1 vol.
Roscoe's Life of Lorenzo de Medici. 1 vol.
" " Leo Xth. 2 vols.
Thierry. History of the Norman Conquests. 1 vol.

Bohn, (H. G.) Catalogue of Books. Vol. I. 8vo. To be completed in 3 vols. London.

Bohn's Antiquarian Library.—$1 25.

Bede's Ecclesiastical History.
Brande's Popular Antiquities, 3 vols.
Chronicles of the Crusaders.
Early Travels in Palestine.
Ellis' Early English Metrical Romances.
Mallet's Northern Antiquities.
Six Old English Chronicles.
William of Malmesbury's Chronicles.
Roger of Wendover's Flowers of History.

—— **Classical Library.**

Herodotus. Translated by Cary. $1 25.
Thucydides. Translated by Dale. 87c.
Plato. Translated by Cary and others.

—— **Scientific Library;** $1 25.

Staunton's Chess-Players' Hand-book.
Lectures on Painting, by the Royal Academicians.
Humboldt's Cosmos. Translated by E. G. Otte. 2 vols.

—— **Standard Library,** in uniform 12mo. vols., with Portraits, Indexes, &c.. bound in cloth, 88c. per vol.

Beckman's History of Inventions. 2 vols.
Benvenuto Cellini, Memoirs of. 1 vol.
Coxe's House of Austria. 3 vols.
" Memoirs of Duke of Marlborough. 3 vols.
Goethe's Autobiography.
Hall, (Robert.) Miscellaneous Works, &c.
Hutchinson, (Col.) Memoirs of; by his Widow Lucy.
Lamartine's History of the Girondists. 3 vols.
Lanzis' History of Painting. 3 vols.
Machiavelli's History of Florence.
Menzel's History of Germany. 3 vols.
Milton's Prose Works. 3 vols.
Miller's Philosophy of History. 3 vols.
Ranke's History of the Popes. 3 vols.
Roscoe's Life of Lorenzo de Medici.
" " Leo Xth. 2 vols.
Schiller's Works; viz. Thirty Years' War and Revolt of Netherlands; Historical Works. 3 vols.
Schlegel's Lectures on Dramatic Literature.
" Lectures on Philosophy of Life.
" Lectures on Philosophy of History.
" Æsthetic and Miscellaneous Works.
Sheridan's Dramatic Works.
Sismondi's History of the Literature of Europe, 2 vols.
Wheatley on Common Prayer.

BOHN'S EXTRA VOLUME.

Grammont's Memoirs of the Court of Charles II.

Boileau-Despreaux. Œuvres Complètes, avec des Notes historiques et littéraires, par M. Amar, avec portrait. 4 vols. in 8vo. demi maroquin, $10 00.

—— Œuvres Complètes, avec des Notes historiques et littéraires, et des recherches sur sa vie, sa famille et ses ouvrages, par M. Berrial Saint Prix, avec portrait, fac-simile, etc. 4 vols. in 8vo. demi veau. $7 50. Paris, 1837.

Boisseau. Treatise on the Cholera Morbus. Translated by Bedford. 8vo. $1 00. New York, 1832.

Boitard. Nouveau Manuel complet des Instruments d'Agriculture et de Jardinage. Ornée de 121 planches, 8vo. broché, $3 25. Paris.

Bojesen, (E. F.) Hand-book of Grecian Antiquities; with plates, &c., by T. K. Arnold. 12mo. $1 00. New York, 1848.

Bolingbroke, Works of, with Life, &c. Portrait. 4 vols. 8vo. cloth, $8 00. Philadelphia, 1841.

Bolton, (James.) Natural History of British Song Birds; illustrated with figures the size of life, of the Birds, both Male and Female, in their most natural attitudes; their Nests and and Eggs, Food, Favorite Plants, Shrubs, Trees, &c.. &c., new edition, revised, and very considerably augmented. Two vols. in 1, 4to. containing eighty beautifully colored plates, half bound, mor. gilt backs and gilt edges, (pub. at £8. 8s.) $17 00. London, 1845.

Bonnycastle, (John.) An Introduction to Algebra. 12mo. $1 00. London, 1846.

The Same. 12mo. sheep, 62c. New York, 1845.

—— (Sir R. H.) Newfoundland in 1842; a Sequel to the Canadas in 1841. Maps. 2 vols. post 8vo. cloth, $2 50. London, 1842.

Book of Ballads. Edited by Bon Gaultier. Illustrated by Crowquill and Doyle. Second edition, enlarged. Square 16mo. cloth, gilt, $1 50. London, 1849.

Book of British Ballads. Edited S. C. Hall. Each page beautifully illustrated with the finest wood-cuts. 2 vols. small 4to. $11 00. London, 1842–43.

Booke of Christmas Carols. Illuminated Borders and Vignettes, in the Missal style. Square post 8vo. $4 00. London.

Book of Costume, from the Earliest Period to the Present Time, by a Lady of Rank. Illustrated with upwards of 200 beautiful engravings on wood, by Linton. 8vo. cloth, gilt edges, $3 25. London, 1847.

Book of Family Crests; comprising nearly every Family Bearing, properly blazoned and explained, accompanied by upwards of four thousand engravings, with surnames of the bearers, Dictionary of Mottoes, &c. 2 vols. 12mo. cloth, $6 00. Lond. 1847.

Book of Gems; or, the Poets and Artists of Great Britain; consisting of Selections from the most eminent Poets, accompanied by original Biographical Notices; embellished with upwards of 150 exquisitely beautiful line engravings, after Turner, Bonington, Landseer, M'Clise, Roberts, Mulready, Paris, &c., &c.; also, numerous engraved Autographs. 3 vols. 8vo. cloth, gilt, $13 50.

The Same. 3 vols. in mor. extra, gilt edges, $20 00. London.

Book of Pearls. Garland of Prose, Poetry, and Verse. Plates. 8vo. $5 00. New York, 1849.

Book of the Court; exhibiting the History, Duties, and Privileges of the several Ranks of the English Nobility and Gentry, particularly of the Great Officers of State, and Members of the Royal Household, &c.; with an Introductory Essay. 8vo. extra cloth, gilt, $2 25. London, 1844.

Book of the Months, and Circle of the Heavens. 28 beautiful illustrations by Harvey. 12mo. cloth, $2 00. London, 1842.

Book of the Poets; from Chaucer to Beattie; with Biographical Notices, &c. 45 beautiful illustrations. 8vo. boards, $2 25. London, 1842.

The Same. Morocco extra, $4 00. London, 1842.

Boone, (Rev. C. T.) Outlines of Man's True Interest. 12mo. cloth, $2 50. Pickering, London, 1844.

Booth, (Abraham.) Essay on the Kingdom of Christ; with Introductory Essay, by Dr. Steane. 12mo. cloth. 75c. London, 1846.

Bopp, (F.) Vergleichende Grammatik des Sanskrit, Zend, Griechisen, Lateinischen, Litthawischen, Altslawischen, Gothischen und Deutschen. Small 4to. half mor. $11 00. Berlin, 1842.

——— (Prof. F.) Comparative Grammar of the Sanscrit, Zend, Greek, Latin, Lithuanian, Gothic, German, and Sclavonic Languages. Translated by Lt. Eastwick. 2 vols. 8vo. cloth, $12 00. London, 1845.

Borrow, (Geo.) The Bible in Spain; or, the Journeys, Adventures, and Imprisonments of an Englishman in an Attempt to circulate the Scriptures in the Peninsula. New edition, 3 vols. post 8vo. cloth, $1 50. London, 1843.

Bossu. Travels through that part of North America called Louisiana. Translated from the French. 2 vols. 8vo. calf, $3 50. London, 1771.

Bossuet. Œuvres completes; portrait. 12 vols. grand in 8vo. demi veau, $30 00. Paris, 1836.

——— Discours sur l'histoire universelle, précédé d'une notice littéraire, par M. Tissot; illustrée par 12 gravures sur acier du plus beau style, d'apres Murrillo, Tony Johannot, H. Rigaud, etc. 2 magnifiques vols. grand in 8vo. demi maroquin. $15 00. Paris.

Boswell. Life of Johnson, with his Tour to the Hebrides, by the Right Hon. J. W. Croker. Second edition, with considerable additions. Also, two supplementary volumes of anecdotes. Illustrated with fifty plates. 10 vols. foolscap 8vo. cloth, $10 00. London, 1839.

——— The Same. 1 vol. royal 8vo. $4 50. London, 1848.

Bosworth, (J.) The Origin of the English, German, and Scandinavian Languages and Nations; with a Sketch of their Early Literature, and Short Chronological Specimens of Anglo-Saxon, Friesic, Flemish, Dutch, German, from the Mæso-Goth to the present time; Icelandic, Norwegian, and Swedish; tracing the Progress of their Languages, and their connection with modern English, &c. Map of European Languages prefixed. Royal 8vo. cloth, $6 00. London, 1848.

——— Compendious Anglo-Saxon and English Dictionary. New and greatly enlarged edition. 8vo. cloth, $3 00. London and New York, 1848.

Bouisson, (F.) De la Bile de ses Variétés Physiologiques de ses altérations morbides. 8vo. $1 25. Paris, 1843.

Bourne, (J.) Catechism of the Steam Engine, illustrative of the Scientific Principles upon which its operation depends, and the Practical Details of its Structure in its Applications to Mines, Mills, Steam navigation, and Railways. edition, 12mo. boards, $1 50. London, 1848.

The Same, (American edition.) 12mo. 75c. New York, 1849.

——— Railways in India. Second edition. With plates. 8vo. sewed, $1 50. London, 1848.

Boussingault, (J. B.) Rural Economy in its Relations with Chemistry, Physics, &c. 12mo. cloth, $1 50. New York, 1845.

Boutell, (C.) Monumental Brasses and Slabs; an Historical and Descriptive Notice of the Incised Monumental Memorials of the Middle Ages, with numerous Illustrations. 8vo. cloth, $3 00. London, 1848.

Bouterwek, (Frederick.) History of Spanish Literature. 12mo. cloth, 87c. (Bogue's European Library.) 1847.

Bowditch. The Mécanique Céleste of La Place. Translated, with Commentary, &c. 4 vols. imperial 4to. $40 00. Boston.

Bourne, (V.) Poemata, Latine partim reddita, partim scripta. In English and Latin. 12mo. cloth, $2 50. Pickering, London, 1836.

Boys, (T. S.) London as It Is; illustrated in a Series of Twenty-six Views, exhibiting the Principal streets of London and Characteristic Accessories, Public Buildings, &c.; with letter-press description in French and English. Royal Atlas, folio. Turkey mor. back. $10 00. London.

Bradley, (Rev. Charles.) Practical Sermons for every Sunday and principal Holydays in the Year. 8vo. cloth, $1 50. New York, 1844.

——— Sermons preached at Glasbury, and in St. James' Chapel, Clapham. 8vo. cloth, $1 25. New York, 1844.

Bradley. Practical Geometry, Linear Perspective, and Projection; with Descriptions of the Principal Instruments used in Geometrical Drawing; with eight plates and numerous wood-cuts. 8vo. cloth, lettered. $1 50. London, 1846.

Braithwaite, (W.) The Retrospect of Medicine. Published half yearly. $1 75 per volume. Vols. 1 to 18, published. London.

The Same. American reprint. 75c. per vol. New York.

Brand, (John.) Observations on the Popular Antiquities of Great Britain; chiefly illustrating the Origin of our Vulgar and Provincial Customs, Ceremonies, and Superstitions. Arranged, revised, and greatly enlarged, by Sir Henry Ellis. New edition, with further additions. 3 vols. foolscap 8vo. cloth, $3 75. (Bohn's Ant. Library.) London, 1849.

Brande, (W. T.) A Manual of Chemistry. Sixth edition, greatly enlarged. 2 vols. 8vo. cloth, $12 50 London, 1848.

——— Dictionary of Science, Literature and Art. One volume, large 8vo. sheep, $4 00. New York.

Brandon, (R. and J. A.) Parish Churches; being Perspective Views of English Ecclesiastical Structures; accompanied by Plans drawn to a uniform scale and Letter-press descriptions. Imperial 8vo. cloth, $8 75. London, 1848.

Brees, (S. C.) Present System of Surveying and Engineering Arithmetic. 8vo. cloth, $3 25. London.

——— Railway Practice; a Collection of Working Plans and Practical Details of Construction in the Public Works of the most celebrated Engineers. First, second, third, and fourth series. 4 vols. 4to. plates. London.

Either series can be purchased separately.

——— Glossary of Civil Engineering; comprising its Theory and Modern Practice. Engravings. 8vo. cloth, $3 25. London, 1844.

Brenton, (Sir L. C.) Septuagint Version of the Old Testament, according to the Vatican Text, translated into English; with the principal various Readings of the Alexandrian copy, and a Table of Comparative Chronology. 2 vols. 8vo. cloth, $6 50. London, 1844.

Breviarum Romanum, ex decreto S. S. Concilii Tridentini restitutum. S. Pii V. jussu editum, Clementis VIII. et Urbani VIII. auctoritate recognitum. 4 vols. 12mo. half mor. $10 00. 1843.

Brewster, (Sir D.) Treatise on Magnetism. Post 8vo. cloth, $1 75. Edinburgh, 1838.

——— Treatise on the Microscope. Post 8vo. cloth, $1 75. Edinburgh, 1837.

——— Treatise on Optics. 12mo. 75c. Philadelphia, 1848.

——— The Martyrs of Science. 12mo. cloth, $1 25. London, 1846.

Bridgens, (R.) Furniture, with Candelabra and Interior Decoration. 4to. half mor. $6 00.

The Same. Plates, colored, half mor. $11 00. London, 1838.

Bridges, in Theory, Practice, and Architecture. Theory of Bridges. General Principles of Construction; Theory of the Arch; Papers on Foundation, &c., &c. 2 vols. in text in 1, and 2 vols. of plates, royal 8vo. half mor. $27 00.

The Same; with the plates in folio. 2 vols. half mor. $33 50. London.

Bridges, (Rev. William.) The Works of; now first collected. Portrait. 5 vols. 8vo. cloth, $8 50. London, 1845.

British Association. Reports of the Annual Meetings of the British Association for the Advancement of Science.

British Butterflies and their Transformations; arranged and illustrated in a Series of Plates, by H. N. Humphreys; with Characters and Descriptions, by J. D. Westwood. Plates, beautifully colored, 4to. cloth, $12 00. London, 1841.

British Dramatists. Moxon's uniform edition, viz.—

Beaumont and Fletcher, 2 vols.
Ben Jonson, 1 vol.
Wycherley, Congreve, Vanbrugh, Farquhar, &c., 1 vol.
Massinger and Ford, 2 vols.
Shakspeare.

in cloth, $4 50 a volume; full calf extra, $6 50

The Same; with Chaucer and Spenser. 7 vols. uniformly bound in calf, antique, $45 00.

British Essays. Modern British Essayists: comprising Macaulay, Wilson, Scott, Carlyle, Talfourd and Stephens, Jeffreys, Sidney Smith, Alison. 9 vols. 8vo. $12 00. Philadelphia.

British Essayists; viz. Spectator, Tatler, Guardian, Rambler, Idler, Adventurer, Connoisseur, Looker In, Lounger, World, &c., with Index. Edited, with Notes, &c., by Chalmers. Portraits. 38 vols. foolscap 8vo. calf extra, $75 00.

The Same; calf, neat, $70 00. London, 1823.

——— viz. Spectator, Tatler, Guardian, Rambler, Idler, Adventurer, Connoisseur. Portraits. 3 vols. 8vo. cloth, $7 00. London, 1829.

The Same; half mor. $12 00.

British Florist; or, Lady's Journal of Horticulture; illustrated by a selection of the most elegant Flowering Plants now cultivated in the English Garden and Green-house. 6 vols. 8vo., with eighty-one beautifully colored plates of Flowers and Groups, green cloth, extra, (published at £4 10s.) $11 00. London, 1846.

British Grasses. Illustrations of British Grasses. Edited by Frederick Hanam; with Description. Illustrated with Dried Specimens of the Plants. Folio mor. $17 00; silk, $15 50. Bath.

British Husbandry, exhibiting the Farming Practice in various parts of the United Kingdom. 3 vols. 8vo. cloth, $4 50. London.

British Museum Marbles and Antiquities; containing 112 engravings of the most remarkable Statuary and Sculpture, Egyptian Antiquities, Vases, &c., with letter-press descriptions, by Sir Henry Ellis. 12mo. cloth, gilt, $1 00. London.

British Poets. Cabinet Edition of Select British Poets. 4 vols. 12mo. cloth, $3 50. London.

——— Edited by Walsh. 50 vols. 12mo. cloth, $25 00. Philadelphia.

——— (The.) From Chaucer to Cowper; including the Series, edited with Prefaces, Biographical and Critical, by Dr. Samuel Johnson, and the most approved translations; the additional Lives, by Alexander Chalmers. 21 vols. royal 8vo. half mor. top edge gilt—in fine condition. $100 00. London, 1810.

British Pulpit. A Collection of Sermons by the most eminent Divines. 6 vols. 8vo. cloth, $9 00. London, 1844.

Broderip, (W. J.) Zoological Recreations. Second edition, with additions. Post 8vo. cloth, $3 00. London, 1848.

Brooke, (J.) Narrative of Events in Borneo and Celebes, down to the occupation of Labuan; from the Journals of Brooke; together with a Narrative of the operations of H. M. S. Iris. By Capt. R. Mundy. Plates, maps, &c. 2 vols. 8vo. cloth, $9 50. Lond. 1848.

Brooks, (J. H.) City, Town, and Country Architecture; being a series of Designs for Street Elevations, Shop Fronts, Buildings for Railway Towers, and Embellishments for Gentlemen's Demenses, &c. Folio, cloth, $12 00. London, 1847.

——— (J. T.) Four Months among the Gold Finders in Alta California; being a Diary of an Expedition from San Francisco to the Gold Districts. Post 8vo. cloth, $2 50. London, 1849.

The Same. 12mo. 75c. New York.

Brougham, (Lord.) Opinions on Politics, Theology, Law, Science, Education, Literature, &c. 8vo. cloth, $2 00. London, 1837.

——— Political Philosophy; containing the Principles of Government; Monarchical Government; Aristocracy; Aristocratic Government; Democracy; Mixed Monarchy. 3 vols. 8vo. cloth, $6 00. London, 1844–46.

——— Speeches upon Questions relating to Public Rights, Duties, and Interests, with a Critical Dissertation upon the Eloquence of the Ancients. 4 vols. 8vo. cloth, $8 00. Edinburgh, 1838.

Broussais. De l'Irritation et de la Folie. 2 vols. 8vo. $4 00. Paris, 1839.

Brown. Book of British Butterflies, Moths, &c. Illustrated by 144 colored plates. 3 vols. 18mo. cloth, gilt, $2 25. London.

——— (William.) Antiquities of the Jews, carefully compiled from Authentic Sources, and their Customs illustrated from Modern Travels. Second edition. 2 vols. 8vo. cloth, $3 75. Edinburgh, 1826.

——— (Capt. Thomas.) Conchologist's Text-book. Engravings. 12mo. cloth, $1 50. Glasgow, 1839.

——— Illustrations of the Land and Fresh-Water Conchology of Great Britain and Ireland, with Figures, Descriptions, and Localities of all the Species; containing, on twenty-seven large plates, 330 figures of all the known British Species in their full size, accurately drawn from nature. Royal 8vo. extra cloth, $3 00.

——— with the plates beautifully colored, extra cloth, $4 50. London, 1845.

This is the only work which gives all the British species in their full size.

——— (Richard.) Rudiments of Drawing Cabinet and Upholstery Furniture. Illustrated by appropriate Figures aud Designs, proportioned upon Architectural Principles, on twenty-five plates; each accompanied with Explanatory Remarks. Second edition, improved. 4to. cloth, $6 00. London, 1835.

——— Domestic Architecture, containing a History of the Science and the Principles of designing Public Edifices, Private Dwelling Houses, &c. Sixty-three plates, containing Diagrams and Examples. 4to. cloth, $7 50. London.

——— (James.) History of the Highlands and the Highland Clans. Illustrated by a series of Portraits, Family Arms, &c. 4 vols. 8vo. cloth, $8 00 London, 1847.

Brown, Sacred Architecture, its Rise, Progress, and Present State; embracing the Babylonian, Indian, Egyptian, Greek, and Roman Temples; the Byzantine, Saxon, Lombard, Norman, and Italian Churches. Sixty-three plates, and a Glossary of Terms. 4to. cloth, $12 00. London.

Browne, (H.) Ordo Sæculorum. A Treatise on the Chronology of the Holy Scriptures. 8vo. cloth, $3 50. London, 1844.

——— (J. Ross.) Etchings of a Whaling Cruise, with Notes of a Sojourn on the Island of Zanzibar; to which is prefixed a History of the Whale Fishery. Illustrated. 8vo. cloth, $2 00. New York, 1846.

——— (D. J.) Trees of America, Native and Foreign, pictorially and botanically delineated, and scientifically described. 8vo. cloth, $3 00. New York, 1846.

——— (Sir Thomas.) Works, complete; including his Vulgar Errors, Religio Medici, Urn Burial, Christian Morals, Correspondence, Journals, and Tracts; many of them hitherto unpublished; the whole collected and edited, with a new Memoir, Notes, and Introduction, by Simon Wilkin, F.L.S., fine portrait, 4 vols. 8vo. extra cloth, (published at £2 8*s.*) $9 00. Pickering, London, 1836.

Browning, (Robert.) Poems. New edition. 2 vols. 12mo. cloth, $4 00. Lond. 1849.

Bryant, (W. C.) Poems. Illustrated with twenty elegant plates, from designs by Leutz. 8vo. cloth, $5 00; mor. $7 00. Philad.

——— Poems. 12mo. cloth, $1 25. Philad.

——— (E.) What I saw in California; being the Journal of a Tour in 1846–7. 12mo. cloth, $1 25. New York, 1848.

Brydges, (Sir Egerton.) Censura Literaria, containing Titles, Abstracts, and Opinions of Old English Books, with Original Disquisitions, Articles of Biography, and other Literary Antiquities. 10 vols. 8vo. $18 00. Lond. 1804.

——— Restituta; or, Titles, Extracts, and Characters of Old Books in English Literature revived. 4 vols. 8vo. $15 00. London, 1814.

——— Archaica, containing a Reprint of several old English Prize Tracts, with Prefaces, Critical and Biographical. 2 vols. 4to. boards, $15 00. London, 1815.

Buchanan, (W. M.) Technological Dictionary, explaining the Terms of the Arts, Sciences, Literature, Professions, and Trades. 12mo. cloth, $1 25. London, 1846.

——— (Robert.) Practical Essays on Mill Work, and other Machinery, with Examples of Modern Tools, &c., improved and edited by Thomas Tredgold, C. E., and now re-edited, with the improvements of the Present Age, by George Rennie, F.R.S., &c.; the text in one large vol. 8vo., and the plates, upwards of 70 in number, in an atlas folio, half morocco, $14 50. London, 1845.

——— Practical Examples of Modern Tools and other Machinery; being a Supplementary volume to Mr. Rennie's edition of Buchanan, "On Mill Work, and other Machinery," by Tredgold; text in royal 8vo., and 20 plates in atlas folio, $5 00. London.

Bucke, (Charles.) Beauties, Harmonies, and Sublimities of Nature; with Notes, Commentaries, and Illustrations; and Occasional Remarks on the Laws, Customs, Habits, and Manners of various Nations. 3 vols. 8vo. cloth, $4 50. London, 1837.

—— Ruins of Ancient Cities; with General and Particular Accounts of their Rise, Fall, and Present Condition. Plates. 2 vols. 18mo. cloth, $2 25. London.

Buckland. Geology and Mineralogy, considered in reference to Natural Theology. 2 vols. 8vo. $4 50. Philadelphia.

Budge, (J.) The Practical Miner's Guide; comprising a set of Trigonometrical Tables, adapted to all the purposes of Oblique, Diagonal, Vertical, Horizontal, and Traverse Drilling. 8vo. cloth, $3 50. London, 1845.

Budinger, (M.) The Way of Faith; or, the Abridged Bible; containing Selections from all Books of Holy Writ. Translated from the 5th German Edition, by D. Asher. Post 8vo. cloth, $2 00. London, 1848.

Buel, (J.) Farmer's Instructor; Essays, Practical Directions, &c., for the Management of the Farm and Garden. 2 vols. 18mo, $1 00. New York.

—— Farmer's Companion; or, Essays on the Principles and Practice of American Husbandry. 12mo, 75 cents. New York.

Buffier. Œuvres Philosoph., éd. F. Bouillier. 12mo. paper, $1 00. Paris.

Buffon. Histoire de ses Travaux et de ses Idées, par P. Flourens. 12mo. paper, $1 00. Paris, 1844.

—— Œuvres Choisies de, précédes d'une notice sur sa vie et ses ouvrages, par D. Saucie, et illustrée par M. Werner. Cr. 8vo, cloth, gilt edges, $2 00. Tours, 1847.

—— Œuvres Complétes, mises en ordre et précédes d'une notice historique, par M. A. Richard; suives de deux volumes sur le progrés des sciences physiques et naturelles, depuis la mort de Buffon; par M. le Baron Cuvier; avec 200 planches. 34 vols. grand in 8vo. demi veau, $50 00. Paris, 1827.

—— Natural History; corrected and enlarged by John Wright. Wood-cuts, &c. 4 vols. 12mo. morocco, $8 50. London, 1833.

Buist, (R.) The Rose Manual; containing accurate descriptions of all the finest varieties of Roses, with engravings. 2d edition, with additions. 12mo, 75 cents. Philadelphia.

—— Flower Garden Directory. 12mo, $1 25. Philadelphia.

Bulfinch, (S. G.) Lays of the Gospel. 12mo. cloth, 75c. Boston, 1845.

Bull, (J.) Hints to Mothers for the Management of Health during Pregnancy. 16mo. cloth, 50c. New York.

—— The Maternal Management of Children, in Health and Disease. 12mo. cloth, 75c. Philadelphia, 1849.

—— (George, D.D.) Works, collected and revised by the Rev. Edward Burton, D.D., to which is prefixed the Life of Bishop Bull, by Robert Nelson, Esq. 8 vols. 8vo cloth, $18 00. Oxford, 1847.

Bullinger. Sermons on the Sacraments. 8vo. cloth, $1 50. Cambridge, 1840.

Bulwer, (Edward Lytton.) Athens, its Rise and Fall; with Views of the Literature, Philosophy, and Social Life of the Athenian People. 2 vols. 8vo. cloth, $4 00. London.

—— Pilgrims of the Rhine; embellished with twenty-seven exquisite line engravings, after David, Roberts, M'Cliss, and Parris, by Goodall, Willmore, and other first-rate artists. 8vo. cloth, full gilt, $4 25. London.

The Same; bound in morocco, gilt edges, $6 50. London.

Bungenes, (L. F.) Trois Sermons sous Louis XV. 3 vols. 12mo. $2 75. Paris, 1849.

Bunsen, (C. C. J.) Egypt's Place in Universal History; an Historical Investigation in Five Books. Plates, &c. Vol. I., 8vo. cloth, $8 50. London, 1848.
To be completed in 3 volumes.

—— The Constitution of the Church of the Future; a Practical Explanation of the Correspondence with the Right Honorable W Gladstone, on the German Church, Episcopacy, and Jerusalem. Post 8vo. cloth, $2 75. London, 1848.

Bunyan, (John.) Pilgrim's Progress, most carefully collated with the edition containing the Author's best Additions and Corrections, and a Life of the Author, by the Rev. Robert Philip. Royal 8vo. illustrated with wood-cuts and steel engravings, cloth, $4 50. London, 1844.

The Same. A new edition, carefully collated with the first edition; with a Life of Bunyan, by Rev. Geo. B. Cheever, D.D.; illustrated with about 300 beautiful engravings on wood, 8vo.; uniform with the illustrated Milton, Cowper, &c., $3 00.

The Same. 1 vol. 12mo, 75 cents. Harpers, New York.

The Same. Royal 8vo. in full morocco, gilt, $8 00.

The Same. Various cheap editions.

Burder, (Samuel.) Oriental Customs; or, an Illustration of the Sacred Scriptures, by Application of the Customs and Manners of the Eastern Nations, etc. 8vo. cloth, $2 00. London, 1840.

—— (William.) Religious Ceremonies and Customs; or, the Forms of Worship practised in the Several Nations of the Known World Plates. 8vo. cloth, $3 00. London, 1841.

Burgess, (T. H.) Eruptions of the Face, Head, and Hands; with the latest Improvements in the Treatment of Diseases of the Skin. Illustrated with colored plates. 8vo. cloth, $4 00. London, 1849.

Burgoyne, (J.) On the Blasting and Quarrying of Stone for Building and other purposes. Numerous engravings. 12mo. 25c. (Weale's Rudimentary Series.) London, 1849

Burke, (Edmund.) Works; beautifully printed on fine paper, in 9 vols. 8vo. cloth, $15 00 neat half calf, $22 50; full calf, gilt, $28 00. Boston, 1839

Burke, (Edmund.) Works; with a Biographical and Critical Introduction, by Rogers. 2 vols. imperial 8vo., closely but handsomely printed, extra cloth, $7 50. London, 1841.

The Same. 3 vols. 8vo. sheep, $5 00. New York, 1847.

——— Correspondence of, between the years 1744 and 1797. Edited by Earl Fitzwilliam and Sir R. Burke. Portrait. 4 vols. 8vo. cloth, $14 00. London, 1844.

——— (J. and J. B.) Encyclopædia of Heraldry; or, General Armory of England, Scotland, and Ireland; comprising a Registry of all Armorial Bearings, Crests, and Mottoes, from the Earliest Period to the Present Time; including the late Grants by the College of Arms. With an Introduction to Heraldry, and a Dictionary of Terms. Embellished with an elaborate frontispiece, richly illuminated in gold and colors; also wood-cuts. Third edition, enlarged. Imperial 8vo. cloth, $7 00. London, 1844.

——— The Royal Families of England, Scotland, and Wales; with their Descendants, Sovereigns, and Subjects. Vol. I., royal 8vo. cloth, $6 50. London, 1848.

——— Genealogical and Heraldic Dictionary of the Peerage and Baronetage of the British Empire. Tenth edition. Royal 8vo. cloth, $9 00. London, 1848.

——— Genealogical and Heraldic Dictionary of the Landed Gentry of Great Britain and Ireland. 2 vols 8vo. cloth, $15 00. London.

——— Supplementary volume to the Same. Sewed, $4 00. London, 1848.

——— (J. B.) The Historic Lands of England. Illustrated. Imperial 8vo. cloth, $2 50. London, 1847.

——— (W.) The Mineral Springs of Western Virginia; with Remarks on their Use. 16mo. cloth, 50c. New York.

Burkitt, (Rev. Wm.) Expository Notes, with Practical Observations on the New Testament. 2 vols. 8vo. sheep, $4 00. Philad. 1844.

Burmeister, (Herman.) Manual of Entomology; translated from the last German edition, by W. E. Shuckard, with considerable additions. Illustrated by thirty-three engravings on steel; in which are represented above five hundred subjects, chiefly Generic Distinctions, Anatomical Sections, Organs, Eggs, Larvæ, &c. 8vo., $4 50. London, 1836.

Burnap, (G. W.) Expository Lectures on the Principal Passages of the Scriptures which relate to the Doctrine of the Trinity. 12mo. cloth, $1 00. Boston, 1845.

——— Lectures to Young Men. 12mo. cloth, $1 50. Baltimore.

——— Sphere and Duties of Woman. 12mo. cloth, $1 00. Baltimore.

Brunet. Manuel du Libraire, et de l'Amateur de Livres. 10 vols. 8vo, $22 50.

The Same. 10 vols. bound in 5; half calf, $27 50. Paris.

——— (Gustave.) Les Evangiles Apocryphes; traduits et annotes, d'apres l'edition de J. C. Thilo. 12mo. broché, $1 00 Paris, 1849.

Burnet, (Bishop.) The History of the Reformation of the Church of England; new edition, with illustrative Notes and Index. 2 vols. imperial 8vo. cloth, $7 00. Lond. 1841.

The Same.. 3 vols. 8vo. boards, $2 50. New York, 1843.

——— History of the Reformation of the Church of England. Illustrated with forty-seven portraits. 2 vols. royal 8vo. cloth, $12 50; calf extra, $17 00. London, 1841.

——— History of His Own Times; with Historical and Biographical Notes. Fifty-one portraits. 2 vols. royal 8vo. cloth, $12 00; calf extra, $16 50. London, 1840.

——— Exposition of the Thirty-nine Articles of the Church of England. 8vo. cloth, $2 00. London, 1841.

——— (Jacob.) Notes on the Early Settlement of the Northwestern Territory. 8vo. cloth, $2 50. New York, 1847.

——— (J.) Practical Essays on various branches of the Fine Arts; to which is added a Critical Inquiry into the Principles and Practice of the late Sir David Wilkie. Post 8vo. cloth, $1 75. London, 1848.

——— Illustrated Edition of Sir Joshua Reynolds on Painting. Twelve fine plates. 4to. cloth, $6 00. London, 1842.

The Same. Large paper, proof-impressions of plates. Royal 4to. cloth, $12 00.

——— Treatise on Painting, in Four Parts. Illustrated by examples from the Italian, Venetian, Flemish, and Dutch Schools. 4to. cloth, $25 00. London, 1846.

——— Rembrandt and his Works; comprising a Short Account of His Life, with a Critical Examination into his Principles and Practice of Design, Light, Shade and Color. Illustrated by Examples of nineteen Etchings. 4to. cloth, $9 00.

The Same. Large paper, proof-impressions, only Fifty printed. $30 00. London, 1848.

Burns, (R.) Statistics of the Cotton Trade. 8vo. cloth, $3 75. London, 1847.

——— (Robert.) Works, with Life, by Allan Cunningham. Plates. 8 vols. 12mo. cloth $9 00; calf extra, $16 00. London, 1835

——— Life and Works; edited by the Ettrick Shepherd and W. Motherwell. 5 vols. 12mo. cloth, $5 00. Glasgow, 1841.

——— Works, complete; with Life by Allan Cunningham, and Notes by Sir W. Scott, Campbell, Wordsworth, Lockhart, &c. Portrait. Royal 8vo. cloth, $4 00; morocco, $7 00. London, 1844.

The Same; with thirty-four beautiful steel engravings; cloth, $5 00; mor. gilt, $7 50; mor. extra gilt, $8 50. Lond. 1844.

——— Poetical Works, with Views and Notes, by Sir H. Nicolas. 3 vols. 12mo. cloth, $4 00; mor. extra, $8 00. Pickering, London, 1843.

——— Poetical Works. 12mo. cloth, $1 50; morocco, $3 25. New York, 1847.

Burr, (D. H.) American Atlas, comprising 13 maps of the United States, on rollers. $50 00. Boston.

Burr, (G. D.) Instructions in Practical Surveying. Second edition. Post 8vo. cloth, $2 25. London, 1847.

Burrough, (Jeremiah.) Exposition of the Prophecy of Hosea; with a Brief Notice of the Author. Imperial 8vo. cloth, $6 00. London, 1843.

Burrow, (E. J.) Elements of Conchology, according to the Linnæan System. Illustrated by twenty-eight plates, containing numerous figures, carefully colored. New edition, 8vo. cloth, $4 50. London, 1840.

The Same. Plates, plain, $2 50.

Burrows, (G.) On Disorders of the Cerebral Circulations, &c. Colored Plates. 8vo. cloth, $1 75. Philadelphia, 1848.

Burton. The Cromwellian Diary of Thomas Burton, during the Protectorate. Published from the Transcript of Edward Hyde, Earl of Clarendon; with Notes by J. T. Rutt. 4 vols. 8vo. cloth, $7 50. London.

——— (Edward.) Lectures upon the Ecclesiastical History of the First Three Centuries. 8vo. cloth, $4 00. Oxford, 1845.

Burton's Anatomy of Melancholy. 8vo. cloth, $2 50. New York.

Bury, (J. T.) Remains of Ecclesiastical Woodwork. Twenty-one plates, folio, $6 50. London, 1847.

Bush, (G.) Anastasis; or, Resurrection of the Body. 12mo. cloth, $1 00. New York.

——— Hebrew Grammar, with Chrestomathy. $1 25. New York.

——— Illustrations of the Scripture. 8vo. cloth, $2 00.

——— (Mrs. Forbes.) Memoirs of the Queens of France; from the second London edition. With portraits. 2 vols. 12mo. Muslin gilt, extra, $2 00. Philadelphia.

Bushe, (G.) On Malformation and Diseases of the Rectum. 8vo., with Atlas, $3 50.

Bushnell, (Horace.) God in Christ: Three Discourses, delivered at New Haven, Cambridge, and Andover; with a Preliminary Dissertation on Language. 12mo. cloth, $1 25. Hartford, 1849.

Bussey's History of Napoleon; illustrated by Horace Vernet. 2 vols. 8vo. cloth, $5 50; published at £2 2*s*. London, 1840.

Butler, (A.) The Lives of the Fathers, Martyrs, and of the principal Saints; compiled from Original Monuments, and other Authentic Records. 12 vols. 8vo. cloth, $18 00. London.

——— (Bp.) Analogy of Religion. 8vo. cloth, 75 cents. New York.

——— Sermons. 8vo. cloth, $1 00. New York.

——— Works. 8vo. cloth, $1 50. New York.

——— The Whole Works of; complete. 12mo. cloth, $1 25. London, 1839.

——— The Analogy of Religion, Natural and Revealed, to the Constitution and Course of Nature. With Life, Notes, and Index, by W. Fitzgerald. 8vo. cloth, $3 00. Lond. 1848.

Butler, (Charles.) Historical Memoirs of the English, Irish, and Scottish Catholics, since the Reformation. 4 vols. 8vo. cloth, $11 00. London, 1822.

——— (Fanny Kemble.) A Year of Consolation. 12mo. cloth, $1 00. New York.

——— (Samuel.) Poetical Works; Aldine edition. 2 vols. foolscap 8vo. cloth, $4 00; or, mor. extra, by Hayday, $6 00. Pickering, London, 1835.

——— Hudibras. Edited by the Rev. T. Nash, D.D., including such of Gray's Notes as are worthy of notice; a new edition, revised by J. Nicol; with 63 engraved portraits, &c., and 27 wood-cuts, with Notes, a Memoir, and Index. 2 vols. crown 8vo. cloth gilt, $6 00. London, 1847.

The Same. Bound in 1 vol. cloth, without the engraved portraits. $3 00. London, 1847.

The Same. With 40 Portraits. 2 vols. 12mo. cloth, 4 50. London, 1845.

The Same. With Notes, by Nash. Illustrated by Portraits. 16mo. cloth, $1 50; mor. extra, $3 00. New York.

Buxton, (Thomas Fowell.) Memoirs of. Edited by his son, Charles Buxton. 2d edition. 8vo. cloth, $4 50. London, 1849.

Bryan, (M.) Biographical and Critical Dictionary of Painters and Engravers; with the Ciphers, Monograms, and Marks used by each engraver. A new edition, with 1000 additional memoirs, and new plates of Ciphers and Monograms. By George Stanley. Royal 8vo. cloth, portrait, $11 00. London, 1849.

Byrne, (J. C.) Twelve Years' Wanderings in the British Colonies; from 1835–47. Maps, Plates, &c. 2 vols. 8vo. cloth, $4 00. London, 1848.

——— (O.) Encyclopædia of Machines, Mechanics, and Engineering; comprising working drawings, and description of every important machine in practical use in the United States, Great Britain, &c; designed for practical working men, and those intended for the engineering profession. In the course of publication in Nos. at 25 cents each; the work will extend to thirty numbers, and when completed will contain nearly 2,000 pages and 1,500 engravings. New York.

——— Practical, Short, and Direct Method of Calculating the Logarithm of any given number, and the number corresponding to any given logarithm. 12mo. 75 c. New York.

——— Doctrine of Proportion clearly developed; or the Fifth Book of Euclid Simplified. 8vo. $1 00.

——— New and Improved System of Logarithms, with a Table. Folio, half mor. $6 50. London, 1838.

——— The First Six Books of the Elements of Euclid; in which colored Diagrams and Symbols are used instead of Letters. Small 4to. $6 25. Pickering, London, 1848.

Byron's (Lord) Works, with his Letters and Journals, and his Life, by Thomas Moore. 17 vols. 12mo., plates, cloth, $17 00; half mor. gilt, $26 00; calf extra gilt, $32 00. Murray, Lond. 1847.

Byron, (Lord.) Complete Poetical Works, with all the Notes; Portrait, and plate of Newstead Abbey. Royal 8vo. cloth, $4 50; calf, $6 50; mor. extra gilt, $8 00. London, 1846.

The Same. Didot's beautifully printed edition, 7 vols. 8vo. paper, $12 00; half calf, gilt, $18 00. Baudry, Paris, 1835.

——— Life, Letters, and Journals, edited by Thomas Moore, with Notes; complete, royal 8vo., with Portraits, vignettes. Cloth, $4 50; calf, $6 50; mor. extra gilt, $8 00. London, 1847.

The Same. Cloth gilt, $5 00; mor. extra, $7 00. Philadelphia.

——— Tales and Poems; a new and splendidly illustrated edition: cloth gilt, $5 00; mor. extra, $7 00. Philadelphia, 1849.

——— Poems. 1 vol. 12mo. mor. $2 50. Lond.

——— Complete Poetical Works; illustrated. 1 vol. royal 8vo. cloth, $4 50; mor. $6 50. New York.

——— Beauties (Gallery of;) a Series of Portraits of the Heroines of Lord Byron's Poems; from Drawings by the most eminent Artists; Imp. 8vo. mor. extra, $8 50. London.

Bythner, (V.) The Lyre of David: or, Analysis of the Psalms, wherein all the Hebrew words are given, also in English, each accented, translated, analyzed, &c. 8vo. cloth, $7 00. London, 1847.

Cabanis. Rapports du Physique et du Moral de l'homme. 12mo. paper, $1 00. Paris, 1843.

Cabinet Portrait Gallery of British Worthies; illustrated with Portraits on steel. 6 vols. 18mo cloth gilt, $5 00. Lond. 1845.

——— Edition of Classic Tales; comprising the most celebrated works of Imagination. 12mo. cloth, $6 00. London, 1847.

Cairns, (William.) Treatise on Moral Freedom; containing Inquiries into the Operations of the Intellectual Principles in connection generally with Moral Agency and Responsibility. 8vo. cloth, $3 50. London, 1844.

Calaynos, a Tragedy. By G. H. Boker. 12mo. 75 cents. Philadelphia, 1848.

Calcott, (Dr.) Grammar of Music; comprising a full explanation of all the Notes and Marks; and Treatises on the Sciences of Melody, Harmony, and Rhythm; illustrated with numerous examples. 12mo. cloth, 75 cents. London, 1849.

Callcott, (Lady.) Scripture Herbal. 120 engravings. Square 8vo. cloth, $7 50. Lond.

——— (Mrs.) Essays towards the History of Painting. Post 8vo. cloth, $1 50. London, 1836.

Calmet. Dictionary of the Bible. Ninth edition, greatly enlarged and improved. By Charles Taylor. 202 plates, 5 vols. 4to. cloth, $26 50. London, 1847.

The Same, abridged. New edition. Royal 8vo. cloth, $4 50. London, 1847.

——— Dictionary of the Bible; revised, with large additions. By E. Robinson, D.D. Royal 8vo. cloth, $4 00. Boston.

Calvert, (G. H.) Scenes and Thoughts in Europe. 12mo. cloth, 50 cents. New York.

Calvin Translation Society's Publications. Four volumes are published annually; subscription to which is $7 50.

BOOKS ALREADY PUBLISHED.

Commentary on the Romans. 8vo. cloth.

" " Acts of the Apostles. 2 vols. 8vo. cloth.

Institutes of the Christian Religion. 3 vols. 8vo. cloth.

The Harmony of the Evangelists. 3 vols. 8vo. cloth.

Tracts on the Reformation. Vol. 1, 8vo.

Commentary on the Book of Psalms. Vols. 1 and 2, 8vo. cloth.

Commentary on the Twelve Minor Prophets. Vols. 1 and 2, 8vo. cloth.

Commentary on the Gospel of St. John. Vols. 1 and 2, 8vo. cloth.

Calvin, (J.) Commentary on the Psalms of David. 3 vols. 8vo. cloth, $5 75. Oxford, 1840.

——— Institutes of the Christian Religion. Third Edition. 2 vols. 8vo. cloth, $3 50. London, 1844.

——— Life and Times, by Henry. Translated by Stebbing. 2 vols. 8vo. cloth, $7 50. London.

Cambridge Classical Examination Papers. 2 vols. 8vo. half cloth, $6 50. Cantab. 1830–31.

——— Prize Poems: being a collection that have obtained the Chancellor's gold medal. 12mo. cloth, $1 25. London, 1847.

——— Mathematics, by Farrar. 2 vols. 8vo. cloth, $4 50. New York.

Camden Society, the Publications of, $7 50 per annum.

Complete sets imported to order.

Campbell, (Thomas.) Life and Letters. By W. Beattie. 3 vols. 8vo. cloth, $13 50.

——— Lives of the Poets; with an Essay on Poetry. Post 8vo. cloth, $2 50. London, 1848.

——— Poetical Works. 12mo. cloth, $1 50; mor. extra, $3 00. New York.

——— Poems. 32mo. 50 cents.

——— The Poetical Works; illustrated by twenty vignettes on steel from designs by Turner, and thirty-seven wood-cuts from designs by Harvey. 8vo. cloth, $6 00; mor. extra, by Hayday, $9 00. London, 1848.

The Same. 12mo. wood-cuts, cloth, $2 50; mor extra, $4 50. London.

——— Specimens of the British Poets; with Biographical and Critical Notices, and an Essay on English Poetry, fine portrait, &c. Royal 8vo. cloth, $5 00. London, 1841.

——— Life of Petrarch. 2 vols. 8vo. cloth, portraits of Petrarch and Laura, $2 50. London, 1841.

(Published at £1 4*s*.)

——— Frederick the Great, his Court and Times. 2 vols. 8vo. cloth, $2 25. London, 1844.

Campbell, (Thomas.) Life of Mrs. Siddons. 12mo. cloth, 75 cents.

——— (John Lord.) Lives of the Lord Chancellors and Keepers of the Great Seal of England. 7 vols. 8vo. cloth, $12 00. Philadelphia, 1847.

The Same. 7 vols. 8vo. cloth, $21 00. London.

——— (J.) Lives of the British Admirals. Many engravings, foolscap 8vo. cloth, $2 00. London.

——— (D.) A Practical Text-Book of Inorganic Chemistry; with Qualitative and Quantitative Analysis. 12mo. cloth, $1 75. London, 1849.

——— (George, D.D.) Works of, complete. 6 vols. 8vo. cloth, $7 50. London.

——— Four Gospels, translated from the Greek, with Preliminary Dissertation, and Notices, Critical and Explanatory. 2 vols. 8vo. cloth, $4 75. London, 1839.

The Same. 2 vols. 8vo. $4 00. New York.

——— Dissertation on the Miracles of our Saviour. 8vo. cloth, $1 50. Lond. 1839.

——— Lectures on Ecclesiastical History. 8vo. cloth, $1 75. London.

The Same. 8vo. $1 25. Philad. 1807.

——— Philosophy of Rhetoric. 12mo. cloth, $1 25. New York.

——— (W. W.) Annals of Tryon County; or, the Border Warfare of New York. 12mo. cloth, $1 25. New York.

——— Life and Writings of De Witt Clinton. 8vo cloth, $1 50. New York, 1849.

——— Dictionary of Military Science; with an Address to Gentlemen entering the Army. 8vo. $1 50. London.

Camus, (M.) On the Teeth of Wheels. 8vo. $3 75. London.

Candolle, (A. P. de.) Icones Selectæ Plantarum, quas in systemate universali descripsit ex archetypis speciminibus a P. G. F. Turpin; delineatæ et editæ B. Delessert; avec 500 planches. 5 vols. 4to. $44 00. Paris, 1820–46.

——— Prodromus Systematis Naturalis Regni Vegetabilis; sive enumeratio contracta ordinum, generum specierumque plantarum hucusque cognitarum. Tomes 1 to 12, $40 00. Paris.

Canning, (George.) Select Speeehes. Edited by Robert Walsh. 8vo. cloth, $1 75. Philadelphia.

Canons and Decrees of the Sacred and Œcumenical Council of Trent. Translated by Rev. J. Waterworth; with Essays on the External and Internal History of the Council. 8vo. cloth, $3 50. London, 1848.

Canons of Discipline and Definitions of Faith of the Six Œcumenical Councils; with the remaining Canons of the Code of the Universal Church; translated, with Notes, &c., by Rev. W. Hammond. 8vo. cloth, $2 00. Oxford, 1843.

Capefigue, (M.) Histoire de Philippe Auguste. 2 vols. 12mo, $2 00. Paris.

Capefigue, (M.) La Reforme et la Ligue. 12mo. $1 00. Paris.

——— La Ligue et Henri IV. 12mo. $1 00. Paris.

——— Henri IV. 12mo, $1 00. Paris.

——— Richelieu. 12mo, $1 00. Paris.

——— Magazine et la Fronde. 12mo, $1 00. Paris.

——— Louis XIV. 12mo, $1 00. Paris.

——— Louis XIV. Son Gouvernement et ses Relations Politiques avec l'Europe. 2 vols. 12mo. $2 00. Paris.

——— Histoire de la Restauration. 4 vols. 12mo. $4 00. Paris.

——— La Société et les Gouvernements de l'Europe. Vol I. 8vo. paper, $1 25. Paris, 1849.

Cardwell, (Edward.) Lectures on the Coinage of the Greeks and Romans. 8vo. cloth, $1 50. Oxford, 1832.

——— Documentary Annals of the Reformed Church of England; being a Collection of Injunctions, Declarations, Orders, Articles of Inquiry, &c., from 1546 to 1716; with Notes, historical and explanatory. 2 vols. 8vo. cloth, $5 50. Oxford, 1844.

——— Synodalia; a Collection of Articles of Religion, Canons, and Proceedings of Convocations, from 1547 to 1717; with notes. 2 vols. 8vo. cloth, $5 50. Oxford, 1842.

——— History of Conferences, and other Proceedings connected with the Revision of the Book of Common Prayer, from 1558 to 1696. 8vo. cloth, $2 50. Oxford, 1841.

——— Two Books of Common Prayer, set forth by Authority of Parliament, in the Reign of Edward VI., compared with each other. 8vo. cloth, $2 50. Oxford, 1841.

Carey, (H. C.) The Past, the Present, and the Future. 8vo. cloth, $2 00. Philadelphia, 1847.

Carleton, (Robert.) Something for Everybody; gleaned from the Old Purchase, from Fields often Reaped. 12mo. cloth, 50 cents. New York, 1846.

——— (W.) Valentine McClutchy, the Irish Agent. Numerous plates, by Phiz. 8vo. cloth, $2 00. Dublin, 1847.

——— The Black Prophet; a Tale of Irish Famine. Six illustrations. 8vo fancy boards, $1 50. London, 1847.

Carlisle, (A.) The Means of Preserving Health and Prolonging Life, applied to Hereditary Diseases, the Affections of Children, and the Disorders of Old Age. 8vo. cloth, $2 00. London, 1841.

Carlyle, (Thos.) Past and Present; Chartism. 12mo. cloth, $1 00. New York.

——— Heroes and Hero Worship; Sartor Resartus. 12mo. cloth, $1 25. New York.

——— The French Revolution; a History. 2 vols. 12mo. cloth, $2 00. New York.

——— The Life, Letters, and Speeches of Oliver Cromwell. 2 vols. 12mo. cloth, $2 00. Fine edition, 2 vols. 8vo. with Portrait, $2 50. New York.

Carlyle, (T.) The Life of Schiller. 12mo. cloth, 75c. New York.

Uniformly bound in half calf, 7 vols., $12 00; calf extra $15 00.

——— Specimens of German Romance. 2 vols. 12mo. cloth, $2 50. Boston, 1848.

——— Miscellanies. 8vo. cloth, $2 00. Philadelphia.

——— (John A.) Dante's Divine Comedy, the Inferno; a literal prose translation, with the text of the original, collated from the best editions, and Explanatory Notes. Portrait. Post 8vo. cloth, $3 25. London, 1849.

The Same. 12mo. cloth, $1 00. N. York, 1849.

Carpenter, (W. B.) Elements of Human Physiology. Plates. 8vo. sheep, $3 25. Philadelphia, 1848.

——— Principles of Human Physiology. 8vo. sheep, $3 75. Philadelphia.

——— Vegetable Physiology. 12mo. cloth, 75 cents. Philadelphia.

——— Zoology: being a Systematic Account of the General Structure, Habits, Instincts, and Uses of the Principal Families of the Animal Kingdom, as well as of the chief forms of Fossil Remains. 2 vols. post 8vo. cloth, $6 00. London, 1845.

——— Mechanical Philosophy, Horology, and Astronomy. 8vo. cloth, $2 00.

Carpentery and Joinery; being a Comprehensive Guide-Book for—with Elementary Rules for the Drawing of Architecture in Perspective, and by Geometrical Rule; also, treating of Roofs, Trussed Girders, Floors, Domes, Staircases, and Hand-Rails, Shop Fronts, Verandas, Window-frames, Shutters, &c., &c.; and Public and Domestic Buildings, with Plans, Elevations, Sections, &c., &c. Illustrated with seventy-four engravings. By P. Nicholson. 2 vols. 4to. cloth, $15 00.

Carpenter's (The) New Guide-Book; edited by Johnson and Nicholson. 4to. sheep, $5 00. Philadelphia.

Carr, (Rev. J.) Synopsis of Practical Philosophy, designed as a Manual for Architects, Surveyors, &c. 18mo. $1 50. London.

——— First Three Sections of Newton's Principia; with copious Notes and Illustrations. 8vo. $1 50.

Carrel, (A.) History of the Counter-Revolution in England for the Re-establishment of Popery under Charles II. and James II. 12mo. cloth, $1 00. London, 1846.

Carriere, (Ed.) Le Climat de l'Italie, sous le Rapport Hygienique et Medical. 8vo. broché, $2 00. Paris, 1849.

Carson, (J.) Illustrations of Medical Botany; consisting of colored figures of the Plants affording the important articles of the Materia Medica. 100 plates, beautifully colored. 2 vols. 4to. cloth, $25 00. Philadelphia, 1848.

Carter, (John.) Ancient Sculpture and Painting in England; Notes by Sir S. R. Meyrick, Dawson, Turner, and John Britton. 120 plates, many highly illuminated. 2 vols. in one, royal folio, half mor., $48 00. London, 1838.

Carter, (John.) Ancient Architecture of England; including the Orders during the British, Roman, Saxon, and Norman Eras; also under the Reigns of Henry III. and Edward III. Illustrated by 103 large engravings; comprising upwards of 2000 specimens, shown in plan, elevation, section, and detail. By J. Britton. Royal folio, half mor. $25 00. London, 1837.

——— Specimens of Gothic Architecture and Ancient Buildings in England. 120 Views, etched by himself. 4 vols. square 12mo. half mor., $6 00. London, 1824.

——— (O. B.) Stained or Painted Glass of Winchester Cathedral. Twenty-eight plates, highly wrought in colors. 4to. half mor., $11 00. London.

Cary, (H. J.) Translation of Dante. New edition, foolscap 8vo. cloth, $2 50. London, 1847.

——— (Rev. H.) Memoir of, with his Literary Journal and Letters. By his Son, Rev. H. Cary. Portrait. 2 vols. post 8vo. cloth, $2 25. London, 1847.

——— (H.) Memorials of the Great Civil War in England, from 1646 to 1652. 2 vols. 8vo. cloth, $3 50. London, 1842.

——— Lives of the English Poets, from Johnson to Kirke White. 12mo. cloth, $1 00. London, 1846.

——— Early French Poets. 12mo. cloth, $1 00. London, 1846.

——— Lexicon to Herodotus, Greek and English. Adapted to the text of Gaisford and Baehr. 8vo. cloth, $2 25. Oxford, 1843.

——— Works of Plato; a new and literal version; chiefly from the text of Stalebaum. Vol. I. foolscap 8vo. cloth, $1 25. (Bohn's Class. Lib.) London, 1849.

——— Testimonies of the Fathers of the First Four Centuries, to the Constitution and Doctrines of the Church of England, as set forth in the XXXIX Articles. 8vo. cloth, $2 25. Oxford, 1835.

Castle, (H. J.) Engineering Field Notes on Parish and Railway Surveying and Levelling; with Plans, Sections, &c., &c. Plates. 8vo. cloth, $3 75. London, 1847.

Castillo, (Diaz Del.) Memoirs, written by by Himself. Containing a true and full Account of the Discovery and Conquest of Mexico and New Spain. Translated by J. I. Lockhart. 2 vols. 8vo. cloth, $3 50. Lond., 1844.

Castlereagh. Memoirs and Correspondence of Viscount Castlereagh, second Marquis of Londonderry. Edited by his brother, Charles Vane. Vols. I. to IV. (Completing the Irish Rebellion.) 8vo. cloth, $17 00. London, 1848–49.

Cathedral; (The) or, the Catholic and Apostolic Church in England. Illustrated with engravings. 12mo. cloth, $2 25. Oxford, 1841.

Cathedral and Architectural Antiquities. Britton's (J.) Historical and Descriptive Account of the Cathedrals of Great Britain; i. e. Canterbury, York, Salisbury, Norwich, Oxford, Winchester, Litchfield, Hereford, Wells, Exeter, Worcester, Peterborough, Gloucester, and Bristol, 5 vols.; and The Architectural Antiquities of Great Britain, 5 vols. The whole represented and illustrated in a series of Views, Elevations, Plans, Sections, and Details of the Cathedrals, and other ancient English edifices; together in 10 volumes, 4to. handsomely bound in half green mor. gilt leaves and backs, $80 00. London, 1835–6.

Catherwood, (Frederick.) Monuments of Central America, Chiapas, and Yucatan. 25 Plates, elegantly colored, mounted on Bristol boards, in portfolio. London.

——— (A.) Treatise on Diseases of the Air Passages. 8vo. cloth, $2 25.

Catlin, (George.) Illustrations of the Manners, Customs, and Conditions of the North American Indians. Illustrated with 360 engravings. 2 vols. imp. 8vo. cloth, $7 25. London, 1846.

——— Indian Portfolio; a Series of twenty-five plates; representing Hunting Scenes, &c., &c., of the North American Indians. Printed in lithotint. Folio, half mor. $20 00.

The Same, colored, mounted on Bristol board in portfolio, $35 00. London.

——— Notes of Eight Years' Travels and Residence in Europe, with his North American Indian Collection. 2 vols. 8vo. cloth, with numerous illustrations. $4 00. London, 1848.

Catlow, (A.) Conchologist's Nomenclator. 8vo. cloth, $6 50. London.

——— Popular Field Botany; containing a Familiar Description of the Plants most common to the British Isles. Illustrated with Twenty plates. Royal 16mo. cloth, $2 25. London, 1848.

The Same. Plates beautifully colored, $3 25. London, 1848.

——— Popular British Entomology. Square 12mo. cloth, colored engravings, $3 00. London, 1848.

Cattermole, (George.) Evenings at Haddon Hall. Twenty-four exquisite engravings on steel, from designs by Himself; the letterpress by the Baroness de Carabella. Royal 8vo. cloth, gilt edges, $4 50. London, 1848.

——— (Rev. R.) Literature of the Church of England. 2 vols. 8vo. cloth, $2 75. London, 1844.

——— Sacred Poetry of the Seventeenth Century. 2 vols. 12mo. cloth, portraits, $3 00. London, 1836.

Caulfield. Portraits, Memoirs, and Characters of Remarkable Persons; from the Reign of Edward III. to the Revolution. 109 curious plates. 3 vols. royal 8vo. cloth, $8 50. London, 1813.

Caussidiere, Memoires de, Ex-préfet de Police, et Representant du Peuple. 2 vols 8vo, $3 50. Paris, 1849.

Cavaignac, (Gen.) Expedition dans le Sahara Algérien, en Avril et Mai, 1847; Relation du Voyage, Exploration Scientifique, Souvenirs, Impressions, &c. Par Felix Jacquot. Illustrée; 1 vol. grand, in 8vo. broché, $4 00. Paris, 1849.

Cave, (W., D.D.) Lives of the Apostles and Evangelists; with an Introductory Discourse concerning the Patriarchal, Mosaical, and Evangelical Dispensations. New edition, by Rev. H. Cary. 8vo. cloth $1 75. Oxford, 1840.

——— Lives of the most eminent Fathers of the Church. A new edition, by Rev. H. Cary. 3 vols. 8vo. cloth, $5 00. London, 1840.

——— (H.) Primitive Christianity; or, the Religion of the Ancient Christians. Edited by Rev. H. Cary. 8vo. cloth, $1 75. Oxford, 1840.

Cecil, (Rev. R.) Works. 3 vols. 12mo. cloth, $2 00. New York.

——— Original Thoughts on Various Passages of Scripture. 12mo. cloth, $1 00. New York, 1849.

Cecil and his Dog; or, the Reward of Virtue; illustrated with wood-cuts. 12mo. cloth gilt, $1 00. New York, 1849.

Cellarius' Drawing-Room Dances. Square 18mo. cloth, $1 00. London.

——— Fashionable Dancing. Square 18mo. cloth, $2 00. London.

Cellini, (Benvenuto,) Memoirs of, translated by T. Roscoe. 12mo. cloth, 87½ cents. London.

Cennini, (C.) Treatise on Painting; translated by Mrs. Merrifield. Royal 8vo. cloth, $3 75 London.

Century of Orchidaceous Plants; consisting of a Hundred of those most worthy of Cultivation. Descriptions by Sir W. J. Hooker; with an Introduction on their culture and general management, by J. C. Lyons. Plates, beautifully colored. 4to. half mor., $32 50. London, 1849.

Cervantes. Don Quixotte de la Mancha; translated. Eighteen engravings on steel. 12mo. cloth, $1 50; mor. extra, $3 00. London.

——— Don Quixotte. Tony Johannot's beautifully illustrated edition. 3 vols. royal 8vo. cloth, $9 00. London.

——— Don Quixotte de la Mancha. Translated by Jarvis; and illustrated by Tony Johannot. 2 vols. royal 8vo. cloth, $7 00; calf, $12 00. London, 1847.

The Same. 2 vols. crown 8vo. cloth, $3 00. Philadelphia.

——— (M. de.) El Buscapie. Crown 8vo. cloth, $1 50. London, 1849.

Chadwick, (John.) Essay on the Use of Alcoholic Liquors in Health and Disease. 12mo. cloth, 75c. London, 1849.

Chalmers, (A.) Works of the English Poets, from Chaucer to Cowper; including the series edited with prefaces, biographical and critical, by Dr. S. Johnson, and the most approved translations. 21 vols. royal 8vo. half green mor. gilt tops, $90 00. [Very scarce.] London, 1810.

——— (Dr. T.) Works. 25 volumes. 12mo. cloth, $25 00. London.

——— Posthumous Works. Edited by the Rev. W. W. Hanna. 6 vols. 12mo. cloth, $6 00. New York, 1848.

Chalmers, (Dr. T.) Miscellanies; embracing Reviews, Essays, and Addresses. 8vo. cloth, $1 50. New York, 1847.

Chambers, (Robert.) Miscellany of Tracts. 20 vols. bound in 10. 12mo. cloth, $7 50; half calf, $10 00. Edinburgh.

——— The Select Writings of. 7 vols. 12mo. cloth, $8 00. Edinburgh.

——— Ancient Sea Margins as Memorials of Changes in the relative Level of Sea and Land. 8vo. cloth, $2 75. Edinburgh, 1848.

——— Cyclopædia of English Literature. 2 vols. 8vo. cloth, $4 00; half calf, $5 00. Edinburgh.

——— Information for the People. 2 vols. 8vo. cloth, $4 50; half calf, $5 50. Edinburgh.

——— Atlas for the People. Thirty-four colored plates. 4to. cloth, $3 50. Edinburgh, 1848.

——— (W. and R.) Treasury of Knowledge. 12mo. half bound, 75 cents. New York, 1849.

——— (Sir W.) Treatise on the Decorative Part of Civil Architecture. Edited, with notes, by J. P. Papworth. Many plates. $20 00.

Champlin, (J. T.) Select Popular Orations of Demosthenes. 12mo. cloth, $1 00. Boston, 1848.

——— Oration of Demosthenes on the Crown, with Notes. 12mo. cloth, $1 00 Boston, 1847.

Channing, (W. E.) Works of. 6 vols. 12mo. cloth, $3 00. Boston.

——— Memoirs of, with Extracts from his Correspondence and Manuscripts. 3 vols. 12mo. cloth, $3 00. Boston, 1848.

——— (Dr. W.) Treatise on Etherization in Childbirth. Illustrated by 581 cases. Royal 8vo. cloth, $2 00. Boston, 1848.

Chants et Chansons Populaires de la France. Choix de chants guerriers, chansons historiques et burlesques, politiques et satiriques, &c., &c. Engraved on steel. 3 vols. 4to. $14 00.

Chapman, (J. R.) Instruction to Young Marksmen on the Improved American Rifle. Plates. 12mo. cloth, $1 25. New York.

Chapone, (Mrs.) Letters on the Improvement of the Mind. 18mo. mor. gilt, $1 25. (Sharpe's beautiful edition, with plates by Westall.) London, 1829.

Charles I., Court and Times of; illustrated by Authentic and Confidential Letters from various Public and Private Collections; with an Introduction and Notes. By the author of "Memoirs of Sophia Dorothea." 2 vols. 8vo. cloth, $8 50. London, 1848.

Charlotte Elizabeth. Chapters on Flowers. 12mo. cloth, $1 50. London, 1841.

——— Works. 2 vols. 8vo. cloth, $5 00. New York.

Charlton, (Foster.) Practical Method of Setting out a Circular Railway Curve. 8vo. 37 cents. London.

Charm, (The.) A Series of graceful and elegantly colored Groups, designed expressly for this work. Folio, cloth gilt, $5 00. Philadelphia, 1848.

Charnock, (Rev. Stephen.) Discourses upon the Existence and Attributes of God. 8vo. cloth, $2 50. London, 1845

——— Works, by Parsons. 9 vols. 8vo. cloth, $30 00

——— (James.) History of Marine Architecture, illustrative of the Naval Architecture of all Nations, from the Earliest Period. Numerous fine plates. 3 vols. 4to. $18 00. London

Chateaubriand, (Le Viscomte.) Les Martyrs. 12mo. broché, $1 00; half mor. marble edges, $1 75. Paris, 1846.

——— Itinéraire de Paris à Jérusalem. 2 vols. 12mo. broché, $1 75.

——— Le Génie du Christianisme. 2 vols. 12mo. broche, $1 75. Paris, 1847.

——— Les Natchez. 12mo. 87 cts.; half mor. $1 75. Paris, 1848.

——— Œuvres complètes; magnifique edition, illustrée, avec plus de 90 gravures. 36 vols grand in 8vo. demi-maroquin, $75 00. Paris, 1827.

——— Atala, René, Les Abencerages, suivis du Voyage en Amérique. 12mo. broché, 87 cts. half mor. marble edges, $1 75. Paris, 1847.

——— The Congress of Verona; comprising a portion of Memoirs of His Own Times. 2 vols. 8vo. cloth, $3 00. London.

——— Mémoires d'outre Tombe. Vols. 1, 2, 3, $2 00 each. [To be completed in 10 vols.] Paris, 1849.

——— Memoirs of; written by Himself. Parts 1, 2, 3, 75 cents each. [To be completed in 10 parts.] London, 1849.

——— Sketches of English Literature; with Considerations on the Spirit of the Times. Men, and Revolutions. 2 vols. 8vo. cloth, $2 50. London, 1837.

Chateauneuf, (A. de) Architectura Domestica; being a series of very tasty Examples of Interiors and Exteriors of Residences of the Gentry, erected in Hamburg, and its neighborhood; principally in the Italian style. Nineteen fine engravings. 4to. cloth, $6 00. London.

Chatham Papers; being the Correspondence of William Pitt, Earl of Chatham. Edited by the Executors of his son, John, Earl of Chatham; and published from the Original Manuscripts in their possession. 4 vols. 8vo. extra cloth, $6 50. London, 1840.

——— (Earl.) The Speeches of; with Memoir, &c. Royal 8vo. cloth, $2 00. London, 1848.

Chatterton, (Thos.) Poetical Works; with Notices of his Life; History of the Rowley Controversy, a selection of his Letters, and Notes, Critical and Explanatory. 2 vols. 12mo. cloth, $3 00. Cambridge, 1842

Chatto, (W. A.) Gems of Wood Engraving principally taken from the London Illustrated News: with a History of the Art. Folio, $6 50. London, 1847

——— Facts and Speculations on the Origin and History of Playing Cards. Plates. 8vo. cloth, $6 00. London, 1848.

Chaucer, (Geoffrey.) Poetical Works, with an Essay on his Language and Versification; and an Introductory Discourse, with Notes and Glossary, by Thomas Tyrwhitt. Portrait, royal 8vo. cloth, $4 00. London, 1847.

The Same. Calf, $7 00; mor. $8 00; mor. extra, by Hayday, $9 50.

——— Canterbury Tales; with an Essay on his Language and Versification; an Introductory Discourse, Notes, and a Glossary, by T. Tyrwhitt, Esq. 5 vols. 12mo. cloth, $15 00. Pickering, London.

——— Selections from: by C. D. Deshler. 12mo. cloth, 63 cents.

Chaumont's Collection de Machines les plus Interessantes et les plus Utiles, accompagnées de Notices descriptives, et précédés d'une Introduction sur les principes Generaux de la Mécanique. 50 planches. Oblong folio, boards, $3 50. Paris.

Cheever, (G. B.) Lectures on the Pilgrim's Progress. 12mo. cloth, $1 00. New York, 1849.

——— The Hill Difficulty, with other Allegories. 12mo. cloth, $1 25. New York, 1849.

——— Wanderings of a Pilgrim to the Jungfrau and Mont Blanc. 12mo. cloth, $1 00. New York.

——— The Journal of the Pilgrims at Plymouth in New England, in 1620; reprinted from the original volume, with notes and illustrations. 12mo. cloth, $1 25; cloth gilt, $1 50. New York, 1849.

Chelius, (T. M.) System of Surgery. Translated, with additional notes and observations, by J. F. South. 2 thick vols. 8vo. cloth, $15 00. London, 1847.

Chemist, (The.) A Reporter of Chemical Discoveries and Improvements. Edited by Charles and James Watt, for 1843, $3 50; for 1844, $2 87; for 1845, $2 87; in 8vo. boards.

Chemistry applied to the Arts. By Porter. 9 vols. 8vo. sheep, $5 00. Philadelphia.

——— of Man. By Simons. 8vo. sheep, $3 50. Philadelphia.

——— of the Four Seasons. By Griffith. 12mo. cloth, $1 25. Philadelphia.

——— Outlines of Qualitative Analysis for the Guidance of Students of Chemistry. 8vo. 75 cents.

Chenier, (André.) Poésies, precédées d'une notice, par H. de Latouche. 12mo. broché, $1 00. Paris, 1849.

——— Poésies Complètes. 12mo. paper, $1 00. Paris.

——— (M. J.) Œuvres choises. 12mo. paper, $1 00.

Cherbulier. Le Potage a la Tortue. 12mo. paper, 32 cents. Paris, 1849.

Cherry, (H. C.) Illustrations of the Saints' Days and other Festivals of the Church 2 vols. in 1, 12mo. cloth, $2 75. London, 1842.

Chesterfield, (P. D. Stanhope, Earl of.) Letters; Edited, with notes, by Lord Mahon, 4 vols. 8vo. half mor. gilt top, ports. $10 00. London, 1847

Chesterfield, (Earl of.) Works; including Letters to his Son. 8vo. cloth, $1 75. New York.

Child, (L. M.) Biographies of Good Wives. 12mo. cloth, 75 cents. New York.

——— Philothea; a Romance. 12mo. cloth, 75 cents. New York.

——— History of the Condition of Women. 2 vols. 12mo. cloth, $1 25. New York, 1845.

——— Letters from New York. First and Second Series. 2 vols. 12mo. cloth, $1 75. New York.

——— (G.) The Advanced Drawing-book; with twenty-four colored plates. Long 4to. $4 50.

——— Drawing-book of Objects. Studies from Still Life, for Young Pupils and Drawing Classes in Schools. Oblong 4to. cloth, $1 50. Philadelphia, 1846.

——— Little Sketch-book, a Course of very Easy Lessons in Landscapes, Figures, &c. 2 vol. oblong 4to. 75 cents.

Chillingworth, (W.) Religion of Protestants, a Safe Way to Salvation. 12mo. cloth, $1 00. London, 1846.

Chippendale's Ornaments and Inferior Decorations, in the Old French style, for the Interior Embellishment of Houses; for Carvers and Decorators; with Designs for Doors, Windows, Fireplaces, Ornamental Furniture, &c. 220 Designs. 4to. half mor. $7 00.

Chivalry, (Modern,) or, a New Orlando Furioso; with Illustrations, by George Cruikshank. 2 vols post 8vo. boards, $2 50. [Published at £1 1s.] London, 1845.

Chomel, (A. F.) Elements of General Pathology. Third edition. Translated by F. E. Oliver and W. W. Morland. 8vo. sheep, $3 00. Boston, 1848.

Choumara, (P. M. Théodore.) Memoires sur la Fortification, ou examen raisonné des Propriétes et des défauts des Fortifications existantes, indiquant de nouveaux moyens très simples pour améliorer, a peu de frais, les places actuelles, et augmenter considerablement la durée des sieges. 1 vol. 8vo. avec Atlas, $5 00. Paris, 1847.

——— (T.) Considerations Militáires sur les Memoires du Marechal Suchet et sur la Bataille de Toulouse. 2 vols. 8vo. $2 50. Paris, 1840.

Chretien, (C. P.) An Essay on Lyrical Method. 8vo. cloth, $2 00. London, 1848.

Christian Evidences. By Watson, Paley, Jenyn, Leslie, Chandler, Lyttelton, Campbell, Sherlock, and West; with Prefatory Remarks, by the Rev. J. S. Memes, LL.D. Royal 8vo. cloth, $3 00. London, 1847.

——— Gentleman's Daily Walk. By Sir Archibald Edmonstone. 12mo. cloth, $1 00. London, 1843

Christian's (The) Half Hour Book. Foolscap 8vo mor. extra, $4 00; 12mo. cloth, illuminated title, $1 50. London, 1847.

Christian Scholar, (The.) By the author of the Cathedral. 12mo. cloth, $3 00. Oxford, 1849.

——— Treasury; containing Original Papers by Begg, Bickersteth, Bonar, Brewster, Bunting, Cox, Fairbairn, Halley, Hamilton, King, Kitto, Landsborough, Lorime, McCrie, Montgomery, Payne, Parsons, Pike, Redford, Smith, Taylor, Thomson, Tweedie, Wardlaw, Winslow, Wood, &c. 3 vols. 8vo. cloth, $4 00. London, 1849.

——— Treasury; consisting of the following Expositions and Treatises, edited by MEMES, viz.—Magee's Discourses and Dissertations on the Scriptural Doctrines of Atonement and Sacrifice; Witherspoon's Practical Treatise on Regeneration; Boston's Crook in the Lot; Guild's Moses Unveiled; Guild's Harmony of all the Prophets; Less's Authenticity, Uncorrupted Preservation, and Credibility of the New Testament; Stuart's Letters on the Divinity of Christ. In 1 vol. royal 8vo. cloth, $2 50. London, 1844.

——— Traité de Mécanique Industrielle, ou Exposé de la Science de la Mécanique, déduite de l'Experience et de l'Observation. 3 vols. in 4to. et Atlas de sixty planches doubles, $22 50.

——— (E.) Architectural Illustrations of Skelton Church, Yorkshire. 4to. $4 50.

——— (P.) La Morale Merveilleuse, Contes de Tous les Temps et de Tous les Pays. Royal 8vo. paper, illustrated with wood-cuts, $2 75. Paris, 1844.

Christison, (R.) Dispensatory; or, Commentary on the Pharmacopœia of Great Britain. 2nd edition, with Supplement, revised and improved. 8vo. cloth, $6 00. Edinburgh, 1848.

——— (R.) and Griffiths, (R. E.) Dispensatory; or, Commentary on the Pharmacopœias of Great Britain and the United States. 8vo. sheep, with 43 illustrations, $4 00. Philadelphia, 1848.

——— On Poisons. 8vo. cloth, $3 00. Philadelphia.

Chronicles of the Crusades; being contemporary Narratives of the Crusade of Richard Cœur de Lion, by Richard of Devizes and Geoffrey de Vinsauf; and of the Crusade of St. Louis, by Lord John de Joinville. Illustrations, Notes, and Index. Foolscap 8vo. cloth, $1 25. (Bohn's Ant. Libr.) London, 1848.

Chronological Tables of Universal History, (called "the OXFORD CHRONOLOGICAL TABLES",) from the Earliest Period to the Present Time; in which all the great Events, Civil, Religious, Scientific, and Literary, of the various Nations of the World are placed, at one view, under the eye of the reader, in a series of Parallel Columns, so as to exhibit the state of the whole Civilized World at any Epoch, and at the same time form a continuous Chain of History, with Genealogical Tables of all the principal Dynasties. Complete in Three Sections, viz.—I. Ancient History. II. Middle Ages. III. Modern History. With a most complete Index to the entire work. Folio, half bound mor. $6 00. Oxford, Talboys, 1835–9

Chrysostom, (St.) Opera omnia quæ exstant (Gr. et Lat.;) vel quæ ejus nomine circumferuntur; opera et studio J. Bernardi de Montfauçon editio Parisina altera, emendata et aucta. 26 vols. imp. 8vo. sewed, $75 00. Paris, Gaume Brothers, 1830.

Church, (W. A.) Patterns of Inlaid Tiles from Churches in the Diocese of Oxford. 4to. paper, $3 00. London, 1845.

Churches of Cambridgeshire, and the Isle of Ely. Published by the Cambridge Camden Society. Beautifully illustrated. 8vo. $3 50.

Churchill, (Charles.) Poetical Works, with Copious Notes, and Life of the Author, by W. Tooke. Portrait. 3 vols. 12mo. mor. gilt leaves, $7 00. (Aldine edition.) London, 1844.

——— (F.) Theory and Practice of Midwifery, with Notes and Additions, by R. M. Huston, M.D., with 128 wood-cuts. 8vo. sheep, $3 25. Philadelphia, 1848.

——— Diseases of Females. 8vo. sheep, $3 00. Philadelphia.

Churchyard Thoughts in Verse; Light in Darkness, or Sermons in Stones. By Joseph Snow. Wood-cuts. 12mo. cloth, $2 25. London, 1847.

Cicero, Life and Letters. By Middleton, Melmoth, and Heberdeen. Royal 8vo. cloth, $4 50. London.

Cities and Towns in Scotland. Illustrated by a View of each City. Engraved by Lizard, and Descriptive Letter-press, by Wilcox. Oblong 8vo. cloth, $1 75.

Civil Engineer and Architect's Journal; Scientific and Railway Gazette. Published monthly.

Civil Engineering. Quarterly Papers on Engineering; comprising several useful Papers on Civil and Mechanical Engineering, &c., &c. Numerous elaborately engraved plates. 6 vols. 4to. cloth, $37 50. London.

Civil Engineers, Transactions of the Institution of. Vol. 14; containing portrait of Telford, 27 plates, and numerous vignette embellishments of portraits of Engineers and their works. $9 00.

——— Vol. I. Containing twenty-three finely engraved plates. $8 50. London.

Clairbois, (M. Vial de.) Elements of Naval Architecture. Translated from the French, by J. N. Strange. 8vo. $1 50.

Clarendon, (Earl of.) Life and Administration of; with Original Correspondence, &c. Edited by J. H. Lister. Portrait. 3 vols. 8vo. cloth, $4 50. London, 1838.

——— The History of the Rebellion and Civil Wars in England. Royal 8vo. cloth, $6 00.

The Same. 56 portraits. 2 vols. royal 8vo. cloth, $12 00; calf extra, $18 00.

The Same. 8 vols. 12mo. cloth, $7 50.

Clarke, (Dr. A.) Commentary on the Old and New Testament. 6 vols. imperial 8vo. $37 50. London.

The Same. 4 vols. 8vo. $12 00. New York.

Clarke, (Dr. A.) Succession of Sacred Literature. 2 vols. 8vo. cloth, $4 00. London.

——— (Hugh.) Introduction to Heraldry; containing the Origin and Use of Arms; rules for Blazoning and Marshalling Coat Armors; a Dictionary of Heraldic Terms; Orders of Knighthood, illustrated and explained, &c.; embellished with 48 engravings, illustrative of upwards of 1000 examples, including the arms of nearly 500 different families. Fourth edition, improved and enlarged. 12mo. cloth, $2 25. London, 1845.

——— (J.) Elements of Drawing and Painting in Water Colors. New edition. Imp. 16mo. cloth, $2 75. London, 1848.

——— (Mrs. C.) Complete Concordance to Shakspeare. Royal 8vo. cloth, $6 00. (London price, $12 00.) London, 1845.

——— Book of Shakspeare Proverbs. 18mo. cloth, 75 cents. London, 1848.

——— Œuvres Philosoph.; ed Jacques. 12mo. paper, $1 00.

Classical Museum, a Journal of Philology, and of Ancient History and Literature. 5 vols. 8vo. cloth, $10 00. London, 1844.

Clater, (F.) and Youatt, (W.) Every Man his own Farrier; containing the Causes, Symptoms, and most approved Methods of Cure, of the Diseases of Horses; with Notes and Additions, by J. S. Skinner. 12mo. 75 cents. Philadelphia.

——— Every Man his own Cattle Doctor; containing the Causes, Symptoms, and Treatment of all the Diseases incident to Oxen, Sheep, and Swine. Wood-cuts. 12mo. 75 cents. Philadelphia.

Claude. Essay on the Composition of a Sermon; with Notes and Illustrations, and One Hundred Skeletons of Sermons, by Rev. C. Simeon. 1 vol. 12mo. cloth, $1 50. London, 1844.

Clegg, (S.) Architecture of Machinery; an Essay on Propriety of Form and Proportion; with a view to assist and improve Design. Numerous cuts. 4to. half mor. $4 75. London.

——— Practical Treatise on the Manufacture and Distribution of Coal Gas; its Introduction and Progressive Improvement. Illustrated by engravings from Working Drawings; with General Estimates. 4to. cloth, $8 50. London, 1841.

Cleghorn, (George.) Ancient and Modern Art, Historical and Critical. Second edition, corrected and enlarged. 2 vols. 12mo. cloth, $3 50. London, 1848.

Clement Lorimer; or, the Book with the Iron Clasps. Plates, in Cruikshank's best style. 12mo. cloth, $2 00. London, 1849.

Clerk, (John.) Essay on Naval Tactics, Systematical and Historical; with explanatory plates. Third edition, with Notes by Lord Rodney, and an Introduction by a Naval Officer. 8vo. boards, $4 50. Edinburgh, 1827.

Clerk of Works, and Young Architects' Guide. By W. D. Haskoll. 12mo. cloth, $1 37½. London, 1849.

Cleveland, (C. D.) Compendium of English Literature from Mandeville to Cowper. 12mo. half bound, $1 25. Philadelphia, 1848.

Clive, (Robert, First Lord.) The Life of. By the Rev. C. R. Gleig. 12mo. cloth, $2 00. London, 1848.

Close, (Rev. F.) Church Architecture, Scripturally considered, from the Earliest Ages to the Present Time. 12mo. $1 25.

Clulow. Aphorisms and Reflections; a Miscellany of Thoughts and Opinions. Thick post 8vo. $1 50. London, 1843.

Cobbett's French Grammar. 12mo. cloth, 75 cents. New York, 1848.

Cobham, (The Good Lord.) The Life and Times of. By Thomas Gaspey. 2 vols. post 8vo cloth, $3 00. London, 1844.

Cockburn, (W.) A New System of Geology; dedicated to Professor Sedgwick. Post 8vo. cloth, $1 12. London, 1849.

Coe, (B. H.) Drawing Cards. Studies in Drawing, in a Progressive Series of Lessons on Cards; beginning with the most Elementary Studies, and adapted for use at Home and in Schools. In Ten Series, each containing about 18 studies. Each Series 25 cents.

Coffin, (J. H.) Elements of Conic Sections and Analytical Geometry. 8vo. cloth, 75 cts. New York, 1848.

Coins of England. Twenty-three Plates; printed in Gold, Silver, and Copper; with descriptions, and a slight sketch of the Progress of Coinage. Post 8vo. fancy boards; $5 50. London, 1848.

Cole, (S. W.) American Fruit Book; with numerous engravings. 18mo. sheep, 50 cents. Boston, 1849.

Coleman, (Rev. L.) Historical Geography of the Bible. Illustrated by maps from the most authentic sources, of the countries mentioned in Scripture. 12mo. half bound, $1 25. Philadelphia, 1849.

——— (Ch.) The Mythology of the Hindus; with notices of the various Mountain and Island Tribes of India; with numerous plates of the Hindu Deities 4to. cloth, $6 50. London, 1832.

Coleridge, (S. T.) Biographia Literaria; edited by his Son. 2 vols. 12mo. cloth, $2 00. New York.

——— Poetical Works. 3 vols. 12mo. cloth, $4 00; mor. $8 25. Pickering, London.

——— Poems. 12mo. cloth, $1 00. New York.

——— Literary Remains. Edited by H. N. Coleridge. 4 vols. 8vo. cloth, $12 00. Lond.

——— Lectures upon Shakspeare, and other Dramatists. 2 vols. 12mo. cloth, $3 25. London, 1849.

——— The Friend; a Series of Essays to aid in the Formation of Fixed Principles in Politics, Morals, and Religion, &c. 3 vols. 12mo. cloth, $4 50. London, 1847.

——— Hints towards the Formation of a more comprehensive Theory of Life. Edited by Seth B. Watson. Post 8vo. cloth, 50 cents. Philadelphia, 1848.

Coleridge, (S. T.) Confessions of an Inquiring Spirit. Edited, from the Author's MS., by H. N. Coleridge, Esq. 12mo. cloth, 50 cts. Boston, 1841.

Coley, (J. M.) Practical Treatise on the Diseases of Children. 8vo. cloth, $4 00. London, 1846.

Collation (A) of the principal English Translations of the Sacred Scriptures; with Memoirs of the principal Translators. By Charles Roger. 4to. cloth, $3 50. London, 1847.

Collier, (J. Payne.) A Book of Roxburghe Ballads. With wood-cuts. Foolscap 4to. boards, $6 00; mor. by Hayday, $12 00. London.

——— (J.) Ecclesiastical History of Great Britain. 9 vols. 8vo. cloth, $30 00. London.

Collings, (J. B.) Gothic Ornaments; being a Series of Examples of Enriched Details, (some superbly colored,) and Accessories of the Architecture of Great Britain. Vol. I. 4to. cloth, $20 00. London, 1848.

Collins, (W.) Memoirs of the Life of; with Selections from his Journals and Correspondence. By his Son, W. Wilkie Collins. 2 vols. post 8vo. cloth, $6 00. London, 1849.

——— Poetical Works; with a Memoir of the Author, and an Essay by Sir E. Brydges. 12mo. cloth, $1 37; mor. $2 75. Pickering, London.

Collis, (J.) Builder's Portfolio of Street Architecture: a Series of Original Designs for Fronts of Houses of all classes. 4to. $6 00.

Colman, (H.) European Life and Manners. 2 vols. 12mo. cloth, $2 00. Boston, 1849.

——— European Agriculture and Rural Economy; from Personal Observation. Illustrated with engravings on steel. 2d edition. 2 vols. 8vo. cloth, $5 00. Boston, 1849.

——— Agriculture and Rural Economy of France, Belgium, Holland, and Switzerland. Crown 8vo. cloth, $1 25. Boston, 1848.

Colombat and De Isere, on Diseases of Females; translated by Meigs. 8vo. sheep, $3 50. Philadelphia.

Colonization, A View of the Art of; with Present Reference to the British Empire. In Letters between a Statesman and a Colonist. Edited by Edward Gibbon Wakefield, one of the Writers. 8vo. cloth, $3 25. London, 1849.

Color. The Principles of Design and Color; together with the Matching of Colors. Illustrated with plates. 4to. cloth, $2 50. London, 1847.

Colton, (C.) Public Economy of the United States. 8vo. cloth, $3 00. New York.

Combe, (A.) The Physiology of Digestion, considered with relation to the Principles of Dietetics. Fifth edition, revised and enlarged. 12mo. paper, 75 cents. Edinburgh, 1845.

——— Treatise on the Physiological and Moral Management of Infancy; with Notes and a Supplementary Chapter, by John Bell, M.D. Third edition. 12mo. cloth, 75 cents. Philadelphia, 1842.

Comber, (Thomas, D.D.) A Companion to the Temple; or, A Help to Devotion, in the Use of Common Prayer. 7 vols. 8vo. cloth, $14 00. Oxford, 1841.

Combes. Traité de l'Exploration des Mines. 3 vols. 8vo. avec une Atlas de 68 planches in folio. $12 50. Paris, 1845.

Comic English Grammar, (The.) A New and Facetious Introduction to the English Tongue. Embellished with 50 characteristic illustrations by Leech. 12mo. cloth. 75 cts. London, 1840.

Commentaries on the Principia of Sir Isaac Newton. Royal 8vo. cloth, $1 25. London, 1846.

Commines, Memoires de; précédés d'une Notice Biographique. 12mo. half mor. marbled edges, $1 75. Paris, 1843

Common Prayer, (The Book of;) Illuminated and Illustrated with engravings, from the Works of the Great Painters. In 1 vol. 8vo. mor. gilt leaves, $12 00. London, 1845.
The Same. Boards, $7 50.

Comptes Rendus Hebdomadaires des Séances de l'Académie des Sciences. 1835 to 1847. 25 vols. 4to. half calf, gilt, $75 00.

Comstock, (J. L.) History of the Precious Metals. 12mo. cloth, 75 cents. Hartford, 1849.

——— Elements of Botany. 12mo. sheep, $1 00. New York.

——— Elements of Chemistry. 12mo. sheep, 75 cents. New York.

——— Elements of Mineralogy. 12mo. sheep, 75 cents. New York.

Conchologist's Nomenclator; or, Catalogue of Recent Species of Shells, with their Authorities, Synonymes, and References to Works where figured or described. By Agnes Catlow, assisted by L. Reeve. Cloth, $6 00; or, interleaved with blank pages for remarks, half calf, $7 50. London.

Concile de Trente (le saint) œcuménique et général, célebre sous Paul III., Jules III., et Pie IV., précédé d'un Essai Historique sur ce Concile et sa reception en France; avec le texte Latin; Traduction nouvelle, par M. l'Abbe Darsance. 2 vols. 8vo. $3 25. Paris, 1842.

Conder's Modern Traveller; a Descriptive, Geographical, Historical, and Topographical Account of the various countries of the Globe. 20 vols. 12mo. red cloth, $18 00. London.

Condie, (D. F.) Practical Treatise on the Diseases of Children. 8vo. sheep, $3 00 Philadelphia, 1847.

Coney, (J.) Fifty-six Architectural Sketches. Large 8vo. $2 50.

——— Beauties of Continental Architecture; in a Series of Views of Ancient Cathedrals and other Remarkable Public Buildings. Folio, half mor. gilt edges. Illustrated with 28 plates and 56 vignettes, $10 00. London, 1843.

——— Foreign Cathedrals, Hotels de Ville, Town Halls, and other Remarkable Buildings in France, Holland, Germany, and Italy. 32 fine large plates, imperial folio, half mor. extra, $22 00. London, 1842

Conquerors of the New World and their Bondsmen. By the Author of Essays in the Intervals of Business, &c. 12mo. cloth, $1 50. London, 1848.

Consolatio; or, Comfort for the Afflicted. Edited by the Rev. C. E. Kennaway; with Preface by Archdeacon S. Wilberforce. 12mo. cloth, $1 50. London, 1844.

Constant, (B.) Adolphe; et d'une Essai sur Adolphe, par M. Gustave. Planche. 12mo. paper, $1 00. Paris, 1845.

——— Cours de Politique Constitutionelle. 3d edition. 8vo. paper, $2 25. Bruxelles, 1837,

Contarini Fleming; by B. D'Israeli. 4 vols. in 2. 12mo. half calf, neat, $2 50. London, 1832.

Cook, (E. W.) Sixty-five plates of Shipping and Craft. 4to. cloth, $5 50. London, 1829.

——— (E.) Poems. 12mo. cloth, $1 25. New York.

——— (Capt. James.) The Voyages of; with an Appendix, giving an Account of the Present Condition of the South Sea Islands. Illustrated with maps, and numerous engravings on wood. 2 vols. imp. 8vo. cloth, $7 00; calf extra, $12 00. London, 1846.

——— (G.) Historical View of Christianity. 3 vols. 8vo. cloth, $3 50. Edinburgh, 1822.

Cookesley, (G. G.) Selections from Catullus, with English Notes; revised, with additional notes, by C. A. Bristed. 12mo. half bd., 63 cents. New York, 1849.

Cooley, (A. J.) The Book of Useful Knowledge; containing 6,000 Practical Receipts in all branches of Art, Manufacture, and Trade. 8vo. sheep, $2 25. New York.

Cooper, (J. F.) Early Works; (uniform with Washington Irving's Works;) in 12mo. cloth, each volume, $1 25.

ALREADY PUBLISHED.

The Spy.
The Pilot.
The Ways of the Hour. (A new work.)

——— Novels and Tales. 23 vols. 12mo. sheep, gilt, $14 00. Philadelphia.

——— Naval History of the United States. 8vo. cloth, $2 00. Philadelphia.

——— Sea Tales. 6 vols. 12mo. cloth, $3 00.

——— Leather-Stocking Tales. 5 vols. 12mo. cloth, $2 50.

——— (Sir A.) Lectures on Surgery. Edited by Tyrrel. 8vo. sheep, $3 00. Philadelphia.

——— On Dislocations and Fractures. 8vo. sheep, $3 50. Philadelphia.

——— On Hernia. 8vo. sheep, $4 00.

——— Anatomy and Diseases of the Breast; with numerous plates. To which are added various Surgical Papers. Imperial 8vo. sheep, $4 00. Philadelphia, 1845.

——— Testis and Thymus Gland. 8vo. sheep, $3 50. Philadelphia.

——— (Samuel.) Dictionary of Practical Surgery. 8vo. $3 88. New York.

——— First Lines in Surgery; with Notes by Parker. 2 vols. 8vo. sheep, $6 00. New York.

Coote, (Holmes.) The Homologies of the Human Skeleton. 8vo. cloth, $1 25. London, 1849.

Copeland, (J.) Dictionary of Practical Medicine. 3 vols. 8vo. sheep, $15 00. New York.

Coquerel, (Athanase.) Christianity; its Perfect Adaptation to the Mental, Moral, and Spiritual Nature of Man. Translated by Rev. Dr. Davison; with an Introductory Notice of the State of the Protestant Church of France, by the Author. Post 8vo. $3 00. London.

Corneille, (P.) Œuvres complètes, avec les Commentaires de Voltaire; avec portrait et gravures. 12 vols. in 8vo, demi maroquin, $24 00. Paris, 1817.

——— Chefs d'œuvre, avec une Histoire abrégée du Theâtre François, et une biographie de l'auteur, et une choix de notes de divers Commentateurs, par M. D. Sancie. Gravures. 1 vol. in 8vo. $1 75. Tours, 1846.

——— Chefs d'Œuvre de. 2 vols. 18mo. broché, $1 00. Paris.

——— (P. et de Theo.) Theâtre avec Notes et Commentaires. 2 vols. 12mo. paper, $1 50. Paris, 1848.

Corner, (Miss.) History of China and India. Pictorial and Descriptive. 180 engravings. 8vo. cloth, gilt edges, $3 50. London.

Cornwall, (Barry.) English Songs, and other small Poems. 18mo. cloth gilt, $1 00. London, 1846.

Corpus Poetarum Latinorum; edidit G. S. Walker, complete in one very thick vol. royal 8vo. cloth, $5 00. London, 1849.

This comprehensive volume contains a library of the poetical Latin classics, correctly printed from the best texts, viz.—

Catullus,	Phædrus,	Statius,
Tibullus,	Lucan,	Silius Italicus,
Propertius,	Persius,	Valerius Flaccus,
Lucretius,	Juvenal,	Calpurnius Siculus,
Virgil,	Martial,	Ausonius,
Ovid,	Sulpicia,	Claudian.
Horace,		

Corpus Juris Canonici Academicum, emendatum et notis P. Lancellotti illustratum usuixue moderno, ad modum C. H. Freiesleben, ita accommodatum ut, uno quasi intuitu, omnes canones, causæ et capitula inveniri possint, accesserunt loci communes et indices titulorum canonumque omnium summa diligentia ac novo methodo concinnati. 2 vols in 1, 4to. half Russia extra, $10 00.

Corson, (Dr. J. W.) Loiterings in Europe or, Sketches of Travel. 12mo. cloth, $1 00. New York, 1848

Cory, (J. P.) Metaphysical Inquiry into the Method, Objects, and Result of Ancient and Modern Philosophy, and Mythological and Chronological Inquiry. 3 vols. in 1, post 8vo. cloth, $2 00. London, 1833–7.

Cosson et Germani's Atlas de la Flore des Environs de Paris. 41 plates, containing 500 figures. 12mo. boards, $2 50. Paris, 1845.

Costello, (L. S.) The Rose Garden of Persia; beautifully printed with Colored Borders and Arabesque Illuminations. 12mo. mor. extra, gilt leaves, $7 50. London, 1845

Costello, (L. S.) Specimens of the Early Poetry of France, from the Time of the Troubadours and Trouveres to the Reign of Henri Quatre. Illustrated with illuminated engravings on vellum paper. 12mo. cloth, $3 75. London, 1835.

——— Pilgrimage to Auvergne, from Picardy to le Velay. Plates. 2 vols. 8vo. cloth, $2 50. London, 1842.

Costume. Beauty's Costume; a Series of Female Figures in the Dresses of all Times and Nations. 12 fine engravings. 4to. cloth. London.

Cottin, (Madame.) Œuvres; accompagnées d'une Notice sur sa Vie et ses Ouvrages. 2 vols. 12mo. broché, $1 75. Paris, 1844.

Cottingham, (L. N.) Gothic Ornaments. Folio, $11 00. London.

——— Grecian and Roman Ornaments. Folio, $7 50.

——— The Smiths', Founders', and Ornamental Metal Worker's Director; comprising a Variety of Designs in the Present Taste for Gates, Piers, Balcony Buildings, Verandahs, &c. &c. Folio, $13 00.

Cottle, (A.) Reminiscences of Coleridge, Southey, Lamb, and others. Portraits. Crown 8vo. cloth, $2 50. London.

The Same. 12mo. cloth, $1 00. New York.

Couch, (T.) Illustrations of Instinct, derived from the Habits of British Animals. Post 8vo. cloth, $2 50. London.

Country House, (The.) With Designs. Edited by Lady Mary Fox. 4to. cloth, $7 50. London, 1843.

Courtenay's Mechanics. 8vo. sheep, $2 25. New York.

——— T. P.) Commentaries on Shakspeare. 2 vols. crown 8vo. cloth, $2 50.

Court and Times of James the First. Illustrated from Authentic and Confidential Letters from various Public and Private Collections. 2 vols. 8vo. cloth, $8 00. London, 1848.

Court Etiquette; a Guide to Intercourse with Royal, or Titled Person, Drawing Rooms, &c. Usages of Social Life, Rules of Precedence, &c., &c. By a Man of the World. 16mo. cloth gilt, $1 25. London, 1849.

Cousin, (V.) The Philosophy of the Beautiful. Translated, with Notes, by Daniel. 12mo. cloth, $1 50. London, 1848.

The Same. 12mo. cloth, 62 cents. N. York, 1849.

——— Elements of Psychology. Translated by C. S. Henry. 12mo. cloth, $1 00. New York.

——— Report on Education in Prussia. Translated by Mrs. Austin. 8vo. cloth, 80 cents. New York, 1835.

——— Cours de l'Histoire de la Philosophie Moderne et Ancienne. 12 vols. 12mo. paper, $12 00. Paris, 1846.

——— Histoire de la Philosophie. 3 vols. 12mo. paper, $2 25. Bruxelles, 1840.

——— Cours de Philosophie—sur le Fondement des Idées Absolues du Vrai, du Beau et du Bien. 12mo. paper, 75 cents. Bruxelles, 1840.

Cousin, (V.) Fragments de Philosophie Cartésienne. 12mo. paper, $1 00. Paris, 1845.

Coventry, (Prof. C. B.) The Epidemic Cholera; its History, Causes, Pathology, and Treatment. 12mo. cloth, 50 cents. Buffalo, 1849.

Cowper, (Wm.) Poetical Works. (Aldine edition.) 3 vols. foolscap 8vo. cloth, $4 00; mor. $7 00; mor. extra, by Hayday, $9 00. Pickering, London.

——— Complete Works, edited by Southey; comprising his Poems, Correspondence, and Translations; with a Life of the Author. Embellished with numerous exquisite engravings, after the designs of Harvey. 15 vols. post 8vo. cloth, $15 00; half mor. $22 00. London, 1835–7.

——— Poems; with Biographical and Critical Introduction, by Dale; with 75 illustrations. 2 vols. 12mo. cloth, gilt edges, $3 75. New York.

The Same. In morocco, elegant, gilt leaves. $5 00.

——— The Task, and other Poems; illustrated with beautiful engravings. 12mo. cloth, $2 25. Philadelphia, 1845.

——— Poetical Works; complete in one volume. Edited by the Rev. H. Carey. Royal 8vo. cloth, $3 00. London, 1839.

The Same. In mor. extra, $6 00. London, 1839.

——— Works of. Edited by T. S. Grimshawe. Royal 8vo. cloth, $4 50. London, 1848.

The Same. Plates. Royal 8vo. cloth, $3 00. New York, 1849.

——— Poetical Works. Edited, with Life, &c., by Grimshawe. 8 vols. 12mo. cloth, $6 50. London.

The Same. Half mor. gilt tops, $8 50.

The Same. 18mo. cloth, $1 25.

The Same. Mor. gilt, $2 50.

The Same. With plates. Royal 18mo. $2 00; mor. gilt, $3 50.

Cowper's Homer's Iliad and Odyssey, in blank verse; edited by Southey. 4 vols. foolscap 8vo. cloth, $4 50. London, 1837.

Cox, (Joseph M.) Practical Observations on Insanity; to which are subjoined, Remarks on Medical Jurisprudence, as connected with Diseased Intellect. Second edition, corrected and greatly enlarged. 8vo. boards, $1 75. London, 1806.

——— (Frances E.) Sacred Hymns. Translated from the German. 24mo. mor. $2 00. Pickering, London, 1841.

Coxe, (W.) History of the House of Austria, from 1218 to 1792. Portrait. 3 vols. 12mo cloth, $2 62. London, 1847.

——— Memoirs of the Duke of Marlborough. New edition, by Wade. Portrait. 3 vols. 12mo. cloth, $2 62. London, 1847.

——— (J. R.) Epitome of the Writings of Hippocrates and Galen. 8vo. sheep, $3 50. Philadelphia.

Cozzen, (J.) Geological History of New York Island. 8vo. cloth, $1 00. New York.

Crabbe, (Rev. G.) English Synonymes; with Copious Illustrations and Explanations; drawn from the best writers. 8vo. sheep, $2 00. New York, 1847.

——— Tales and Poems. 2 vols. 12mo. mor. $5 00. London, 1846.

——— Poetical Works, complete in one handsome volume. Portrait and vignette. Royal 8vo. cloth, $4 25. London.

——— An Outline of a System of Natural Theology. 8vo. cloth, $2 00. Pickering, London, 1840.

Cradock, (Thos.) Chemistry of the Steam Engine Practically Considered. Illustrated with ten large plates. 8vo. cloth, $2 25. London, 1847.

——— Description of Cradock's Patent Universal Condensing Steam Engine. 8vo. sewed, 31 cents. London, 1847.

Craig, (Rev. R.) Theocracy; or, the Principles of the Jewish Religion and Polity adapted to all Nations and Times. Post 8vo. cloth, $1 50. London, 1848.

Craik's Pursuit of Knowledge under Difficulties. 3 vols. 18mo. cloth, $1 25.

——— Do. Do. Female Examples. 18mo. cloth, 30 cents. London.

——— Spenser and his Poetry. 3 vols. 18mo. cloth, $1 25. London.

——— History of British Commerce. 3 vols. 18mo. cloth, $1 25. London.

——— History of Literature, &c., in England. 6 vols. 18mo. cloth, $2 70.

——— (G. L.) The Romance of the Peerage, and Curiosities of Family History. Portraits. Vols. 1 and 2. $6 00. London, 1848–9.

Crawfurd, (J.) Journal of an Embassy to the Courts of Siam and Cochin China. Plates. 2 vols. 8vo. cloth, $3 50. London, 1830.

——— Journal of an Embassy from the Governor-General of India to the Court of Ava; with an Appendix, containing a Description of Fossil Remains, by Professor Buckland and Mr. Clift. 2 vols. 8vo. cloth, $3 50. Lond. 1834.

Cresy's Encyclopædia of Civil Engineering; Historical, Theoretical, and Practical; 3000 illustrations. In one thick volume, royal 8vo. cloth, $18 00. London, 1847.

Creswell, (D.) Elements of the Theory of Mechanics; to which is added a Selection of Problems in Mechanics. 8vo. $1 25.

reuze, (A. J. B.) Treatise on the Theory and Practice of Naval Architecture. 15 plates. 4to. cloth, $3 50. Edinburgh, 1848.

richton, (Sir A.) Commentaries on Some Doctrines of a Dangerous Tendency in Medicine, and on the General Principles of Safe Practice. 8vo. cloth, $2 75. London, 1842.

Crichton and Wheaton. A History of Denmark, Sweden, and Norway; comprehending a Description of those Countries; with illustrations of their Natural History. Map and 12 engravings. Thick 12mo., cloth, $1 25. Edinburgh.

Crisp, (E.) Treatise on the Structure, Diseases, and Injuries of the Blood Vessels. 8vo. cloth, $4 50. London, 1847.

Critchet, (George.) Lectures on the Causes and Treatment of Ulcers of the Lower Extremities. 8vo. cloth, $1 50. London, 1849.

Critic, (The) In Parliament and in Public. 12mo. cloth, $1 London, 1841.

Crocker. Elements of Land Surveying. 5th edition, corrected throughout, and considerably improved and modernized, by T. G. Bunt. To which are added Tables of Six Figure Logarithms, &c., superintended by R. Farley. Post. 8vo. cloth, $3 75. London.

——— (Charles.) Vale of Obscurity, the Lavant, and other Poems. 8vo. paper, 50 cents. Chichester, 1830.

Croly, (Rev. G.) Divine Providence; or, the Three Cycles of Revelation; showing the Parallelism of the Patriarchal, Jewish, and Christian Dispensations. 8vo. cloth, $1 50. London, 1834.

Cromwell, (O.) Letters and Speeches. Edited by Carlyle. 2 vols. 8vo. cloth, $2 50. New York, 1845.

Crosby, (A.) Tables, illustrative of Greek Inflection. 12mo. cloth, 38c. 1841.

Crowe, (E.) Night-Side of Nature; or, Ghosts and Ghost-Seers. 2 vols. crown 8vo. bds. $6 50. London, 1849.

Cruikshank, (G.) Illustrations of Smollet, Fielding, and Goldsmith. Containing 41 plates by that Original Artist. 12mo. cloth, 87 cents. London, 1836.

——— Three Courses and a Desert. Illustrated with plates and wood-cuts, by George Cruikshanks. Crown 8vo. half bound, $1 75.

——— Table Book. Edited by Gilbert à Becket; with Twelve steel and wood engravings, by George Cruikshanks. Imperial 8vo extra cloth, $3 50. London, 1845.

——— At Home. A new Family Album of Endless Amusement; with numerous illustrations on wood. 2 vols. in 1, 12mo. cloth, $2 50. London, 1845.

Crusius, (G. C.) Complete Greek and English Lexicon of the Poems of Homer and the Homeridæ. Translated by Hy. Smith. 8vo. sheep, $3 00. Hartford, 1844.

Cruveilhier, (J.) Anatomy of the Human Body. 8vo. cloth, $3 00. New York.

Cudworth, (Ralph, D.D.) The True Intellectual System of the Universe; with a Treatise concerning Eternal and Immutable Immortality; with the Notes and Dissertations of Dr. J. L. Moshiem. Translated by J. Harrison. 3 vols. 8vo. cloth, $6 50. London, 1845.

——— Intellectual System of the Universe. 2 vols. 8vo. cloth, $4 50. New York.

Cuitt's Wanderings of a Pen and Pencil among the Ruins of Olden Time. Comprising numerous Picturesque Views. Large folio, half bound mor. $20 00. London, 1848

Cullum, (G. W.) Description of a System of Military Bridges, with India Rubber Pontons; prepared for the Use of the United States Army. 8vo. cloth, $2 00. New York, 1849.

Culverwell, (R. J.) Porneiapathology; or, the Green Book. The Modern Treatment of Syphilis, &c. 12mo. paper, $1 50. London, 1842.

Cumming, (Rev. J. G.) The Isle of Man; its History, Physical, Ecclesiastical, Civil, and Legendary. Plates. 8vo. cloth, $3 25. London, 1848.

——— (Rev. J.) Apocalyptic Sketches; or, Lectures on the Book of Revelations, delivered in 1847–8. Foolscap 8vo. cloth, $2 75. London, 1848.

——— (J.) Manual of Electro-Dynamics; with Notes and Additions, comprehending the latest Discoveries and Improvements. 8vo. cloth, $3 50.

Cundall, (Joseph.) On Ornamental Art, applied to Ancient and Modern Bookbinding. Illustrated with Col'd Plates. 4to. bds. $5 00. London, 1848.

Cunningham, (J. D.) A History of the Sikhs, from the Origin of the Nation to the Battles of the Sutlej. Maps. 8vo. cloth, $4 50. London, 1849.

——— (A.) Cabinet Gallery of Pictures, by the First Masters of the English and Foreign Schools. 73 line engravings. 2 vols. royal 8vo. half mor. gilt tops, $12 00. London, 1836.

——— Lives of the most Eminent British Painters, Sculptors, and Architects. Portraits. 6 vols. 12mo. cloth, $7 00.

The Same. 5 vols. 18mo. cloth, $2 25. New York.

——— (Peter.) A Hand-Book for London, Past and Present. 2 vols. post 8vo. cloth, $7 00. London, 1849.

Curiosities of Glass-Making; by Apsley Pellat. Illustrated with Colored plates and engravings. Small 4to. cloth, $3 50. London, 1849.

Curling, (T. B.) On the Testis. 8vo. cloth, $3 00. Philadelphia.

Curr, (J.) On Railway Locomotion and Steam Navigation. 8vo. cloth, $3 50 Lond.

Curtis's Flora Londinensis; Revised and improved by George Graves; extended and continued by Sir W. Jackson Hooker; comprising the History of Plants indigenous to Great Britain; their Uses, Economy, and various interesting Particulars, with Alphabetical, Linnæan, and other Indexes, the Drawings made by Sydenham Edwards and Lindley. 647 plates, exhibiting the full natural size of each plant; with magnified dissections of the parts of fructification, &c., all beautifully colored. 5 vols. folio, $156 00. London, 1835.

The Same. Elegantly half bd. mor. top edges gilt. $180 00.

——— Botanical Magazine. Commenced in 1786; continued by Sir .W. Jackson Hooker. Illustrated by Fitch. Published in monthly numbers, each containing 7 plates, beautifully colored. $12 00 per annum.

Curzon, (Hon. R.) Visits to Monasteries in the Levant. Illustrated with numerous woodcuts. Crown 8vo. cloth, $1 50; half calf neat. $2 25; whole calf gilt, marbled leaves, $2 75. New York, 1849.

Cust, (Sir E.) Noctes Dominic; or, Sunday Night Readings. 8vo. cloth, $4 50. London.

Cuvier, (Baron.) The Animal Kingdom arranged according to its Organization; serving as a Foundation for the Natural History of Animals. 4 vols. letter press, 4 vols., Colored plates, 8vo. cloth, $25 00.

——— Animal Kingdom Described and Arranged in conformity with its Organization. By Griffith, Lieut. Col. H. Smith, Pidgeon, Gray, and others. 814 plates. 16 vols. 8vo. cloth, $70. London.

The Same. Colored plates. Royal 8vo. cloth, $140 00.

——— The Animal Kingdom, arranged according its Organization. New edition, with Additions, by W. B. Carpenter and J. O. Westwood. Illustrated by 300 engravings on wood and 34 on steel. Royal 8vo. cloth, $6 50. London, 1849.

——— Animal Kingdom. The Classes Annelida, Crustacea, and, Arachnida, as arranged by Cuvier; with Additions by Griffith and Pidgeon. Illustrated with 60 colored plates. In one thick volume, royal 8vo. cloth, $5 00. Lond. 1835.

——— Animal Kingdom, arranged according to its Organization. (The Crustacea, Arachnida, and Insecta, by P. A. Latreille. Translated ftom the French by H. M'Murtrie, M.D. Illustrated with plates. 4 vols. 8vo. boards, $7 50. New York, 1831.

——— Animal Kingdom. Fishes as arranged by Cuvier; with Additions by Griffith and Smith. 64 plates. In 1 large vol. royal 8vo. $5 00. London, 1834.

Cuvier and Zoology. A Popular Biography, with an Historical Introduction and Sequel. 12mo. cloth, 63 cents. London, 1844.

Cyprian, (St.) The Life and Times of; by G. A. Poole. 8vo. cloth, $2 75. Oxford, 1840.

Daille, (Rev. John.) Exposition of the Epistle of Paul to the Philippians; translated by the Rev. J. Sherman. Imperial 8vo. cloth, $3 75. London, 1841.

——— Treatise on the Right Use of the Fathers, in the Decision of Controversies at this day existing in Religion. Translated by Smith; new edition, edited by Rev. G. Jekyll. 8vo. cloth, $1 50. London, 1841.

Dale, (Thomas.) Poetical Works. New edition. Foolscap 8vo. cloth, $2 25; mor. $3 50. London.

Dallaway, (Rev. J.) A Series of Discourses upon Architecture in England; with Notes and Illustrations. 8vo cloth, $3 50.

Dalton, (John.) Meteorological Observations and Essays. Second edition. 8vo. $2 00. London.

——— Chemical Philosophy. 2 vols. 8vo. cloth, $9 50. London.

Dalrymple, (D.) Annals of Scotland. 3 vols. 8vo. cloth, $9 50. London.

Dalyell, (J. G.) Rare and Remarkable Animals of Scotland. Plates. 2 vols. 4to. $38 00. London, 1848.

Dalzel, (A.) Lectures on the Ancient Greeks. 2 vols. 8vo. cloth, $7 25. London.

Dammii Lexicon, Homericum et Pindaricum. Edited by Duncan. 4to cloth, $3 50. London.

Dana, (James D.) System of Mineralogy, comprising the most Recent Discoveries; with numerous wood-cuts and four copper plate engravings. Third edition, greatly enlarged and improved. 8vo. cloth, $3 50. New York, 1850.

——— Manual of Mineralogy; including Observations on Mines. 260 illustrations. 12mo. sheep, $1 00. New Haven, 1849.

——— Geology of the United States Exploring Expedition; with an Atlas of plates in folio. Royal 4to. $15 New York, 1849.

——— On Zoophytes. Being vol. 8 of the United States Exploring Expedition. 4to. cloth, $15 00. Philadelphia, 1848.

——— Atlas to Do. folio, half mor. gilt top, cloth sides, 61 plates, many beautifully colored. $30 00. Philadelphia, 1849.

——— (R. H.) Seaman's Manual; containing a Practical Treatise on Seamanship. Plates. 12mo. 75 cents. Boston.

Daniels, (W.) Picturesque Delineations of the most Interesting Subjects from all branches of Natural History. 125 engravings, with letter-press descriptions 2 vols. small folio. hlf. mor. (Published at 15 guineas.) $19 00. London.

——— (S. and W.) Oriental Scenery and Antiquities; 150 splendid Colored Views on the largest scale, of the Architecture, Antiquities, and Landscape scenery of Hindostan. 6 vols. in 3, elephant folio, elegantly half bound mor. with full gilt backs and gilt edges. (Published at £210.) $300 00.

The Same. 3 vols. small folio, reduced from the above, and uncolored; half mor. gilt. (Published at 18 guineas.) $40 00.

Daniel, (George.) Merrie England in the Olden Time. 2 vols. post 8vo. cloth, $2 75. London, 1842.

Daniell, (J. Frederic.) Introduction to the Study of Chemical Philosophy; being a Preparatory View of the Forces which concur to the Production of Chemical Phenomena. 2d edition, revised and enlarged. 8vo. clf. $6 00. London, 1843.

——— Elements of Meteorology; being the 3d edition, revised and enlarged, of Meteorological Essays. 2 vols. 8vo. cloth, $9 50. London.

Dante. Poems. Translated by Cary. Illustrated. 16mo. cloth, $1 50; mor. $3 00. New York.

——— The Inferno. A Prose Translation. By J. Carlyle. 12mo. cloth, $1 00. N. York, 1849.

D'Arblay, (Madame.) Diary and Letters of. Including notices of most of her contemporaries. 3 vols. 8vo. cloth, $5 50. Philadelphia, 1842.

The Same. 7 vols. post 8vo. cloth, $12 00. London, 1842–46.

Darbyshire, (G. C.) Tables for setting out Curves for Railways, &c.; with Appendix, containing Demonstrations and Rules. Oblong 12mo. $1 25. London.

Darlington's Agricultural Chemistry. 12mo. cloth, $1 00. Philadelphia.

——— Agricultural Botany. 12mo. cloth, $1 00. Philadelphia.

Darwin, (Charles.) Journal of Researches into the Natural History and Geology of the Countries visited during the Voyage of H. M. S. Beagle round the World. 2 vols. 12mo. cloth, $1 00. New York, 1846.

——— The Structure and Distribution of Coral Reefs. With colored maps. 8vo. cloth, $4 75. London, 1842.

——— Volcanic Islands. 8vo. cloth, $3 25. London.

Das Nibelungen Lied; or, Lay of the Last Nibelungers. Translated into English Verse, after Professor Carl Lachmann's collated and corrected text. By J. Birch. 8vo. $2 00; half mor. $3 50. Berlin, 1848.

Daubeny, (Charles.) Description of Active and Extinct Volcanoes, of Earthquakes, and of Thermal Springs. Second edition, enlarged. 8vo. cloth, $6 00. London, 1848.

D'Aubigne, (J. H. M.) History of the Great Reformation of the Sixteenth Century, in Germany and Switzerland. 4 vols. 12mo $1 75. New York, 1846.

The Same. 2 vols. 12mo. $1 50. New York, 1846.

——— The Protector. A Vindication. 12mo. cloth, $1 00. New York, 1848.

Davenport's Dictionary of Biography. 8vo. cloth, $2 00. Boston.

Davidson's Universal Melodist; consisting of the Music and Words of Popular, Standard, and Original Songs. 2 vols. royal 8vo. cloth, $4 50. London, 1848.

——— Songs of Charles Dibdin, Chronologically Arranged, with Notes and the Music to the best and most popular of the Melodies, with new Piano Forte accompaniments. Portrait. 2 vols. royal 8vo. cloth, $4 50. London, 1848.

——— (John.) Practical Mathematics. 8vo. cloth, $4 50.

——— Key to Do. 8vo. cloth, $2 12. London.

——— (Samuel.) Introduction to the New Testament. Vol. 1, 8vo. cloth, $3 75. London, 1848.

——— The Ecclesiastical Polity of the New Testament Unfolded, and its Points of Coincidence or Disagreement with Prevailing Systems indicated. 8vo. cloth, $3 00. London, 1848.

———(Lucretia) Poetical Remains. Edited by Miss Sedgwick. 12mo. cloth, 75 cents. Philadelphia.

——— (Margaret.) Memoirs and Writings. Edited by W. Irving. 12mo. cloth, 75 cents. Philadelphia.

——— (Mrs.) Memoirs, &c. 12mo. 75 cents. Philadelphia.

Davies, (Rev. J.) Supremacy of the Scriptures, the Divine Rule of Religion; with a Recommendatory Letter, by Rev. J. P. Smith. 12mo. cloth, $1 50. London 1846.

Davies, (Edward.) The Mythology and Rites of the British Druids, ascertained by National Documents; and compared with the General Traditions and Customs of Heathenism; as illustrated by the most eminent Antiquaries of our Age; with an Appendix, containing Ancient Poems and Extracts; with some Remarks on Ancient British Coins. Royal 8vo. calf, $5 00. London, 1809.

Davinci, (L.) Treatise on Painting. Translated by Rigaud. Crown 8vo. cloth, $3 00. London.

Davis, (J. F.) The Chinese; a General Description of China and its Inhabitants. 3 vols. 18mo. half calf, neat, wood-cuts. $2 25. London, 1844.

The Same. 2 vols. 12mo. cloth, $1 50. Lond.

——— (A. J.) The Principles of Nature, her Divine Revelations, and a Voice to Mankind. Thick 8vo. cloth, $2 50. New York, 1847.

Davis's Elements of Obstetric Medicine. 8vo.; plates 4to. $8 25. London.

Davison's Poetical Rhapsody; to which are added several other pieces; with Memoir and Notes, by Sir Harris Nicolas. 2 vols. post 8vo. cloth, $2 75. London, 1826.

Davy, (Sir Humphrey.) Collected Works; edited by his brother, J. Davy; with Memoir of his Life. 9 vols. 8vo. cloth, $13 50. London.

——— Elements of Agricultural Chemistry. New edition, with Notes by J. Shier. 8vo. cloth, $2 00. London.

——— Memoirs of the Life of; by Dr. Davy. 2 vols. 8vo. cloth, $3 50. London.

——— On the Safety Lamp. 8vo. cloth, with folding plate, $1 50. London.

——— (C.) The Architect, Engineer, and Operative Builder's Constructive Manual. 8vo. cloth, $3 25. London.

——— Architectural Precedents; with Notes and Observations. 8vo. cloth, $4 00. London.

Day, (G. F.) On Diseases of Advanced Life. 8vo. cloth, $1 25. Philadelphia, 1849.

——— (J.) Practical Treatise on the Construction and Formation of Railways. Illustrated with Diagrams, and Original Useful Tables. 12mo. cloth, $2 50.

Deakin, (Rd.) Florigraphia Britannica. 4 vols. 8vo. cloth, plates, plain, $13 50; colored, $19 50. London, 1848.

De Barante. Tableau de la Litterature. 12mo. paper, $1 00.

Debrett. Genealogical Peerage of Great Britain and Ireland. Revised and Corrected to January, 1849, by Henry Collen. Thick 8vo. half mor. $8 00. London, 1849.

De Burtin. A Treatise on the Knowledge Necessary to Amateurs of Pictures. Translated and Abridged, from the French of M. Francis Xavier de Burtin, by Robert White, Esq. with four plates. 8vo. cloth, $3 75. Lond. 1847.

De Candolle, (A.) Prodromus Systematis Naturalis Regni Vegetabilis, sive enumeratio Contracta Ordinum, Generum, Specierumque, Plantarum, &c. 12 vols. 8vo. paper, each $4 50. Paris, 1848.

Decker, (Col. C.) Petite Guerre (la) ou Traite des Operations Secondaires de la Guerra. 18mo. $1 25. Bruxelles, 1838.

Decorator, (The.) By J. Page. 48 plates. 12mo. cloth, $1 75.

De Foe's Life and Times, by Wilson. 3 vols. 8vo. cloth. London.

——— Novels and Miscellaneous Works. 20 vols. foolscap 8vo. cloth, $15 00. London.

——— Life and Adventures of Robinson Crusoe. Foolscap 8vo. cloth, $1 25. London.

——— New edition, printed in Old Style. Six illustrations, from Designs by Stothard. 4to. cloth, $2 25. London.

——— Complete Works; with Memoir of his Life and Writings, by William Hazlitt 3 vols. royal 8vo. cloth. $12 00. London.

De Graff's Stairbuilder's Guide. 8vo. cloth, $3 00. New York.

De Hart on Courts Martial. 8vo. law sheep, $3 00. New York.

De Hell, (Xavier.) Travels in the Steppes of the Caspian Sea. 8vo. cloth, $3 50. London, 1848.

D'Israeli, (I.) Amenities of Literature; consisting of Sketches and Characters of English Literature. Second edition. 3 vols. 8vo. cloth, $5 00. London, 1842.

The Same. 2 vols. 12mo. cloth, $1 50. N. York.

——— Curiosities of Literature. 8vo. cloth, $2 50. New York.

——— Miscellanies of Literature. 2 vols. 8vo. calf neat, $4 50. Paris, 1840.

——— (B.) Novels, in 1 vol. 8vo. cloth, $2 00. Philadelphia.

De La Beche's Report on the Geology of Cornwall, Devon, and West Somerset. 8vo. cloth, $4 25. London.

——— Geological Manual. 8vo. sheep, $3 50. Philadelphia, 1832.

——— Selection of the Geological Memoirs contained in the Annales des Mines, written by Brongniart, Humboldt, Von Buch, &c.; together with a Synoptical Table of Equivalent Formations, and Table of the Classification of Mixed Rocks. Translated, with Notes and Additions; illustrated by 11 folding plates, including a Geological map of France. 8vo. extra cloth boards, $2 25. 1836.

Delavigne, (C.) Œuvres Dramatique. 3 vols. 12mo. paper, $3 00. Paris.

——— Messéniennes et Poésies Diverses. 12mo. paper, $1 00. Paris.

Delecluze, (E. J.) Romans, Contes et Nouvelles. 12mo. broché, $1 00. Paris, 1835.

Delessert, (M. Eugene.) Voyages dans les deux Océans, Atlantic et Pacifique, 1844–47; Bresil, Etats Unis, Cap de Bonne-Esperance, Nouvelle Hollande, Nouvelle Zélande, Taiti, Philippines, Chine, Java, Indes Orientales, Egypt. Illustré. 1 vol. grand in 8vo. $6 00. Paris, 1849.

Delagardette. Ruines de Pæstum, ou Posidonia. ancienne ville de la Grande Grèce, mesurées, dessinées et restaurées, par Delagardette, architecte. 1 vol. in folio, de 14 planches. $6 00.

De Leuze. Treatise on Animal Magnetism. Translated by Hawthorne. 12mo. cloth, $1 00. New York.

De Lolme On the Rise and Progress of the English Constitution. With an Introduction, and Notes, by A. J. Stephens. 2 vols. 8vo. cloth, $3 50. London

Demaguy. Science des Armoiries. Royal 4to. colored, $30 00. Paris, 1848.

De Morgan, (A.) Trigonometry and Double Algebra. Post 8vo. cloth, $2 25. London, 1849.

——— Differential and Integral Calculus. Thick 8vo. cloth, $2 50. London, 1842.

——— Elements of Arithmetic. Post 8vo. cloth, $2 00. London, 1848.

——— Essay on Probabilities. 12mo. cloth, $2 00. London, 1848.

——— Formal Logic; or, the Calculus of Inference. 8vo. cloth, $3 75. London, 1847.

——— Notices of Arithmetical Books. Post 8vo. cloth, $2 00. London, 1848.

——— Treatise on the Globes. 8vo. cloth. $1 50. London, 1847.

Dempsey, (G. D.) The Practical Railway Engineer. Examples of the Mechanical and Engineering Operations and Structures combined in the making of a Railway. Fifty engravings. 4to. half mor. $11 00. London, 1847.

Dendy, (W. C.) Phenomena of Dreams. 12mo. cloth, $1 25. London.

——— Philosophy of Mystery. 12mo. cloth, 50 cents. New York, 1845.

Denison, (W.) Cricketer's Companion; containing the Scores of the Grand and Principal Matches of Cricket, played at Lord's, and other Grounds, in the Season 1844. 12mo. cloth, $1 00. London, 1845.

Denman, (T.). Midwifery. 8vo. sheep, $3 50. Philadelphia.

Dennis, (George.) Cities and Cemeteries of Etruria; with illustrations. 2 vols. 8vo. cloth, $12 00. London, 1848.

Denon's Antiquities of Egypt. 2 vols. 4to. Text; 1 vol. folio, 109 plates, $38 00.

De Pambour, (Comte.) The Theory of the Steam Engine. 8vo. cloth, $3 25. Lond. 1839.

——— Practical Treatise an Locomotive Engines. 8vo. cloth, $5 50. London, 1840.

De Quincy, (M. Q.) Essay on the Nature, the End, and the Means of Imitation in the Fine Arts. 8vo. cloth, $2 00.

——— Confessions of An Opium Eater. 12mo. 50 cents. Boston, 1848.

De Retz, (Cardinal.) Memoirs du Edition Collationnée, sur les Manuscrits authentiques de la Bibliothèque Royale. 2 vols. 12mo. paper, $2 00; half mor. $3 50. Paris, 1846.

Descartes. Œuvres, edition Jules Simon 12mo. paper, $1 00. Paris.

Description of a Series of Geological Models, illustrating the Nature of Stratification, Denudation, Coal Seams, Faults, or Dislocations of Strata, Intersection of Mineral Veins, &c. 12 lithographic drawings. $1 00.

Desdouits, (M.) Leçons élémentaires D'Astronomie. Crown 8vo. mor. gilt edges, $2 25. Tours, 1844.

De Senancour. Obermann. 12mo. paper, $1 00. Paris.

Deshler, (C. O.) Selections from Chaucer. 12mo. cloth, 50 cents. New York, 1847.

De Tocqueville's Democracy in America. One vol. thick 8vo. cloth, $3 00. New York, 1848.

Detournelle. Nouveau Traité des cinq Ordres d'Architecture, d'après J. A. de Vignole, dessiné par Detournelle, Architecte. 1 vol in 4 de 21 planches, avec texte. $1 50.

——— Grand Prix d'Architecture. 120 plates. Folio, half calf, $22 00.

De Wette, (M. W. L.) Human Life; or, Practical Ethics. 2 vols. 12mo. cloth, $2 00. Boston.

——— Theodore; or, the Sceptic's Conversion. 2 vols. 12mo. cloth, $2 00. Boston.

——— Introduction to the Canonical Books of the Old Testament. Translated by Theodore Parker. 2 vols. 8vo. cloth, $4 50. Boston.

Dewey, (Orville.) Works. 3 vols. 12mo. cloth, $3 00. New York.

——— (L. D.) Wisdom for the Young; being the Advice of Chief Justice Hale; with the Opinions of Distinguished Americans. 12mo. cloth, 75 cents. New York, 1847.

Deyeux. La Chassomanie, Poeme, ornée de Seize Grands Dessins a deux Teintes. 8vo. hf. mor. gilt, gilt top, $5 00. Paris, 1844.

Diary of the Times of Charles the Second; by the Hon. Henry Sidney. To which are added. Letters illustrative of the Times of James II. and William III. Edited, with Notes, by R. W. Blencowe, Esq., A.M. Portraits. 2 vols. 8vo. cloth, $3 75. London, 1843.

Diary of the Times of George the Fourth, interspersed with Original Letters from the late Queen Caroline, and from various other Distinguished Persons, (by Lady Charlotte Bury, Maid of Honor to Queen Caroline, Miss Sheridan, and John Galt.) New edition. Beautiful portrait of the Queen. 4 vols. post 8vo. extra cloth, $4 75. London, 1839

Diary of Lady Willoughby; (so much of the) as relates to her Domestic History, and the Eventful Period of the Reign of Charles I. 12mo. cloth, 50 cents. New York, 1848.

The Same. Original edition; second part. 4to. $5 00. London.

Dibdin, (T. F.) Introduction to the Classics. 2 vols. 8vo. cloth, $3 50. London.

——— Bibliomania; or, Book-Madness; a Bibliographical Romance, new edition, with considerable Additions; including a Key to the Assumed Characters in the Drama, and a Supplement. Handsomely printed; embellished by numerous wood-cuts. 2 vols. royal 8vo. $8 00.

——— (Charles.) Selected Songs, with Notes and Memoirs of the Author. Thick 18mo. cloth gilt, $1 00. London, 1845

Dick, (R.) On the Treatment of Dyspepsia. 8vo. cloth, $1 75. Philadelphia.

——— (Thos. LL.D.) Complete Works. 2 vols. 8vo. Philadelphia.

——— Celestial Scenery. 12mo. cloth, 50 cents. New York.

——— Sidereal Heavens. 12mo. cloth, 50 cts. New York.

——— Practical Astronomer; with a Particular Account of the Earl of Rosse's Telescopes. 100 engravings. 12mo. cloth, 50 cents. New York, 1846.

——— Christian Philosopher; or, the Connection of Science and Philosophy with Religion. Illustrated with engravings. 2 vols. 12mo. cloth, $1 25. London.

Dickens, (Charles.) Works. 3 vols. 8vo. cloth, $3 50. Philadelphia.

——— Dealings with the Firm of Dombey and Son. Illustrations by H. K. Browne. 8vo. cloth, $5 00. London, 1848.

The Same. 2 vols. 12mo. cloth, $2 00.

The Same; without the plates. 2 vols. 12mo. cloth, $1 25. New York.

——— Pictures from Italy. Wood-cuts. 12mo. cloth, $1 25. London, 1846.

American Edition. 38 cents.

——— Personal History and Experience of David Copperfield the Younger. Now publishing in Nos. each 12½ cents. New York.

——— Works; uniform in 12mo. cloth, each $1 50.

ALREADY PUBLISHED.

Pickwick Papers.
Old Curiosity Shop.
Nicholas Nickleby.
Barnaby Rudge. London, 1849.

——— Martin Chuzzlewit. Cloth, 75 cents. New York.

———Nicholas Nickleby. 8vo. cloth, $1 50. Philadelphia.

——— Oliver Twist. 8vo. cloth, $1 25. Philadelphia.

——— Pickwick Papers. 8vo. cloth, $1 50. Philadelphia.

——— Christmas Stories. 12mo. cloth, $1 00. New York.

Dickson, (J. H.) Letters on the Improved Mode in the Cultivation and Management of Flax; with various Rules and Instructions. 12mo. cloth, $1 12. London, 1846.

——— (S.) Chrono-Thermal Practice of Medicine. 8vo. cloth, $1 00. New York.

——— (S. H.) Manual of Pathology. $1 50. New York.

——— Practice of Medicine. 2 vols. 8vo. $8 00. New York.

Difficulties of a Young Clergyman in Times of Division. 12mo. cloth, $1 00, London, 1844.

Digby, (R. H.) Broad Stone of Honor, in Three Parts. 3 vols. 12mo. cloth, $7 50. London, 1848.

Divers Works of Early Masters in Christian Decoration; with an Introduction, containing the Biography, Journal of Travel, and contemporaneous Associations in Art, of Albert Durer, notices of his master, Wohlgemuth, and his friend Pirckheymer; Adam Krafft, and his Sacrament-house at Nuremburg; some English Examples of Painted and Stained Glass of an Earlier Date; the ancient Church and Sacrament-House at Limbourg; the Works of Dirk and Wouter Crabeth, &c. Numerous specimens of richly Painted and Stained Glass Windows, and Ecclesiastical Decoration. 2 vols. folio, half mor. $55 00. London.

Dix, (W. G.) Pompeii, and Other Poems. 12mo. boards, 75 cents. Boston, 1848.

——— (John H.) Treatise upon the Nature and Treatment of Morbid Sensibility of the Retina, or Weakness of Sight. 12mo. cloth, 75 cents. Boston, 1849.

Doane, (A. S.) Magrière's Midwifery. 8vo. cloth, $5 00. New York.

——— Magrière's Anatomy. 8vo cloth, $4 75. New York.

——— Surgery. 8vo. cloth, $4 50. N. York.

Dobson, (E.) Rudiments of the Art of Building. 12mo. cloth. Illustrated with 118 cuts. 25 cts. London, 1849.

——— Builder's and Architect's Instructor. 8vo. cloth, $2 25. London.

——— Historical, Statistical, and Scientific Account of the Railways of Belgium, from 1834 to 1842. Royal 8vo. cloth boards, $1 75.

——— (Rev. W.) Subjects and Selections for Latin and Greek Composition, in Prose and Verse. 12mo. cloth, 63 cts. London, 1845.

Dodd. Beauties of Shakspeare; a new edition, with two engravings. 18mo. cloth, $1 00. London.

——— (G.) Chemical Manufactures of Great Britain. 18mo. half calf neat, 75 cents. London, 1844.

——— Textile Manufactures of Great Britain. 6 vols. 18mo. half calf, cloth sides, and lettered. $5 00. London, 1844.

——— (Charles R.) The Peerage, Baronetage, and Knightage of Great Britain and Ireland for 1839, including all the Titled Classes. 12mo. cloth, $3 00. London, 1849.

——— Annual Biography. 12mo. cloth, $1 00, London, 1843.

——— (C.) Manual of Dignities, Privileges, and Precedents; including Lists of the Great Public Functionaries, from the Revolution to the Present Time. Thick 12mo. cloth, $1 25. London, 1844.

Dodd's Church History of England, from the Commencement of the Sixteenth Century to the Revolution in 1688. With Notes, Additions, and a Continuation by Rev. M. Tierney. 5 vols. 8vo. cloth, $18 00. London, 1839.

Doddridge's Rise and Progress of Religion in the Soul. 18mo. cloth, 42 cents. New York.

——— (Dr.) Miscellaneous Works. Imperial 8vo. cloth, $5 00. London.

Dodo and its Kindred; Or, the History, Affinities, and Osteology of the Dodo, Solitaire, and other extinct Birds of the islands

Mauritius, Rodriguez, and Bourbon. By H. E. Strickland and A G. Melville. Eighteen plates and numerous wood illustrations. Royal 4to cloth, $6 50. London, 1848.

Dog-Fancier's Guide. Plain Instructions for Breeding and Managing the Several Varieties of Field, Sporting, and Fancy Dogs. 12mo. cloth, 25 cents. London.

Dollman, (F. C.) Examples of Ancient Pulpits existing in England, drawn from actual measurement, with Descriptions. 4to. $8 00. London.

Dollinger's History of the Church, by Cox. 4 vols. 8vo. cloth, $10 25. London.

Domestic Scenes; by the Author of the Baroness, &c. 12mo. cloth, $2 25. London, 1848.

Don Quixotte. (See Cervantes.)

Don's General System of Gardening and Botany, containing a complete Enumeration and Description of all Plants hitherto known; with their Generic and Specific Characters, Places of Growth, Time of Flowering, Mode of Culture, and their Uses in Medicine and Domestic Economy, &c. founded upon Miller's Gardener's Dictionary; and arranged according to the Natural System. Numerous wood-cuts. 4 vols. royal 4to. cloth, (published at £14 8s.) London, 1331–38.

Donaldson's Treatise on Manures; their Nature, Preparation. and Application. With wood-cuts, and plans of Farm Buildings. 2d edition. 8vo. cloth, lettered, $1 00. London, 1846.

——— (J. W.) Complete Greek Grammar, for the Use of Learners. 12mo. bound, $1 25. London, 1848.

——— New Cratylus. 8vo. cloth, $5 12. London

——— Greek Theatre. 8vo. cloth, $3 50. London.

——— Examples of Doorways, from Ancient Buildings in Greece and Italy. Plates. 4to. cloth, $9 50.

——— Modern Doorways. Plates. 4to cloth, $9 50.

——— (Thos. L.) Architectural Maxims and Theorems. 8vo. cloth, bds. $1 75.

Donegan, (James.) Greek and English Lexicon. 8vo. sheep, $5 00. Philadelphia.

Donne, (Dr. John.) Works; including his Sermons, Devotions, Poems, Letters, &c., edited, with a new Memoir, by the Rev. Henry Alford. With fine portrait. 6 handsome vols. 8vo. cloth, (pub. at £3 12s.) $12 00. Parker, 1839.

The Same. 6 vols. 8vo. calf extra, $18 00.

——— Devotions, with Two Sermons. To which is prefixed his Life, by Isaac Walton. 12mo. morocco, gilt edges, $4 00; cloth, $1 75. London, 1840.

Donovan, (Edward.) Natural History of the Insects of India. New edition, by J. O. Westwood. 58 plates, containing upwards of 120 exquisitely colored figures. 4to. cloth, gilt, $13 50. London, 1842.

Donovan, (E.) Natural History of the Insects of China. New edition, by J. O. Westwood. 50 plates, containing upwards of 120 exquisitely colored figures. 4to. cloth gilt, $13 50. Lond. 1842.

——— Works on British Natural History, viz. Insects, 16 vols.; Birds, 10 vols.; Shells, 5 vols.; Fishes, 5 vols.; Quadrupeds, 3 vols.; together 39 vols. 8vo. bds. plates colored, $144.

The Same. Bound in 21 vols. half green mor. gilt edges and gilt backs, $180 00.

——— British Birds. 244 colored plates. 11 vols. royal 8vo. bds. $38 00.

——— British Fishes. 126 colored plates. 5 vols. royal 8vo. bds. $19 00.

——— British Quadrupeds. 72 colored plates. 3 vols. royal 8vo. bds. $9 00.

——— Natural History of British Quadrupeds; consisting of colored figures, accompanied with Scientific and General Descriptions. 8vo. half mor. $5 00.

——— (M.) A Treatise on Chemistry. 4th edition. Foolscap 8vo. cloth, $1 87. London.

D'Ormoy, (Louis.) Histoire de Paris en 1843, d'apres les Publications Officielles les Révélations de l'Enquête et les Discussions de l'Assemble Nationale. 12mo. broché, 75 cts. Paris, 1849.

Doubleday, (Edward.) Butterflies. The Genera of Diurnal Lepidoptera: comprising their Generic Characters; a Notice of the Habits and Transformations, and a catalogue of each Genus. Illustrated with 75 colored plates, by W. C. Hewitson, Esq. Imperial 4to. cloth, about $63 00.

(Publishing in parts at $1 50 each; to be completed in 40 parts, 31 of which have appeared)

——— (Thos.) A Financial, Monetary, and Statistical History of England, from the Revolution, 1688, to the Present Time. 8vo. cloth, $3 25. London, 1847.

Douce, (F.) Illustrations of Shakspeare, and of Ancient Manners; with Dissertations on the Clowns and Fools of Shakspeare. Forty engravings. 8vo. cloth, $2 25. London.

Douglas, (Major General Sir Howard.) On Military Bridges. Plates. 8vo. $6 00.

Douling, (W.) A Popular Natural History of Quadrupeds and Birds. 12mo. cloth, $1 25.

Dover, (Lord.) Life of Frederic the Great. 2 vols. 8vo. cloth, $8 50. London.

Downing, (A. J.) Fruits and Fruit-Trees of America; or, the Culture, Propagation, and Management in the Garden and Orchard, of Fruit-Trees generally. Illustrated with many engravings. 12mo. $1 50. New York, 1849.

——— Cottage Residences; or, a Series of Designs for Rural Cottages and Cottage Villas. 8vo. cloth, $2 00. New York.

——— Treatise on the Theory and Practice of Landscape Gardening; with Remarks on Rural Architecture. Second edition, enlarged, revised, and newly illustrated. 8vo. cloth, $3 50. New York.

Downing, (A. J.) Country Houses; or, New Designs for Rural Cottages, Farm-Houses, and Villas, with Interior and Furniture. New York.

Doyle. Cyclopædia of Practical Husbandry and Rural Affairs. Edited by Rham. 8vo. cloth, $2 75. London, 1843.

Drake, (N.) Memorials of Shakspeare; or, Sketches of his Character and Genius; by Various Writers. Now first Collected, with Prefatory Essay and Notes. 8vo. cloth, $3 00. London, 1848.

——— Shakspeare and his Times; including a Biography of the Poet. Royal 8vo. calf, neat marble edges, $4 50. Paris, 1838.

——— (S. G.) Tragedies of the Wilderness. 12mo. cloth, $1 00.

——— Book of the Indians. 8vo. cloth, $3 00.

Draper, (J. W.) Chemistry of Plants. 4to. cloth, plates, $2 50. New York.

——— Text-book of Natural Philosophy. 12mo. sheep, 75 cents. New York.

——— Elements of Chemistry. 12mo. sheep, illustrated, 75 cents. New York.

Dramatic (American) Library, Containing Athenia of Damascus, a tragedy, by Rufus Dawes; Bianca Visconti, by N. P. Willis; and Tortesa, the Usurer, by N. P. Willis. 12mo. cloth, 75 cents. New York, 1839.

Drawing-Room Scrap-Book. Edited by Mrs. Norton. 4to. cloth, $4 50. London, 1849.

Dredge, (J.) Suspension Bridge explained, upon the Principles of the Lever, by W. Turnbull; with a Specification, &c. of the Suspension Bridge at Balloch Ferry, Dunbartonshire, and an Isometrical Projection. 8vo. cloth. Plate and wood-cuts, $1 50.

Druitt, (Robert,) The Principles and Practice of Modern Surgery. A new American edition, from the last and improved London; edited by F. W. Sargent. Illustrated with 193 wood engravings. 8vo. sheep, $3 25. Philadelphia, 1848.

Drummond, (Sir William.) Origines, or Remarks on the Origin of Empires, States, and Cities. 4 vols. 8vo. maps and plates, cloth, $9 50. 1824–29.

——— (J. L.) Observations on Natural Systems of Botany. 12mo. cloth, $1 00. London, 1849.

Drury, (Miss.) Friends and Fortune. 12mo. cloth, $1 00. New York, 1849.

——— (D.) Illustrations of Foreign Entomology. New edition, by J. O. Westwood. 600 figures, engraved by Moses Harris, correctly and beautifully colored; in 3 vols. 4to. half mor. neat, $41 00. London, 1837.

Dryden, (John.) Works of, in verse and prose, with a Life, by Rev. John Mitford. 2 vols. 8vo. sheep, $3 75. New York, 1847.

Dubourg, (M.) Views of the Remains of Ancient Buildings in Rome and its Vicinity, with a Descriptive and Historical Account of each subject. 4to. cloth, colored plates, $10 00. London, 1844

Dublin Dissector; or, Manual of Anatomy, by Harrison. 12mo. cloth, $2 75. London.

The Same. 12mo. cloth, $2 00. New York.

Ducatel's Toxicology. 12mo. cloth, $1 00. Baltimore.

Ducoin-Girardin. Entretiens sur la Physique et ses Applications les plus curieuses; orne de 2 portraits. 1 vol. in 8, $1 75.

Duckett, (G. J.) Technological Military Dictionary; German, English, French. New Edition, German part. 8vo. cloth, $6, 50. London, 1849.

Dufief. Nature displayed in the Teaching of French. 2 vols. 8vo. bds., $5 00. Philadelphia.

——— Nature displayed in the Teaching of Spanish. 2 vols. 8vo. bds., $7 00. Philadelphia.

Duffin, (G. W.) On Deformity of the Spine, cloth, 50 cents. New York.

Dufton, (William.) The Nature and Treatment of Deafness and Diseases of the Ear, and the Treatment of the Deaf and Dumb. 12mo. cloth, 63 cents. Philadelphia, 1848.

Dugdale's Monasticon Anglicanum. New edition, with the whole of the Plates and Text as originally published, by Caley, Ellis, Bandinel, and others, with every needed correction. 8 vols. folio. half mor. gilt, $189 00.

Duke, (E.) Druidical Temples of the County of Wilts. 12mo. $1 50. London.

Duke of Argyll's Essay on the Ecclesiastical History of Scotland, since the Reformation. Second edition. 12mo. cloth, $1 50.

Dumas, (M. T.) Memoires de Chimie. 8vo. paper, $2 00. Paris 1843.

——— (A.) Isabel de Bavière. 2 vols. 12mo. broché, $1 50. Paris, 1848.

——— Le Maitre D'Armes. 12mo. broché, 75 cents. Paris, 1848.

——— Fernande. 12mo. broché, 75 cents. Paris, 1848.

——— Un Fille du Régent. 12mo. broché, 75 cents. Paris, 1848.

——— Le Comte de Monte Cristo. bds. 12mo. broché, $4 50. Paris, 1847.

——— Une Fille du Régent. 3 vols. 12mo. paper, $1 75. Bruxelles, 1849.

——— Les Trois Mousquetaires. 2 vols. 12mo. paper, $1 50. Paris, 1847.

Dumont's Plans, Elevations, and Sections of St. Peter's at Rome. 96 plates, folio, $13 50.

Duncan, (J. F.) Clinical Lectures, Dublin. 8vo. cloth. $1 50. London, 1848.

——— (H.) Sacred Philosophy of the Seasons. 4 vols. 12mo. cloth, $3 00. New York.

——— (W.) Select Orations of Cicero. Translated into English, with Notes Historical, Critical, and Explanatory. 8vo. cloth, $1 75. Oxford, 1841

Dunglison, (R.) Medical Student. post, 8vo. cloth, $2 00. New York.

——— Materia Medica, and Therapeutics. 2 vols. 8vo. sheep, $5 50. Philadelphia.

Dunglison's Physiology. 2 vols. 8vo. sheep $6 00. Philadelphia.

——— On Human Health. 8vo sheep, $2 50. Philadelphia.

——— The Practice of Medicine; a Treatise on Special Pathology and Therapeutics. Third edition, 2 vols. 8vo. sheep, $6 25. Philadelphia, 1848.

——— New Remedies. Fifth edition; with extensive additions. 8vo. sheep, $3 00. Philadelphia, 1846.

——— Dictionary of Medical Science. Seventh edition, carefully revised, and greatly enlarged. thick 8vo. sheep, $4 00. Philadelphia, 1848.

Dunham. History of Europe during the Middle Ages. 4 vols. 12mo. cloth, $6 75. London.

——— History of the Germanic Empire, to the French Revolution. 3 vols. 12mo. cloth, $5 00. London.

——— History of Spain and Portugal, to the French Revolution. 5 vols. 12mo. cloth, $8 50. London.

——— History of Denmark, Sweden, and Norway. 3 vols. 12mo. cloth, $5 00. London.

——— History of Poland. 12mo. cloth, $1 75. London.

Dunham. (Dr.) **Bell,** (R.) The Lives of British Dramatists. 2 vols. foolscap 8vo. cloth, $3 62. London.

——— The Lives of the Early British Writers of Great Britain. Foolscap 8vo. cloth, $1 75. London.

Dunlop, (John.) Memoirs of Spain, during the Reign of Philip IV. and Charles II. 1621–1700. 2 vols. 8vo. cloth, $3 50.

——— History of Fiction; being a Critical Account of the most celebrated Prose Works of Fiction from the earliest Greek Romances to the Novels of the Present Age. Third edition. 8vo. cloth. $4 50. London.

——— (Robert G.) Travels in Central America; with a Journal of nearly Three Years' Residence in the Country. To which is added a Short Sketch of the History of the Republic, and an Account of its Climate, Productions, Commerce, &c., &c.; with Map. Post 8vo. cloth, $3 50. London.

Dunn, (M.) Treatise on the Winning and Working of Collieries. Illustrated by Plans and Engravings. 8vo. cloth, $4 00.

Dupin, (C.) Mathematics, practically applied to the useful and Fine Arts. Adapted to the state of the Arts in England, by Geo. Birkbeck, Esq., M.D. 8vo, cloth, $1 25. London, 1827.

Dupuyten, (Baron.) Surgery. Translated by A. S. Doane. 8vo. cloth, $1 25. Philadelphia.

Durand. Recueil et Parallele des Edifices de tout genré, Anciens et Moderns, remarquables par leur beauté, &c.; above 100 fine large detailed folio plates, half bound, $37 50.

Durer, (A.) Married Life of; by Schefer. 12mo. cloth, 75 cents, plain, gilt, $1 00. Boston, 1849.

Durer, (A.) Passion of Our Lord Jesus Christ, from the thirty-eight original woodcuts. Small 4to. mor. $8 00. London.

Duval, Kaufman, Renaud, et autres architectes.—Petites maisons de villes et de campagne, choisies dans les quartiers neufs de la capitale et aux environs de Paris. $16 00.

Premiere partie, composée de 60 pl. in-folio, avec texte. $8 00.

La Deuxieme Partie a pour titre; Fermes modèles.—Recueil de constructions rurales et communales, comprenant un choix d'exemples des bâtiments nécessaires aux divers degrés de l'exploitation agricole; des motifs ou modèles d'édifices et établissements d'utilite publique, appropriés nux besoins des communes suivant leur importance, &c. $8 00.

Dwight, (T.) Theology. 4 vols. 8vo. cloth, $6 00

——— Travels in New England and New York. 4 vols. 8vo. cloth, $7 50. New York.

——— (M. A.) Grecian and Roman Mythology; with an Introduction by Taylor Lewis, Professor of Greek, in the University of New York. 12mo. half bound, $1 50; Large paper, with illustrations. $3 00; cloth gilt, $3 50; half mor. top edge gilt, $3 75. New York, 1849.

Dwyer, (J.) Principles and Practice of Hydraulic Engineering. 8vo. cloth, $3 25. London, 1848.

Dyce, (A.) Remarks on Collier's and Knight's Shakspeare. 8vo. cloth, $2 75. London.

Dyer, (The) and Color Maker's Companion; containing upwards of 200 Receipts for making Colors on the most Approved Principles, for all the various styles and fabrics now in existence. 12mo. cloth, gilt edges, $2 25. Glasgow, 1849.

Dyeing, Calico Printing; including the latest Inventions and Improvements, with an Appendix, comprising Definitions of Chemical Terms, with Tables of Weights, Measures, Thermometers, Hydrometers, &c. By an Experienced Dyer; and assisted by several Scientific Gentlemen. Illustrated with Engravings on wood and steel. 8vo. cloth, $3 50. New York.

Eadie, (John, LL.D.) Biblical Cyclopædia; or, Dictionary of Eastern Antiquities, Geography, Natural History, Sacred Annals, and Biography, Theology, and Biblical Literature. Illustrative of the Old and New Testaments; with Maps and Pictorial Illustrations, drawn from the most Authentic Sources. 8vo. cloth, $3 00.

Earnshaw, (S.) Treatise on Dynamics. 8vo cloth, $4 25. London.

——— Treatise on Statics; containing the Theory of the Equilibrium of Forces, and numerous Examples, illustrative of the General Principles of the Science, &c. 8vo. $2 75.

Eastern Arts and Antiquities. Cloth, 75 cents. Philadelphia.

Eastlake, (C. L.) Contributions to the Literature of the Fine Arts. 8vo. cloth, $3 75. London, 1848.

——— (E. E.) Materials for a History of Oil Painting. 8vo. cloth, $3 75. London, 1848.

Eaton and Wright's North American Botany. 8vo. cloth, $3 75. London.

Eaton's Engineering and Surveying. 4to. hf bound, $1 75. New York.

Eberle. (J.) Notes and Lectures for Students. 8vo. sheep, $1 13.

——— Practice of Medicine. 2 vols. in 1, 8vo. sheep, $5 00.

——— Therapeutics. 2 vols. in 1. 8vo. sheep, $4 00.

——— On Children. 8vo. sheep, $3 00.

Ecclesiastes: The Words of the Preacher; magnificently illuminated by Owen Jones; curiously bound, in massive carved wood covers. Royal 8vo. $12 00. London, 1849.

Eccleston, (J.) Manual of English Antiquities. 8vo. cloth, $6 50. London.

Ecclesiologist, (The.) With many Plates, illustrative of Churches and Church Decorations. First and Second Series. 10 vols. 8vo. $20 00.

Eckerman, (J. P.) Conversations with Goethe. 12mo. cloth, $1 00. Boston.

Eckfeld and Du Bois. Manual of Coins. 4to. half bound, $5 00. Philadelphia.

Eddy, (Rev. D. C.) Lectures to Young Ladies on Subjects of Practical Importance. 12mo. cloth, 63 cents. Lowell, 1845.

Eden, (T. E.) Search for Nitre, and the True Nature of Guano; being an Account of a Voyage to the South West Coast of Africa. 12mo. cloth, 87 cents. London, 1846.

Edgar, (Samuel.) The Variations of Popery. Second edition. 8vo. $2 00. Lond. 1838.

Edgeworth, (Miss.) Tales and Novels. New edition; in 9 vols. 12mo. cloth. Frontispieces and Vignettes. $12 00. London, 1849.

——— Tales and Novels. Complete in 10 vols. 12mo. cloth, $7 50. New York.

——— Castle Rackrent; an Essay on Irish Bulls 12mo. mor. gilt, $2 00. London, 1832.

Edinburgh Cabinet Library. 38 vols. 12mo. cloth, $34 25.

Edinburgh Review, (The.) From the commencement to October, 1849. 93 vols including the 2 vols. of Indexes. half calf, neat, $130 00. A very fine set.

——— Selections from; comprising the best Articles from that Journal, from its commencement to the present time; with Preliminary Dissertation, &c. Edited by M. Cross. 6 vols. 8vo. sewed, $4 50. Paris, 1835.

Edward's Materia Medica. 8vo. sheep, $2 75. Philadelphia,

——— (Jonathan.) Works. 2 vols. impl. 8vo. cloth, lettered, $12 50. 1840.

——— (J.) On the Will. 12mo. cloth, $1 00. New York.

——— (H. M.) Anatomy and Physiology. 8vo. cloth, $1 75. Boston.

——— Voyage up the River Amazon. 12mo. cloth, $1 00. New York.

Egan, (Ch.) Observations on the New French Law relative to Patents for Inventions. 4to. cloth, $1 50. London.

Egypt under Mahomet Ali; by Prince Puckler Muskau. 3 vols, post, 8vo. cloth, $4 50.

Egyptian Antiquities in the British Museum, drawn by Arundale and Bonomi, with letter-press descriptions, by S. Birch, of the British Museum, royal 4to., containing several hundred figures of interesting subjects, represented on 57 elaborate plates, many colored; gilt cloth, with Egyptian devices in gold on back and sides, $6 50. London, 1844.

Egypt and the Pyramids. Colonel Vyse's great work on the Pyramids of Gizeh, containing a detailed account of his extraordinary Operations and Discoveries on the opening of these interesting Monuments of Antiquity, with an account of his voyage into Upper Egypt; to which is added an Appendix, by J. S. Perring, Esq., (the engineer,) on the Pyramids at Abou Roash, the Fayoum, &c., &c. 3 vols. impl. 8vo. with 125 plates, lithographed by Haghe, cloth, bds. $13 00. 1840–42.

Ekin, (Ch.) Naval Battles from 1744 to 1814. 4to. cloth, $12 75. London.

——— Naval and Universal Signals, in Symbols of Black and White. 8vo. cloth, $1 00.

Eldon, (Life of.) By Horace Twiss. 3 vols. crown, 8vo. $12 75. London.

Elementary Book of Drawing, Shading, and Coloring, $4 50. Philadelphia.

Elizabeth, (Charlotte.) The English Martyrology; abridged from Fox. 2 vols. 12mo. cloth, illustrated, $3 37. London, 1835.

——— Wrongs of Woman. Milliners and Dressmakers. 18mo. cloth, 50 cents. New York, 1843.

——— Second Causes; or, Up and Be Doing. 18mo. cloth, 50 cents. New York, 1843.

Elkington on Land Draining. 8vo. cloth, plates, $3 12. London.

Ellet, (Mrs. E. F.) Family Pictures from the Bible. 12mo. paper, 75 cents, cloth $1 25. N. Y., 1849.

The Same. Fine edition, roy. 8vo. cloth, gilt $3 00.

The Same. Handsomely bound in mor. gilt $5 00.

——— Women of the American Revolution. 2 vols. 12mo. cloth, $2 25. New York, 1848.

Elliott, (Rev. G. B.) Horæ Apocalypticæ; or, Commentary on the Apocalypse, Critical and Historical, third edition, revised and corrected. 4 vols. 8vo. cloth, $12 00. London, 1847.

——— (S.) Roman Liberty: a History, with a View of the Liberty of other Ancient Nations. 2 vols. 8vo. cloth. $4 50. New York.

Elliotson's Practical Medicine. By Roger Lee. 8vo. cloth, $7 50. London.

Ellis, (George Viner.) Demonstrations of Anatomy; being a Guide to the Knowledge of the Human Body by Dissection. Second edition, rewritten. 12mo. cloth, 2 parts, $3 75. London, 1843.

——— (G.) Specimens of Early English Metrical Romances. 12mo. cloth, $1 50. London, 1848.

Ellis, (Sir W. C.) On the Nature, Symptoms, Causes, and Treatment of Insanity; with Practical Observations on Lunatic Asylums, and a Description of the Pauper Lunatic Asylum for the County of Middlesex, at Hanwell, with a Detailed Account of its Management. 8vo. extra, cloth, boards, $1 50. 1838.

——— Specimens of Early English Poets, with an Historical Sketch of the Rise and Progress of the English Poetry and Language. Fifth edition. 3 vols. small 8vo. cloth, gilt. $3 75. London, 1845.

The Same. Half mor. $4 50.

The Same. Mor, antique, $15 00.

The Same. 3 vols. 12mo. cloth, $2 75.

——— (Sir H.) Original Letters, Illustrative of English History, with Notes and Illustrations 4 vols. 12mo. cloth, $4 00. London, 1846.

——— Townley Gallery of Classic Sculpture. 2 vols. 12mo. cloth, $1 37. London.

Ellis's Laws and Regulations of the Customs, for 1846. 12mo. cloth, $2 00. Lond. 1846.

Elliston, (R. W.) Memoirs of; by George Raymond; with illustrations by George Cruikshank. Portrait. 8vo. cloth, $2 50. London, 1844.

Elmes, (J.) Memoirs of the Life of Sir Christopher Wren. 4to. calf, plates, $6 00.

——— A General and Biographical Dictionary of the Fine Arts. 8vo. cloth, $4 50.

Elphinstone, (Hon. M.) History of India. 8vo. cloth, $6 50. London.

——— Account of the Kingdom of Caubul and its Dependencies in Persia, Tartary, and India, &c. 2 vols. 8vo. cloth, plates and maps, $3 00. London, 1842.

Elsley, (Rev. J.) Annotations on the Four Gospels and the Acts of the Apostles. New edition, revised by R. Walker. Map, 8vo. cloth, $3 00. Oxford, 1844.

Elsemere, (Earl.) Guide to Northern Archæology. 8vo. cloth, $2 25. London.

Elwood, (Mrs) Memoirs of the Literary Ladies of England, from the commencement to the last Century. 2 vols. post, 8vo. cloth, $3 London, 1848.

Emerson. Trees of Massachusetts. 8vo. cloth, $3 00. Boston, 1846.

——— (R. W.) Poems. Fourth edition, 12mo. $1 00. Boston, 1847.

——— Essays. First and Second Series. 2 vols. 12mo. cloth $1 50. Boston, 1848.

Emmon's Works, Complete. 6 vols. 8vo. sheep, $12 00. Boston.

Enny on Hydraulic Maritime Works. 1 vol. 4to. and an Atlas of Plates, $6 00. London.

Encyclopædia Britannica. Last edition, handsomely bound in half Russia, 21 vols. 4to. $145 00. 7th edition. Edinburgh, 1842.

——— Metropolitana. Complete in 27 volumes. 4to. half Russia, marble edges, $160 00. London, 1845.

——— Americana. A Popular Dictionary of Arts, Sciences, Literature, History, Politics, and Biography. A new edition; including a Copious Collection of Articles in American Biography—on the Basis of the German Conversations Lexicon. Edited by F. Lieber, assisted by E. Wigglesworth. 14 vols. 8vo. cloth, $16 00. Philadelphia, 1848.

——— Methodique—Repertoire universel de tout ce qui l'esprit humain a recueil de connaissances dans les temps anciens et modernes divise par ordre de matières, par une societe de gens de lettres. 164 vols. avec 6,439 planches, $300, au lieu de 4,206 francs.

——— Des Gens Du Monde. Repertoire universel des sciences, des lettres, et des arts, avec des notices sur les principales families historiques et sur les principaux personnages, morts et vivants, par une societe de savants. 22 vol. 8vo. demi maroquin, $65. Paris, 1833.

——— Of Arts, Manufactures, and Machinery. By Peter Barlow; to which is prefixed an Introductory View of the Principles of Manufactures, by Charles Babbage. Illustrated by 550 figures of Machinery and Implements. 4to. cloth, $12 50.

——— Of Religious Knowledge. royal 8vo. sheep, $5 00. Brattleboro.

——— Of Useful Knowledge. 8vo. calf, $5 00. New York.

——— Of Civil Engineering; Historical, Theoretical, and Practical. Illustrated by upwards of 3000 Engravings on wood, explanatory of the Principal Machinery and Constructions which come under the direction of the Civil Engineer. By E. Cresey. Thick 8vo. cloth, $18.

Endless Amusements. 18mo. cloth, 62 cents. London.

Engineer's Manual of Geology and Mineralogy. 12mo. plates, $1 00. London.

——— Pocket Guide. By Kelt. 18mo. cloth, 75 cents. Boston.

Engineer's and Contractor's Pocket-Book. 12mo. mor. $1 87. London, 1849.

Engineer and Mechanic's Companion. By Scribner. $1 13. New York.

Engineering, Architectural and Mechanical Drawing-Book; a series of Instructive Examples, illustrated by 30 large folio Engravings, with descriptive letter-press. $5 00. London.

——— From the French of Sganzin, $1 38. Boston.

Englishman's Greek Concordance of the New Testament; being an Attempt at a Verbal Connection between the Greek and the English Texts; including a Concordance of Proper Names, with Indexes, Greek-English and English-Greek. Second edition, with a new Index. royal 8vo. sheep, $5 00. New York.

——— Hebrew and Chaldee Concordance of the Old Testament; being an Attempt at a Verbal Connection between the Original and the English Translations, with Indexes; a List of the Proper Names, and their occurrences, &c. &c. 2 vols. royal 8vo. cloth, $22 00. London.

Englefield, (Sir H.) Collection of Vases; drawn and engraved by H. Moses. Impl. 8vo. half mor. $2 50. London, 1819.

Enigmas, Charades, Transpositions, &c. 12mo. cloth, 50 cents. London, 1810.

Ensamples of Railway Making. 28 plates. royal 8vo. cloth, $4 75. London.

Entertaining Naturalist. Edited and enlarged by Mrs. Loudon. 12mo. cloth. $2 25. London.

Eothen; or, Traces of Travel brought Home from the East. 12mo. cloth, 50 cents. New York.

The Same. Beautifully illustrated with Engravings on Steel. 12mo. cloth, gilt, $1 50. New York, 1848.

Ephemera. A Hand-Book of Angling; Teaching Fly-Fishing, Trolling, Bottom-Fishing, Salmon-Fishing, the Natural History of River Fish, and the best Modes of Catching them; with numerous wood engravings. Foolscap, 8vo cloth, $2 75. London.

Episodes of Insect Life. A Discourse on the Instincts and Habits of Insects, combining an Admixture of the Real and Ideal of Entomological Life, in a Series of Essays, adapted to the Months of the Year. By Acheta Domestica, Author of "Floral Fancies." Numerous illustrations. 8vo. cloth, $4 50. London, 1848.

The Same. Colored plates, silk, $6 50.

Equestrian, (The.) A Hand-Book of Horsemanship, containing Practical Rules for Riding, Driving, and the Management of Horses, with illustrations by Frank Howard. 12mo. cloth, plates, $1 00. London.

Eschenberg, (J. J.) Manual of Classical Literature. Translated by N. W. Fish. 8vo. cloth, $4 00. Philadelphia.

Esdaile, (J.) Mesmerism in India, and its Application in Surgery, 12mo. cloth, $2 00. London.

Espy, (James P.) The Philosophy of Storms. 8vo. cloth. $2 00. Boston.

Esquirol, (E.) On Mental Maladies and their Treatment. Translated, with additions, by Dr. Hunt. 8vo. cloth, $4 25. London, 1849.

——— On Insanity. 8vo. cloth, $2 00. Philadelphia.

Esquiros, (Alphonse.) Histoire des Montagnards; avec portraits et gravures sur acier. 2 vols. in 8vo. demi maroquin, $5 50.

Essays; Written in the Intervals of Business. 12mo. $1 50. Pickering, London, 1847.

Essay on the Military Policy and Institutions of the British Empire. 8vo. cloth, $3 75. London.

Essays on Education,—viz. Hill's National Education, 2 vols. 1836. The Schoolmaster, 2 vols. Central Society of Education's Essays, 3 vols., and Prize Essays on Education, 1 vol.; together 8 vols. 12mo. cloth, $7 50. London, 1836–39.

Essay on the Credibility of the Existence of the Kraken, Sea-Serpent, and other Sea Monsters; with illustrations. 8vo. pamphlet, 75 cents. London, 1849.

Euclid, (Dr. Lardner's.) The Six Books, with a Commentary and Geometrical Exercises; to which are Annexed a Treatise on Solid Geometry, and Short Essays on the Ancient Geometrical Analysis, and the Theory of Transversals. 8vo. ninth edition, cloth, $1 75. 1846.

Euler. Lettres à une Princesse éd. Laistet. 12mo. paper, $1 00.

Euripides, (The Tragedies of.) Translated by Potter. 3 vols. 18mo. cloth, $1 50. New York.

Eusebius' Ecclesiastical History. Translated by Rev. C. F. Cruize. 8vo. cloth, $2 50.

Evagrius' Ecclesiastical History. 8vo. cloth, $2 25. London.

Evangelia Sacra Slavice, quibus olim in regum Francorum oleo Sacro inungendorum solemnibus uti solebat exclesia Remensis Vulgo Texte du sacre. Editit J. B. Silvestre, &c. 4to. whole bound in mor. richly blind tooled, edges gilt, and embossed, $25 00. Paris, 1843.

Evans, (W. J.) The Sugar Planter's Manual; being a Treatise on the Art of obtaining Sugar from the Sugar-Cane. 12mo. cloth, $1 25. Philadelphia.

——— (Arthur B.) Leicestershire Words, Phrases, and Proverbs. 12mo. cloth, $1 50. Pickering, London, 1847.

——— (Rev. R. W.) Day in the Sanctuary; with an Introductory Treatise on Hymnology. 12mo. oloth, $1 38. London, 1843

——— Bishoprick of Souls. 12mo. cloth, $1 75. London. 1844.

——— Sketch of all Religions. New Edition; improved, by the Rev. J. H. Bransby. 12mo cloth, $1 25. London, 1841.

——— (O. L.) The Young Millwright aud Miller's Guide. 28 plates. 8vo. sheep, $2 50. Philadelphia.

Evening Bell, (The;) Or, The Hour of Relating Entertaining Anecdotes. By Caroline Reinhold. German and English. $1 75.

Evenings with the Old Story Tellers. 12mo cloth gilt, $1 00; plain, 50. cents. New York, 1848.

Evelyn, (J.,) Sylva; or, a Discourse on Forest Trees, and the Propagation of Timber; to which is added the Terra, a Philosophic Discourse of Earth. 2 vols. royal 4to. cloth, $12 00. London, 1825.

Everett, (A. H.) Critical and Miscellaneous Essays. 2 series, 12mo. cloth, $3 00. Boston.

Ewald, (G. H. A.) Grammar of the Hebrew Language of the Old Testament. Translated by John Nicholson. 8vo. bds, $3 12.

Ewell's Medical Companion. 8vo. sheep, $3 75. Philadelphia.

Ewbank, (T.) Descriptive and Historical Account of Hydraulic and other Machines for Raising Water; with Observations on various subjects connected with the Mechanic Arts; including the Progressive Development of the Steam Engine. 8vo. $2 50. New York.

Examples in Architectural Engineering. 12mo. folio Atlas, $5 00. London.

Examples of Ancient Stained Glass Windows; comprising Accurate Fac-Similes in colors of the Windows of St. Margaret's, Westminster; St. Dunstan's in the East; St. Dunstan's in the West; Lincoln's Inn Chapel. folio, $6 00. London.

Exley, (Thos.) Principles of Natural Philosophy. 8vo. cloth, $4 25. London.

——— Physical Optics; or, the Phenomena of Optics Explained according to Mechanical Science, and on the known Principles of Gravitation. 8vo. bds. 75 cents. London, 1834.

Experimental Philosophy, (The Encyclopædia of.) Comprising Magnetism, Electro-Magnetism, Electricity, Galvanism, Heat, Chemistry, and Meteorology. Illustrated by numerous engravings. 4to. cloth, $9 00. London, 1848.

Exterior and Interior Finishings and Decorations, chiefly selected from Examples at Paris; consisting of Doors, Windows, Shop-Fronts, Sides of Rooms, Ceilings, Library Fittings, Iron Railings, &c.; with details. folio, $9 00. Paris.

Exton, (Rev. R. B.) Sixty Lectures on the Several Portions of the Psalms. 8vo. cloth, $3 50. London, 1847.

Eysenbach, (G.) Histoire du Blason et Science des Armoiries. Planches, 8vo., $2 00. Tours, 1848.

Fables of Æsop, (The.) A new version, chiefly from original sources, by Rev. Thomas James, with more than 100 illustrations, designed by John Tenniel. 8vo. cloth, $3 00. London, 1848.

Fairborn, (H.) Treatise on the Political Economy of Railroads; in which the new mode of Locomotion is considered in its Influence upon the Affairs of Nature. 8vo cloth, $2 00.

Fairfax, (The) Correspondence. Memoirs of the Reign of Charles the First. Edited by G. W. Johnson. 2 vols. 8vo. cloth, portraits, $9 00. London, 1848.

Fairholt, (F. W.) Home of Shakspeare. Illustrated and described. 12mo. 75 cents. London.

——— Costume in England. A History of Dress from the Earliest Period till the Close of the 18th Century. Illustrated with above 600 engravings on wood. 8vo. cloth, $8 00. London, 1846.

Falconer, (W.) Poetical Works. Complete in 1 vol. 12mo. mor. gilt edges, $3 00. London, 1836.

——— A New Universal Dictionary of the Marine, to which is added a Vocabulary of French Sea Phrases and Terms of Art, collected from the best authorities 4to. cloth. Published at $24 00; reduced to $8 00. Lond. 1815.

Falkner's Farmer's Manual. A Practical Treatise on the Nature and Value of Manures, &c., &c. 12mo. cloth, 50 cents. New York.

Family Joe Miller. A Drawing-Room Jest Book. Illustrated. 12mo. cloth, $1 50. London, 1847.

Fanny Hervey; or, the Mother's Choice. 2 vols. cr. 8vo. cloth, $5 00. London, 1849.

Faraday, (Michael.) Chemical Manipulation; being Instructions to Students in Chemistry on the Methods of performing Experiments of Demonstration or Research, with accuracy and success. Third edition, revised, 8vo. cloth, $5 50. London, 1842.

——— Experimental Researches in Electricity. 2 vols. 8vo. cloth, $7 50. London.

Farey, (John.) A Treatise on the Steam Engine, Historical, Practical, and Descriptive. 4to. illustrated by numerous wood-cuts and 25 copper-plates. bds. $31 50. London.

Farmer's Treasure, (The.) Containing Falkner's Farmer's Manual, and Smith's Productive Farming, bound together, 75 cents. New York.

Farming for Ladies; or, a Guide to the Poultry-yard, Dairy, and Piggery. 16mo. cloth, $2 00.

Farnham, (E. W.) Life in Prairie Land 12mo. cloth, 50 cents. New York, 1847.

Farquhar's Plays. The Dramatic Works of Farquhar, Congreve, Wycherley, and Vanburgh, with Biographical and Critical Notices, by Leigh Hunt. Beautifully printed in royal 8vo. cloth. Portrait and Vignette, $4 50. London, 1846.

Faulkner's Designs for Rural Monuments Tombs, and Tablets, 4to. $3 00.

——— (T.) Designs for Organs. Impl. 4to. 20 plates, $2 50.

Featherstonhaugh, (G. W.) A Canoe Voyage up the Minnay Sotor; with an Account of the Lead and Copper Deposits in Wisconsin; of the Gold Region in the Cherokee country; and Sketches of Popular Manners. 2 vols. 8vo. cloth, $2 50. London, 1847.

Fellows, (Sir Charles.) Discoveries in Ancient Lycia. roy. 8vo. cloth, plates. $12 75. London.

——— Excursion in Asia Minor, roy. 8vo. plates $7 50. London.

Feltham. Resolves; Divine, Moral, and Political. 12mo. $1 50. Pickering, Landon, 1840.

The Same. 4to. half mor. $3 00. Pickering, London, 1845.

Felton, (C. C.) Iliad of Homer, from the Text of Wolf, with English Notes. Illustrated with Portrait and Flaxman's Designs. 8vo. cloth, $3 00. Boston, 1847.

——— Panegyricus of Isocrates, from the Text of Bremi, with English Notes, 12mo. cloth, 75 cents. Cambridge, 1847.

——— Greek and Roman Metres. Translated from the German of Munk. 12mo. sheep, $1 50. Boston, 1844.

——— Iliad of Homer, from the Text of Wolf; with English Notes. 12mo. sheep. $1 50. Boston, 1848

Felton, (C. C.) The Agamemnon of Æschylus; with notes. 12mo. $1. Boston, 1847.

—— Greek Reader, containing Selections in Prose and Poetry; with English notes and a Lexicon. 12mo. cloth, $1 25. Hartford, 1842.

Fenelon. Œuvres completes, precedes d'une notice sur sa vie et sur ses ecrits; avec portrait. 12 vols. in 8vo. demi veau, $20 00. Paris, 1826.

—— Œuvres Philosophiques de, nouvelle edition, par M. A. Jacques. 12mo. paper, $1 00. Paris, 1845.

—— De l'Education des Filles. 12mo. $1 00. Paris, 1845.

—— Aventures de Télémaque. 12mo. $1 00. Paris, 1846.

Fenn, (J.) Paston Letters, written during the Time of Henry VI. to Richard III. Edited by Ramsay. 2 vols. 12mo. cloth, $3 London.

Fenwick, (H.) Essays on Field Fortification. 18mo. cloth, $1 75. London.

—— (Thos.) Treatise on Subterranean Surveying. 8vo. cloth, $3 50. London.

Fergusson, (J.) An Essay on a Proposed new System of Fortification. Imp. 8vo. cloth, $3 75. London, 1849.

—— An Historical Inquiry into the True Principles of Beauty in Art; more especially with reference to Architecture. Plates. Colombier, 8vo. $9 00. London, 1849.

—— Illustrations of the Rock cut Temples of India, with Descriptive Text. 8vo. cloth, folio atlas of plates, $15 00.

—— Essay on the Ancient Topography of Jerusalem, with restored plans of the Temple, &c. &c. Imperial 8vo. cloth, bds, $4 75.

—— Astronomy Explained upon Sir I. Newton's Principles; with Notes, &c., by Sir David Brewster. 2 vols. 26 plates, $3 50.

Ferguson, (R.) Essay on the most Important Diseases of Women. Part I. Puerperal Fever. crown 8vo. bds., $2 50. London, 1839.

—— (A.) History of the Progress and Termination of the Roman Republic. Portrait. 8vo. cloth, $1 50. New York, 1849.

—— (W.) System of Practical Surgery. 74 engravings. 8vo. sheep, $3 25. Philad. 1848.

Ferry's Christ Church, Hampshire. Plates. 4to. $6 50.

Festus. A Poem, by Philip James Bailey. 12mo. cloth gilt, gilt edge, $1 00. Bost. 1849.

Fichte, (J. G.) Memoirs of; by W. Smith. Second edition. Post 8vo. cloth. $1 25. London, 1848.

The Same. 12mo. 50 cents. Boston.

—— Popular Works. Translated by William Smith. Portrait. Vols. 1 and 2; post 8vo. each, cloth, $3 50. London, 1848, 9

—— Vocation of Man. Post 8vo. cloth, $1 37. London.

—— The Nature of the Scholar. Post 8vo. cloth, $1 09. London.

—— Characteristics of the Present Age. Post 8vo. cloth, $2 12. London.

Fichte, (J. C.) Vocation of the Scholar. Post 8vo. cloth, 60 cents. London.

—— The Way towards the Blessed Life; or, the Doctrine of Religion, and Outlines of the Doctrine of Knowledge. Post 8vo. cloth, $1 75. London, 1849.

Field, (G.) Chromatics; or, the Analogy, Harmony, and Philosophy of Colors. $6 50. Lond.

—— Chromatography; or, a Treatise on Colors and Pigments, and of their Powers in Painting. New edition. $4 00.

—— (Rev. H. M.) The Good and the Bad in the Roman Catholic Church, 12mo. paper, 12½ cents. New York, 1849.

—— (J. T.) Poems. Square 12mo. cloth, 50 cents. Boston, 1849.

Fielding, (T. H.) On the Knowledge and Restoration of Oil Paintings. 12mo. cloth, $1 25. London.

—— Theory and Practice of Painting in Oil and Water Colors, for Landscapes, Portraits, &c. Illustrated with plates, some colored 4th. edition. 8vo. $8 50. London..

—— Synopsis of Practical Perspective, Lineal and Ærial; with Remarks on Sketching from Nature. Plates. 8vo. cloth, $6 50. London, 1843.

—— Works, (Tom Jones, Amelia, Jonathan Wild, Joseph Andrews, Plays, Essays, and Miscellanies,) complete in one thick volume, medium 8vo. with 20 capital plates by Cruikshank, extra red cloth, richly gilt, $4 25. London, 1848.

Fincham, (J.) Directions for Laying off Ships. Royal 8vo. plates in folio, $7 50.

—— Treatise on Masting Ships. Royal 8vo. plates in folio, $7 50. London.

Findlay's Outline Geographical Atlas, with the lines of Latitude and Longitude; intended as Practical Lessons for Pupils to fill up. 4to paper, $1 37. London.

First of the Knickerbockers. A Tale of 1673. 12mo. cloth, 75 cents. New York, 1848.

Fisher, (P.) Angler's Souvenir. Post 8vo. mor. gilt, $4 75. London.

Fishbourne, (E. G.) Lectures on Naval Architecture. 8vo. $1 75. London.

Fisk, (W.) Travels in Europe. 8vo. sheep, $3 25. New York.

—— (N. W.) Classical Antiquities. Sheep, $2 00. Philadelphia.

—— Manual of Classical Literature. 8vo sheep, $3 00. Philadelphia

Fitch's Dental Surgery. 8vo sheep, $3 25. Philadelphia

Fitzgerald, (James E.) An Examination of the Charter and Proceedings of the Hudson's Bay Company, with reference to the Grant of Vancouver's Island. 12mo. cloth, $1 75. London, 1849.

Fitzroy and Darwin's Zoology of the Voyage of H. M. S. Beagle. Numerous plates, many colored. 3 vols. 4to. cloth, $30 00. London, 1840.

Flaxman. Sou Œuvres. Recueil de ses Compositions gravées au trait par Reveil, contenant Iliade d'Homère, 39 planches. Odyssée, 34 pl. Tragedies d'Eschyle, 34 pl. L'Enfer du Dante. 34 pl. Le Purgatoire. 39 pl. Le Paradis. 33 pl. Hesiode. 37 pl. Statues et Cas Reliefs, 14 pl. Oblong 8vo. half mor. gilt, $12 00. Paris.

——— Compositions from Dante. Oblong 4to. half mor. $12 75.

——— Studies of Anatomy for Artists. Royal folio, cloth, $6 50.

——— Outlines, illustrative of Homer's Iliad, Odyssey, Ovid, and Æschylus. 4 vols oblong folio, $30 00. London, 1805.

——— Lectures on Sculpture. Numerous plates. 8vo. cloth, $6 50.

——— Book of Prayer. Folio, cloth, $6 50.

Fleming, (A.) Inquiry into the Physiological and Medicinal Properties of the Aconitum Napellus; to which are added Observations on several other species of Aconitum. 8vo. cloth, $1 50. London, 1845.

——— (John.) Exposition of the Structure, Systematic Arrangement, Physical Distribution, and Dietetical Uses of Moluscous Animals, including Shell Fish. Plates. 12mo. cloth, $1 75. Edinburgh, 1837.

Flemming and Tibbins' French and English Dictionary. 8vo. sheep, $5 00. Philadelphia.

Fletcher's, (J.) Dramatic Works. The Complete Dramatic Works of Francis Beaumont and John Fletcher; with Biographical and Critical Notices, by John Darley. Beautifully printed, with portraits and vignettes. 2 vols. royal 8vo. cloth, $8 00. London, 1840.

——— (Rev. John.) Works. 4 vols. 8vo. sheep, $10 00. New York.

——— Rudiments of Physiology. 8vo. cloth, $5 75.

Fleury. Histoire Ecclesiastique; nouvelle edition augmentée de quatre livres comprenant l'histoire du XV. Siècle, avec une table alphabetique. 6 vols. royal 8vo. $15 00. Paris, 1843.

Florence Gallery; containing more than 200 line engravings of the Paintings and Sculpture of this splendid collection. 4 vols. folio, original binding, $113 50.

Florian. Œuvres complètes; nouvelle edition, ornee d'un portrait, et de 42 gravures. 13 vol. in 8, demi veau, $18. Paris, 1823.

——— Fables, precedes d'une notice par Ch. Nodier, et suivies des poemes de Ruth et de Tobie. 1 magnfique vol. grand in 8, illustre par Victor Adam de 120 gravures en taille-douce, et de 200 gravures sur bois, $3 50.

——— Fables, &c. 12mo. $1 00. Paris, 1846.

Flugel's Complete Dictionary of the English and German Languages, with Additions and Improvements, by C. Feiling and A. Heimann, in 2 parts. 2 vols. 8vo. bds. $7 50. London, 1845.

Follen, (Chas.) Works. 5 vols. 12mo. cloth, $4 00. Boston.

Follen, (Mrs.) Sketches of Married Life. 12mo. cloth, $1 00. Boston

Folsom, (G.) Letters and Despatches of Cortez, 8vo. bds. $2 00. New York.

Fontana, Trattato dell Acque Correnti. Folio, cloth, $6 00.

Forbes, (E.) History of British Star Fishes. 8vo. cloth, $4 50. London.

——— (Lieut. F. E.) Five Years in China; from 1842 to 1847, with an Account of the Occupation of the Islands of Labaun and Borneo by Her Majesty's Forces. 8vo. cloth, wood-cuts, $2 00. London, 1848.

——— (J. L) The Danger of Superficial Knowledge; an Introductory Lecture to the Course of Natural Philosophy in the University of Edinburgh. 8vo. bds. 60 cents. London, 1849.

Ford, (John.) Dramatic Works. The Dramatic Works of Philip Massinger and John Ford, with Biographical and Critical Notices. By Henry Nelson Coleridge. Beautifully printed in 1 vol. royal 8vo. cloth, portrait and vignette, $4 00. London, 1848.

——— (R.) Hand-Book for Spain, Andalusia, &c. 2 vols. post 8vo. cloth, $4 75. London.

——— (J.) Spaniards and their Country. 12mo. cloth, $1 00. New York.

Foreign Quarterly Review, from its commencement in 1827, to June, 1846. 37 vols. 8vo. half calf, neat, $50 00.

Formby, (Rev. H.) A Visit to the East; comprising Germany and the Danube, Constantinople, Asia Minor, Egypt, and Idumea. 12mo. cloth, wood-cuts, $2 00. London, 1843.

Form and Sound. Can their Beauty be dependent on the same Physical Laws? A Critical Inquiry, by Thomas Purdie. 8vo. cloth, plates, $2 25. Edinburgh, 1849.

Forrester, (Fanny.) Alderbrook. 2 vols. in 1, thick 12mo. cloth, $1 63. Boston, 1849.

Forster, (John.) The Life and Adventures of Oliver Goldsmith, a Biography in Four Books. Plates, 8vo. cloth, gilt, $6 00. London, 1848.

——— The Statesmen of the Commonwealth of England; with an Introductory Treatise on the Popular Progress in English History. 5 vols. foolscap, 8vo. with original Portraits of Pym, Eliot, Hampden, Cromwell, and an Historical Scene of a Picture by Cattermole, cloth, $9 00. London.

The Same. 8vo. sheep, $2 00. New York, 1848.

Forsyth, (W.) Treatise on Fruit-Trees. 8vo. cloth, $4 00. London.

——— Hortensius; or, the Advocate. An Historical Essay. Post 8vo. cloth, $3 75. London, 1849.

Fosbrooke's British Monachism; or, the Manners and Customs of the Nuns and Monks of England. Royal 8vo. cloth, plates and cuts, $4 50. London

——— Encyclopædia of Antiquities and Archæology. 2 vols. 8vo. cloth, 145 plates, $9 50.

Fosbrooke, (Rev. T. D.) A Treatise on the Arts, Manners, Manufactures, and Institutions of the Greeks and Romans. 2 vols. foolscap, 8vo. cloth, $3 75. London.

Fosdick, (David.) German and English Pocket Dictionary. Square 12mo. sheep, $1 75. Boston, 1847.

Foss, (Edward.) The Judges of England; with Sketches of their Lives and Miscellaneous Notices connected with the Courts at Westminster from the time of the Conquest. vols. 1 and 2. 8vo. cloth, $8 00. London, 1848.

Foster, (J.) Essays on Decision of Character. 12mo. cloth, 75 cents. New York.

Foulston's Public Buildings of the West of England. 100 detailed plates. Royal 4to. cloth, $12 50.

Fountains of Paris. 84 plates. Folio, cloth. $12 50.

Fouque, (F. de La Motte.) Undine and Sintram and his Companions. 12mo. cloth gilt, gilt edges, $1 00; plain, 50 cts. N. York, 1848.

Fowler's Illustrations of the most Remarkable Examples of Ancient Stained Glass and Mosaic Pavements. 2 vols. atlas folio, 54 colored plates, $126 00.

——— (R.) Observations on the Mental State of the Deaf and Dumb. 12mo paper, 75 cts. Salisbury, 1843.

Fowne, (G.) Elementary Chemistry, Theoretical and Practical. Edited, with Additions, by Robert Bridges. Numerous Illustrations. 12mo. sheep, $1 50. Philadelphia. 1847.

——— Rudimentary Chemistry, for the Use of Beginners; to which is added an Essay on the Application of Chemistry to Agriculture. 32mo. 25 cents. Philadelphia, 1848.

Fox, (John.) Acts and monuments of matters most special and memorable, happening in the Church, with an universal historie of the same, wherein is set forth the bloody times, horrible troubles, and great persecutions against the true martyrs of Christ, as well by heathen Emperors as now lately practised by Romish Prelate, especially in this Realme of England and Scotland. A new edition, with Preliminary Dissertation, by Rev. G. Townsend; edited by Rev. S. R. Cattley. 8 vols. 8vo. cloth, $23 00. Philadelphia.

——— Book of Martyrs. 8vo. sheep, $2 00. Philadelphia.

——— (Right Hon. Charles James.) Speeches in the House of Commons. Portrait. Royal 8vo. cloth, $5 75. London, 1848.

——— (Jos.) On the Teeth. 4to. cloth, $7 50. New York.

——— **and Harris** on the Teeth. 8vo. sheep, $5 00. Philadelphia.

Francais Peints Par Eux-Memes (les) Encyclopêdie morale de la France au XIX. siècle, par toutes les sommités littéraires de l'epoque; dessins par MM. Gavarni, Grandville, Tony Johannot, etc. 8 vols. grand in 8vo.—illustrées, gravures coloriées, $24 00. Paris, 1841.

France and the French Revolution; consisting of,—I. The Reign of Terror, a Collection of Authentic Narratives of the Horrors committed by the Revolutionary Government of France, under Marat and Robespierre; written by Eye-witnesses of the Scenes, 2 vols.—II. Sketch of the History of France, from the Suspension of the Monarchy in 1792 to its re-establishment in 1815; with illustrative Official Papers. Together, 3 vols. 8vo. portrait, &c., cloth lettered, $4 00. London, 1817–26.

Francis's Chemical Experiments; illustrating the Theory, Practice, and Application of the Science of Chemistry; and containing the Properties, the Uses, Manufacture, Purification, and Analysis of all Inorganic Substances. Numerous engravings. $1 75. London.

——— (G.) Manual of Practical Levelling. 12mo. cloth, $1 25. London.

——— Dictionary of Receipts in Manufactures, &c. 8vo. cloth, $2 25. London.

——— (John.) History of the Bank of England; its Times and Traditions. 2 vols. 12mo. cloth, $5 75. London, 1848.

——— (G. W.) Analysis of the British Ferns and their Allies. Plates. 8vo. cloth, $1 75. London, 1842.

Franklin, (B.) Autobiography, with a Narrative of his Public Life and Services. By Rev. H. Weld; with numerous Designs, by J G. Chapman. 8vo. cloth, $3 50. New York, 1848.

——— Complete Works; with Life, by Jared Sparks. 10 vols. 8vo. cloth, $20 00. Boston.

Franks, (A. W.) A Book of Ornamental Glazing Quarries, collected and Arranged from Ancient Examples. Colored plates, 8vo. $4 00 London, 1849.

Freeman, (E. A.) History of Architecture. Plate. 8vo. cloth, $4 25. London, 1849.

Fremont, (Col. J. C.) Expedition to Oregon. 8vo. 75 cents. Syracuse.

——— Tour through the Rocky Mountains, California, and Oregon. 12mo. cloth, $1 25. Buffalo.

French, (B. F.) Historical Collections of Louisiana; embracing many rare and valuable Documents, relating to the Natural, Civil, and Political History of that State. Compiled with Historical and Biographical Notes. 8vo. cloth, $1 50. New York, 1846.

Fresenius, (Dr. G. Remigius.) Instruction in Chemical Analysis (Qualitative;) with a Preface by Prof. Liebig. Edited by J. Lloyd Bullock. 2d edition, 8vo. cloth, $2 75. London, 1846.

The Same. American edition. $1 00.

——— Quantitative Analysis. 8vo. cloth, $4 00.

——— New Methods of Alkalimetry, and of Determining the Commercial Value of Acids and Manganese. $1 00.

Frey, (J. S. C. F.) Hebrew Grammar, with a Vocabulary. 8vo. cloth, $1 50.

Friendship's Offering and Winterss Wreath. A Christmas and New Year's Present. 12mo. cloth, gilt edges, $1 12. London

Friends in Council. Part I. Post 8vo. cloth, $1 75. Pickering, Lond. 1847.

The Same. Part II. Foolscap 8vo. cloth, $2 50. London, 1849.

Frithiof's Saga. A Legend of Norway, by Esaias Tegner. Translated from the Swedish, by George Stephens, with Life of the Author, &c. 8vo. silk, portrait and plates, $3 50. London, 1839.

Froissart, (Sir John.) Chronicles of England, France, Spain, and the adjoining Countries. 2 vols. royal 8vo. cloth, illustrated with wood-cuts, $7 50. London, 1844.

——— Illuminations. Illustrations of Froissart, selected from MSS. in the British Museum, and the Bibliotheque du Roi; comprising 75 fine plates, printed in colors and gold, being exact fac-similes of the originals. 2 vols. royal 8vo. half mor. cloth sides, $18 00. Lond. 1844–5.

——— Ballads of England, France, and Spain. 8vo. cloth, $4 00.

Frome, (Capt.) Outline of the Method of conducting a Trigonometrical Survey. Engravings and wood-cuts. 8vo. cloth, $3 75. London.

Froude, (J. A.) The Nemesis of Faith. post 8vo. cloth, $2 00. London, 1849.

Frost, (J.) History of the United States. 400 illustrations, 8vo. sheep, $6 00. Philadelphia.

Fry, (Rev. J.) New Translation and Exposition of the very Ancient Book of Job; with Notes. 8vo. cloth, $2 50. London, 1827.

——— (C.) An Autobiography and Letters. 12mo. cloth, $1 00. Philadelphia, 1849.

——— (Elizabeth.) Memoirs of the Life of; with Extracts from her Letters and Journals. Edited by two of her daughters. 2 vols. 8vo. cloth, $3 50. Philadelphia, 1847–8.

Fuerbach, (A. R. Von.) Narratives of Remarkable Criminal Trials. Translated by Lady Duff Gordon. 12mo. cloth, 50 cents. New York, 1846.

Fuller, (Thomas.) The History of the Holy War. 12mo. cloth, $1 63. London, 1840.

——— Memorials of the Life and Works of Rev. A. T. Russell. 12mo. cloth, portrait. $1 50. London, 1844.

——— (Thomas, D. D.) The Church History of Britain, from the Birth of Jesus Christ to the year 1648. New edition, by Nichols. Plates, 3 vols. 8vo. cloth, $6 50. London, 1843.

——— History of Cambridge and Waltham Abbey, and Defence of Church History against Dr. Heylyn. New edition. Plates, 8vo $3 25. London, 1840.

——— The History of the Worthies of England. New edition, edited by Dr. Nuttall. 3 vols. 8vo. $6 50. London, 1840.

——— Holy and Profane State; with Notes by Nicholls. Plates, 8vo cloth, $2 25. London, 1847.

The Same. 8vo. calf, extra, $3 00.

——— (Rev. Andrew.) Complete Works; with a Memoir of his Life, by his Son. 1 large vol. impl. 8vo. new edition, portrait, extra cloth, bds. $7 50.

Fuller, (A.) Works. Edited by Joseph Belcher. 3 vols. 8vo. sheep, $7 50. Philadelphia.

——— (S. M.) Papers on Literature and Art. 12mo. cloth, $1 25. New York.

——— Summer on the Lakes in 1843. 12mo cloth, 75 cents. Boston.

Fullerton, (Col.) Views in the Himalaya. folio, plates, $7 75. London.

Furnivall, (Dr. J. J.) Diagnosis, Prevention, and Treatment of Diseases of the Heart, and of Aneurism; with Observations on Rheumatism. 8vo. cloth, $2 50. London, 1845.

Fuseli, (Hen.) Lectures on Painting. 4to. cloth. 1st and 2d series, $9 00. London.

Gabourd, (A.) Histoire de Napoléon Bonaparte. cr. 8vo. cloth, gilt, gilt edges, plates, $1 75. Tours, 1845.

Gaertner's Works; consisting of Plans Elevations, and Sections of the Public Buildings erected by this celebrated Architect in Bavaria. Large folio, numerous plates, $25 50.

Gairdner, (W.) Essay on Mineral and Thermal Springs. 12mo. cloth, $2 50. Edinburgh.

——— Essay on the Effects of Iodine. 8vo. cloth, $1 25. London.

——— (W. T.) Contributions to the Pathology of the Kidneys. 24 engravings, 8vo. sewed, 75 cents. London, 1849.

Gailhabaud. Ancient and Modern Architecture; consisting of Views, Plans, Elevations, Sections, and Details of the most remarkable Edifices in the World; giving examples of the Hindoo, Egyptian, Persian, Grecian, Roman, Italian, Byzantine, Gothic, and Modern Styles. 3 vols. 4to. steel plates, $60 00. Lond.

Galbraith, (G.) Cotton-Spinner's Companion. 12mo. cloth, $1 25. London.

Gallaudet, (Rev. T. H.) Class-Book of Natural Theology for Common Schools and Academies. 18mo. bds. 50 cents. Hartford, 1837.

Gallery of Pictures by the First Masters of English and Foreign Schools; with Biographical Notices, by Allan Cunningham. 2 vols. royal 8vo. half mor. gilt tops and back 73 plates, $12 00. London, 1836.

Gallery of Portraits; with Memoirs. By E. Lodge. 8 vols. small 8vo. half mor. gilt edges, $14 00. London.

Galli, (C.) Essai sur le nom et la Langue des Anciens Celtes. cr. 8vo. paper, $1 50. Sainte Etienne, 1843.

Gall, (J. J.) System of Phrenology. 12mo. cloth, $1 00. Philadelphia, 1835.

——— Works. 6 vols. 12mo. cloth, $4 80. Boston.

Galland, (A.) Les Mille et une Nuits contes Arabes; avec un Dissertation par M. Le Baron Sylvestre de Sacy. 3 vols. royal 8vo. numerous wood-cuts, $9 00. Paris, 1840.

Gallatin, (A.) The Right of the United States of America to the North-Eastern Boundary claimed by them; principally extracted from the statements laid before the King of the Netherlands. 8vo. bds. illustrated with 8 maps, $1 25. New York, 1840.

Gallier, (J.) American Builder's Price Book and Estimator. 8vo. cloth, 50 cents. New York.

Galloway and Herbert. History and Progress of the Steam Engine; to which is added an extensive Appendix, containing minute descriptions of all the various improved Boilers, with upwards of 200 Engravings. 8vo. cloth, $5 00. London.

Galloway, (T.) Treatise on Probability. Cr. 8vo. cloth, $1 75. Edinburgh.

Galt, (Dr.) Treatment of Insanity. 8vo. cloth, $1 50. New York.

——— Practical Medicine, illustrated by Cases. 8vo. sheep, $2 50. Philadelphia.

——— (John.) The Provost and other Tales. 12mo. cloth, frontispiece, $1 50. Edinburgh, 1842.

——— Life of Cardinal Wolsey. 12mo. portrait, 88 cents. London, 1846.

Game of Natural History. A Series of Cards carefully drawn and colored, representing the most important and interesting of the Animal Creation; with Questions—in a case. 50 cents.

Gammer Grethel; or, German Popular Fairy Tales. Translated by E. Taylor, and illustrations by Cruikshank. $1 25. London, 1848.

Garstin, (Major-General John.) Treatise on Rivers and Torrents; with an Essay on Navigable Canals. 4to. cloth, plates, $4 50.

Gardner, (D. P.) Medical Chemistry, for the use of Students and the Profession; being a Manual of the Science, with its Application to Toxicology, Physiology, Therapeutics, Hygiene, &c. Post 8vo. bound, $1 50. Philadelphia, 1849.

——— Farmer's Dictionary; a Vocabulary of the Technical Terms recently introduced into Agriculture and Horticulture, from various Sciences; and also a Compendium of Practical Farming; with numerous illustrations. 12mo. sheep, $1 75. New York, 1846.

——— New Medical Dictionary. 8vo. sheep, $2 50. New York.

——— (E. W.) Elementary Principles deduced into Rules of Practice, for the Calculation of all kinds of Railway Work. Plates. Royal 8vo. $3 00.

——— An Easy Introduction to Railway Mensuration. Illustrated by Drawings from Original Works, that have been carried out upon various English Railway Lines. Royal 8vo. $4 50.

Gardener's Monthly Volumes, viz. 1. The Potato. 2. The Cucumber and the Gooseberry. 3 and 4. The Grape Vine. 5. The Auricular and Asparagus. 6 and 7. The Pine Apple. 8. The Strawberry. Together 8 vols. 12mo. cloth, $4 00. London, 1847.

Garnier, (J.) Eléments de l'Economie Politique exposé des Notions Fundamentales de cette Science. 12mo. paper, $3 50. Paris, 1848.

——— et Guillaumin Annuaire de l'Economie Politique et de la Statistique pour 1849. 12mo. broché.

Gasc, (M.) Le Livre des Pères de Famille et des Instituteurs ou de l'Education Publique, au 19th Siècle. 12mo. paper, $1 00. Paris, 1843.

Gaskin, (T.) Selections of the Trigonometrical Problems proposed at St. John's College, Cambridge, from 1829 to 1845. 8vo cloth, $2 50.

Gatty, (A.) Origin, History, and Uses of the Bell. 12mo. cloth, $1 00. London.

Gau, (F. C.) Antiquities de la Nubie, ou Monuments inédits des bords du Nil. Folio, 63 planches. $36 00. Paris, 1821–7.

Gaudin, (T.) Traité complet de Photographie. Exposé complet des procédés relatifs du Daguerreotype. 8vo. paper, $1 25. Paris, 1845.

Gauthier's Le Plus Beaux Edifices de la Ville de Gênes et des Environs. 2 vols. folio. 200 plates. $63 00. 1826–30.

——— (Theophile.) Mademoiselle de Maupin. 12mo. broché, $1 00. Paris, 1845.

——— Nouvelles. 12mo. broché, $1 00. Paris, 1845.

——— Voyage en Espagne. 12mo. broché, $1 00. Paris, 1845.

Gavard. Interior Views of the Palace of Versailles. Thirty plates. Folio, cloth, $12 50.

Gavarni. Œuvres choisies de, Revues, Corrigées et nouvellement Classées par l'auteur. Avec des Notices en tête de chaque serie, par M.M. Theophile Gautier and Laurent Jan. 4 vols. in 2, small folio, half mor. gilt tops, $14 00. Paris, 1846.

Geddes, (W.) Clinical Illustrations of Diseases of India. 8vo. cloth, $4 75. London.

Geiger, (F. C.) History of the Swedes. Translated from the Swedish, by J. H. Turner, Esq. 8vo. cloth, $2 25. London.

Gell et Gandy. Vues des Ruines de Pompei, par William Gell et J. P. Gandy, architectes. 1 vol. gr. in 4 de 125 pl. sur papier vélin, gravées, par Roux ainé, avec texte historique et descriptif. Prix: 150 fr. réduit à $12 50.

——— Pompeiana; or, the Topography, Edifices, and Ornaments of Pompeii, Original Series, containing the Result of the Excavations previous to 1819, best edition, with upwards of 100 beautiful line engravings by Goodall, Cooke, Heath, Pye, &c. 2 vols. imp. 8vo cloth, $15 00. London, 1824.

Gell, (Sir William.) Topography of Rome and its Vicinity. An improved edition, complete in 2 vols. 8vo. with map and several plates, cloth, lettered, $6 50. 1840–40.

Goethe. Correspondence with a Child. 2 vols. 12mo. bds. $1 50. New York.

——— Reinecke Fuchs, mit Zeichnungen ven W. Kaulbach. 4to. cloth, 72 plates, $12 50. München, 1847.

Geldart's Halifax. Analysis of the Civil Law, in which a Comparison is occasionally made between the Roman Laws and those of England. 8vo. cloth, $2 50. Cambridge, 1836.

Gems of Art; a Collection of Thirty-six Engravings, after the most celebrated Paintings by Rembrandt, Cuyp, Sir Joshua Reynolds, Poussin, Murillo, Teniers, Corregio, Vandervelde, Gainsborough, Northcote, &c., executed in mezzotint, by Reynolds, Turner, Bromley, &c. Folio, proof impressions, in a portfolio, lettered, $9 50. London.

Gems of European Art. Edited by Mrs. S. C. Hall. 2 vols. 4to. cloth, $30 00. London.

Gems of Epistolary Correspondence; selected from the best English Authors, from the time of Sir Philip Sidney to the present day. By R. A. Willmot. Post 8vo. cloth, $1 00; published at 7*s.* 6*d.* London, 1846.

Geometry without Axioms; or, the Book of Euclid's Elements; with alterations and familiar notes. 8vo. cloth, 75 cents.

Georgian Era; or, Modern British Biography; comprising Memoris of the most Eminent Persons who have flourished in Great Britain, from the Accession of George the First to the Demise of George the Fourth. 4 vols. small 8vo. portraits on steel; cloth, elegantly gilt, $4 75. 1832.

George IV. Diary, illustrative of the Life and Times of George IV.; interspersed with Original Letters from the late Queen Caroline, and from various other Distinguished Persons. Portraits. 4 vols. post 8vo. cloth. $3 75. London, 1838.

George II. Memoirs of the Reign of; from his succession to the Death of Queen Caroline. By John Lord Hervey. Edited, from the Original MSS., by the Right Hon. J. W. Croker. 2 vols. 12mo. cloth, $3 00. Philadelphia, 1842.

Gerber, (Fr.) Elements of the General and Minute Anatomy of Man and the Mammalia; with Notes and Appendix, by G. Gulliver. 2 vols. 8vo. cloth, $7 00. London, 1842.

Gerstæcher, (J.) Wanderings and Fortunes of some German Emigrants. 12mo. cloth, 75 cts. New York, 1848.

Gerey's Monumental Tablets. 12mo. $3 25.

Gervinus, (G. G.) Geschichte der Poetischen National-Literatur der Deutschen. 5 vols. 8vo. paper, $19 00. Leipsig, 1838–44.

Gesenius' Hebrew Grammar, by Roediger. 8vo. $2 00. New York.

——— Hebrew Grammar and English Lexicon, by Professor Robinson. 8vo. cloth, $6 00. Boston.

Gessert, (Dr. M. A.) Art of Painting on Glass, or Glass Staining; comprising the Mode of preparing the Pigments and Fluxes; their manipulation, and the process for burning the Colors in; with description of Furnace and Apparatus used for the same. 4to. boards, $1 50.

Getty, (J. A.) Art of Rhetoric; or, the Elements of Oratory. 12mo. cloth. $1 00. Philadelphia, 1849.

Gibbs, (G.) Memoirs of the Administration of Washington and John Adams. Edited from the Papers of Oliver Wolcott, Secretary to the Treasury. Portraits. 2 vols. 8vo. cloth. $4 50. New York, 1849.

Gibbon, (E.) History of the Decline and Fall of the Roman Empire. 4 vols. 8vo. sheep, $5 00. New York.

The Same. Royal 8vo. cloth, $5 50. London, 1840.

The Same. Edited, with Notes, &c., by Rev. H. H. Millman. 6 vols. 8vo. calf extra, $28 00. London, 1846.

The Same. 8 vols. 8vo. tree marbled calf, $25. London, 1848.

Gibbons, (B.) On the Ventilation of Mines. 8vo. cloth, $1 25. London.

Gibney, (J.) Treatise on the Properties and Medical Application of the Vapor Bath. 8vo. bds. $2 25. London, 1829.

Gibson, (W.) Surgery. 2 vols. 8vo. sheep. $7 00. Philadelphia.

——— (R.) Surveying. 8vo. sheep, $1 25. Baltimore.

Gidde, (W.) Book of Sundry Draughts for Glaziers, and not impertinent for Plasterers and Gardeners. Edited by Shaw. 8vo. bds. 117 plates. $5 00. London, 1848.

Giessen. Outlines of Qualitative Analysis. By Henry Will; with a Preface by Baron Liebig. 8vo. cloth, $1 63. London, 1846.

Gifford, (I.) Marine Botanist. An Introduction to the Study of Algology; containing descriptions of the commonest British Sea-weeds and the best method of preserving them, with accurate drawings of some of the most remarkable species, and some of the most beautiful in colors. 12mo. cloth, $1 50. Bath, 1849.

Gilbart, (J. W.) The History and Principles of Banking. Third edition, 8vo. bds. $2 75. London.

Gilbert, (H.) Pulmonary Consumption, its Prevention and Cure established on new views of the Pathology of the Disease. 8vo. cloth, $2 00. London, 1842.

——— (J.) Stained Glass of Canterbury Cathedral, and Fragments towards the History of Stained Glass and the Sister Arts of the Middle Ages 4to. bds. 10 plates, $1 50.

——— Modern Atlas of the Earth; with an Introduction to Physical and Historical Geography, and a copious consulting Index of 45,000 places. By Robert Mudie. 4to. cloth, 56 maps, colored, $7 00. London, 1844.

Gil Blas. Translated by Smollett. Pictorial Edition, illustrated by upwards of 500 beautiful wood Engravings, after the celebrated designs of Gigoux. 2 vols. royal 8vo. extra cloth, bds. $7 00. London.

Gil Blas, with illustrations by George Cruikshank. 2 vols. 12mo. cloth, $2 50. Lond.

——— 1 vol. 12mo. cloth, $1 50. Lond.

The Same. mor. $3 00. Lond.

Gill, (C.) Application of the Angular Analysis to the Solution of Indeterminate Problems of the Second Degree. Post 8vo. cloth, $2 25. New York.

—— (John, D. D.) Complete Body of Doctrinal and Practical Divinity; a System of Evangelical Truths, deduced from Sacred Scriptures. 2 vols. 8vo. cloth, $5 00. London, 1839.

Gilchrist. English and Hindostanee Dictionary; with a Grammatical Introduction. 4to. cloth, $9 75. London, 1825.

Gillies, (J.) History of Ancient Greece; its Colonies and Conquests from the earliest accounts, including the History of Literature, Philosophy, and the Fine Arts. 8 vols. 8vo. cloth, $10 00. London.

—— (Rev. J.) Historical Collections relating to Remarkable Periods of the Success of the Gospel. Royal 8vo. cloth, $2. London, 1845.

Gilman. (C.) Verses of a Lifetime 12mo. cloth, 87 cents. Boston, 1849.

—— (Mrs.) The Sibyl; or, New Oracles from the Poets; a Fanciful Diversion for the Drawing-Room. 12mo. cloth, extra gilt, $1 50 New York, 1849.

Gillespie, (W. M.) Manual of the Principles and Practice of Road-Making; comprising the Location, Construction, and Improvement of Roads, (common, Mac Adam, paved, plank, &c.) and Railroads. 8vo. cloth; with Supplement, $1 50. New York, 1848.

Gilpin, (W. S.) Practical Hints upon Landscape Gardening, with some Remarks upon Domestic Architecture. Roy. 8vo. cloth, $1 75. London, 1835.

—— (W.) Works, viz.: Highlands of Scotland, 2 vols. Lakes of Cumberland, 2 vols. Observations on the Western Part of England, 1 vol. Southern Tour, 1 vol. River Vye, 1 vol. Essays on Picturesque Subjects, 1 vol.; together, 8 vols. 8vo. bds. colored plates, $12 00. London, 1808.

Gilray's Caricatures, complete in one large folio volume, handsomely half bound in mor. gilt, and gilt edges, $50 00. London, 1849.

Gilroy, (C. G.) On Weaving. 8vo. cloth, $5 00. New York.

Girard on the Teeth of the Horse. By Gauly. 12mo. colored plates, $1 37. London.

Giradin, (E. de.) Le Droit au Travail au Luxembourg et a l'Assemblée Nationale. 2 vols. 12mo. paper, $1 50. Paris, 1849.

—— (Madame de.) Poésies Complètes. 12mo. paper, $1 00.

—— Lettres Parisiennes. 12mo. paper, $1 00 Paris

—— (S. M.) Cours de Littèrature Dramatique. 12mo. paper, $1 00 Paris

Giraud, (J. P.) Birds of Long Island. 8vo. cloth, $2 00. New York.

Giulani, (N.) Introduction au Code d'Harmonie Pratique et Théorique, ou Nouveau Systême de basse fondamentale. 8vo. sewed, $2 00. Paris, 1847.

Gladstone, (Hon. W. E.) Church Principles considered in their Results. 8vo. cloth, $1 75. London, 1840.

Gladstone, (Hon. W. E.) The State in its Relation with the Church. 2 vols. 8vo. cloth, $3 50. London, 1841.

Glasgow Infant School Magazine. 18mo. cloth, $1 00. London, 1844.

—— Practical Mechanic; containing numerous illustrations. 6 vols. small folio, cloth, $15 00.

A very useful and valuable book to all Mechanics and Engineers.

Gladwin's Elevation of Stephenson's Patent Locomotive Engine. Columbier size, 3*s.* 6*d.*, printed on hard paper, for coloring.

Glascock, (W. N.) Naval Officer's Manual. Post 8vo. cloth, $6 50. London.

Glass-Painting. An Inquiry into the Difference of Style observable in Ancient Glass-Painting, with Hints on Glass-Painting. By an Amateur. Colored plates. 2 vols. $7 50. Oxford, 1847.

Gleig, (Rev. G. R.) Memoirs of the Life of Right Hon. Warren Hastings. Portrait. 3 vols. 8vo. cloth, $6 00. (Scarce.) London, 1841.

—— Lives of the Most Eminent British Military Commanders. 3 vols. foolscap 8vo. cloth, $5 50. London.

Glendenning, (R.) Hints on the Culture of the Pineapple. 12mo. cloth, $1 50. London.

Gliddon, (G. K.) Otia Ægyptiaca. Discourses on Egyptian Archæology and Hieroglyphical Discoveries. 8vo. cloth, $2 25. London, 1849.

Glimpses of the Wonderful. An Entertaining Account of Curiosities of Nature and Art. 1st, 2d, and 3d Series. Square 16mo. cloth, each 75 cents. New York, 1846.

Glossary of Terms used in British Heraldry. 8vo. cloth, $5 00. London.

—— **of Architecture.** Several hundred wood-cuts. 3 vols. 8vo. cloth, $14 50. London, 1848.

The Same. Abridged. $2 25.

Godman, (J. D.) Natural History. 8vo. cloth, $3 00. Philadelphia.

Godwin, (W.) Lives of the Necromancers. 12mo. cloth, 65 cents. New York.

Goethe. Faust. Translated by Lewis Filmore. 12mo. cloth, 75 cents. London, 1847.

The Same. Part the Second. Translated into English verse. 12mo. cloth, $1 00. Pickering, London, 1842.

—— Werther. Traduit et précédé d'une préface par Pierre Leroux et accompagne d'un Travail Littèraire, par George Sand. Imperial 8vo. paper. Illustrated with ten beautiful engravings by Tony Johannot. $2 75. Paris, 1845.

—— Le Faust de, Traduction Revue et complète, précédée d'un Essai sur Goëthe, par M. Henri Blaze. Imperial 8vo. paper. Illustrêe par M. Tony Johannot. $3 25. Paris, 1847.

—— Affinitês Electives. Traduction nouvelle, par Madame de Carlowitz. 12mo. broché, $1 00. Paris, 1844.

—— Wilhelm Meister. Translated by Thos. Carlyle. 3 vols. post 8vo. cloth, $5 50. London

Goethe. Conversations with Eckerman. Translated by S. M. Fuller. 12mo. cloth, $1 00. Boston.

——— Essays on Art. Translated by S. G. Ward. 12mo. cloth, 75 cents. Boston.

——— Egmont. Translated. 12mo. bds. 38 cts. Boston.

——— Theory of Colors. Translated by Eastlake. 8vo. bds. $3 50. London, 1840.

——— Faust. Translated by Heyward. 12mo. cloth, $1 00. New York.

——— and Schiller's Correspondence. 12mo. cloth, $1 00. New York.

——— Select Minor Poems. Translated. 12mo. cloth, $1 00. Boston.

——— Autobiography; by Parke Godwin. 2 vols. 12mo. cloth, $2 25. New York, 1846–7.

Goldfinch, (J.) Builder's Concomitant; containing Tables of Superficial and Cubic Measure. 12mo. cloth, $1 50.

Goldsmith, (Oliver.) The Life and Adventures of; a Biography, in Four Books, by John Foster. Illustrated. 8vo. cloth gilt, $6 00. London, 1848.

——— The Life of; from a variety of Original Sources. By James Prior. Portrait. 2 vols. 8vo. cloth, $3 50. London, 1839.

——— Life of. By Washington Irving. Illustrated with numerous engravings. Royal 8vo. cloth, $3 50; cloth gilt, $4 00; morocco, $5 00.

The Same. 12mo. cloth, (uniform with Washington Irving's Works,) $1 25. New York, 1849.

——— Miscellaneous Works; with Life and Notes. Illustrated from Designs by Stothard and Cruikshank. 4 vols. 12mo. cloth, $4 00. London, 1845.

——— Poetical Works. Illustrated from Designs by the Etching Club. Square 8vo. cloth, $2 75. New York.

——— Vicar of Wakefield. Illustrated from Designs by Mulready. 12mo. cloth gilt, $1 00; plain cloth, 50 cents. New York, 1849.

——— Letters from a Citizen of the World to his Friends in the East. Square 12mo. cloth, $1 00. London, 1840.

——— History of the Earth and Animated Nature. 2 vols. 8vo. cloth, $8 00. London.

The Same. $4 00. Philadelphia

Golovine, (Ivan.) L'Europe Révolutionnaire. 12mo. paper, $1 00. Paris, 1849.

Golownin, (Capt.) Memoirs of a Captivity in Japan in 1811, 1812, and 1813. 3 vols. 8vo. cloth, $2 75.

Good, (J. M.) Study of Medicine. By Cooper. 4 vols. 8vo. cloth, $19 00. London.

The Same. 2 vols. 8vo. sheep, $5 00. N. York.

——— The Book of Nature; with a Sketch of the Author's Life. Complete in 1 vol. 8vo. sheep, $1 25. Hartford, 1847.

Goodman, (Dr. G.) Court of King James the First; in a series of Letters—now first published from the Original MSS. 2 vols. 8vo. cloth, port, $3 50. London, 1839.

Goodwin, (Thos.) Child of Light walking in Darkness. 12mo. cloth, 63 cents. London, 1840.

Goodwin's Domestic Architecture; a Series of New Designs for Mansions, Villas, Rectory-Houses, Parsonage-Houses; Bailiffs', Gardeners', Gamekeepers', and Park-Gate Lodges; Cottages, and other Residences, in the Grecian, Italian, and Old English style of Architecture; with Estimates; new edition, with twelve supplementary plates, plain. 2 vols. royal 4to. ninety-six plates, cloth, $15 00. Lond. 1845.

——— Expositions on part of the Epistle to the Ephesians, and on the Book of Revelations. 8vo. cloth, $3 00. London, 1842.

——— (John.) Redemption Redeemed; a Discussion of the great questions of Election, Reprobation, and the Perseverance of the Saints. New edition. 8vo. $2 00. London, 1840.

——— Collection of Problems and Examples, adapted to the Elementary Course of Mathematics. 8vo. $1 50.

——— (Rev. H.) An Elementary Course of Mathematics. 8vo. cloth, $4 50.

Gordon, (Thomas.) History of the Greek Revolution, and of the Wars and Campaigns arising from the Struggle of the Greek Patriots in emancipating their country from the Turkish yoke. Second edition. 2 vols. 8vo. $2 75. London, 1842.

——— Economy of the Marine Steam Engine. 8vo. cloth, plates, $3 25. London.

Gore, (J.) Evolutions of Field Battery. 12mo. cloth, $1 00. London.

Gorton, (J.) Biographical Dictionary. 3 vols. 8vo. cloth, $12 50. London.

Gosse, (P. H.) Birds of Jamaica. 12mo. cloth, $2 75.

——— Natural History—Birds. Foolscap 8vo. cloth, $1 25. London, 1849.

——— Popular British Ornithology; containing a familiar and technical Description of the Birds of the British Isles. Colored plates, square 12mo. cloth, $2 75. London, 1849.

Gostick, (J.) The Spirit of German Poetry. Royal 8vo. paper, $1 25. London, 1845.

Gouin and Chatelier. Experiments on the Locomotive Engine. 4to. cloth, $2 12. London.

Grace Leslie; a Tale. 12mo. cloth, $1 00. New York, 1848.

Graham, (G. F.) An Essay on the Theory and Practice of Musical Composition. 4to. cloth, $2 75. Edinburgh.

Grahame, (James.) History of the United States of North America. 2 vols. 8vo. cloth, portrait, $5 00. Philadelphia, 1848.

——— (J. J.) The Cold Water System, an Essay exhibiting the real merits, &c. 8vo. cloth, $2 25. London, 1843.

——— Modern Domestic Medicine. 8vo. cloth, $4 75. London.

——— (T.) Elements of Chemistry, 8vo. cloth, $2 50. Philadelphia.

——— (S.) Lectures on Human Life. 2 vols. 8vo. cloth, $3 00. Boston.

Grant, (B. E.) Outlines of Comparative Anatomy. 8vo. cloth, $7 50. London.

Grant, (A.) History of the Nestorians. 12mo. cloth, $1 00. New York.

Grantham, (John.) Iron as a Material for Ship-Building. 8vo. cloth, 5 plates, $1 75.

Granville, (A. B.) On Counter-Irritation, &c. 8vo. $1 50. Philadelphia.

Grattan's Speeches; to which are added his Letter on the Union, and a Memoir. One thick vol. 8vo. portrait, cloth, $1 75. London, 1847.

——— (H.) Memoirs of the Life and Times of Hon. H. Grattan, by his Son. 5 vols. 8vo. cloth, portrait, $6 50. London, 1849.

Graves, (Dean.) Whole Works of; including his Lectures on the Pentateuch, Essay on the Apostles and Evangelists: with a Memoir of his Life and Writings, by his son, Richard H. Graves. Portrait, 4 vols. 8vo. cloth, $9 00. London, 1840.

——— (R. J.) Clinical Lectures on the Practice of Medicine. 2 vols. 8vo. cloth, $7 25. London.

Graviere, (E. J. de la.) Guerres Maritimes sous la République et L'Empire. 2 vols. 12mo. paper, $2 00. Paris, 1847.

Gray and Percy's Key to the Old Testament and Apocrypha. 8vo. cloth, $2 00. London, 1842.

Gray, (S. F.) Operative Chemist. 2 vols. 8vo. $5 00. Philadelphia.

——— (Mrs. H.) History of Etruria. Parts 1 and 2, post 8vo. cloth, extra, each $2 50.

——— Tour to the Sepulchres of Etruria in 1839. Post 8vo. cloth, $6 50. London.

——— (A.) Elements of Chemistry; containing the Principles of the Science. Illustrated with Engravings. 12mo. sheep, 75 cents. New York, 1849.

——— Genera of the Plants of the United States. Illustrated by Figures and Analyses from Nature, by Isaac Sprague. 2 vols. royal 8vo. cloth, 186 plates, $12 N. York. 1849.

The Same. Vol. 2, royal 8vo. cloth, 86 plates, $6 00. Boston, 1849.

——— Hand-Book of Botany. Plates. 12mo. cloth, $1 75. New York.

——— Manual of Botany of the Northern United States. Plates, 12mo. cloth, $2 00. Boston, 1847.

——— (M. E.) Figures of Molluscous Animals. Etched, for the use of Students. Vol. 1, 8vo. 88 plates, $3 75. London, 1842.

——— (Thomas.) Poetical Works, English and Latin; with Introductory Stanzas, by Rev. J. Moultrie, and a Life, by Rev. J. Mitford. Illustrated, 8vo. cloth, $3 50. London, 1847.

The Same. Mor. extra, $6 00.

——— The Aldine edition, 5 vols. foolscap, 8vo. mor. $12 00. Pickering, London, 1841.

——— Elegy in a Country Churchyard. Illustrated by the Etching Club. Proofs on India Paper. Colombier 8vo. mor. extra, $20 00.

The Same. Illuminated in the Missal style, by Owen Jones. Imp. 8vo. elegantly bound in patent relievo leather, $9 50. London.

Gray, (W.) Historical Sketch of the Origin of English Prose Literature, and its Progress till the Reign of James I. 8vo. cloth, $1 00. Oxford, 1835.

——— (James.) The Earth's Antiquity in Harmony with the Mosaic Record of Creation. 12mo. cloth, $1 50. London, 1849.

——— (Peter.) Tables and Formulæ for the Computation of Life Contingencies. 8vo. cloth, $4 50. London, 1849.

——— Supplement to the Pharmacopœia, by Theophilus Redwood. Second edition, thick 8vo. cloth, $7 00. London, 1848.

Graydon, (A.) Memoirs of his own Time; with Reminiscences of the Men and Events of the Revolution. Edited by John Stockton Little. 8vo. cloth, $2 50. Philadelphia, 1846.

Great Britain. The Atlantic Steam Ship of 3,500 Tons, constructed of Iron, with Engines of 1000 to 2000 Horse-power, and the Screw Propeller. 25 engravings, folio, $5 00. London.

Greave's Essays for Sabbath Reading. 12mo. cloth, $1 50. 1840.

Greek Ecclesiastical Historians. Eusebius. Ecclesiastical History to the 324th Year of the Christian Era; a new translation, with Life of Eusebius, &c. 8vo. cloth, $2 25. London, 1842.

Theodoret. A History of the Church, in Five Books, from A. D. 322 to 427, with Memoir of the Author, &c. 8vo. cloth, $2 25. London, 1843.

Socrates. A History of the Church, in Seven Books, from the Accession of Constantine to A. D. 445, translated from the Greek, with Life of the Author, &c. 8vo. cloth, $2 25. London, 1844.

Eusebius Pamphilus. The Life of the Emperor Constantine, in Four Books. A new translation. 8vo. cloth, $2 25. Lond. 1845.

Sozomen. A History of the Church, in Nine Books, from A. D. 324 to A. D. 440. A new translation, with Life of the Author. 8vo. cloth, $2 25. London, 1846.

Evagrius. A History of the Church, in Six Books, from A. D. 431 to A. D. 594. A new translation, with Life of the Author. 8vo. cloth, $2 25. London, 1846.

The Same. Complete set. 6 vols. 8vo. calf, extra, $21 50.

Green, (J. H.) Vital Dynamics. 8vo. cloth, $1 63. London, 1840.

——— Mental Dynamics, or Groundwork of a Professional Education. 8vo. cloth, $1 13. London, 1847.

——— (J.) On the Skin. Cloth, $1 25. Philadelphia

——— (H.) Treatise on Diseases of the Air-Passages; comprising an Inquiry into the History, Causes, and Treatment of those Affections of the Throat called Bronchitis, Chronic Laryngitis, Clergyman's Sore Throat, &c. 8vo. colored plates, $3 00. New York, 1846.

——— Observations on the Pathology of Croup, with Remarks on its Treatment by Topical Medications. 12mo. cloth, 75 cents. New York, 1849

Greene, (R.) Dramatic Works; with Life, by A. Dyce. 2 vols. post 8vo. cloth, $6 50. London.

Greener, (William.) The Science of Gunnery, as applied to the Use and Construction of Fire-Arms. Plates, 8vo. cloth, $2 50. London, 1841.

——— The Gun; or, a Treatise on the Various Descriptions of Small Arms. 8vo. with illustrations, bds. $4 50. London.

Greenhill's Exposition of the Prophet Ezekiel, with a brief Notice of the Author; one large vol. impl. 8vo. extra cloth, bds. $6 50. 1839.

Greenhow, (R.) History of Oregon and California. 8vo. cloth, $2 50. New York.

Greenleaf, (S.) Examination of the Testimony of the Evangelists. 8vo. cloth, $3 75. Boston.

Greenwood, (F. W. P.) Sermons of Consolation. 12mo. cloth, $1 00. Boston, 1847.

——— Sermons on Various Subjects. 2 vols. 12mo. cloth, $2 50. Boston.

——— Lives of the Twelve Apostles; with a Life of John the Baptist. 12mo. cloth, 75 cents. Boston, 1846.

——— (Col. G.) The Tree-Lifter; or, a New Method of Transplanting Forest-Trees 8vo. $2 00. London.

Grecian Ornaments. A Series of Examples of Grecian Ornaments. 21 plates, finely engraved from drawings. Royal folio, $4 50. London.

Gregory, (O.) Mathematics for Practical Men; being a Common-place Book of Pure and Mixed Mathematics. Revised and enlarged by Henry Law. 8vo. half mor. neat, $6 00. London, 1848.

——— Mathematics for Practical Men. $1 75. Philadelphia.

——— (Dr. G.) Elements of the Theory and Practice of Medicine. Designed for the Use of Students and Junior Practitioners. 8vo. cloth, $5 00. London, 1839.

——— (J.) Conspectus Medicinæ Theoreticæ; or, a View of the Theory of Medicine. Translated from the original Latin. 12mo. cloth, $1 87. Edinburgh, 1844.

——— (D. F.) Examples of the Processes of the Differential and Integral Calculus. Second Edition. 8vo. cloth, $5 00. London.

——— (W.) Outlines of Chemistry, for the Use of Students. 2 vols. 12mo. cloth, illustrated with wood-cuts, $3 25. London, 1846.

——— Treatise of Mechanics. 2 vols. 8vo. 45 large plates, $12 50. London.

Grey, (Geo.) Journals of Discovery in Australia, 1837–39. 2 vols. 8vo. plates, $11 00. London.

Greville, (R. K.) Algæ Britannicæ; or, a Description of the Marine and other Articulated Plants of the British Islands. 8vo. cloth, $12 50 Edinburgh, 1830.

Grier's Mechanical Calculator. 12mo. cloth, $2 75. London.

——— Pocket Dictionary. 12mo. cloth, 200 cuts, $2 75.

Griesselich, (Dr.) Manuel pour Servir a l'étude Critique de la Médécine Homœopathique. Traduit par Schlesinger-Rahier. 12mo. broché, $1 50. Paris, 1849.

Griffin, (J. J.) Chemical Recreations. A Popular Compendium of Experimental Chemistry. 16mo. cloth, $2 00.

——— (W. N.) Treatise on the Motion of a Rigid Body. 8vo. cloth, $1 75.

Griffith, (F. A.) Artillerist's Manual. 18mo. cloth, $2 12. London.

——— (T.) Chemistry of the Four Seasons. 12mo. cloth, wood-cuts, $3 00. London, 1846.

——— (R. E.) Medical Botany; or, Descriptions of the more important Plants used in Medicine, with their History, Properties, and Mode of Administration. 8vo sheep, 300 illustrations, $3 50. Philadelphia, 1847.

——— Natural System of Architecture. 4to. cloth, $3 25. London.

——— Proportions of Greek Architecture. 4to. cloth, $2 25. London.

——— (Thomas.) Leading Idea of Christianity. 12mo. cloth, $1 12. London, 1838.

Grimboldt, (P.) Letters of William III. and Louis XIV., and of their Ministers. Illustrating the Domestic and Foreign Policy during the Period which followed the Revolution of 1688. Extracted from the Archives of France and England, and from Family Papers. 2 vols. 8vo. $9 00. London.

Grimm's Tales from Eastern Land. Translated from the German, with four colored illustrations. Square, cloth, gilt, 75 cents. London, 1847

Griswold, (R.) Prose Writers and Literature of America. Royal 8vo. cloth, portraits, $3 75. Philadelphia

——— Female Poets of America. 8vo. mor. gilt, $4 50. Cloth, gilt, $3 00. Philadelphia.

——— Poets and Poetry of America. 8vo. cloth, gilt, $3 50. Cloth, $3 00. Philadelphia.

——— Poets and Poetry of England. Cloth, extra, $3 50. Cloth, $3 00. Philadelphia.

Grohmann. Series of Views of Garden Houses, Temples, &c. 4to. cloth, 37 plates, $6 50. London.

Grose, (F.) Glossary of Provincial and Local Words used in England, with Supplement, by Samuel Pegge. Cr. 8vo. cloth, $1 25. London, 1839.

Gross, (S. D.) Elements of Pathological Anatomy. Illustrated by colored engravings and wood-cuts. Royal 8vo. sheep, $5 00. Philadelphia, 1849.

——— General Anatomy. 8vo. sheep, $3 00. Philadelphia, 1828.

——— On Wounds of the Intestines. Cloth, $2 00. Philadelphia.

Grote, (George.) The History of Greece. Vols. 1 to 6, $3 00 each. London, 1846–49.

Grotius de Veritate Religionis Christianæ. 12mo. bds. $1 00. Boston.

Grouvelle et Jaunez, (MM.) Guide du Chauffeur et du Proprietaires de Machines a Vapeur. 8vo. paper, with atlas and plates, $3 00. Paris, 1840.

Gruner, (L.) Decorations of the Pavillion at Buckingham Palace. Folio cloth, $9 50. Colored plates. $31 50. London.

——— Fresco Decorations and Stuccoes of the Churches and Palaces in Italy, during the 15th and 16th Centuries; with English Descriptions. 45 plates, folio, plain and colored. London, 1845.

Guenon, (M. F.) A Treatise on Milch Cows, whereby the Quality and Quantity of Milk which any Cow will give may be determined. Translated from the French, by N. P. Trist. 8vo. cloth, 63 cents. New York.

Guerin. Manuel de l'Histoire des Conciles, ou Traité Théologique, Critique, Historique, Analytique, et Chronologique des Conciles et des Synodes, depuis le Concile de Jérusalem, par les Apotres, jusqu'aux derniers Synodes tenus de nos juors. 8vo. $2 50. Paris, 1846.

Guesses at Truth, by Two Brothers. 1st and 2d Series. 12mo. cloth, $3 75. London, 1847.

Guest, (R.) Treatise on Spinning Machinery. 8vo. cloth, $2 25. London.

Guicciardini, (F.) The Maxims of. Translated by Emma Martin, with Notes and Parallel Passages from the Works of Machiavelli, Lord Bacon, Pascal, Rochefoucault, Montesquieu, Burke, Talleyrand, M. Guizot, &c., and a Sketch of the Life of Guicciardini. Square foolscap, 8vo. with portrait, bds. $2 25. Bound in morocco, $4 50. London.

Guide to Northern Archæology. For the Use of English Readers, by the Earl of Ellesmere. Royal 8vo. cloth, $2 25. London, 1848.

Guizot. History of the English Revolution of 1640. 12mo. cloth, $1 25. New York.

——— History of Civilization. 4 vols. 12mo. cloth, $3 50. New York.

——— Histoire de la Civilization en France. 4 vols. 12mo. broché, $4 00. Paris, 1847.

——— Civilization en Europe. 12mo. $1 00. Paris, 1848.

——— Essais sur l'Histoire de France. 12mo. $1 00. Paris, 1847.

——— Histoire de la Civilization en France. 5 vols. 12mo. paper, $2 50. Bruxelles, 1839.

Gulliver's Travels into several Remote Nations of the World. By Jonathan Swift; with a Life of the Author. Embellished with numerous engravings, by first-rate artists. 8vo. cloth, $1 50. London, 1848.

Gully, (J. M.) On Water-Cure in Chronic Diseases. Post 8vo. cloth, $2 12. London.

Gummere's Astronomy. 8vo. sheep, $3 00. Philadelphia.

Gunther, (F. H.) New Manual of Homœopathic Veterinary Medicine, 8vo $3 00.

Gurney, (J. J.) A Winter in the West Indies, described in Familiar Letters to Henry Clay of Kentucky. 18mo. cloth, $1 25. London, 1841.

Gurwood, (Lieut. Col.) General Orders of the Duke of Wellington in Portugal, Spain, and France, from 1809 to 1814, in the Low Countries and France in 1815, and in France, Army of Occupation, from 1816 to 1818. 8vo. bds. $3 75. London.

Gutch, (J. W. G.) The Literary and Scientific Register and Almanac for 1849. 32mo. tuck. $1 00. London, 1849.

Guthrie, (W.) Universal Geography. 2 vols. 8vo. and atlas, $8 00. Phila. 1821.

——— (G. J.) Lectures on Operative Surgery of the Eye. 8vo. cloth, $7 50. London.

Guy, (W. A.) Principles of Medical Jurisprudence. 8vo. sheep, $3 00. New York.

Guyot, (Prof.) The Earth and Man. Lectures on Comparative Physical Geography, in its Relation to the History of Mankind. Translated by Felton. 12mo. plates, $1 25. Boston, 1849.

Gwilt's Encyclopædia of Architecture. Upwards of 1000 wood-cuts, thick 8vo. $15 75. London.

——— Notitia Italiana; or, Notices of the most remarkable Buildings in Italy. 8vo. $3 75. London.

——— Rudiments of Architecture 17 plates, of the orders, with their parts and proportions. 8vo. cloth, $3 75. London.

——— Elements of Architectural Criticism, for the Use of Students, Amateurs, and Reviewers. 8vo. cloth, $1 50. London.

——— Sciography; or, Examples of Shadows. 24 plates, $3 25. London.

——— Treatise on the Equilibrium of Arches. 8vo. plates, $1 50. London.

——— (Josh.) Rudiments of a Grammar of the Anglo-Saxon Tongue. 8vo. cloth, $1 75. London, 1829.

Habershon's Half-timbered Houses. 4to. cloth, numerous plates, $15 00. London.

Hackle, (Palmer.) Hints on Angling; with Suggestions for Angling Excursions in France and Belgium. 8vo. cloth, $1 25. London, 1846.

Hackley, (C. W.) Elements of Geometry. 12mo. sheep, 75 cents. New York.

——— Treatise on Algebra. 8vo. sheep, $1 50. New York.

——— Elements of Trigonometry. 8vo. sheep, $1 25. New York.

Haddock, (J. W.) Somnolism and Psycheism; otherwise, Vital Magnetism or Mesmerism, considered Physiologically and Philosophically. Foolscap 8vo. 37 cents. London, 1849.

Hadfield, (James.) The Ecclesiastical, Castellated, and Domestic Architecture of England, from the Norman Conquest to the 16th Century. Illustrated by the best existing examples, with Plans, Elevations, Sections, Details, and Exterior and Interior Views, from a Series of original measured drawings. Folio, cloth, $15 00. London, 1848.

Haghe's Sketches in Belgium, Holland, &c. 2 vols. folio, of Exterior and Interior Views, tinted, each $25 00. London.

Hahn Hahn, (Ida, Countess.) Adventures and Travels in Turkey, Egypt, and the Holy Land. 3 vols. cr. 8vo. cloth, $3 00. Lond.

Hahneman, (Sam.) Organon of Homœopathic Medicine. 8vo. cloth, $1 25. New York.

——— On Chronic Diseases and Homœopathic Treatment. 5 vols. 8vo. cloth, $7 00. New York.

Hakewill, (Jas.) Picturesque Tour in Italy, from drawings by Turner, and beautiful outlines of the chief Museums of Sculpture and Painting. 4to. cloth, $12 50. London.

——— An Attempt to Determine the Exact Character of Elizabethan Architecture. 8vo. cloth, 8 plates, $1 25. London.

Hakluyt Society's (The) Publications. 8vo. cloth. Yearly Subscription, $7 50. Works already published: Raleigh's Discovery of the Empire of Guiana. Sir Francis Drake—his Voyage, 1595. The Observations of Sir Richard Hawkins. The Select Letters of Christopher Columbus. 1847–8.

Hale, (H.) The Ethnography and Philology of the United States Exploring Expedition; containing the Languages of the Pacific Islands and the Western Coast of America generally. Imperial 4to. cloth, $10 00. Philadelphia, 1846.

——— (Mrs. C. V. R. M.) Saturday Evenings, a Series of Moral and Religious Essays. 12mo. cloth, 75 cents. New York, 1845.

Half Hours with the Best Authors; selected and arranged with Biographical and Critical Notices, by Charles Knight. 4 vols. 12mo. $4 00. New York.

Halfpenny, (Jos.) Gothic Ornaments of the Cathedral Church of York. 4to. cloth, $31 50. London.

Hall, (Rev. A.) Treatise on the Faith and Influence of the Gospel; with Introductory Essay, by Thomas Chalmers. 12mo. cloth, post, $1 00. Glasgow, 1831.

——— (James.) The Palœontology of New York. Vol. I. 4to. cloth, 100 plates, $6 00. New York, 1848.

——— Wilderness and the War-Path. 12mo. cloth, 50 cents. New York, 1849.

——— (Mrs. James.) Phantasia, and other Poems. 8vo. plates, $1 50. Cloth, gilt, $2 00. New York.

——— (John.) Select and Original Modern Designs for Dwelling-Houses, for the Use of Carpenters and Builders. 4to. cloth, 24 plates, $2 50. Baltimore, 1848.

——— (Rev. T. G.) A Treatise on the Differential and Integral Calculus, and the Calculus of Variation. 8vo. cloth, $3 50. London.

——— (S. F.) Land-Owner's Manual. 8vo. cloth, $2 00. Buffalo.

——— (Marshall.) The Principles of Diagnosis with Notes, by John A. Sweet. 8vo. sheep, $2 00. New York, 1839.

Hall, (Mrs. S. C.) The Book of British Ballads. 2 vols. 4to. cloth, fancy binding. Profusely illustrated with exquisite engravings on wood, by the first artists, $11 00. London, 1847.

——— (Mr. and Mrs. S. C.) Ireland, its Scenery, Character, Manners, &c. 3 vols. royal 8vo. cloth, illustrated with wood-cuts and plates, $19 00. London, 1841–43.

——— (Mrs. S. C.) Sketches of Irish Character. Royal 8vo. cloth, gilt, 5 engravings by Maclise, and numerous wood-cuts, $3 25. Lond. 1849.

——— (Bp.) The Whole Works of; with some Account of his Life and Sufferings, by himself. A new edition, revised and corrected. 12 vols. 8vo. cloth, $28 00. London, 1837.

——— Contemplations on the Principal Passages of the Old and New Testaments. 6 vols. post 8vo. calf, extra, $6 00. London, 1836.

The Same. Complete, 8vo. $2 25. Lond. 1842.

——— (Rev. Robert.) The whole Works of; with Life by Gregory. 6 vols. 8vo. cloth, $10 00. London, 1843.

The Same. Foolscap, 8vo. cloth, $7 00. London, 1844.

——— Miscellaneous Works, with Life by Gregory, &c. Post 8vo. cloth, 88 cents. Lond.

——— (Captain Basil.) Patchwork; a new Series of Fragments of Voyages and Travels. Second edition, 12mo. handsomely printed, extra cloth, with the back very richly and appropriately gilt with patchwork devices, $2 25. Moxon, 1842.

Hallam, (H.) Works Complete, viz: History of Literature of Europe, 3 vols. History of the Middle Ages, with Supplemental Volume of Notes, 3 vols., and Constitutional History of England, 2 vols., together, 8 vols. 8vo. calf, gilt marbled leaves, $40 00. London, 1846.

——— Historical Works. 4 vols. 8vo. sheep, $7 00. New York, 1847.

Halleck, (Fitzgreen) Poems. Cr. 8vo. cloth, beautifully printed and illustrated with engravings on steel, mor. gilt, $6 00; cloth, gilt, $4 00. New York, 1848.

——— Elements of Military Art and Science. Plates, 12mo. cloth, $1 25. New York.

Halley, (R.) Inquiry into the Nature of the Symbolic Institutions of the Christian Religion usually called the Sacraments. 8vo. cloth, $4 00. London, 1844.

Halliwell, (J. O.) Dictionary of Archaic and Provincial Words. 2 vols. 8vo. cloth, $12 50. London, 1846.

——— The Nursery Rhymes of England. 4th edition, with illustrations. 12mo. bds. $1 50. London, 1848.

——— Collection of Letters Illustrative of the Progress of Science in England from the Reign of Elizabeth to that of Charles II. 75 cents. London, 1841.

——— Letters of the Kings of England; now first collected from the originals. 2 vols. post 8vo. cloth, $3 75. London, 1848.

Halsted, (Caroline A.) Life and Times of Richard the Third, as Duke of Gloucester and King of England; in which all the Charges against him are Carefully Investigated and Compared with the Statements of Cotemporary Authorities. With an original portrait and other illustrations. 2 vols. 8vo. cloth, $9 00. London.

The Same. American edition, 8vo. cloth, $1 50. Philadelphia, 1844.

Hamilton, (Jos.) A Treatise on the Cultivation of the Pineapple. 12mo. cloth, $1 50. London.

——— (W.) A Hand-Book or Concise Dictionary of Terms used in the Arts and Sciences. 12mo. bds. $2 50. London, 1825.

——— (Count A.) Fairy Tales and Romances. Portrait, 12mo. cloth, 88 cents. London, 1849.

——— (W. J.) Researches in Asia Minor, Pontus, and Armenia; with some Account of their Antiquities and Geology. 2 vols. 8vo. cloth, $3 00. London, 1842.

——— Vases. Collection of Engravings from Ancient Vases, mostly of pure Greek Workmanship, now in the possession of Sir William Hamilton, with letter-press in English and French. 3 vols. super-royal folio, containing upwards of 200 fine large engravings, capitally executed in outline by Tischbein, Director of the Academy of Painting in Naples; stiff covers, with lettered backs, $12 50. 1791.

Hammond, (H., D. D.) A Paraphrase and Annotations on all the Books of the New Testament. 4 vols. 8vo. cloth, $9 00. London, 1845.

——— (J. D.) Political History of New York. 3 vols. 8vo. sheep, $6 00. New York.

Hampden, (R. D.) Sermons Preached before the University of Oxford. 8vo. bds. $3 50. London, 1848.

Hand, (The) Phrenologically Considered; being a Glimpse at the Relation of the Mind with the Organization of the Body. 12mo. cloth, plates. $1 25. London, 1848.

Hand-Book of Angling. By Ephemera. 12mo. cloth, wood-cuts, $2 75. London, 1848.

Hand-Book for Young Artists and Amateurs in Oil Painting; with a new Explanatory and Critical Vocabulary. 12mo. cloth, $1 25. New York, 1848.

Hand-Book for London. Past and Present. By Peter Cunningham. 2 thick vols. 12mo. cloth, $6 50. London, 1849.

Hand-Book of Water-Colors. A Brief Treatise on their Qualities and Effects when Employed in Painting. 12mo. 37 cents. London, 1849.

Hann (J.) Theoretical and Practical Mechanics. Designed principally for practical men. 8vo. cloth, $2 50. London.

——— Short Treatise on the Steam Engine; adapted to the Use of Schools, in which are given Practical Rules for the Use of Engineers. 12mo. cloth, $1. London, 1849.

Hanham, (F.) Natural Illustrations of British Grasses. Folio, cloth, $18 00. London.

Hannay, (James.) King Dobbs. Sketches in Ultra-Marine. 12mo. cloth, $2 00. London, 1849.

Hannett, (J.) Bibliopegia; or, the Art of Book-Binding in all its branches. 12mo. cloth, $1 75. London, 1843.

Hansard's Pocket Peerage for 1845. 12mo. cloth, $1 50. London.

——— (T. C.) Treatise on Printing and Type Founding. Post 8vo. cloth, $1 75. London.

——— (G. A.) Book of Archery; being the Complete History and Practice of the Art, interspersed with numerous Anecdotes; forming a complete Manual for the Bowman. 8vo. cloth, engravings on steel, $3 25. London, 1840.

Happy Home, (The.) Affectionately Inscribed to the Working People, by the Author of "Life in Earnest." 32mo. cloth, 75 cents. London, 1848.

Harcourt, (Rev. Vernon) The Doctrine of the Deluge. 2 vols. 8vo. $3 50. London, 1838.

Hare, (Julius Charles.) The Duty of the Church in Times of Trial. 8vo. bds. $1 50. London, 1848.

——— Sermons Preached in Herstmonceux Church. Vol. II. $3 50. London, 1849.

——— (C. and J.) Guesses at Truth. 2 vols. 12mo. cloth, $3 50. London, 1847.

Harding, (G. D.) Lithographic Drawing-Book. sm. folio, $3 25. London.

——— Sketches of Park and Forest Scenery. Royal folio, 26 plates in the tinted style, $15 75 London.

——— Lessons on Art. Royal folio, cloth. plates, $7 50. London, 1849.

——— Principle and Practice of Art. 4to. cloth, plates, $18 00.

——— Elementary Art. Folio, cloth, plates, $12 50. London, 1849.

Hardwick, (Lord Chancellor.) The Life of; with selections from his Correspondence, Diary, Speeches, &c. By G. Harris. 3 vols. 8vo. cloth, $6 00. London, 1847.

Hardy and Mc Clintock, (Drs.) Practical Observations on Midwifery and the Diseases incident to the Puerperal State. 8vo. cloth, $3 25. Dublin, 1848.

Harlan, (R.) Medical and Physical Researches. Cloth, $5 00. Phila. 1835.

Harness, (Rev. W.) Parochial Sermons. 8vo. cloth, $1 50. London, 1838.

Harris, (Chapin A.) Dissertation on the Diseases of the Maxillary Sinus. 8vo. cloth, $1 50. Philadelphia, 1843.

——— (W. S.) On the Nature of Thunder storms, and on the means of Protecting Buildings and Shipping against the Destructive Effects of Lightning. 8vo. cloth, $3 25. London, 1843.

——— (G.) Life of Lord Chancellor Hardwicke, with Selections from his Correspondence, Diaries, Speeches, and Judgments. 3 vols. 8vo. cloth, portrait, $6 00. London, 1847.

——— (John.) The Pre-Adamite Earth; Contributions to Theological Science. 12mo. cloth, 88 cents. Boston, 1849

Harris, (C. A.) The Principles and Practice of Dental Surgery; with 156 illustrations. 3d edition, royal 8vo. cloth, $4 00. New York, 1848.

——— (W. C.) Wild Sports of Southern Africa. Royal 8vo. cloth, beautifully colored, plates, $12 50. London, 1841.

——— (T. W.) Treatise on the Insects of New England. 8vo. cloth, $2 50. Cambridge.

——— (Sir W. S.) Rudimentary Electricity. Illustrated with wood-cuts, 12mo. cloth, 25 cents. London, 1849.

——— On the Nature of Thunder-Storms, and on the Means of Protecting Buildings and Shipping against the Destructive Effects of Lightning. 8vo. cloth, $2 50. London.

Harrison, (John.) On the Nervous System. 8vo. sheep, $2 00. Philadelphia.

Harry Lorrequer. 12 plates. By Lever. 8vo. cloth, $1 25. Philadelphia.

Hart. Essay on Spenser's Faery Queen. 8vo. cloth, $3 00. New York.

——— (J.) Practical Treatise on the Construction of Oblique Arches, 8vo. cloth, $3 00. London.

——— (J. C.) Romance of Yachting; Voyage the First. $1 00. New York, 1848.

——— (Rev. Richard.) Ecclesiastical Records of England, Ireland, and Scotland, from the Fifth Century till the Reformation. 8vo. cloth, $2 25. Cambridge, 1846.

Hartley, (R. M.) Essay on Milk as an Article of Human Sustenance. 12mo. cloth, $1 00. New York, 1842.

Hartshorn's Clinical Surgery. 12mo. sheep, $1 50. Philadelphia.

Hartman, (F.) Homœopathic Remedies, translated by A. H. Okie. 12mo. cloth, $1 75. Philadelphia.

——— Acute Diseases. Translated by C. J. Hempel. 2 vols. 12mo. cloth, $2 00. New York.

Harvey, (W. H.) Neresis Australis; or, Illustrations of the Algæ of the Southern Ocean. To be completed in 4 parts. Part 1, published, $5 00. London.

——— Phycologia Britannica; or, History of the British Sea-Weeds; containing colored figures, Generic and Specific Characters, Synonymes, and Descriptions of all the Species of Algæ inhabiting the shores of the British Islands. (Now publishing in parts; to be completed in sixty parts.) Plain, 75 cents each; colored, $1 50 each. London.

Haskell, (M. D.) Assistant Engineer's Railway Guide in Boring, Stumping, and Striking out Centre Lines and Curves, setting out Slopes and Foundations of Works, Working Sections and Land Plans, &c. &c. 60 wood-cuts and 3 plates. 2 vols. 8vo. $11 00. London, 1846–48.

——— Clerk of the Works; or, Young Architect's Guide. 12mo. $1 50. London, 1848.

Haskell and Smith's Gazetteer of the United States. 8vo. sheep, $3 00. New York, 1846.

Hastings, (John.) Lectures on Yellow Fever, its Causes, Pathology, and Treatment. 8vo cloth, 50 cents. Philadelphia, 1848.

Haswell, (C. W.) Engineer and Mechanic's Pocket-Book; containing United States and Foreign Weights and Measures; Mensuration of Surfaces and Solids, Steam, and the Steam Engine. 12mo. $1 25. New York.

Hatcher, (W. H.) An Account of the Electric Telegraph now in use for Railway and other purposes. 12mo. wood-cuts, 25 cents. London.

Hatfield, (R. G.) The American House-Carpenter; a Treatise upon Architecture, together with the most Important Principles of Practical Geometry. Illustrated by more than 300 engravings. 8vo. $2 50. New York.

Hattersley, (John.) First Course of Mathematics. 8vo. cloth, $3 25. London.

Haviland, (James.) Tables of Specific Gravities of all Substances. 8vo. cloth, $1 50. London.

——— The Improved Portable Measurer; containing New Sets of Tables for Solid and Superficial Measurement, &c. Long, narrow size, suited for the Pocket, bound, 75 cents. Lond.

Haweis, (J. O. W.) Sketches of the Reformation and Elizabethan Age, taken from the Contemporary Pulpit. 12mo. cloth, $1 75. London, 1844.

Hawks, (Rev. F. L.) Monuments of Central and Western America; with Comparative Notices of those in Egypt, India, and Assyria. 8vo. cloth, with illustrations.

——— Egypt and its Monuments, as illustrative of Scripture History. 8vo. cloth, illustrated with engravings New York, 1849.

Hawker. Instructions to Young Sportsmen in all that Relates to Guns and Shooting. 8vo. plates and wood-cuts, $6 50. London, 1844.

The Same. To which is added the Hunting and Shooting of North America, with Descriptions of the Animals and Birds. By W. T. Porter. 8vo. red cloth gilt, plates, $2 75. Philadelphia, 1846.

Hawker, (Dr.) Spiritual Reflections on the Chapters of Holy Scripture. 2 vols. 12mo. $1 00. London, 1845.

Hawkesworth, (John.) Account of the Voyages undertaken by the Order of his Present Majesty, for making Discoveries in the Southern Hemisphere, and successively performed by Com. Byron, Capts. Wallis, Carteret, and Cook. 3 vols. 4to. full Russia, $10 00. London. 1783.

Hawkins' Treatise on the Teeth of Wheels. 8vo. cloth, 18 plates, $3 75. London.

Hawthorne, (N.) Twice Told Tales. 2 vols. 12mo. cloth, $2 25. Boston, 1845.

Hay, (Sir A. L.) Castellated Architecture of Aberdeenshire. Royal 4to. with 37 lithographic illustrations, cloth, $12 75. Edinburgh, 1849.

——— (D. R.) Original Geometrical Diaper Designs, for the Use of Decorative Painters, Calico Printers, &c. 4 parts, folio, $4 00.

——— Proportion; or, the Geometric Principle of Beauty Analyzed. 4to. cloth, 17 plates, $6 75. Edinburgh, 1843

Hay, (D. R.) A Nomenclature of Colors, Hues, Tints, and Shades, applied to the Arts and Natural Sciences. 8vo. 40 colored plates, $6 50. Edinburgh, 1845.

——— Laws of Harmonious Coloring, adapted to Interior Decoration, with Observations on the Practice of House Painting. $2 00.

——— The Principles of Beauty in Coloring Systemized. 8vo. $6 50.

——— First Principles of Symmetrical Beauty. 12mo. plates, $2 00.

——— The Natural Principle and Analogy of the Harmony of Form. 4to. $5 00.

——— On the Science of those Proportions by which the Human Head and Countenance, as represented in Works of Ancient Greek Art, are distinguished from those of Ordinary Nature. 4to. cloth, 26 plates, $11 00. Edinburgh, 1849.

Haydon, (B. R.) Lectures on Painting and Design. 2 vols. 8vo. cloth, $7 50. 1844–46.

Haydn. (Joseph) Dictionary of Dates and Universal Reference, relating to all Ages and Nations. 8vo. calf, gilt, m. e. $6 00. London, 1847.

Hayter, (C.) Introduction to Perspective, Practical Geometry, Drawing, and Painting. 8vo. cloth, $4 50. London, 1844.

——— A New Practical Treatise on the Three Primitive Colors. 8vo. $2 75. London.

Hazlitt, (W.) Characters of Shakspeare's Plays. 12mo. cloth, 50 cents. N. Y. 1846.

——— English Comic Writers. 12mo. cloth, 50 cents. New York, 1848.

——— English Poets. 12mo. cloth, 50 cents. New York, 1845.

——— Dramatic History of the Age of Elizabeth. 12mo. cloth, 50 cents. N. Y. 1845.

——— The Spirit of the Age. 12mo. cloth, 50 cents. New York.

——— The Life of Napoleon Buonaparte. 3 vols. 12mo. cloth, $3 00. Phila. 1848.

——— Miscellanies. 5 vols. 12mo. cloth, $5 00. half mor. $7 00. Philadelphia.

Head, (Sir E.) A Hand-Book of the History of the Spanish and French Schools of Painting, intended as a Sequel to Kugler's Hand-Book. 12mo. cloth, $3 25. London.

——— (Sir G.) Tour of Many Days in Rome. 3 vols. 8vo. cloth, $10 00. London, 1849.

——— (Francis B.) Stokers and Pokers on the London and North-Western Railway, the Electric Telegraph and the Halfway Clearing-House. 12mo. paper, 75 cents. Lond. 1849.

Headley, (J. T.) The Life of Oliver Cromwell. Thick 12mo. portrait. New York, 1848.

——— The Adirondack; or, Life in the Woods. 12mo. cloth, 8 illustrations, $1 25. New York, 1849.

Headlong Hall and Nightmare Abbey—Evenings with the Old Story-Tellers. Together, in 1 vol. 12mo. cloth, $1 00. New York, 1845.

Heald, (G.) Complete and Most Improved System of Setting Out Railway Curves. 4to. paper, wood-cuts, $1 00. London.

Hearn, (E. M.) "The Man of Sin." 12mo. cloth, 87 cents. London, 1844.

Hearn, (G. W.) Researches on Curves of the Second Order; also on Cones and Spherical Conics, treated Analytically. 8vo. $1 50. London, 1846.

Heather, (J. F.) Treatise on Mathematical Instruments. Illustrations, 25 cents. (Weale's Series.) London, 1849.

Heat: its Sources, Influence, and Results. Square cloth gilt, plates, $1 00. Lond. 1841.

Heber, (R.) Narrative of a Journey through the Upper Provinces of India in 1824–25. 2 vols. 12mo. calf, neat, $5 00. London, 1844.

Hebert, (J.) Engineer's and Mechanic's Encyclopædia. 2 vols. 8vo. cloth, $9 00. London.

Hecker, (J. F. C.) The Epidemics of the Middle Ages. 8vo. cloth, $1 00. Phila. 1837.

Hedge, (F. H.) Prose Writers of Germany. Royal 8vo. cloth, portraits, $3 50; cloth, extra, $4 00; mor. gilt, $5 50. Phila. 1848.

Heeren's Historical Works, viz.: African Nations. Asiatic Nations. European States and Colonies. Ancient Greece and Historical Treatises. Ancient History. 7 vols. 8vo. calf, extra, $32 50. London.

Heideloff, (C.) Collection of Architectural Ornaments of the Middle Ages in the Byzantine and Gothic Styles. 4to. 128 plates, $24 00. Nuremburg, 1844–46.

Heliconia; comprising a Selection of English Poetry of the Elizabethan Age; written or published between 1575 and 1604. Edited by J. Park. 3 vols. 4to half Russia, top edge gilt, $25 00. London, 1815.

Hemans, (Mrs.) Complete Poetical Works. Reprinted entire from the last London Edition. Edited by her Sister. 2 vols. 12mo. cloth, $3 50. New York, 1847.

The Same. Bound in morocco, gilt edges, $5 00.

Hemming, (G. W.) Treatise on the Differential and Integral Calculus. 8vo. cloth, $2 75. London.

Hempel, (C. J.) Homœopathic Domestic Physician. 18mo. cloth, 50 cents. N. York.

——— Organon of Homœopathic Medicine. 8vo. cloth, $1 25. New York.

Henderson, (W.) Inquiry into the Homœopathic Practice. $1 50. New York.

Henderson and Forbes on Homœopathic Practice. $1 00. New York.

Hendric, (R., Jr.) Encyclopædia of the Fine Arts in the Tenth and Eleventh Centuries. Translated from the MS. of the Monk Theophilus, with Notes. 8vo. cloth, $4 75. London, 1843.

Henry, (Matthew.) Commentary on the Bible. Bickersteth's Edition, in 6 vols. 4to. new edition, printed on fine paper, $28 00. London, 1846.

The Same. 6 vols. 4to. strongly bound in purple calf, grained and lettered, $38 00.

——— (Capt. W. S.) Campaign Sketches of War with Mexico. 12mo. cloth, $1 00. New York.

——— Chemistry. Edited by Dr. Hare. 2 vols. 8vo. sheep, $5 00. Philadelphia.

——— (Rev. C. S.) Epitome of Philosophy. 2 vols. 18mo. cloth, 90 cents. New York.

Henry, (Paul.) The Life and Times of John Calvin, the great Reformer. Translated from the German, by Henry Stebbing. 2 vols. 8vo. cloth, $7 00. London, 1849.

Henshall, (J.) A Practical Treatise on the Cultivation of Orchidaceous Plants; with Remarks on their Geographical Distribution. 8vo. cloth, $3 50. London.

Henshaw, (Dr. J.) Meditations, Miscellaneous, Holy and Humane. 12mo. cloth, 50 cents. Oxford, 1841.

Henslow, (Rev. J. S.) The Principles of Descriptive and Physiological Botany. 12mo. cloth, $1 75. London.

Henfrey, (A.) Outlines of Structural and Physiological Botany. 12mo. cloth, $2 75. London.

Herberden, (Wm.) On Cure of Diseases. 8vo. sheep, $1 50. Philadelphia.

Herbert, (G.) Works in Prose and Verse. 2 vols. 8vo. mor. gilt, $13 00. Lond. 1846.

——— The Temple. Sacred Poems and Private Ejaculations, with the Country Parson. 18mo. cloth, neat, 75 cents. London, 1849.

——— The Poems and Remains of; with his Life. by Walton, &c. 2 vols. 12mo. cloth, $3 00. Mor. extra, $5 50. London, Pickering, 1842.

——— (L.) The Engineer's and Mechanic's Encyclopædia; comprehending Practical Illustrations of the Machinery and Processes employed in every Description of Manufacture of the British Empire; with upwards of 2000 engravings. New edition, with considerable additions and improvements. 2 vols. 8vo. cloth, $9 00. London, 1849.

Herepath, (J.) Mathematical Physics; or, the Mathematical Principles of Natural Philosophy; with a Development of the Causes of Heat, Gaseous Electricity, Gravitation, and other great Phenomena of Nature. 2 vols. 8vo. with Tables and Diagrams, $9 00. London, 1847.

Herder's Spirit of Hebrew Poetry. 2 vols. 12mo. cloth, $1 25. Burlington.

Hering, (G. E.) Mountains and Lakes of Switzerland. 4to. cloth, plates, $6 50. Lond.

Hermann's Manual of the Political Antiquities of Greece, Historically Considered. Translated from the German. 8vo. extra cloth, $3 00. Oxford, Talboys, 1836.

Herodotus. A New and Literal Version. From the Text of Baehr, with a Geographical and General Index, by Henry Carey. 12mo. cloth, portrait, $1 50. London, 1848.

Herrick, (R.) Hesperides—his Works, both Humane and Divine. 2 vols. 12mo. cloth, portrait, $3 50; morocco, gilt edges, $8 00. London, 1846.

Herschel, (Sir John.) Outlines of Astronomy; comprising a View of the Actual State of Knowledge in the Departments of Astronomy, both Descriptive and Physical; an Elementary Exposition of its Principles, and a Rational Elucidation on the Theory of Gravity, of the Chief Lunar and Planetary Perturbations. 8vo. with steel plates, cr. 8vo. cloth, $5 50. London, 1849.

——— American edition, 12mo. cloth, $1 75. Philadelphia.

Herschel, (Sir J. F. W.) Manual of Scientific Enquiry, prepared for the Use of Her Majesty's Navy, and adapted for Travellers in general. Post 8vo. wood-cuts, &c. $3 25. London, 1849.

——— A Preliminary Discourse on the Study of Natural Philosophy. New edition, foolscap, 8vo. cloth, $1 75. London.

——— 12mo. cloth, 60 cents. New York.

——— Observations at the Cape of Good Hope, 1834–38. 4to. bds. $25 00. Lond. 1848.

Hervey, (Thos. K.) Book of Christmas; descriptive of the Customs, Ceremonies, Traditions, Superstitions, Fun, Feeling, and Festivities of the Christmas Season. 12mo. cloth, 63 cents; cloth, gilt edges, $1 00. New York, 1848.

Hetherington, (Rev. W. M.) The History of Rome. 12mo. cloth, $1 37. Edinburgh, 1839.

Heugh, (H.) Notices of the State of Religion in Geneva and Belgium. $1 25. Glasgow, 1844.

Heurtly, (Charles A.) Bampton Lectures, delivered at Oxford. 8vo. cloth, $2 50. Oxford, 1846.

Heustis on Diseases of Louisiana. 12mo. cloth, 50 cents. New York.

Hewitt, (Rev. O.) Problems and Theories in Plane Trigonometry. 8vo. $1 75.

Hewitson, (W. C.) Illustrations of the Eggs, &c. of British Birds. 2 vols. 8vo. cloth, colored plates, $27 00. London.

Hickok, (L. P.) Rational Psychology; or, the Subjective Idea and the Objective Law of all Intelligence. 8vo. cloth, $2 50. Auburn, 1848.

Hieronymus, (St.) Opera omnia, post monachorum S. Mauri, sed potissimum Joannis Martinæi reconsionem quibusdam ineditis monumentis aliisque lucubrationibus aucta, notis et observationibus illustrata, studio et labore Valarsii et Maffæii. 11 vols. in 9, royal 8vo. $16 50. Paris, 1845.

Higgins, (W. M.) The Book of Geology; being an Elementary Treatise on that Science, &c. 12mo. cloth, $1 75. London.

——— The House Painter, or Decorator's Companion; being a complete Treatise on the Origin of Color, Laws of Harmonious Coloring, Manufacture of Pigments, Oils, and Varnishes, and the Art of House Painting, Graining, and Marbling. Plates, 4to. cloth, $9 00. London, 1841.

Hildreth, (R.) History of the United States, from the Discovery of the Continent to the Organization of Government under the Federal Constitution. 3 vols. royal 8vo. cloth, top edge gilt, $6 00. New York, 1849.

Hill, (W.) An Essay on the Theory and Practice of Setting out Railway Curves. 8vo. plates and cuts, 50 cents. London.

Hillyard. Practical Farming and Grazing. Post 8vo. cloth, $3 50. London.

Hind's Farriery. 12mo. sheep, $1 00. Philadelphia.

Hind, (J.) The Elements of Algebra; designed for the Use of Students in the University. Fifth edition, 8vo. $3 50. London.

Hind, (Rev. S.) The Three Temples of the One God contrasted. 8vo. bds. $1 75. London, 1846.

Hindostan; its Landscapes, Palaces, Temples, Tombs, the Shores of the Red Sea, and the Scenery of the Himalaya Mountains. Illustrated in a Series of Views drawn by Turner, Stanfield, Prout, &c. 2 vols. 4to. cloth, gilt, $12 50. London.

Hints on Glass Painting: an Inquiry into the Difference of Style observable in Ancient Glass Painting. By an Amateur. 8vo. with an 8vo. volume of plates, $7 50. Oxford, 1849.

Hirschfeld. Théorie de l'Art des Jardins. 5 vols. 4to. plates, $19 00. Paris.

Historic Gallery of Portraits and Paintings; with brief Mémoirs of the most celebrated Men of every Age and Country, with engravings in outline. 2 vols. 8vo. half mor. $5 00. London.

History of Infusoria, Living and Fossil. 8vo. cloth, $3 75. London.

Historical Pictures of the Middle Ages in Black and White, made on the spot, by a Wandering Artist. 2 vols. 12mo. cloth, $3 London, 1846.

Histoire de la Vie des Saints des Pères et des Martyrs, composée par une société d'Ecclésiastiques et de Gens de Lettres. 400 plates. 2 vols. royal 8vo. half mor. $8 50. Paris.

History (A) of Wonderful Inventions. 12mo. cloth, illustrated with spirited wood-cuts, 75 cents. New York.

History of England. By Hume and Smollett; with Continuation by Hughes. 17 vols. 12mo. calf extra, $50 00.

——— American edition, 6 vols. 12mo. cloth, $4 50. Boston, 1849.

Hitchcock, (Prof.) Elements of Geology. 12mo. sheep, $1 25. New York.

Hittorf et Zanth. Architecture Moderne de la Sicily. Folio, half bound, 8vo. plates, $30 00. Paris, 1835.

Hoare, (Rev. W. H.) Harmony of the Apocalypse with other Prophecies of Holy Scripture; with Notes, and an Outline of the various Interpretations. $2 75. London, 1848.

——— (Prince.) Epochs of the Arts, including Hints on the Rise and Progress of Painting and Sculpture in Great Britain. 12mo. cloth, $1 75. London.

——— (C.) A Practical Treatise on the Cultivation of the Grape Vine on Open Walls; to which is added, a Treatise on the Planting and Managing of the Roots of Grape Vines. 12mo. bds. 75 cents. Boston, 1845.

Hobart, (Rev. J. H.) An Apology for Apostolic Order and its Advocates. 12mo. cloth, bds. 50 cents. New York, 1844.

——— (Bishop) Posthumous Works; with a Memoir of his Life, by Rev. William Berrian, D. D. 3 vols. 8vo. cloth, $4 00. N. Y. 1833.

Hobbes, (J. R.) Picture Collector's Manual, adapted to the Professional Man and the Amateur; being a Dictionary of Painters, containing 1500 more names than any other Work; with an Alphabetical Arrangement of the Scholars, Imitators, and Copyists of the various Masters, and a Classification of Subjects. 2 vols. 8vo. cloth, $9 75. Lond. 1849.

Hobbes, (Thomas of, Malmesbury.) English Works of. Now first collected, by Sir William Molesworth. 16 vols. 8vo. cloth, $50 00. London.

Hoblyn, (R. D.) A Dictionary of Scientific Terms. 12mo. cloth, $3 00. Lond. 1849.

——— 12mo. sheep, $1 50. Phila. 1846.

Hodge, (P. R.) Hydraulic Table for the use of Engineers, showing the Weight in Pounds and the Number of Imperial Gallons and Cubic Feet contained in Six Feet Cylindrical Pipe, with counterpart column, showing the same Quantities for One Foot, and a column of Circular Areas, &c., &c., on a sheet, $1 00. London, 1849.

——— The Steam Engine; its Origin and Gradual Improvement from the Earliest to the Present Time. Illustrated with 48 plates in detail. 8vo. with folio atlas of plates, $10 00. New York.

——— Analytical Principles and Practical Application of the Expansive Steam Engine. 4to. half mor. plates, $18 00. London, 1849.

Hodgkin, (Thos.) Lectures on the Morbid Anatomy of the Serous and Mucous Membranes. 2 vols. 8vo. cloth, $7 00. Lond. 1836.

Hodgkinson, (E.) Experimental Researches on the Strength and other Properties of Cast Iron. 8vo. cloth, $3 75. Lond. 1842.

Hoefer, (F.) Histoire de la Chimie. 2 vols. 8vo. $4 25. Paris, 1843.

——— Dictionnaire de Chimie et Physique. 12mo. $1 00. Paris, 1846.

Hoffland, (T. C.) Specimens of Garden Decorations and Scenery. Folio, cloth, plates, $3 50. London.

——— Specimens of Garden Decorations and Ornamental Scenery, appropriate to Pleasure-Grounds, &c. Folio, 23 plates, $9 50. London, 1846.

——— British Angler's Guide: new and enlarged Edition, revised and edited by Jesse. Illustrated with wood-cuts and fine engravings on steel. Thick 12mo. cloth, $3 50. Lond. 1848.

Hoffman. Contes Fantastiques Traduits par P. Christian. 12mo. $1 00. Paris, 1846.

Hogarth, (William.) Works. 150 steel engravings. 2 vols. 4to. cloth, $13 50. mor. $20 00. London, 1849.

——— Memoirs of the Musical Drama. 2 vols. 8vo. illustrated by capital portraits, including Madame Mara, Farinelli, Dr. Arne, Mrs. Billington, Catalani, &c. Extra cloth, $2 50. 1838.

Hogg's Practical Treatise on the Culture of the Carnation, Pink, Auricula, Polyanthus, Tulip, Hyacinth, Rose, and other Flowers, with a Dissertation on Soils and Manures, and Catalogues of Esteemed Varieties. Foolscap 8vo. sixth edition, colored plates, extra cloth, $1 50. 1839.

Holbein's Dance of Death, with an Historical and Literary Introduction. By an Antiquary; with 54 engravings, being the most accurate copies ever executed of these Gems of Art. Square post 8vo. cloth, $2 50. London, 1849.

Holbrook, (J. E.) North American Herpetology; or, a Description of the Reptiles inhabiting the United States. 5 vols. 4to. plates, $50 00. Philadelphia, 1842.

Hole, (Rev. Matthew.) Practical Discourses on all the Parts and Offices of the Liturgy of the Church of England. Edited by the Rev. I. A. Giles. 4 vols. 8vo. cloth, $10 00. Pickering, London, 1837.

Holland, (J.) Manufactures in Metal. 3 vols. small 8vo. cloth, $5 50. Lond. 1834.

——— Records; Biographical and Literary, of upwards of One Hundred and Fifty Authors who have rendered the whole or parts of the Books of Psalms into English Verse. 2 vols. 8vo. cloth, $6 00. London, 1843.

——— Cruciana. Illustrations of the most striking Aspects under which the Cross of Christ and Symbols derived from it have been contemplated by Piety, Superstition, Imagination, and Taste. Plates, 12mo. half mor. $2 50. London, 1835.

——— (H.) Medical Notes and Reflections. 8vo. sheep, $1 50. Philadelphia.

——— (G. C.) Philosophy of Animated Nature. 8vo. cloth, $3 75. London.

Hollis on Electricity and Magnetism. 8vo. cloth, 2 50. Boston.

Holmes, (A.) Annals of America from 1492 to 1826. 2 vols. 8vo. cloth, $4 00. Boston.

——— (Oliver Wendell.) Poems. New and enlarged edition, illustrated with wood-cuts. 12mo. cloth, gilt, $1 50; cloth, plain, $1 13. Boston, 1849.

——— (J.) Art of Rhetoric; or, the Elements of Oratory. A new edition, edited by John A. Getty. 12mo. cloth, $1 00. Philadelphia, 1849.

——— (W. R.) Sketches on the Shores of the Caspian, Descriptive and Pictorial. 8vo. cloth, plates, $1 50. London, 1845.

——— (E.) The Life of Mozart, including his Correspondence. 12mo. cloth, 50 cents. New York, 1845.

Holtzapffel, (C.) Turning and Mechanical Manipulation; intended as a work of General Reference and Practical Instruction on the Lathe, and the various Mechanical Pursuits followed by Amateurs. 2 vols. 8vo. cloth, 1000 wood-cuts, $10 50. (To be completed in 6 vols.) London, 1846–7.

Holy Gospels, (The) with numerous illustrations on wood, engraved under the superintendence of Mr. Charles Heath. Folio, $9 50.

Holz, (F. W.) Architectonische Detail, zum prakt Gebrauch. 4to. plates, $10 00. Berlin, 1844–45.

Homassel. Cours Théorique et Pratique sur l'Art de la Teinture. 8vo. broché, $1 50. Paris.

Home, (Sir Everard.) Great Work on Comparative Anatomy, being the Substance of his numerous Lectures, and including Explanations of nearly all the Preparations in the Hunterian Collection; with a General Index. 6 vols. royal 4to. portrait and 361 fine plates after drawings by Bauer and others. Extra cloth boards, $25 00. 1814–28.

Homer's Iliad. Translated by William Cowper, with Notes for the use of the Higher Classes in Schools and Academies. 12mo. cloth. $1 25.

——— Translated by T. S. Brandreth, Esq. 2 vols. 12mo. cloth, $3 00. London, 1846.

——— and Odyssey. Translated by A. Pope, Esq. 2 vols. 18mo. cloth, $2 00. Lond. 1845.

Homer. The Prince of Poets. Translated by George Chapman. 2 vols. cr. 8vo. cloth, Flaxman's Designs, $3 25. London, 1843.

Homilies. Certain Sermons or Homilies appointed to be read in Churches in the Time of Queen Elizabeth. 8vo. cloth, $2 25. Oxford, 1844.

Hood, (Thos.) Prose and Verse. 12mo. cloth gilt, gilt edges, $1 50; cloth, plain, $1 00. New York, 1848.

——— (George.) A History of Music in New England, with Biographical Sketches of Reformers and Psalmists. 12mo. cloth, 75 cents. Boston, 1846.

Hook, (T. G.) Life and Remains. By Rev R. H. Dalton. 2 vols. 12mo. cloth, portrait, $6 50. London, 1849.

——— (Dr.) Holy Thoughts and Prayers; arranged for Daily Use on each Day of the Week, according to the Stated Hours of Prayer. Square 18mo. cloth, 63 cents. Lond. 1849.

——— A Companion to the Altar; being Prayers, Thanksgivings, and Meditations, to assist the Devout Christian in his Preparation for and Attendance at the Lord's Supper. 32mo. cloth, 75 cents. London, 1849.

——— Church of England Vindicated against Romanism and Ultra Protestantism. 12mo. cloth, $1 37. London, 1845.

——— The Cross of Christ; or, Meditations on the Death and Passion of our Blessed Lord and Saviour. 12mo. cloth, 63 cents. New York, 1845.

——— Short Meditations for Every Day in the Year. Part II. Lent to the Fourth Sunday after Easter. 12mo. cloth, $1 75. London, 1849.

Hooker and Greville. Icones Filicum, or Figures and Descriptions of Ferns, many of which have been altogether unnoticed by Botanists, or have not been correctly figured. 2 vols. folio, with 240 beautifully colored plates, half bound, green morocco, gilt edges, $75 00. 1829–31.

Hooker, (Rev. H.) The Christian Life a Fight of Faith. 18mo. cloth, 38 cents. Philadelphia, 1848.

——— (Dr. J. D.) Rhododendrons of the Sikkim-Himalaya. From Drawings and Descriptions made on the Spot. Imperial folio, 10 highly-finished colored plates, $6 50. London, 1849.

——— Exotic Flora: containing Figures and Descriptions of Rare or othewise Interesting Exotic Plants, especially of such as are deserving of being cultivated in our gardens; together with Remarks upon their Generic and Specific Characters, Natural Orders, History, Culture, Time of Flowering, &c., complete in 3 vols. imperial 8vo. containing 232 large and beautifully colored plates, extra cloth, gilt bands, $38 00; elegantly half bound green morocco, gilt edges, $40 00. Lond. 1823–27.

Hooker, (Sir W. J.) Journal of Botany; being a Second Series of Botanical Miscellany, containing Figures and Descriptions of such Plants as recommend themselves by their Novelty, Variety, or by the Uses to which they are applied in the Arts, Medicine, &c. 4 vols. 8vo. cloth, $4 50. London, 1834.

——— (Sir W. J.) Century of Orchidaceous Plants, selected from the Botanical Magazine, with an Introduction and Practical Instructions on their Culture. By J. C. Lyons. 100 beautifully colored plates, 4to. cloth, $31 50. London, 1849.

——— Flora Boreali-Americana; or the Botany of British North America; compiled principally from the Plants collected by Dr. Richardson and Mr. Drummond on the late Northern Expeditions, under the command of Captain Sir John Franklin; to which are added, by Permission of the Horticultural Society, those of Mr. Douglas and other Naturalists. Illustrated by 240 plates, 2 vols. royal 4to. extra cloth, $35 00. 1829–40.

——— (Rev. Richard.) The Works of; with Account of his Life and Death, by Isaac Walton. Edited and arranged by Rev. John Keble. 3 vols. 8vo. cloth, $10 00. Oxford, 1841.

——— 2 vols. 8vo. cloth, $4 00. New York, 1844.

——— The Works of; with Life by Walton. 2 vols. 8vo. cloth, $4 50. Calf, extra, $6 50. Oxford, 1843.

Horner, (Leonard.) Memoirs of Francis Horner, M. P.; with Selections from his Correspondence. 12mo. cloth, 88 cents. Edinburgh, 1849.

Howell, (James.) Epistolæ Ho-Elianæ; Familiar Letters, Domestic and Foreign. cr. 8vo. old calf, $1 50. London, 1737.

Hooper, (Miss Lucy.) The Complete Poetical Works of. 8vo. cloth, handsomely printed and bound, $2 00. New York, 1848.

——— (R.) Lexicon Medicum; or, Medical Dictionary. Thick 8vo. sheep, $3 00. New York, 1848.

Hope, (J.) A Treatise on the Diseases of the Heart and Great Vessels, and on the Affections which may be mistaken for them. Thick 8vo. sheep, plates, $3 00. Phila. 1846.

——— Designs for Household Furniture and Interior Decoration. Imperial folio, bds. $12 75. London, 1807.

——— (T.) Historical Essay on Architecture. 2 vols. 8vo. cloth, many engravings, $9 00. London, 1840.

——— Analytical Index to an Historical Essay on Architecture. 8vo. cloth, $1 25. Lond.

——— (Rev. W.) Coleopterist's Manual, the Predaceous Land and Water Beetles. 8vo. beautifully colored plates, cloth, $2 00. 1845.

——— Costume of the Ancients, illustrated in upwards of 320 beautifully engraved plates, containing representations of Egyptian, Greek, and Roman Habits and Dresses. 2 vols. royal 8vo. new edition, with nearly 20 additional plates, bds. $13 50. London, 1841.

Hopkins, (Bp.) The Works of; with Memoir of his Life and copious Indices. 2 vols. imperial 8vo. cloth, $5 50. Edin. 1844.

Hopkin, (J. D.) Scrap-Book of Elizabethan Ornaments. 4to. cloth, plates, $6 00. Lond.

Hopper, (T.) Designs for the Houses of Parliament. Oblong folio, beautiful plates. $31 50. London.

Hoppus, (E.) Practical Measuring made Easy by a New Set of Tables. 88 cents. Derby, 1846.

Horace. The Works of Quintus Horatius Flaccus. Illustrated chiefly from the Remains of Ancient Art, with a Life by the Rev. H. H. Milman. 8vo. Etruscan boards, $6 50. London, 1849.

Horne, (R. H.) History of Napoleon. Illustrated by Raffet and Horace Vernet. 2 vols. royal 8vo. cloth, $5 00. London, 1844.

Horne, (Rev. T. H.) A Compendious Introduction to the Study of the Bible; being an Analysis of his "Introduction to the Critical Study and Knowledge of the Holy Scriptures." New edition, corrected and enlarged. 12mo. with maps and other engravings, bds. $2 75. London.

——— An Introduction to the Critical Study and Knowledge of the Holy Scriptures. A new edition, revised and corrected. 5 vols. 8vo. with numerous maps and fac-similes of Biblical Manuscripts, bound in calf, half extra, $19 00.

——— An Introduction to the Critical Study and Knowledge of the Holy Scriptures. 2 vols. imp. 8vo. bds. $3 50. New York, 1844.

——— A Manual of Biblical Bibliography. 8vo. cloth, $3 25. London, 1839.

Horsley, (Sam.) Biblical Criticism, or the First Fourteen Historical Books of the Old Testament; also on the First Nine Prophetical Books. 2 vols. 8vo. cloth, $8 75. London, 1844.

Hosking, (Wm.) Guide to the Proper Regulations of Building in Towns, as a Means of Promoting and Securing the Health, Comfort, and Safety of the Inhabitants. 12mo. cloth, $2 00. London, 1848.

——— Treatise on Architecture, Building, Masonry, Joinery, and Carpentry, from the Encyclopædia Britannica. 4to. cloth, $4 00.

Hoste, (Paul.) Treatise on Naval Tactics. Translated by Captain Boswall. 4to. 52 plates. $7 25; handsomely bound in mor. gilt, and gilt leaves, $11 25. London, 1834.

Hotel de Ville de Paris. A complete Restoration of this Celebrated Building of the Renaissance Style; containing most beautiful outline engravings of the Exterior and Interior, Plans, Elevations, Sections, Ceilings, Details, and Ornaments. Imp. folio, $42 00.

Hovey, (C. M.) Fruit-Trees of America, containing richly-colored engravings, accompanied with the Wood and Foliage of all the choicest Fruits of the United States, from Paintings from Nature, by W. Sharp. Royal 8vo. Boston, 1847.

Howard, (Frank.) The Spirit of the Plays of Shakspeare, exhibited in a series of outline plates Illustrative of the Story of each Play; with Quotations and Descriptions. 5 vols. 8vo. cloth, $12 00. London, 1833.

Howard, (F.) The Science of Drawing; being a Progressive Series of the Characteristic Forms of Nature. 3 vols. $3 75. Lond.

——— (H.) Course of Lectures on Painting, delivered at the Royal Academy of Fine Arts. 12mo. cloth, $1 25. London.

——— On Color as a Means of Art, being an Adaption of the Experience of Professors to the Practice of Amateurs. Illustrated by 18 colored plates. Post 8vo. extra cloth gilt, $2 50. 1838.

Howse, (J.) Grammar of the Cree Language, with which is combined an Analysis of the Chieppewa Dialect. 8vo. cloth, $2 75. London, 1844.

Howship, (J.) On the Discrimination and Appearances of Surgical Diseases. 8vo. $3 25. London, 1840.

Howitt, (W.) Homes and Haunts of the most Eminent British Poets; with illustrations by W. and G. Measom. 2 vols. 8vo. cloth, $6 50; morocco gilt, gilt leaves, $12 00. London, 1847.

——— 2 vols. 8vo. cloth, $3 00. New York, 1847.

——— The Rural Life in England. Third edition, corrected and revised, with engravings. Medium 8vo. cloth, $6 50. London.

——— American edition, $1 00. Phila.

——— The Rural and Social Life of Germany; with Characteristic Sketches of its Chief Cities and Scenery; with above 50 illustrations. Medium 8vo. cloth, $6 50. Lond. 1849.

——— The Student Life in Germany; from the Unpublished MSS. of Dr. Cornelious. 8vo. with 24 wood engravings, and 7 steel plates, cloth, $2 25. London, 1849.

——— American edition, $1 00. Phila.

——— Visits to Remarkable Places; Old Halls, Battle-Fields, and Scenes Illustrative of Striking Passages in English History and Poetry. New edition, with 40 illustrations. Medium 8vo. cloth, $6 50. Second Series, chiefly in the Counties of Durham and Northumberland, and a Stroll along the Border. Medium 8vo. cloth, $6 50. London.

——— American edition, 2 vols. $3 50. Philadelphia.

——— (Mary.) Ballads and other Poems; with a portrait, from a picture by Miss Gillies, engraved by W. H. Egleton. Cloth, $5 50. London.

——— American edition, 12mo. cloth, 75 cents; with portrait, cloth, gilt, $1 25. 1849.

——— The Peasant and his Landlord. Translated from the Swedish of the Baroness Knorring. 12mo. cloth, 75 cents. N. Y. 1848.

Hoyau, Ingénieur-Mécanicien. Art du serrurier, comprenant les moyens de reconnaître les qualités des matières, etc. 1 vol. in-folio de 17 pl. renfermant plus de 400 fig. et 36 pages de texte explicatif, $5. Paris, 1845.

Hoyt, (Rev. R.) Sketches of Life and Landscape. 8vo. cloth, wood engravings, plain, 75 cents; gilt extra, $1 25. New York.

Huber, (V. A.) The English Universities. Translated and abridged by F. W. Newman. 3 vols. 8vo. cloth, plates, $7 50. Lond. 1843.

Hufeland, (C. W.) Enchiridion Medicum; or Manual of the Practice of Medicine. Translated from the German. 8vo. cloth, $2 50. New York, 1843.

Hughes, (W.) On the Construction of Maps. 8vo. bds. plates, $1 50. London.

——— (T.) Practice of Making and Repairing Roads. 8vo. cloth, $1 25. London.

——— Comprehensive Tables for Calculations of Earthwork. 4to. $8 00. London.

——— (S.) On Making Roads. 12mo. cloth. wood-cuts, 25 cents. London, 1849.

Hugo, (Victor.) The Rhine and Father Ripa's Memoirs of a Thirteen Years' Residence at the Court of Peking, in the Service of the Emperor of China, together in one volume. 12mo. cloth, $1 25. New York, 1845–6.

Huguenin, (Gen.) Déscription de la Fabrication des Bouches a feu en font de fer et des projectiles a la fonderie de Liége, traduit par Capt. Neusus. 8vo. 13 planches, $3 00. 1839.

Huish on Bees; their Natural History and General Management. New and greatly improved edition, containing all the latest Discoveries and Improvements in every Department of the Apiary, with a Description of the most approved Hives now in use. Thick 12mo. port. and numerous wood-cuts, extra cloth gilt, $1 50. London, 1844.

Hulmandel, (C.) Manual of Lithography, or the Art of Drawing on Stone. 8vo. plates, $2 25. London, 1835.

Humble, (Wm.) Dictionary of Geology and Mineralogy. 8vo. cloth, $1 50. London, 1843.

Humboldt, (Von.) Cosmos; a Sketch of a Physical Description of the Universe. Translated from the German, by E. C. Otte. 2 vols. 12mo. cloth, $1 75. London.

——— Authorized edition. Translated under the direction of Lieut. Colonel Sabine. 2 vols. 12mo. paper, $1 50. London, 1849.

Hume, (A.) The Learned Societies and Printing Clubs of the United Kingdom; being an Account of their Respective Origin, History, Objects, and Constitution, &c. 8vo. cloth, $2 50. London, 1847.

——— (D.) Life and Correspondence, by J. H. Burton. 2 vols. 8vo. cloth, $7 50. London.

Humfrey, (Lieut. Col. J. H.) An Essay on the Modern System of Fortification, &c. Roy. 8vo. cloth, plans, &c. $2 25. London.

Humphreys, (H. N.) Illuminated Books of the Middle Ages. Printed in colors an gold, folio cap $100 00. London, 1850.

——— Coins of England. Printed in gold, &c., post 8vo. $4 50. London.

——— The Art of Illumination; being a Guide to Modern Students in the Art of Illuminating Books. Illustrated by exquisite Fac-Similes from Illuminated MSS. of different Periods, and other embellishments, in an ornamental cover, $6 00. London, 1849.

——— (J. H.) An Essay on the Modern System of Fortification adopted on the Rhine and Danube, and followed in all the Works constructed since the Peace of 1815. Royal 8vo. $2 25. London.

Humphrey and Westwood. British Moths and their Transformation. Arranged and illustrated in a Series of Plates, by H. N. Humphreys; with Characters and Descriptions, by J. O. Westwood. 2 vols. 4to. cloth, 56 colored plates, $33 00. London, 1843.

Hundertpfund, (L.) The Art of Painting restored to its simplest and surest principles. Translated from the German. Illustrated with colored plates. Post 8vo. $3 00. London, 1849.

Hunt, (F. K.) Book of Art; or Cartoons, Frescoes, Sculptures, &c. Royal 4to. cloth, $4 25. London.

——— (I. F.) Architectura Campestra. 4to. cloth, $4 50. London.

——— Designs for Parsonage Houses, Alms-Houses, &c. Royal 4to. 21 plates, half mor. $3 75. London, 1841.

——— Designs for Gate Lodges, Gamekeepers' Cottages, &c. Royal 4to. 13 plates, half mor. $3 50. London, 1841.

——— Examples of Tudor Architecture, adapted to Modern Habitations. Royal 4to. 37 plates, half mor. $6 50. London, 1836.

——— (Leigh.) Imagination and Fancy; or Selections from the English Poets, illustrative of those First Requisites of their Art; with Markings of the best Passages, Critical Notices, &c. 1 vol. 12mo. cloth, 62 cents; cloth gilt, and gilt edges, $1 00. New York, 1848.

——— Stories from the Italian Poets; being a Summary in Prose of the Poems of Dante, Pulci, Boiardo, Ariosto, and Tasso, with Comments throughout, occasional Passages Versified, and Critical Notices of the Lives and Genius of the Authors. 1 thick vol. cloth, $1 25; cloth gilt, gilt edges, $1 75. N. Y. 1848.

——— Wit and Humor; selected from the English Poets, with an illustrative Essay and Critical Comments. 12mo. cloth gilt, $1 00. New York, 1847.

——— A Book for a Corner; being Selections in Prose and Verse from Authors the best suited to that mode of enjoyment, with Comments on each, and a general Introduction. Illustrated with 80 wood engravings from designs by F. W. Holmes and J. Franklin. 2 vols. 12mo. cloth, $3 50. London, 1849.

——— Indicator; a Miscellany for the Fields and Fireside. 12mo. cloth, $1 25. N. Y. 1849.

——— (R.) Researches on Light; an Examination of all the Phenomena connected with the Chemical and Molecular Changes produced by the Influence of the Solar Rays, embracing all the known Photogenic Processes and New Discoveries in the Art. 8vo. cloth, $3 25. London, 1844.

——— The Poetry of Science; or, Studies of the Physical Phenomena of Nature. 8vo. cloth, $3 50. London, 1848.

Hunter, (Wm.) An Anglo-Saxon Grammar and Derivatives, and an Analysis of the Style of Chaucer, Douglas, and Spenser. 8vo. cloth, $1 50. London, 1832.

——— (H.) Sacred Biography; or, History of the Patriarchs. 8vo. cloth, $1 75. New York, 1844.

Huntington, (Countess.) The Life and Times of; with Index, &c. Portrait, 2 vols. 8vo. cloth, $3 50. London, 1844.

——— (Rev. W.) Works; with Additions and Corrections by his Son, Ebenezer Huntington. 6 thick vols. 8vo. portraits and plates, cloth, lettered, $13 50.

Huntingdon, (J. B.) Tables and Rules for Facilitating the Calculation of Earthwork, Land, Curves, Distances, and Gradients. 8vo. bds. $5 00. London.

——— Tables of Gradients. 8vo. paper, $1 00. London.

Hurcourt, (R. D.) De l'éclairage au gaz; dévelloppements sur la composition des gaz destinêes a l'éclairage, sur la construction des fourneaus et des cheminés la pose des treyaus et les phénomenes de la lumière. 8vo. plates, $2 00. Paris, 1845.

Hurd, (Richard, Bishop of Worcester.) The Complete Works of. 8 vols. 8vo. calf, portrait, $11 75. London, 1811.

Hussey, (Mrs. T. J.) Illustrations of British Mycology; containing figures and descriptions of the Funguses of interest and novelty, indigenous to Britain; with handsome colored drawings. Publishing in monthly parts, $1 50 each.

Hutchinson, (John.) Experiments on Building Materials. 8vo. cloth, $1 00. Lond.

——— (G.) Treatise on the Causes and Principles of Meteorological Phenomena; also two Essays, the one on Marsh Fevers, the other on Mr. Owen's System of Equality. 8vo. cloth, $2 50. Glasgow, 1843.

——— (Lieut. Col.) Dog-Breaking. Plates, 12mo. cloth, $1 75. London, 1848.

Hutton, (Charles.) Mathematical Tables by Gregory. Royal 8vo. cloth, $5 50. Lond.

——— Mathematics by Rutherford. 8vo. cloth, $5 00. London.

——— Mathematics. Key to Rutherford's edition of. By James Hickie. 8vo. cloth, $2 25. London, 1849.

Huxtable, (Rev E.) Ministry of St. John the Baptist, &c. 8vo. bds. $1 13. Lond. 1848.

Hymer, (Rev. W.) The Theory of Algebraic Equations. 8vo. cloth, $1 75. Cambridge, 1849.

——— (J.) A Treatise on the Integral Calculus, &c. 8vo. $3 50.

——— A Treatise on Trigonometry and Trigonometrical Tables and Logarithms. 8vo. cloth, $2 75.

——— A Treatise on Differential Equations and on the Calculus of Finite Differences. 8vo. $3 50. Cambridge, 1839.

Illuminated Illustrations of the Bible, copied from Select MSS. of the Middle Ages. By. T. O. Westwood. $17 00. London, 1846.

——— Of Froissart, Selected from MSS. in the British Museum and the Bibliothèque du Roi, Paris. By R. N. Humphreys, Esq 2 vols. royal 8vo. half mor. comprising 72 illuminations, beautifully executed, $20 (former price $35.) London, 1844–5.

Illustrated Commentary on the Old and New Testaments, chiefly explanatory of the Manners and Customs mentioned in the Sacred Scriptures, and also of the History, Geography, Natural History, and Antiquities; being a republication of the Notes of the Pictorial Bible. 5 vols. post 8vo. with upwards of 600 fine wood-cuts, gilt cloth, $7 50. London, 1840.

Illustration, (l') Journal universel, paraissant, tous les samedis, orne de gravures sur tous les sujets actuels, formant chaque six mois 1 vol. in folio. Souscription a l'anne courante $9 00.

Illustrations of the Public Buildings of London. 165 engravings, originally edited by the late Augustus Pugin, J. Gwilt, Britton, and others; newly edited and enlarged by W. H. Leeds. 2 vols. 8vo. half mor. $18 00. London.

Imitations of Celebrated Authors; or, Imaginary Rejected Articles, in Prose, by Lamb, James, and Horace Smith, Professor Wilson, Hazlitt, Leigh Hunt, &c. Fourth edition, post 8vo. extra cloth, $1 25. London, 1844.

Inchbald, (Mrs.) The British Theatre; or a Collection of Plays which are Acted at Theatres Royal, Drury Lane, Covent Garden, Haymarket, and Lyceum. 12 vols. 18mo. cloth, $6 00. London.

Incidents of Missionary Enterprise, illustrative of the Progress of the Gospel among the Heathen. 12mo. cloth, $1 00. Edinburgh, 1841.

Index Expurgatorius Vaticanus; an Exact Reprint of the Roman Index Expurgatorius; the only Vatican Index of the kind ever published. Edited, with a Preface, by R. Gibbings. Thick 12mo. cloth, $1 25. Dublin, 1837.

Index to the Principal Places in the World, (Modern,) with Reference to the Maps of the Society for the Diffusion of Useful Knowledge. By Rev. James Mickleburgh. 8vo. cloth, $1 75. London, 1844.

——— (An) of Subjects in Reviews and Periodicals. To which no Index has been published. 8vo. paper, $1 00; half bound, $1 25. New York, 1848.

Indicator (The) and Dynamometer, with their Practical Application to the Steam Engine. 8vo. cloth, plate, $1 50. Lond. 1847.

Infantry Sword Exercise. 12mo. paper, 37 cents. London, 1842.

Ingpen, (A.) Instructions for Collecting, Rearing, and Preserving British and Foreign Insects. 16mo. $1 25.

Ingram, (J.) Memorials of Oxford. 3 vols. 8vo. cloth, with 248 engravings. By J. Le Keux, from drawings by F. Mackenzie. $17 50. London, 1834–37.

Infinity (The) of Geometric Design Exemplified, by R. W. Billings. 4to. cloth, illustrated with 40 plates, $8 00. Lond. 1849.

Inman, (W.) An Essay on Symbolic Colors in Antiquity, the Middle Ages, and Modern Times. Translated from the French of De Portal. 4to. cloth bds. with illustrative engravings, $3 25. London.

Inman, (W. S.) Report on Ventilation, Warming, and Transmission of Sound. 8vo. cloth, plates, $2 25. London.

——— (J.) Formulæ and Rules for Making Calculations on Plans of Ships, with an Example on their Application. Royal 8vo. paper, $1 00. London, 1849.

Innis, (T.) The Skin in Health and Disease; a Concise Manual, with Cases and Colored Explanatory plates. 8vo. cloth, $2 50. London, 1849.

Insect Miscellanies. 12mo. cloth, wood-cuts, 75 cents. London, 1847.

Instructions for Establishing and Conducting Regimental Schools. 18mo. paper, 25 cents. London, 1812.

——— and Regulations for the Service and Management of Heavy Ordnance, $1 50. Woolwich, 1835.

Integral Calculus. A Collection of Examples on the Integral Calculus; in which every Operation of each Example is completely effected. By a Member of the University. 8vo. $1 35.

Introductory Lectures delivered at Queen's College, London. 12mo. cloth, $1 50. London, 1849.

Introduction (An) to the Geometry and Science of Form; prepared from the Russian Text-Books. 12mo. sheep, plates, 84 cents. Boston, 1846.

Instrumenta Ecclesiastica; a Series of Working Designs for the Furniture, Fittings and Decorations of Churches and their Precincts. Edited by the Ecclesiological Society. 4to. 72 plates, $10 00. Lond. 1847.

Inwood, (W.) Tables for the Purchasing of Estates, &c. Small 8vo. for the pocket. $2 25. London.

——— (H. W.) The Erectheion at Athens. Fragments of Athenian Architecture, and a few Remains in Attica, Megara, and Epirus. Illustrated with outline plates, folio, $7 00.

Ionian Antiquities, published by the Dilettante Society. 2 vols. folio, half mor. $31 50. London.

Isle of Wight. Illustrated in a Series of colored Views in aqua-tint, by Mr. Percy Roberts, from the original Drawings of the late Mr. F. Calvert, accompanied by a succinct Historical, Geographical, and Topographical Description of the Island. 4to. cloth, gilt, plates, $3 00. London, 1846.

Isnard, (Dr. J. A.) Aide Mêmoire de l'opérateur, comprenant les opérations élémentaires, les ligatures d'artérés les amputations dans la contiquité et dans la continuité des membres, et les résections des extremités articulaires, avec 60 planches. 12mo. broché, $1 50. Paris, 1849.

Italian School of Design; containing 100 plates, chiefly engraved by Bartolozzi, after original paintings by the Great Masters, in the Collection of her Majesty. Imperial 4to. half mor. $19 00. London.

Irving, (Washington.) Works; a new and complete edition, beautifully printed and uniformly bound. 12mo. cloth. New York, 1848–9.

Irving, (Washington.) Works.

THE FOLLOWING WORKS HAVE ALREADY APPEARED, ANY OF WHICH MAY BE HAD SEPARATELY.

The Sketch-Book, 1 vol. $1 25.

Knickerbocker's History of New York, 1 vol. $1 25.

Bracebridge Hall, 1 vol $1 25.

Columbus and his Companion, 3 vols. $4 00

Astoria, 1 vol. $1 50.

The Crayon Miscellany, 1 vol. $1 25.

Bonneville's Adventures, 1 vol. $1 25.

Tales of a Traveller, 1 vol. $1 25.

Oliver Goldsmith; a Biography, 1 vol. $1 25.

Either volume, or complete sets may also be had, substantially bound in half calf, 75 cents extra; in half morocco, $1 00 extra; or full calf, $1 25 extra.

THE FOLLOWING WILL APPEAR IN DUE COURSE.

George Washington, a Biography, 1 vol.

The Alhambra, 1 vol.

Mohammed and his Successors, 2 vols.

The Conquest of Granada, 1 vol.

Miscellanies, 1 vol.

——— The Book of the Hudson 18mo. cloth, illustrated with 4 lithograph engravings, 50 cents; without plates, 38 cents. New York, 1849.

——— The Crayon Reading-Book; comprising selections from the various Writings of Washington Irving, prepared for the use of schools. 12mo. half bound, 75 cents. N. Y. 1849.

——— Life and Voyages of Christopher Columbus, to which are added those of his Companions. Library edition, in 3 vols. 8vo. cloth, $6 00; half mor. $8 50; full calf, $10 00. New York, 1848.

ILLUSTRATED SERIES.

——— The Sketch-Book. Illustrated with a series of highly-finished engravings on wood, from Designs by Darley and others, engraved in the best style by Childs, Herrick, &c. Square 8vo. cloth, $3 50; cloth gilt and gilt edges, $4 00; mor. in an original style, gilt and gilt leaves, $6 00. New York, 1848.

——— Oliver Goldsmith, a Biography; with about 40 illustrations, selected by the Publisher from Forster's Life of Goldsmith, beautifully engraved on wood by W. Roberts. 8vo. cloth, $2 50; cloth, gilt, $3 00; elegantly bound in mor. gilt leaves, $5 00.

——— Knickerbocker's History of New York. Illustrated with 15 superior engravings on wood, by the most eminent artists, from designs by Darley. 8vo. cloth, $3 50; extra gilt, $4 00; calf, in antique style, $5 00; elegantly bound in mor. gilt leaves, $6 00. In progress, to be followed by

——— Tales of a Traveller. Illustrated with 15 designs by Darley, engraved on wood in the first style, by Childs, Herrick, Leslie, Bobbet, Edmonds, &c. 1 vol. 8vo. cloth, $3 50; extra gilt, $4 00; elegantly bound in mor. gilt leaves, $6 00.

——— (Prof. Theodore.) The Conquest of Florida. 12mo. cloth, $1 00. New York, 1849.

Jacob's Historical Inquiry into the Production and Consumption of the Precious Metals. 2 vols. 8vo. cloth, $3 50. London, 1831.

Jacobi, (Dr. M.) On the Construction and Management of Hospitals for the Insane, with a Particular Notice of the Institution at Siegburg. Translated by John Kitching. $3 00. London, 1841.

Jacob-Petit. Ornements, Décorations, Intérieurs, Meubles et objets de goût dans le style de la renaissance, composés, desinés et gravés. Folio, 75 planches, $12 50. Paris.

Supplement to Do. Folio, 25 planches, $4 50. Paris.

Jacocks, (A. B.) General Features of the Moral Government of God. 12mo. cloth, 31 cents. Boston, 1848.

Jackson, (J. R.) Minerals and their Uses, in a Series of Letters to a Lady. 12mo. cloth, colored plates, with 17 figures, $2 25. London, 1849.

——— (I.) A Treatise on Wood Engraving, Historical and Practical. Royal 8vo. half bound, 300 Illustrations, $14 00. (Scarce.) London, 1839.

——— (Mrs.) The Practical Companion to the Work-Table; containing Directions for Knitting and Netting. 18mo. cloth, 50 cents. London.

——— (E.) Practical Companion to the Work-Table; containing Directions for Knitting, Netting, and Crotchet-work. 12mo. cloth, gilt, 75 cents. London, 1845.

Jahn, (J.) Biblical Antiquities. Translated by Upham. Royal 8vo. cloth, $1 75. Lond.

——— History of the Hebrew Commonwealth. Royal 8vo. cloth, $2 00. London.

Jahr, (G. H.) Manual of Homœopathic Medicine. 2 vols. post 8vo. cloth, $9 75. Lond.

James I. The Court and Times of James the First. Illustrated by Authentic and Confidential Letters. 2 vols. 8vo. cloth, $8 00. London, 1848.

——— (J. A.) The True Christian Exemplified in a Series of Addresses from a Pastor to his own People. 18mo. cloth, 32 cents. New York, 1849.

——— (C.) A Collection of Charges, Opinions, and Sentences of General Courts Martial. 8vo. cloth, $5 00. London, 1821.

——— (G. P. R.) A History of the Life of Edward the Black Prince, and of various Events connected therewith, which occurred during the Reign of Edward III. King of England. Second edition, 2 vols. foolscap 8vo. map, cloth, $4 50. London.

——— William the Third; comprising the History of his Reign, illustrated in a Series of unpublished Letters, addressed to the Duke of Shrewsbury, by James Vernon, Secretary of State, with Introduction and Notes. 3 vols. cloth, $5 00. London, 1841.

——— (John Angell.) The Widow directed to the Widow's God. 18mo. cloth, 32 cents. New York, 1849.

——— Pastoral Addresses. 18mo. cloth, 50 cents. New York, 1841.

Jameson, (Mrs.) Sacred and Legendary Art. 2 vols. 8vo. cloth, illustrated with plates etched by the Author, and wood engravings of the most exquisite character, $12 00. London, 1848.

Jameson, (Mrs.) Lives of the Early Italian Painters. 2 vols. 18mo. cloth, $1 00. London, 1846.

——— Characteristics of Women 12mo. cloth, $1 00. Boston, 1846.

——— Legends of the Monastic Orders. 8vo. cloth, (shortly.)

——— Beauties of the Court of Charles II. Large paper copy, proof impressions. Folio, mor. extra, $30 00. London.

——— Memoirs and Essays illustrative of Art, Literature, and Social Morals. 12mo. cloth, 50 cents. New York.

——— Companion to the Private Picture Galleries in London; containing accurate Catalogues arranged alphabetically, preceded by an Historical and Critical Introduction, and an Essay on Art, Artists, Collectors, and Connoisseurs. 1 thick vol. post 8vo. extra cloth, $1 50. London, 1844.

Jamieson, (A.) Manual of Map-Making. 12mo. cloth, 75 cents. Glasgow.

——— Mechanics for Practical Men; being Treatises on the Composition and Resolution of Forces, the Centre of Gravity, and the Mechanical Power. Fourth edition, 8vo. $2 25.

——— Mechanics of Fluids. 8vo. cloth, $3 50.

——— Etymological Dictionary of the Scottish Language. Second edition, enlarged, including the Supplement. 4 vols. 4to. cloth, lettered, $25 00. London, 1840.

Jane Eyre. An Autobiography, edited by Currer Bell. 12mo. cloth, $1 00. Boston, 1848.

Janin, (Jules.) L'Ane mort et la Femme Guillotinée; illustre par Tony Johannot. 1 beau vol. grand in 8, orne de 140 gravures et de 12 vignettes tirées séparêment, $2 50.

——— Un Hiver a Paris, tableau des mœurs contemporaines, illustre par 18 splendides gravures sur acier par M. Heath, de Londres, d'après les tableaux de M. Eugene Lami, et par des nombreuses gravures sur bois imprimées dans le texte. 1 vol. grand in 8, gilt extra, $5 50.

——— La Normandie historique, pittoresque et monumentale, illustre par MM. Morel-Fatio, Tellier, Daubigny, Gigoux, H. Bellange, J. Debon, Outhewaite, Alfred Johannot. 1 vol. grand in 8, orne de 180 gravures, 23 vignettes sur acier et 2 cartes, $5.

——— The American in Paris. Illustrated with 18 engravings from Designs by M. Eugene Lami. Royal 8vo. cloth, $2 50. Lond. 1843.

Jardin des Plantes, (Le.) Déscription complète, Historique et Pittoresque du Museum d'Histoire Naturelle, de la Ménagerie, des serres, des Galleries de Minéralogie et d'Anatomie et de la vallée suisse par MM. P. Bernard, L. Couailhac, Gervais et Emm. Lemaout et une Société de Savants attachés au Museum d'Histoire Naturelle. 2 vols. small folio, half mor. gilt tops, illustrated profusely with engravings, many colored, on steel and wood, $16 00. Paris, 1842.

Jardine's Naturalist's Library. 40 vols. 12mo. colored plates, cloth lettered, top edges gilt, $50 00. 1834–43

Or separately, $1 50 per vol. viz.:

1. Humming Birds, vol. 1.
2. Monkeys.
3. Humming Birds, vol. 2.
4. Lions, Tigers, &c.
5. Peacocks, Pheasants, &c.
6. Birds of the Game kind.
7. Fishes, vol. 1.
8. Coleopterous Insects (Beetles.)
9. Columbidæ (Pigeons.)
10. British Diurnal Lepidoptera (Butterflies.)
11. Ruminating Animals (Deer, Antelopes, &c.)
12. Ruminating Animals (Goats, Sheep, Cattle, &c.)
13. Pachidermata (Elephants, Rhinosceroses, &c.)
14. British Nocturnal Lepidoptera (Moths, Sphinx, &c.)
15. Parrots.
16. Whales.
17. Birds of Western Africa, vol. 1.
18. Foreign Butterflies.
19. Birds of Western Africa, vol. 2.
20. British Birds, vol. 1.
21. Fly-catchers.
22. British Quadrupeds.
23. Amphibious Carnivora (Walrus, Seals, &c.)
24. British Birds, vol. 2.
25. Dogs, vol. 1.
26. Honey Bees.
27. Fishes, vol. 2.
28. Dogs, vol. 2.
29. Introduction to Entomology.
30. Marsupialia, or Pouched Animals.
31. Horses.
32. Fishes of Guiana, vol. 1.
33. Foreign Moths.
34. British Birds, vol. 3.
35. Introduction to Mammalia.
36. Sun Birds.
37. British Fishes, vol. 1.
38. Fishes of Guiana, vol. 2.
39. British Fishes, vol. 2.
40. British Birds, vol. 4.

Jarret, (Rev. T.) An Essay on Algebraical Development, &c. 8vo. cloth, $2 50. London, 1831.

Jarves, (J. J.) History of the Hawaiian or Sandwich Islands. 8vo. cloth, portraits and illustrations, $2 25. Boston, 1844.

Jay, (William.) A Review of the Causes and Consequences of the Mexican War. 12mo. cloth. Boston, 1849.

——— (Rev. W.) Jubilee Memorial; being the Sermons, Meetings, Presentations, and full Account of the Jubilee Commemorating his Fifty Years' Ministry. 37 cents. New York, 1841.

——— The Christian Contemplated, in a Course of Lectures. 18mo. cloth, 50 cents. New York, 1846.

Jean, (H. W.) Solutions of Problems in Trigonometry. Part 1. Designed as an Introduction to Nautical Astronomy. 12mo. cloth, $1 25. Portsea, 1843.

Jean Paul. Samtliche Werke in vier Banden. Royal 8vo. half mor. marbled leaves, with a beautifully engraved portrait, $12 00. Paris, 1843.

——— Richter's Flower, Fruit, and Thorn Pieces. Translated by E. H. Noel. 2 vols. 12mo. cloth, $1 50. London, 1845.

——— Life of Jean Paul Fr. Richter, compiled from various sources, together with his Autobiography. Translated from the German, by Mrs. Lee. 2 vols. 12mo. cloth. Boston.

——— Richter's Walt and Vult; or, the Twins. Translated from the German, by Mrs. Lee. 2 vols. 12mo. cloth, $2 00. Boston

——— Campaner Thal; or, the Immortality of the Soul. Translated by Miss Bauer. 12mo. paper, 75 cents. London, 1848.

——— Richter's Levana; or, the Doctrine of Education. Translated from the German. Post 8vo. cloth, $3 25. London, 1848.

——— Reminiscences of the Best Hours of Life for the Hour of Death, &c. 32mo. cloth, gilt edges, 37 cents. Boston.

Jebb, (Bp.) Pastoral Instructions on the Character and Principles of the Church of England. 12mo. cloth, $1 63. London, 1844.

——— (J.) Treatises on Attack and Defence. 30 plates, third edition, 8vo. cloth, $4 25. London, 1843.

——— (Rev. J.) Literal Translation of the Book of the Psalms. 2 vols. 8vo. cloth, $6 25. London, 1846.

——— (Major.) Modern Prisons, their Construction and Ventilation. 4to. paper, 10 plates, $3 50. London.

——— and **Knox**, (Alexander.) Thirty Years' Correspondence between. Edited by the Rev. Charles Forster. Second edition, 2 vols. 8vo. cloth, $8 50. London.

——— A Literal Translation of the Book of Psalms; intended to illustrate their Poetical and Moral Structure: to which is added Dissertations on the word "Selah," and on the Authorship, Order, Titles, and Poetical Features of the Psalms. 2 vols. 8vo. cloth, $6 50. London.

Jefferson, (Thomas.) Memoirs, Correspondence, and Private Papers. Edited by Thomas Jefferson Randolph. Portrait, 4 vols. 8vo. half calf, $7 50. London, 1829.

Jeffrey, (Fra.) Miscellaneous Essays. 8vo. cloth, $2 00. Philadelphia.

Jehan, (L. F.) Botanique et Physiologie Végétale. Cr. 8vo. Fr. calf gilt, and gilt edges, $2 25. Tours, 1847.

Jelf, (W. E.) Twelve Sermons Preached at the Chapel Royal, Whitehall. 8vo. cloth, $2 00. Oxford, 1848.

Jenks, (B.) Prayers and Offices of Devotion. Altered and improved by Rev. Charles Simeon. 12mo. cloth, 50 cents. London, 1847.

Jenkins, (J. S.) History of the War between the United States and Mexico, from the commencement of Hostilities to the Ratification of the Treaty of Peace. Thick 8vo cloth gilt, many plates, 12mo. cloth, $1 25. Auburn, 1848.

Jenkyn, (Rev. W.) An Exposition upon the Epistle to St. Jude; new edition, by the Rev. J. Sherman. Imp. 8vo. cloth, $2 50. London, 1839.

Jennings, (Rev. David.) Jewish Antiquities; with a Dissertation on the Hebrew Language. 8vo. cloth, $2 00. London, 1839.

Jennour, (Rev. Alfred.) The Book of the Prophet Isaiah. Translated from the Hebrew. 2 vols. 8vo. $3 00. London, 1830.

Jenyns, (Rev. L.) Observations in Natural History; with an Introduction on Habits of Observing. 12mo. cloth, $3 00. London.

Jerrold, (Douglas.) Chronicles of Clovernook and the Hermit of Bellyefulle. 12mo. cloth, $1 37. London.

——— Mrs. Caudle's Curtain Lectures. 12mo. cloth, 75 cents. London.

——— Man made of Money. Illustrated with 12 plates on steel, from designs by J. Leach. Post 8vo. cloth, $2 00. London, 1849.

Jermyn, (J.) Book of English Epithets, Literal and Figurative; with Elementary Remarks and Minute References to abundant Authorities. Imp. 8vo. cloth, $2 50. London, 1849.

Jerome Paturot. A la recherche de la Meilleure des Républiques, par Louis Reybaud. Edition illustrée, par Tony Johannot. 1 vol. grand in 8, $6. Paris, 1849.

Jesse, (John H.) Memoirs of the Chevalier, Prince Charles Edward, and their Adherents. 2 vols. 8vo. cloth, portraits, $2 50. London, 1846.

——— Memoirs of the Court of England from the Revolution in 1688 to the Death of George II. 3 vols. 8vo. portraits, $4 50. London, 1846.

——— Memoirs of the Court of England during the Reign of the Stuarts, including the Protectorate. 4 vols. 8vo. cloth, portraits, $6 50. London, 1846.

——— (E.) Favorite Haunts and Rural Studies, including Visits to Spots of Interest in the Vicinity of Windsor and Eton. Post 8vo. paper, wood-cuts, 75 cents. London, 1847.

——— Anecdotes of Dogs. Small 4to. cloth, with illustrations on steel, $3 50. Lond. 1846.

Jeumont, (Dr. F. F. De.) Mémoires de Médecine Pratique. 8vo. paper, 63 cents. Paris, 1845.

Jews, (Letters of Certain) to M. Voltaire; containing an Apology for their own People, and for the Old Testament. Translated by Rev. Philip Lefranc. 2 vols. in 1, 8vo. cloth, $3 00. Philadelphia, 1848.

Jewel, (Dr. J.) Works. Edited by Richard W. Jelf. 8 vols. 8vo. cloth, $19 50. Oxford, 1848.

Jobert, (Dr.) Traité de Chirurgie Plastique. 2 vols. folio, with atlas of colored plates, $15 00.

Johnes, (J.) Philological Proofs of the Origin of the Human Race. 8vo. cloth, $1 75. London.

Johnson, (C. W.) On Fertilizers. 8vo. cloth, $4 25. London, 1844.

——— (T. B.) The Sportsman's Encyclopædia; comprising a complete Elucidation of the Science and Practice of Hunting, Shooting, Coursing, Racing, Fishing, Hawking, Cock-Fighting, and other Sports and Pastimes of Great Britain. Illustrated with engravings on steel and wood. 8vo. cloth, $5 75. London, 1848.

——— (C. W.) A Dictionary of Modern Gardening. 12mo. cloth, $3 00. London.

——— American edition, $1 75.

——— Farmer's Encyclopædia and Dictionary of Rural Affairs; embracing all the most Recent Discoveries in Agricultural Chemistry. Large 8vo. $10 00. London.

——— Adapted to the United States. By Governeur Emerson. 8vo. $4 00. Phila.

——— The Farmer's Medical Dictionary, for the Diseases of Animals. 12mo. cloth, $1 75. London.

——— (Samuel.) The Works of; with an Essay on his Life and Genius, by Arthur Murphy. Portrait, 2 vols. 8vo. cloth, $3 50; half mor. $6 50. London, 1835.

Johnson, (Samuel.) Life of. By James Boswell; including the Tour to the Hebrides. Edited by J. W. Croker. A new edition, with portraits, royal 8vo. cloth, $4 00. London, 1848.

——— Life of. By James Boswell. Edited by Malone. 1 vol. 8vo. cloth, $2 25. London, 1848.

——— Diamond Dictionary. 32mo. very neat edition, 38 cents. London, 1848.

——— (Dr. E.) Results of Hydropathy; or, Constipation not a Disease of the Bowels; Indigestion not a Disease of the Stomach, &c. 12mo. cloth, 50 cents. New York.

——— (W.) Essays on the Diseases of Young Women. Post 8vo. cloth, $1 50. Lond. 1849.

——— (Cuthbert.) The Farmer's Encyclopædia and Dictionary of Rural Affairs; embracing all the Recent Discoveries in Agricultural Chemistry; adapted to the Comprehension of Unscientific Readers. 8vo. illustrated by wood engravings, cloth, $15 00. London.

——— (James, Dr.) A Tour in Ireland, with Meditations and Reflections. Cr. 8vo. cloth, portrait, $1 50. Lond. 1849.

Johnsoniana; a Collection of Miscellaneous Anecdotes and Sayings, gathered from nearly a hundred different Publications, and not contained in Boswell's Life of Johnson. Edited by J. W. Croker, M. P., complete in one thick vol. foolscap, 8vo. portrait and frontispiece, extra cloth, gilt, $1 25. 1845.

Johnston's Universal Atlas. A new edition of the Maps transferred from stone; with the addition of a copious and useful Index of 40,000 names. Half bound in mor. gilt edges, $20 00.

——— (A. K.) Index to the National Atlas. Folio sewed, $2 25. London, 1849.

——— (James.) A Discourse on the Phenomena of Sensation, as connected with the Mental, Physical, and Instinctive Faculties of Man. 8vo. cloth, $2 50. London, 1841.

——— (Charles.) Travels in Southern Abyssinia, through the Country of Adal to the Kingdom of Shoa. 2 vols. 8vo. cloth, plates, $2 50. London, 1844.

——— (J. F. W.) The Use of Lime in Agriculture. 12mo. cloth, $1 75. London, 1849.

——— Lectures on the Application of Chemistry and Geology to Agriculture. 12mo. $1 50. New York.

Joigneaux, (P.) Organisation du Travail Agricole. 18mo. broché.

Jomini, (Baron de.) Traité des Grandes Opérations Militaires, ou Histoire Critique et Militaire des guerres de Frédéric II. comparées au Système Moderne avec un recueil des Principes les plus importants de l'art de la guerre. 2 vols. royal 8vo. with an atlas of 26 plates. $12 00. Brux. 1840.

——— Histoire Critique et Militaire de la Revolution. 4 vols. royal 8vo. atlas de 38 cartes et plans, $27 50. Bruxelles, 1840.

——— Précis de l'art de la Guerre, ou Nouveau tableau analytique des principales combinaisons de la stratégie, de la grand tactique et de la politique Militaire. 8vo. orne de plans et de cartes, $2 00. Bruxelles, 1838.

Jomini, (Baron de.) Precis politique et Militaire de la Campagne de 1815. 12mo. broche, 75 cents.

——— Principes de la stratégie, dévellopés par la relation de la campagne de 1796 in Allemagne, par S. A. I. et R. L'Archiduc Charles; ouvrage traduit de l'Allemand. 1 vol. royal 8vo. with an atlas of plans on a large scale, $6 00. Bruxelles, 1841.

——— Vie politique et Militaire de Napoleon, racontee par lui-meme au tribunal de Cesar, d'Alexandre et de Frederic, faisant suite a l'Histoire des guerres de la Revolution. 2 vols. royal 8vo. with an atlas of 36 plates, $12 00. Bruxelles, 1840.

Jones and Newman's American Architect; comprising original Designs of Cheap Country and Village Residences, with details, &c. 4to. sheep, $3 50. New York, 1848.

Jones, (T. R.) Natural History of Animals; being the Substance of Three Courses of Lectures delivered before the Royal Institution of Great Britain. 12mo. cloth, $3 25.

——— (T. W.) Manual of Ophthalmic Medicine and Surgery. 12mo. cloth, $3 75. Lond.

——— The Principles and Practice of Ophthalmic Medicine and Surgery, with 102 illustrations. Thick 12mo. cloth, $2 00. Philadelphia, 1847.

——— (H. B.) On Gravel, Calculus, and Gout; being an Application of Professor Liebig's Physiology to the Prevention and Cure of these Diseases. 8vo. cloth, $1 50. London, 1842.

——— (Maj. Gen. Sir J. T.) Journal of the Sieges carried on by the Army under the Duke of Wellington in Spain from 1811 to 1814. 3 vols. 8vo. cloth, 26 plates, $12 50. Lond.

——— (O.) and **Goury,** (M. J.) Plans, Elevations, Sections, and Details of the Alhambra, from Drawings taken on the Spot in 1834 and 1837. 2 vols. royal folio, half mor. $150 00. London, 1842.

——— Scenery of the Nile, from Cairo to the Second Cataract, from drawings made on the spot; with Historical Notices of the Monuments, by Samuel Birch, Senior in the Department of Antiquities in the British Museum, and Honorary Member of the Egyptian Societies of Cairo. Royal folio, containing 30 large and very fine tinted engravings, drawn on stone by George Moore, (the Artist of Gally Knight's Works) and a colored frontispiece. Half mor. $17 00. London, 1843.

——— (Rev. R.) Essay on the Distribution of Wealth, and on the Sources of Taxation. 12mo. $2 50. London, 1844.

——— (William.) An Autobiography of the late. Edited by his Son. 8vo. cloth, $1 50. London, 1846.

——— (E.) Principles and Practice of Levelling. 12mo. cloth, 75 cents. London.

——— (Rev. J.) Chronological and Analytical View of the Holy Bible. 8vo. cloth, $2 00. Oxford, 1836.

——— The Book of the Young; an Invitation to Early Christian Piety. 12mo. cloth, $1 00. Oxford, 1837.

Jonson, (Ben.) Dramatic Works. Complete, with Biographical Memoir, by William Gifford. Royal 8vo. cloth, portrait and vignette, $4 00; handsomely bound in calf, marbled leaves, $6 00. Lond. 1845.

Jopling, (J.) Practice of Isometrical Perspective. 8vo. bds. 3 plates and 173 diagrams. $1 50. London, 1842.

——— Taylor's Principles of Linear Perspective. 8vo. plates and diagrams, $3 25. London.

Jortin, (John, D. D.) Remarks on Ecclesiastical History; with Life of the Author. 3 vols. 8vo. calf gilt, $7 00. Lond. 1805.

——— Edited by Rev. W. Trollope. 2 vols. 8vo. cloth, $4 50; calf extra, $6 50. Lond. 1846.

Josephine. Historical and Secret Memoirs of the Empress Josephine. By Mademoiselle M. A. Le Normand. Translated from the French, by Jacob M. Howard, Esq. 2 vols. post 8vo. cloth, $2 00. New York, 1849.

Josephus, (Flavius.) Works; with the Three Dissertations concerning Jesus Christ, John the Baptist, James the Just, God's Command to Abraham, &c.; with an Index. Translated by William Whiston. 3 vols. 8vo. cloth, $6 50. Oxford, 1839.

——— 1 vol. 8vo. cloth, $2 50. Lond. 1843.

——— Translated by Whiston. 52 plates. 2 vols. 8vo. cloth, $5 50.

Josselyn, (R.) The Faded Flower and other Songs and little Poems. 12mo. bds. 50 cents. Boston, 1849.

Jouffroy. Introduction to Ethics; including a Critical Survey of Moral Systems. Translated by W. H. Channing. 2 vols. 12mo. cloth, $2 00. Boston, 1848.

Journal of Design, (The.) A new Periodical devoted to Ornamental Art and Design. The first part has ten actual Fabric Patterns inserted and 30 wood engravings. (To be published monthly.)

——— Vol. 1, 8vo. cloth, with 44 Fabric Patterns inserted and upwards of 200 engravings, $2 25. London, 1849.

——— of the Proceedings of the Philomathic Institution; or, Lectures, Essays, and Discussions. 4 vols. 8vo. cloth, $4 00. London, 1826.

——— of a Few Months' Residence in Portugal and Glimpses of the South of Spain. 2 vols. post 8vo. cloth, $4 00. London, 1847.

——— of a Voyage to the Levant. 2 vols. 8vo. paper, $3 50. Paris, 1848.

——— of the American Oriental Society; comprising Original Papers Relating to the East. Nos. 1 to 4, already published.

Jousse's Piano-Forte Preceptor, with Examples and Exercises from celebrated Composers. Oblong 4to. paper, 75 cents. Lond. 1848.

Jowett, (Rev. W.) Scripture Characters, from Adam to Abraham. 12mo. cloth, 60 cents. London, 1847.

Joyce, (Jer.) Scientific Dialogues, by Gregory and Walker. 12mo. cloth, wood-cuts, $1 75. London.

Junkin, (Rev. D. X.) The Oath a Divine Ordinance and an Element of the Social Constitution, &c. 12mo. cloth 50 cents. New York.

Junius. The Authorship of the Letters of Junius Elucidated; including a Memoir of Lieut. Col. Isaac Barre. By John Britton. Portraits, 8vo. cloth, $2 75. London, 1848.

——— Letters. 2 vols. 12mo. calf, Woodfall's edition. London.

Jurgensen. Principes de l'exact mesure du temps par horologes, ou Résume des principes de construction des horologes pour la plus exact mesure du temps. 4to. 17 planches, $6 25. Paris.

Jurieu, (Peter.) The Accomplishment of the Scripture Prophecies; or, the Approaching Deliverance of the Church. 8vo. calf, $2 00. London, 1687.

——— A Critical History of the Doctrines and Worships of the Church. 2 vols. 8vo. calf, $3 50. London, 1705.

Jussieu, (H. De.) Elements of Botany. Translated by Wilson. 12mo. cloth, $3 75. London, 1848.

Kallenbach's Atlas of the Germanic Middle Age Architecture. Oblong folio, cloth, $25 00.

Kames, (Lord.) Elements of Criticism. $2 50. London, 1840.

Kane, (Sir R.) Elements of Chemistry; including the most recent Discoveries and Applications of the Science to Medicine and Pharmacy, and to the Arts, with additions and corrections, by J. W. Draper. 8vo. cloth, $1 75. New York.

——— Second edition, enlarged. 8vo. cloth, $8 00. London.

Kant, (J.) Critick of Pure Reason. Translated from the Original of Immanuel Kant. Second edition, with Notes and Explanation of Terms, by Francis Haywood. 8vo. $5 50. London, 1849.

Kater and Lardner's Treatise on Mechanics. 12mo. cloth, $1 75. Lond. 1830.

Kean, (Edmund.) The Life of. 12mo. cloth, $1 00. New York, 1835.

Keats, (John.) Poetical Works. 12mo. cloth, $1 00. New York, 1846.

——— Life, Letters, and Literary Remains, by Monckton Milnes. 12mo. cloth, portrait, $1 25. New York, 1846.

Keble, (J.) Lyra Apostolica. 18mo. cloth, $1 00. Derby, 1841.

——— Lyra Innocentium. 12mo. cloth, 50 cents. New York, 1848.

——— The Christian Year. Thoughts in Verse for the Sundays and Holydays throughout the Year. Illustrated edition. Square 12mo. cloth, $1 00. Philadelphia, 1848.

Another edition. 12mo. cloth, 75 cents. Philadelphia, 1842.

——— Selections from Hooker. 18mo. cloth, 75 cents. Oxford, 1845.

Keeling, (Wm.) Liturgiæ Britannicæ; or, the several editions of the Book of Common Prayer; from its compilation to its last revision, arranged to show their respective variations. 8vo. cloth, $5 00. Pickering, 1842.

Keepsake des Jeunes Personnes. Par Mme. La Comtesse Dash. Illustre par Ernest Girard. Royal 8vo. cloth gilt and emblazoned, $5 00. Paris.

Keightley, (Thos.) History of England. 2 vols. 8vo. cloth, $4 00. New York.

——— History of Greece. 8vo. cloth, $1 75. New York.

——— History of Rome. 8vo. cloth, $1 75. New York.

——— History of the Roman Empire. 8vo. cloth, $1 75. New York.

———Mythology of Greece and Rome. 50 cents. New York.

Keith, (A.) Demonstration of the Truth of the Christian Religion. 12mo. cloth, $1 38. New York.

——— The Signs of the Times, as denoted by the Fulfilment of Historical Predictions 2 vols. 12mo. cloth, $1 50. New York, 1842.

——— On the Prophecies. 12mo. cloth, 75 cents. New York.

——— Evidence of the Truth of the Christian Religion, derived from the Fulfilment of Prophecy. 12mo. mor. $3 50. Edin. 1845.

——— (Sir Robert M.) Memoirs and Correspondence of; with a Memoir of Queen Carolina Matilda of Denmark, and an Account of the Revolution in 1772. Edited by Mrs. G. Smyth. Portrait, 2 vols. post 8vo. cloth, $7 50. London, 1849.

Kelland, (P.) Theory of Heat. 8vo. cloth, $2 63. Cambridge, 1837.

Kellogg, (E.) Labor and other Capital. The Rights of each Secured, and the Wrongs of both Eradicated, &c. 8vo. cloth, $1 50. New York, 1849.

Kelly's Universal Cambist and Commercial Instructor. Second edition, corrected to 1835. 2 vols. in 1, 4to. cloth lettered, $4 75. 1835.

——— (Walter K.) History of the Year 1848. 12mo. cloth, $1 50. London, 1849.

Kelt's Engineer's Pocket Guide. 18mo. cloth, 75 cents. New York.

Kemble, (Fanny.) A Year of Consolation. 12mo. cloth, $1 00. New York.

——— (John Mitchell.) Saxons in England; a History of the English Commonwealth till the Period of the Norman Conquest. 8vo. cloth, $8 00. London, 1849.

Kendall, (G. W.) Narrative of Texan Santa Fê Expedition across the great Southwestern Prairies to the City of Mexico. 2 vols. 12mo. plates, $2 00. New York.

——— (H. E.) Designs for Schools and School-Houses, Parochial and National, in the Gothic, Old English, Tudor, and Elizabethan Styles. Illustrated by a series of 21 plates of Plans, Elevations, and Perspective Views, with Estimates and Descriptive letter-press. Folio, cloth, $16 00. London.

——— (Otis.) Monography; or, Description of the Heavens, and atlas, $1 25. Phila.

Kennedy, (J. P.) Memoirs of the Life of William Wirt, Attorney-General of the United States. 2 vols. 8vo. cloth, portrait, $3 50. Philadelphia, 1849.

Kennish, (W.) A Method for Concentrating the Fire of a Broadside of a Ship of War, with an Appendix, containing several important subjects connected with the Naval Service. 4to. cloth, 19 plates, $6 50. Lond.

Keppel, (G.) Narrative of Journey from India to England in 1824. 8vo. cloth, $1 50. Philadelphia, 1827.

——— Expedition to Borneo. 12mo. cloth, 50 cents. New York.

Kidd, (John.) On the Physical Condition of Man. 12mo. cloth, 60 cents. Phila.

Kidder, (D. P.) Sketches of a Residence and Travels in Brazil. 2 vols. post 8vo. cloth, 50 engravings, $2 50. New York.

Kindersley, (E. C.) The very Joyous, and Pleasant, and Refreshing History of the Feats, Exploits, Triumphs, and Atchievements of the Good Knight without Fear and without Reproach, the Gentle Lord De Bayard. Square 8vo. bds. $3 00. London, 1848.

King's Munimenta Antiqua; or, Observations on Ancient Castles in Great Britain. 4 vols. folio, 166 plates, $63 00.

King, (T.) Working Ornaments and Forms. Full size, for the use of the Cabinet Manufacturer, Chair and Sofa Maker, Carver and Turner, &c. 3 parts, folio, paper.

——— (Col. J. A.) Twenty-four Years in the Argentine Republic. 12mo. cloth, $1 00. New York.

Kingsborough, (Lord.) Antiquities of Mexico, comprising fac-similes of Ancient Mexican Paintings and Hieroglyphics, preserved in the Royal Libraries of Paris, Berlin, Dresden, Vienna; the Vatican and the Borgian Museum, at Rome; the Institute at Bologna; the Bodleian Library at Oxford; and various others; the greater part inedited. Also, the Monuments of New Spain, by M. Dupaix. Illustrated by upwards of one thousand elaborate and highly interesting plates, accurately copied from the originals, by A. Aglio. 9 vols. impl. folio, very neatly half bound mor. gilt edges, $200 00.

The Same, 9 vols. with the plates beautifully colored, half bound mor. gilt edges, $350 00.

Kinglake. Eothen; or, Traces of Eastern Travel. 12mo. cloth, 50 cents; illustrated, cloth extra, $1 50. New York, 1849.

Kingston, (W. H. G.) Lusitanian Sketches of the Pen and Pencil. 2 vols. post 8vo. $2.

Kip, (Rev. W. J.) Early Jesuit Missions in North America. 12mo. cloth, map, $1 00. New York.

Kirby, (W.) and **Spence**, (W.) An Introduction to Entomology; or, Elements of the Natural History of Insects; comprising an Account of Noxious and Useful Insects, of their Metamorphoses, Food, Stratagems, Habitations, Societies, Motions, Noises, Hybernation, Instinct, &c. Sixth edition, corrected and enlarged. 2 vols. 8vo. cloth, $9 50. London.

——— An Introduction to Entomology; or, Elements of the Natural History of Insects. 8vo. colored plates, $2 50. Philadelphia.

Kirby's Wonderful Museum; or, Magazine of Remarkable and Eccentric Characters, including Curiosities of Nature and Art, from the remotest period to the present time, drawn from every authentic source. 6 vols. 8vo. 124 curious portraits and plates, cloth lettered, $7 50.

Kirkaldy, (Sir William, of Grange.) Memoirs and Adventures of. 12mo. cloth, $3 25. Edinburgh, 1847.

Kirkland, (Mrs.) A New Home, Who'll Follow? or, Glimpses of Life in the Far West or New Settlements of America. 12mo. cloth, $1 00. New York.

——— Western Clearings. 12mo. cloth, 50 cents. New York.

——— Holidays Abroad; or, Europe from the West. 2 vols. 12mo. cloth, $2 25. New York, 1849.

Kirke White's Poems. 32mo. cloth, 63 cents. Philadelphia.

——— Remains. 18mo. mor. gilt, port. $1 50. Glasgow, 1848.

Kirke, (W. S.) Hand-Book of Physiology. Assisted by James Paget, with illustrations on steel and wood. 12mo. cloth, $3 75. London, 1849.

——— and **Paget**, (J.) Manual of Physiology. 12mo. sheep, 118 wood-cuts, $2 00. Philadelphia, 1849.

Kit Bam's Adventures; or, the Yarns of an Old Mariner. By Mary Cowden Clarke. 12mo. cloth, Cruikshank's plates, $1 50. London, 1849.

Kitchener, (Dr.) The Cook's Oracle and Housekeeper's Manual. 12mo. cloth, 88 cents. New York.

Kitto, (J.) Cyclopædia of Biblical Literature. 2 vols. 8vo. cloth, with maps, 7 50. New York.

——— History of Palestine. 12mo. cloth, 75 cents. New York, 1844.

Kleuze's Works; containing the Pinnacotheca and other Public Buildings of Bavaria. Folio, half bound, $31 50.

Kling, (Herr.) Chess Euclid: a Collection of 200 Chess Problems and End Games. 8vo. cloth, $2 50. London, 1849.

Klipstein, (L. F.) Study of Modern Languages. Imperial 8vo. cloth, $1 00. New York, 1849.

——— Grammar of the Anglo-Saxon Language. 12mo. cloth, $1 25. New York, 1848.

——— Analecta Anglo-Saxonica; with an Introductory Ethnological Essay and Notes, Critical and Explanatory. 2 vols. 12mo. cloth, $3 50. New York, 1849.

——— A Glossary to Do. (In preparation.)

——— Ælfric's Anglo-Saxon Homily on the Birthday of St. Gregory; with a full rendering into English, and Notes, &c. 12mo. cloth, 50 cents. New York, 1849.

Klopstock's Odes from 1747 to 1780. Translated from the German, by W. Nind. 12mo. cloth, $1 63. London, 1848.

Knapen, (D. M.) The Mechanic's Assistant; a thorough Practical Treatise on Mensuration and the Sliding Rule. 12mo. half bound, wood-cuts, $1 00. New York, 1848.

Knapp, (Dr. F.) Chemical Technology; or, Chemistry applied to the Arts and to Manufactures. Translated and edited by Drs. Ronalds and Richardson, with Notes and Additions, by Prof. W. R. Johnson. 2 vols. 8vo. cloth, and upwards of 400 engravings, $7 50. Philadelphia, 1848.

Knight, (Charles.) William Shakspeare; a Biography. Royal 8vo. half calf, gilt, profusely illustrated with wood-cuts, $8 00. (Scarce.) London, 1843.

——— Penny Magazine; the last 2 vols. published together in 1 vol. 12mo. cloth, wood-cuts, 75 cents. London, 1846.

——— Pictorial London. 6 vols. bound in 3 thick handsome vols. imperial 8vo. illustrated by 650 wood engravings, extra cloth, gilt backs, very elegant, $10 00. 1841–44.

The Same. 6 vols. in 3, elegantly half bound mor. extra, gilt backs and gilt edges, $16 00.

——— Pictorial Shakspeare. A few sets of the choice original copies (now very scarce), complete in 8 vols. royal 8vo. calf extra, $35 00.

The Same, half mor. neat, $33 00.

——— (C.) Half Hours with Best Authors. 4 thick vols. 12mo. cloth, $6 00. New York.

——— (Henry Gally.) Ecclesiastical Architecture of Italy. 2 vols. folio, half mor. 81 plates, $63 00. London, 1844.

——— Saracenic and Norman Remains, to illustrate the Normans in Sicily. Imp. folio, half mor. 30 plates, $22 00. London, 1840.

——— (F.) Scroll Ornaments; designed for the use of Silversmiths, Chasers, Die-Sinkers, Modellers, &c. 4to. cloth, $12 00.

Kock, (Paul De.) La Grande Ville, nouveau tableau de Paris, comique, critique et philosophique; illustrations de Gavarni, Gigoux, Victor Adam et Daumier. 2 vols. grand in 8, $5 00.

Knowles, (J.) The Elements and Practice of Naval Architecture; or, a Treatise on Ship Building. Illustrated with a series of 39 large draughts and numerous smaller engravings. 4to. cloth, plates, folio, $35 00. London.

Kohl, (J. G.) Scotland: Glasgow, the Clyde, Edinburgh, the Forth, Stirling Drummond Castle, Perth, Taymouth Castle, and the Lakes. 8vo. paper, 50 cents. London, 1844.

——— Travels in Russia, Austria, Scotland, England, and Wales. 8vo. cloth, $1 25. Philadelphia.

Kohlrausch's History of Germany, from the earliest period to the present time. Thick 8vo. $1 50.

Koran. Translated from the original Arabic, with Explanatory Notes, and a Preliminary Discourse, by George Sale. Maps and plates, 8vo. cloth, $2 50. London, 1838.

Krafft. Portes cochères et portes d'entrée des maisons particulières et édifices publics. Partie séparée de l'ouvrage ci-dessus dénommé. 1 vol. in folio, de 60 planches graves au trait, $7 00.

——— Modèles de Dessin lineaire, appliqués a l'architecture, intitules: Ornementation de l'architecture antique et moderne. 1 vol. in-fol. de 72 planches dessineés par J-Ch. Krafft, graveés au trait, avec texte, $7 50.

Krafft, (J.-Ch.), Architecte. Maisons de campagne, habitations rurales, chateaux, fermes, plans de jardins de France, d'Angleterre, d'Allemagne; decorations de jardins, etc. Cet ouvrage, du format grand in-folio de 292 planches avec texte explicatif, renfermé dans son ensemble tout ce qui concerne la distribution, l'arrangement, l'embellissement et la decoration des maisons de campagne, parcs et jardins, classes en trois parties. 3 vols. in 1, folio, $30 00.

——— Traité de l'Art de la charpente. Plans, coupes et elevations de diverses productions executés tant en France que dans les pays etrangers; publié par J.-Ch. Krafft, architecte. Troisieme edition, mise en ordre et augmentée de 40 planches par Rondelet et Thiollet, architectes et professeurs. 2 vol. fol. $35 00.

——— et **Thiollet.** Choix des plus jolies maisons de Paris et de ses environs. Edifices et monuments publics presentes en plans, elevations, coupes et details de constructions. Nouvelle edition, revue et mise en ordre, format grand in-fol. contenant: Maisons particulières et petits hotels; maisons à loyer et à boutiques; maisons de commerce, magasins et hotels garnis; pavillons, galeries, passages, restaurants, cafés, bains, glacieres et lavoirs; corps-de-garde, prisons, theatres, hopitaux, eglises, etc. Leves, mesures et dessines par J.-Ch. Krafft et Thiollet, architectes, 153 pl. gravées au trait, accompagnées d'un texte; ouvrage terminé par 60 planches gravées, representant les portes cocheres et portes d'entrées des maisons particulieres et edifices publics de Paris, levées, mesurées et dessinées par le mêmes. 1 vol. grand in-folio de 218 pl.

Kramer, (W.) On Diseases of the Ear. 8vo. cloth, $1 25. Philadelphia.

Krudner, (Mme. de.) Valerie avec preface de S. Beuve. 12mo. paper, $1 00.

Kughler, (Dr. F.) Hand-Book of the Dictionary of Painting: German, Flemish, and Dutch Schools, with Notes, by Sir F. Head. 12mo. cloth, $3 25.

Kuhner, (Dr. R.) Grammar of the Greek Language for the use of High Schools and Colleges. Translated from the German, by Professors Edwards and Taylor. 8vo. boards, $3 00. Andover.

——— Elementary Grammar of the Latin Language. Translated by Champlin. 12mo. half roan, $1 50. Boston.

Kynaston, (Lieut. A. F.) Casualties Afloat, with Practical Suggestions for their Prevention and Remedy. 8vo. cloth, $2 25. London, 1849.

Labedolliere, (E. de.) Histoire de la Garde Nationale recit complet de tous les Faits qui l'ont Distinguée depuis son origine jusqu'en 1848. 12mo. paper, illustrée par dix dessins colories, $1 00. Paris, 1848.

Laborde, (Le Comte de.) Les Ducs de Bourgoyne etudes sur les Lettres, les Arts et l'Industrie pendant le XVe Siècle. Seconde Parte. Tome I. Preuves, $2 00. Paris, 1849.

——— Voyage Pittoresque et Historique en Espagne. 4 vols. grand en folio, half bound, with numerous engravings, $125 00. Paris, 1806.

Lacroix, (S. F.) Elements of Algebra Translated by J. Farrar. 2 vols. 8vo. sheep, $4 00. Boston.

Lactantius, (St.) Opera omnia, cum emendationibus tum disquisitionibus criticis aucta; editio novissima, precedunt S. Marcellini, S. Eusebii, S. Melchiadis, Anonymi, Celsi, omnia quæ exstant Fragmenta. 2 vols. royal 8vo. $4 50. Paris, 1844.

Lafever, (M.) The Beauties of Modern Architecture. Large 8vo. 58 plates, $5 00. New York.

La Fontaine, (Jean de.) Œuvres completes, mises en ordre, accompagnées de notes et augmentées de plusieurs pieces inedites et de variantes, par M. Walckenaer, avec portrait. 6 vols. grand in 8, veau, $12 00. Paris, 1822.

——— Le meme ouvrage, demi veau. $10 50. Paris, 1822.

——— Œuvres completes avec les notes de tous les commentateurs, et des notices historiques en tête de chaque ouvrage: avec portraits et gravures. 6 vols. in 8, demi veau, $12 00. Paris, 1826.

——— Fables et Œuvres diverses, avec des notes et une nouvelle notice sur sa vie par Walckenaer. 12mo. broché, 1 vol. half mor. $1 75. Paris, 1846.

Laharpe. Abrege de l'histoire generale des voyages, contenant ce qu'il y a de plus remarquable, de plus utile et de mieux avere dans les pays ou les voyageurs out penetre, les mœurs des habitants, la religion, les usages, arts et sciences, commerce et manufactures—ornes de 24 gravures et d'un bel atlas in folio. 24 vol. grand in 8, demi maroquin, $30 00. Paris, 1825.

——— Lycée ou Cours de Litterature, ancienne et moderne—Philosophie du dix huitieme siecle. 16 vol. grand in 8, demi veau, $16 00. Paris, 1825.

Laing, (S.) National Distress, its Causes and Remedies. 8vo. cloth, 75 cents. Lond. 1841.

——— (D.) Hints for Dwellings; consisting of original designs for Cottages, Farm-Houses, Villas, &c. 4to. cloth, plates, $6 00. London, 1841.

——— (Samuel.) The Chronicles of the Kings of Norway, from the earliest period of the History of the Northern Sea-Kings to the Middle of the Twelfth Century, commonly called the Heimskringla. 3 vols. 8vo. cloth, $10 75. Lond.

Laisne, (J.) Aide-memoire portatif a l'usage des officiers du Genie. 12mo. paper, $2 75. Bruxelles, 1841.

Lajolais, (Mle. N. de.) Le Livre des Mères de Famille. 12mo. paper, $1 00. Paris, 1844.

Lallemand, (M.) A Practical Treatise on the Causes, Symptoms, and Treatment of Spermatorrhœa. Translated by H. J. McDougal. 8vo. cloth, $1 50. Phila. 1848.

——— (F.) Revolutions Politiques et Sociales de 1848. Predites en 1843. 12mo. 38 cents. Paris, 1848.

Lamarck's Conchology; containing a complete Translation of his Descriptions of both the Recent and Fossil Genera, illustrated by nearly 400 accurate Figures of Shells, drawn by J. Mawe, edited by E. A. Crouch. Royal 4to. extra cloth boards, $3 25. 1827.

The Same, with the plates beautifully colored, elegantly bound in gilt cloth, $9 50.

Lamartine, (Alphonse de.) Œuvres completes; nouvelle edition illustrée, ornée du portrait, de 30 vignettes, vues ou portraits graves sur acier d'apres les dessins de MM. Alfred et Tony Johannot, de 500 vignettes, culs-de-lampe, fleurons, graves sur bois; de titres graves avec grandes vignettes, et la musique de plusieurs pieces. 21 vol. in 8, demi maroquin, $55 00. Paris, 1839–48.

——— Histoire des Girondins. 8 vols. 12mo. half mor. marbled edges, $14 00. Paris, 1848.

——— La meme ouvrage. Imp. 8vo. broché. Bruxelles.

——— Histoire des Girondins. 8 vols. 12mo. paper, $8 00. Paris, 1848.

——— Raphaël. Pages de la vingtième année. 8vo. paper, $1 50. Paris, 1849.

——— History of the Girondists. Translated by H. T. Ryde. Portraits, 3 vols foolscap, extra cloth, $2 63. London.

——— Pilgrimage to the Holy Land. 2 vols. 12mo. cloth, $1 75. New York, 1848.

——— Raphael; or, Pages of the Book of Life at Twenty. Translated with sanction of Author. Post 8vo. cloth, $2 00. Lond. 1849.

——— Confidential Disclosures. Translated from the French, by E. Plunkett. 12mo. cloth, 50 cents. New York, 1849.

——— Histoire de la Revolution de 1848. 2 vols. 8vo. broché, $3 50. Paris, 1849.

The Same. Translated. 12mo. cloth, 75 cents. Boston, 1849.

Lamb, (Charles.) Complete Works. 1 vol. royal 8vo. cloth, portrait and vignette, $3 50; calf gilt, $6 00. London, 1840.

——— Complete Works; to which are prefixed his Letters and a Sketch of his Life, by Thos. Noon Talfourd. 2 vols. 12mo. cloth, portrait, $2 00. New York, 1849.

——— Literary Sketches and Letters; being the final Memorials of Charles Lamb, never before published, by Thomas Noon Talfourd. 12mo. cloth, 75 cents. New York, 1849.

——— Essays of Elia. 12mo. cloth, $1 00; cloth gilt, $1 25. New York, 1849.

——— Specimens of the English Dramatic Poets. 12mo. cloth, $1 25; cloth gilt, $1 50. New York, 1848.

——— (C. and M.) Tales from Shakspeare. 12mo. cloth, 75 cents. New York.

——— (E. B.) Studies of Ancient Domestic Architecture. Imperial 4to. half calf, 20 fine plates, $7 50. London.

Lambert, (Miss.) The Hand-Book of Needlework, with numerous illustrations, engraved by O. J. Butler. 8vo. cloth, $1 50. New York, 1847.

Lamennais, (F. De.) Œuvres complètes. Nouvelle edition. 10 vols. broché, $9 00. Paris, 1844.

——— Amschaspands et Darvands. 12mo. paper, 75 cents. Bruxelles, 1843.

——— De L'Esclavage Moderne. 12mo. paper, 25 cents. Bruxelles, 1840.

——— Affaires de Rome. 12mo. paper, $1 00. Bruxelles, 1837.

——— Le Pays et le Gouvernement. 18mo. broché, 25 cents.

Landais, (N.) Lettres a Amelie sur le Mariage. 12mo. paper, $1 00. Paris, 1845.

Landor, (Walter Savage.) Works. 2 vols. royal 8vo. cloth, $9 50; Russia gilt, marbled leaves, $12 00. London, 1846.

——— (E. W.) Lofoden; or, the Exiles of Norway. 2 vols. post 8vo. cloth, $6 00. Lond. 1849.

Landseer, (C.) The Mother; a series of Pen and Ink Sketches, etched by Charles Lewis. 8 plates, folio prints, $6 50; India proofs, $13 00; artist's proofs, $26 00. London, 1849.

Lane, (E. W.) Selections from the Kur-an, commonly called the Koran; with an interwoven Commentary. 8vo. cloth, $1 50. London, 1843.

——— Translation of the Thousand and One Nights; or, the Arabian Nights' Entertainments, with Explanatory Notes. A new edition. 3 vols. 12mo. cloth, illustrated with 600 wood-cuts, by Harvey, and illuminated titles, by Owen Jones, $6 00. London, 1847.

——— Manners and Customs of the Modern Egyptians; a new and enlarged edition, with great improvements. 2 vols. 8vo. numerous wood-cuts, printed to match Wilkinson's Ancient Egyptians, cloth, richly gilt backs, $4 00. 1842.

——— (Rev. B.) Mysteries of Tobacco. 12mo. paper, 38 cents. New York.

Lang, (J. D.) An Historical and Statistical Account of New South Wales, both as a Penal Settlement and as a British Colony. 2 vols. cr 8vo cloth, $3 00. London, 1840.

Langley's Ancient Masonry. 2 vols. folio, plates, $9 50. London.

Lanman, (C.) Letters from the Alleghany Mountains. 12mo. cloth, 75 cents. New York.

——— Canoe Voyage up the Mississippi. 12mo. 50 cents. New York.

——— Letters from a Landscape Painter. 12mo. cloth, 75 cents. Boston.

——— Summer in the Wilderness. 12mo cloth, 63 cents. New York.

——— Tour on the Sanguanay. 12mo. cloth, 63 cents. Philadelphia.

La Place, (P. S.) Precis de l'Histoire de l'Astronomie. 8vo. paper, $1 00. Paris, 1821.

——— (Le Marquis De.) Œuvres. 7 vols. in 4to. papier vellin, $30 00. Paris, 1843.

——— Mecanique Celeste. Translated, with a Commentary, by Bowditch. 4 vols 4to. bds. $35 00. Boston, 1829–39.

——— The System of the World. Translated from the French and elucidated with Explanatory Notes, by Rev. Henry H. Blake. 2 vols. 8vo. boards, $7 25. London.

Lapide, (Cornelius A.) Commentarii in Scripturam Sacram. 20 vols. imp. 8vo. $37 50. Lugduni.

Lappenberg, (Dr. J. M.) History of England under the Anglo-Saxon Kings. Translated from the German, by Benjamin Thorpe. 2 vols. 8vo. cloth, $4 00. London, 1845.

Lardner, (Dr.) Cabinet Cyclopædia; comprising a series of original Works on History, Biography, Literature, the Sciences, Arts, and Manufactures. The series complete in 133 vols $200 00; separately, per vol. $1 75. London.

Lardner, (Dr.) On the Steam Engine. 12mo. cloth, wood-cuts, 25 cents. Lond. 1849.

——— Steam Engine Explained and Illustrated, with an Account of its Invention and Progressive Improvement, and its application to Navigation and Railways. Seventh edition, 8vo. numerous engravings on wood, cloth, $2 00.

——— Treatise on the Differential and Integral Calculus. 8vo. $2 00. London, 1825.

——— A Treatise on Arithmetic. Foolscap 8vo. cloth, $1 75. London.

——— A Treatise on Geometry and its Application to the Arts. Foolscap 8vo. upwards of 200 figures, cloth, $1 75. London.

——— A Treatise on Hydrostatics and Pneumatics. New edition, foolscap 8vo. cloth, $1 75. London.

——— A Treatise on Heat. 12mo. cloth, $1 75. London, 1833.

——— and **Walker's** Manual of Electricity, Magnetism, and Meteorology. 2 vols. 12mo. $3 50.

——— Works; containing Credibility of the Gospel History, Jewish and Heathen Testimonies, History of Heretics, and Sermons and Tracts, with Life of the Author, by Dr. Kippis. 10 vols. 8vo. best edition, extra cloth, lettered, $20 00. 1838.

Larned, (Rev. S.) Life and Eloquence, by R. R. Gurley. 12mo. cloth, portrait, $1 25. New York.

Larrey, (Baron D. J.) Surgical Memoirs of the Campaigns of Russia, Germany, and France. Translated by J. C. Mercer. 8vo. boards, $1 50. Philadelphia, 1832.

Lassaigne, (M. J. L.) Dictionnaire des Réactifs chimiques employés dans toutes les expériences dans les cours publics et particulières. 8vo. broché, $2 75. Paris, 1839.

Latham, (R. Y.) The English Language. Second edition, revised and enlarged. 8vo. cloth, $4 50. London, 1848.

Latimer, (Hugh.) Sermons and Remains. 2 vols. 8vo. cloth. Cambridge, 1845

Latour, (A. de.) Poesies complètes. 12mo. paper, $1 00.

Laud, (Archbishop.) Conference between, and William Fisher, a Jesuit, by command of King James. 8vo. $2 25. Oxford, 1839.

——— Liturgy, Episcopacy, and Church Ritual. 12mo. cloth, $1 25. Oxford, 1840.

——— The Private Devotions of. 12mo. cloth, $1 25. Oxford, 1839.

Laurence, (L.) Perspective Simplified. 8vo. cloth, 10 plates, $2 25. London.

Lavater, (John Caspar.) Essays on Physiognomy, designed to promote the Knowledge and the Love of Mankind. Translated by Holcroft. 8vo. cloth, many plates, $3 00. London, 1848.

——— Physiognomy; or, the Corresponding Analyses between the Conformation of the Features and the Ruling Passions of the Mind. 12mo. cloth, 7 engravings, 75 cents. London, 1844.

Lavallee, (Th.) Histoire des Française 4 vols. 12mo. paper, $4 00.

——— Histoire des Français depuis le Temps des Gaulois Jusqu'en 1830. 2 vols. small folio, half mor. gilt tops, illustrated with 80 superb engravings on steel, forming a complete gallery of portraits of the Kings of France and other celebrated men, $15 00. Paris, 1847.

Lavergne, (A. de.) Chateaux et Ruines Historiques de France. Imperial 8vo. paper, with illustrations by Theodore Frère, $2 75. Paris.

Law, (Henry.) Examples of the Modes of Setting out Railway Curves. Plates, 8vo. 75 cents. London.

——— Rudiments of Civil Engineering. Parts 1 and 2. 12mo. 50 cents. London, 1849.

Lawrence, (Sir Thos.) Engravings from the choicest works of. Folio, half mor. gilt, gilt edges, 50 engravings, with accompanying letter-press descriptions and portrait, $25 00. London, 1841.

——— Life and Correspondence, by Williams. 2 vols. 8vo. fine portrait, cloth, $3 75. London, 1831.

——— (W.) Treatise on the Diseases of the Eye. Third edition, revised, corrected, and enlarged, 1 thick vol. 8vo. 820 closely printed pages, extra cloth boards, $3 25. 1844.

Lawson, (Peter.) The Agriculturist's Manual; being a Familiar Description of the Agricultural Plants cultivated in Europe. 8vo. cloth, $2 25. Edinburgh.

Layard, (Austen Henry.) Nineveh and its Remains, with an Account of a Visit to the Chaldean Christians of Kurdistan and the Yeridis, or Devil-Worshippers; and an Inquiry into the Manners and Arts of the Ancient Assyrians. 2 vols. 8vo. $10 50. Lond. 1849.

American edition. 2 vols. 8vo. cloth, plates and cuts, $4 50; 2 vols. in 1, half mor. $5 00. New York, 1849.

——— Monuments of Nineveh, from drawings made on the spot. Folio, 100 plates in portfolio, $60 00. London, 1849.

Lays of the Western World; containing "Love's Requiem," by C. F. Hoffman; "The Mother of Moses," by Mrs. Osgood; "The Land of Dreams," by W. C. Bryant; "Lees in the Cup of Life," by Mrs. S. G. Howe; "The Night Cometh," by Mrs. Embury; "The Tournament of Acre," by W. H. Herbert; "Greenwood," by Miss Pindar; "Worship," by Miss Bayard; "The Child's Mission," by Mrs. Embury. Beautifully printed in colors and gold, designs by Mapleson, with borders and vignettes after the manner of the illuminated books of the Middle Ages. 4to. handsomely bound in morocco, in antique style, gilt, and gilt leaves, $12 00. New York, 1849.

Lays of Ancient Babyland; to which are added divers small Histories not known to the Ancients. Dedicated, with much respect, but without permission, to the Babies of England. 12mo. cloth, $1 00. Pickering, 1849.

Leaflets of Memory; an Illuminated Annual for 1849. Edited by Reynell Coates, M. D. 8vo. mor. gilt, $6 00. Phila. 1849.

Leahy, (E.) A Practical Treatise on Making and Repairing Roads. Cr. 8vo. cloth, plates, $1 50. London.

Le Bealle, (A.) Cours Elementaire Theorique et Pratique de dessin Lineaire. 2 vols. 4to. boards, many plates, some colored, $5 50. Paris.

Le Canu, (Louis-Rene.) Etudes Chimiques sur le Sang Humain. 4to. paper, $1 00. Paris, 1837.

Le Comte's Gothic Ornaments, and of the Renaissance Style. Folio, 76 plates, $15 75.

Leconte. Ornements Gothiques de toutes les epoques, et choix d'ornements de la Renaissance et des differents siecles, à l'usage des peintres, decorateurs et architectes. 1 vol. in fol. de 72 planches, avec description, cartonné, $15 00.

——— Variete ou choix d'ornements tires des œuvres des maitres des seizieme, dix septieme et dix-huitieme siecles. 1 vol. in fol. de 72 planches, avec description, cartonné, $12 50.

Lecount's Practical Treatise on Railways. 8vo. cloth, plates, $2 75.

Lectures on Subjects connected with Prophecy, delivered at the request of the Edinburgh Association for Promoting the Study of Prophecy. 12mo. cloth, $1 00. Edin. 1843.

——— on Painting, by the Royal Academicians, Barry, Opie, and Fuseli. Edited, with Notes, by R. N. Warner. 12mo. cloth, $1 25. London, 1848.

Lee, (R.) Clinical Midwifery; comprising the Histories of 545 Cases of Difficult, Preternatural, and Complicated Labor. 12mo. cloth, $1 00. Philadelphia, 1849.

——— Researches on the Pathology and Treatment of some of the most important Diseases of Women. 8vo. cloth, $2 00. Lond. 1833.

——— (Edwin.) Animal Magnetism and Homœopathy; with Notes illustrative of the Influence of the Mind on the Body. 12mo. cloth, $1 50. London, 1843.

——— (Samuel.) An Inquiry into the Nature, Progress, and End of Prophecy, in Three Books. I. On the Covenants. II. An Exposition of the Visions of the Prophet Daniel. III. An Exposition of the Revelation of St. John. With Preface and Introduction. 8vo. cloth, $4 00. Cambridge, 1849.

——— (Mrs. R., formerly Mrs. J. E. Bowditch.) Taxidermy; or, the Art of Collecting, Repairing, and Mounting Objects of Natural History. For the use of Museums and Travellers. Sixth edition, improved, with an Account of a Visit to Walton Falls, and Mr. Waterton's Method of Preserving Animals. Foolscap 8vo. with wood-cuts, cloth, $3 00. London.

Leeds, (W. H.) Illustrations of the Public Buildings of London. 2 vols. 8vo. half mor. gilt tops, 165 Engravings, $19 00. London.

——— Rudimentary Architecture for Beginners. The Orders and their Asthetic Principles. 12mo. cloth, 25 cents. London, 1849.

Lefevre, (M. A.) D'Asthme, Recherches Medicalés sur la Nature, les Causes et le Traitement de cette Maladie. 8vo. paper, 75 cents. Paris, 1847.

——— (Sir George.) An Apology for the Nerves; or, their Influence and Importance in Health and Disease. Cr. 8vo. cloth, $2 50. London, 1844.

Legrew, (James.) A Few Remarks on the Sculpture of the Nations referred to in the Old Testament, deduced from an Examination of some of their Idols. 12mo. cloth, $1 25. London, 1845.

Leibnitz. Œuvres, édition amendée Jacques. 2 vols. 12mo. paper, $2 00. Paris.

Leichhardt, (Dr. Ludwig.) Journal of an Overland Expedition in Australia, from Moreton Bay to Port Essington, a distance of three thousand miles, during the Years 1844–45. $4 00. London, 1847.

Leighton, (Archbishop.) The Whole Works; with a Memoir, by Aikman. 8vo. cloth, $2 00. Edinburgh, 1840.

——— with Life, by Rev. J. Pearson. Portrait, 2 vols. 8vo. cloth, $5 00; calf, $7 50. London, 1846.

——— Commentary on Peter; with Life, by Pearson. Complete in one thick handsomely printed volume, 8vo. portrait, extra cloth, $2 75. 1846.

Le Keux's Memorials of Cambridge. 2 vols. 4to. $25 00. London, 1842.

——— Memorials of Oxford. Text by Dr. Ingram. 2 vols. 4to. $25 00. Lond. 1834–7.

Leland, (John, D. D.) The Divine Authority of the Old and New Testaments asserted. 8vo. cloth, $2 50. London, 1837.

——— The Advantage and Necessity of the Christian Revelation shown from the State of Religion in the Ancient Heathen World. 2 vols. 8vo. calf, $3 50. Philadelphia, 1818.

——— View of the Principal Deistical Writers that have appeared in England, etc. 8vo. cloth, $2 50. London, 1837.

Le Monde. Histoire de tous les peuples. Grèce et Italie, France, Allemagne. Prusse, etc., Russie, Pologne, etc., Terre Sainte. Angleterre, Chine, Amerique et Oceanie, Espagne. 10 vol. in 8, demi veau, $15 00. Paris, 1844–46.

Lemon, (Mark.) The Enchanted Doll; a Fairy Tale for Little People, with Illustrations by Richard Doyle. 12mo. boards, $1 00. London, 1849.

Lempriere, (T.) A Classical Dictionary; containing a copious Account of all the Proper Names mentioned in Ancient Authors; with Value of Coins, Weights, and Measures used amongst the Greeks and Romans, and a Chronological Table. Twentieth edition, corrected. 8vo. cloth, $2 75. London.

——— Classical Dictionary. Miniature edition. One very thick vol. 18mo. cloth lettered, neatly bound, $1 37. 1845.

——— (F. D.) Lectures upon the Collects of the Book of Common Prayer. 8vo. cloth, $3 50. London, 1845.

Lenoir, (A.) Nouvelle Collection D'Arabesques propres a la Décoration des Apartemens; dessinées à Rome, par L. Poussin et centres célèbres artistes. 4to. cloth, $3 25.

Leone, (The Abbate.) The Jesuit Conspiracy. The Secret Plan of the Order. 12mo. cloth, $3 00. London, 1848.

Lequeux. Manuale Compendium Juris Canonici ad usum seminariorum juxta temporum circumstantias accommodatum. 4 vols. 12mo. $4 50. Paris, 1843

Lerebour, (N. P.) Treatise on Photography; containing the latest Discoveries and Improvements appertaining to the Daguerreotype. Translated by J. L. Egerton. Post 8vo. cloth, $2 25. London, 1843.

Le Sage. Gil Blas de Santillane, precede d'une notice sur l'auteur, par M. Charles Nodier; ornée de 600 dessins par Gigoux, graves sur bois et imprimes dans le texte. 1 vol. grand in 8, $4 50.

——— Histoire de Gil Blas de Santillane. 12mo. broché, $1 00; half mor. $1 75. Paris, 1847.

Les Hindoos, ou Description de leurs Mœurs, Coutumes, et Ceremonies. Par Baltarand Solryns. 4 large folio vols. with several hundred colored plates, $150 00. Paris, 1808.

Leslie, (Rev. Charles.) The Theological Works of. 7 vols. 8vo. cloth, $17 50. Oxford, 1832.

——— (John.) Rudiments of Plane Geometry, including Geometrical Analysis and Plane Geometry. 8vo. boards, $1 37. Edin. 1828.

——— (Miss.) Directions for Cookery in its various branches. 12mo. sheep, $1 00. Philadelphia, 1848.

——— The House-Book; or, a Manual of Domestic Economy for Town and Country. 12mo. sheep, $1 00. Philadelphia, 1845.

Lester, (C. Edwards.) The Artists of America; a series of Biographical Sketches of American Artists, with portraits and designs on steel. 8vo. cloth, $1 25. New York, 1846.

Letters on Entomology, intended for the Amusement and Instruction of Young Persons. 12mo. half bound, colored plates, $1 75. London, 1825.

Leverton-Donaldson. Collection des exemples les plus estimés des portes monumentales de la Grece et de l'Italie, mesurés et dessinés exprès pour cet ouvrage. 1 vol. in 4, de 86 planches, avec texte, $4 00.

Levy, (Michel.) Traité d'Hygiene publique et Privée. 2 vols. 8vo. paper, $3 63. Paris, 1844.

Lewes, (G. H.) The Life of Maximilien Robespierre; with Extracts from his Unpublished Correspondence. Post 8vo. cloth, $2 75. London, 1849.

——— American edition, $1 00. Phila. 1849.

Lewis' Illustrations of Kilpeck Church, with an Essay on Ecclesiastical Design. Imp. 4to. $12 50.

——— Early Fonts of England; containing Illustrations of the Font at Little Walsingham Church, Norfolk. 4to. $6 50. London.

——— (W.) A Treatise on the Game of Chess; containing an Introduction to the Game, and an Analysis of the various Openings of Games, with several new Modes of Attack and Defence, to which are added 25 new Chess Problems. 8vo. cloth, $4 87. London, 1844.

——— (G. C.) An Essay on the Influence of Authority in Matters of Opinion. 8vo. $3 00. London, 1849.

Lexicon. A new Hebrew-English Lexicon; containing all the Hebrew and Chaldee Words in the Old Testament Scriptures, with their Meanings in English. 12mo. cloth, $1 75. London, 1844.

Library of the Fathers of the Holy Catholic Church, anterior to the Division of the East and West. Translated by Members of the English Church.

VOLUMES PUBLISHED.

1. St. Augustine's Confessions. Third edition, $2 50.
2. St. Cyril's Lectures. Third edition, $3 00.
3. St Cyprian's Treatises, $3 00.
4 and 5. St. Chrysostom on 1 Corinthians. 2 vols. $5 00.
6. St. Chrysostom on Galatians and Ephesians, $3 00.
7. St. Chrysostom on Romans, $4 25.
8. St. Athanasius against the Arians, $2 50.
9. St. Chrysostom, Homilies on the Statues, $3 50.
10. Tertullian, vol. 1, $4 50.
11. St. Chrysostom, Homilies on St. Matthew, Part I. $3 50.
12. St. Chrysostom, Homilies on 1 and 2 Timothy, Titus, and Philemon, $3 50.
13. St. Athanasius' Historical Tracts, $3 00.
14. St. Chrysostom, Homilies on Philippians, &c. $4 50.
15. St. Chrysostom, Homilies on St. Matthew, Part II. $3 50.
16. St. Augustine's Sermons, vol. 1, $4 25.
17. St. Cyprian's Epistles, $3 50.
18. St. Gregory the Great, Morals on the Book of Job, vol. 1, $4 50.
19. St. Athanasius against the Arians, Part II. $3 00.
20. St. Augustine's Sermons, vol. 2, $4 25.
21. St. Gregory the Great, Morals, &c. vol. 2, $4 50.
22. St. Augustine's Short Treatises, $4 75.
23. St Gregory the Great, Morals, &c. vol. 3, Part I. $3 00.
24. St. Augustine on the Psalms, vol. 1, $3 00.
25. St Augustine on the Psalms, vol. 2, $3 00.
26. St. Augustine on St. John, vol. 1, $4 25.

BIBLIOTHECA PATRUM.

S. Augustini Confessiones (Latin Text), $2 75.

S. Chrysostomi Homiliæ in Matthæum (Greek Text), cum notis edit. F. Field, 3 vols. $12 00.

S. Chrysostomi Homiliæ in S. Pauli Epist. ad Corinthios, (the Greek Text,) 2 vols. $7 50.

Libri, (M.) Reponse de, au Rapport de M. Bouchy. 8vo. broché, 25 cents. Paris, 1848.

Liebig, (J.) Annual Report of the Progress of Chemistry and the Allied Sciences, Physics, Mineralogy, and Geology. Part I. 8vo. paper, $1 50. London, 1849.

——— Researches on the Chemistry of Food and the Motion of the Juices. 12mo. cloth, 75 cents. New York.

——— Chemistry and Physics in Relation to Physiology and Pathology. 8vo. cloth, $1 00. London.

——— Animal Chemistry; or, Chemistry in its Application to Physiology and Pathology. Edited by Gregory. 12mo. paper, 50 cents. New York, 1848.

——— Chemistry in its Applications to Agriculture and Physiology. 12mo. cloth, $1 00. New York.

——— Familiar Letters on Chemistry and its Relation to Commerce, Physiology, and Agriculture. 12mo. cloth, 25 cents. New York.

——— Agricultural Chemistry; or. Chemistry in its Applications to Agriculture and Physiology. Edited by Playfair and Gregory. 12mo. paper, 75 cents; cloth, $1 00. N. York, 1848.

Life Assurance, Friendly Societies, and Savings' Banks, by A. Burt. 8vo. cloth, $2 25. London, 1849.

Life in California during a Residence of Several Years in that Territory. 12mo. cloth, $1 00. New York.

Ligori, (St. A. M.) Compendium Theologiæ Moralis sive Medulla Theologiæ Moralis Hermanni Busembaum, Societatis Jesu. 2 vols. $2 25.

Lindley, (John.) Flora Medica; a Botanical Account of the most important Plants used in Medicine in different parts of the World. 8vo. cloth, $5 50.

——— (G.) Guide to Orchard and Kitchen Garden: or, an Account of the most valuable Fruits and Vegetables cultivated in Great Britain, with Calendars of the Work required in the Orchard and Kitchen Garden during every Month in the Year. Edited by John Lindley. 8vo. boards, $4 75. London.

——— An Introduction to Botany, with six copper-plates and numerous wood engravings. Fourth edition, with corrections and numerous additions. 2 vols. 8vo. cloth, $6 50. London, 1848.

——— Pomologia Britannica: or, Figures and Descriptions of the most important Varieties of Fruit cultivated in Great Britain. 3 vols. half calf, plates beautifully colored after Nature, $27 00. London, 1841.

——— and **Hutton,** (Wm.) The Fossil Flora of Great Britain; or, Figures and Descriptions of the Vegetable Remains found in a Fossil State in this Country. 3 vols. 8vo. calf, illustrated with numerous plates, $30 00. London, 1831–33.

——— Medical and Œconomical Botany. 8vo. cloth, with numerous illustrations, $2 00. London, 1849.

——— Elements of Botany, Structural and Physiological. 8vo. cloth, numerous wood-cuts, $3 50. London, 1848.

——— The Theory of Horticulture; or, an Attempt to explain the Principal Operations of Gardening upon Physiological Principles. 8vo. with illustrations on wood, cloth, $3 50. Lond.

——— A Synopsis of the British Flora; arranged according to the Natural Orders. Third edition, with numerous additions, corrections, and improvements. 12mo. cloth, $3 25. Lond.

——— (J.) The Vegetable Kingdom; or, the Structure, Classification, and Uses of Plants. 8vo. cloth, 500 engravings, $6 50. Lond. 1846.

Lingard, (John, D. D.) The History and Antiquities of the Anglo-Saxon Church. 2 vols. 8vo. cloth, $7 00. London, 1845.

——— A History of England from the First Invasion by the Romans to the Commencement of the Reign of William III. 13 vols. 12mo. cloth, portraits and vignettes, $17 00. London, 1844.

Lindsay, (Lord.) Lives of the Lindsays; or, Memoirs of the Houses of Crawford and Balcarres. 3 vols. 8vo. cloth, $12 00. London, 1849.

——— Letters on Egypt, Edom, and the Holy Land. Fourth edition, revised. Post 8vo. cloth, $2 25. London, 1849.

Linnaeus and Jussieu; or, the Rise and Progress of Systematic Botany. 12mo. 50 cents. New York.

Linwood, (W.) Anthologia Oxoniensis, sive Florilegium, e lusibus poeticis diversorum Oxoniensium Græcis et Latinis decerptum. 8vo. cloth, $4 25. London.

Lister, (T. H.) Life and Administration of Edward First, Earl of Clarendon, with original Correspondence and Authentic Papers, never before published. 3 vols. 8vo. cloth, portrait, $6 00. London, 1838.

Livermore, (A. A.) Lectures to Young Men on their Moral Dangers and Duties. 12mo. cloth, 50 cents. Boston, 1847.

——— The Four Gospels, with Commentary. 2 vols. 12mo. cloth, $2 25. Boston, 1847.

——— The Acts of the Apostles, with a Commentary. 12mo. cloth, $1 00. Boston, 1844.

Liverseege's Works, complete in 1 vol. folio, 37 plates in mezzotint, half mor. $16 00. London.

Lizars, (A. J.) Elements of Anatomy; intended as a Text-Book for Students. Thick 12mo. cloth, $3 25. Edinburgh, 1844.

Lloyd, (R.) Translation of MM. Gouin and Chatelier's Experimental Researches upon the Locomotive Engine on the Versailles and Paris Railway. 4to. paper, engravings, $2 25. London.

Locke, (John.) Philosophical Works, with a Preliminary Discourse and Notes, by J. A. St. John, Esq. Imp. 8vo. cloth, port. $3 50. London, 1843.

Locke and Dodd. Common-Place Book of the Holy Scriptures. 8vo. cloth, $2 50. London, 1842.

Lockhart's History of the Conquest of Mexico and New Spain, and Memoirs of the Conquistador, Bernal Diaz del Castillo, written by himself, and now first completely translated from the original Spanish, $3 75. 1844.

——— (J. G.) The Life of Sir Walter Scott, Bart. 10 vols. 12mo. half mor. gilt backs and marbled leaves, portraits and vignettes, $15 00. Edinburgh, 1848.

Locomotive Engines. The Student's Guide to the Locomotive Engine; containing full detailed representations of every feature of Locomotive Engines, as constructed by different Engineers. Illustrated on 72 copper-plate engravings. 1 vol. 8vo. cloth, $6 00. London, 1849.

Lodge, (Edmund.) Portraits of Illustrious Personages of Great Britain, with Biographical and Historical Memoirs of their Lives and Actions. 12 vols. imperial 8vo. cloth, an original copy, with early impressions, $45 00. London, 1835

——— Portraits of Illustrious Personages of Great Britain, with Biographical and Historical Memoirs of their Lives and Actions. Cabinet edition. 8 vols. 12mo. cloth, $10 00. Lond.

——— Illustrations of British History, Biography, and Manners, from Henry VIII. to James I., in original Papers, selected from the MSS. of the Noble Families of Howard, Talbot, and Cecil. 3 vols. 8vo. cloth, $5 00. Lond. 1838

Lombardie, (Les Monumens de la) from the Seventh to the Fourteenth Century, by F. Osten. In parts, 6 large folio plates, each $5 50.

Londina Illustrata; or, Graphic Illustrations of the most interesting and curious Architectural Monuments of the City and Suburbs of London, by Wilkinson. 2 vols. imperial 4to. 207 Plates, half mor. $31 50. London, 1819–25.

London Chemical Pocket-Book; or, Memoranda Technica, arranged for the use of the Student. 12mo. half bound, 75 cents. London.

London Interiors; a series of beautiful Engravings of the Interiors of the great Public Buildings of the Metropolis, with Costumes and Ceremonies. 50 plates, with Description. 4to. cloth, $6 50. London.

Longet, (F. A.) Anatomie et Physiologie du Système Nerveux de l'Homme et des Animaux Vertibrés. 2 vols. 8vo. paper, $4 50. Paris, 1842.

Longfellow, (H. W.) The Poets and Poetry of Europe. Royal 8vo. cloth, $5 00; mor. $7 00. Philadelphia, 1847.

——— Poems. Illustrations by D. Huntingdon, and engraved by American Artists. 8vo. cloth, $3 50; mor. gilt, $5 00. Phila. 1848.

——— Complete, cheap edition. 8vo. paper, 63 cents. New York, 1849.

——— Hyperion; a Romance. 12mo. cloth, $1 00. Boston.

——— Outre Mer; a Pilgrimage beyond the Sea. 12mo. cloth, $1 00. Boston, 1848.

——— The Estray; a Collection of Poems. 12mo. cloth gilt, $1 00. Boston, 1847.

——— The Waif; a Collection of Poems. 12mo. cloth, 87 cents. Boston, 1846.

——— Voices of the Night. 12mo. cloth, 87 cents. Boston, 1848.

——— Belfry of Bruges, and other Poems. 12mo. cloth, 87 cents. Cambridge, 1846.

——— Ballads and other Poems. 12mo. cloth, 87 cents. Boston, 1848.

——— Poems on Slavery. 12mo. paper, 25 cents. Boston.

——— Evangeline; a Tale of Acadie. 12mo. boards, 75 cents. Boston, 1849.

——— The Spanish Student; a Dramatic Poem. 12mo. cloth, 87 cents. Boston.

——— Kavanagh; a Tale. 12mo. cloth, 75 cents. Boston, 1849.

Longchene, (M. de.) Le Monde souterrain ou Merveilles Géologiques. 12mo. paper, plates, 50 cents. Tours, 1846.

Loomis, (E.) Tables of Logarithms, of Numbers, and of Lines and Tangents for every Ten Seconds of the Quadrant, with other useful Tables. 8vo. sheep, $1 00. New York.

L'Orleanais. Histoire des Ducs et du Duché D'Orleans par M. V. Philipon de la Madelaine. Illustrée par MM. Baron, Francis, &c. Royal 8vo. paper, $3 75. Paris, 1845.

Lothian, (James.) Practical Hints on the Culture and General Management of Alpine or Rock Plants. 12mo. cloth, illustrated with colored plates, $1 00. London.

Louis Le Masson, Ingénieur en chef des Ponts-et-Chaussées. Projet d'un palais abbatial pour l'abbaye de Royaument. 1 vol. gr. atlas de 17 planches, dont trois doubles, et texte, $4 00.

Loudon, (J. C.) Encyclopædia of Gardening. Illustrated with several hundred engravings, thick 8vo. cloth, $10 00. London.

——— Suburban Horticulturist; an Attempt to Teach the Science and Practice of the Culture of the Kitchen, Fruit, and Forcing Garden. 8vo. illustrated, $4 50. London.

Loudon, (J. C.) Suburban Gardener and Villa Companion. 8vo. 300 cuts, $5 50. London.

——— Magazine; embracing many valuable communications on various subjects relating to Gardening, Agriculture, &c. 10 vols. 8vo. cloth, $18 00.

——— An Encyclopædia of Agriculture; comprising the Theory and Practice of the Valuation, Transfer, Laying out, Improvement, and Management of Landed Property, and of the Cultivation and Economy of Animal and Vegetable Productions of Agriculture; including all the latest improvements, a general History of Agriculture in all Countries, a Statistical View of its present state, with Suggestions for its future Progress in the British Isles, and Supplement, bringing down the Work to the Year 1844. Fifth edition, 8vo. with upwards of 1,100 engravings on wood, cloth, $10 00. Lond.

The Supplement, separately, sewed, $1 50.

——— An Encyclopædia of Plants; including all the Plants which are now found in or have been introduced into Great Britain; giving their Natural History, accompanied by such descriptions, engraved figures, and elementary details, as may enable a beginner, who is a mere English reader, to discover the name of every Plant which he may find in Flower, and acquire all the information respecting it which is useful and interesting. The Specific Characters by an eminent Botanist; the drawings by L D. C. Sowerby. A new edition, with Supplement and a new General Index. 8vo. with nearly 10,000 wood engravings, cloth, $20 00.

The Supplement, separately, 8vo. cloth, $4 50. London.

——— Hortus Britannicus; a Catalogue of all the Plants indigenous to or introduced into Great Britain. Third edition, with a new Supplement, prepared under the direction of Mr. Loudon, by W. H. Baxter, and revised by George Don. 8vo. cloth, $9 50.

The Supplement, separately, 8vo. sewed, 75 cents.

Later do. do. $2 50.

——— Encyclopædia of Trees and Shrubs; being the Arboretum et Fructicetum Britannicum abridged; containing the Hardy Trees and Shrubs of Britain, with engravings of nearly all the Species. 8vo. $14 00. London.

A new edition of the original Work. 8 vols. 8vo. with above 400 octavo plates of Trees, and upwards of 2,500 wood-cuts, cloth, $28 00. London.

——— An Encyclopædia of Cottage, Farm, and Villa Architecture and Furniture; containing numerous designs, from the Villa to the Cottage and the Farm, including Farm-Houses, Farmeries, and other Agricultural Buildings, Country Inns, Public Houses, and Parochial Schools; with the requisite Fittings up, Fixtures, and Furniture, and appropriate Offices, Gardens, and Garden Scenery; each design accompanied by Analytical and Critical Remarks. New edition, edited by Mrs. Loudon. 8vo. with more than 2,000 engravings on wood, cloth, $15 00. London.

——— Hortus Lignosis Londinensis: or, a Catalogue of all the Ligneous Plants cultivated in the neighborhood of London; to which are added their usual prices in Nurseries. 8vo. cloth, $2 25. London.

Loudon, (J. C.) Self-Instruction for Young Gardeners, Foresters, Bailiffs, Land Stewards, and Farmers, in Arithmetic, Book-Keeping, Geometry, Mensuration, Practical Trigonometry, Mechanics, Land Surveying, Levelling, Planning, and Mapping, Architectural Drawing, and Isometrical Projection and Prospective; with Examples showing their Applications to Horticulture and Agricultural purposes. With a portrait of Mr. Loudon, and a Memoir by Mrs. Loudon. 8vo. with wood engravings, cloth, $2 25. London.

——— and **Westwood's** Treatise on Insects Injurious to Gardens, Forests, and Farms. Translated from the German of Kollar, illustrated by 60 wood-cuts. Foolscap 8vo. extra cloth, $1 25. 1840.

——— (Mrs.) Ladies' Flower Garden of Ornamental Bulbous Plants. 58 colored plates, 4to. cloth gilt, $14 00. London.

——— Ladies' Flower Garden of Ornamental Perennials. 96 colored plates, 2 vols. 4to. cloth, gilt, $22 00.

——— British Wild Flowers. 60 colored plates, 4to. $14 00.

——— Amateur Gardener's Calendar; being a Monthly Guide as to what should be avoided as well as what should be done in a Garden in each Month, with Plain Rules to do what is requisite. Numerous illustrations. 12mo. cloth, $2 50. London.

——— The Lady's Country Companion; or, How to Enjoy a Country Life Rationally. New edition, foolscap 8vo. with a steel plate and wood engravings, cloth, $2 25. Lond.

——— Gardening for Ladies, and the Ladies' Companion to the Flower Garden. Edited by A. J. Downing. 12mo. illustrated, $1 25. New York.

——— London edition, $1 75.

——— The Ladies' Flower Garden of Ornamented Annuals. 4to. cloth, 48 colored plates, $11 00. London, 1842.

——— Flower Garden of Ornamental Greenhouse Plants. 4to. cloth, gilt, 42 plates, $12 00. London, 1848.

Lover, (Samuel.) Songs and Ballads; including those sung in his Irish Evenings, and hitherto unpublished. 12mo. cloth, 75 cents. New York.

Low, (Hugh.) Sarawak; its Inhabitants and Productions; being Notes during a Residence in that Country with his Excellency, Mr. Brooke, $3 50. London, 1848.

——— (David.) An Inquiry into the Nature of the Simple Bodies of Chemistry, $3 00. London, 1848.

——— The Breeds of the Domesticated Animals of Great Britain described. The plates from drawings by W. Nicholson, reduced from a series of oil paintings executed for the Agricultural Museum of the University of Edinburgh, by W. Shiels. 2 vols. atlas quarto, with 56 plates of Animals, beautifully colored after Nature. Half bound in mor. $100 00; or in four separate portions, as follows: the Ox atlas, 4to. half bound in mor. $41 00; the Sheep atlas, 4to. half mor. $41 00; the Horse atlas, 4to. half mor. 8 plates, $18 00; the Hog atlas, 4to. 5 plates, half mor. $12 50. London.

Low, (D.) On the Domesticated Animals of Great Britain; comprehending the Natural and Economical History of the Species and Breeds; Illustrations of the Properties of External Form, and Observations on the Principles and Practice of Breeding. 8vo. with engravings on wood, cloth, $7 50. London.

——— Elements of Practical Agriculture; comprehending the Cultivation of Plants, the Husbandry of Domestic Animals, and the Economy of the Farm. Fifth edition, with alterations and additions, and an entirely new set of above 200 wood-cuts. 8vo. cloth, $6 50. London.

——— On Landed Property and the Economy of Estates; comprehending the Relation of Landlord and Tenant, and the Principles and Forms of Leases; Farm Buildings, Enclosures, Drains, Embankments, and other Rural Works; Minerals and Woods. 8vo. with numerous wood engravings, cloth, $6 50. London.

Lowell, (James Russell.) Poems. First and Second Series. 12mo. boards, $2 00. Cambridge.

——— A Year's Life. (Earlier Poems.) 12mo. boards, $1 00. Cambridge.

——— Conversations on the Old Poets. 12mo. boards, $1 00. Cambridge.

——— The Vision of Sir Launfal. 12mo. bds. 25 cents. New York.

——— The Bigelow Papers. 12mo. boards, 75 cents. New York, 1849.

——— Fable for Critics; being a Glance at a few of our Literary Progenies. 12mo. boards, 50 cents. New York, 1848.

Lower, (M. A.) English Surnames; an Essay on Familiar Nomenclature, Historical, Etymological, and Humorous. Enlarged, with several new chapters. 2 vols. post 8vo. cloth, $3 75. London, 1849.

——— Curiosities of Heraldry, with illustrations from old English writers, by Mark Antony Lower. Numerous wood engravings. 8vo. cloth gilt, $2 50. London, 1845.

Lowne, (B. T.) Lectures on Animal Physiology; or, the Physical Condition of Man. 6 plates, 12mo. paper, 75 cents. Lond. 1842.

Lowth, (Bishop.) The Works of. 3 vols. 8vo. cloth, $5 00; calf extra, $8 00. Lond. 1843.

——— Isaiah, with a Preliminary Dissertation and Notes. Portrait, 8vo. cloth, $1 75. London, 1839.

——— Lectures on the Sacred Poetry of the Hebrews, with the Notes of Michaelis and others. Portrait, 8vo. cloth, $1 75. London, 1839.

Luby, (Rev. J.) The Elements of Geometry in general Terms; with Notes, &c.; also, a variety of Problems and Theorems, carefully arranged with Analysis, $2 25.

Lugar, (R.) Sketches for Cottages, Rural Dwellings, &c. 4to. cloth, $7 25. Lond.

——— Ornamental Domestic Buildings. Imp. 4to. half bound, $10 25. London.

——— Villa Architecture; a Collection of Views, with Plans of Building executed in England, Scotland, &c. Imp. 4to. cloth, $15 00. London.

——— Country Gentleman's Architect. 4to. cloth, $6 50. London.

Lugol, (J. G.) Researches and Observations on the Causes of Scrofulous Diseases. Translated, with an Introduction and Essay, by W. H. Ranking. 8vo. cloth, $3 00. Lond. 1844.

Luther, (Dr. M.) Geistliche Lieder. 12mo. cloth, portrait, $1 25. Lond. 1845.

Lyell, (Sir Charles.) Principles of Geology; or, the Modern Changes of the Earth and its Inhabitants, considered as illustrative of Geology. 8vo. cloth, maps and plates, $5 50. London, 1847.

——— Travels in North America, in the Years 1841, '42, with Geological Observations on the United States, Canada, and Nova Scotia. 2 vols. 12mo. cloth, maps, $1 50. New York.

——— Second Visit to the United States. 2 vols. post 8vo. cloth, $5 50. London, 1849.

American edition, 2 vols. 12mo. cloth, $1 50. New York, 1849.

Lynch, (W. F.) Narrative of an Exploring Expedition to the Dead Sea and Source of the Jordan. 8vo. cloth, with numerous engravings, $3 00. Philadelphia, 1849.

——— (Miss A. C.) Poems. 8vo. cloth, illustrated by Durand, Huntingdon, Darley, &c., &c., $1 50; cloth gilt, $2 00; mor. extra, $3 00. New York, 1849.

Lyson's Environs of London; being an Historical Account of the Towns, Villages, and Hamlets in the Counties of Surrey, Kent, Essex, Herts, and Middlesex, within 12 miles of that Capital; including the Middlesex Parishes, interspersed with Biographical Anecdotes. 5 vols. royal 4to. cloth, $19 00. Lond.

McCartney, (W.) Origin and Progress of the United States. 12mo. cloth, $1 00. Philadelphia.

Macaulay, (Thomas Babington.) Critical and Historical Essays contributed to the Edinburgh Review. Fourth edition, 3 vols. 8vo. cloth, $10 75. London, 1848.

American edition, complete in 1 vol. with Lays of Ancient Rome. 8vo. cloth, $2 00; boards, $1 50. Philadelphia, 1849.

——— Miscellaneous Writings. 5 vols. 12mo. cloth, $5 00; half mor. $7 00. Phila. 1843-4.

——— Lays of Ancient Rome, with Ivry and the Armada. Post 8vo. cloth, $1 50. London, 1848.

——— History of England, from the Accession of James II. 2 vols. 8vo. cloth, $5 50. London, 1849.

——— 2 vols. 8vo. cloth, $1 50. (Harpers' edition.) New York, 1849.

——— 2 vols. 8vo. cloth, portrait, $2 00. (Butler & Co.'s edition.) Philadelphia, 1849.

——— 2 vols. 12mo. cloth, $1 25. Phillips, Boston, 1849.

——— History of England. Vols. 1 and 2, complete in 1 vol. 8vo. cloth, 75 cents; boards, 60 cents; paper, 50 cents; or in 2 vols. paper, each 25 cents. Philadelphia, 1849.

——— (J. S.) Treatise on Field Fortifications. Second edition, 12mo. with a folio Atlas of plates, $6 00. London, 1848.

——— (A.) Medical Dictionary. 8vo. cloth, $4 25. London.

Maccall, (W.) Elements of Individualism; a Series of Lectures. Cr. 8vo. cloth, $2 00. London, 1847.

M'Cheyne, (Rev. R. M.) A Basket of Fragments; being the Substance of Sermons delivered. 12mo. cloth, $1 25. Aberdeen, 1848.

M'Clellan, (G.) Principles and Practice of Surgery. 8vo. sheep, $3 50. Phila.

M'Clintock, and Hardy. Practical Observations on Midwifery and the Diseases incident to the Puerperal State. 8vo. cloth, $3 25. London, 1848

M'Cormac, (Dr.) Philosophy of Human Nature in its Physical, Intellectual, and Moral Relations. 8vo. cloth, $1 75. Lond. 1837.

——— Translation of the Meditations of Marcus Aurelius Antoninus, with the Manual of Epictetus, and a Summary of Christian Morality. 12mo. cloth, 75 cents. London, 1844.

M'Crie's Life of John Knox, with illustrations of the History of the Reformation in Scotland, Biographical Notices of the Principal Reformers, Sketches of the Progress of Literature during the Sixteenth Century, and an Appendix of original Papers. New edition, with numerous corrections, additions, and a Memoir, &c., by Andrew Crichton. 1 thick vol. foolscap 8vo. (560 pages), cloth, lettered, $1 00. 1847.

M'Culloch, (G. R.) An Account, Descriptive and Statistical, of the British Empire; exhibiting its extent, Physical Capacities, Population, Industry, and Civil and Religious Institutions. Third edition, corrected, enlarged, and greatly improved. 2 thick vols. 8vo. cloth, $12 50. London.

——— The Literature of Political Economy; being a classified Catalogue of the principal Works in the different Departments of Political Economy, with Historical, Critical, and Biographical Notices. 8vo. cloth, $4 25.

——— A Dictionary, Geographical, Statistical, and Historical, of the various Countries, Places, and Principal Natural Objects in the World. A new edition. 2 vols. 8vo. with six large maps, cloth, $24 00. The new articles have been printed separately, as a Supplement to the former edition; they comprise a full Account of the Present State of the United Kingdom, the Oregon Territory, &c. 8vo. sewed, $1 50. London.

——— A Dictionary, Practical, Theoretical, and Historical, of Commerce and Commercial Navigation. Illustrated with maps and plans. An entirely new edition, corrected, enlarged, and improved, with a Supplement. 8vo. cloth, $15 00.

The Supplement to editions published in 1844-46 may be had separately, sewed, $1 50. Lond.

American edition. 2 vols. 8vo. cloth, $7 50. Philadelphia.

——— Treatise on the Principles and Practical Influence of Taxation and the Funding System. New edition, 8vo. cloth, $3 00. Lond. 1848.

——— Treatise on the Succession to Property vacant by Death. 8vo. cloth, $2 00. London, 1848.

——— Universal Gazetteer. 2 vols. 8vo. cloth, $6 00. New York.

——— (J. H.) Researches in the Aboriginal History of America. 8vo. cloth, $2 00. Baltimore

Macculloch, (John.) Essay on Malaria. 8vo. cloth, $4 75. London.

——— On Marsh Fever, &c. 2 vols. 8vo. $9 00. London.

——— Proofs and Illustrations of the Attributes of God. 3 vols. 8vo. cloth, $6 50. London, 1843.

Maccullagh's Industrial History of Free Nations; considered in Relation to their Domestic Institutions and External Policy. 2 vols. 8vo. $6 00. 1846.

——— Use and Study of History. 8vo. cloth, $3 25. London.

Mac Farlane, (C.) Our Indian Empire, from its earliest Settlement to 1843. 2 vols. 12mo. cloth, $2 25.

——— Glance at Revolutionized Italy; a Visit to Messina, &c. 2 vols. 8vo. cloth, $5 75. London, 1849.

M'Gavin, (W.) Scots Worthies. 8vo. cloth, portraits, $3 00. Glasgow, 1846.

Macgillivray, (W.) A History of British Birds, Indigenous and Migratory; including their Organization, Habits, &c. Illustrated by numerous engravings. 3 vols. 8vo. cloth, $5 00. London.

——— Descriptions of the Rapacious Birds of Great Britain. Post 8vo. plates and numerous fine wood-cuts, cloth gilt. 1836.

Mac Gregor, (J.) Commercial Statistics. 4 vols. royal 8vo. cloth, $38 00. Lond. 1844–8.

——— Progress of America. 2 vols. royal 8vo. cloth, $8 00. London, 1847.

Machiavelli. History of Florence. 12mo. cloth, $1 00. London.

——— Florentine Histories. 2 vols. 12mo. cloth, $1 25. New York.

Mc Intosh, (C.) The Greenhouse, Hothouse, and Stove; including selected Lists of the most beautiful Species of Exotic Flowering Plants, and Directions for their Cultivation. 12mo. cloth, gilt leaves, illustrated with several beautifully colored plates, $3 00. Lond. 1840.

——— The Orchard; including the Management of Wall and Standard Fruit-Trees, and the Forcing Pit; with Groups of Fruit beautifully colored. 12mo. cloth, gilt leaves, $3 00. London, 1839.

M'Ivor, (James.) Essay upon the Versification of Homer and his Digamma. 8vo. cloth, $1 75. Dublin, 1839.

Mackay, (A.) The Western World; or, Travels in the United States in 1846–7; including a Chapter on California. 3 vols. post 8vo. cloth, $9 00. London, 1849.

——— (Chas.) History of London, with some Account of the Progress of its Institutions. 8vo. cloth, $1 50. London.

——— Memoirs of Extraordinary and Popular Delusions. 3 vols. 8vo. $12 50. London.

——— The Thames and its Tributaries. 2 vols. 8vo. wood-cuts, $7 50. London.

Mackenzie, (M.) Marine Surveying, by Horsburg. 8vo. cloth, $2 50. London.

——— (F.) An Account of the Roof of King's College Chapel, Cambridge. 4to. plates, $2 25. London.

——— (Henry.) Novels and Miscellaneous Works. 12mo. cloth, $1 25. New York.

——— Complete Works. Portrait, 8 vols. 12mo. calf, $10 00. Edinburgh, 1838.

Mackernan's Treatise on Silk Dyeing. 8vo. cloth, $2 25. London.

Mackinnon, (W. A.) History of Civilization. 2 vols. 8vo. cloth, $7 00. London.

——— (Col.) Origin and Services of the Coldstream Guards. 2 vols. 8vo. cloth, $3 00. London.

Mackintosh, (Sir James.) Dissertation on the Progress of Ethical Philosophy, with a Preface, by Rev. W. Whewell. 8vo. cloth, $2 00. Edinburgh, 1837.

——— American edition, $1 25. Phila.

——— The History of England. 10 vols. foolscap 8vo. cloth, $16 00. London.

——— History of England. 3 vols. 12mo. cloth, $1 50. New York.

——— The Life of Sir Thomas More. Reprinted from the Cabinet Cyclopædia, and intended as a Present Book or School Prize. Foolscap 8vo. with Portrait, $1 50; cloth, or bound in vellum gilt, $2 50. London.

——— Miscellaneous Works of; including his Contributions to the Edinburgh Review. 3 vols. 8vo. cloth, $12 50. London.

——— Miscellanies. 8vo. cloth, $1 75. Philadelphia.

Mc Lean, (R.) Illustrations of Teething. Royal 8vo. $3 00; colored, $3 75. Lond.

Macleod, (N.) and **Dewar,** (D.) A Dictionary of the Gaelic Language, in two parts, Gaelic and English, and English and Gaelic. Thick 8vo. cloth, $3 25. Lond. 1845.

——— Voyage of H. M. S. Alceste. 8vo. cloth, $2 75. London.

Maclise, (J.) Comparative Osteology. Folio, cloth, $15 75. London.

Mc Mahon, (B.) American Gardener. 8vo. cloth, $3 50. Philadelphia.

Mc Neile, (Rev. Hugh.) The Church and the Churches; or, the Church of God in Christ, and the Churches of Christ Militant here on Earth. 8vo. cloth, $3 63. London, 1840.

Mc Neill, (Sir J.) Tables for Cutting, &c., of Canals, Railroads, &c. 4to. cloth, $9 00. London.

——— On Railways and Locomotive Engines. 8vo. cloth, $1 50. London.

——— On the Resistance of Water in Canals. 4to. cloth, $2 25. London.

Mackness, (J.) The Moral Aspects of Medical Life, with Biographical Notices and Illustrative Remarks. 8vo. cloth, $1 75. London.

——— Dysphonia Clericorum; or, Clergyman's Sore Throat, its Pathology, Treatment, and Prevention. 8vo. cloth, $1 50. Lond. 1848.

Macnish's Modern Pythagorean; a Series of Tales, Essays, and Sketches. 2 vols. 12mo. half calf, $3 25.

Mc Sherry, (James.) History of Maryland from 1634 to 1848. 8vo. cloth, $2 00. Baltimore, 1849.

Mc Williams, (Robert.) Essay on Dry Rot and Forest Trees. 4to. $9 50. Lond.

Madagascar, Past and Present, by a Resident. 12mo. cloth, $2 75. London.

Madge, (Rev. Thomas.) Analytical View of Puseyism. 8vo. cloth, $1 38. Lond. 1844.

Madison Papers, (The.) Edited by H. D. Gilpin. 3 vols. 8vo. cloth, $9 00. New York.

Magee, (Archbishop.) Works; comprising Discourses and Dissertations on the Scriptural Doctrines of Atonement and Sacrifice, Sermons, and Visitation Charges, with a Memoir of his Life, by the Rev. A. H. Kenny, D. D. 2 vols. 8vo. extra cloth, $5 50. 1842.

Magendie, (F.) Human Physiology. 8vo. sheep, $2 25. New York.

——— Lectures on the Blood. 8vo. half sheep, $1 25. Philadelphia.

——— Formulary of New Remedies. 8vo. sheep, 50 cents. Philadelphia.

Magoon, (E. L.) Orators of the American Revolution. 12mo. cloth, $1 25. N. Y. 1848.

——— Living Orators of America. 12mo. cloth, $1 25.

——— Republican Christianity. 12mo. cloth, $1 25. Boston.

——— Proverbs for the People. 12mo. cloth, 87 cents.

Magoivar, (J. G.) On the Beautiful, the Picturesque, and Sublime. 8vo. cloth, $2 50.

Magrier's Anatomy, by Doane. 8vo. $1 50. New York.

Mahan, (Prof. D. H.) Field Fortifications; containing Instructions on the Methods of Laying Out, Constructing, and Attacking Intrenchments, &c., &c. 16mo. cloth, many plates, $1 00. New York, 1848.

——— An Elementary Course of Civil Engineering. 8vo. cloth, wood-cuts, $3 00. New York, 1848.

——— Advanced Guard Outpost, and Detachment Service of Troops, and the Manner of Posting and Standing them in Presence of the Enemy, &c. 16mo. cloth, 75 cents. N. York.

Mahon, (Lord.) Historical Essays. Square 12mo. cloth, $1 50. London, 1849.

——— Life of Louis, Prince of Conde, surnamed The Great. 12mo. cloth, $1 00. N. Y. 1848.

Main, (J.) Village and Cottage Florist's Directory; particularly the Management of the best Stage, Bed, and Border Flowers usually cultivated in Britain. Second edition, foolscap 8vo. extra cloth, bds. $4 00. 1835.

——— The Villa and Cottage Florist's Directory. 12mo. cloth, $1 00.

——— Hortus Dietica; or, Plants useful for Food. 18mo. cloth, $1 00. London.

——— Treatise on Breeding, Rearing, &c. Poultry. 12mo. cloth, $1 75. London.

Mainwaring, (R.) Gleanings on Painting, &c. 8vo. cloth, $1 75.

Maistre, (X. de.) Œuvres complètes. 12mo. paper, $1 00.

——— Du Pape. 12mo. paper, $1 00. Paris.

Maitland, (T. R.) Essays on Subjects connected with the Reformation in England. 8vo. cloth, $4 50. London, 1849.

——— Dark Ages; a Series of Essays intended to illustrate the state of Religion and Literature in the Ninth, Tenth, Eleventh, and Twelfth Centuries. Reprinted from the British Magazine, with corrections, and some additions. Second edition, 8vo. cloth, $3 50. Lond. 1849.

Maitland, (Dr. Charles.) The Church in the Catacombs; a Description of the Primitive Church of Rome. Illustrated by its Sepulchral Remains. New edition, corrected, 8vo. with numerous wood engravings, cloth, $4 25. London.

Major's Treatise on Insects prevalent to Fruit-Trees. 8vo. cloth, $3 25. London.

Malcolm, (H.) Travels in South Eastern Asia. 8vo. cloth, $1 50. Boston.

——— Memoir of Central India, including Malwa and adjoining Provinces, with the History and copious illustrations of the Past and Present Condition of that Country. 2 vols. 8vo. third edition, with large map, gilt cloth, $5 50. 1832.

Malan, (S. C.) Catalogue of the Eggs of British Birds. 8vo. cloth, $2 50. London.

Male, (G. E.) Elements of Forensic Medicine. 8vo. cloth, $2 75. London.

Malebranche. Œuvres. Nouvelle edition, par J. Simon. 2 vols. 12mo. foolscap, half mor. $3 50. Paris, 1846.

Malherbe, Rousseau, Lebrun, Œuvres Choises poetiques. 12mo. $1 00; half mor. $1 50. Paris, 1844.

Maliphant, (G.) Designs for Sepulchral Monuments, Mural Tablets, &c. 4to. cloth, 31 plates, $6 00. London, 1836.

Malkin, (B. H.) Classical Disquisitions and Curiosities, Critical and Historical. 8vo. cloth, $2 50.

Mallet, (D.) Ballad of Edwin and Emma, with Notes and Illustrations, by F. T. Dinsdale. 12mo. cloth, plates, $1 50. Lond. 1849.

——— Northern Antiquities. 12mo. cloth, colored frontispiece, $1 25. Lond. 1848.

——— (R.) Three Reports upon improved Methods of constructing and working Atmospheric Railways. 4to. paper, 10 plates, $2 25. London.

Malorti, (C. M.) Treatise on Permanent Fortification. 8vo. $7 25. London.

——— Treatise on Trigonometrical Surveying. 2 vols. 8vo. cloth, $6 50. London.

——— Instructions for Military Plan Drawing. 4to. cloth, $4 50. London.

——— Practical Field Fortification. 8vo. cloth, $1 75. London.

——— Theory of Field Fortification. 8vo. cloth, $4 50. London.

Malte-Brun, (C.) Universal Geography. 6 vols. 8vo. sheep, $10 00. Philadelphia.

Manesca, (J.) Oral System of Teaching the French Language. Fourth edition, royal 8vo. $3 00. New York.

Mangall, (R.) Historical and Miscellaneous Questions, adapted for Schools in the United States, by Mrs. Julia Lawrence. 12mo. half bound, wood-cuts, $1 00. New York, 1848.

Mangan, (J. C.) German Anthology; a Series of Translations from the most Popular of the German Poets. 2 vols. 12mo. cloth, $1 75. Dublin, 1845.

Mann, (H.) Lectures on Education. 12mo. cloth, 75 cents. Boston.

Manning, (H. G.) Sermons. 3 vols. 8vo. cloth, $4 50. New York.

Mansfield, (E. D.) Legal Rights, Liabilities, and Duties of Women, with an Introductory History, &c. 12mo. cloth, $1 00. Boston.

—— History of the Mexican War. 12mo. cloth, $1 25. New York.

—— Silk-Grower's Manual, by G. Robbins. 12mo. 38 cents. Hartford.

Mansion, (L.) Letters on Miniature Painting. 18mo. cloth, $2 00. London.

Mant, (Bp.) and **D'Oyley.** Bible. 3 vols. 4to. calf, m. e. $15 00. London.

—— Primitive Christianity exemplified and illustrated by the Acts of the Primitive Christians. 8vo. cloth, $3 00. London, 1842.

—— Book of Psalms in an English Metrical Version, with Critical Notes. 8vo. bds. $2 00. Oxford, 1824.

Mantell, (G. A.) Wonders of Geology. Edited by Prof. Silliman. 2 vols. 12mo. cloth, $3 75. New Haven.

—— Thoughts on Animalcules; or, a Glimpse of the Invisible World revealed by the Microscope. Small 4to. cloth, colored plates, $2 25. London, 1849.

—— Medals of Creation; or, First Lessons in Geology, and in the Study of Organic Remains; including Geological Excursions to the Isle of Sheppy, Brighton, Lewes, Tilgate Forest, Charnwood Forest, Faringdon, Swindon, Calne, Bath, Bristol, Clifton, Matlock, Crich Hill, &c., by Gideon Algernon Mantell, Esq., LL.D., F.R.S., &c. 2 thick vols. foolscap 8vo. with colored plates and several hundred beautiful wood-cuts of Fossil Remains, cloth, elegantly gilt, $5 50. London, 1844.

—— Wonders of Geology; or, a Familiar Exposition of Geological Phenomena. Sixth greatly enlarged and improved edition. 2 vols. post 8vo. colored plates, and upwards of 200 wood cuts, many of which are now first added, gilt cloth, $4 75. London, 1848.

—— Fossils of the South Downs; or, Illustrations of the Geology of Sussex. Royal 4to. 42 plates, cloth bds. $12 50. 1822.

—— Geological Excursions round the Isle of Wight, and along the adjacent Coast of Dorsetshire, illustrative of the most interesting Geological Phenomena and Organic Remains, with Hints to Visitors, &c. One very elegantly printed vol. post 8vo. (430 pages,) illustrated by upwards of 100 fine wood engravings, and a Geological Map of the Isle of Wight, extra cloth, richly gilt with Geological devices, $3 50. 1847.

—— Thoughts on a Pebble; or, First Lessons in Geology. Illustrated. Seventh edition, $1 00. London.

Manton, (Thomas, D. D.) One hundred and ninety Sermons on the Hundred and Nineteenth Psalm. New edition, with a Life of the Author, by Dr. Harris. 3 vols. 8vo. cloth, $6 50; half calf, neat, $7 50. London, 1842.

—— A Practical Exposition on St. James. Revised and corrected by Rev. J. Sherman. Imp. 8vo. cloth, $1 75. Lond. 1840.

The Same, with Jenkin on Jude. Imp. 8vo. cloth, $4 25. London, 1840.

Manuel de l'Architecte des Jardins, ou l'art de les composer et de les decorer in-18, avec atlas de 132 planches, $3 75. Paris.

—— du Banquier agent de change et courtier in-18, 63 cents. Paris.

—— des Fleurs Emblématiques, ou leur Histoire, leur Symbole, leur Langage, etc. avec les figures coloriées, in-18, $1 50. Paris.

—— du Fondeur en tous metaux. 2 vols. in-18, ornés d'un grand nombre de planches, $1 75. Paris.

—— du Mouleur, ou l'art de mouler en plâtre, carton-pierre, carton-cuir, cire, plomb, argile, bois, ecaille, corne, etc. 1 vol. in-18, orne de figures, 63 cents. Paris.

—— du fabricant de Papiers carton et Art du formaire. 2 vol. in-18, avec atlas, $2 63. Paris.

—— du Graveur ou Trait complet de l'art de la gravure en tous genres. 1 vol. in-18, orne de planches, 75 cents. Paris.

—— de l'Horologer, ou guide des ouvriers qui s'occupant de la construction des machines propres à mesurer le temps. 1 vol. in-18, orne de planches, 88 cents. Paris.

—— du Fleuriste artificial, ou l'art d'imiter d'apres nature toute espèce de fleurs; suivi de l'art du plumassier, in-18, orne de figures, 75 cents. Paris.

—— du Teinturer, contenant l'art de teindre en laine, soie, coton, fil, etc. 1 gros vol. in-18, 75 cents. Paris.

—— du Verrier et du Fabricant de glaces, cristaux, pierres precieuses factices, verres colores, yeux artificiels. 1 gros vol. in-18, orne de planches, 75 cents. Paris.

—— du Cordier, contenant la culture des plantes textiles, l'extraction de la filasse et la fabrication de toutes sortes der cordes, in-18, 63 cents. Paris.

—— du Distillateur et Liquoriste, in-18, 88 cents. Paris.

—— du fabricant de Tabac, son histoire, sa culture et sa fabrication. 1 vol. in-18, 63 cents. Paris.

—— du Tanneur, corroyeur Hongroyeur et Boyandier. 1 vol. in-18, orne de planches, 88 cents. Paris.

—— Chamoiseur, (du.) Maroquinier, peaussier et parcheminier. 18mo. paper, plates, 75 cents. Paris.

—— du Coloriste, contenant le mélange et l'emploi des couleurs ainsi que les differents travaux de l'enluminure. 18mo. broché, 63 cents. Paris.

—— de Blanchiment, et Blanchissage, nettoyage et dégraissage des fil, lin, coton, laine, soie, etc. 2 vol. in-18, $1 25. Paris.

—— du Bottier et du Cordonnier, in-18, 75 cents. Paris.

—— de l'essayeur de Metaux, in-18, 75 cents. Paris.

—— de l'Exploitation des mines Houilles, fer, plomb, cuivre, etain, argent, or, zinc, diamant, etc. 2 vol. in-18, $1 75. Paris.

Manual for the Study of Monumental Brasses. 8vo. cloth, 56 wood-cuts, $3 25. Lond.

—— of Gold and Silver Coins, by Eckfeldt and Dubois. 4to. half roan, $5 00. Phila.

Manual of Heraldry; being a concise Description of the several Terms used. Illustrated by 400 engravings on wood. 12mo. cloth, $1 75. London.

——— of Ancient History, particularly with regard to the Constitutions, the Commerce, and the Colonies of the States of Antiquity. Third edition, corrected and improved, 8vo. extra cloth, $3 50. Oxford, Talboys, 1840.

Manzoni, (A.) Novels. The Betrothed Lovers and the Column of Infamy. 1 thick vol. post 8vo. cloth, $1 50. Lond. 1845.

Maps of the Society for the Diffusion of Useful Knowledge; containing 112 Maps, colored, with Index. Folio, half Russia, cloth sides, $40 00. London, 1848.

Marbois, (B.) History of Louisiana. 8vo. cloth, $2 00. Philadelphia.

Marcet, (Mrs.) Conversations on Chemistry; in which the Elements of that Science are familiarly explained and illustrated by Experiments. New edition, enlarged and improved 2 vols. foolscap 8vo. cloth, $4 25. London.

——— Conversations on Land and Water. New edition, revised and corrected. Foolscap 8vo. with colored map, showing the comparative altitude of Mountains, cloth, $1 63. Lond.

——— Conversations on Natural Philosophy; in which the Elements of that Science are familiarly explained. New edition, enlarged and corrected. Foolscap 8vo. with 23 plates, cloth, $3 50. London.

——— Conversations on Political Economy; in which the Elements of that Science are familiarly explained. New edition, revised and enlarged. Foolscap 8vo. cloth, $2 25.

——— Conversations on Vegetable Physiology; comprehending the Elements of Botany, with their application to Agriculture. New edition. Foolscap 8vo. with 4 plates, cloth, $2 75. London.

Marco-Polo's Travels; greatly amended and enlarged, with copious Notes, by Hugh Murray. 18mo. cloth, maps, 50 cents. New York, 1845.

Margaret; a Tale of the Real and Ideal, Blight and Bloom; including Sketches of a Place, not before described, called Mons Christi. Post 8vo cloth, $1 00. Boston, 1847.

Marie Stuart. Lettres, Instructions et Mémoirs of. Publies sur les originaux et les Manuscrits du State Paper Office de Londres, accompagnées d'un Resumé Chronologique. Par le Prince Alexandre Labanoff. 7 vols. 8vo. paper, $6 50. London, 1845.

Marine Steam Engine, designed chiefly for the use of Naval Officers and Engineers. 8vo. cloth, $3 50. Lond. 1849.

Marivaux. Marianne. Nouvelle edition, précedée d'une notice par J. Janin. 12mo $1 00. Paris, 1846.

Markham, (Mrs.) A History of Germany from the Invasion by Marius, to the Battle of Leipsic, 1823. 12mo. $1 75. New York.

——— History of England. Edited by Miss E Robbins. 12mo. sheep, 75 cents. New York.

Markland, (T. H.) Remarks on English Churches, and on the Expediency of rendering Sepulchral Memorials subservient to Pious and Christian uses. 12mo. cloth, $1 75.

Marks, (Rev. R.) Danger and Duty; or, a few Words on Popery, Puseyism, and the Present State of the Times. 18mo. cloth, 31 cents. New York, 1844.

——— Sermons, with an accompanying Prayer to each, intended for Reading in Families and Sick Rooms. 12mo. cloth, $1 50. London, 1845.

Marlborough Correspondence. Private Correspondence of Sarah, Duchess of Marlborough, illustrative of the Court and Times of Queen Anne; with her Sketches and Opinions of her Contemporaries, and the Select Correspondence of her Husband. Portrait, 2 vols. 8vo. cloth, $3 75. London.

——— (Duke of.) Memoirs of. By William Coxe. New edition, revised by John Wade. 3 vols. foolscap 8vo. cloth, $2 62. (Bohn's Standard Library.) London, 1848.

——— Atlas to. 4to. cloth, $3 00. London.

Marmont, (Maréchal.) De L'Esprit des Institutions Militaires. 8vo. broché, $1 50. Paris, 1846.

Marriotti, (L.) Italy, Past and Present. 2 vols. post 8vo. cloth, $3 50. Lond. 1848.

Marriage Offering, (The.) A Selection from the best Writers. 12mo. cloth, 50 cents. Boston, 1848.

Marryatt, (Capt.) Poor Jack. Royal 8vo. cloth, 46 beautiful wood-cuts, from designs by Stanfield, $2 75. London, 1842.

——— Diary in America. First and Second Series. 6 vols. post 8vo. cloth, $4 50. London, 1839.

The Same. 2 vols. 8vo. $1 25. Phila.

——— (Francis T.) Borneo and the Indian Archipelago. Richly illustrated with numerous lithographic drawings and engravings on wood, from original sketches, by Mr. Marryatt. Imp. 8vo. cloth, $9 50. London.

Marsden, (Rev. J. H.) Hulsean Lectures. 8vo. cloth, $1 63. London, 1844.

Marsh, (C. C.) Book-Keeping. 8vo. cloth, 63 cents. New York.

——— (Rev. J.) The Remains of the late President and Professor of Moral and Intellectual Philosophy in the University of Vermont, with a Memoir of his Life. 8vo. cloth, $1 50. Burlington.

Marshall, (B.) Royal Naval Biography; or, Memoirs of the Services of all the Flag-Officers, Superannuated Rear Admirals, Retired Captains, &c., who have been promoted since the present Year; with an Account of all the Naval Actions and other important events, from the commencement of the late Reign, in 1790, to the present period. 12 vols. 8vo. cloth, $16 00. London, 1823-35.

——— (J. T.) The Farmer's Hand-Book; being a full and complete Guide for the Farmer and Emigrant. Illustrated, $1 00. New York.

——— (T. W.) Notes on the Episcopal Polity of the Holy Catholic Church. 12mo. cloth, $1 25. New York, 1844.

——— (G.) Silver Coinage of Great Britain to 1837. Royal 8vo. $3 75. London.

——— (John) Mode of Mounting and Working Ships' Guns. 4to. cloth, $3 75. London.

Marshall, (John.) Mode of Classification of Ships. 8vo. cloth, $2 00. London.

——— Writings upon the Federal Constitution. 8vo. cloth, $3 50. Boston, 1839.

——— (W.) The Art of Reading Church Music; founded on a Simple Explanation of the First Principles of Music. 12mo. cloth, 62 cents.

——— on Diseases of the Heart, Lungs, &c. Half sheep, $1 00. Philadelphia.

Martelli, (Chas.) The Naval Officer's Guide for Preparing Ships for Sea. 12mo. cloth, $2 00. London.

Martin, (M.) China, Political, Commercial, and Social. 2 vols. 8vo. maps, &c. cloth, $4 25. London, 1847.

——— (L. and C.) Civil Costume of England from the Conquest to the present period. 4to. cloth, 61 plates, printed in gold and colors, $16 00. London, 1842.

——— (R. M.) Hudson's Bay Territories, and Vancouver's Island. 8vo. cloth, $2 25. Lond.

——— History of the British Colonies. Royal 8vo. cloth, $3 50. Lond.

——— History, &c. of Eastern India. 3 vols. 8vo. cloth, plates and maps, $6 00. Lond.

——— Statistics of the Colonies of the British Empire. Royal 8vo. cloth, $12 50. Lond.

——— (P. J.) Geological Memoir on Part of Sussex. 4to. cloth, $6 00. Lond.

——— (W. L.) Treatise on the Ox. Imp. 8vo. cloth, $2 25. Lond.

——— (G. A.) The Undercliff, Isle of Wight; its Climate, History, and Natural Productions, with Panoramic View. Post 8vo. cloth, $3 25. London, 1849.

——— Bible Illustrations; a Series of splendid designs, with descriptions. 4 vols. folio, cloth, $30 00. Lond.

——— (W. C.) Natural History of Man and Monkeys. 8vo. cloth, $4 75. Lond.

——— (F. P.) The History of North Carolina, from the earliest period. 2 vols. cr. 8vo. cloth, $3 00. New Orleans, 1829.

——— (Montgomery.) British Colonial Library; forming a popular and Authentic Description of all the Colonies of the British Empire, and embracing the History, Physical Geography, Geology, Climate, Animal, Vegetable, and Mineral Kingdoms, Government, Finance, Military Defence, Commerce, Shipping, Monetary System, Religion, Population, White and Colored, Education and the Press, Emigration, Social State, &c., of each Settlement. Founded on Official and Public Documents, furnished by Government, the Hon. East India Company, &c. Illustrated by original maps and plates. 10 vols. foolscap 8vo. extra cloth, boards, $8 00. 1848.

CONTENTS.

Vol. I The Canadas, Upper and Lower.
Vol. II. New South Wales, Van Dieman's Land, Swan River, and South Australia.
Vol. III. The Cape of Good Hope, Mauritius, and Seychelles. New and enlarged edition, just published.
Vol. IV. The West Indies. Vol. I. Jamaica, Honduras, Trinidad, Tobago, Granada, the Bahamas, and the Virgin Isles.
Vol. V. The West Indies. Vol. II. British Guiana, Barbadoes, St. Lucia, St Vincent's, Demerara, Essequibo, Berbice, Anguilla, Tortola, St. Kitt's, Barbuda, Antigua, Montserrat, Dominica, and Nevis.
Vol. VI Nova Scotia, New Brunswick, Cape Breton, Prince Edward's Isle, the Bermudas, Newfoundland, and Hudson's Bay.
Vol. VII Gibraltar, Malta, the Ionian Islands, &c.
Vol. VIII. The East Indies. Vol I. containing Bengal, Madras, Bombay, Agra, &c.
Vol. IX. Ditto, Vol. II.
Vol. X. British Possessions in the Indian and Atlantic Oceans, viz.: Ceylon, Penang, Malacca, Singapore, Sierra Leone, the Gambia, Cape Coast Castle, Accra, the Falkland Islands, St. Helena, and Ascension.

Martineau, (Harriet.) Tales. Life in the Wilds; Hill and the Valley; Brooke and Brooke Farm; Briery Creek; Three Ages; Farrers of Budge Row; Moral of many Fables; Charmed Sea; Berkeley the Farmer, parts 1 and 2; Demerara; Ella of Garveloch; Weal and Woe in Garveloch; Homes Abroad; For Each and for All; French Wines and Politics; Vanderput and Snoek; Loom and the Lugger, 2 parts; Manchester Strike; Cousin Marshall; Ireland; Sowers not Reapers; Cinnamon and Pearls; Tales of the Tyne. 8 vols. 16mo. cloth, gilt, $6 00. London.

——— The History of England during the Thirty Years' Peace, 1814–1846, plates; being the Continuation of Knight's Pictorial History. Vol. 1, imp. 8vo. $7 00. Lond. 1849.

——— Eastern Life, Past and Present. 12mo. cloth, $1 25. Philadelphia, 1848.

——— Household Education. 12mo. cloth, 75 cents. Philadelphia, 1849.

——— Forest and Game Law Tales. 3 vols. 12mo. cloth gilt, $1 75. London, 1848.

——— Life in the Sick-Room, with an Introduction, by E. L. Follen. 12mo. cloth, 75 cents. Boston, 1845.

——— (James.) Endeavors after the Christian Life. 2 vols. 12mo. cloth, $4 50. Lond. 1849.

——— Rationale of Religious Enquiry. 12mo. cloth, $1 25. Lond.

Marvel, (Ik.) Fresh Gleanings; or, a New Sheaf from the Old Fields of Continental Europe. 12mo. cloth, $1 25. New York.

Maskell, (Rev. Wm.) The Ancient Liturgy of the Church of England, according to the uses of Sarum, Bangor, York, and Hereford, and the Modern Roman Liturgy. 8vo. cloth, $4 00. London, Pickering, 1846.

——— Holy Baptism; a Dissertation. 8vo. cloth, $4 75. London, 1848.

——— Monumenta Ritualia Ecclesiæ Anglicanæ 2 vols. 8vo. cloth, $8 00. Pickering, 1846

Mason, (R.) The Gentleman's New Pocket Farrier; comprising a general Description of the Noble and Useful Animal, the Horse, with an Essay on Mules, and a Supplement, by J. S. Skinner. 12mo. sheep, wood-cuts, $1 25. Philadelphia, 1848.

——— Practical Astronomer. 8vo. cloth, $1 50. New York.

Masse, (J. N.) Anatomie Synoptique ou resumè complet D'Anatomie descriptive du Corps Humain, comprenant L'Exposition succinta de toutes les Aponeroses. 12mo. cloth, $1 00. Paris, 1844.

Massilon, (John-Baptist.) Sermons; to which is prefixed the Life of the Author. 8vo. cloth, $2 00 London, 1849.

——— Sermons et Morceaux choises precedes de son eloge. 12mo. $1 00. Paris, 1845

Massinger, (P.) Plays adapted for Family Reading and the use of Young Persons. 3 vols. 12mo. cloth, $1 25. London, 1830.

——— Plays, with Notes, Critical and Explanatory, by Gifford. Portrait, royal 8vo. $3 25.

Masson, (Charles.) Narrative of various Journeys in Balochistan, Afghanistan, the Punjab, and Kalat, during a Residence in those Countries: to which is added an Account of the Insurrection at Kalat, and a Memoir of Eastern Balochistan. 4 handsome vols. 8vo. with 20 illustrations on stone and wood from drawings by the Author, and a large map, extra cloth, $7 50. 1844.

Master's Ice-Book, and everything connected with Ice. 8vo. cloth, $2 25. London.

Mathematician, (The.) Edited by W. Rutherford and S. Fenwick. Vols. 1 and 2. 8vo. cloth, each $6 00. London, 1843.

Matthews, (C.) Miscellaneous Writings. 8vo. cloth, $1 00. New York.

——— (W.) An Historical and Scientific Description of the Mode of Supplying London with Water. 8vo. boards, 19 plates, $2 75. London.

——— Compendium of Gas Lighting. 12mo. cloth, $1 50. London.

——— Historical Sketch of Gas Lighting. 12mo. cloth, $2 25. London.

——— (P.) Treatise on Naval Timber, &c. 8vo. cloth, $3 75. London.

Matteucci, (C.) Lectures on the Physical Phenomena of Living Beings. Translated by Pereria. 12mo. cloth, wood-cuts, $1 25. Philadelphia, 1848.

Maund, (B.) The Book of Hardy Flowers; or, Gardener's Edition of the Botanic Garden. 4to. cloth, $2 75. London.

Maunder, (Samuel.) The Biographical Treasury; consisting of Memoirs, Sketches, and brief Notices of above 12,000 eminent Persons of all Ages and Nations, from the Earliest Period of History. Foolscap 8vo. cloth extra, $3 00; roan gilt, $3 50. Lond. 1847.

——— The Treasury of History; comprising a general Introductory Outline of Universal History, Ancient and Modern, and a Series of separate Histories of every Principal Nation that exists; their Rise, Progress, and Present Condition, the Moral and Social Character of their respective Inhabitants, their Religion, Manners, and Customs, &c. New edition, foolscap 8vo. cloth, $3 00; roan, $3 50. Lond.

——— The Scientific and Literary Treasury; a new and popular Encyclopædia of Science and the Belles-Lettres; including all Branches of Science, and every Subject connected with Literature and Art. Foolscap 8vo. cloth, $3 00; roan, $3 50. London.

——— The Treasury of Knowledge, and Library of Reference, in two parts. New edition, thoroughly revised and enlarged. Foolscap 8vo. cloth, $3 00; roan, $3 50. Lond.

——— The Treasury of Natural History; or, a popular Dictionary of Animated Nature; in which the Zoological Characteristics that distinguish the different Classes, Genera, and Species, will be found, combined with a variety of interesting information, illustrative Habits, Instincts, and General Economy of the Animal Kingdom. Foolscap 8vo. with 800 engravings on wood, designed expressly for this Work, $3 00; roan gilt, $3 50. London.

Maurice, (F. D.) The Prayer-Book Considered, especially in Reference to the Romish System. 12mo. cloth, $1 75. Lond. 1849.

——— (H. D.) The Kingdom of Christ; or, Hints respecting the Principles, Constitution, and Ordinances of the Catholic Church. 8vo. cloth, $2 50. New York, 1843.

Maury's Treatise on the Dental Art, founded on Actual Experience. Translated from the French, with Notes and Additions, by T. B. Savier. 8vo. cloth, 241 lithographic figures and 54 wood-cuts, $2 25. Philadelphia.

Mawe, (John.) Travels into the Interior of Brazil. 8vo. cloth, $5 50. London.

——— Treatise on Diamonds and other Precious Stones. 8vo. cloth, $4 50. London.

Maxims and Hints for an Angler, and Miseries of Fishing. Illustrated with wood-cuts. 12mo. cloth, 50 cents.

Maximes de Guerre de Napoleon. 32mo. broché, 50 cents. Bruxelles, 1837.

Maximilian, (Prince.) Travels in Brazil in the Years 1815, '16, '17. 4to. cloth, $7 50. London, 1843.

Maxwell, (W. H.) Field-Book; being a complete Dictionary of Field Sports. Illustrated with numerous spirited wood-cuts. 8vo. cloth, $7 50. London.

——— (J. S.) Czar, his Court and People. 12mo. cloth, $1 00. New York, 1848.

——— Life of the Duke of Wellington. 3 handsome vols. 8vo. embellished with numerous highly finished line engravings by Cooper and other eminent artists, consisting of battle pieces, portraits, military plans, and maps; besides a great number of fine wood engravings. Elegant, in gilt cloth, $10 75. 1841.

May, (Sir J.) Observations on Mode of Attack, &c. of Heavy Artillery. 8vo. cloth, $1 75. London.

——— (C.) American Female Poets, with Biographical and Critical Notices. Cr. 8vo. cloth, $2 00. Philadelphia, 1848.

——— (R. C.) New Method of Setting out Railway Curves. 12mo. 75 cents. London.

Maycock, (J. D.) Flora and Geology of Barbadoes. 8vo. cloth, $5 50. London.

Mayer, (Brantz.) A History of the Mexican War, with a View of the Causes that led to it.

——— (J.) The Sportsman's Directory, and Park and Gamekeeper's Companion. 12mo. cloth, $1 25.

Mayhew, (Brothers.) The Magic of Kindness; or, the Wondrous Story of the Good Huan. Illustrated by Cruikshank and Kenny Meadows. 12mo. cloth gilt, $1 75. London, 1849.

The Same. 12mo. cloth, 50 cents. New York, 1849.

——— (Edward.) On the Horse's Mouth; showing the Age by the Teeth, &c. Colored engravings. 8vo. cloth, $3 25. Lond. 1849.

Mayne, (Capt.) Military Reconnoissance. 8vo. boards, $1 75. London.

——— (John.) A Dispensatory and Therapeutical Remembrancer, &c. Revised, with the Addition of the Formulæ of the United States Pharmacopœia, by R. S. Griffith. 12mo. cloth, $1 00. Philadelphia, 1848.

Mayo, (E.) Lessons on Objects as taught in the Pestalozzian Schools. 12mo. boards, $1 00. London.

——— Lessons on Shells. 12mo. boards, $1 75. London.

——— (H.) On the Nervous System. 12mo. cloth, $1 00. New York.

——— (W. S.) Kaloolah; or, Journeyings to the Djébel Kumri. 12mo. cloth, with two fine and spirited illustrations, by Darley. Second edition, $1 50. New York, 1849.

——— (Herbert.) Letters on the Truths contained in Popular Superstitions. Post 8vo. cloth, $1 50. Frankfort, 1849.

Meason, (G. L.) Landscape Architecture of Italian Painters. 4to. $25 00. Lond.

Meckel, (J. F.) Manual of Anatomy. 3 vols. 8vo. sheep, $5 00. Phila. 1832.

Mechanical Problems, adapted to the Course of Reading pursued in the University of Cambridge. 8vo. boards, $1 75. London, 1828.

Medhurst, (W. H.) Chinese Dictionary; (Hek-keen dialect.) Royal 4to. $13 00. London.

——— Japanese and English Vocabulary. 8vo. cloth, $3 00. London.

Medwin, (T.) Angler in Wales; or, Days and Nights of Sportsmen. 2 vols. 8vo. cloth, $4 00. London.

Meikle, (J.) The Traveller; or, Meditations on various Subjects. Written on board a Man-of-War. 12mo. cloth, 87 cents. Aberdeen, 1844.

Meigs, (C.) Females and their Diseases. 8vo. sheep, $3 50. Phila. 1848.

——— Puerperal Fevers and Cural Plebitis. 12mo. sheep, $1 75. Philadelphia.

——— Velpeau's Midwifery. 8vo. sheep, $3 50. Philadelphia.

——— (J. F.) Practical Treatise on Diseases of Children. 12mo. sheep, $1 50. Phila. 1848.

——— (Charles D.) Obstetrics; the Science and the Art. With 120 illustrations. 8vo. $3 50. Phila. 1849.

Mellen, (G.) Book of the United States, its Geography, History, Government, &c. 8vo. $2 75. Hartford.

Mellingen on Management and Treatment of the Insane. 12mo. 75 cents. Phila. 1841.

Melville, (Herman.) Typee; a Peep at Polynesian Life during a Four Months' Residence in a Valley of the Marquesas. 12mo. cloth, $1 00. New York.

——— Omoo; or, a Narrative of Adventures in the South Seas. 12mo. cloth, $1 25. New York, 1847.

——— Mardi, and the Voyage thither. 2 vols. 12mo. cloth, $1 75. New York, 1849.

Memoirs of the Kit Cat Club, with Kneller's portraits. Royal 4to. $25 00. London.

——— of the Generals, Commodores, and other Commanders of the American Revolution. Royal 8vo. cloth, $3 50.

——— of the Geological Society of Great Britain. 2 vols. royal 8vo. cloth, plates, $19 00. London, 1847–8.

Memoirs of Jeanne d'Arc, surnamed La Pucelle d'Orleans; with the History of her Times. Post, 2 vols. 12mo. half calf, neat, $5 00. London, 1824.

Memoria Technica; or, the Art of Abbreviating Difficult Studies. 12mo. boards, 50 cents. Boston, 1849.

Memorial de l'Officier du Genie ou recueil de Memoires, Experiences, Observations, et Procédés Géneraux propres a perfectionner les Fortifications et les Constructiones Civiles et Militaires. 8 vols. 8vo. paper, $16 00. Liege, 1844.

——— de l'Artillerie ou recueil Memoires, Expériences, Observations et procédés relatifs au service de l'artillerie, redigé par les soins du Comité avec l'approbation du Ministre de la Guerre. 5 vols. 8vo. broché, $10 00. Bruxelles, 1839.

Memorials of the Rebellion of 1569. 8vo. cloth, portrait, $5 50. Lond. 1844.

Memoires de Caussidere ex-Prefet de Police et representant du Peuple. 2 vols. 8vo. paper, $3 50. Paris, 1849.

MEMOIRES DE L'INSTITUT NATIONAL DES SCIENCES ET DES ARTS.

Sciences Physiques et Mathematiques, 14 vols. Litterature et Beaux Arts, 5 vols. Sciences Morales et Politiques, 5 vols. Base du Systeme Metrique, 3 vols. Savants Etrangers, vols. 1 and 2. Académies des Sciences, 21 vols. Memoires presentes par divers savans, 1e serie, 2 vols. The Same, 2d serie, 9 vols. Academie des Inscriptions et Belles Lettres, 15 vols. Academie des Savans Etrangers, 1 vol. Academie des Sciences Morales et Politiques, 2d series, 5 vols. Notices et Extraits des Manuscrits de la Bibl. du roi, 14 vols.

In all 96 volumes quarto, handsomely bound, half red morocco, $350 00.

Mendham, (Rev. J.) The Literary Policy of the Church of Rome. 8vo. cloth, $2 75. London, 1830.

——— Acta Concilii Tridentini; anno 1572 et 1573. 8vo. cloth, $3 00. London, 1842.

——— Life and Pontificate of Pope Pius V. 8vo. cloth, $2 00. London, 1832.

——— An Index of Prohibited Books, by Command of Pope Gregory XVI., in 1835; exhibiting the Literary Policy of the Church of Rome, $12 75. 1840.

——— Index Librorum Prohibitorum a Sixto V. Papa. 4to. cloth, $1 50. Lond. 1835.

Mendenhall, (G.) Medical Vade Mecum. 12mo. cloth, $1 75. Phila. 1848.

Menzel's History of German Literature. Translated by C. C. Felton. 3 vols. 12mo. cloth, $3 00. Boston.

——— (W.) History of Germany, from the earliest period to the present time. Translated by Mrs. G. Horrocks. 3 vols. 12mo. cloth, portraits, $2 63. London, 1848.

Meredith, (W. G.) Memorials of Charles John, King of Sweden and Norway; illustrative of his Relations with the Emperor Napoleon, &c. 8vo. cloth, $1 75. Lond. 1829.

——— (H.) Account of the Gold Coast of Africa. 8vo. cloth, $2 75. Lond.

Merrifield's Ancient Practice of Oil Painting, Original Treatises from the Twelfth to the Eighteenth Century, on the Art of Painting in Oil, Mosaic, &c., with Notes, &c., &c. 2 vols. 8vo. $8 00. London, 1849.

——— (Mrs.) The Art of Fresco Painting, as practiced by the old Italian and Spanish Masters, with Observations and Notes. 8vo. cloth, $2 25. London.

Merimee. Chronique de Charles IX., etc., etc. 12mo. paper, $1 00.

——— Colomba, la Mosaique, etc., etc. 12mo. paper, $1 00.

——— Théâtre de Clara Gazul, etc., etc. 12mo. paper, $1 00.

——— (M. J.) The Art of Painting in Oil and in Fresco. 8vo. cloth, $3 75. London.

Merry Mount; a Romance of Massachusetts Bay. 12mo. cloth, $1 25.

Merivale, (J. H.) Poems, Original and Translated. 2 vols. 12mo. cloth, $4 00. London, 1838.

Merryweather, (F. Somner.) Bibliomania in the Middle Ages; or, Sketches of Bookworms, Collectors, Bible Students, Scribes, and Illuminators, from the Anglo-Saxon and Norman Periods, to the Introduction of Printing into England, with Anecdotes, &c. 12mo. cloth, $1 50. London, 1849.

Metcalf, (Samuel L.) New Theory of Terrestrial Magnetism. 8vo. cloth, $1 00. London, 1833.

Methuen, (H. H.) Life in the Wilderness; or, South Africa. Post 8vo. cloth, plates, $3 25. London.

Meurer, (M.) The Life of Martin Luther, related from original authorities, with 16 engravings. 8vo. cloth, portrait, $2 00. New York, 1848.

Meyer's Illustrations of British Birds; consisting of colored figures of Birds indigenous to Great Britain, with fac-similes of their Eggs. Numerous plates, beautifully colored after Nature. 78 parts, 4to. containing 327 plates, $180 00. London, 1835–41.

Meyrick's Painted Illustrations of Ancient Arms and Armor; a Critical Inquiry into Ancient Armor as it existed in Europe, but particularly in England, from the Norman Conquest to the Reign of Charles II., with a Glossary, &c., by Sir Samuel Rush Meyrick, LL.D., F.S.A., &c., new and greatly improved edition, corrected and enlarged throughout by the Author himself, with the assistance of Literary and Antiquarian Friends (Albert Way, &c.) 3 vols. imp. 4to. illustrated by more than 100 plates, splendidly illuminated, mostly in gold and silver, exhibiting some of the finest specimens existing in England, also a new plate of the Tournament of Locks and Keys. Neatly half bound mor. gilt extra, full gilt backs and edges, $60 00. 1844.

Michelet, (M.) Life of Martin Luther. 12mo. cloth, $1 00. New York, 1846.

——— History of the Roman Republic. 12mo. cloth, $1 00. London, 1847.

——— (J.) Du Prétre de la Femme de la Famille. 12mo. paper, 75 cents. Brux. 1846.

——— History of the French Revolution. Translated by C. Cocks. 12mo. cloth, $1 25. London, 1848.

Michaud. Histoire des croisades, 6e edition, revue, corrigée et augmentée par M. Poujoulat, ornes de 14 vignettes sur acier et de 3 cartes des differents itine rares des croises. 6 vol. in 8, demi veau, $14 00. Paris, 1841.

Michaux, (F. A.) The North American Sylva; or, a Description of the Forest Trees of the United States, Canada and Nova Scotia, &c. 3 vols. roy. 8vo. cloth. Illustrated with colored plates, $22 00. Philadelphia, 1841.

Microscopic Objects, Animal, Vegetable, and Mineral, with Instructions for Preparing and Viewing them. 12mo. cloth, colored plate, $1 50. Lond. 1847.

Middleton, (Thomas.) Works, (Dramatic) and Life, with Notes, by Rev. A. Dyce. 5 vols. cr. 8vo. bds. $12 50. London.

——— Life of Cicero; Letters to several of his friends, by Melmoth; Letters to Atticus, by Heberden. Complete in 1 thick vol. imp. 8vo. portrait, cloth lettered, $3 75. Lond. 1841.

Midshipman's (The) Friend; or, Hints for the Cockpit, by A. P. E. Wilmot. 12mo. cloth, 87 cents. London, 1845.

Mier's Travels in Chili and La Plata; including Accounts respecting the Geography, Geology, Statistics, Government, Finances, Agriculture, Manners, Customs, and the Mining Operations in Chili. Maps and plates, 2 vols. 8vo. cloth, $2 50. London, 1826.

Mignet, (A. P.) History of the French Revolution from 1789 to 1814. 8vo. cloth, $1 38. New York, 1827.

——— (A. P.) History of the French Revolution. 12mo. cloth, $1 00. London.

——— (M.) Antonio Perez and Philip II. Translated by C. Cocks. Post 8vo. cloth, $2 63. London, 1846.

Milburn, (W.) Oriental Commerce, by Thornton. Royal 8vo. cloth, $11 00. Lond.

Miles, (W.) The Horse's Foot, and how to keep it sound, with Illustrations. 12mo. cloth, 37 cents; paper, 25 cents. New York.

——— (E.) An Epitome, Historical and Statistical, descriptive of the Royal Naval Service of England. 8vo. cloth, colored plates, $3 00. London.

——— (Pliny.) Statistical Register and Book of General Reference. 8vo. half roan, 75 cents. New York.

——— (H. A.) The Gospel Narratives, their Origin, Peculiarities, and Transmission. 12mo. cloth, 50 cents. Boston, 1848.

——— (William.) The Horse's Foot, and how to keep it sound. New edition, with an Appendix on Shoeing in General, and Hunters in particular. Imp. 8vo. with illustrations, cloth, $2 75. London.

The Appendix separately, 75 cents.

Four casts or Models of Shoes may be had, displaying the different kinds of Shoeing, $1 00 each, or $3 50 the set.

No. 1, Shod for general purposes.
No. 2, Shod for Hunting.
No. 3, Shod with Leather.
No. 4, Foot prepared for Shoeing.

Mill, (J. S.) Principles of Political Economy, with some of their Applications to Social Philosophy. 2 vols. 8vo. cloth, $8 50. London, 1848.

Mill, (J. S.) Principles of Political Economy, with some of their Applications to Social Philosophy. 2 vols. 8vo. cloth, $4 50. Boston, 1848.

——— (Chas.) Crusades and Chivalry. 8vo. cloth, $1 25. Philadelphia.

Mill, (James.) History of British India. 6 vols. 8vo. cloth, $25 00. London.

——— Continuation of, by H. N. Wilson. 3 vols. 8vo. cloth, $12 50. London.

——— Logic, Ratiocinative and Inductive. 8vo. cloth, $2 00. New York.

Millard, (S. W.) British Entomology. 12mo. cloth, $2 75. London.

Mills, (G.) Treatise on the Cultivation of the Cucumber. 12mo. cloth, $3 00. Lond.

——— Treatise on the Culture of the Pine Apple. 12mo. cloth, $1 50. London.

Millengen, (Dr.) History of Duelling, including Narratives of the most remarkable Personal Encounters that have taken place from the earliest period to the present time. 2 vols. 8vo. cloth, $2 75. London, 1841.

——— Ancient Inedited Monuments of Grecian Art. Imp. 4to. half mor. gilt top, fine plates, $28 00. London.

——— The Passions; or, Mind and Matter. Illustrated by Considerations on Insanity. 8vo. $2 50.

Miller, (Von.) Leçons sur la Tactique des Trois Armes Traduction par Lieut. Col. Huybrecht. 8vo. paper, with folio atlas of 32 plates, $7 50. Bruxelles, 1846.

——— (T.) Treatise on Water Color Painting as applied to Landscapes, and the Figure for the use of the Amateur and Student. Illustrated by 8 plates, imp. 8vo. cloth, $6 00. London, 1848.

——— (G.) History Philosophically Illustrated from the Fall of the Roman Empire to the French Revolution. 4 vols. 12mo. cloth, $3 50. London, 1849.

——— (J. S.) History of the Crinoidea. 4to. cloth, plates, $16 00. London.

——— (W. H.) Treatise on Crystallography. 8vo. cloth, $2 25. London.

——— (Hugh.) The Old Red Sandstone; or, New Walks in an Old Field. 12mo. cloth, $2 25. Edinburgh, 1847.

——— (W. H.) An Elementary Treatise on the Differential Calculus. 8vo. cloth, $1 75.

——— (Thos.) Treatise on Water Color Painting. Imp. 8vo. $6 50. London

——— (James.) Practice of Surgery. 8vo. sheep, $2 75. Philadelphia.

——— (Thos.) Rural Sketches. 12mo. cloth, $1 00. Philadelphia.

Millevoy. Poesies avec Notice. 12mo. paper, $1 00.

Millington, (J.) Treatise on Civil Engineering. Royal 8vo. cloth, with numerous illustrations, $2 50. Philadelphia, 1839.

Military Bridges. Description of a System of, with India Rubber Pontoons. Prepared for the use of the United States Army, by Capt. George W. Cullum. 8vo. cloth, plates, $2 00. New York, 1849.

Milizia, (F.) The Lives of Celebrated Architects, Ancient and Modern. Translated from the Italian, by Mrs. E. Gray. 2 vols. 8vo. cloth, $3 50. London.

Milman, (Rev. H. H.) Poetical Works. 3 vols. 12mo. cloth, portrait, $8 00; mor. gilt leaves, $9 00. London, 1839.

——— History of Christianity. 8vo. cloth, $2 00. New York.

——— History of the Jews. 3 vols. 18mo. cloth $1 25.

Milne, (D.) Essay on Comets, 4to. cloth, $3 25. London.

——— Plan for Floating Stranded Vessels. 8vo. cloth, $1 00. London.

——— (Josh.) Treatise on Annuities. 2 vols. 8vo. cloth, $9 00.

——— (R. M.) Poems of Many Years. 12mo. cloth, 88 cents. Boston, 1846.

Milner, (Rev. T.) The Gallery of Nature; a Pictorial and Descriptive Tour through Creation, illustrative of the Wonders of Astronomy, Physical Geography, and Geology. 8vo. plates, $5 00; mor. gilt, $8 00. London.

Miltitz, (A. de.) Manuel des Consuls. 2 vols. 12mo. broché, $2 00. Paris.

Milton, (John.) Prose Works, with a Biographical Introduction, by R. W. Griswold. 2 vols. 8vo. cloth, $4 00. New York, 1847.

——— L'Allegro. Illustrated by the Etching Club. Imp. 8vo. mor. gilt leaves.

——— Poetical Works. Edited by Todd. 4 vols. 8vo. cloth, $15 00. London.

——— Poetical Works. 12mo. cloth, plates, $2 25. London.

——— Poetical Works. Edited by Sir E. Brydges. Plates from designs by Turner. 6 vols. 12mo. cloth, $9 00. London.

——— Complete in 1 vol. 8vo. cloth, Turner's designs, $4 50. London.

——— Paradise Lost. Small folio, beautifully printed in large type, neatly half bound in morocco, and illustrated with numerous plates, by John Martin, $10 00. London, 1849.

——— Life of, by Todd. 8vo. cloth, $3 00. London.

——— Practical Bee-Keeper. 12mo. cloth, $1 37. London.

Minard, (M.) Cours de Construction des ouvrages Hydrauliques des ports de mer professê a L'Ecole des ponts et Chaussées. 2 vols. 4to. paper, plates, $6 00. Paris, 1846.

Miner, (T. B.) American Bee-Keeper's Manual; a Practical Treatise. 12mo. wood-cuts, $1 25. New York, 1849.

——— (Charles.) History of Wyoming, in a Series of Letters to his Son, W. P. Miner. 8vo. cloth, maps, $2 50. Phila. 1845.

Mingaud's Game of Billiards. Translated by Thurston. Royal 8vo. plates, $6 50. Lond.

Minifie, (W.) A Text-Book of Geometrical Drawing for the use of Mechanics and Schools. 8vo. half bound, 56 plates, $3 00. Balt. 1849.
School Edition, 12mo. sheep, $1 25. Balt. 1849.

Minot, (G. R.) History of the Insurrection in Massachusetts. 12mo. cloth, 67 cents. Cambridge.

Minutes of the Committee of Council on Education, with Appendices. 2 vols. cr. 8vo. cloth, $3 50. London, 1848.

Mirabeau. A Life History. 2 vols. 12mo. cloth, portrait, $3 50. London, 1848.
The Same, 12mo. cloth, $1 00. Phila. 1849.

Mirabeau. Œuvres, précédées d'une notice sur sa vie et ses ouvrages, par M. Mérilhon. 8 vol. in 8, demi veau, $12 00. Paris, 1834.

Miracles of Our Saviour. Profusely Illuminated on every page with elaborate Borderings of original and appropriate design, composed from the works of the Old Illuminators. Square foolscap, 8vo. uniform in size with "The Sermon on the Mount," and "Parables of Our Lord;" in a binding of novel character, designed and modelled expressly for this work, $6 50. London.

Mitchell, (J.) Treatise on the Falsification of Food, and the Chemical Means employed to detect them. 12mo. cloth, $2 00. London, 1848.

—— Manual of Practical Assaying, for the use of Metallurgists, &c.; with copious Tables, &c. 12mo. cloth, $3 00. Lond. 1846.

—— (T. L.) Expeditions into Eastern Australia. 2 vols. 8vo. cloth, plates, $12 00. London, 1839.

—— Outlines of a System of Surveying. Post 8vo. cloth, $1 50. London.

—— Expedition into the Interior of Tropical Australia. 8vo. cloth, $6 50. Lond.

—— (Colonel) Life of Wallenstein, Duke of Friedland. Cr. 8vo. cloth, portrait, $3 00. London.

—— (Colonel.) Fall of Napoleon, an Historical Memoir. 3 vols. post 8vo. cloth, $8 00. London.

—— (O. M.) The Planetary and Stellar Worlds. 12mo. cloth, 17 engravings, $1 25. New York, 1848.

—— (John.) Dendrologia, or Treatise on Forest Trees. 8vo. cloth, $4 50. London.

—— Thoughts on Tactics and Military Organization. 8vo. cloth, $3 25. Lond.

—— (T.) Translation of the Comedies of Aristophanes. 2 vols. 8vo. bds. $7 50. London, 1822.

—— The Knights of Aristophanes, with Notes, Critical and Explanatory, adapted to the use of Schools and Universities. 8vo. cloth, $2 75. London, 1836.

Mitford, (M. R.) The Works of—Prose and Verse. 8vo. cloth, $1 50. Philadelphia.

—— (Miss.) Our Village. New Edition. 2 vols. 12mo. cloth, $3 00. Lond.

—— History of Greece, by Lord Redesdale, the Chronology corrected and compared with Clinton's Fasti Hellenici, by King, (Cadell's last and much the best edition.) 8 vols. 8vo. gilt cloth, $12 00. Lond. 1838.

The Same, tree-marbled calf extra, by Clarke, $28 00.

Moberly, (G.) Sermons preached at Winchester College. 12mo. cloth, $2 00. London, 1848.

Modern Architecture. First Series. Examples of Villas in the neighborhood of London. Colored plates. Oblong folio, cloth, $6 00.

—— Second Series. Examples of Architecture in the Suburbs of London. Colored plates. Folio, cloth, $6 00. London, 1848.

Modern Orator. Roy. 8vo. cloth. Burke's Speeches, $3 00. Erskine's Speeches, $1 75. Fox's Speeches, $6 00. Pitt's (E. of Chatham.) Speeches, $1 75. Lond. 1845–7.

Modern Painters. By a Graduate of Oxford. Parts 1, 2, 3. 2 vols. 12mo. cloth, $1 87. New York, 1847–8.

Moehler, (J. A.) Athanase le grand et l'église de son temps en lutte avec l'Arianisme. 3 vols. 8vo. $4 00. Paris, 1840.

—— Symbolism; or, Exposition of the Doctrinal Differences between Catholics and Protestants. 8vo. cloth, $2 25.

Moench. Ornements d'architecture pour l'étude. 1 cahier de 20 planches in folio lithographiées, $4 00.

Morenhaut, (J. A.) Voyages aux îles du Grand Ocean contenant des documens nouveaux sur la Geographie physique et politique, la Langue, la Littérature, la Religion, les mœurs, les usages, et les coutumes de leurs habitans, &c. &c. 2 vols. 8vo. paper, $5 50. Paris, 1837.

Mofras, (M. D. de.) Exploration du Territoire de l'Orégon, des Californies et de la mer mermeille. 4 vols. roy. 8vo. paper, with atlas of maps, $25 00. Paris, 1844.

Mohr and Redwood's Practical Pharmacy; the Arrangements, Apparatus and Manipulations of the Pharmaceutical Shop and Laboratory. Illustrated by four hundred engravings on wood. 8vo. cloth, $3 75. Lond. 1849.

—— Practical Pharmacy, by Proctor. Cr. 8vo. sheep, $3 50. Philadelphia, 1848.

Mohs, (F.) Characters of the Classes, &c. in Mineralogy. 8vo. cloth, $2 00. Lond.

—— Treatise on Mineralogy, by Haidinger. 3 vols. post 8vo. cloth, $11 00. London.

Moigno. Traité de Telegraphique Electrique, renfermant son histoire, sa théorie et la description des appareils. Enriche de seize planches. 8vo. $3 00. Paris, 1849.

Moliere. Œuvres de, avec des Notes de tous les Commentateurs. 2 vols. $1 50. Paris, 1847.

—— Œuvres complètes, avec des remarques grammaticales, des avertissemens et des observations sur chaque pièce, par Bret; précédés de la vie de Molière, par Voltaire, et de son éloge, par Chamfort; avec planches. 6 vols. grand in 8, demi veau, $20. Paris, 1821.

—— Œuvres, avec des remarques grammaticales; des avertissemens et des observations sur chaque pièce, par M. Bret. 6 vol. in 8, $15 00. Paris, 1773.

—— Œuvres complètes, avec les Notes de tous les Commentateurs; edition publiée par L. Aime-Martin, ornes de 18 gravures et d'un portrait, d'apres les dessins de Desenne. 8 vol. in 8, veau, $27 50.

—— Le meme ouvrage, demi veau, $22 00. Paris, 1824.

—— Théâtre, avec des Notes de tous les Commentateurs. 2 vols. 12mo. $2 00. Paris, 1848.

Moller, (De G.) An Essay on the Origin and Progress of Gothic Architecture, $1 50.

—— (George.) Memorials of Ancient German Gothic Architecture, with a Description of each Edifice, and an Essay on the Origin and Progress of Gothic Architecture, &c. &c. 130 plates. 2 vols. folio in one, $25 00. London.

Monastic and Social Life in the Twelfth century. 8vo. paper, 63 cents. This Book furnished the Text for Carlyle's "Past and Present."

Monette, (J. W.) History of the Discovery and Settlement of the Valley of the Mississippi. 2 vols. 8 vo. cloth, $5 00. New York.

Mon Journal. Evênements de 1815, par Louis Philippe d'Orleans. 2 vols. 12mo. $1 50. Paris, 1849.

Money, (W.) Vade Mecum of Morbid Anatomy. 8vo. sheep, $4 00. New York.

Monumenta Historica Britannica; or, Materials for the History of Britain from the earliest period. Vol. 1, extending to the Roman Conquest. Prepared and Illustrated, with Notes, by the late Henry Petrie—assisted by the Rev. J. Sharpe; finally completed for publication, and with an Introduction, by Thomas Duffus Hardy. Numerous plates, folio, half-bound, $30 00. Lond. 1849.

Montaigne, (Michel Sieur de.) Works (comprising his Essays and Travels) newly translated, with Life, Preface, and Bibliographical Introduction by William Hazlitt. Roy. 8vo. cloth, portrait, $4 50. Lond. 1843.

The Same. Roy. 8vo. cloth, $2 50. Phil.

——— Essais. Nouvelle edition précédé d'une lettre à M. Villemain sur l'eloge de Montaigne, par P. Christian. 12mo. paper, $1 00. Paris, 1848.

Montagu, (G.) Ornithological Dictionary, by Rennie. 8vo. cloth, $6 50. Lond.

——— (J. A.) Guide to the Study of Heraldry. 4to. cloth, $5 50.

——— (B.) Selections from the Works of Taylor, Latimer, Hall, Milton, Barrow, South, Brown, Fuller and Bacon. 12mo. cloth, 50 cents; cloth, gilt, $1 00. New York, 1848.

Montalba, (A. R.) Fairy Tales from all Nations. Illustrated by Richard Doyle. Square 12mo. boards, $2 50. Lond. 1849.

Monteath, (R.) Forester's Guide and Profitable Planter. 8vo. cloth, $4 75. Lond.

Montesquieu. Esprit des Lois. 12mo. broché, $1 00. Paris, 1846.

——— Grandeur et Decadence des Romans, Lettres Persanes. 12mo. $1 00. Paris, 1845.

Montfalcon, (T. B.) et **Poliniere,** (A. P. I. de.) Traité de la Salubrité dans les Grandes Villes. 8vo. paper, $1 87. Paris, 1846.

Montgomery, (James.) Poetical Works. 4 vols. 12mo. cloth, portrait and vignettes, $6 00. Lond.

——— (Jas.) Poems. Edited by Griswold. 2 vols. 12mo. $3 00. Philadelphia.

——— (G. W.) Narrative of a Journey to Guatemala in 1838. 8vo. cloth, $1 00. New York.

Montholon, (Count.) Account of Napoleon's Captivity at St. Helena. 8vo. cloth, $2 50. Phila. 1848.

Montmorency. Exercise of the Lance. 4to. cloth, plates, $6 00.

Montpensier, (Mad.) Memoirs of, written by herself. Edited from the French. 3 vols. post 8vo. cloth, $9 00. Lond. 1848.

Moore, (J. B.) Memoirs of American Governors. Vol. 1, 8vo. cloth, $2 00. New York.

Moore, (Thos.) Poetical Works, complete in one volume, $4 00. New York,

——— Lalla Rookh. 8vo. cloth, extra, $5 00. Philadelphia.

——— English Edition. Square 12mo. cloth, $1 25. Lond. 1849.

——— Irish Melodies. Square 12mo. cloth, $1 25. London, 1849.

——— Life of Lord Byron 2 vols. 12mo. cloth, $2 00. Philadelphia.

——— Letters and Journal of Lord Byron. 2 vols. 12mo. cloth, $2 75. New York.

——— Epicurean, a Tale; and Alciphron, a Poem. 12mo. cloth, with 4 illustrations, by Turner, $1 00. London, 1839.

——— (G.) Man and his Motives. 12mo. cloth, 50 cents. New York.

——— Use of the Body in Relation to the Mind. 12mo. cloth, 50 cents. New York, 1848.

——— Power of the Soul over the Body. 12mo. cloth, 50 cents. New York, 1848.

——— (Rev. D.) The Christian System Vindicated against the more Popular Forms of Modern Infidelity. 12mo. cloth, $1 00.

——— (H.) Dictionary of Quotations. Post 8vo. cloth, $3 50. London.

——— (J. B.) Lives of the Governors of New Plymouth and Massachusetts Bay. 8vo. cloth, $2 50. New York.

——— Laws of Trade in the United States. 12mo. sheep, 75 cents. New York.

Moorsom, (C. R.) Principles of Naval Tactics. 8vo. cloth, $1 50. London.

Morale en Action (la) illustrée, ou Recueil d'anecdotes propres a former le cœur et l'esprit des jeunes gens; redige sur un nouveau plan, d'apres les meilleures histoires et nouvelles. 1 vol. in 8, illustre de 300 vignettes dessinées par Camille Roqueplan, Lorentz, Girardet, etc. $1 75. Paris.

——— Merveilleuse (la), contes de tous les temps et de tous les pays, illustres par MM. Cel. Nanteuil, Français, Lorentz, Seguin. 1 magnifique vol. grand in 8, orne de 150 vignettes, $3 00.

More, (Sir Thomas.) Life of, by Sir James Mackintosh. 12mo. cloth, portrait, $1 50. London.

——— Utopia; or, the Happy Republic with the New Atlantis, by Lord Bacon. 1 vol. 12mo. cloth, $1 25. London, 1845.

——— (Hannah.) The Complete Works of; with a Memoir and Notes. Portrait, 9 vols. 12mo. cloth, $10 00. London, 1846.

The Same. 7 vols. 12mo. $6 50. New York.

——— Christian Morals. 18mo. mor. gilt leaves, $1 00. London, 1841.

Moreau, (F. J.) Practical Treatise on Midwifery; exhibiting the Present Advanced State of the Science. Translated by Thomas F. Breton, M. D., and edited by P. B. Goddard, A. M., M. D. 30 plates. 4to. cloth, $10 00; colored, $20 00. Philadelphia.

——— Fragments et Ornements d'Architecture dessines à Rome d'apres l'antique, par Ch. Moreau, architecte, contenant simples fragments avec le trait à côté, chapiteaux, entablements, bases, corniches, details, frises, coupes, vases, trepieds, autels, etc. 1 cahier de 36 planches in-folio, $6 00.

Morell, (J. D.) On the Philosophical Tendencies of the Age. 8vo. cloth, $1 62 London, 1848.

——— Historical and Critical View of the Speculative Philosophy of Europe in the Nineteenth Century. 8vo. cloth, $3 00. New York, 1848.

——— Philosophy of Religion. 12mo. cloth, $1 00. New York, 1849.
The Same. $3 50. London.

——— (L. A.) American Shepherd; being a History of Sheep, their Breed, Management, &c. 12mo. cloth, $1 00. New York.

——— (Capt. B.) Four Voyages to the South Seas. 8vo. cloth, $1 50. New York.

Morewood, (S.) History of Inebriating Liquors. 8vo. cloth, $4 75. London.

Morfit, (C.) Chemistry applied to the Manufacture of Soap and Candles. 170 Engravings. 8vo. cloth, $5 00. Phila.

——— Perfumery, its Manufacture and Use. From the French of Celnart and others. 12mo. cloth, wood-cuts, $1 00. 1847.

——— Chemical and Pharmaceutic Manipulations; a Manual of the Mechanical and Chemico-Mechanical Operations of the Laboratory. 12mo. cloth, $2 00. Philadelphia.

Morgan, (J.) Lectures on Diseases of the Eye. Second edition, carefully revised and enlarged, with Notes, by J. J. France. 8vo. cloth, $5 00. London, 1848.

Morin, (A.) Aide Mémoire de Mécanique Pratique à l'usage des Officiers d'Artillerie et des Ingénieurs Civils et Militaires. 8vo. paper, $1 75. Bruxelles, 1845.

Morison, (Rev. J.) The Protestant Reformation in all Countries, including Sketches of the State and Prospects of the Reformed Churches. 8vo. cloth, $1 63. London, 1843.

——— (Sir A.) Outlines of Lectures on the Nature, Causes, and Treatment of Insanity. 8vo. cloth, portrait, $6 00. Lond. 1848.

——— Lectures on Mental Diseases. 8vo. cloth, $3 50. London, 1829.

——— Physiognomy of Mental Disease. Royal 8vo. cloth, 100 plates, $21 00. Lond. 1840.

Morrice, (A.) Treatise on Brewing. 8vo. cloth, $2 50. London.

Morris, (R.) Flora Conspicua. Royal 8vo. cloth, $12 50. London.

——— (J.) Catalogue of British Fossils. 8vo. cloth, $3 00. London.

——— (Rev. J. B.) Select Works of. S. Ephrem the Syrian. Translated out of the original Syriac, with Notices and Indices. 8vo. cloth, $2 75. Oxford, 1847.

Morrison. Memoirs of the Life and Labors of. Compiled by his Widow. 2 vols. 8vo. cloth, $5 00. London.

——— (Robert.) Chinese and English Dictionary. 6 vols. royal 4to. bds. $95 00.

——— Chinese and English Grammar. 4to. cloth, $6 50.

Morse, (S. E.) North American Atlas. Folio, half bound, $2 75. New York.

——— School Geography. 4to. half bound, 50 cents. New York.

Morton, (W. J.) Manual of Veterinary Pharmacy. 12mo. cloth, $3 00. London.

——— (Rev. James.) The Monastic Annals of Teviotdale; or, the History and Antiquities of the Abbeys of Jedburgh, Kelso, Melros, and Dryburgh. 4to. half mor. fine steel engravings on India paper, $9 00. Edinburgh, 1832.

——— (S. G.) Human Anatomy. 391 illustrations. 8vo. sheep, $8 00. Philadelphia.

——— On Pulmonary Consumption. 8vo. cloth, $3 00. Philadelphia, 1837.

——— Crania Egyptica; or, Observations on Egyptian Ethnography, derived from Anatomy, History, and the Monuments. 4to. plates, $3 50. Philadelphia, 1839.

——— Crania Americana; or, a Comparative View of the Skulls of various Aboriginal Nations of North and South America, with an Essay on the Varieties of the Human Species. Imp. folio, 78 plates and colored maps, $20 00. Philadelphia, 1839.

——— (John.) The Nature and Property of Soils, the Best Means of Permanently increasing their Productiveness, and on the Rents and Profits of Agriculture. 8vo. cloth, $2 75.

Moseley, (Prof.) Mechanics. Edited by Professor Renwick. 12mo. cloth, 50 cents. New York.

——— The Mechanical Principles of Engineering and Architecture. 8vo. with wood-cuts and diagrams, cloth, $6 50.

——— Illustrations of Practical Mechanics; being the first volume of the Illustrations of Science by the Professors of King's College. New edition, foolscap 8vo. with numerous wood-cuts, cloth, $2 50. London.

Moses' Antique Vases, Candelabra, Lamps, Tripods, Pateræ, Tazzas, Tombs, Mausoleums, Sepulchral Chambers, Cinerary Urns, Sarcophagi, Cippi, and other Ornaments. 170 plates, several of which are colored, with historical and descriptive letter-press, by Hope. Small 4to. cloth, $7 50. 1814.

Mosheim, (J. L.) Ecclesiastical History, by Murdock. 3 vols. 8vo. sheep, $7 00. New York.

——— By Maclain. 2 vols. 8vo. sheep, $3 50. New York.

Moss, (J. W.) Manual of Classical Biography. 2 vols. 8vo. cloth, $4 50. Lond.

Motherwell, (William.) The Poetical Works of, with Memoir, by James M'Conechy. 12mo. bds. 75 cents. Boston, 1847.

Moule, (T.) An Essay on the Roman Villas of the Augustan Age. 8vo. cloth, $2 00.

Mount Auburn Illustrated in highly finished line engravings, from drawings taken on the spot, by James Stillie, with descriptive Notices, by C. W. Walter. 4to. mor. gilt leaves, $7 00; cloth, $5 00. New York, 1847.

Mountford, (W.) Euthanasy; or, Happy Talk towards the End of Life. 12mo. cloth, $1 00. Boston, 1849.

Mudie, (R.) Natural History of Birds. 18mo. cloth, $1 25. London.

——— The Feathered Tribes of the British Islands. 2 vols. cr. 8vo. cloth, colored plates, $5 00. London.

Muhlenberg, (H. A.) The Life of Major-General Peter Muhlenberg, of the Revolutionary Army. 12mo. cloth, portrait, $1 00. Philadelphia, 1849.

Mulder, (G J.) Chemistry of Vegetable and Animal Physiology, with an Introduction by J. F. W. Johnstone. 8vo. cloth, 20 plates, $9 00. London, 1849.

Muller, (C. O.) Introduction to a Scientific System of Mythology. Translated by John Leitch. 8vo. cloth, $4 00. Lond. 1844.

——— History and Antiquities of the Doric Race. Translated by Henry Tufnell. 2 vols. 8vo. bds. maps, $7 00. London, 1839.

——— Francis the First. Twenty-five fac-similes of original drawings of the Costumes, Fetes, and Ceremonies of the Renaissance Period. Mounted as drawings, in folio, and colored, $63 00. London, 1841.

——— (K. O.) History of the Literature of Ancient Greece. 8vo. cloth, $2 25. Lond.

——— Ancient Art and its Remains; or, a Manual of the Archæology of Art. Translated by J. Leitch. 8vo. cloth, $4 00. Lond.

——— (J.) Embryology, with the Physiology of Generation. Translated by Baly. 8vo. cloth, plates and wood-cuts, $2 25. Lond. 1849.

——— The Physiology of the Senses, Voice, and Muscular Motion with the Mental Faculties. Translated, with Notes, by W. Baly. Illustrated with numerous wood engravings. 8vo. cloth, $2 25. London, 1849.

Mundy, (Lieut. Gen.) The Life of Rodney. 12mo. 75 cents. London.

Munsell, (Joel.) Every Day Book of Chronology and History. 2 vols. 12mo. sheep, $2 00. Albany.

Murphy, (A.) Translation of Tacitus. 8vo. cloth, $2 50. New York.

——— (E. W.) Lectures on Parturition. 8vo. sheep, $2 75. New York.

——— Arabian Antiquities of Spain, representing in 100 very highly finished line engravings by Le Keux, Finden, Landseer, G. Cooke, &c., the most remarkable Remains of the Architecture, Sculpture, Paintings, and Mosaics, of the Spanish Arabs, now existing in the Peninsula, including the magnificent Palace of Alhambra; the celebrated Mosque and Bridge at Cordova; the Royal Villa of Generaliffe; and the Casa de Carbon; accompanied by letter-press. 1 vol. atlas folio, plates, half mor. $75 00. 1813.

Murchison, (R. J.) Silurian System of Geology. 2 vols. royal 4to. maps, $50 00. London, 1839.

——— Geology of Russia and the Ural Mountains. 2 vols. 4to. cloth, maps, $50 00. London, 1840.

Murray, (H.) Encyclopædia of Geography 3 vols. 8vo. sheep, $8 00. Phila.

——— (Hugh.) Encyclopædia of Geography: comprising a complete Description of the Earth: Exhibiting its Relation to the Heavenly Bodies, its Physical Structure, the Natural History of each Country, and the Industry, Commerce, Political Institutions and Civil and Social State of all Nations. New Edition. 8vo. with 82 maps, and upwards of 1,000 other wood-cuts, cloth, $18 00. London.

Murray, (John.) Memoir on the Diamond. 12mo. cloth, $1 50. London.

——— (J.) Materia Medica. 8vo. sheep, $2 00. New York.

——— (Lindley.) English Grammar. 8vo. sheep, $2 00. New York.

——— (Hugh.) Historical Account of British America. 2 vols. 12mo. cloth, $1 00. New York.

——— (J. F.) The World of London. 12mo. cloth, $1 25. London, 1844.

——— Hand-Book of Travel Talk, a Collection of Dialogues and Vocabularies intended to serve as Interpreter to Travellers in Germany, France, or Italy. Royal 18mo. cloth, $1 50. London, 1847.

——— Hand-Book for Travellers in Switzerland and the Alps of Savoy and Piedmont. 12mo. cloth, map and plates, $3 00. London, 1846.

——— Hand-Book to Northern Italy. Thick 12mo. cloth, map and plans, $3 50. London, 1847.

——— Hand-Book for Travellers in France. 12mo. cloth, 5 maps, $3 50. London, 1848.

——— Hand-Book for Egypt and Thebes, with all the necessary Information for the Overland Passage to India. 12mo. cloth, maps, $4 00. London.

——— Hand-Book for Spain, Andalusia, Granada, Madrid, &c. 2 vols. 12mo. cloth, maps, $4 50. London.

——— Hand-Book for Northern Europe, Russia, Norway, Sweden, and Denmark. 2 vols. 12mo. cloth, maps, $7 00. London.

——— Hand-Book for London, Past and Present, a complete Guide for Strangers visiting the Metropolis. 2 vols. 12mo. cloth, $7 25. London, 1849.

——— Hand-Book for North Germany and the Rhine, Holland, Belgium, and Prussia. 12mo. cloth, maps, $3 50. London.

——— Hand-Book for South Germany and the Tyrol, Bavaria, Austria, Salzburgh, Austrian and Bavarian Alps and the Danube. 12mo. cloth, maps, $3 00. London.

——— Hand-Book for Central Italy and Rome. 12mo. cloth, maps, $4 00. London.

——— Hand-Book for Malta and the East, the Ionian Islands, Turkey, Asia Minor, and Constantinople. 12mo. cloth, maps, $4 00. London

Musaus. Legends of Rubezahl. Translated from the German. 12mo. cloth, gilt, plates, $1 00. Lond. 1845.

Museum Criticum; or, Cambridge Classical Researches, a Series of Philological Papers, Criticisms, Essays, Fragments of Greek and Roman Authors, unpublished Notes of Scholars, learned Correspondence and Memoirs, &c. by many of the most talented Critics of the University, including Bishops Bloomfield and Maltby, Professor Monk, Elmsley, Dr. Burney, Hare, &c. &c. 2 vols. 8vo. cloth, $4 75. Cambridge, 1826.

The Same, tree-marbled, calf extra, for College Prizes, $7 50.

Mushet, (D.) Papers on Iron and Steel, Practical and Experimental, with copious Illustrative Notes. Plates, thick 8vo. cloth, $9 00. Lond.

Musical Library, (The) a Selection of the best Vocal and Instrumental Music, both English and Foreign, edited by W. Ayrton, Esq. of the Opera House. 8 vols. folio, comprehending more than four hundred pieces of Music, beautifully printed with metallic types, $9 50. London, 1846.

——— 8 vols. in 4, neatly half-bound morocco, emblematically gilt on the sides, $16 75. The Vocal and Instrumental may be had separately, each in 4 vols· $4 75.

Musset, (Alf. de.) Poésies complètes. 12mo. paper, $1 00.

——— Comédies et Proverbes. 12mo. paper, $1 00.

——— La Confession d'un Enfant du Siècle. 12mo. broché, $1 00. Paris, 1848.

——— Nouvelles. Les deux Maîtresses, Emmeline, Le Fils du Titien, Frederic et Bernerette, Croisilles, Margot. 12mo. broché, $1 00. Paris, 1848.

Mutiny at Spithead and the Nore. A History of, with an Inquiry into its Origin and Treatment. 12mo. cloth, $1 25. Lond. 1842.

Mutter on Club Foot. 12mo. cloth, $1 25 Philadelphia.

Myers, (P. H.) The First of the Knickerbockers. 12mo. cloth, 75 cents. New York, 1848.

——— The Young Patroon; or, Christmas in 1690. 12mo. cloth, 75 cents. New York, 1849.

Napier, (Capt.) Florentine History, from the earliest Authentic Records to the present time. 6 vols. post 8vo. cloth, $17 00. Lond.

——— (W. F. P.) History of the Peninsular War. 4 vols. 8vo. cloth, $6 50. Phila.

The Same. 8vo. sheep, $3 25. New York.

——— Montrose and the Covenanters. Illustrated from original Documents. 2 vols. 8vo. cloth, $4 25. London, 1838.

Napoleon's Invasion of Russia; a History of. From the French of Eugene Labaume. 12mo. cloth, 75 cents. London, 1844.

Napoleon and the Marshals of the Empire. 2 vols. post 8vo. cloth, 16 portraits on steel, $2 50. New York, 1848.

——— (M.) Précis des Guerres ecrite a l'Ile Sainte Hélène sous la dictée de l'Empereur, par M. Marchand. 8vo. $1 00. Paris, 1836.

——— Maximes de guerre de Napoleon. 18mo. broché, 83 cents. Bruxelles, 1837.

——— Maxims of War. Translated from the French, by Col. D'Aguilar. 18mo. cloth, 50 cents. New York, 1845.

——— Œuvres Choises, precedes d'une etude litteraire. 12mo. broché, $1 00. Paris, 1844.

——— Gallery; or, Illustrations of the Life and Times of the Emperor, in a Series of Sketches, by some of the most distinguished Authors, with 99 remarkably clever etchings on steel, by Reveil and other eminent artists, from all the most celebrated pictures produced in France during the last forty years. Thick post 8vo. extra cloth, gilt edges, $2 50. London, 1846.

Nare's Life and Times of Lord Burleigh. 3 vols. 4to. cloth, portraits, $22 00. London, 1828–31.

——— (E.) Glossary of Words, Phrases, &c., in old Authors. 4to. $15 00. Lond. 1822.

The Same. 8vo. $7 50. Stralsund, 1825.

Narrien, (J.) Analytical Geometry, with the Properties of Conic Sections, and an Appendix. 8vo. cloth, $2 50.

——— Treatise on Architecture. 4to. paper, 23 plates, $3 25. London, 1849.

——— Elements of Geometry; consisting of the First Four and the Ninth Books of Euclid, with the Principal Theorems in Proportion. 8vo. cloth, $3 00.

——— (Prof.) Practical Astronomy and Geodesy. 8vo. cloth, $4 25. London.

Nash. Picturesque Views of Paris. 2 vols. 4to. cloth, $11 50. London.

——— Mansions of England in the Olden Time. Three Series, colored and mounted in portfolio, $63 00. London.

Nasology; or, Hints towards a Classification of Noses, by Eden Warwick. Cr. 8vo. cloth, wood-cuts, $1 50. Lond. 1848.

National Cyclopædia of Useful Knowledge. Vols. 1 to 8. 8vo. cloth, each $1 50. London

Natural History of New York State. 14 vols. 4to. cloth, colored copy.

CONTENTS.

Part I. ZOOLOGY.—Mammalia. By James E. De Kay. 4to. cloth, 33 colored plates.

——— Ornithology. By James E. De Kay. 4to. cloth, 141 colored plates.

——— Reptiles and Amphibia. By James E. De Kay. 2 vols. 4to. cloth, 79 colored plates.

——— Mollusca. By James E. De Kay. 4to. cloth, 53 colored plates.

Part II. BOTANY.—Flora. By John Torrey, M. D. F. L. S. 2 vols. 4to. cloth, 158 colored plates.

Part III. MINERALOGY.—By Lewis C. Beck. 4to. cloth, with above 500 figures and 10 plates.

Part IV. GEOLOGY.—By W. W. Mather, comprising the Geology of the first Geological District. 4to. cloth, 146 plates, some colored.

——— Comprising the Survey of the Second Geological District. By Ebenezer Emmons, M. D. 4to. cloth, 15 plates.

——— Comprising the Survey of the Third Geological District. By Lardner Vanuxem. 4to. cloth, wood-cuts.

——— Comprising a Survey of the Fourth Geological District. By James Hall. 4to. cloth, with nearly 200 Illustrations, Maps, Views, Sections, &c.

Part V. AGRICULTURE.—By Ebenezer Emmons. 4to. cloth, 24 plates, Maps and Views.

Part VI. PALÆONTOLOGY.—By James Hall. Vol. I. 4to. cloth, upwards of 100 plates.

Natural Philosophy, by the Society for the Diffusion of Useful Knowledge, with copious Indexes. 4 vols. 8vo. wood-cuts, cloth, $6 00.

Nautical Almanac and Astronomical Ephemeris. Published yearly, three years in advance, for the convenience of Mariners and Travellers. Royal 8vo. paper, per year, $2 00. London.

Nautical Routine and Stowage, with Short Rules in Navigation. By John McLeod Murphy and W. N. Jeffers, Jun. Royal 8vo. cloth, plates, $3 00. New York, 1849.

Neal, (Rev. D.) History of the Puritans, from the Reformation to the Revolution in 1686. New edition, with Dr. Toulmin's Notes. 3 vols. 8vo. cloth, $6 50. London, 1838.

——— American edition. 2 vols. 8vo. sheep, $4 00. New York.

Neale. Views of the Seats, Mansions, and Castles of England. 2 vols. 4to. 400 views, India paper, $22 00. London, 1818.

—— and **Le Keux's** Views of the Churches of Great Britain, with Historical and Architectural Descriptions. 2 vols. royal 4to. $25 00. London, 1824–5.

Neander, (Dr. A.) General History of the Christian Religion and Church. Translated from the German, by Professor Joseph Torrey. 2 vols. 8vo. portrait, $6 00. Boston.

—— Life of Christ. 8vo. sheep, $2 25. New York.

—— The Life of St. Chrysostom. Translated from the German, by Rev. J. C. Stappleton. 8vo. cloth, $1 75. London, 1845.

Neill, (H.) The Cure of Cataract, with a Practical Summary of the best Modes of Operating. 8vo. cloth, $2 00. London.

—— on the Arteries, Nerves, Veins, and Lymphatics. 12mo. cloth, $2 50. Phila.

—— and **Smith's** Compend of Medicine, Surgery, &c. 12mo. sheep, many cuts, $3 00. Philadelphia.

Neison, (T. G.) Contributions to Vital Statistics. 4to. cloth, $6 50. Lond.

Neligan, (J. M.) Uses and Modes of Administering Medicines. 8vo. cloth, $3 75. London, 1847.

—— American edition. 8vo. sheep, $2 00. New York.

Nelson's Letters and Dispatches. Edited by Sir Harris Nicolas. 7 thick vols. 8vo. (uniform with the Wellington Dispatches), cloth lettered, $21 00. 1845–46.

—— (Lord.) The Life and Naval Memoirs of. Compiled from original Documents and Authentic Sources, by Col. J. M. Tuck. 8vo. cloth, portrait and numerous wood-cuts, $1 25. London, 1848.

—— Memoirs of the Life of Vice-Admiral, by Thomas Joseph Pettigrew. 2 vols. 8vo. cloth, $10 00. London, 1849.

—— (Robert.) A Companion for the Festivals and Fasts of the Church of England. 8vo. cloth, $2 25. Oxford, 1843.

Nesbit's Practical Mensuration and Land Surveying. 12mo. cloth, $1 75. Lond.

Neuman, (H.) Spanish Dictionary. 2 vols. 8vo. sheep, $3 75. Boston.

—— Abridged edition. 12mo. sheep, $1 25. Philadelphia.

—— and **Baretti's** Spanish-English and English-Spanish Dictionary. Greatly improved and enlarged by Dr. Seoane. 2 thick vols. 8vo. extra cloth, $8 50. 1845.

—— Abridged edition. 12mo. pearl, new edition, roan lettered, $2 50. 1843.

—— **Baretti y Seoane.** Diccionario de las lenguas Española é Inglesa. 2 vols. 8vo. broché, $6 50. Paris and Lyons.

Neville, (J.) An Inquiry into the Fall Necessary in the Cross Section of Roads, and the Best Form of Cross Sections. 4to. paper, plates, 75 cents. London.

—— (W. B.) On Insanity, its Nature, Causes, and Cure. 8vo. cloth, $3 00. London.

Newbold, (T. J.) British Settlements in Malacca. 2 vols. 8vo. cloth, $7 75. Lond. 1839.

Newell, (Rev. C.) History of the Revolution in Texas and War of 1835–6. 12mo. cloth, 75 cents. New York, 1838.

New England Gazetteer, by John Hayward. 8vo. sheep, $3 00. Concord, 1839.

New Hampshire. History of, by Geo. Barstow. 8vo. sheep, $2 00. Concord.

New Haven. History and Antiquities of, by J. W. Barber. 12mo. cloth, $1 00. New Haven.

Newman, (J. W.) The Soul and her Aspirations; an Essay towards the Natural History of the Soul, as the basis of Theology. Post 8vo. cloth, $1 75. Lond. 1849.

—— (Dr. F.) History of the Hebrew Monarchy. From the Administration of Samuel to the Babylonish Captivity. 8vo. cloth, $2 50. London, 1848.

—— (J. H.) Sermons bearing on Subjects of the Day. 8vo. cloth, $3 50. London, 1843.

—— American edition. 12mo. cloth, $1 00. New York, 1844.

—— (Charles.) Practical Hints on Land Draining. 8vo. $1 00. London.

—— (E.) History of British Ferns. 8vo. cloth, illustrated by wood-cuts of the most beautiful kind, $7 50. London.

—— Introduction to a History of Insects. 8vo. cloth, $3 75. London.

—— System of Nature. 8vo. cloth, $3 00. London.

Newnham, (W.) Human Magnetism. Its claims to Dispassionate Inquiry, being an attempt to show the utility of its application for the relief of Human Suffering. 12mo. cloth, $1 00. New York.

New Testament. Translated by John Wycliffe, circa 1380, now first printed from a contemporary MS. formerly in the Monastery of Sion, Middlesex. Small 4to. half mor. black letter, $12 00. London, 1848.

Newton, (Rev. John.) Works. 2 vols. 8vo. cloth, $3 00. New York.

—— The Works of, with Memoirs of his Life, by the Rev. B. Cecil. 8vo. cloth, $2 50. London, 1840.

—— (Sir I.) Principia. Translated by A. Motte, with Life, by N. W. Crittenden. Royal 8vo. bound, $4 50. New York, 1848.

—— (Thos., D. D.) Dissertations on the Prophecies, which have been remarkably fulfilled, and are now fulfilling. 8vo. cloth, $2 50. London, 1840.

—— **and Son,** (Messrs.) List of all Patents for Inventions granted in England. Alphabetically arranged. Published annually in 8vo. cloth, 75 cents. London.

—— (W.) Display of Heraldry, with 700 engravings on wood. 8vo. cloth, $4 25. London, 1846.

New World, (The Conquerors of,) and their Bondsmen; being a Narrative of the Principal Events which led to Negro Slavery in the West Indies and America. Vol. 1, 12mo. cloth, $1 75. Pickering, 1848.

New York Gazetteer, by Thomas Gordon. 8vo. sheep, $3 00. Phil. 1846.

New York. History of, by Dunlap. 2 vols. 18mo. cloth, $1 00. New York.

Nichols, (J. B.) Illustrations of Literary History. 6 vols. 8vo. cloth, $48 50. Lond.

——— Vol. 7, 8vo. boards, $6 00. Lond. 1849.

——— Literary Anecdotes of the 18th Century. 9 vols. 8vo. cloth, $70 00. London.

Nichol, (Prof.) Architecture of the Heavens. 12mo. cloth, $3 25. Edin. 1845.

——— Neptune—being a Critical Account of the Discovery of the New Planet. 12mo. cloth, $1 75. Edin. 1848.

——— The Stellar Universe; Views of its Arrangement, Motions, and Evolutions. 12mo. cloth, $1 50. Edin. 1848.

——— Thoughts on some Important Points in the System of the World. Illustrated. 12mo. cloth, $3 75. Edin. 1847.

Nicholson, (P.) Principles of Architecture: comprising Fundamental Rules of the Art; also Rules for Shadows, and for the Five Orders. 8vo. cloth, 218 Engravings, by Lowry. Edited by Gwilt. $7 50. London, 1848.

——— Carpentry; being a Comprehensive Guide-Book for Carpentry and Joinery. 2 vols. 4to. plates, $15 00. London, 1849.

——— Architectural Dictionary. 2 vols. 4to. plates, $25 00. London, 1810.

——— Builder and Workman's Director, 141 copperplates, and numerous wood-cuts. 2 vols. 4to. cloth, $17 00. Lond.

——— Cabinet-maker's Guide. 4to. cloth, $12 00. London.

——— Art of Masonry and Stone-cutting. 4to. 43 plates, $3 50. London, 1839.

——— Treatise on the Construction of Staircases and Hand-rails. 39 Engravings, 4to. cloth, $3 50. London, 1847.

——— On Projection. Numerous plates, 8vo. cloth, $4 75. London.

——— (J.) Builder's Guide. 8vo. cloth, $2 25. London.

——— Millwright's Guide. 8vo. cloth, $2 25. London.

——— Operative Mechanic. 8vo. cloth, $9 50. London.

——— (John.) Carpenter's Guide. 4to. sheep, $5 00. Philadelphia.

——— Operative Mechanic, and British Machinist. 2 vols. 8vo. cloth, $4 50. Phil.

——— Mechanic's Companion. 8vo. sheep, $2 25. Philadelphia.

——— (F.) Practice of Drawing and Painting Landscapes. 4to. cloth, $7 50. Lond.

Nicolas, (Sir N. Harris.) A History of the Royal Navy from the Earliest Times to the Wars of the French Revolution. 2 vols. 8vo. cloth, $3 00. London, 1847.

——— History of the Orders of Knighthood of the British Empire, &c. 4 vols. 4to. cloth, many plates, $25 00. London, 1840–41.

Nicol, (J.) Manual of Mineralogy; or, the Natural History of the Mineral Kingdom, containing a General Introduction to the Science and Descriptions of the Separate Species, including the more recent Discoveries and Chemical Analyses. Post 8vo. cloth, $3 75. Lond. 1819.

Niebelungen Lied; or, the Lay of the Last Niebelungers. Translated into English verse, after Prof. C. Lachman's Collated and Corrected Text, by Jonathan Birch. 8vo. sewed, $2 25; half mor. gilt, $3 50. London, 1848.

Niebuhr, (B. G.) Lectures on the History of Rome from the Earliest Times to the Fall of the Western Empire. Edited by Dr. L. Schmitz. 2d Edition, with every addition derivable for Dr. Isler's German Edition. 3 vols. 8vo. cloth, $5 50. London, 1849.

——— History of Rome. 5 vols. in 2, 8vo. cloth, $4 00. Philadelphia.

Niles, (Hon. J. M.) History of South America and Mexico, and a View of Texas. 8vo. cloth, $2 00. Hartford.

Nimrod. Hunting Reminiscences; comprising Memoirs of Masters of Hounds, Notices of Crack Riders, and Characteristics of the Hunting Counties of England. 8vo. cloth, $4 00.

——— Remarks on the Condition of Hunters, the Choice of Horses, and their Management. 8vo. cloth, $3 00. Lond.

——— The Chase, the Turf, and the Road, with spirited illustrations by Alken and Gilbert. 12mo. cloth, $1 25. London, 1843.

Noad, (H. M.) Lectures on Electricity; comprising Galvanism, Magnetism, Electro-Magnetism, Magneto and Thermo-Electricity. A new edition, 8vo. cloth, 300 wood-cuts, $3 75. London, 1849.

——— Chemical Manipulation and Analysis, Qualitative and Quantitative. 8vo. cloth, $2 00. Phila. 1848.

Noble, (James.) The Professional Practice of Architects and that of Measuring Surveyors. 8vo. cloth, frontispiece, $3 25. London.

Nodier, (Chas.) Romans. 12mo. paper, $1 00. Paris.

——— Contes. 12mo. paper, $1 00.

——— Nouvelles. 12mo. paper, $1 00.

——— Souvenirs de la Revolution. 12mo. paper, $1 00. Paris.

——— Contes Choisies; Trilby—La Fee aux Miettes—La Songe d'or—Baptiste Montauban, La Tombe de l'homme mort. Edition illustrée de jolies vignettes. 1 vol. grand in 8, demi maroquin, $6 00. Paris, 1846.

Noehden's German Grammar. 12mo. sheep, $1 50. Boston.

Nolan, (Frederick.) The Egyptian Chronology analyzed, its Theory developed, and Practically applied and confirmed in its Dates and Details, from its Agreement with the Hieroglyphic Monuments and the Scripture Chronology. 8vo. cloth, $4 50. London, 1848.

Noland, (Robert.) The Legacy of an Etonian. Cr. 8vo. cloth, $2 87. Cambridge, 1846.

Nollekens and his Times, by C. T. Smith. 2 vols. 8vo. cloth, portrait, $7 50. London.

Norden's Travels in Egypt and Nubia. Translated by Templeman. 2 vols. royal folio, portrait and 160 plates, $20 00. Lond. 1757.

Nordheimer, (I.) Critical Grammar of the Hebrew Language. 2 vols. 8vo. cloth, $3 00. New York.

——— Chrestomathy; or, a Grammatical Analysis of Selections from the Hebrew Scriptures, with an Exercise in Hebrew Composition. 8vo. half bound, $1 00. New York.

Normand, (M. A. Le.) Historical and Secret Memoirs of the Empress Josephine. Translated by J. M. Howard. 2 vols. 12mo. cloth, $2 00. 1849.

Normand's Arabesque Ornaments. Folio, 36 plates, $9 00.

——— (Ch.) et **Queverdo.** Nouveau recueil d'ornements et d'objets propres à la décoration des bâtiments, tels que plafonds, frises, panneaux, vases, candelabres, autels, trepieds, cassoiettes, sarcophages, coupes, camées, bas reliefs, masques, lits, chaises, fauteuils, bergeres, tables, bureaux, etc., etc. 3d edition, composee de 48 planches gravees au trait, precedees d'une introduction à l'etude et à la composition des ornements. 1 vol. in fol. cartonne, $6 00.

——— Arcs de triomphe eleves à l'Etoile, au Carrousel et autres lieux, graves à l'eau forte par Normand fils, accompagnes, d'un texte historique et descriptif. In 4-oblong, $1 50.

Normandy, (A.) Practical Introduction to H. Rose's Treatise on Chemical Analysis. Illustrated by Synoptic Tables and numerous Formulæ. 8vo. cloth, $2 00. Lond. 1849.

Norrie, (J. W.) Epitome of Practical Navigation. 8vo. bds. $4 75. London.

——— Linear Tables for Correcting Refraction. 8vo. cloth, $4 50. London.

——— Nautical Tables. Royal 8vo. cloth, $3 75. London.

——— Naval Gazetteer. 12mo. cloth, $3 25. London.

——— Seaman's Daily Assistant. 8vo. cloth, $1 50. London.

North, (Hon. R.) Memoirs of Music, now first printed from the original Manuscript. 4to. cloth, $4 50. London.

——— (I. W.) Sermons on the Liturgy. Cr. 8vo. cloth, $2 50. London, 1844.

Northcote, (James.) The Life of Titian, with Anecdotes of the Distinguished Persons of his Time. 2 vols. 12mo. cloth, portrait, $2 50. London, 1830.

Norton, (A.) On the Genuineness of the Gospel. 3 vols. 8vo. cloth, $4 50. Cambridge, 1846–48.

——— Statement of Reasons for not Believing the Doctrines of Trinitarians concerning the Nature of God and the Person of Christ. 12mo. cloth, $1 00. Boston, 1833.

——— Treatise on Astronomy. A new edition, enlarged and illustrated, $2 00. New York.

Notes on the Four Gospels and the Acts of the Apostles. 2 vols. 12mo. cloth, $6 00. Pickering, 1838.

Novum Testamentum Græcum. Editio Hellenistica. E. G. Grinfield, M. A. 2 vols. 8vo. cloth, $12 00. London, 1843.

Noyes, (G. R.) New Translation of the Hebrew Prophets, arranged in Chronological order. 3 vols. 12mo. cloth, $3 38. Boston.

——— New Translation of the Book of Job, with an Introduction and Notes, chiefly Explanatory. 12mo. cloth, $1 13.

——— Psalms, with an Introduction and Notes, chiefly Explanatory. 12mo. cloth, $1 13.

——— New Translation of the Proverbs, Ecclesiastes, and the Canticles, with Introductions and Notes, chiefly Explanatory. 12mo. cloth, $1 13.

Nugent, (Thos.) French and English Dictionary. 12mo. sheep, 62 cents. Phila.

Nursery Rhymes, Tales, and Jingles. Small 4to. cloth, $2 25; colored, $3 25. London.

Nuts and Nut-crackers. 12mo. cloth, gilt edges, plates and cuts, by Phiz, $1 75. London, 1845.

Nuttall's Classical and Archæological Dictionary of the Manners, Customs, Laws, Institutions, Architecture, Arts, &c. of the celebrated Nations of Antiquity, and particularly of the Middle Ages; to which is prefixed a Synoptical and Chronological View of Ancient History. 8vo. extra cloth, bds. $2 00. 1840.

——— (Thos.) United States and Canada. 2 vols. 12mo. $5 00. Boston, 1834.

O'Brien, (John.) Treatise on American Military Laws, and the Practice of Courts Martial, with Suggestions for their Improvement. 8vo. bds. $3 50. Phila.

——— (Rev. M.) A Treatise on Plane Coordinate Geometry; or, the Application of the Method of Co-ordinates to the Solution of Problems in Plane Geometry. 8vo. bds. $2 31. Cambridge, 1844.

——— (J.) Irish and English Dictionary, by Daly. Royal 8vo. cloth, $5 50. London.

Observations on a General Iron Railway. 8vo cloth, $2 50. London.

——— on the Influence of Climate upon Wool. 8vo. cloth, $2 25. London.

——— on the Construction and Fitting up of Meeting-Houses, &c. for Public Worship. Illustrated by Plans, Sections, and Descriptions. 4to. plates, $3 25. London.

O'Byrne, (W. R.) A Naval Biographical Dictionary; comprising the Life and Services of every Living Officer in her Majesty's Navy, from the rank of Admiral to that of Lieutenant. 1 thick vol. imp. 8vo. cloth, $11 00. London, 1849.

O'Callaghan, (Dr. E. B.) History of New Netherlands; or, New York under the Dutch. 2 vols. 8vo. cloth, maps and fac-similes, $5 00. New York, 1848–9.

Ockley. History of the Saracens. Revised, enlarged, and completed, with a Life of Mohammed. 12mo. cloth, post, 88 cents. London, 184-

Oehlenschlœger's Gods of the North. Translated by W. E. Fry. Royal 8vo. cloth $4 25. London

Ogilby, (Dr. J. D.) Catholic Church in England and America. 12mo. cloth, 50 cents. London.

Okouneff, (N.) Considerations sur les grand Opérations de la Campagne de 1812 in Russia, etc. avec Bulow's Histoire de la Campagne in 1800 en Allemagne et en Italie, etc. etc. Royal 8vo. paper, $5 00.

Old Alphabets, Monograms, Architectural Ornaments, Sacred Illustrations, &c. 20 beautifully colored and illuminated plates. 4to. half mor. $7 50. London.

——— English and French Ornaments for the Interior Embellishment of Houses, for Carvers and Decorators, with Designs for Doors, Windows, &c. &c., by Chippendale, Johnson, Inigo, Jones, Locke, and others. 200 Designs in 100 Engravings. 4to. half mor. $7 50. Lond.

Old England's Worthies: a Gallery of Portraits from Authentic Sources of the most Eminent Statesmen, Sages, Warriors, Men of Letters and Science, with Illuminated Engravings, and Illustrative Wood-Cuts. Folio, cloth, $6 00. London, 1847.

Olin, (Rev. S.) Travels in the East, Holy Land, &c. 2 vols. 8vo cloth, $2 50. New York.

Oliphant, (Thos.) La Musa Madrigalesca; or, a Collection of Madrigals, Ballets, Roundelays, &c., chiefly of the Elizabethan Age, with Remarks and Annotations. Cr. 8vo. half calf, (scarce,) $3 00. London, 1837.

Oliver, (Steph.) Scenes and Recollections of Fly Fishing. 12mo. cloth, $2 50. London.

Ollendorff's New Method of Learning to Read, Write, and Speak a Language in Six Months. Adapted to the German, for the use of Schools and Private Teachers. Edited by G. J. Adler. 12mo. half bound, $1 50. New York.

——— Do. do. Adapted to the French. Edited by J. L. Jewett. 12mo. half bound, $1 00.

——— Do. do. Adapted to the Spanish. Edited by M. Velasquez and Simonne. 12mo. half bound, $1 50. New York.

——— Do. do. Applied to the Italian. Edited by Prof. Felix Foresti. 12mo. half bound, $1 50. New York.

Olmsted, (Prof.) Letters on Astronomy. 12mo. cloth, with numerous engravings, 75 cents. New York.

——— System of Astronomy, with Supplement. 8vo. cloth, $2 00. New Haven.

——— School Astronomy. 12mo. bds. 75 cents. New York.

——— Natural Philosophy. 8vo. cloth, new edition, $3 00. New Haven.

——— Student's Common Place Book. 12mo. cloth, $1 75. New Haven.

Olmstead, (F. A.) Incidents of a Whaling Voyage. 12mo. cloth, $1 50. New York.

Olshausen, (H.) Commentary on the Epistle of Paul to the Romans. 8vo. cloth, $3 25. Edinb. 1849.

Omerod, (E. L.) Clinical Observations on the Pathology and Treatment of Continued Fever. 8vo. cloth, $2 50. Lond. 1848.

O'Neil's Dictionary of Spanish Painters. 2 vols. roy. 8vo. cloth, $4 75. London, 1834.

Onderdonk, (H. K.) Documents and Letters intended to Illustrate the Revolutionary Incidents of Queen's County, with Connecting Narratives, Explanatory Notes, and additions 12mo. cloth, 75 cents. New York, 1846.

——— Revolutionary Incidents of Suffolk and King's Counties, with an Account of the Battle of Long Island, and the British Prisons, and Prison-Ships at New York. 12mo. cloth, map, $1 25. New York, 1846.

On the State of Man before the Promulgation of Christianity. 12mo. cloth, $1 00. London, 1848.

Open Timber Roofs of the Middle Ages. Illustrated by Perspective and Working Drawings of some of the best varieties of Church Roofs, with Descriptive Letter-Press. By Raphael and J. Arthur Brandon. 4to. cloth, 43 plates, $18 00. Lond. 1849.

Orators (The) of France. Translated by J. T. Headley, and edited by G. H. Colton. 12mo. cloth, portraits, $1 25. New York, 1848.

Oratory, (Library of.) Embracing Select Speeches of Celebrated Orators of America, Ireland, and England. 4 vols. 8vo. cloth, $5 00. Philadelphia.

Oram, (W.) Precepts and Observations on the Art of Coloring in Landscape Painting. 4to. cloth, $1 50. London, 1810.

Oregon and California in 1848, by J. Q. Thornton. 2 vols. 12mo. cloth, $1 75. New York, 1849.

Oregon County, History of, by Twiss. 8vo. cloth, 75 cents. New York.

Oregon and California Trail, by Parkman. 12mo. cloth, $1 25. New York, 1849.

Orfila, (M. P.) Treatise on Poisons, with Supplement. 3 vols. 8vo. cloth, $12 75. London.

——— Elements of Modern Chemistry. 8vo. cloth, $3 25. London.

——— Remedies Against Poison, by Black. 12mo. cloth, $1 50. London.

Oriental Album. Characters, Costumes, and Modes of Life in the Valley of the Nile. Illustrated from Designs taken on the Spot, by E. Prisse. With Letter-Press Descriptions, by J. A. St. John. 32 Plates, and 35 Wood-Cuts. Imp. folio, half mor. $30 00. Plates Tinted, $60 00. Colored and printed on Bristol Board, in portfolio, $80 00. Lond. 1848.

Oriental Outlines; or, a Rambler's Recollections of a Tour in Turkey and Greece, in 1838. By William Knight. 12mo. cloth, map, $1 00. Lond. 1839.

Original Letters Relative to the English Reformation. Edited for the Parker Society. By Rev. H. Robinson. 8vo. cloth, $2 25. Cambridge, 1847.

Orme, (Rev. William.) The Life and Times of the Rev. Richard Baxter, with a Critical Examination of his Writings. 2 vols. 8vo. $2 00. Boston, 1831.

Ornaments Displayed on a full size for Working, proper for all Carvers, Painters, &c. containing a variety of Accurate Examples of Foliages and Friezes. 33 folio plates, $4 50. London.

Ornamentist; (The,) or, Artisan's Manual. Imp. 4to. cloth, $19 50. Lond.

Orr's Pictorial Guide to Niagara. 18mo. cloth, 75 cents. Buffalo.

Orton, (Rev. Job.) Practical Works: consisting of Discourses, Sacramental Meditations, and Letters. 2 vols. 8vo. cloth, $5 00. London, 1842.

——— (J. W.) The Miner's Guide. 18mo. cloth, 50 cents. New York, 1849.

Osburn, (W.) Ancient Egypt; her Testimony to the Truth of the Bible, being an Interpretation of the Inscriptions and Pictures which remain upon her Tombs and Temples. Illustrated by Engravings and Colored Plates. 8vo. cloth, $4 00. London, 1846.

Osgood, (Mrs.) Letter about the Lions, in Envelope. 13 cents. New York, 1849.

——— Poems. Illustrated by Darley. 8vo. cloth, gilt, $5 00; mor. extra, $7 00. Philadelphia, 1849

Osgood, (Mrs. F. S.) Floral Offering. 4to. cloth, colored plates, $4 50. Phila. 1848.

——— (Mrs.) Book of Poetry and Flowers. 12mo. cloth extra, $2 00. New York.

Osmond, (W.) Christian Memorials. 4to. cloth, 23 plates, $4 50. London, 1848.

Ossian's Poems. Translated by Macpherson. 8vo. cloth, $2 00. Philadelphia.

The Same. 12mo. cloth, $1 25. New York.

Ottley, (W. C.) A Treatise on the Differential Calculus, with a Collection of Examples. 8vo. cloth, $2 00. London.

Otto, (J. A.) Treatise on the Violin. Translated by Bishop. 8vo. paper, $1 00. Lond.

——— (Dr. F.) History of Russian Literature, with a Lexicon of Russian Authors. Translated by George Cox. 8vo. cloth, $3 00. Oxford, 1839.

Otway, (Rt.) Treatise on Steam Navigation. 8vo. cloth, $2 25. London.

——— (T.) Dramatic Works. 2 vols. 8vo. cloth, $7 25. London.

Our Young Men, their Importance and Claims. A Prize Essay, by F. A. Cox. 75 cents. New York.

Ouseley, (Sir W.) Travels in various Countries in the East, more particularly Persia. 3 vols. 4to. bds. 80 plates, $22 00. London, 1823.

Outline of Social Systems and Communities, by Chas. Bray. 12mo. cloth, $1 50. Lond.

Ovidii Opera, cum Notis, Burmanni, Bentleii et Variorum. 5 vols. royal 8vo. cloth, $12 50. Oxon, 1825.

——— Metamorphoses. Ed. by N. C. Brooks. 8vo. bds. illustrated with notes and wood-cuts, $2 75. Philadelphia.

Ovid's Fasti, with Introduction, and Notes, and Exercises, by Thos. Keightley. 12mo. cloth, $2 00. London.

——— Metamorphoses and Epistles. Translated by Dryden, Pope, Addison, Congreve, and others. 2 vols. 12mo. cloth, $1 00. New York.

Owen, (Richard.) On the Nature of Limbs; a Discourse delivered before the Royal Institution of Great Britain. Plates, 8vo. cloth, $1 75. London, 1849.

——— History of British Fossil Mammals and Birds. 8vo. illustrated by 237 wood-cuts, cloth, $8 50. London, 1846.

——— On the Archetype and Homologies of the Vertebrate Skeleton. 8vo. cloth, plates, $3 00. London, 1848.

——— On Parthenogenesis; or, the Successive Production of Procreating Individuals from a Single Ovum. Plates, 8vo. cloth, $1 50. London, 1849.

——— (R. D.) Hints on Public Architecture. 4to. cloth, 113 illustrations, $6 00. New York, 1849.

——— (J.) Anabasis of Xenophon, according to the Text of Dindorf, with Notes, &c. 12mo. half bound, $1 25. New York.

——— Cyropædia. 12mo. bds. $1 50. New York.

——— Odyssey of Homer, according to the Text of Wolfe, with Notes. 12mo. bds. $1 50. New York.

Owen, (J. J.) Thucydides, from the Text of Dindorf. 12mo. bds. $2 00. New York

——— (Capt. W. F. W.) Narrative of Voyages to Explore the Shores of Africa, Arabia, and Madagascar. 2 vols. 12mo. cloth, $1 12. New York.

——— (John, D. D.) Exposition of St. Paul's Epistle to the Hebrews. New edition. 4 vols. 8vo. cloth, $12 00. London, 1840.

——— Preliminary Exercitations to the Exposition of Hebrews. 8vo. cloth, $2 50. London, 1840.

Oxford Chronological Tables of Ancient History, Synchronistically and Ethnographically arranged. Compiled from the best authorities. Folio, half mor. $6 75. Oxford, 1836.

——— Classics.

Euripides.	Square 12mo.	cloth,	$1 25.
Homeri Ilias.	do.	do.	1 25.
Horatius.	do.	do.	63.
Sophocles.	do.	do.	75.
Thucydides.	do.	do.	1 25.

——— English Prize Essays. New edition, brought down to 1836. 5 vols. cr. 8vo. cloth, $7 50. Oxford, 1836

——— Tracts. 3 vols. 8vo. cloth, $6 00. New York.

——— A Guide to the Architectural Antiquities in the Neighborhood of Oxford. 8vo. numerous cuts, $5 50. Oxford.

——— Original Views in Oxford, its Colleges Chapels, and Gardens; comprising 26 tinted drawings on stone. By V. Gaucci, with historical and descriptive Notices, by Chas Ollier. Royal atlas folio, Turkey mor. backs, $10 00. London.

Oxley, (John.) Two Expeditions in New South Wales. 4to. cloth, $15 00. London.

——— (T.) Gem of the Astral Sciences. 8vo. cloth, $3 25. London.

Page, (J.) History and Guide for Drawing the Acanthus and other Descriptions of Ornamental Foliage. 12mo. cloth, $3 00. Lond.

——— Decorator and Mechanic's Assistant. Oblong, cloth, $1 63. London.

——— (D. P.) Theory and Practice of Teaching; or, the Motives and Methods of Good School Keeping. 12mo. cloth, $1 25. New York.

Paget, (J.) Travels in Hungary and Transylvania. 2 vols. 8vo. cloth, $9 00. Lond.

——— (F. E.) Sermons on Duties of Daily Life. 12mo. cloth, $1 75. Rugeley, 1844.

Pain, (W.) The Practical House Carpenter; or, Youth's Instructor. 4to. cloth, $5 50. London.

Paine, (M.) Institutes; or, Philosophy of Medecine. 8vo. cloth, $2 75. New York.

——— Medical and Physiological Commentaries. 2 vols. 8vo. cloth, $8 50. New York, 1840.

Paixhan, (H. J.) Nouvelle Force Maritime, et Application de Cette force á quelques parties du service de l'armée de terre. 4to. $4 00. Paris, 1822.

Palais Farnese. Details of. By M. Letarouilly. Folio, plates, $13 50.

Paley, (W.) The Works of, with Notes and Illustrations, by James Paxton. 5 vols. 8vo. half calf, $9 50. London, 1845.

Paley, (W.) Horæ Paulinæ; or, the Truth of the Scripture History of St. Paul Evinced. 12mo. cloth, 75 cents. New York, 1849.

——— Works, i. e. Evidences of Christianity, Moral and Political Philosophy, Natural Theology, and Horæ Paulinæ. 8vo. cloth, portrait $1 50. London, 1844.

——— Natural Theology. By Brougham and Bell. 4 vols. 18mo. cloth, $2 00. Lond.

——— (F. A.) Illustrations of Baptismal Fonts. 8vo. cloth, 124 engravings, with descriptions, $6 00. London, 1844.

——— Manual of Gothic Mouldings; a Practical Treatise on their Formations, Gradual Developments, Combinations, and Varieties. 8vo. cloth, $2 50. London, 1849.

——— Manual of Gothic Architecture. Foolscap, 8vo. 70 illustrations, $2 00. Lond. 1847.

Palfrey, (J. G.) Academical Lectures on the Jewish Scriptures and Antiquities. 2 vols. royal 8vo. cloth, $5 00. Boston, 1838.

——— Lowell Lectures on the Evidences of Christianity, with a Discourse on the Life and Character of John Lowell, by Edward Everett. 2 vols. 8vo. cloth, $2 75. Boston, 1843.

Palgrave, (Sir F.) History of the Anglo-Saxons. 12mo. cloth, $1 00. Lond. 1842.

——— Rise and Progress of the English Commonwealth, Anglo-Saxon Period, containing the Anglo-Saxon Policy, and the Institutions arising out of Laws and Usages which prevailed before the Conquest. 2 vols. 4to. $15 00. London, 1832.

——— The Merchant and Friar. 12mo. cloth, 50 cents. London.

Palladio's Architecture. Translated by Ware. Folio, half bound, $8 50. Lond.

Pallavicini. Histoire du Concile de Trent traduit pour la premiere fois, en Français sur l'original Italien, réedité par La Propaganda en 1833; publiée par M. l'Abbé Migne. 3 vols. royal 8vo. $4 50. 1844.

Palliser, (Sir Hugh.) The Life of, Admiral of the White, and Governor of Greenwich Hospital. 8vo. cloth, portrait, $4 50. Lond. 1844.

Palmer, (S.) A Pentaglot Dictionary of the Terms employed in Anatomy, Physiology, Pathology, Practical Medicine, Surgery, Obstetrics, Medical Jurisprudence, Materia Medica, Pharmacy, Medical Zoology, Botany, and Chemistry, &c. 8vo. cloth, $2 25. Lond. 1845.

——— (Major.) Detail of Line Movements, &c. 8vo. cloth, $4 25. London.

——— (Rev. William.) Origines Liturgicæ; or, Antiquities of the English Ritual. 2 vols. 8vo. bds. $5 00. London, 1845.

Pambour, (Comte de.) The Theory of the Steam Engine; a Series of Practical Formulæ to Determine the Velocity of any Engine with a given Load, &c. 8vo. bds. $3 50. London, 1839.

——— A Practical Treatise on Locomotive Engines, with Appendix. 8vo. cloth, $5 50. London, 1840.

Pancoast, (Dr. J.) Treatise on Operative Surgery; comprising a Description of the Various Processes of the Art, including all the new Operations. 4to. cloth, 80 plates, $10 00. colored, $20 00. New York.

Pap with a Hatchet; being a Reply to Martin Mar-Prelate. Reprinted with an Introduction and Notes, by John Petherham. 12mo. cloth, 75 cents. London, 1844.

Papers on Engineering. 6 vols. 4to. numerous Mechanical and Civil Engineering plates, $44 00.

——— Part XII., very recently published, to complete Sets, $5 50.

——— on Subjects connected with the Duties of the Corps of Royal Engineers. 4to. cloth, illustrated with many engravings. Vol. 1, $4 75; Vol. 2, $7 50; Vol. 3, $7 50. Vol. 4, $8 50; Vol. 5, $10 75; Vol. 6, $10 75; Vol. 7, $9 00; Vol. 8, $9 00; Vol. 9, $10 75.

——— on Naval Architecture. 3 vols. 8vo. cloth, $20 00. London.

Papworth, (J. B.) Rural Residences; consisting of Designs for Cottages, Decorated Cottages, Small Villas, &c. Imp. 8vo. 27 colored plates, $4 50. Lond. 1832.

——— A Series of Designs for Garden Buildings, Gates, Fences, Railings, &c. 4to. cloth, $4 50. London.

——— Hints on Ornamental Gardening. Imp. 8vo. $4 50. London.

——— (J. and W.) Specimens of Decoration. 4to. cloth, $3 00.

Parables of our Lord, Richly Illuminated with Appropriate Borders, printed in Colors and in Black and Gold, with a Design from one of the Early German Engravers. Square foolscap. 8vo. bound in mor. in Missal style, $8 00. London, 1847.

——— Richly Illuminated with Appropriate Borders, printed in Colors and Gold. Square cr. 8vo. binding in antique style, $3 50. New York.

Paraguay. Four Years in, by J. P. and W. P. Robertson. 2 vols. 12mo. cloth, $1 00. Philadelphia.

Pardoe, (Miss.) River and the Desert; or, Recollections of the Rhone and the Chartreuse. 2 vols. post 8vo. extra cloth boards, $1 75. 1838.

——— City of the Magyar; or, Hungary and her Institutions in 1839–40. 3 vols. 8vo. cloth, $3 25. Lond. 1840.

——— The Court and Reign of Francis the First, King of France. 2 vols. 12mo. cloth, $2 00. Phila. 1849.

——— Louis XIV. and the Court of France in the 17th Century. 2 vols. 12mo. cloth, $3 50. New York.

Pardon. The Universal Picture Gallery, comprising 40 Engravings from the Works of the best Masters, Ancient and Modern, beautifully executed on wood. 4to cloth, $2 50.

Paris Moderne. The Street Architecture of Paris. 2 vols. 4to. 300 plates, $29 00.

——— in 1841. By Mrs. Gore, with 21 highly finished Engravings from Original Drawings, by Thos. Allom. Royal 8vo. cloth, gilt edges, $3 50. London, 1842.

——— and its Historical Scenes, with an Account of the Revolution of 1830, and the Abdication of the King. Plates, 2 vols. 12mo. $1 50. London, 1848.

Parish, (W.) Buenos Ayres, and Provinces of Rio de la Plata. 8vo. cloth. $4 25. Lond.

Park, (J. R.) Inquiry into the Laws of Animal Life. Royal 8vo. cloth, $4 25. Lond.

——— (T.) Heliconia, comprising a Selection of English Poetry of the Elizabethan Age, written or published between 1575 and 1604. 3 vols. 4to. half Russ. gilt tops, $30 00. (Fine copy, newly bound.) London, 1815.

Parkes, (Josiah.) Essays on Philosophy and Art of Land Drainage. 8vo. paper, 75 cents. London.

Parker, (Theodore.) Discourse of Matters Pertaining to Religion. 12mo. cloth, $1 25. Boston, 1847.

——— Critical and Miscellaneous Writings. 12mo. cloth, $1 25. Boston.

——— (C.) Villa Rustica; selected from Buildings and Scenes in the Vicinity of Rome and Florence, and arranged for Rural and Domestic Dwellings, with Plates and Details, publishing in Parts, each $1 00. New York.

——— (R. G.) Aids to English Composition. Foolscap 8vo. cloth, 80 cents. New York.

——— A School Compendium of Natural and Experimental Philosophy. 12mo. sheep, 87 cents. New York, 1848.

——— (Rev. S.) Journal of an Exploring Tour beyond the Rocky Mountains in 1835–6 and 7. 12mo. cloth, $1 25. Ithaca.

Parkinson. Organic Remains of a Former World; or, Examination of the Mineralized Remains of the Animals and Vegetables of the Antediluvian World. 3 vols. 4to. cloth, 54 colored plates, by Sowerby, $15 75. London, 1833.

Parkman, (Fr.) California and the Oregon Trail, being Sketches of Prairie and Rocky Mountain Life. 12mo. cloth, with Illustrations, by Darley, $1 25. New York, 1849.

——— Offering of Sympathy for the Afflicted. 18mo. cloth, 63 cents. Boston.

Parnell, (Thos.) Poetical Works, with Life, by Rev. J. Mitford. 12mo. mor. gilt leaves, portrait, $2 25. Pickering, 1833.

——— (Sir H. T.) A Treatise on Roads, wherein the Principles on which Roads should be made are Explained and Illustrated. 8vo. cloth, $5 75. London, 1838.

——— (E. A.) Elements of Chemical Analysis, Qualitative and Quantitative. 8vo. cloth, $4 00. London.

——— Applied Chemistry, in Manufactures, Arts, and Domestic Economy. 12mo. cloth, illustrated, $1 00. New York.

Parrot, (Dr. F.) Journey to Ararat. Translated by W. D. Cooley. 12mo. cloth, with maps and wood-cuts, 50 cents. New York, 1846.

Parry, (W. E.) Nautical Astronomy by Night. 4to. cloth, $2 75. London.

——— (Capt.) Voyages to the Arctic Regions. The first, with Appendix and Supplement, 2 vols.: the Second, with Appendix, 2 vols.; the Third, 1 vol.; the Fourth, 1 vol.; altogether 6 vols. 4to. illustrated with numerous fine engravings, from $50 00 to $70 00. London, 1821–27.

Parry, (Capt.) Three Voyages for the Discovery of a North-west Passage from the Atlantic to the Pacific, and Narrative of an Attempt to reach the North Pole. 2 vols. 12mo. cloth, $1 00. New York.

——— (Thos.) On Diet, with its Influence on Man. 8vo. cloth, $1 50. London.

——— (H.) Art of Bookbinding. 12mo. cloth, $1 50. London.

——— Cambrian Plutarch; being Lives of Eminent Welshmen. 8vo. cloth, $1 50. London, 1834.

Parsey, (A.) Art of Miniature Painting on Ivory. 12mo. cloth, $2 25. London.

——— Perspective Rectified. 4to. cloth, $3 75. London.

Parsons. The Rose, its History, Poetry, Culture, and Classification, with two large colored plates and other engravings. 1 vol. royal 8vo. cloth, $1 50. New York.

——— (U.) Physician for Ships. 12mo. cloth, $1 00. Boston.

Parterre, (The); or, Universal Story Teller; a Collection of Original Tales, Romances, and Historical Relations. Illustrated. 4 vols. 8vo. cloth, $3 75. London, 1840.

——— or, Beauties of Flora, by Andrews. Imp. 4to. cloth, $5 50. London.

——— or, Whole Art of Forming Flower Gardens. 12mo. cloth, $2 00. London.

Partington, (C. F.) The Mechanic's Library; or, Book of Trades, comprehending a Series of Distinct Treatises and Practical Guides on every Subject. 1 thick vol. 8vo. cloth, plates, $2 00. London.

Pascal. Pensées. 12mo. paper, $1 00; half mor. $1 50. Paris, 1848.

——— Lettres écrites a un Provincial. 12mo. $1 00; half mor. $1 50. Paris, 1846.

——— (Blaise.) The Provincial Letters of. A new Translation, with Introduction and Notes, by Thos. McCrie. 12mo. cloth, portrait, $1 00. Edinburgh, 1848.

——— (M.) The Miscellaneous Writings of; consisting of Letters, Essays, Conversations, and Thoughts. Newly Translated by M. P. Faugère, with Introduction and Notes, by G. Pearce. Post 8vo. cloth, $2 50. Lond. 1849.

Pasley, (Sir C. W.) Essay on the Military Policy and Institutions of the British Empire. 8vo. cloth, $3 75. London, 1847.

——— Complete Course of Practical Geometry and Plan Drawing. 8vo. cloth, $5 00. Lond.

——— Rules, chiefly deduced from Experiments for conducting the Practical Operations of a Siege. 8vo. cloth, $3 75. Lond.

——— Observations on the Expediency and Practicability of Simplifying and Improving the Measures, Weights, and Money used in this Country. 8vo. bds. $1 50. London.

——— A Course of Elementary Fortification, including Rules, deduced from Experiment, for Determining the Strength of Revetments, Treated on a Principle of Peculior Perspicuity. 8vo. plates and cuts, (nearly ready.)

——— Observations on Limes, Calcareous Cements, Mortars, Stuccoes, and Concrete, and on Puzzolanas, Natural and Artificial, together with Rules deduced from numerous Experiments for making an Artificial Water Cement. Part 1, 8vo. cloth, $2 75. Lond. 1847.

Passaic. A Group of Poems, touching that River, by Flaccus. 12mo. bds. $1 00. New York.

Pastor Fido. Italian, by Zotti. 12mo. $2 25. London.

Paton, (A. A.) Servia, the Youngest Member of the European Family; or, a Residence in Belgrade in 1843–44. 8vo. cloth, $3 75. London, 1845.

Patrick, (Simon.) Advice to a Friend. Royal 18mo. cloth, 75 cents. Oxford, 1840.

Patrick, Lowth, Arnald, Whitby, and Lowman's Commentary and Paraphrase on the Old and New Testament, and the Apocrypha. A new edition, with the Text at large. 4 vols. imp. 8vo. cloth, $15 00. Phila. 1844.

Patterson, (R.) Letters on the Natural History of the Insects mentioned in Shakspeare's Plays. 12mo. cloth, $1 25. Lond.

——— Introduction to Zoology. 12mo. cloth, illustrated with excellent wood engravings, $1 75. Belfast, 1848.

Pattison, (William.) Sketches for Cottage Villas, Country Residences, Parsonage Houses, Lodges, &c., &c., with Plans, Details, and Estimates. 31 plates, imp. 4to. cloth, $7 50. London.

Paulding, (J. K.) American Comedies. 12mo. bds. 75 cents. Phila. 1847.

Paul and Virginia. By Bernardin de Saint Pierre, with a Memoir of the Author. Embellished with illuminations and engravings in Tint, by Devereux. Square 12mo. cloth, $3 00. Phila. 1849.

Paul, (A.) Essay on Ringworm. 8vo. cloth, $1 75. London.

——— Observations on Piles and Prolapsus. 8vo. cloth, $1 50. London.

——— Remarks on Costiveness. 8vo. cloth, $1 50. London.

Pauli, (C. W. H.) Analecta Hebraica, with Critical Notes and Tables of Paradigms of the Conjugations of the Regular and Irregular Verbs. 8vo. cloth, 2d edition, with a key, $3 25. Oxford, 1842.

Paul Jones. The Life of, by A. S. Mackenzie. 2 vols. 12mo. cloth, portrait, $1 00. New York, 1845.

Paxton, (Joseph.) A Pocket Botanical Dictionary: comprising the Names, History, and Culture of all Plants known in Britain; with a full Explanation of Technical terms. New edition, with Supplement containing all the new Plants since its appearance. 12mo. cloth, $4 50. London, 1849.

——— Treatise on the Cultivation of the Dahlia. 12mo. cloth, 75 cents. London.

Payen. Précis de Chimie Industrielle, à la usage des Ecoles Prèparatoires aux Professions Industrielles et des Fabricants. 8vo. paper, $4 50. Paris, 1849.

Payne, (G.) The Doctrine ot Original Sin; or, the Nature, State, and Character of Man Unfolded. 8vo. cloth. Lond. 1845.

——— (J. H.) Bee-Keeper's Guide. 12mo. cloth, $1 25. London.

Payne's Universum; or, Pictorial World: being a Collection of engravings of Views in all countries, Portraits of Great Men, and Specimens of Works of Art, of all Ages, and of every Character. 3 vols. 4to. cloth, $12 00. London.

Payson, (Rev. E.) Memoir, Select Thoughts, and Sermons. Compiled by Rev. A. Cummings. 3 vols. royal 8vo. cloth, portrait, $6 75. Portland, 1846.

Peabody, (A. P.) Lectures on Christian Doctrine. 12mo. cloth, 81 cents. Boston, 1844.

Peacock. Headlong Hall and Nightmare Abbey. 12mo. cloth, 50 cents. New York.

Peacocke, (R. A.) Practical and Experimental Researches in Hydraulics. 4to. paper, plates, $2 25. London.

Pearls of American Poetry, Illuminated, by T. W. G. Mapleson. 4to. mor. gilt leaves, in antique style, $12 00. New York, 1848.

Pearson, (Bp.) The Minor Theological Works of; collected, with Memoir of the Author, by Edward Churton. Portrait. 2 vols. 8vo. cloth, $7 00. Oxford, 1844.

——— An Exposition of the Creed. New Edition, Revised and Corrected. 8vo. cloth, $2 75. Lond. 1845.

——— An Exposition of the Creed, with an Appendix containing the Latin and Greek Creeds. Edited by Rev. W. S. Dobson. 8vo. cloth, $2 00. New York, 1844.

——— (W.) An Introduction to Practical Astronomy. 2 vols. 4to. cloth, only $20 00, (published at $37 00.) Lond. 1824–1829.

Peckston, (Thomas S.) A Practical Treatise on Gas-Lighting, in which the Gas Apparatus generally in use is Explained and Illustrated by 22 Appropriate Plates. 3d edition, carefully corrected and adapted to the present Manufacture of Gas. 8vo. cloth, $7 50. London, 1841.

Peele, (G.) Dramatic Works, collected and Edited, with some Account of his Life and Writings, by the Rev. A. Dyce. 3 vols. cr. 8vo. cloth, $8 50. Pickering.

Peile, (T. W.) Annotations on St. Paul's First Epistle to the Corinthians, designed chiefly for the use of Students of the Greek Testament. 8vo. cloth, $2 00. Lond. 1848.

Peirce, (B.) A History of Harvard University from its Foundation in the year 1636 to the Period of the American Revolution. Cr. 8vo. cloth, $2 50. Cambridge, 1833.

——— An Elementary Treatise on Sound, being the Second Volume of a Course of Natural Philosophy, designed for the use of Schools, &c. 8vo. cloth, $1 50. Boston, 1836.

Pellatt, (Apsley.) Curiosities of Glass-making, with Details of the Processes and Productions of Ancient and Modern Ornamented Glass Manufacture. Plates, small 4to. $3 50. Lond. 1849.

Pellew, (Hon. G.) Sermons on many of the Leading Doctrines and Duties taught by the Church of England. 2 vols. 8vo. cloth, $6 00. London, 1848.

Pellico, (Silvio.) Memoirs of Ten Years' Imprisonment, in Italian, with an English Translation, by Thos. Roscoe. 8vo. portrait, paper, 75 cents. Paris, 1837.

Pelouze, (T.) and E. Frewen. Cours de Chimie Générale. 3 vols. 8vo. with an Atlas of 46 plates, paper, $8 50. Paris, 1848–9.

Pen and Ink Sketches of Poets, Preachers, and Politicians. Cr. 8vo. cloth, portrait, $2 25. London, 1846.

Penfold, (J. W.) Madeira Flowers, Fruit and Ferns. Royal 4to. $6 50. London.

Penn, (Sir W.) Memorials of the Professional Life and Times of, from 1644 to 1670, by Granville Penn. 2 vols. 8vo. portrait. $3 50. London, 1833.

Penny, (The,) Cyclopædia, published by the Society for the Diffusion of Useful Knowledge, with Supplement. 29 vols. half calf, cloth sides, marbled leaves, $75 00. London, 1833–1848.

The Same in 16 vols. half mor. cloth sides, marbled leaves, $70 00.

——— **Magazine.** Published by the Society for the Diffusion of Useful Knowledge. New Series. 5 vols. imp. 8vo. cloth, $7 50. London.

Pennsylvania, Historical Collections of, by Sherman Day. 8vo. cloth, $3 00. Lond.

People's, (The,) Music Book, comprising Anthems, by the most Eminent English and Foreign Composers, from the Period of the Reformation to the Present Time, with an Accompaniment for the Organ and Piano-forte. Edited by J. Turle and E. Taylor. 3 vols. royal 8vo. cloth, $9 75. Lond. 1844.

——— Dictionary of the Bible. Edited by Dr. Beard. 2 vols. 8vo. cloth, maps and woodcuts, $6 50. London, 1848.

——— **Journal**, (The.) A Magazine Illustrated with excellent Wood-Cuts, Portraits of Celebrated Men, Copies of new and beautiful Paintings and Engravings, with Literary Articles, by some of the ablest living authors. 5 vols. roy. 8vo. cloth, $5 00. London.

Pepe, (General.) Memoirs of, comprising the Principal Military and Political Events of Modern Italy, written by himself. 3 vols. post 8vo. cloth, $3 00. Lond. 1846.

Pepys, (Samuel.) Diary and Correspondence of, with a Life and Notes, by Richard Lord Braybrooke. Vols. 1 to 5, cr. 8vo. cloth, portraits. A new edition, each $3 00. London, 1848–9.

——— The Life, Journals, and Correspondence of, including a Narrative of his Voyage to Tangier. 2 vols. 8vo. cloth, portraits, $3 00. London, 1841.

Percier et Fontaine. Choix de Maisons de Plaisance de Rome Moderne. Folio, 75 plates, $41 00.

——— Palais, Maisons, et autres Edifices de Rome Moderne. 100 plates in 1 vol. folio, $15 00.

Percivall, (W.) Lectures on the Veterinary Art. 3 vols. 8vo. $14 00. Lond.

——— Lameness in the Horse, with Colored Lithographic Plates. 8vo. cloth, $6 25. London, 1849.

Percy, (Bp.) Reliques of Ancient English Poetry. New Edition, with Illuminated Titles. 3 vols. 12mo. cloth, $4 50. Beautifully bound in morocco, in old style, with embossed gilt edges, $18 00. London, 1847.

——— Do. do. 3 vols. 18mo. cloth, $2 50. Moxon, 1844.

——— 8vo. cloth, frontispiece and vignette, $2 50. London, 1844.

——— **Anecdotes** on a variety of Subjects. 20 vols. 18mo. cloth, $18 00. Lond.

——— (Sholto and Ruben) **Anecdotes**, in 1 vol. 8vo. sheep, $2 00. New York.

Perdonnet et Polonceau. Portfeuille de l'ingénieur des Chemins de fer. Recueil de dessins, notes, Documents et devis relatifs à la construction des chemins de fer. 11 livraisons in 8, avec un atlas in folio, de 132 planches, $22 00. Paris.

Pereira, (Jonathan.) Elements of Materia Medica and Therapeutics. Third edition, enlarged and improved, including Notices of most of the Medical Substances in use in the Civilized World, and forming an Encyclopædia of Materia Medica. Vol. 1, royal 8vo. cloth, $7 00. London, 1849.

——— The Elements of Materia Medica and Therapeutics, with Notes and Additions, by Joseph Carson. 2 vols. 8vo. sheep. Philadelphia, 1846.

——— Lectures on Polarized Light. 8vo. cloth, $1 75. London.

——— Treatise on Food and Diet. 8vo. cloth, $4 75. London.

Pere le Chaise. Monuments, Tombs, and Tablets from this celebrated Cemetery. 4to. cloth, $21 00. Paris.

Perkin's Eight Years in Persia. 8vo. cloth, $3 50. Boston.

Pering, (R.) Treatise on the Anchor. 8vo. bds. $3 75. London.

Perrault, (Ch.) Les Contes des fées, illustres par un grand nombre de gravures sur bois et 10 vignettes sur acier, coloriées avec le plus grand soin, d'apres les dessins de MM. Pauquet freres. 1 beau vol. grand in 8, $2 50; gilt, extra, $3 50. Paris.

——— Contes du temps passe, contenant le Petit Chaperon rouge, les Fées, Barbe-Bleu, La Belle au bois dormant, Cendrillon, le Petit Poucet, Riquet a la houppe et Peau d'ane; precedes d'une notice litteraire sur Charles Perrault, par M. E. de la Bedolliere; illustres par 100 magnifiques gravures sur acier, avec un texte grave, destine a apprendre aux enfants a lire les manuscrits. 1 vol. grand in 8, $4 50. Paris, 1843.

Perrone. Prælectiones Theologicæ; accurante Migne, cursuum completorum in singulos scientiæ ecclesiasticæ ramos editore. 2 vols. royal 8vo. $4 50. Paris, 1842.

Perrussel, (F.) Critique de l'Homœopathie et de l'Allopathie. 8vo. paper, 75 cents. Paris, 1843.

Persoz, (J.) Traité Théorique et Pratique de l'Impression des Tissus. 4 vol. in-8, avec 165 figures et 429 echantillons dans le texte et accompagnes d'un atlas in-4 de 20 pl. dont 4 coloriées, $18 00. Paris, 1846.

Peschel, (C. E.) Elements of Physics. Translated from the German, with Notes, by E. West. 3 vols. 12mo. cloth, profusely illustrated with wood-cuts, $5 75. Lond. 1845-8.

Peter, (W.) The Poets and Poetry of the Ancients. 8vo. cloth, $3 00; mor. $5 00. Philadelphia, 1848.

Peter Wilkins. Life and Adventures of. 12mo. cloth, $1 00. London.

——— American edition. 12mo. cloth, 50 cents. Hartford.

Peter Schlemihl. German, with English Version, by William Howitt. 16mo. cloth, $2 25. London.

——— In America. Thick 12mo. cloth, $1 25. Philadelphia, 1848.

Peters, (J. G.) Treatise on the Art of Horsemanship. Royal 8vo. cloth, $6 50. London.

Peterson's Military Heroes of the American Revolution. 2 vols. 8vo. cloth, $3 00. Philadelphia.

Petit's Remarks on Church Architecture, with illustrations. 2 vols. 8vo. cloth, $10 75. London, 1841.

——— Remarks on Architectural Character, with 44 etchings. Folio, cloth, $6 50. Oxford, 1846.

Petites Miseres de la Vie Humaine par old Nick et Grandeville. 8vo. half mor. gilt top, illustrated with numerous engravings, $5 50. Paris, 1846.

Petrarca. Le Rime, con le opere di Poliziano, e note di diversi. 2 vols. 8vo. portrait, $2 50. Parigi, 1836.

Petrarch's Life, by Thomas Campbell. 2 vols. 8vo. cloth, portraits of Petrarch and Laura, $2 50. London.

Petrie, (G.) Round Towers of Ireland. Imp. 8vo. cloth, $8 50. London.

Petherham, (John.) Historical Sketch of Anglo-Saxon Literature. 8vo. cloth, $1 50. London.

Pettigrew, (T. J.) On Superstitions connected with the History and Practice of Medicine and Surgery. 8vo. cloth, $1 75. London, 1844.

Petzholdt, (A.) Lectures to Farmers on Agricultural Chemistry. 12mo. $1 25. Lond.

——— American edition. 50 cents. New York.

Phœdrus, Fabulæ, in usum Delphinum. 8vo. bds. $1 37. London.

Phantasmagoria of Fun. Edited and Illustrated by Alfred Crowquill. 2 vols. post 8vo. cloth, wood-cuts, by Leech, Cruikshank, &c. $2 75. London, 1843.

Pharmacopœia Londonensis. By Phillips. 8vo. cloth, $3 25. London.

Philidor. Studies of Chess. 8vo. cloth, $3 50. London.

——— Analysis of Chess, by Walker. 12mo. cloth, $2 25. London.

Philip, (A. W.) Inquiry into the Laws of the Vital Functions. 8vo. cloth, $3 75. London.

——— American edition. 8vo. sheep, $1 50. Philadelphia, 1818.

——— Inquiry into the Nature of Sleep and Death. 8vo. cloth, $2 50. London.

Phillips, (Chas.) Recollections of Curran. 8vo. cloth, $3 25. London.

——— De la Ténotomie sous-cutanee, ou des operations qui se pratiquent pour la Guerison des pieds-bots, du Torticolis, de la Contracture de la main et des Doights, &c. accompagne de 12 planches. 8vo. paper, $1 63. Paris, 1841.

——— (G.) Theory, &c. of Painting in Water Colors. 4to. cloth, $7 50. London.

——— Elements of the Syriac Grammar. 8vo. cloth, $3 00. London.

——— (H.) Sylva Florifera; the Shrubbery. 2 vols. 8vo. cloth, $6 50. London.

——— The True Enjoyment of Angling. 12mo. cloth, $3 25. London.

——— (H. C.) Code of Universal Naval Signals. 8vo. cloth, $3 25. London.

——— (J.) Palœozoic Fossils of Cornwall, Devon, &c. 8vo. cloth, $2 75. London.

——— A Treatise on Geology. 12mo. cloth, $1 75. Edinburgh.

——— (Sir R.) A Million of Facts. Thick 12mo. cloth, $3 75. London.

——— (R.) Translation of the Pharmacopœia of the Royal College of Physicians of London, in 1836, with Notes and Illustrations. Cloth, $3 50. London.

——— The Eternal; or, the Attributes of Jehovah, &c. 12mo. cloth, $1 25. Lond. 1846.

——— (Thos.) Lectures on Painting. 8vo. cloth, $4 00. London.

——— (Sir Thos.) Wales, the Language, Social Condition, Moral Character, and Religious Opinions of the People, considered in their Relation to Education, with some Account of the Provision made for Education in other parts of the Kingdom. 8vo. cloth, $4 25. London, 1849.

——— Lectures on the History and Principles of Painting. 8vo. cloth, $2 50. Lond. 1833.

——— (W.) Introduction to Mineralogy, by Allan. Edited by Alger. Thick 12mo. cloth, $3 00. Boston, 1848.

——— Outlines of the Geology of England and Wales. 8vo. cloth, $4 75. London.

——— Inventor's Guide; comprising the Rules, Forms, and Proceedings for Securing Patent Rights. 12mo. sheep, $1 00. Boston, 1837.

——— Principles of Effect and Color, as applicable to Landscape Painting, &c. 4to. 10 colored plates, $2 50. London, 1838.

——— Curvilinear Designs for Ornaments. Folio, plates, some colored, $19 00. Lond.

Philip Quarl's Life and Adventures. Square 18mo. cloth, 63 cents. London.

Philip Randolph; a Tale of Virginia, by Mary Gertrude. 12mo. cloth, $1 50. London, 1844.

Philosophical Transactions of the Royal Society, from its first Formation to the Year 1800. Abridged by Shaw, Hutton, and Pearson. 18 vols. 4to. calf, from $60 00 to $70 00. London.

——— Abstract of Papers, from the Year 1800 to 1843. 4 vols. 8vo. bds. $9 00. Lond. 1844.

Philosophy in Sport Made Science in Earnest. 12mo. cloth, $2 25. Lond.

Philpott, (Lieut. Col.) Report on the Canal Navigation of the Canadas. 4to. map and plates, $2 50. London.

Phipps, (E.) Guide to the Commerce of Bengal. 4to. cloth, $15 00. London.

——— Treatise on Indigo, &c. Royal 8vo. cloth, $2 75. London.

Picket, (W. V.) New System of Architecture, founded on the Forms of Nature, $2 25. London.

Pickering, (John.) Greek and English Lexicon. Royal 8vo. sheep, $3 75. Boston.

——— (Chas.) The Races of Men and their Distribution, being the 9th vol. of the United States Exploring Expedition. 4to. cloth, colored plates and map, $10 00. Boston, 1848.

Pickton, (H.) Introduction to Lineal Drawing and Mensuration, with Hints on the Arrangement of Drawing Classes. Second edition, 12mo. cloth, 75 cents. London, 1849.

Pictorial (The) Book of Ballads, Traditional and Romantic, with Introductory Notices, Glossary, and Notes. Edited by T. S. Moore. 8vo. half mor. illustrated with numerous engravings, $3 50. London, 1849.

——— Dictionary of the Holy Bible; or, a Cyclopædia of Illustrations, Graphic, Historical, and Descriptive, of the Sacred Writings, by reference to the Manners, Customs, Rites, Traditions, Antiquities, and Literature of Eastern Nations. 2 vols. 4to. with upwards of 1000 illustrative wood-cuts, extra cloth, $7 50. London, 1846.

——— History of Napoleon, by G. M. Bussey. 2 vols. imp. 8vo. cloth, with 500 beautiful engravings, by Horace Vernet, $6 50. London, 1840.

——— History of London. Edited by Charles Knight. 6 vols. in 3, royal 8vo. cloth, $9 50; half mor. gilt backs and edges, $13 50. London, 1841–44.

——— History of England; being a History of the People as well as a History of the Kingdom to the end of the Reign of George III. Illustrated with some thousand wood-cuts, by G. L. Craik and Chas. McFarlane, assisted by other Contributors. 8 vols. imp. 8vo. handsomely bound in calf, gilt backs, marbled leaves, $45 00; cloth, $30 00. Lond. 1838–44.

The Same. First 4 vols. imp. 8vo. cloth, $14 00. New York.

——— History of Germany during the Reign of Frederick the Great, including a complete History of the Silesian Campaigns and the Seven Years' War, by F. Kugler. Illustrated with 500 wood-cuts, by Adolph Menzel. Royal 8vo. cloth, $3 50. London, 1845.

——— History of France and of the French People, from the establishment of the Franks in Gaul to the period of the French Revolution, by G. M. Bussey and T. Gaspey. 2 vols. royal 8vo. cloth, with 500 engravings on wood, $7 00. London, 1843.

——— History of Palestine, the Holy Land, and the Jews, by John Kitto, Editor of the Pictorial Bible. 2 vols. royal 8vo. cloth, above 500 wood-cuts, $7 50. London.

——— Illustrations of New Zealand, from a Series of original drawings, by S. C. Brees, Engineer to the New Zealand Company from 1841 to 1845. 4to. cloth, with 2 maps and 60 plates, $12 50. London.

Pictorial Museum of Animated Nature; containing some thousands of figures beautifully engraved on wood, and accompanied with Letter-press, descriptive and illustrative. 2 vols. folio, cloth, $10 25. London, 1846.

Picture Bible; or, a Pictorial History of the Old and New Testament, by Rev. H. Caunter, with 144 lignographic illustrations, by J. Martin and R. Westall. 8vo. cloth, $3 25. London, 1846.

Pictures of the French; a Series of Literary and Graphic Delineations of French Character, by Jules Janin, Balzac, Connenin, and other celebrated French Authors. Royal 8vo. cloth, 230 engravings, by distinguished Artists, $3 50. London, 1840.

Picturesque Tour on the River Thames in its Western Course, including particular Descriptions of Richmond, Windsor, and Hampton Court. By John Fisher Murray. Illustrated with upwards of 100 highly finished wood engravings. Royal 8vo. cloth, $3 25. Lond. 1845.

Piscator. The Practical Angler. 8vo. cloth, plates, $2 75. London.

Piddington. (H.) The Sailor's Horn-Book; being a Practical Exposition of the Law of Storms, and its uses to Mariners of all classes in all parts of the World. 8vo. cloth, $2 50. New York, 1848.

Pierce, (B.) An Elementary Treatise on Algebra, to which are added, Exponential Equations and Logarithms, 83 cents. Boston, 1846.

——— An Elementary Treatise on Plane and Solid Geometry. 12mo. sheep, 83 cents. Boston, 1847.

——— An Elementary Treatise on Sound. 8vo. cloth, plates, $1 50. Boston, 1836.

——— On Trigonometry. 12mo. sheep, $1 50. Boston.

——— On Curves, Functions, and Forces. 12mo. sheep, $1 25. Boston.

Piers Ploughman's Vision and Creed. Edited by Wright. 2 vols. 12mo. cloth, $6 50. Pickering.

Pigault Lebrun. Mon Oncle Thomas. 12mo. broché, $1 00.

——— Angelique et Jeanneton suivi de Garçon sans souci. 12mo. broché, $1 00. Paris, 1843.

——— Monsieur Botte. 12mo. broché, $1 00.

——— Les Barons de Felsheim. 12mo. broché, $1 00. Paris, 1843.

——— L'Enfant du Carnaval. 12mo. broché, $1 00. Paris, 1843.

——— L'Homme à Projets. 12mo. broché, $1 00. Paris, 1834.

Pigott, (Grenville.) Manual of Scandinavian Mythology; containing a Popular Account of the two Eddas, and of the Religion of Odin. Illustrated by Translations from Oehlenschlager's Danish Poem, the Gods of the North. 8vo. cloth, $3 75. Pickering, 1839.

Pike, (B.) Illustrated Descriptive Catalogue of Optical, Mathematical, and Philosophical Instruments. 2 vols. 12mo. cloth, $2 00. New York.

Pilgrim's, (The,) Progress, with a Life of John Bunyan, by Robert Southey. 12mo. cloth, illustrated with 50 wood-cuts, 75 cents. New York, 1847.

Pilgrim's, (The,) Progress; a beautiful edition, printed in the old-fashioned type of the Seventeenth Century, with Red Letter Title, Marginal Glosses and References. Embellished with an accurate portrait, engraved on steel. 8vo. cloth, $3 00. Pickering, 1849.

Pilgrims, (The,) of the Rhine. By the Author of Pelham, Eugene Aram, &c. 8vo. mor. gilt leaves, illustrated with beautiful engravings, $6 00. London, 1840.

Pilkington, (M.) Dictionary of Painters. New edition, by Allan Cunningham, with 26 new Lives. 8vo. cloth, $4 50. Lond. 1840.

Pilpay's Fables, with wood-cuts. 12mo. cloth, $1 75. London.

Pindar. Translated by Rev. C. A. Wheelwright. 12mo. 75 cents.

——— and **Anacreon's** Odes. Translated by Wheelwright and Bourne. 12mo. cloth, 50 cents. New York.

Pinelli's Etchings of Italian Manners and Costume. Imp. 4to. half mor. 27 large and spirited etchings, $4 50. Rome, 1840.

——— and **Cooke's** Views in Rome. Roy. 8vo. cloth, 27 fine plates, $2 25. Lond. 1834.

Pinnock's Improved edition of Dr. Goldsmith's History of England from the Invasion of Julius Cæsar to the Year 1845. 12mo. half bound, 88 cents. Phila. 1848.

——— Pictorial History of England from the Invasion of Julius Cæsar to the Death of George Third. 12mo. cloth, map and plates, $2 00. London.

Piobert, (G.) Cours D'Artillerie, partie Theorique. 8vo. orne de planches, $1 50.

——— Traite D'Artillerie Theorique et Pratique. 2 vols. 8vo. avec planches, $3 25. Bruxelles, 1838–44.

Piranesi, Opere. 28 vols. atlas folio, $750 00. Roma, 1756–83.

Vol. 1–4. Antichita Romane.
5–6. Monumenti degli Scipio-Antiquies Romane.
7. Manificenza ed Architectura de Romani.
8. Differens ouvrages d'Architecture.
9–10. Differens ouvrages d'Architecture Campus Martius.
11. Antichite d'Albano e di Castel Gandolfo.
12–13. Vasi, Candelabri, Sarcofagi, Tripoda, etc.
14. Colona Trajana e Antonia.
15. Antichita di Paestum.
16–17. Vedute di Roma.
18–19. Statues Antiques-Teatro d'Ercolano.
20–21. Maniere d'Adornaire J. Cammini-Disegni Guericino.
22–23. Scholia Italica Picturæ Diverses Gravures.
24–28. Various.

Piscatorial Reminiscences and Gleanings. 12mo. cloth, $2 25. Pickering.

Pitcairn's Criminal Trials in Scotland, 1488 to 1624. 4 vols. 4to. $41 00. Lond.

Pitkin, (T.) Political and Civil History of the United States, from 1763 to 1797. 2 vols. 8vo. $5 00. New Haven, 1828.

——— Statistics of the United States, $3 00. New Haven, 1835.

Pitman, (Rev. J. R.) Sermons on the Book of Psalms. 8vo. cloth, $2 25. Lond. 1846.

——— (R. B.) On the Junction of the Atlantic and Pacific Oceans. 8vo. cloth, $2 50. Lond.

——— (J.) Manual of Phonography; or, Art of Writing by Sound. 12mo. 50 cents. London, 1848.

Pitman, (J.) Phonography adapted to Verbatim Reporting. 8vo. paper, 75 cents. London.

Plain Sermons, by Contributors to the Tracts for the Times. 10 vols. 8vo. bds. each $2 00. London.

Place, (F.) Principle of Population. 8vo. cloth, $2 50. London.

Planck, (G. J.) Introduction to Sacred Philology and Interpretation. Translated by S. H. Turner. 12mo. cloth, $1 25. New York, 1834.

Platonis. Scripta Græce omnia ad Codicis Manuscriptos recensuit variasque inde Lectiones diligenter enotavit Immanuel Bekker annotationibus integris Stephani, Heindorfii, Wyttenbachii, etc., etc. 11 vols. 8vo. cloth, $25 00. London, 1826.

Plato's Works. Translated by Sydenham and Taylor. 5 vols. 4to. $50 00. Lond. 1804.

——— Divine Dialogues, with the Apology of Socrates. Translated, with Notes, from the French of M. Dacier. 12mo. cloth, $1 75. London.

——— The Phœdrus, Lysis, and Protagoras of Plato. New and Literal Translation, mainly from the Text of Bekker. By J. Wright. 12mo. cloth, $1 50. London, 1848.

——— The Works of. Translated by Carey. Vols. 1 and 2, each $1 50. London, 1849.

——— His Life, Works, Opinions, and Influence, by E. Pond. 32mo. cloth extra, 38 cents. Portland.

Plattner, (Prof. C. F.) Use of the Blowpipe in the Examination of Minerals, &c. Translated by Musprat, with Preface, by Liebig. 8vo. cloth, wood-cuts, $3 25. Lond. 1845.

Plautus, English Notes, by Dillaway. 18mo. cloth, 60 cents. Philadelphia.

——— Translated by Proudfit. 18mo. paper, 38 cents. New York.

Playfair's Euclid. Revised by James Ryan. 8vo. sheep, $1 00. New York.

Plinii, ex editione Gabrielis Brotier cum notis et interpretatione in usum Delphini, etc. 12 vols. 8vo. cloth, $20 00. Valpy, 1826.

Plough, (The), the Loom, and the Anvil. Vol. 1, 8vo. sheep, $3 50. Phila. 1848–9.

Plutarchus. Ed Schæfer. 6 vols. 12mo. fine paper, $11 00. Leips.

——— Vitæ parallelæ et Moralia. 15 vols. 12mo. paper, $7 25. Tauchnitz, Leips.

——— Moralia ed Dübner, Græce et Latine. 2 vols. royal 8vo. paper, $7 50. Paris.

Plutarch's Lives. Translated by J. and W. Langhorne. 4 vols. 12mo. sheep, $3 50. New York.

——— 8vo. sheep, $2 00. New York.

Pocket-Book for Architects, Builders, Contractors, &c. 12mo. cloth, $1 87. Lond.

Pocket and the Stud; or, Hints for the Stable, by Harry Hieover. 12mo. cloth, $1 50. London.

Pocock, (W. F.) Modern Finishings for Rooms. 4to. cloth, $6 50.

——— Designs for Churches and Chapels. 4to. cloth, $6 50.

——— Designs for Cottages, &c. 4to. cloth, $9 50. London.

Poe, (E. A.) Tales. 12mo. cloth, 50 cents. New York.

——— The Raven, and other Poems. 12mo. cloth, 50 cents. New York.

——— Eureka; or, the Universe, a Prose Poem. 12mo. cloth, 75 cents. New York.

Poetæ Scenici Græci, Dindorfi. Royal 8vo. cloth, $7 25. London.

Poems and Pictures. A Collection of Ballads, Songs, and other Poems. Illustrated with wood engravings of the most exquisite kind, from designs by eminent English Artists, with borders, &c. Small 4to. bound in mor. in Antique style, gilt leaves, $15 00. London, 1846.

Poetical Language of Flowers. Edited by E. O. Smith, and illustrated with colored plates, $4 50. New York.

Poet's Pleasaunce, (The;) or, Garden of all Sorts of Pleasant Flowers, which our Poets have, in Past time, for Pastime Planted. By Eden Warwick. Cr. 8vo. with ornamental borders of Flowers and Insects, engraved on wood and elegantly bound in mor. gilt backs and leaves, $12 00. London, 1847.

Points and Pickings; or, Information about China and the Chinese, with engravings. 12mo. cloth, $1 75. London.

Pole, (W.) The Art of Painting on Glass; or, Glass Staining. 4to. $1 25. London.

——— (Wm.) Investigation of the Comparative Loss by Friction in Beam and Direct Action Steam Engines. 4to. $1 00. London.

——— Cornish Pumping Engine. 4to. cloth, with plates in folio, $9 50. London.

Political Dictionary, Constitutional and Legal. 4 vols. 12mo. cloth, $4 50. Lond. 1848.

——— History of New York, with Portraits of the Twelve Governors. 8vo. sheep, $1 50. Auburn.

——— and Social Economy, its Practical Applications, by John Hill Burton. 12mo. cloth, 75 cents. Edinburgh, 1849.

Pollet, architecte. Recueil d'edifices d'architecture, grecque, romaine, gothique et de la renaissance, suivi d'un essai sur la decoration et l'ameublement des monuments de ces diverses epoques, grave par Roux aine. 1 vol. in-folio, de 60 planches, avec texte, $12 50.

Pollok, (R.) Course of Time; a Poem. 12mo. cloth, $1 00. New York.

——— Life, Letters, and Remains. By Rev. James Scott, with portrait. 12mo. cloth, $1 00. New York.

——— (Thos.) An Attempt to Explain the Phenomena of Heat. 8vo. cloth, $1 50. Lond.

Polybii Opera. Gr. et Lat. cura Sceweighœuser. 5 vols. 8vo. cloth, $16 00. Lond.

——— Historia. 4 vols. 12mo. paper, $2 50. Tauchnitz, Leipsic.

——— History Translated. Royal 8vo. bds. $2 50. London.

Pontey, (W.) Profitable Planter. 8vo. cloth, $3 25. London.

——— Rural Improver. 4to. cloth, $12 75. London.

——— Forest Pruner's Assistant. 8vo. $3 75. London.

Poole, (Matthew.) Annotations upon the Holy Bible, wherein the Sacred Text is inserted, and various Readings annexed, together with the Parallel Scriptures; the more difficult Terms in each Verse are explained, seeming Contradictions reconciled, Questions and Doubts resolved, and the whole Text opened. 3 large vols. imp. 8vo. extra cloth, $19 00. London, 1842.

——— (G. A.) History of Ecclesiastical Architecture in England. 8vo. cloth, $3 75. London, 1849.

——— Index to Subjects in all the Reviews and Periodicals that have not Indexes. 8vo. paper, $1 00; half bound, $1 25. New York, 1848.

Poore, (B. P.) The Rise and Fall of Louis Philippe, giving an Account of the French Revolution, from its commencement in 1789. 12mo. cloth, plates, $1 00. Boston, 1848.

Pope, (A.) Works complete, with Notes and Illustrations, by himself and others, to which are added a new Life of the Author, by William Roscoe.. 8 vols. 8vo. beautifully bound in tree calf, by Riviere, marbled leaves, full gilt backs, portrait, $28 00. Lond. 1847.

——— Aldine edition, with Memoirs, by Dyce. 3 vols. 12mo. cloth, $3 75; mor. gilt edges, $6 75; sup. extra, $9 00. London, 1840.

——— Works, complete in 1 vol. with Notes, by Dr. Warburton, with illustrations on steel. 12mo. cloth, $1 50. London.

Popp et Buleau. L'Architecture gothique et son origine, demontrees par la cathedrale, l'eglise Saint-Jacques, l'ancienne paroisse, et quelques autres restes de l'architecture germanique à Ratisbonne. L'ouvrage fait connaitre successivement le style germanique proprement dit, le style byzantin, le style de transition, enfin le style gothique pur. Prix du vol. grand in-folio, de 50 pl. complet, cartonne, $20 00. Paris.

Popular Errors. Explained and Illustrated, by John Timbs. Foolscap 8vo. $1 50. London, 1841.

Popular Flowers, their Cultivation, Propagation, and General Treatment in all Seasons, with Lists of Choice and Favorite Varieties. Illustrated with beautifully colored plates. 12mo. cloth, $1 75. London.

Porcelain, (The,) Tower; or, Nine Stories of China. Compiled from original Sources. Cr. 8vo. cloth. plates, 75 cents. London, 1841.

——— and Glass. A Treatise on. 12mo. cloth, 50 cents. Philadelphia.

Porson, (Rd.) Adversaria. 8vo. bds. $5 50. London.

——— Opera Philologica et Critica, Bloomfield et Kidd. 5 vols. 8vo. cloth, $16 50. Lond.

——— Tracts and Criticisms, by Kidd. 8vo. cloth, $4 25. London.

Portal, (F. de.) An Essay on Symbolic Colors in Antiquity, the Middle Ages, and Modern Times. Translated by W. Inman. 4to. cloth, plates, $3 25. London, 1845.

Porter's Progress of the Nation in its various Social and Economical Relations, from the beginning of the Nineteenth Century to the present time. 2d edition, 1 vol. 8vo. $8 25. London, 1846.

——— (J. S.) Principles of Textual Criticism, with their application to the Texts of the Old and New Testaments, with 13 lithographed and colored fac-similes of interesting Biblical MSS. 8vo. cloth, $4 75. London, 1849.

——— (G. R.) Treatise on the Manufacture of Porcelain and Glass. 12mo. cloth, $1 75. London.

——— Nature and Properties of the Sugar Cane. 8vo. cloth, $3 75. Lond.

——— (A. L.) Chemistry of the Arts, on the Basis of Gray. 8vo. cloth, $5 00. Phila.

Portlock, (Col.) Rudimentary Geology. 12mo. cloth, wood-cuts, 25 cents. Lond. 1849.

Ports, Arsenals, and Dockyards of France. Post 8vo. cloth, $3 25. Lond.

Portwine, (E.) The Steam Engine, from the earliest to the present time. 18mo. cloth, wood-cuts, 25 cents. London, 1847.

Post, (A. C.) On the Cure of Strabismus and Stammering. 12mo. cloth, 50 cents. N. Y.

Potter's Remains of the Monastic Architecture of England. Folio, half mor. 78 plates, $29 00. London.

——— Specimens of Ancient English Architecture, chiefly Parish Churches. 4to. 42 plates, $11 00. London.

——— (R.) An Elementary Treatise on Mechanics, for the Use of Junior University Students. 8vo. cloth, $2 25. Lond. 1846.

——— (A.) Science applied to the Domestic Arts. 12mo. cloth, wood-cuts, 75 cents. N. Y.

Poujoulat. Histoire de la Revolution Français, gravures sur acier. 2 vol. in 8, demi veau, $3 50. Tours, 1848.

Poussin, (N.) Life of, by Lady Calcott. 8vo. cloth, $3 25. London.

——— (G. T.) De la Puissance Americane, origine, Institutions, esprit politique, ressources Militaires Agricoles, Commerciales et Industrielles des Etats-Unis. 2 vols. 8vo. $3 00. Paris, 1848.

Powell, (C. F.) Life of Maj. Gen. Zachary Taylor. 8vo. paper, 25 cents. New York.

——— (Thos.) Living Authors of England. 12mo. cloth, $1 00. New York, 1849.

Poynder, (John.) Literary Extracts from English and other Works, collected during half a Century, together with some original Matter. First and Second Series. 3 vols. 8vo. cloth, $8 00. London.

Practice of Architecture. By Asher Benjamin. 4to. sheep, $4 50. Boston.

Practical, (A,) Guide to the First Study of the Greek Testament. 12mo. cloth, $1 00. London, 1849.

——— Mechanic and Engineer's Magazine. 6 vols. 4to. cloth, plates, $15 00. Glasgow.

——— Pharmacy, the Arrangements, Apparatus, and Manipulations of the Pharmaceutical Shop and Laboratory. By Mohr and Redwood. 8vo. $8 75. London.

Practical Sermons, by Dignitaries and other Clergymen of the United Church of England and Ireland. Vols. 1 to 3. 8vo. cloth, $2 37 each. London, 1845–7.

Pratt, (Anne.) The Field, the Garden, and the Woodland; or, interesting Facts respecting Flowers and Plants in general. 12mo. cloth, $1 00. London.

——— (J. H.) Principles of Mechanical Philosophy. 8vo. cloth, $6 50. London.

Precis Politique et. Militaire de la Campagne de 1815 pour servir de supplement et de rectification a la vie Politique Militaire de Napoleon. 8vo. $2 00. Paris, 1839.

Prescott, (W.) History of Ferdinand and Isabella. 3 vols. 8vo. cloth, portraits, $6 00; calf, full gilt backs and marbled leaves, $11 00. New York, 1847.

——— History of the Conquest of Mexico. 3 vols. 8vo. cloth, $6 00; calf, uniform with the above, $11 00. New York, 1847.

——— History of the Conquest of Peru. 2 vols. 8vo. cloth, portraits, $4 00; calf, uniform with the above, $8 00. New York, 1848.

Prevost, (l'Abbe.) Histoire de Manon Lescaut, illustree de 100 vignettes, par Tony Johannot; precedee d'une notice historique sur l'auteur, par M. Jules Janin. 1 magnifique vol. grand in 8, avec titre et frontispiece en couleur, rehausses d'or, $2 50.

——— Histoire de Manon Lescaut et du Chevalier Desgrieux. 12mo. broché, $1 00. Paris, 1846.

Price, (Uvedale.) On the Picturesque in Scenery and Lancscape Gardening, with an Essay on Taste, &c., by Sir Thos. Dick Lauder. 8vo. cloth, 60 engravings, $3 75. Lond. 1842.

——— Treatise on the Differential Calculus, and its Application to Geometry. 8vo. cloth, $3 50. London.

——— History of the Mohammedan Empire. 4 vols. 4to. cloth, $11 00. Lond. 1821.

Prichard, (J. C.) Researches into the Physical History of Mankind. 5 vols. 8vo. plates, $25 00. London, 1841–7.

——— The Natural History of Man; comprising Inquiries into the Modifying Influence of Physical and Moral Agencies, on the different Tribes of the Human Family. Third edition, with 50 colored and 5 plain illustrations engraved on steel, and 97 engravings on wood. Royal 8vo. cloth, $9 00. London, 1848.

——— Ethnographic maps to accompany the above. Large folio, cloth, bds. $7 50. London, 1848.

——— (A.) A History of Infusoria, Living and Fossil, with colored engravings. 8vo. cloth, second edition, $3 50. London, 1849.

Pridden, (W.) History and Condition of Australia. 12mo. cloth, $1 50. London.

Prideaux, (Humphrey, D. D.) The Old and New Testament connected in the History of the Jews and neighboring Nations, from the declension of the Kingdoms of Israel and Judah, to the time of Christ. Maps and plates. 2 vols. cloth, $4 50; calf extra, $7 00. Oxford, 1839

Pridham, (Charles.) An Historical, Political, and Statistical Account of Ceylon and its Dependencies. Map, &c. 2 vols. 8vo. cloth, $8 00. London, 1849.

——— History of the Mauritius. 8vo. cloth, $4 50. London.

Priest, (Josiah.) American Antiquities and Discoveries in the West. 8vo. cloth, $1 50. Albany, 1841.

Priestley, (Rev. J.) Life of, by John Towhill Rutt. 8vo. bds. $1 25. Lond. 1832.

——— (Joseph.) A Course of Lectures on the Theory of Language and Universal Grammar, and on Oratory and Criticism. 8vo. bds. $1 25. London, 1824.

——— Lectures on History and General Policy. Royal 8vo. bds. $2 00. London, 1840.

Prince, (W. R.) Manual of Roses. 12mo. cloth, 75 cents. New York.

Princeton Essays, Theological and Miscellaneous, reprinted from the Princeton Review. First and Second Series. 8vo. cloth, $5 00. New York.

Prinsep, (G. A.) Account of Steam Vessels, &c. in India. Royal 4to. $6 50. London.

Prior, (M.) Poetical Works, with Life, by Rev. J. Mitford. 2 vols. 12mo. cloth, portrait, $3 00. Pickering, 1835.

——— (J.) Life of Burke, with numerous unpublished Letters, Anecdotes, &c. 8vo. cloth, portrait, $2 75. London, 1839.

——— Life of Goldsmith. 2 vols. 8vo. cloth, $3 75. London, 1837.

Pritchard, (A.) Notes on Natural History, selected from the Microscopic Cabinet. 10 colored plates, second edition, 12mo. cloth, 75 cents. London, 1849.

Prize Cartoons Exhibited at Westminster Hall. Folio, cloth, $30 00. London.

——— Second Exhibition. Folio, cloth, $6 50; proofs, $8 00. London.

Proceedings of the Electrical Society, 1841–3. Edited by Walker. 8vo. cloth, $6 50. London.

Proctor, (Col.) The History of Italy from the Fall of the Western Empire to the commencement of the Wars of the French Revolution. Royal 8vo. cloth, $1 87. Lond. 1844.

Progress of Machinery and Manufactures in Great Britain. 4to. bds. $6 50. London.

Prout, (S.) Hints on Light and Shadow, Composition, &c., as applicable to Landscape Painting. Illustrated by Examples. 4to. cloth, $7 50. London, 1838.

——— Sketches in France, Switzerland, and Germany. Imp. folio, 26 plates, half mor. $21 00. London, 1841.

——— Sketches at Home and Abroad: being Examples of the Interiors and Exteriors of Gothic Buildings. Imp. 4to. 48 plates, $12 50. London.

——— (W.) On the Nature and Treatment of Stomach and Renal Diseases. Fifth edition, revised. 8vo. cloth, $6 00. London, 1848.

——— American edition. 8vo. cloth, $2 50. Philadelphia.

——— On Chemistry, Meteorology, &c. 63 cents. Philadelphia.

Provis, (John.) Tables for the Copper Trade. 8vo. cloth, $9 00. London.

Pruen, (Rev. Thos.) View of the Church of the Living God, its Ministry and Service. 2 vols. 8vo. bds. $2 50. London, 1823.

Public Works of the United States practically Elucidated, by Detailed Drawings of the Aqueducts, Breakwaters, Bridges, Canals, Floating Dry Docks, Gas Works, Harbors, Locomotive Engines, Steam Engines, and Steamboats, Water Works, &c., the Architecture, Banks at Philadelphia, New York, Girard College, and other Public Edifices. Edited by W. Strickland, E. H. Gill, and H. R. Campbell. 1 vol. 8vo. with folio atlas of Plates, $10 00. London, 1841.

——— of Great Britain; consisting of Railways, Tunnels, Oblique Arches, Docks, Cast Iron Bridges, &c., &c. Edited by F. W. Simms. 153 plates, folio, half mor. $25 00. London.

Pugin, (A. W.) The True Principles of Pointed or Christian Architecture. 4to. half mor. 130 illustrations, $4 50. Lond. 1841.

——— The Present State of Ecclesiastical Architecture in England. 8vo. cloth, 36 illustrations, $2 75. London, 1843.

——— Contrasts; or, a Parallel between the Noble Edifices of the Middle Ages and corresponding Buildings of the present, showing the present Decay of Taste. Accompanied by appropriate Text. 4to. cloth, $9 00. Lond. 1841.

——— Examples of Gothic Architecture, selected from Ancient Edifices in England, consisting of Plans, Elevations, Sections, and parts at large, with Historical and Descriptive letter-press. Illustrated by 235 engravings, by Le Keux. 3 vols. 4to. cloth, $48 00. Lond. 1838.

——— and **Le Keux.** Specimens of the Architectural Antiquities of Normandy. 80 plates, 4to. cloth, $15 75. London, 1828.

——— Glossary of Ecclesiastical Ornament and Costume; setting forth the Origin, History, and Signification of the various Emblems, Devices, and Symbolical Colors, peculiar to Christian Design of the Middle Ages, with especial reference to the Decoration of the Sacred Vestments and Altar Furniture, formerly used in the English Church. Illustrated by nearly 80 plates, splendidly printed in gold and colors. By A. Welby Pugin, Architect. New edition, 1 magnificent vol. royal 4to. half mor. extra, top edges gilt, $38 00. 1846.

——— Gothic Ornaments, selected from various Ancient Buildings both in England and France. 4to. half mor. $12 00. London, 1844.

——— Paris and its Environs displayed in a Series of Picturesque Views. 4to. cloth, $5 00. London.

——— Ornamental Timber Gables, selected from Ancient Examples in England and Normandy. Royal 4to. 30 plates, $6 50. London, 1839.

——— An Apology for the Revival of Christian Architecture in England. 4to. half mor. $3 50. London.

——— and **Britton's** Illustrations of the Public Buildings of London, with Historical and Descriptive Accounts of each Edifice. Edited by W. H. Leeds. 2 vols. large 8vo. half mor. $19 00. London, 1838.

Pulpit Cyclopædia and Minister's Companion. 8vo. cloth, $2 50. New York.

Purdie, (Thomas.) Form and Sound; Can their Beauty be dependent on the same Physical Laws? Plates, 8vo. cloth, $2 25. Edinburgh, 1849.

Pure Gold from the Rivers of Wisdom. 18mo. cloth, 31 cents. New York.

Pure Mathematics, (Encyclopædia of.) Being Treatises from the Encyclopædia Metropolitana. 4to. cloth, $9 00. London.

Pursh's Flora Americana. 2 vols. 8vo. cloth, 24 plates, colored, $6 50. London, 1814.

Pusey, (Dr.) Scriptural Views of Holy Baptism. 12mo. cloth, 50 cents. New York, 1843.

——— (E. B.) Sermons for the Season, from Advent to Whitsuntide. 8vo. cloth, $3 00. London, 1848.

Putnam, (G. P.) American Facts; Statistics of the United States. 12mo. cloth, portraits and map, $1 00. New York.

——— Library of American History; being rare Tracts illustrative of American History. Edited, with Notes, by Rev. F. L. Hawks. 8vo. cloth. (In press.)

——— (Mrs.) Receipt-Book and Young Housekeeper's Assistant. 12mo. cloth, 50 cents. Boston, 1849.

Putz, (W.) Manual of Ancient Geography and History. Translated from the German, with Notes, by Rev. T. K. Arnold. 12mo. cloth, $1 00. New York.

Pym, (A. G.) Narrative of Mutiny on board Brig Grampus, by E. A. Poe. 12mo. cloth, 63 cents. New York.

Pyne, (Geo.) Elements of Perspective Parts 1 and 2. 12mo. cloth, plates and woodcuts, 50 cents. London, 1849.

——— Microcosm; a Series of 1000 Subjects of Rural and Domestic Scenery, Shipping, Craft, Sports, &c. Royal 4to. half bound, $12 75. London.

Quain, (Rich.) Anatomy of the Arteries, with its applications to Pathology and Operative Surgery, in lithographic drawings, the size of and drawn from Nature, with Practical Commentaries. Elephant folio, 87 plates, finely colored, half mor. with an 8vo. volume of letter-press, $70 00. London, 1844.

——— and **Wilson**. The Vessels of the Human Body. Royal folio, 50 plates, plain, cloth, $13 50; colored, $18 50. Lond. 1837.

——— The Nerves of the Human Body. Royal folio, 38 plates, plain, $12 50; colored, cloth, $20 00. London, 1839.

——— The Viscera of the Human Body, including the Organs of Digestion, Respiration, Secretion, and Excretion. Royal folio, 32 plates, plain cloth, $10 50; colored, $18 00. London, 1840.

——— The Bones and Ligaments. Royal folio, 30 plates, plain, cloth, $10 50; colored, $13 50. London, 1842.

——— The Muscles of the Human Body. Roy. folio, 51 plates, plain, cloth, $16 00; colored, $37 00. London, 1836.

——— Anatomical Plates, with References and Physiological Comments, illustrating the Structure of the different parts of the Body. Third edition, revised, with Notes, by Joseph Pancoast. 4to. cloth, $15 00; colored, $30 00. Philadelphia, 1845.

Quarle, (Francis.) Emblems, Divine and Moral. Cuts. 16mo. cloth, $1 00. London, 1845.

——— The School of the Heart. Cuts. 16mo. cloth, $1 50; together, unique binding, $3 00. London, 1845.

Quarterly Papers on Architecture. 4 vols. 4to. cloth, with about 500 wood, steel, and copper engravings, some highly and expensively colored, $38 00. London.

Quarterly Review, complete from its commencement in 1809 to 1846, with Indexes. 77 vols. 8vo. half calf, neat, $125 00. Lond.

Quarterly Journal of the Chemical Society of London. Edited by Dr. E. Ronalds. Vol. 1, 8vo. cloth, $4 00. London, 1847.

Quatremere de Quincy. Hist. de la vie et des ouvrages des plus celebres architectes du XIe siecle jusqu'à la fin du XVIIIe. 2 vols. 8vo. 47 plates, $9 00. Paris, 1830.

——— Dictionnaire Historique d'Architecture. 2 vols. 4to. $15 00. Paris, 1833.

Quekett's Practical Treatise on the Microscope; including the different Methods of Preparing and Examining Animal, Vegetable, and Mineral Structures. Illustrated with 9 plates and 241 wood engravings. 8vo. cloth, $6 00.

Quested, (J.) Treatise on Railways, Surveying, and Levelling. 8vo. cloth, $1 75. London.

Quetelet, (M. A.) Letters on the Theory of Probabilities as applied to the Moral and Political Sciences. Translated by O. G. Downs. 8vo. cloth, $3 50. Lond. 1849.

——— Popular Instructions on the Calculations of Probabilities. 12mo. cloth, $1 37. Lond.

Quin's Steam Voyages on the Moselle, the Elbe, and Lakes of Italy, with Notices of Thuringen and Saxon Switzerland, &c. 2 vols. post 8vo. cloth, $2 75. London, 1843.

Quincy, (J.) Life of Josiah Quincy. Imp. 8vo. bds. $2 00. Boston, 1825.

——— History of Harvard University. 2 vols. royal 8vo. plates, $5 00. Cambridge, 1840.

Quinet, (E.) Ultramontanism; or, the Roman Church and Modern Society. 12mo. cloth, $1 50. London, 1845.

Quintiliani Instit. Oratoriæ cura Ingram. 8vo. cloth, $3 25. London.

Rabelais. Œuvres de completes. 12mo. paper, $1 00. Paris.

——— Œuvres, edition variorum, augmentee de pieces inedites, de songes drolatiques de Pantagruel, ouvrage posthume, avec l'explication en regard; des remarques de Le Duchat, de Bernier, de Le Motteux, de l'abbe de Marsy, de Voltaire, de Ginguene, etc.; et d'un nouveau commentaire historique et Philologique, par Esmangart et Eloi Johanneau, avec 10 vignettes, 2 portraits, 120 figures grotesques, etc. 9 vols. in 8, demi veau, $18 00. Paris, 1823.

——— Works. Translated from the French, by Sir Thomas Urquhart, Motteux, and Ozell, with Explanatory Notes, by Duchat and others. 2 vols. foolscap 8vo. cloth, $1 75. 1849.

Racine. Theatre complet precede d'une Notice par M. Anger. 12mo. broché, $1 00; half mor. $1 50. Paris, 1848.

——— (J.) Œuvres choisies avec la vie de l'auteur et des notes de tous les commentateurs, par M. D. Sancie, gravures. 1 vol. in 8, maroquin, $1 75. Tours, 1847.

Radcliffe, (E. P. D.) The Noble Science; a few General Ideas on Fox Hunting, for the use of the Rising Generation. 8vo. cloth, plates, $4 50. London, 1839.

Rae, (J.) Principles of Political Economy. 8vo. cloth, $1 80. Boston.

Raffaelle. The Cartoons of, from the originals in Hampton Court Palace. Drawn and etched on steel, by John Burnet, accompanied by a Critical Dissertation on each plate. Elephant folio, $10 00; colored after the originals, $18 00. London, 1849.

Raffles, (Sir Stamford.) The History of Java. 2 vols. and his Life and Journals, 2 vols., together, 4 vols. 8vo. and atlas of plates, &c. $12 00. London, 1835.

Raguet, (Condy.) Principles of Free Trade. 8vo. cloth, $2 00. Philadelphia.

Railway Locomotive Management, in a Series of Letters. 8vo. cloth, $1 50. London.

Railway Works; Portfolio of Views of some of the most important Works on the Principal Railroads in England. Oblong folio, cloth, $6 00. London, 1846.

Ralfs, (J.) British Desmidieæ; or, Fresh Water Algæ. Royal 8vo. cloth, $10 75. London.

Ralph, (T. S.) Icones Carpologicæ; or, Figures and Descriptions of Seeds, after the manner of Gaertner. Part 1, Leguminosæ, containing 40 plates, with about 200 figures. 4to. bds. $5 00. London, 1849.

Rambles in Sweden and Gottland, with etchings by the Wayside. By Sylvanus. 8vo. cloth, portrait and etchings, $1 25. Lond. 1847.

Rammelsberg, (Dr. C. F.) Leitfaden für die qualitative chemische analyse. 8vo. paper, 87 cents. Berlin, 1843.

Ramsbotham, (F. H.) Principles and Practice of Obstetric Medicine and Surgery. 8vo. sheep, $5 00. Philadelphia.

Ramshorn, (Lewis.) Dictionary of Latin Synonymes, for the use of Schools and Private Students. From the German, by F. Lieber. 12mo. half bound, $1 25. Boston, 1839.

Randall, (H. S.) Sheep Husbandry in the South. 8vo. cloth, $1 25. Phila. 1849.

Ranke, (L.) History of the Popes of Rome during the Sixteenth and Seventeenth Centuries. Translated by Sarah Austin. 3 vols. 8vo. cloth, $9 00. London, 1841.

——— History of the Popes of Rome. Translated by E. Foster. 3 vols. foolscap 8vo. cloth, $2 63. London, 1848.

——— History of the Popes. Translated by W. Kelly. 8vo. cloth, $1 50. Philadelphia.

——— Memoirs of the House of Brandenburg, and History of Prussia, during the Seventeenth and Eighteenth Centuries. Translated from the German, by Sir Alexander and Lady Duff Gordon. 3 vols. 8vo. cloth, $10 00. Lond. 1849.

Ranke, (L.) A History of Servia and the Servian Revolution. Translated from the German, by Mrs. A. Kerr. 8vo. cloth, $4 50. London.

——— History of the Reformation in Germany. Translated by Sarah Austin. 3 vols. 8vo. cloth, $12 00. London, 1845.

Rankin, (R.) Treatise on Life Assurances and Annuities. 8vo. cloth, $1 75. London.

——— Half Yearly Abstract of Medical Science. 8vo. paper, per No. 75 cents. Phila.

Ranlett, (W. A.) The Architect; a Series of original designs, adapted to the United States. Illustrated with Elevations, Plans, Ground Lots, &c. 2 vols. 4to. $12 00. New York.

Ransome, (J. A.) The Implements of Agriculture. Royal 8vo. cloth, plates, $2 25. London, 1843.

Ransom's Military Tactics. 12mo. cloth, 50 cents. Concord.

Raper, (Lieut. H.) The Practice of Navigation and Nautical Astronomy. 8vo. with Supplement, $5 00. London, 1840.

——— Tables of Logarithms. Royal 8vo. cloth, $1 75. London.

Raphael. Collection d'Arabesques et de tableaux antiques des bains de Titus et de Livie, peints par Raphael, dessines, graves et decrits par N. Ponce. Ouvrage utile aux peintres et decorateurs. 1 vol. in-fol. de 73 planches, avec texte, cartonne, $12 50. Paris.

——— Cartoons, Book of, by R. Cattermole. 8vo. cloth, portrait of Raphael and 7 highly finished engravings, $1 75. Lond. 1845.

——— Life, by Duppa, with Life of Michael Angelo, by Q. de Quincey. Post 8vo. cloth, 88 cents. London, 1847.

Rask, (E.) Danish Grammar for Englishmen, by Repp. 8vo. $1 50. London.

Raspail. Nouveau systeme de chimie organique. 3 vols. 8vo. paper et atlas, $9 00. Paris, 1838.

Rau, (G. L.) Organnon; or, the Specific Healing Art. 8vo. cloth, $1 25. New York.

Raumer, (Von.) England in 1841; being a Series of Letters written to Friends in Germany. Translated from the German, by H. E. Lloyd. 2 vols. Post 8vo. cloth, $2 75. Lond. 1842.

——— America and the American People. 8vo. cloth, $2 00. New York.

Ray, (John.) Collection of Proverbs. 12mo. cloth, $2 25. London.

Rayer, (P.) A Theoretical and Practical Treatise on the Diseases of the Skin. Translated by R. Willis. 4to. cloth, plates, $15 00. Philadelphia.

Reach, (A. B.) Clement Lorimer; or, the Book with the Iron Clasps; a Romance. Illustrated with several fine plates, by George Cruikshank. 12mo. cloth, $2 00. Lond. 1849.

Read, (T. B.) Female Poets of America. 8vo. cloth, $4 50; mor. gilt, $5 50. Philadelphia, 1848.

Readings for the Young, from Sir Walter Scott. 3 vols. 12mo. cloth gilt, $3 50. London, 1848.

——— American edition. 2 vols. 12mo. $2 00. Philadelphia.

Record of Edward, the Black Prince. Illuminated by Humphreys. Post 8vo. unique binding, $6 50. Lond. 1848.

Recreations of Christopher North. 8vo. cloth, $1 00. Philadelphia, 1848.

——— in Science and Natural Philosophy, by Dr. Hutton. A new edition, revised, with additions, by Edward Riddle. 8vo. cloth, 400 wood-cuts, $3 50. London.

——— in Shooting, by Craven. Post 8vo. cloth, $3 50. London.

Redhead, (T. W.) History of the French Revolution. 3 vols. 12mo. cloth, $2 25. Edinburgh, 1849.

Rees, (James.) Mysteries of City Life; or, Stray Leaves from the World's Book. 12mo. cloth, $1 00. Philadelphia, 1849.

Reed, (Joseph.) Life and Correspondence, by his Grandson, W. B. Reed. 2 vols. 8vo. cloth, portrait, $4 50. Philadelphia.

Reeve, (L.) Conchologia Systematica; or, Complete System of Conchology, in which the Lepades and Mollusca are described and classified according to their Natural Organization and Habits. Illustrated with 300 plates of upwards of 1500 figures of Shells. 2 vols. 4to. cloth, $36 00; plates elegantly colored, $60 00. London, 1843.

——— Conchologia Iconica; or, Figures and Descriptions of the Shells of Molluscous Animals, with Critical Remarks on their Synonymes, Affinities, and Circumstances of Habitation. Publishing in monthly parts, each containing 8 plates beautifully colored, $3 00 each; uncolored, containing 6 plates, 75 cents.

——— Elements of Conchology; or, Introduction to the Natural History of Shells and their Molluscous Inhabitants, their Structure, Calcifying Functions, and Habits, Geographical Distribution, Affinities, Arrangement, and Enumeration of Species. Numerous illustrations, colored. Royal 8vo. cloth, $12 00. London, 1849.

Regnard, (J. F.) Theatre suivi de ses voyages en Lapoine en Pologne, &c. et de la Provençale. 12mo. $1 00. Paris, 1845.

——— Œuvres de, suivies des Œuvres choisies de N. Destouches. Imp. 8vo. paper, $2 50. Paris, 1836.

Regnault, (M. V.) Elementary Course of Crystallography. 8vo. cloth, $1 00. Lond.

——— Cours Elementaire de Chimie, avec planches intercales, dans le texte. 4 vols. 12mo. $6 50. Paris, 1849.

Reid, (T., D. D.) Essays on the Intellectual Powers of Man, and Analysis of Aristotle's Logic, &c., by Wright. 8vo. cloth, $2 50. London, 1843.

——— (T.) Philosophical Works. Edited by Sir William Hamilton. Royal 8vo. cloth, $7 50. London.

——— (Lieut. Col.) An Attempt to Develop the Law of Storms. Royal 8vo. bds. with 11 charts, $2 75. London, 1849.

——— (John.) Young Surveyor's Preceptor. 4to. cloth, $5 75. London.

——— Bibliotheca Scoto Celtica, with Notes. 8vo. cloth, $3 75. London.

——— (H.) The Steam Engine popularly described, with illustrations. 12mo. cloth, $1 25. London.

Reid, (D. B.) Rudiments of Chemistry. Edited by Dr. M. Reese. 12mo. half bound, 70 cents. New York.

——— Illustrations of the Theory and Practice of Ventilation, with Remarks on Warming, &c. 8vo. cloth, $5 00. London.

——— (A.) Dictionary of the English Language, with a Preface, by H. Reid. 12mo. sheep, $1 00. New York, 1846.

——— (Thos.) Treatise on Clock and Watchmaking. Royal 8vo. cloth, plates, $6 50. Glasgow, 1847.

——— (Lieut. Col.) Short Account of the Failure of a part of the Brighton Chain Pier, in the Gale of November 30, 1836. (Papers, R. E. vol. 1, 4to.) London.

——— On Assaults, and Hints for the Compilation of an Aide-Memoire for the Corps of Royal Engineers. (Papers, R. E. Vol. 1, 4to.) Lond.

——— Description of the Concrete Sea Wall at Brighton, and the Groins which Defend the Foot of it. (Papers, R. E. vol. 1, 4to.) Lond.

——— On Intrenchments as Supports in Battle, and on the Necessity of completing the Military Organization of the Royal Engineers. Further Observations on Removing the Shingle along the Coast. On Hurricanes. (Papers, R. E. vol. 2, 4to.) London.

——— On the Decomposition of Iron in Salt Water, and of its Reconstruction in a Mineral Form. (Papers, R. E. vol. 3, 4to.) Lond.

——— On Lodging Troops in Fortresses at their Alarm Posts. (Papers, R. E. vol. 4, 4to.) Lond.

Reinhold, (Caroline.) The Evening Bell; or, the Hour of Relating Entertaining Anecdotes for Dear Young People. Translated by Rev. C. S. Mangan. 12mo. cloth, plates, $1 75. Dublin, 1848.

Relfe, (I.) Principles of Harmony. Folio, half bound, $6 50. London.

——— Studies in Musical Science. 4to. cloth, $4 75. London.

Remarks and Experiments on various Woods, both Foreign and Domestic, by Lieuts. Nelson and Denison, Capts. Young, Smyth, and Sir R. Seppings. (Papers, R. E. vol. 5, 4to.) London.

Rembrandt and his Works; comprising a Short Account of his Life, with a Critical Examination into his Principles and Practice of Design, Light, Shade, and Color. Illustrated with Examples from the Etchings of Rembrandt, by John Burnet, F. R. S. 4to. numerous plates, $9 00: proof impressions, (only 50 printed,) folio, $30 00.

Remusat, (Mme. de.) Education des femmes. 12mo. paper, $1 00.

Rendell, (J. M.) Particulars of the Construction of the Floating Bridge lately established across the Hamoaze, between Tor Point, in the County of Cornwall, and Devonport, in Devonshire. (Trans. I. C. E. vol. 2, 4to.) Lond.

——— Particulars of the Construction of the Lary Bridge near Plymouth. (Trans. I. C. E. vol. 1, 4to.) London.

Rennie, (J.) Conspectus of Butterflies and Moths. 18mo. cloth, $2 25. London.

——— (Sir John.) Account of the Breakwater at Plymouth. Folio, half bound, $25 00. London.

——— (Jas.) Bird Architecture and Miscellanies. 3 vols. 18mo. cloth, $1 37. Lond.

Rennell, (Major.) Currents of the Atlantic Ocean. 8vo. cloth, with charts in folio, $19 00. London, 1832.

——— Geographical Illustrations of Xenophon. 4to. cloth, $6 50. London.

——— Geography of Herodotus. 2 vols. 8vo. $8 50. London.

Renwick, (J.) First Principles of Chemistry. 18mo. half sheep, 75 cents. New York.

——— First Principles of Natural Philosophy. 18mo. cloth, wood-cuts, 75 cents.

——— Practical Mechanics. 18mo. half bound, plates, $1 00. New York.

——— (Prof.) Life of De Witt Clinton. 18mo. cloth, 50 cents. New York.

Report of the Railroad constructed from Kingston to Dalkey, upon the Atmospheric System. 4to. paper, $2 50. London.

——— of Experiments made with a Shot Furnace at Malta. (Papers, R. E. vol. 6, 4to.) London.

Repton, (H.) On Landscape Gardening and Architecture, by J. C. Loudon. 8vo. cloth, 250 engravings, $4 00. Lond. 1840.

Retzsch, (Moritz.) Outlines to Shakspeare's Dramatic Works, with Explanations in English. Oblong 4to. paper, $10 00. Leipsic, 1836–45.

——— Outlines to Shakspeare's Othello, King Lear, and Merry Wives of Windsor. 4to. cloth, each $4 00. Lond. 1838–44.

——— Illustrations to Schiller's Fridolin. Roy. 4to. containing 8 plates, engraved by Moses, stiff covers, $1 38.

——— Outline Illustrations to Schiller's "Fight with the Dragon." Royal 4to. containing 16 plates, engraved by Moses, stiff covers, $2 25.

Revere, (J. W.) Tour of Duty in California. 12mo. cloth, plates, $1 00. New York, 1849.

Revised Statutes of New York State. By Duer, Butler, and Spencer, late Revisers of the Statutes, and published under their Superintendence, pursuant to an Act of the Legislature. 3 vols. 8vo. sheep, $12 50. Albany, 1846.

Revue des Deux Mondes. Subscription per year, $12 50.

——— Generale de l'Architecture et des Travaux Publics. Journal des Architects, des Archeologues, des Ingenieurs et des Entrepreneurs: Publiee sous la Direction du M. Cesar Daly, elucide par des gravures sur bois, et accompagne de magnifiques planches gravees sur acier. 4to. 6 vols. published at $9 00 each. Paris, 1840–46.

——— Pittoresque Anne 1848; containing Tales by the best French Writers, and illustrated with 150 engravings. 1 handsome vol. imp. 8vo. paper, $2 00. Paris, 1848.

Reybaud, (Louis.) Jerome Paturot a la recherche de la Meilleure des Republiques. 4 vols. 12mo. broché, $3 00. Paris, 1849.

——— Jerome Paturot a la recherche d'une position sociale. 2 vols. 16mo. $1 00. Paris.

Reynard, the Fox: a renowned Apologue of the Middle Ages, reproduced in Rhyme, by Samuel Naylor. 4to. printed in black letter, with red letter Initials, &c. $6 00. London, 1844.

——— Reinecke Fuchs, mit Zeichnungen Von W. Kaulbach. 4to. cloth, 72 fine engravings on steel, $12 50. München, 1847.

Reynolds, (John.) On the Principle and Construction of Railways of Continuous Bearings. (Trans. I. C. E. vol. 2, 4to.) Lond.

——— (Sir Joshua.) Graphic Works. 300 beautiful engravings, comprising nearly 400 subjects, engraved on steel, by S. W. Reynolds. 3 vols. folio, elegantly half bound mor. gilt edges, $65 00. London.

——— Literary Works; comprising his Discourses delivered at the Royal Academy, on the Theory and Practice of Painting, also his Journey to Flanders and Holland, with Criticisms on Pictures—Du Fresnoy's Art of Painting, in English Verse, with Latin Text subjoined, and Notes. A Tabular View of Painters, from the Revival of the Art to the beginning of the last Century, to which is prefixed a Memoir of the Author, with Remarks on his Professional Character, illustrative of his Principles and Practice, by Henry William Beechey. New edition, 2 vols. foolscap, 8vo. with portrait, gilt cloth, $3 00. London, 1846.

——— The Discourses of. Illustrated by Explanatory Notes and plates, by John Burnet. 4to. cloth, $5 50. London.

——— Discourses on Painting. 12mo. cloth, $1 25. London.

——— (J. N.) Pacific and Indian Oceans. 8vo. cloth, $1 50. New York.

——— Voyage of the United States Frigate Potomac around the Globe in 1831–34. 8vo. cloth, $3 50. New York.

Rhine, (The,) Italy, and Greece; in a Series of Drawings by Cockburn, Titon, Bartlett, Leitch, and Wolfsenberger. 2 vols. 4to. cloth, gilt, $9 00. London.

Ruhlman, (M.) On Horizontal Water-wheels, especially Turbines or Whirl-wheels, their History, Construction, and Theory. Illustrated for the use of Mechanics. 4to. paper, $2 25. Dublin, 1846.

Ricardo, (D.) Principles of Political Economy and Taxation. 8vo. cloth, $3 75. Lond.

——— Political Works, with a Notice of the Life and Writings of the Author, by J. R. McCulloch. 8vo. cloth, $4 50. Lond. 1846.

Ricauti, (T. J.) Sketches for Rustic Work; including Bridges, Park and Garden Buildings, Seats, and Furniture, with descriptions and Estimates of the Buildings. 4to. $3 50. London, 1848.

Rich, (Anthony.) Illustrated Companion to the Latin Dictionary and Greek Lexicon; forming a Glossary of all the Words representing visible objects connected with the Arts, Manufactures, and every-day Life of Greeks and Romans, with representations of nearly two thousand objects from Antique. Post 8vo. cloth, $6 00. London, 1849.

——— Narrative of a Journey to the Site of Babylon, with Remarks on Topography of Ancient Babylon, by Major Rennell. Also, Narrative of a Journey to Persepolis, &c. 8vo. maps and plates, $3 25. Lond. 1839.

——— (C. H.) Specimens of Ornamental Turning. 4to. cloth, $3 75. London.

Richards, (Rev. James.) Sermons, with an Essay on his Character, by W. B. Sprague. 12mo. cloth, portrait. Albany, 1849.

——— (T.) Welsh and English Dictionary. 8vo. cloth, $4 00. London.

Richardson, (W.) Catalogue of 7,385 Stars, (Southern Hemisphere.) 4to. $4 50. London.

——— and **Ronalds**. Metallurgy and the Chemistry of Metals. 3 vols. 8vo. cloth, illustrated with numerous wood engravings.

——— (Dr.) Dictionary of the English Language. 2 vols. 4to. $12 00. Philadelphia.

——— (C.) A new Dictionary of the English Language; combining Explanations, with Etymology. New edition, 8vo. cloth, $4 50. London, 1849.

——— and **Gray's** Zoology of the Erebus and Terror. 4to. parts 1 to 18, each $3 00. London, 1844–48.

——— (John.) Fauna-Boreali Americana; or, the Zoology of the Northern Parts of British America. 4 vols. 4to. cloth, plates, $36 00. London, 1829–36.

——— Arabic Grammar. 4to. $5 50. Lond.

——— Persian, Arabic, and English Dictionary. Imp. 4to. cloth, $57 00. London, 1829.

——— (H. D.) Dogs, their origin and varieties, Directions as to their General Management, with numerous original Anecdotes. 12mo. 25 cents. New York.

——— Geology for Beginners; comprising a Familiar Explanation of Geology and its associate Sciences, Mineralogy, Physical Geology, Fossil Conchology, Fossil Botany, and Palæontology: including Directions for forming Collections, &c. by G. F. Richardson, F. G. S., formerly with Dr. Mantell, now of the British Museum. Second edition, considerably enlarged and improved. 1 thick vol. post 8vo. illustrated by upwards of 260 wood-cuts, cloth lettered, $2 25. 1846.

——— (Josh.) On the Prevention of Accidents in Mines. 8vo. cloth, $1 25. Lond.

——— (J.) Travels in the Great Desert of Sahara, in 1845–46. Numerous plates and maps. 2 vols. 8vo. cloth, $8 50. Lond. 1848.

——— Specimens of the Architecture of the Reigns of Elizabeth and James I. 4to. half mor. 60 plates, $10 50. Lond.

——— Studies of old English Mansions. 4 vols. 4to. cloth, $50 00. London.

——— (C. J.) Popular Treatise on the Warming and Ventilation of Buildings, showing the Advantages of the Improved System of Heated Water, Circulation, &c. Plates, second edition, 8vo. $2 00. London.

——— (W. A.) Reprints of Rare Tracts and Imprints of Ancient Manuscripts, chiefly illustrative of the History of the Northern Counties. Biography, 2 vols. Historical Tracts, 4 vols. Miscellaneous Tracts, 1 vol. Complete in 7 vols. 12mo. bds. $40 00. Newcastle, 1847–49.

Richmond, (Rev. Legh.) Annals of the Poor A new edition, 12mo. cloth, portrait and engravings, 75 cents. Philadelphia.

Richter, (J. P. T.) Levana; or, the Doctrine of Education. Translated from the German. Post 8vo. cloth, $3 25. Lond. 1848.

Rickman, (Thos.) Attempt to Discriminate the different Styles of Architecture in England. 8vo. cloth, 30 plates, 465 wood-cuts, $6 00. London, 1848.

Riddell, (J. L.) Monograph of the Silver Dollar. 8vo. cloth, $4 00. New Orleans, 1845.

Riddle, (Rev. J. E.) Ecclesiastical Chronology; or, Annals of the Christian Church from its foundation to the present time. 8vo. cloth, $4 00. London, 1840.

——— Luther and his Times; or, a History of the Rise and Progress of the German Reformation. 12mo. cloth, $1 75. London, 1837.

——— Manual of Christian Antiquities; or, an Account of the Constitutions, Ministers, Worship, &c., of the Ancient Church, with an Analysis of the Writings of the Anti-Nicene Fathers. Thick 8vo. cloth, $3 50.

——— and **Scott's** English and Latin Lexicon. 8vo. cloth, $5 00 New York.

Rider, (W.) Principles of Perspective. 8vo. cloth, $2 25. London.

Ridgley, (Thomas, D D.) A Body of Divinity, wherein the Doctrines of the Christian Religion are Explained and Defended. 4 vols. 8vo. $4 50. Phila. 1814.

Ridley, (Bp.) The Works of. 8vo. cloth, $3 75. Cambridge, Parker Society, 1841.

Rigby, (E.) Midwifery. 8vo. sheep, $2 81. Philadelphia.

Rigg, (R.) Experimental Researches, Chemical and Agricultural, showing Carbon to be a Compound Body made by Plants, and Decomposed by Putrefaction. 8vo. bds. $1 75. London, 1844.

Riggs, (E.) Manual of the Chaldee Language. 8vo. cloth, $1 75. Boston.

Rimbault, (Dr. E. T.) Bibliographical Account of the Musical and Poetical Works published in England in the Sixteenth and Seventeenth Centuries. 8vo. cloth, $1 25. London, 1847.

——— American edition. 8vo. 75 cents. New York, 1848.

——— (E. F.) Book of Christmas Carols, with Melodies. Small 4to. $1 25. London.

——— Nursery Rhymes, with the Ancient Tunes. Small 4to. $1 75. London.

Rio, (A.) Collection of Tables for Navigation. 4to. cloth, $19 00.

Ripa, (Father.) Memoirs of, during Thirteen Years' Residence at the Court of Peking, in the Service of the Emperor of China, &c. Translated from the Italian, by F. Prandi. 12mo. cloth, 50 cents. New York.

Ripley, (H. J.) Sacred Rhetoric; or, Composition and Delivery of Sermons. 12mo. cloth, 75 cents. Boston, 1849.

——— (G.) Specimens of Foreign Standard Literature. 14 vols. 12mo. each $1 00. Boston.

Cousin, Jouffroy. and Constant's Philosophical Miscellanies, 2 vols.
Goethe and Schiller's Select Minor Poems, translated, 1 vol.
Eckerman's Conversations with Goethe, 1 vol.
Jouffroy's Introduction to Ethics, 2 vols.
Menzel's German Literature, 3 vols.
De Wette's Theodore; or, the Skeptic's Conversion, 2 vols.
De Wette's Human Life; or, Practical Ethics, 2 vols.
Brooks' Songs and Ballads, 1 vol.

Ritch, (J. W.) The American Architect; comprising original designs of cheap Country and Villa Residences. 4to. cloth, $3 50. New York.

Ritchie, (Robt.) Rise, Progress, &c. of Railways. 12mo. cloth, $2 75. London.

Ritter, (Dr.) History of Ancient Philosophy. Translated by Morrison. 4 vols. 8vo. $10 00. London.

Ritson's Various Works, as published by Pickering, the set, viz.: Robin Hood, 2 vols.; Annals of the Caledonians, 2 vols.; Ancient Songs and Ballads, 2 vols.; Memoirs of the Celts, 1 vol.; Life of King Arthur, 1 vol.; Ancient Popular Poetry, 1 vol.; Fairy Tales, 1 vol.; Letters and Memoirs of Ritson, 2 vols.; together, 12 vols. post 8vo. cloth, $17 50. Lond. 1827–33.

River Dove, (The,) with some Quiet Thoughts on the Happy Practice of Angling. 12mo. cloth, printed in the old style, $2 00; mor. gilt, $3 50. Pickering, 1847.

Roads and Railroads, (Vehicles and Modes of Travelling of,) of Ancient and Modern Countries, with Accounts of Bridges, Tunnels, and Canals, in various parts of the World. 12mo. cloth, $1 00.

Robin, (C.) Galerie des Gens de Lettres au XIXe Siecle, avec portraits, d'apres nature. Imp. 8vo. paper, $4 00. Paris, 1848.

——— Du Microscope et des Injections. 8vo. avec planches, $3 25. Paris, 1849.

——— Des Vegetaux qui croissent sur l'Homme et sur les Animaux vivants. Royal 8vo. paper, avec trois planches, $1 25. Paris, 1847.

Robinson Crusoe, (Life and Adventures of.) 8vo. cloth, 300 cuts, $1 75. New York.

——— A fine edition, with plates, after Stothard's Designs. Cr. 8vo. cloth, $2 25. London, 1848.

Robinson, (Thos.) Scripture Characters; or, a Practical Improvement of the Principal Characters of the Old and New Testament. Portrait, 8vo. cloth, $2 50. Lond. 1839.

——— (Dr.) Bibliotheca Sacra. Tracts and Essays connected with Biblical Literature and Theology. Complete in 1 vol. 8vo. cloth, $3 00. New York.

——— (E.) and **Smith's** Biblical Researches in Palestine, &c. 3 vols. 8vo. cloth, $8 00. Boston.

——— Complete Series of Cottage Architecture. 6 vols. 4to. with 390 plates, half bound, mor. $54 00.

Or separately:

——— Rural Architecture, being a Series of Designs for Ornamental Cottages, in 96 plates, with Estimates. Fourth greatly improved edition, royal 4to. half mor. $13 50. 1837.

——— New Series of Ornamental Cottages and Villas. 56 plates, by Harding and Allom. Royal 4to. half mor. $12 50. 1838.

——— Ornamental Villas. 96 plates, half mor. $13 50. 1836.

——— Farm Buildings. 56 plates, half mor. $9 50. 1837.

——— Lodges and Park Entrances. 48 plates, half mor. $9 50. 1837.

——— Village Architecture. Fourth edition, with additional plate. 41 plates, half bound, uniform, $7 00. 1837.

——— (R.) Art of Curing, Pickling, &c. Meat and Fish. 12mo. $1 37. London.

Robinson, (E.) Greek Lexicon of the New Testament. 8vo. half Russia, $5 50. Boston.

——— Gesenius's Hebrew Lexicon. 8vo. half Russia, $6 00. Boston.

——— and **Britton's** Vitruvius Britannicus History of Woburn Abbey, Hatfield House, Hardwicke Hall, and Cassiobury Park. Illustrated by Plans, Elevations, and Internal Views of the Apartments. Imp. folio, half mor. 44 plates, $25 00. Lond. 1847

Robison, (J.) Mechanical Philosophy, by Brewster. 4 vols. 8vo. cloth, $14 00. Lond.

Robley, (A. J.) Selection of Madeira Flowers. Folio, $6 50. London.

Roberts, (Joseph.) Oriental Illustrations of the Holy Scriptures, collected from the Customs, Rites, Literature, &c. of the Hindoos. 8vo. cloth, $2 50. London, 1844.

——— (W. H.) Scottish Ale Brewer. 8vo. cloth, $3 25. London.

——— (Emma.) East India Voyager; or, Ten Minutes' Advice to the Outward Bound. 12mo. cloth, $2 00. London, 1839.

——— (Mary.) The Seaside Companion; or, Marine Natural History. 12mo. cloth, woodcuts, $1 50. London, 1835.

——— (W.) History of Letter-Writing, from the earliest period to the Fifth Century. 1 vol. 8vo. $3 50. London.

Robertson, (J. P. and W. P.) Letters on South America. 3 vols. post 8vo. $7 50. London.

——— Four Years in Paraguay. 2 vols. 12mo. $1 00. Philadelphia.

——— (W.) History of America. 8vo. sheep, $1 75. New York.

——— Treatise on the Teeth. 8vo. cloth, $1 75. Philadelphia.

——— Dictionary of Latin Phrases, comprehending a Methodical Digest of the various Phrases from the best Authors, which have been collected in all Phraseological Works hitherto published, for the more speedy progress of Students in Latin Composition. New edition, with considerable Additions, Alterations, and Corrections, by Dr. Valpy. Post 8vo. roan lettered, $2 75. London.

——— American edition. 8vo. sheep, $1 75. New York.

——— Historical Works; containing the History of Scotland, History of the Reign of the Emperor Charles V., History of America, and Historical Disquisition concerning Ancient India, with an Account of the Life and Writings of the Author, by Dugald Stewart. 1 large vol. imp. 8vo. portrait, cloth lettered, $6 50. 1840.

——— (Dr. W.) Works, with Life, by Dugald Stewart. 8 vols. 8vo. calf gilt, marbled leaves, portrait, $23 25; cloth, $16 00. Lond. 1840.

——— 3 vols. 8vo. $3 00. New York.

Robespierre, (M.) The Life of, with a Selection from his Correspondence, by G. H. Lewis. 12mo. cloth, $2 50. London.

——— 12mo. cloth, $1 00. Phila. 1849.

Robson, (Thos.) British Herald; an enlarged Dictionary of Armorial Bearings of the Nobility and Gentry of Great Britain and Ireland. 3 vols. 4to. $60 00. London.

Roby, (I) Popular Traditions of Lancashire. 3 vols. 12mo. cloth, portrait, $4 00. Lon. 1843.

Rodham, (H.) Treatise on Land Surveying. 8vo. cloth, $1 50. London.

Roger of Wendover. Flowers of History; comprising the History of England, from the Descent of the Saxons to A. D. 1235. Formerly ascribed to Matthew Paris. To be completed in 2 vols. Vol. 1, foolscap 8vo. cloth, $1 37. London, 1849.

Rogers, (Samuel.) Poems. 8vo. mor. gilt leaves, beautifully illustrated by Turner, $7 00. London.

——— Italy, a Poem. 8vo. mor. fine illustrations, by Turner, $7 00. London.

——— Poetical Works. Complete in 1 vol. 18mo. paper, 75 cents. Lond. 1846.

——— (J.) Fruit Cultivator. 12mo. cloth, $1 75. London.

——— Vegetable Cultivator. 12mo. cloth, $2 25. London.

——— American Biography. 8vo. sheep, $3 50. Philadelphia.

Roget, (P. M.) Animal and Vegetable Physiology. 2 vols. 8vo. cloth, $2 50. Phila.

Rohner, (G. W.) Treatise on Musical Composition. Post 4to. cloth, $4 75. Lond.

——— Key to Treatise on Musical Composition. $1 50. London.

Roland Cashel. By Lever. 8vo. cloth, with illustrations by Phiz, $1 00. New York.

Rolando's Art of Fencing, by Forsyth. 18mo. cloth, $2 75. London.

——— Introductory Course of Fencing. Royal 8vo. half bound, $1 00. London.

Rollin, (C.) Ancient History. 2 vols. 8vo. sheep, $3 75. New York.

——— 6 vols. 8vo. half calf gilt, $11 00. London, 1847.

Rome, as seen by a New Yorker in 1843–44, with a map of Modern Rome. 12mo. cloth, 75 cents. New York.

Romilly, (Sir Samuel.) Life of, written by himself, with his Letters and Political Diary. Edited by his Sons. Third edition, 2 vols. foolscap 8vo. cloth, portrait, $2 50. London, 1841.

Ronald's Fly Fisher's Entomology. Illustrated by colored representations of the Natural and Artificial Insect, &c. 8vo. cloth, 20 copperplates, $3 50. Lond. 1839.

——— (Hugh.) Pyrus Malus Brentfordiensis; or, a concise Description of Selected Apples, with a Figure of each sort drawn from Nature on stone, by his Daughter. 4to. cloth, 42 plates, containing some hundreds of beautifully colored figures, $15 00. Lond. 1831.

Rondelet, (J.) Traite Theorique et pratique de l'art de Bâtir. 6 vols. 8vo. with atlas of plates, $25 00. Paris.

Roorbach, (O. A.) Bibliotheca Americana; a Catalogue of American Publications, including Reprints and original Works from 1820 to 1848, inclusive. Royal 8vo. cloth, $4 00. New York, 1849.

Rose, (H.) Practical Treatise of Chemical Analysis; including Tables for Calculations in Analysis. Translated from the French, and from the fourth German edition, with Notes and Additions, by A. Normandy. Qualitative and Quantitative. 2 vols. 8vo. cloth, $8 50. London, 1848.

Rose, (Rev. H. J.) A new General Biographical Dictionary. Vols. 1 to 12, 8vo. cloth, $65 00. London.

——— (The.) Memoirs of the Rose, Queen of Flowers. Square 18mo. cloth gilt, colored plates, $1 00. London, 1840.

——— Garden of Persia: Poems. Translated from the Persian, by Louisa Costello. Beautifully illuminated. 8vo. mor. gilt, $6 00. London.

Rosenmuller, (E. F.) Mineralogy and Botany of the Bible. 12mo. cloth, $1 75. London.

Roscoe's Life of Leo X. and Lorenzo de Medici. 3 vols. 8vo. tree-marbled calf, $14 00.

——— (Thomas.) Life of William the Conqueror. Now first published from Official Records, &c. Post 8vo. cloth, $1 50. London, 1848.

Ross, (Sir J. C.) Memoirs and Correspondence of Admiral Lord de Saumarez, from original Papers in the Possession of the Family. 2 vols. 8vo. cloth, portrait, $3 50. Lond. 1838.

——— A Voyage of Discovery and Research in the Southern and Antarctic Regions during the Years 1829–43. 2 vols. 8vo. cloth, maps, plates, and wood-cuts, $10 00. Lond. 1847.

——— (A.) Adventures of the First Settlers on the Oregon or Columbia River; being a Narrative of the Expedition fitted out by John Jacob Astor to establish the Pacific Fur Company, with an Account of some Indian Tribes on the Coast of the Pacific. Post 8vo. cloth, $3 25. London, 1849.

Rossignon, (Jules.) Guide Pratique des emigrants en Californie et des Voyageurs dans l'Amerique Espagnole. 12mo. paper, 32 cents. Paris, 1849.

Rotteck, (C.) History of the World. Translated by J. Jones. 4 vols. 8vo. cloth, $6 00. Philadelphia.

Roujoux et Alfred Mainguet. Histoire d'Angleterre depuis les temps les plus recules jusqu'a nos jours; nouvelle edition, entierement refondue, augmentee de plus d'un tiers, ornee de 500 gravures sur bois, et accompagnee de tableaux synoptiques, plans, cartes geographiques, etc. 2 beaux vol. grand in 8, mor. gilt top, $9 00. Paris.

Rousseau, (J. B.) Œuvres completes, avec une commentaire historique et litteraire, precede d'un nouvel essai sur la vie et les ecrits de l'auteur; avec portrait, rare. 5 vols. in 8, demi veau, $11 00. Paris, 1820.

——— (J. J.) Œuvres completes avec des eclaircissements et des notes historiques par P. R. Auguis. 27 vols. grand in 8, demi veau, $40 00. Paris, 1824–25.

——— La Nouvelle Heloise, edition illustree par MM. Tony Johannot, Em. Hattier, Lepoitevin, Girardet, Guerin, de 250 beaux dessins, dont 25 a 30 tires sur papier de Chine, et d'un superbe frontispice avec portrait. 3 vol. grand in 8, demi maroquin, $12 00. Paris, 1845.

——— Le meme ouvrage broche, $6 50.

——— La Nouvelle Heloise. 12mo. broché, $1 00; half mor. $1 50. Paris, 1847.

Rousseau, (J. J.) Emile ou de l'Education. 12mo. paper, $1 00. Paris, 1848.

——— Les Confessions. Edition illustree par Tony Johannot, Baron, Girardet, de 28 magnifiques vignettes. 1 vol. grand in 8, demi maroquin, $6 00. Paris, 1845.

——— Le meme ouvrage broché, $4 00.

——— Les Confessions. 12mo. broché, $1 00; half mor. $1 50. Paris, 1846.

——— Confessions Translated. 4 vols. 12mo. cloth, $6 50. London.

Roussel. Systeme Physique et Moral de la Femme. 12mo. paper, $1 00. Paris, 1845.

Routh's Reliquæ Sacræ; sive auctorum fere jam Perditorum secundi tertiique seculi post Christum natum, quæ supersunt accedunt Synodi, et Epistolæ Canonicæ, Nicæno Concilio Antiquiores. 5 vols. 8vo. cloth, $15 75. Oxford, 1846.

Roux de Luicy, (Le.) Les Cent nouvelles Nouvelles. 2 vols. 12mo. paper, $2 00. Paris, 1841.

Rowan, (F.) New Modern French Reader. Edited by J. L. Jewett, 75 cents. New York.

Rowbotham, (I.) Diamond Pocket Dictionary of the French and English Languages. 24mo. bound, $1 75.

Rowe, (J.) New Principles of Political Economy. 8vo. $1 00. Boston.

Rowton, (Frederic.) The Female Poets of Great Britain, Chronologically arranged, with Selections and Critical Remarks. 8vo. cloth, $3 50. London, 1848.

——— The Same, illustrated. 8vo. cloth gilt, $5 00; mor. $7 00. Phila. 1849.

Royal Engineers. Papers on Subjects connected with the Duties of the Corps of. Vol. 1, second edition, plates and cuts. 4to. cloth, $4 75.

——— Vol. 2, second edition, plates and cuts. 4to. cloth, $7 25.

——— Vol. 3, several plates and cuts· 4to. cloth, $7 25.

——— Vol. 4, 40 plates and numerous cuts. 4to. cloth, $8 50.

——— Vol. 5, 60 plates and numerous cuts. 4to. cloth, $11 00.

——— Vol. 6, 62 plates and 30 wood-cuts. 4to. cloth, $11 00.

——— Vol. 7, plates and wood-cuts. 4to. cloth, $9 00.

——— Vol. 8, plates and wood-cuts. 4to. cloth, $9 00.

——— Vol. 9, plates and wood-cuts. 4to. cloth, $11 00. London.

Royle, (J. F.) Materia Medica and Therapeutics, by Carson. 8vo. sheep, $3 50. Philadelphia.

——— Botany of the Himalayan Mountains. 2 vols. 4to. cloth, $70 00. London.

Roxburgh, (W.) Description of Indian Plants. 2 vols. 8vo. cloth, $15 50. Lond.

Roxburghe Ballads, (The Book of.) Edited by J. Payne Collier. Printed in imitation of the old style. Small 4to. half mor. $6 50. Lond. 1847.

Rubens, (P. P.) His Life and Genius. Translated from the German of Dr. Waagen, by R. R. Noel. 12mo. cloth, $2 75. Lond.

Ruckert, (E. F.) Therapeutics of Homœopathy. Translated by Kempel. $3 50. New York.

Ruding, (Rev. R.) Annals of the Coinage of Great Britain and its Dependencies, from the earliest period of Authentic History to the Reign of Victoria. 3 vols. 4to. cloth, numerous plates, $26 00. Lond. 1840.

Rues de Paris, (Les.) Paris, Ancien et Moderne. 2 vols. imp. 8vo. paper, profusely illustrated with steel and wood engravings, $6 50. Paris, 1844.

Ruoff's Repertory of Homœopathic Medicines. $1 50. New York.

Rupp, (J. D.) History of all Religious Denominations in the United States. 8vo. sheep, $3 50. New York.

Rural Cemeteries of America. 4to. mor. $11 00. New York.

Rural Architecture. A Series of Drawings in the Italian style, for Villas, &c., made out practically as Working Plans, for the use of Gentlemen Building, with Forms of Contract, Specifications, &c. Folio, bds. $6 00. London, 1843.

Ruschenberger's Voyage round the World in 1835–37. 2 vols. 8vo. cloth, $6 50. London.

——— (W. S. W.) Natural History. 2 vols. 12mo. half mor. $3 25. Phila.

Rush, (J.) On the Voice. 8vo. cloth, $3 00. Philadelphia.

——— (R.) Memoranda of a Residence at the Court of London; comprising Incidents, Official and Personal, from 1819 to 1825. 8vo. cloth, $1 50. Philadelphia.

Ruskin, (John.) Modern Painters and Landscape Painting. 2 vols. 12mo. cloth, $1 88. New York, 1848.

——— Seven Lamps of Architecture. Imp. 8vo. embossed cloth, gilt top, 14 etchings, $6 50. London, 1849.

——— 12mo. cloth, 14 etchings, $1 25. New York, 1849.

Russell, (W.) History of Modern Europe to 1763, continued to 1825, by W. Jones. 3 vols. 8vo. sheep. New York.

——— (J. S.) Treatise on Steam and Steam Navigation. Post 8vo. cloth, $2 25. Edinburgh, 184

——— Do. on Steam Engine, $2 25.

——— (Jos.) A Treatise on Practical an. Chemical Agriculture, with a Dissertation on the Cultivation of the Soil. 8vo. $2 00.

——— Life of Oliver Cromwell. 2 vols. 18mo. cloth, $1 00. New York.

Russian and English Dictionary. 18mo. bds. $1 50. London.

Ruxton's Adventures in the Rocky Mountains. 12mo. cloth, 63 cents. New York.

——— Life in the Far West. 12mo cloth, 63 cents. New York, 1849.

Ryder, (A. P.) Practical Rules for Steering from a Hurricane. 8vo. cloth, 63 cents. Lond.

Ryland, (J. E.) Life of John Foster. 2 vols. in 1, 12mo. cloth, $1 25. New York.

Saavedra, (Duc de Rivas.) Insurrection de Naples en 1847, traduite et precede d'une Introduction par Le Baron Leon D'Hervey. 2 vols. 8vo. broché, $3 00. Paris, 1849.

Sabbath, (The); or, an Examination of the Six Texts commonly adduced from the New Testament in Proof of a Christian Sabbath. 8vo. cloth, $2 50. London, 1849.

Sabine, (L.) American Loyalists; or, Biographical Sketches of Adherents to the British Crown in the War of the Revolution. 8vo. cloth, $2 75. Boston.

——— (Lieut. Col. E.) Observations on Days of unusual Magnetic Disturbance. Part 1, 4to. cloth, $4 00. London, 1843.

——— (Major E.) Report on the Magnetic Isoclinical and Isodynamic Lines in the British Islands. 8vo. cloth, $1 50. Lond. 1839.

——— Observations on Days of unusual Magnetic Disturbance, made at the British Colonial Observatories, under the Departments of the Ordnance and Admiralty. 8vo. bds. $3 50. London.

Sacred Hymns. Translated from the German, by Frances E. Cox. 12mo. mor. gilt, $2 00. London, 1841.

Sacred and Legendary Art. By Mrs. Jameson. With numerous illustrations. 2 vols. 8vo. $12 00. Lond. 1848.

Sadler, (M. T.) Memoir of the Life and Writings of. 8vo. cloth, portrait, $1 25. London, 1842.

——— (Thos.) The Silent Pastor; or, Consolations for the Sick. 18mo. cloth, 50 cents. Boston, 1848.

Sainte-Beuve, Poesies completes. 12mo. paper, $1 00.

——— Volupte. 12mo. paper, $1 00.

——— Poesie française au Seizieme siecle. 12mo. paper, $1 00. Paris.

Saintes, (Arnaud.) A Critical History of Rationalism in Germany, from its origin to the present time. Translated and edited by Rev. Dr. Beard. 8vo. cloth, $3 00. London, 1849.

Saint Edme. Repertoire generale des causes celebres anciennes et modernes. 15 vol. in 8, demi veau, $16 00. Paris, 1834.

Saintine, (X.) Picciola, edition illustree; 120 gravures sur bois, gravees par Porret, sur les dessins de Johannot, Nanteuil, etc. 1 vol. grand in 8, $2 50.

——— (X. B.) Picciola. 12mo. $1 00. Paris, 1849.

——— Picciola. Imp. 8vo. paper, illustrated with beautiful engravings, $3 00. Paris, 1847.

Saint-Pierre, (B. de.) Paul et Virginie la chaumiere Indienne. Imp. 8vo. paper, illustrated with a profusion of engravings on steel and wood, $7 50. Paris, 1839.

Saint Simon, (Le Duc de.) Memoirs complets et authentiques sur le siecle de Louis XIV. et la regence, publies sur le manuscrit original entierement ecrit de la main de l'auteur par le marquis de Saint Simon; nouvelle edition, revue et corrigee; avec 38 portraits. 40 vol. en 39, demi veau, $25 00. Paris, 1840.

Salambier. Principes d'Ornements pour l'architecture, depuis les fragments jusqu'aux chapiteaux. Cours d'etudes dessines et graves a la maniere du crayon, par Salambier Grand in 4 de 40 planches, $4 00.

Sale, (Sir R.) Note on the Defensive Works in Jellalabad. (Papers, R. E. vol. 6, 4to.) London.

Salmon, (Geo.) Treatise on Conic Sections. 8vo. cloth, $3 75. London.

Salt, (H.) Voyage to Abyssinia, and Travels into the Interior of that Country, with an Account of the Portuguese Settlements on the East Coast of Africa. 4to. cloth, maps, charts, and plates, $5 50. London, 1844.

——— (Sam.) Statistics and Calculations regarding Railways or Canals. 8vo. cloth, $2 12. Manchester, 1845.

Salter, (S. F.) Angler's Guide; being a Plain and Complete Practical Treatise on the Art of Angling, &c. 12mo. cloth, 88 wood-cuts, $2 50. London, 1841.

Salverte, (E.) Philosophy of Magic, &c. Translated by A. T. Thomson. 2 vols. 8vo. cloth, $2 50. London, 1841.

——— Philosophy of Magic. 2 vols. 12mo. cloth, $1 00. New York, 1847.

Samuel, (E.) Historical Account of the British Army and of the Law Military. Commentary on the Mutiny Act. Rules and Articles of War. Decisions of Courts Martial. 8vo. half calf, $2 00. London, 1816.

Sand, (G.) Jeannic. 2 vols. 12mo. paper, $1 50. Bruxelles, 1845.

——— Le Meunier D'Angibault. 2 vols. 12mo. paper, $1 75. Bruxelles, 1842.

——— Leone Leoni. 12mo. paper, 63 cents. Bruxelles, 1842.

——— Les Maitres Mosaistes. 12mo. paper, 63 cents. Bruxelles, 1842.

——— Melchior, Mouny, Robin. 12mo. paper, 50 cents. Bruxelles, 1843.

——— Consuello. 4 vols. broché, $3 50. Paris, 1845.

——— Teverino. 12mo. paper, 63 cents. Bruxelles, 1845

——— The Works of. Translated by Matilda M. Hays, viz.: The Last Aldini. Simon. Mauprat. The Miller of Angibault. Letters of a Traveller. Andre. Mosaic Masters. Oreo. Fanchette. The Companion of the Tour of France. 6 vols. 12mo. cloth, $7 50. London, 1847.

——— (Me. Dudevant.) Consuelo. 2 vols. 12mo. bds. $1 50. Boston.

——— The Countess of Rudolstadt; a Sequel to Consuelo. 2 vols. 12mo. $1 00. Boston.

Sands, (R. C.) The Writings of, in Prose and Verse, with a Memoir of the Author. 2 vols. 8vo. cloth, $2 50. New York, 1835.

Sand and Canvas. A Narrative of Adventures in Egypt, with a Sojourn among the Artists in Rome. 8vo. cloth, colored plates, $3 25. London.

Sandby's Mesmerism and its Opponents. 12mo. cloth, $1 50. London, 1848.

Sanderson, (Bp.) Sermons, with Life of the Author, by Izaac Walton, and Essay, by Rev. R. Montgomery. 2 vols. 8vo. cloth, $3 75.

Sandford and Merton, (The History of,) by Mr. Thomas Day. 16mo. mor. gilt, plates, $1 50. London.

Sandham, (Capt.) On the Coast Defences of Holland. (Papers, R. E. vol. 2, 4to.) Lond.

——— Mode of Curing Smoky Chimneys, with Remarks on Count Rumford's System. (Papers, R. E. vol. 2, 4to.) London.

Sandey, (Archbishop.) The Sermons and Miscellaneous Pieces of. 8vo. cloth, $3 00. London, Parker Society, 1841.

Sanier. Recueil complet de chiffres offrant une collection de plus de 400 exemples a deux ou trois lettres au moyen desquels il est facile d'en composer d'autres et de les varier a l'infini. 34 pl. in-4o avec texte explicatif, 75 cents. Paris,

Santi. Modeles de meubles et de decorations interieures, tels que tables, secretaires, commodes, bureaux, fauteuils, chaises, lits, alcoves, draperies de croisees, etc., dessines par Santi. Nouvelle edition composee de 86 pl. epresentant un grand nombre de meubles de tout les genres, a l'usage des ebenistes, tapissiers, fabricants de bronze, etc. 1 vol. in-fol. avec texte, $12 50. Paris.

Sartorius, (E.) The Person and Work of Christ. Translated by Rev. O. S. Stearns. 18mo. cloth. Boston, 1848.

Sargeant, (F. W.) Minor Surgery. 12mo. sheep, $1 50. Philadelphia.

——— (Epes.) Songs of the Sea and other Poems. 12mo. bds. 75 cents. Boston.

Savage, (Capt.) Description of the Landing Wharf erected at Hobbs' Point, Milford Haven, for the Accommodation of Steam Packet Service at that Station, and of the Diving Bells and Machinery used in the Erection. (Papers, R. E. vol. 1, 4to.) London.

——— (W.) A Treatise on the Preparation of Printing Inks, both Black and Colored. 8vo. cloth, $12 50. London, 1832.

——— Practical Hints on Decorative Printing. Folio, half mor. gilt tops, illustrated with colored plates and specimens, $12 00. London, 1842.

Say, (J. B.) Political Economy. 8vo. sheep, $1 75. Philadelphia.

Saurin, (Rev. J.) Sermons. Translated, with additional Sermons, by Rev. S. Burder. 3 vols. 8vo. half calf neat, $7 50. Lond. 1836.

Scarron. Le Roman Comique. Nouvelle edition precedee d'une Notice sur l'auteur et sur l'etat des lettres en France au dix-septieme siecle par P. Christian. 12mo. broché, $1 00. Paris, 1846.

Scenes on the Lakes; being a complete Guide to the Lakes, with Mr. Wordsworth's Description of the Scenery of the Country. 12mo. cloth, plates and maps, $1 50. Kendal, 1842.

Scenes in the Life of our Saviour. Edited by R. W. Griswold. Royal 8vo. cloth gilt, plates, $3 00. Phila. 1848.

——— Lives of the Patriarchs and Prophets. Edited by the Rev. H. H. Weld. Royal 8vo. cloth gilt, plates, $3 00. Phila. 1848.

Scenes and Thougts in Europe. By an American. 12mo. cloth, 50 cents. New York, 1848.

Schayes, (A. G. B.) Treatise on the Pointed Style of Architecture in Belgium. Translated by H. Austin. 4to. bds. engravings, $3 25. Lond. 1845.

Schefer, (L.) The Artist's Married Life; being that of Albert Durer. Translated by Mrs. J. R. Stoddart. 12mo. cloth, $1 00. Boston, 1849.

Schelling. Ecrits philosophiques et morceaux propres a donner un idee generale de son systeme. Trans. par Renard. 8vo. broché, $2 50. Paris, 1847.

Scheult. Recueil d'Architecture levee et mesuree en Italie, par L.-F. Scheulte, architecte a Nantes. Un volume in-folio de 72 planches avec texte, $12 00. Paris.

Schill's Outlines of Pathological Seminology. 8vo. sheep, $1 75. Phila.

Schiller, (F.) Works Translated. Vols. 1 to 4. 12mo. cloth, each 88 cents. London, 1847–49.

——— Werke. 10 vols. 8vo. paper, beautifully printed and illustrated with portrait, $9 00. Leipsic, 1844.

——— History of the Revolt of the Netherlands. Trial and Execution of Counts Egmont and Horn, and the Siege of Antwerp. 12mo cloth, 50 cents. New York, 1847.

——— History of the Thirty Years' War. Translated by Rev. A. J. W. Morrison. 12mo. cloth, 50 cents. New York, 1846.

——— The Bride of Messina. Translated by A. Lodge. 8vo. cloth, $1 37. Lond. 1841.

——— Philosophical and Æsthetic Letters and Essays. Translated, with an Introduction, by J. Weiss. Post 8vo. cloth, $1 25. Boston.

——— Homage of the Arts. Translated by C. T. Brooks. 12mo. bds. 63 cents. Boston.

——— and **Korner.** Correspondence of; comprising Sketches and Anecdotes of Goethe, the Schlegels, Wieland, and other contemporaries, with Biographical Sketches and Notes, by Leonard Simpson, Esq. 3 vols. 8vo. cloth, $9 50. London, 1849.

Schlegel's Lectures on the Philosophy of History. Translated from the German, by J. B. Robertson. 12mo. cloth, portrait, 88 cents. London, 1847.

——— Lectures on Dramatic Literature. Post 8vo. cloth, 88 cents. London.

——— Philosophy of Life and Language. 12mo. cloth, 88 cents. London.

——— Lectures on the History of Literature. 12mo. cloth, $1 50. London.

Schleiden, (J. M.) Principles of Scientific Botany; or, Botany as an Inductive Science. Translated by E. Lankester. 8vo. cloth, $6 00. London, 1849.

——— The Plant; a Biography, in a Series of Popular Lectures. Translated by Arthur Henfrey. 5 colored plates and 13 engravings. 8vo. cloth, $4 50. London, 1848.

Schlosser, (F. C.) History of the Eighteenth and Part of the Nineteenth Centuries. Translated, with Notes, by D. Davidson. 6 vols. 8vo. cloth, $18 00. Lond. 1843–46.

Schmit. Cours elementaire du dessin d'ornement, d'apres les types originaux de l'antiquite et du moyen-age, a l'usage des artistes, des eleves et des ouvriers, par J. P. Schmit. Un cahier de 27 planches petit in folio lithographiees, $4 00. Paris.

Schmitz, (Dr. L.) History of Rome. 12mo. cloth, 75 cents. New York.

——— Grammar of the Latin Language. 12mo. cloth, $1 00 Edinburgh, 1849.

Schmucker's Modern Infidelity. 12mo. cloth, $1 00. Philadelphia.

——— Psychology. 12mo. cloth, $1 00. New York.

Schmitzler, (J. H.) Statistique generale methodique et complete de la France. 4 vols. 8vo. paper, $9 00. Paris, 1846.

Schoen. L'Homme et son Perfectionnement. 8vo. paper, $2 25. Paris, 1845.

Schomburg, (R. H.) History of Barbadoes. Royal 8vo. cloth, $9 50. Lond.

——— Map to do. $6 50. London.

Schomann, (G. F.) A Dissertation on the Assemblies of the Athenians. 8vo. cloth, $2 25. Cambridge, 1838.

Schoolcraft, (H. R.) Notes on the Iroquois; or, Contributions to American History, Antiquities, and General Ethnology. 8vo. cloth, colored plates, $2 50. Albany, 1848.

——— Oneota; or, the Red Race of America. 8vo. cloth, $1 50. New York.

Schramke, (T.) Description of the New York Croton Aqueduct, in English, German, and French. 4to. 20 plates, $2 50. N. York.

Scituate, Mass. History of, to 1831, by Thomas Dean. 8vo. cloth, $1 75. Boston.

Sclavonic, or Glagolitic Gospels. Evangelia Sclavice: a singularly exact and beautiful fac-simile of a very Ancient Manuscript of the Sclavonic Gospels used at the Coronation of the French Kings at Rheims, by M. Silvestre, with a Latin Translation opposite. 4to. containing 63 finely engraved plates, colored and illuminated, with a large plate of the Sclavonic Characters; olive mor. richly blind tooled in the old Style, leather joints and tooled edges, $30 50. Paris, 1843. (Only 100 copies printed.)

Scoffern, (John.) The Manufacture of Sugar in the Colonies and at Home Chemically considered. 8vo. cloth, $3 00. Lond. 1849.

——— Chemistry no Mystery. 12mo. cloth, $1 50. London.

Scoresby, (Rev. W.) Zoistic Magnetism. 12mo. cloth, $1 75. London, 1849.

Scott, (D.) The Engineer and Machinist's Assistant; being a Series of Plans, Sections, and Elevations of Steam Engines, Spinning Machines, Mills for Grinding, Tools, &c., taken from Machines of Approved Construction at present in Operation, with Descriptions and Instructions for Drawing Machinery. 2 vols. folio, half Russia, $20 00. London.

——— Elements of Arithmetic and Algebra, for the use of the Royal Military College. 8vo. cloth, $4 25. London.

——— Plane Trigonometry and Mensuration, for the use of the Royal Military College. 8vo. cloth, $2 75. London.

——— (R.) Practical Cotton Spinner; or, Manufacturer's, or Manager's, Overlooker's, and Mechanic's Companion; being a comprehensive System of Calculations of Mill Gearing and Machinery, with the most recent Improvements in Machinery. 8vo. cloth, plates, $4 00. London, 1846.

Scott, (Gen.) Infantry Tactics. 3 vols. 12mo. cloth, plates, $2 50. New York.

——— And his Staff. Compiled from Public Documents and Private Correspondence. 12mo. cloth, portraits, $1 00. Phila. 1848.

——— (James.) The Life, Letters, and Remains of the Rev. Robert Pollok. 12mo. cloth, portrait, 63 cents. New York, 1848.

——— (Rev. Thos.) Family Bible. 6 vols. 8vo. sheep, $12 00. Boston.

——— 3 vols. imp. 8vo. cloth, $13 50. Lond.

——— Theological Works. 8vo. cloth, $1 50. Edinburgh, 1838.

——— (W. B.) Ornamentist; or, Artisan's Manual, in the various Branches of Ornamental Art, being a Series of Designs selected from the best French and German Ornamentalists, &c. 4to. cloth, $16 00. Lond. 1845.

——— (Sir Walter.) Works complete, with Life, by Lockhart. 98 vols. foolscap 8vo. cloth, 198 engravings, best edition, $90 00; or half mor. lettered, $130. London, 1829–39.

——— Complete Works, with Life. (Abbottsford edition.) 17 vols. royal 8vo. cloth, numerous wood-cuts and steel Engravings, $80 00. Edinburgh, 1842–47.

——— Waverly Novels. (Abbottsford edition.) 12 vols. royal 8vo. cloth, numerous plates and wood-cuts, $50 00; calf gilt, marbled leaves, $80 00. Edin. 1842–46.

——— Complete Works, i. e., Novels, Tales, Prose, Poetry, Criticism, and Biography. 10 vols. 8vo. cloth, $10 00. Phila. 1847.

——— Novels and Tales. 48 vols. foolscap 8vo. cloth, 96 plates, $36 00 Edin. 1829–33.

——— Novels, Tales, and Romances. 25 vols. 12mo. cloth, $20 00; half mor. $25 00. Edinburgh, 1841–2.

——— Do. do. 5 vols. royal 8vo. cloth. (The People's edition,) $15 00. Edin. 1846.

——— Waverly Novels and Tales. 27 vols. 12mo. half roan, cloth sides, $18 00. Boston.

——— Waverly Novels and Tales. 5 vols. 8vo. cloth, $5 00. Phila. 1847

——— Poetical Works. 12 vols. foolscap 8vo. cloth, 24 engravings, $12 00. Edin. 1834.

——— Do. do. 6 vols. 12mo. cloth, $6 00. Edin. 1843.

——— Poetical Works, containing The Lay of the Last Minstrel; Marmion; Lady of the Lake; Don Roderick; Rokeby; Ballads, Lyrics, and Songs. 1 vol. 16mo. cloth, $1 25; mor. $2 50. New York.

——— Poetical Works. Royal 8vo. cloth, 28 engravings from Turner, $4 50; mor. extra, $8 00. Edinburgh, 1848.

——— Miscellaneous Prose Works. 28 vols. foolscap 8vo. cloth, 56 plates, $20 00. Edinburgh, 1834–36.

——— Miscellaneous Prose Works. 7 vols. 8vo. paper, $5 25. Paris, 1837.

——— Critical and Miscellaneous Essays. 3 vols. 12mo. cloth, $3 50. Phila.

——— Letters on Demonology and Witchcraft, addressed to J. G. Lockhart. 12mo. cloth, $1 00. London, 1831.

——— The Lady of the Lake. 32mo. cloth, 50 cents; mor. $1 25. New York.

Scottish Banker, (The.) A Popular Exposition of the Practice of Banking in Scotland, by W. H. Logan. 18mo. cloth, 87 cents. Edin. 1845.

Scoutetten, (H.) On the Club Foot, &c. 8vo. sheep, $2 00. Philadelphia.

Scribner, (J. M.) Engineer's, Contractor's, and Surveyor's Pocket-Book. 12mo. $2 00.

——— Engineer's and Mechanic's Companion. 12mo. $1 50. New York.

Scriptural Instruction for the Least and the Lowest; or, the Bible History in its Simplest Form. 3 vols. 18mo. cloth, $1 50. Bath, 1842.

Scrivener, (F. H.) A Supplement to the Authorized English Version of the New Testament. Vol. 1, 8vo. cloth, $2 75. Pickering, 1844.

——— (H.) A Comprehensive History of the Iron Trade throughout the World, with an Appendix, containing Official Tables and other Public Documents. 8vo. cloth, $5 00. Lond.

Scrope, (W.) Days and Nights of Salmon Fishing, with a short Account of the Natural History and Habits of the Salmon, &c. Royal 8vo. cloth, illustrated with plates from Landseer, &c. $10 00. London, 1843.

——— Days of Deer Stalking in the Forest of Atholl, with some Account of the Nature and Habits of the Red Deer. Illustrated by engravings and wood-cuts, from Designs by the Landseers. 8vo. cloth, $6 50. Lond. 1847.

Scudamore on the Production of Early Swarms of Bees. 12mo. cloth, 75 cents. London.

Sears, (R.) Scenes and Sketches in Continental Europe, embracing Descriptions of France, Portugal, Spain, Italy, Sicily, Switzerland, Belgium, and Holland. 8vo. cloth, illustrated with numerous engravings, $2 50. New York, 1848.

——— Bible Biography; or, the Lives and Characters of the Principal Personages recorded in the Sacred Writings, &c. 8vo. cloth, with several hundred engravings on wood, $2 50. New York, 1848.

Seaman, (E. C.) Essays on the Progress of Nations. 8vo. cloth, $2 00. New York.

Sedgwick, (Miss.) Clarence; or, Twenty Years Since. 12mo. cloth, (uniform with Irving's Works,) $1 25. New York, 1849.

——— Redwood. Author's revised edition, complete in 1 vol. $1 25. New York.

——— A New England Tale. 12mo. (In press.) New York, 1850.

——— Stories for Young Persons. 18mo. cloth, 50 cents. New York.

——— The Morals of Manners; or, Hints for our Young People. Square 18mo. cloth, woodcuts, 25 cents. New York.

——— Facts and Fancies for School Day Reading; a Sequel to Morals of Manners. Square 18mo. cloth, 50 cents. New York, 1848.

——— Means and Ends. 18mo. cloth, 50 cents. New York.

——— The Boy of Mount Rhigi. 18mo. cloth, 50 cents.

——— The Poor Rich Man and the Rich Poor Man. 18mo. cloth, 50 cents. New York.

——— Home. 18mo. cloth, 50 cents. Boston.

——— Hope Leslie. 2 vols. 12mo. cloth, $1 25. New York.

Sedgwick, (Miss.) Letters from Abroad. 2 vols. 12mo. cloth, $2 00. New York.

——— Live and Let Live. 18mo. cloth, 50 cents. New York.

——— The Linwoods. 2 vols. 12mo. cloth, $1 50. New York.

Seguin, (E.) Notice sur la vie et les Travaux de Pereire Premier Instituteur des Sourds et Muets en France. 12mo. broché, $1 00. Paris, 1847.

Selby, (P. J.) A History of British Forest Trees Indigenous and Introduced. Illustrated by nearly 200 engravings. 8vo. cloth, $10 00. London, 1842.

Selden, (John.) Table Talk, with Preface, Notes, and Life, by Singer. 12mo. cloth, $1 75. London, 1848.

——— Another edition. 18mo. cloth, 75 cents. London, 1847.

Selecta Praxis Medico-Chirurgicæ quam Mosquæ exercet Alexander Auvert, Augustissimi omnium Russiarum Imperatorio Consiliarus Status, Medicinæ et Chirurgiæ Doctor, etc. Typis et Figuris expressa Parisiis Moderante Ambr. Tardieu, Medicæ Facultatis Parisiensis Professore, Nosoconisorum Civitatis Medico, Anatomicæ Societatis, ex-Preside, etc. L'ouvrage complet se composera de 24 livraisons distribuees en 4 parties. Chaque partie comprend 6 livraisons de 5 planches chacune avec texte. Une livraison paraitra tous les deux mois. The first two parts, comprising 12 livraisons, are now ready; price $60 00. Paris.

Select British Poets; containing the Poetical Works of Milton, Cowper, Goldsmith, Thomson, Falconer, Akenside, Collins, Gray, Somerville, Kirke White, Gay, Beattie, Burns, Shenstone, Butler, Selections from Byron, Hannah More, Pope, Isaac Watts, Hayley, Mason, Prior, Grahame, Logan, Dryden, Lyttleton, Hammond, Charlotte Smith, Richardson, Bloomfield, Gifford, and Canning. 4 vols. 12mo. cloth, portraits and vignettes, $4 50. London, 1838.

Select Christian Authors, with Introductory Essays. 2 vols. 8vo. cloth, $3 00. New York, 1849.

Senecæ Opera Philosophica. Ed. M. N. Bouillet. 3 vols. 8vo. $6 00. Paris, 1827.

Senefelder, (A.) Complete Course of Lithography, and Art of Lithographic Printing, with clear and explicit Instructions in all the Branches of the Art, &c. 4to. plates, $4 50. London, 1819.

Series of Instructive Examples in Architectural Engineering and Mechanical Drawing. 30 plates in folio and 12mo. vol. of descriptive Text, $5 00. London.

Sermon on the Mount Illuminated. Paper, $2 00; mor. $4 00. Phila.

Sermons. The Scottish Pulpit, a Series of Sermons by the most eminent Divines of the Scottish Church, forming a complete body of Practical Divinity. 5 vols. 8vo. cloth, $7 50. Aberdeen, 1841.

Servetus, (M.) The Life of, by W. H. Drummond. 12mo. cloth, $1 00. Lond. 1848.

Sevigne, (Mme. de.) Nouveau choix des Lettres. Cr. 8vo. calf, gilt, portrait and vignette, $2 00. Tours, 1846.

—— Lettres choix nouveau tres complet, contenant 318 lettres precede d'une notice et de l'essai sur le style epistolaire par M. Suard. 12mo. broché, $1 00. Paris, 1847.

—— Lettres a su famille et a ses amis, augmentee de plusieurs lettres inedites, des 105 lettres publiees en 1814, des notes et notices de Gronvelle, et des reflexions de l'Abbe de Vauxcelles; precedees d'une nouvelle notice biographique sur Mme. de Sevigne, accompagnees de notes geographiques et historiques, par M. Gault de Saint Germain. 25 portraits avant la lettre, desines par Deviera. 12 vols. in 8, veau, $30 00.

—— Lettres avec les Notes de tous les commentateurs. 6 vols. 12mo. $6 00. Paris, 1844.

Sewall, (R. K.) Sketches of St. Augustine. 12mo. cloth, plates, 63 cents. New York.

Seward, (John.) On Procuring Supplies of Water for Cities and Towns, by Boring. (Trans. I. C. E. vol 1, 4to.)

Sewell, (Miss.) Gertrude. 12mo. cloth, 75 cents. New York, 1848.

—— Margaret Percival. 2 vols. 12mo. cloth, $1 50. New York, 1847.

—— Walter Lorimer and other Tales. 12mo. cloth, plates, 75 cents. New York, 1849.

—— Amy Herbert; a Tale. 12mo. cloth, 75 cents. New York, 1848.

—— (Rev. Wm.) Christian Morals. 12mo. cloth, $1 00. London, 1842.

—— History of the Quakers. 2 vols. 8vo. sheep, $3 50. New York.

Seymour's Humorous Sketches; comprising 86 exceedingly clever and amusing Caricature etchings, on steel. Illustrated by Alfred Crowquill. 2 vols. in 1, royal 8vo. cloth extra, gilt edges, $5 50. 1843.

Sganzin, (M. J.) An Elementary Course of Civil Engineering, with Notes and Applications adapted to the United States. Translated from the French. 8vo. cloth, $2 00. Boston.

Shakespear, (J.) Hindustani Grammar. Royal 8vo. bds. $4 25. London.

—— Hindustani Selections. 2 vols. 4to. bds. $10 75. London.

—— Introduction to Hindustani. Royal 8vo. cloth, $7 25. London.

Shakespeare. A Reprint of the First Folio Edition of Heminge and Condell, in 1623. Folio, whole bound in calf, fine copy, portrait, $15 00. London, 1808.

—— Knight's Pictorial edition, with Biography. Best edition. 8 vols. imp. 8vo. calf extra, $40 00; half mor. $38 00. Lond. 1839–42.

—— New edition. 7 vols. imp. 8vo. cloth, numerous engravings, $18 00; half mor. $24 00; calf, $25 00. Lond. 1848.

—— Plays and Poems. Valpy's Cabinet Pictorial edition, with Life, Glossarial Notes, and Historical Digests of each Play, &c. 15 vols. foolscap 8vo. with 171 plates engraved on steel, cloth, $13 50. 1843.

Shakespeare's Plays. 7 vols. 8vo. cloth, $10 00. Boston.

—— Works, with a Life, and a History of the Stage, by Alexander Chalmers. 8 vols. 8vo. cloth, portrait, $18 00. London, 1847.

—— Plays, with his Life. Illustrated with many hundred wood-cuts. Edited by G. C. Verplanck, with Critical Introductions, Notes, &c., original and selected. 3 vols. imp. 8vo. half calf neat, $20 00; mor. extra, $25 00; cloth, $18 00. New York, 1847.

—— Dramatic Works. Edited, with Life, by Thos. Campbell. Royal 8vo. cloth, portrait, $4 00; calf, gilt backs, marbled edges, $5 00; mor. gilt, $9 50. London.

—— Bowdler's Family edition, reprinted from the Sixth London edition. 8vo. cloth, $3 00. New York.

—— Dramatic Works. Complete in 1 vol. with Glossary. 12mo. cloth, gilt, $1 75. London, 1849.

—— Poems. 32mo. cloth, 75 cents. Phila.

—— Songs. Illustrated by the Etching Club. 4to. cloth, $8 00. London.

—— Seven Ages of Man. Illustrated by wood engravings, from original Designs, by Mulready. 8vo. cloth, gilt, $1 75. London.

—— Autobiographical Poems; being his Sonnets clearly developed with his Character, drawn chiefly from his Works. By Charles A. Brown. Post 8vo. cloth, 88 cents. London, 1838.

—— Portfolio; a Series of 96 graphic Illustrations, after Designs by the most eminent British Artists, including Smirke, Stothard, Stephanoff, Cooper, Westall, Hilton, Leslie, Briggs, Corbould, Clint, &c., beautifully engraved by Heath, Greatbach, Robinson, Pye, Finden, Engleheart, Armstrong, Rolls, and others, in a case, with leather back. Imp. 8vo. $6 50.

—— The Book of Shakspeare Gems; a Series of 45 Landscape Illustrations, finely engraved on steel, of some of the most interesting localities of Shakespeare's Dramas. 1 elegant 8vo. vol. rich Turkey mor. $7 00.

—— Gallery of Female Characters, engraved by Heath. Royal 8vo. mor. gilt edges, $9 00. New York.

—— Novels. 3 in 1 vol. 8vo. cloth, $2 00. New York.

Shadwell, (C. F. A.) Tables for Facilitating the Approximate Prediction of Occultations and Eclipses for any Particular Place. 8vo. bds. $1 75. London.

Shaw, (Thos. B.) Outlines of English Literature. 12mo. cloth, $1 25. Phila. 1849

—— (S) The Chemistry of the several Natural and Artificial Heterogeneous Compounds used in Manufacturing Porcelain, Glass, and Pottery. Royal 8vo. half calf, neat, $3 50. (Only 250 copies of this work were printed.) London, 1837.

—— (Edward.) Rural Architecture. 4to. sheep, $5 00. Boston.

Shaw, (H.) Illuminated Ornaments, selected from Manuscripts of the Middle Ages. 4to. half bound, colored plates, $35 00. Lond. 1833.

—— and **Bridgen's** Designs for Furniture, with Candelabra and Interior Decoration. 60 plates, royal 4to. half bound mor. uncut, $8 50. London, 1838.

—— Encyclopædia of Ornaments. 4to. half bound, plates, $8 50. London, 1842.

—— Dresses and Decorations of the Middle Ages from the Seventh to the Seventeeth Century. 2 vols. imp. 8vo. cloth, beautifully illuminated plates, $38 00. Lond. 1840–43.

Sharpe, (Thomas, D. D.) The Rubric in the Book of Common Prayer, and the Canons of the Church of England. 8vo. cloth, $2 25. Oxford, 1834.

—— (Archbishop.) The Life and Times of, by Henry Stephens. 8vo. cloth, $3 50. Lond.

—— Corresponding Atlas; comprising 54 maps, constructed upon a System of Scale and Proportion, from the most recent Authorities, with a copious Consulting Index. Folio, half mor. $10 00; colored, $15 00. 1849.

—— (C.) Architectural Parallels; or, the Progress of Ecclesiastical Architecture traced through the Twelfth and Thirteenth Centuries, exhibited in a Series of Parallel Examples. Folio, 121 tinted plates, half mor. $72 00. London, 1849.

Sharpey, (W.) and **Quain,** (J.) Anatomy. Edited by Joseph Leidy. 2 vols. 8vo. sheep, 500 illustrations, $6 50. Phila. 1849.

Sheil, (Hon. R. L.) Speeches, with a Memoir. Edited by Thomas McNevin. 8vo. cloth, $1 75. Dublin, 1845.

Sheldon, (F.) The Minstrelsy of the Scottish Border; being a Collection of Scottish Ballads, Ancient, Remodelled, and Original, founded on well known Border Legends. Small 4to. beautifully printed in old style, $4 50. London, 1847.

Shelley, (Percy Bysshe.) Poetical Works. Edited by Mrs. Shelley. 3 vols. foolscap 8vo. cloth, $4 00. London, 1846.

The Same. 1 vol. royal 8vo. cloth, $4 50; half calf, gilt, $6 00.

—— Essays, Letters, Translations, and Fragments. Edited by Mrs. Shelley. 2 vols. 8vo. cloth, $3 50. Moxon, 1840.

—— Works. Edited by Foster. 12mo. $1 50. New York.

—— Life of, by Captain Medwin. 2 vols. 12mo. cloth, $4 50. London, 1848.

Shepherd, (C. U.) Treatise on Mineralogy. 2 vols. 12mo. cloth, $1 50. London.

Sheridan, (Rt. Hon. B.) Speeches, with a Sketch of his Life. 3 vols. 8vo. cloth, $6 00. London, 1842.

—— (R. B.) Dramatic Works. Complete in 1 vol. 12mo. cloth, portrait, 88 cents. London, 1848.

Sherlock, (Thos.) Discourses and Dissertations. 4 vols. 8vo. cloth, $7 75. Oxford, 1842.

Sherwood, (Mrs.) Works. Complete in 16 vols. 12mo. cloth, $13 50. New York

Shew, (Joel.) Water Cure. 12mo. cloth, $1 00. New York.

—— Hand-Book of Hydropathy. 12mo. cloth, 75 cents. New York, 1844.

—— (Mrs.) Water Cure for Ladies; a Popular Work on the Health, Diet, &c. of Females and Children, with a full Account of the Processes of the Water Cure. Revised by Dr. J. Shew. 12mo. cloth, 50 cents. New York.

Ship-Master and Merchant's Assistant, by Blunt. 8vo. cloth, $4 50. New York.

Shirley, a Tale, by Currer Bell, Author of Jane Eyre. 12mo. cloth, $1 00. New York, 1850.

Shirley's Dramatic Works and Poems, with Notes, by W. Gifford, and an Account of Shirley's Life and Writings, and Additional Notes, by A. Dyce. 6 vols. 8vo. cloth, $9 00. large paper. London, 1833.

Shoberl, (F.) Persecutions of Popery. 2 vols. 8vo. cloth, $2 00. London, 1844.

—— Excursions in Normandy, illustrative of the Character, Manners, Customs, and Traditions of the People, &c., selected from the Journal of a Traveller, by F. Shoberl. Plates, 2 vols. post 8vo. cloth, $3 00. Lond. 1841.

Shooter's Hand-Book; a Treatise on Shooting. Post 8vo. cloth, $1 75. London.

Shores, (The,) and Islands of the Mediterranean. Drawn by Temple, Leitch, Irton, and Allen. 3 vols. 4to. cloth gilt, $18 00.

Short, (Thos. V.) Sketch of the History of the Church of England to the Revolution in 1688. 8vo. cloth, $4 00. Lond. 1840.

Shuckard, (W. E.) The British Coleoptera delineated, consisting of Figures of all the Genera of British Beetles. Drawn in outline, by W. S. Spring. 8vo. cloth, $5 50. London, 1840.

Sibley, (C. K.) and **Rutherford,** (W.) Tables for Estimating the Contents in Cubic Yards of the Earthwork of Railways and other Public Works. 4to. cloth, $4 25. Lond. 1847.

Siborne, (Capt. W.) Waterloo Campaigns. 8vo. cloth, maps, $2 00. Phila. 1845.

—— War in France and Belgium in 1815. 8vo. cloth, with folio atlas of maps, $9 50. London.

Siddons, (Mrs.) The Life of, by Thomas Campbell. 12mo. cloth, portrait, $1 50. London.

Sidney, (Rev. E.) Life of Rev. Rowland Hill. 12mo. cloth, 75 cents. New York, 1834.

—— (Hon. H.) Diary of the Times of Charles II.; including his Correspondence with the Countess of Sutherland, &c. 2 vols. 8vo. cloth, $2 75. London, 1843.

—— (Algernon.) Discourses concerning Government. 2 vols. 8vo. cloth, $3 50. Phila.

Sigourney, (Mrs.) Scenes in my Native Land. 12mo. cloth, $1 25. Boston, 1843.

—— Pleasant Memories of Pleasant Lands. 12mo. cloth, $1 25. Boston, 1844.

Sigourney, (Mrs.) Poems, with 14 splendid illustrations from Designs by Darley. 8vo. cloth gilt, $4 50; mor. $6 00. Phila. 1849.

Silk, Cotton, Linen, and Wool. History of Manufacture of, &c. 8vo. cloth, $3 00. New York.

Silliman, (B. Jr.) First Principles of Chemistry, for the use of Colleges and Schools. 12mo. sheep, $1 00. Phila. 1848.

Silvestre's Great Work of Ornamental Alphabets. Collection d'Alphabets Histories et Fleuronnes, tires des diverses Bibliotheques de l'Europe. 60 beautiful plates, many of which are colored, atlas folio, (uniform with the same author's great work, the Paleographie Universelle,) $12 50. Paris, 1843.

——— Paleographie Universelle, ou Collection de fac-simile d'Ecritures de tous les Peuples et de tous les temps, tires des plus Authentiques Manuscrits existant dans les Archives et les Bibliotheques de France, d'Italie, d'Allemagne, et d'Angleterre; par M. Silvestre. Accompagnes d'Explications, Historiques et Descriptives, par MM. Champollion Figeac et Aime Champollions fils. 4 vols. atlas folio, containing upwards of 300 large and most beautifully executed fac-similes, on copper and stone, of the finest and most interesting manuscripts of every age and nation, drawn and painted by J. B. Silvestre, Calligraphist to the King of France, from the most authentic Documents, Missals, and other MSS. existing in France, Italy, Germany, and England, most richly illuminated in the finest style of art. Unbound, in parts, $315 00. Paris, 1841.

——— The Same. 4 vols. atlas folio, splendidly half bound mor. gilt edges, $360 00.

——— The Same. 4 vols. atlas folio, splendidly bound in mor. gilt edges, by Wright, $420 00.

Simcoe's Military Journal; a History of the Operations of a Partisan Corps called the Queen's Rangers, commanded by Lieut. Col J. G. Simcoe during the War of the American Revolution, with Memoir of the Author. Imp. 8vo. bds. illustrated with 10 maps and plans of Battles, colored, $2 00. New York, 1844.

Simeon's Works, including his Skeletons of Sermons and Horæ Homileticæ; or, Discourses digested into one continued Series, and forming a Commentary upon every Book of the Old and New Testament; to which are annexed an improved edition of Claude's Essay on the Composition of a Sermon, and very comprehensive Indexes. Edited by Rev. Thomas Hartwell Horne. 21 vols. 8vo. extra cloth, $35 00. London, 1836.

Simms, (F. W.) Treatise on the Principles and Practice of Levelling Plates. Third edition. 8vo. cloth, $2 25. London.

——— Railways. Illustrated by 83 engravings, with explanatory Text, containing the Specifications of the Works as executed. Folio, half mor. $15 00. London.

——— A Treatise on the Principal Mathematical and Drawing Instruments employed by the Engineer, Architect, and Surveyor. Third edition, with a description of the Theodolite, together with instructions in Field-work. Compiled for the use of Students on commencing Practice, with numerous wood-cuts. 12mo. cloth, $1 75. London, 1849.

Simms, (F. W.) Rules for Making and Repairing Roads. 8vo. 75 cents. Lond.

——— Public Works of Great Britain; Railways, Tunnels, Bridges, Stations, Gas Works, Canals, Locks, Canal Boats, Docks, Quays, Harbors, &c. Imp. folio, half mor. 153 plates, some colored, $32 00. London.

——— (W. G.) History of South Carolina. 12mo. sheep, $1 00. New Haven.

——— Geography of South Carolina. 12mo. 75 cents. New Haven.

——— Life of Capt. John Smith. 12mo. cloth, wood-cuts, $1 13. New York.

——— Life of the Chevalier Bayard. 12mo. cloth, $1 00. New York.

——— The Wigwam and the Cabin. 12mo. cloth, $1 25. New York, 1845.

——— Views and Reviews in American Literature, History, and Fiction. 12mo. cloth, $1 00. New York, 1845.

——— Life of General Marion. 12mo. cloth, $1 13. New York.

——— Mellichampe; a Legend of the Santee. 2 vols. 12mo. cloth, $1 50. New York.

——— Martin Faber and other Tales. 2 vols. 12mo. cloth, $1 25. New York.

——— The Partisan. 2 vols. 12mo. $1 25. New York.

Simmons, (T. F.) Remarks on the Constitution and Practice of Courts Martial, with a Summary of the Laws of Evidence as connected with such Costs. 8vo. cloth, $5 00 Lond.

——— Ideas as to the Effect of Heavy Ordnance directed against and applied by Ships of War, particularly with reference to the use of Hollow Shot and Loaded Shells. 8vo. plates, bds. $2 50. London, 1837.

Simon, (J. F.) The Chemistry of Man. 8vo. sheep, $3 50. Philadelphia.

Simpson, (J. Y.) Anæsthesia; or, the Employment of Chloroform and Ether in Surgery, Midwifery, &c. 8vo. cloth, $1 25. Phila. 1849.

——— (F.) A Series of Ancient Baptismal Fonts, Norman, Early English, Decorated English, and Perpendicular English. Imp. 8vo. cloth, 40 plates, $4 75. London.

——— Narrative of the Discoveries on the North Coast of America, effected by the Officers of the Hudson's Bay Company. 8vo. cloth, maps, $1 25. London, 1843.

——— (A.) Life and Travels of Thomas Simpson, the Arctic Discoverer. 8vo. cloth, portrait, London, 1845.

——— (Thos.) Select Exercises for Young Proficients in the Mathematics. 12mo. half bound, $1 00. Lond. 1792.

——— (Sir George.) Narrative of a Journey round the World, during the Years 1841, '42. 2 vols. 8vo. cloth, portrait and map, $8 50. London, 1847.

——— American edition. 8vo. cloth, $1 75. Philadelphia.

Simson, (R) The Elements of Euclid, (the parts read at the University of Cambridge,) with Geometrical Problems for Solution. 12mo $1 75. London.

Sinclair, (Cath.) Holliday House; a Series of Tales. 12mo. cloth, 75 cents. New York.

——— Scotland and the Scotch. 12mo. cloth, 75 cents. New York.

——— Shetland and the Shetlanders. 12mo. cloth, 88 cents. New York.

——— Modern Accomplishments. 12mo. cloth, 75 cents.

——— Modern Society. 12mo. cloth, 75 cents. New York.

Sinnet, (Mrs. P.) By-Ways of History from the Twelfth to the Sixteenth Century. 2 vols. post 8vo. cloth, $2 50. London.

Sinnott, (J.) Manual of Light Infantry and other Duties. 12mo. cloth, $1 25. Lond. 1849.

Sirr, (Henry Charles) China and the Chinese: their Religion, Character, Customs, and Manufactures; the Evils arising from the Opium Trade, with a Glance at our Religious, Moral, Political, and Commercial Intercourse with the Country. Plates. 2 vols. 8vo. cloth, $7 50. London, 1849.

Sismondi, (Simonde de.) Histoire des Republiques Italiennes du moyen age; nouvelle edition, ornes de belles gravures sur acier. 10 vol. in 8, demi veau, $18 00. Paris, 1840.

——— Histoire des Français. 31 vols. in 8, demi veau, $70 00. Paris, 1821–42.

——— History of the Fall of the Roman Empire; comprising a View of the Invasion and Settlement of the Barbarians. 2 vols. foolscap 8vo. cloth, $3 50. London, 1832.

——— History of the Literature of the South of Europe. Translated by Roscoe, with Notes, by Cary, and a Memoir of the Author, and an enlarged Index. 2 vols. post 8vo. cloth, $1 75. London, 1846.

——— Political Economy and the History of Government; a Series of Essays selected from the Works of M. de Sismondi, with an Historical Notice of his Life and Writings, by M. Mignet. Translated by Roscoe, and illustrated by Extracts from an unpublished Memoir, and M. de Sismondi's Private Journals and Letters. 8vo. cloth, $3 50. London, 1847.

——— History of the Italian Republics, or of the Origin, Progress, and Fall of Freedom in Italy, A. D. 476 to 1805. Foolscap 8vo. cloth, $1 75. London, 1834.

——— 12mo. cloth, 63 cents. New York.

Six Dramas, Illustrative of German Life, from the original of Princess Amelia of Saxony. Illustrated with 6 outline plates. 8vo. cloth, $3 00. London, 1848.

Sketches, by Boz. 8vo. cloth, $1 25. Philadelphia.

——— (The.) Three Tales; Walter Lorimer. The Emblems of Life, and the Lost Inheritance. 12mo. cloth, $1 00. New York, 1849.

Skinner, (J. S.) The Dog and the Sportsman; embracing the Uses, Breeding, Training, Diseases, &c., &c.; also, Hints to Shooters, with various useful Receipts. Illustrations, 12mo. 75 cents. Philadelphia.

Slick, (Sam.) Clockmaker; or, the Sayings and Doings of Sam Slick of Slickville; to which is added, the Letter Bag of the Great Western, or Life in a Steamer. 8vo. paper, 75 cents. Paris, 1841.

Sluice-Gate. Investigation of the Position of the Horizontal Axis of a Self-Acting Sluice-Gate. Translated from the Memorial du Genie. (Papers, R. E. vol. 1, 4to.) Lond.

Small Books on Great Subjects. 3 vols. 12mo. cloth, $2 50. Philadelphia.

Smedley, (E.) History of Reformation in France. 3 vols. 12mo. cloth, $1 50. New York.

——— Sketches from Venetian History. 2 vols. 12mo. cloth, $1 00. New York.

——— History of France from A. D. 843 to 1529. 8vo. cloth, with map, $1 75. London, 1835.

Smee, (A.) The Sources of Physical Science. 8vo. cloth, $3 25. London, 1843.

——— Elements of Electro-Biology; or, the Voltaic Mechanism of Man; of Electro-Pathology, especially of the Nervous System, and of Electro-Therapeutics. Numerous engravings on wood. 8vo. cloth, $3 25. Lond. 1849.

——— Elements of Electro-Metallurgy. New edition, 8vo. cloth, $4 50. London, 1849.

——— The Potato Plant, its uses and Properties, together with the Causes of the Present Malady, the Extension of that Disease to other Plants, the Question of Famine arising therefrom, and the best Means of Averting that Calamity. 8vo. cloth, $2 00. Lond. 1846.

——— American edition. 12mo. cloth, 75 cents. New York.

Smellie, (W.) Philosophy of Natural History. 12mo. cloth, $1 00. Boston.

Smirke's Specimens of Continental Architecture. Folio, colored plates, $4 50. Lond.

——— Illustrations of the Architectural Ornaments and Embellishments, and Painted Glass of the Temple Church, London, from Drawings by W. R. H. Essex. 4to. half mor. colored plates, $13 50. London, 1845.

Smith, (Miss Ann) Drawing-Book of Flowers. 15 plates, 8vo. cloth, $3 50. Baltimore.

——— (Albert.) Pottleton Legacy; a Story of Town and Country Life, with Illustrations, by H. K. Browne. 12mo. cloth, $2 00. London, 1849.

——— (Augustus W.) An Elementary Treatise on Mechanics, embracing the Theory of Statics and Dynamics, and its Application to Solids and Fluids. 8vo. cloth, $1 50. N. York, 1849.

——— (A.) An Inquiry into the Wealth of Nations. Edited by Macculloch. 8vo. cloth, $5 50. London.

——— Cheap edition. 12mo. cloth, $1 00.

——— Do. with a Commentary by the Author of "England and America." 4 vols. 12mo. cloth, $4 00. London, 1848.

——— (C. H.) Lithology; or, Observations on Stone used for Building. 4to. plates, $1 75. London, 1845.

——— The Natural History of the Human Species; its Typical Forms, Primeval Distributing Filiations and Migrations. 12mo. cloth, 34 colored plates, $2 50. London, 1848.

——— The Ancient Costume of Great Britain and Ireland, from the Sixth to the Sixteenth Century. Folio, half mor. gilt, colored plates, $25 00. London, 1848.

Smith, (C. J.) Historical and Literary Curiosities; consisting of fac-similes of Original Documents and Autographs, Scenes of Remarkable Events and Interesting Localities, Birthplaces, Residences, Portraits, and Monuments of Eminent Literary Characters, &c. 4to. half mor. top gilt, 100 curious and interesting plates, $14 00. London, 1840.

——— (E.) Account of a Journey through North-Eastern Texas, undertaken in 1849, for the purposes of Emigration, &c. 12mo. cloth, 2 maps, 88 cents. London, 1849.

——— (Mrs. E. O.) Salamander; a Legend for Christmas. 12mo. cloth, 75 cents. New York, 1848.

——— (D.) The Practical Dyer's Guide; comprising Practical Instructions in the Dyeing of Shot Cobourgs, Silk Striped Orleans, colored Orleans, from Black Warps, White Warps, &c., &c., with Patterns; to which the Art of Padding is annexed. 8vo. cloth, $19 00. London, 1849

——— (J. T.) On the Methods of Illuminating Light-Houses, with a Description of a Reciprocating Light. (Trans. I. C. E. vol. 2, 4to.) London.

——— Essay on the Method of Illuminating Light-Houses, with a Description of a Reciprocating Light.—On a New System of Fixed Lights. (Papers, R. E. vol. 5, 4to.) Lond.

——— Madras Light-House. Report of Progress in the Execution of the New Machinery and Illuminating Apparatus for the Madras Light. Description of a New Hydro-Pneumatic Lamp. (Papers, R. E. vol. 5, 4to.) London.

——— (F. H.) Biot's Analytical Geometry. 8vo. cloth, $1 25. New York.

——— (Rev. G.) The Consular Cities of China. 12mo. cloth, $1 25. New York.

——— (John.) History of Virginia. 2 vols. 8vo. cloth, $6 00. Richmond.

——— Memoirs of the Marquis of Pombal, with Extracts from his Writings. 2 vols. 8vo. cloth, $6 50. London, 1843.

——— (J. and H.) Rejected Addresses; or, the new Theatrum Poetarum. Foolscap 8vo. bds. Twentieth edition, portraits, $1 50. London, 1841.

——— (J. V. C.) Natural History of the Fishes of Massachusetts. $1 50. Boston.

——— (J. M.) Elements of Etiology and Philosophy of Epidemics. 12mo. cloth, $1 00. New York.

——— (J. P.) The Relation between the Holy Scriptures and some parts of Geological Science. Fifth edition, greatly enlarged. 8vo. cloth, $2 75. London, 1848.

——— On Scripture and Geology. 12mo. cloth, $1 25. New York.

——— and **Horner's** Anatomical Atlas. 8vo. cloth, $5 00. Philadelphia.

——— (Major J. T.) Observations on the Duties and Responsibilities involved in the Management of Mints. 8vo. bds. $2 25. Madras, 1848.

——— (J. A.) Productive Farming; a Familiar Digest of the most Recent Discoveries of Liebig, Davy, Johnstone, and other celebrated Writers on Vegetable Chemistry, &c. 12mo. paper, 50 cents. New York.

Smith, (Rev. Sidney.) Miscellanies. 8vo. cloth, $1 00. Philadelphia.

——— Sermons. 12mo. cloth, $1 00. Phila.

——— (W.) Dictionary of Greek and Roman Biography and Mythology. Illustrated with numerous engravings on wood. 3 vols. royal 8vo. cloth, $15 00. Lond. 1844–49.

——— Dictionary of Greek and Roman Antiquities. Second edition, illustrated with numerous wood engravings. Thick royal 8vo. cloth, $5 00. London, 1849.

——— Chronological Tables of Greek and Roman History, Civil and Literary, from the First Olympiad, B. C. 776, to the Fall of the Western Empire, A. D. 476, with Tables of Greek and Roman Measures, Weights, and Money. 8vo. cloth, $1 50. Lond. 1849.

——— (W. T.) Parturition and the Principles and Practice of Obstetrics. 12mo. sheep, $1 50. Philadelphia, 1849.

Smollett, (T.) Complete Works. 8vo. cloth, $1 50. Philadelphia.

——— Roderick Random. 12mo. sheep, 88 cents. New York.

——— Peregrine Pickle. 8vo. paper, 50 cents. Philadelphia.

Smyth, (Capt.) Cycle of Celestial Objects, for the use of the Naval, Military, and Private Astronomers. 2 vols. 8vo. cloth, $11 00. London.

——— On the Construction of Barracks for Tropical Climates. (Papers, R. E. vol. 2, 4to.) London.

——— (Mrs. Gillespie.) Memoirs and Correspondence of Sir Robert Murray Keith. 2 vols. cr. 8vo. cloth, portraits, $7 50. Lond. 1849.

——— (J. W.) An Exposition of various Passages of Scripture for the use of Families for every Day in the Year. 3 vols. 8vo. cloth, $2 50. London, 1842.

——— (W.) Lectures on Modern History, from the Irruptions of the Northern Nations to the close of the American Revolution, with a Preface, List of Books on American History, &c., by Professor Sparks. A new edition, 8vo. cloth, $3 50. Boston, 1849.

——— Lectures on the French Revolution. 3 vols. 8vo. cloth, $9 50. London.

——— Evidences of Christianity. Second edition, foolscap 8vo. cloth, $1 50. Lond. 1848.

Snell, (J.) Guide to Operations on the Teeth. 8vo. sheep, $1 00. Phila.

Snelling, (H. H.) The History and Practice of the Art of Photography; or, the Production of Pictures by the Agency of Light. 12mo. cloth, wood-cuts, $1 00. N. York, 1849.

Snow, (Jos.) Light in Darkness; or, Sermons in Stones, Churchyard Thoughts in Verse. Square cr. 8vo. with designs for Headstones, $1 50. London, 1845.

——— (R.) Observations on Imitation. 12mo. cloth, 75 cents. London.

Snowball, (J. C.) The Elements of Plane and Spherical Trigonometry. 8vo. bds. $3 00. London.

——— Elements of Mechanics. 8vo. cloth, $2 25. London.

Soames, (Rev. H.) The Latin Church during Anglo-Saxon Times. 8vo. cloth, $4 50. London, 1848.

Soane, (Sir John.) Public and Private Buildings. Folio, 56 plates, etched by Coney, $12 50. London.

Solly, (E.) Syllabus of a complete Course of Lectures on Chemistry, including its Applications to the Arts, Agriculture, and Mining. 8vo. cloth, $1 50. London, 1848.

——— (Sam.) On the Brain. 8vo. sheep, $2 75. Philadelphia.

Somerville, (Mary.) Connection of the Physical Sciences. 12mo. cloth, 50 cents. New York.

——— Physical Geography. 12mo. cloth, $1 25. Philadelphia, 1848.

Songs in the Desert; or, Bible Gleanings. 18mo. mor. gilt, 50 cents. London.

Songs, Madrigals, and Sonnets. A Gathering of some of the most Pleasant Flowers of Old English Poetry. Set in borders of colored ornaments and vignettes. Square 16mo. fancy binding, $3 00. Lond. 1849.

Song of Solomon. Illustrated by Owen Jones. Post 8vo. embossed calf, gilt leaves, $6 London.

Sophia Dorothea, (Consort of George I.) Memoirs of; including a Diary of the Conversations of Illustrious Personages of those Courts. Second edition. 2 vols. 8vo. cloth, $6 00. London, 1848.

Sophocles. The Antigone of, in Greek and English, with an Introduction and Notes, by J. W. Donaldson. 8vo. cloth, $3 00. Lond. 1848.

——— Tragædiæ, cum Scholiis bet. versione Latina et Notis ex. ed. R. F. B. Brunck. 2 vols. royal 8vo. bds. $6 00. Oxon, 1808.

——— Ed. G. Dindorfii. 2 vols. 8vo. cloth, $5 00. Oxon, 1836.

——— Translated by Thomas Francklin. 1 vol. 12mo. cloth, 50 cents. New York.

——— The Oxford Translation into English Prose 12mo. cloth, portrait, $1 25. London, 1849.

Sopwith, (Thos.) Treatise on Isometrical Drawing. 8vo. cloth, $3 75. London.

——— Geological Plans and Sections of Lead Mines in Alston Moor and Teesdale. 4to. 3 plates, $3 25. London.

——— Description of a Series of Geological Models. 12 plates, $1 00. London.

——— Account of the Mining Districts of Alston Moor, Weardale, and Teesdale. 12mo. cloth, $1 50. London.

——— Plans of Coal and Iron Mines in H. M. Forest of Dean. 16 copperplates, 20 inches square, $7 50. London.

——— The Award of the Dean Forest Mining Commissioners as to the Coal and Iron Mines in Her Majesty's Forest of Dean, and the Rules and Regulations for Working the same, &c. 8vo. cloth, $1 50. London.

——— Projecting and Parallel Rulers for Constructing Plans and Drawings in Isometrical and other Modes of Projection, with Descriptive letter-press, and a Specimen Sheet of Drawing Paper. $1 00. London.

Soulie, (Fr.) Sathaniel. 12mo. paper, 75 cents. Paris, 1842.

South, (I. F.) Household Surgery; or, Hints on Emergencies. 12mo. cloth, $1 50. London.

——— (Theophilus.) Illustrated Fly-Fisher's Text-Book. A complete Guide to the Science of Trout and Salmon Fishing, with 23 beautiful steel engravings. 8vo. cloth, $3 00. London, 1845.

——— (Robert.) Sermons. 4 vols. 8vo. cloth, $8 00. Philadelphia.

——— Sermons Preached on several Occasions, including the Posthumous Discourse. 5 vols. 8vo. cloth, $15 00. Oxford, 1842.

Southgate, (Bp.) Narrative of a Visit to the Syrian Church of Mesopotamia, &c. 12mo. cloth, with maps, $1 00. New York.

——— Narrative of a Tour through Armenia, Kurdistan, Persia, and Mesopotamia. 2 vols. 12mo. cloth, $1 50. New York.

Southey, (Caroline.) Poetical Works. 12mo. cloth, $1 00. New York.

——— Chapters on Churchyards. 12mo. paper, 50 cents. New York.

——— (Robert.) Complete Poetical Works. 1 vol. royal 8vo. cloth, portrait and vignette, View of Keswick, $6 00. London, 1845.

——— Poetical Works. 8vo. cloth, $3 50; mor. $6 00. New York.

——— Oliver Newman; a New England Tale, (unfinished,) and other Poetical Remains. 12mo. cloth, $1 50. Lond. 1845.

——— Chronicle of the Cid, from the Spanish. 8vo. cloth, $2 00. Lowell, 1846.

——— Common-Place Book. First Series, choice passages. Square cr. 8vo. cloth, $3 75. London, 1849.

——— American Edition. 8vo. cloth, $1 25. New York, 1849.

——— The Doctor. A new edition, edited by his Son-in-Law, J. W. Warter. Royal 8vo. cloth, portrait, $5 50. London, 1849.

——— The Book of the Church. 8vo. calf extra, $5 00. London, 1$41.

——— The History of Brazil. 3 vols. 4to. cloth, $12 00. London, 1810–19.

——— The Life of Wesley, and Rise and Progress of Methodism. 2 vols. 8vo. cloth, $8 00. London.

——— (Rev. C. C.) Life and Correspondence of the late Robert Southey. 6 vols. cr. 8vo. cloth, portrait, per vol. $3 25. Lond. 1849–50.

Souza, (Mme. de.) Romans Choisis. 12mo. paper, $1 00. Paris.

——— Œuvres, avec une notice par M. Sainte-Beuve. 12mo. $1 00. Paris, 1545.

Souvestre, (E.) Les Derniers Bretons. 12mo. paper, $1 00. Paris, 1843.

Sowerby, (G. B.) The Conchological Manual. A new edition, considerably enlarged, with many plates. 8vo. cloth, $5 00; colored, $10 00. London, 1846.

——— Conchological Illustrations; or, Colored Figures of all the hitherto Unfigured Shells. Complete in 200 parts, 8vo. comprising several thousand Figures of Shells, all beautifully colored, $45 00. 1841–45.

——— (James.) English Botany. 12 vols. royal 8vo. cloth, $170 00. London.

Soyer, (A.) The Modern Housewife; or, Ménagère, comprising nearly 1000 Receipts for the Economic and Judicious Preparation of every Meal of the Day. 12mo. cloth, portrait and engravings, $2 25. Lond. 1849.

——— The Gastronomic Regenerator; a simplified and entirely new System of Cookery, containing 2000 Practical Receipts for all Classes. 8vo. cloth, wood-cuts, $6 50. Lond. 1849.

Spalding, (W.) History of Italy and the Italian Islands. 3 vols. 18mo. cloth, $1 37. New York.

Spanish Poetry. Early Spanish Poetry and Romances, edited by Riego. Las Doze Triumphos de los doze Apostoles, Poema Heroico Christiano, por el Cartuxano (Don Juan de Padilla, el Homer y Dante Espanol,) and various other Pieces, some accompanied by English Poetical Translations, by Dr. Bowring. 4to. large paper, portraits, bds. $2 25. 1841–2.

Sparks, (Jared.) Life of George Washington. Royal 8vo. cloth, illustrated with portraits, plans, views, fac-similes, &c. $3 00. Boston.

——— Life of Benjamin Franklin; containing the Autobiography, with Notes, and a Continuation. 8vo. cloth, $3 00. Boston.

——— Life and Writings of Benjamin Franklin. 10 vols. 8vo. cloth, portraits and plates, $25 00. Boston.

——— Life and Writings of George Washington. 12 vols. 8vo. cloth, portraits and plates, $18 00. New York.

——— American Biography. 25 vols. 12mo. cloth, plates, each $1 00. Boston, 1844–47. (For Contents, see page 4.)

Specimens of the Architecture of the Reigns of Queen Elizabeth and James I. 60 plates, printed in colors and gold, from drawings by Richardson, Moore, and others. 4to. half mor. $11 00. London.

Spectator, (The.) 8vo. cloth, portrait, $2 50; mor. elegant, gilt edges, $6 50. London, 1847.

Speechley, (W.) Treatise on the Vine and Pine. 8vo. cloth, $5 50. London.

Spencer, (Rev. J. A) The East; a Visit to Egypt, the Holy Land. 8vo. cloth, illustrated from original drawings.

——— On the Patent American Steam Pile-Driving Machines. (Papers, R. E. vol. 6, 4to.) London.

——— On the System of combining Mechanical Ventilation with Warming by Steam Heat, as adapted to Public Buildings. (Papers, R. E. vol. 6, 4to.) London.

Spenser, (E.) Poetical Works, with a Selection of Notes, from various Commentators and a Glossarial Index, with Life, by Rev. H. J. Todd. Royal 8vo. cloth, with portrait, $4 00; calf, gilt backs and marbled leaves, $6 00. London, 1845.

——— Poetical Works, with Life, by Rev. J. Mitford. 5 vols. 12mo. cloth, portrait, $6 50; mor. neat, gilt leaves, $15 00. (Aldine edition.) London, 1839.

——— Poetical Works. Edited by G. S. Hillard. 5 vols. 12mo. portrait and Illuminated Title-Pages, cloth, $7 50. Boston, 1845.

Spiers, (A.) Manual of Commercial Terms, in French and English. 12mo. cloth, $1 00. Philadelphia, 1847.

——— General French and English Dictionary, newly composed. 8vo. sheep, $4 50. Paris, 1849.

Spinoza. Œuvres, traduites par Saisset. 2 vols. 12mo. paper, $2 00. Paris.

——— Opera Omnia, Ex. Edit. princ. denuo ed et praef. est C. H. Bruder. 3 vols. 16mo. $2 75. Leipsic, 1846.

Spirit of the Woods, (The.) 8vo. half mor. gilt top, illustrated with colored engravings, $7 50. London, 1837.

Sportsman in France; comprising a Sporting Ramble through Picardy and Normandy, and Boar-Shooting in Lower Brittany. By F. Tolfrey. Plates, 2 vols. post 8vo. cloth, $2 25. London, 1841.

Sprague, (Chas.) Poetical and Prose Writings. 12mo. cloth, 83 cents; bds. 75 cents. Boston, 1850.

——— (Capt.) History of the Florida War. 8vo. cloth, $2 50. New York, 1843.

Spring, (Gardiner.) The Power of the Pulpit; or, Thoughts addressed to Christian Ministers and those who hear them. 12mo. cloth, portrait. New York, 1848.

Sproule, (J.) Elements of Practical Agriculture, comprehending the Nature, Properties, and Improvements of Soils, the Structure, Functions, and Cultivation of Plants, and the Husbandry of the Domestic Animals of the Farm. 8vo. $3 50. London.

Spry's British Coleoptera Delineated; containing Figures and Descriptions of all the Genera of British Beetles. Edited by Shuckard. 8vo. with 94 plates, comprising 638 figures of Beetles, beautifully and most accurately drawn, cloth, lettered, $6 50. 1840.

Spurzheim, (J. G.) Anatomy of the Brain. 8vo. cloth, plates, $2 50. Boston.

——— Phrenology. 8vo. cloth, $1 50. New York, 1846.

——— Physiognomy. 8vo. cloth, plates, $2 88. Boston.

——— Observations on the Deranged Manifestations of the Mind; or, Insanity, with an Appendix, by A. Brigham. 8vo. cloth, $1 50. Boston, 1833.

Squier, (E. G.) and **Davis,** (E. H.) The Ancient Monuments of the Mississippi Valley, comprising the Results of extensive original Surveys and Explorations. 4to. cloth, plates and numerous wood-cuts, $10 00. New York, 1848.

Stack, (Rich.) Lectures on the Acts of the Apostles. 8vo. cloth, 75 cents. Lond. 1805.

Stackhouse, (Rev. Thos.) A History of the Bible from the beginning of the World to the Establishment of Christianity. New edition, with Notes, &c., by Dr. Dewar. Portrait, imp. 8vo. cloth, $6 0. Lond. 1846.

Stael, (Mad. de.) De l'Allemagne. 12mo. broché, $1 00; half mor. $1 50. Paris, 1849.

——— Corinne ou L'Italie. 12mo. $1 00; half mor. $1 50. Paris, 1846.

——— Corinne. Paper, 50 cents. New York.

Stael, (Mad. de.) Delphine. 3 vols. 12mo. cloth, $1 25. Philadelphia.

——— Delphine. 12mo. paper, $1 00. Paris.

——— De la Litterature.* 12mo. paper, $1 00.

——— Revolution Francais. 12mo. paper, $1 00.

——— Œuvres Completes. 17 vols. 8vo. broché, portrait, $12 75. Paris.

——— De L'Influence des Passions. 12mo. broché, 63 cents. Paris.

——— Lettres sur les ecrits et le caractere de J. J. Rousseau. 12mo. broché, 25 cents. Paris.

——— Memoirs (dix ans d'exit), etc. 12mo. paper, $1 00. Paris.

Stalkartt, (M.) Naval Architecture; or, the Rudiments and Rules of Ship Building exemplified in a Series of Draughts and Plans, with Observations tending to the Improvement of that important Art. 2 vols. folio, 14 plates, $25 00. London, 1812.

Stallo, (J. B.) The General Principles of the Philosophy of Nature. 12mo. cloth, $1 00. Boston.

Stanhope, (Lady Hester.) Memoirs related by herself. 3 vols. post 8vo. cloth, $6 50.

——— Travels. 3 vols. post 8vo. cloth, $5 50. London.

Stanfield, (Chas.) Coast Scenery. Royal 8vo. cloth, $3 75. London.

——— Sketches on the Moselle, the Rhine, and the Mense. Imp. folio, half mor. 27 plates, $22 50. London, 1838.

Stanley, (A. D.) An Elementary Treatise of Spherical Geometry and Trigonometry. 12mo. cloth, 63 cents. New Haven, 1848.

——— Logarithms of Numbers and Mathematical Tables. 8vo. cloth, $2 00. New Haven.

——— Treatise on Diseases of the Bones. 8vo. cloth, $1 50. Phila. 1849.

——— (W.) The Faith and Practice of a Church of England Man, with Notes, by Rev. Dr. Eden. 12mo. cloth, $1 50.

——— (Bp.) Familiar History of Birds. 12mo. cloth, $1 50. London.

Stanton, (H. B.) Sketches of Reforms and Reformers. 12mo. cloth, $1 00. New York, 1849.

Stapf, (E.) Homœopathic Materia Medica. 8vo. $1 50. New York.

Staples, (Rev. G.) Macedonia; or, a Voice to the Christian Church. 18mo. cloth, 50 cents. London, 1847.

Stars, (The,) and the Earth; or, Thoughts on Space, Time, and Eternity. 18mo cloth, 25 cents. Boston, 1849

State, (The,) of Man before the Promulgation of Christianity. 12mo. cloth, $1 00. London, 1848.

Statesman's, (The,) Manual. Presidents' Messages, Inaugural, Annual, and Special, from 1789 to 1846, compiled from Official Sources, by Edwin Williams. 2 vols. 8vo. cloth, portraits, $5 00. New York, 1848.

Statii Opera omnia ex editione Bipontina cum notis et interpretatione in usum Delphina, &c. 4 vols. 8vo. bds. $8 00. Valpy, London, 1824.

Staunton, (H.) Chess-Player's Text-Book. Square paper, cloth, $1 00. Lond. 1849.

Staunton, (H.) Chess-Player's Hand-Book; a Popular and Scientific Introduction to the Game of Chess, exemplified in Games actually played by the greatest masters. 12mo. cloth, illustrated with numerous diagrams, $1 25. London, 1847.

——— Chess-Player's Companion; comprising a New Treatise on Odds, and a Collection of Games contested by the Author, with various distinguished Players during the last Ten Years, &c., &c. 12mo. cloth, $1 25. London, 1849.

Staveley, (T. K.) On Posen. Instructions concerning the Model Towers approved of by Napoleon. Translated by Lieut. Laffan. Report on the Demolition of the Revetments of some of the old Works at Sheerness in 1827. (Papers, R. E. vol. 3, 4to.) London.

——— Notes on Brixen and Verona in 1838. (Papers, R. E. vol. 4, 4to.) London.

Steam Engine. By the Artisan Club. Edited by Bourne. Third edition, 4to. cloth, $8 00. London, 1849.

——— The Marine Steam Engine, designed chiefly for the use of Naval Officers and Engineers. Plates, 8vo. cloth, $3 50. Lond.

Steel's Ship-master's Assistant. Edited by Graham Wilmore, George Clements, and William Tate. Thick 8vo. cloth, plates, $8 50. London, 1846.

——— Book of Niagara Falls. 50 cents. Buffalo.

——— (W. E.) Hand-Book of Field Botany; comprising the Flowering Plants, Ferns, &c. 12mo. cloth, $2 25. London.

Stehelin, (Capt.) Memorandum descriptive of the Alterations made in a Cast Iron Pump at the Jesuits' Barracks, Quebec, to enable it to resist the Action of Frost. (Papers, R. E. vol. 9, 4to.) London.

Steiner, (Ignace.) German and English Reader. 12mo. cloth, $1 00. New York.

Steinitz, (F.) The Ship, its Origin and Progress; being a General History, from its first Invention to the Latest Improvements; forming a complete Account of the Naval Events of the Ancients, the Middle Ages, and the Modern Epoch, to the close of 1848, &c. 4to. half bound, 24 plates, $15 00. Lond. 1849.

Steinmetz, (A.) History of the Jesuits, from their Foundation to their Suppression, by Pope Clement XIV. 2 vols. 8vo. cloth, $3 00. Philadelphia.

Sterne, (L.) Works; containing Tristram Shandy, Sentimental Journey through France and Italy, Sermons, Letters, &c., with a Life of the Author, written by himself. Royal 8vo. cloth, portrait, $3 75. London, 1843.

——— Works, with Life. 8vo. cloth, $2 25. Philadelphia.

Stephanus Byzantinus, cum annotationibus Holstenii, Berkelii, et de Pinedo cum G. Dindorfii Præfatione, cui insunt Lectiones, libii vratislav. 4 vols. 8vo. bds. $6 50. Leipsic, 1825.

Stephens, (H.) The Book of the Farm; detailing the Labors of the Farmer, Steward, Ploughman, &c., with numerous illustrations. 3 vols. 8vo. cloth, $26 00. Edinburgh.

Stephens, (H.) Manual of Practical Draining. 8vo. cloth, $1 00. Edinburgh.

——— Practical Irrigator and Drainer. 8vo. cloth, $1 50. Edinburgh.

——— (Sir James.) Essays in Ecclesiastical Biography. 2 vols. 8vo. cloth, $7 00. London, 1849.

——— Critical and Miscellaneous Essays. 12mo. cloth, $1 25. Phila. 1843.

——— (Thomas.) The History of the Church of Scotland from the Reformation to the present time. Portraits, 4 vols. 8vo. half calf, neat, $11 00; cloth, $7 50. London, 1843.

——— Illustrations of British Entomology, with several hundred colored figures. 12 vols. royal 8vo. half bound, $36 00. Lond. 1828.

——— (J. F.) Systematic Catalogue of British Insects; being an attempt to arrange the Indigenous Insects with their Natural Affinities, &c. 8vo. cloth, $4 75. Lond. 1829.

——— (J. L.) Incidents of Travel in Egypt, Arabia Petræa, &c. 2 vols. 12mo. cloth, $1 75. New York.

——— Incidents of Travel in Greece, Turkey, &c. 2 vols. 12mo. cloth, $1 75. New York.

——— Incidents of Travel in Yucatan. 2 vols. 8vo. cloth, $5 00. New York.

——— Travels in Central America, Chiapas, and Yucatan. 2 vols. 8vo. map and 88 engravings, $5 00. New York.

Stephenson, (Robert.) Description of Locomotive Steam Engines. 4 elaborately engraved plates and numerous wood-cuts. 4to. cloth, $6 00. London.

——— Report on the Atmospheric Railway System. 27 tabular engraved plates. Medium 4to. $2 25. London.

Stevens, (F.) Views of Cottages and Farm Houses in England and Wales. 4to. plates, $5 00. London.

——— (William.) History of the High School of Edinburgh. 12mo. cloth, $2 50. Lond. 1849.

——— (W. B.) A History of Georgia from its First Discovery to the Adoption of the Constitution in 1798. Vol. 1, 8vo. cloth, $2 50. (To be completed in 2 volumes.) New York.

Stevenson, (R.) A Treatise on the Nature and Properties of Algebraic Equations. 8vo. bds. $1 63. Cambridge, 1835.

——— (A.) Account of Skerryvore Light-House. 4to. cloth, plates, $19 00. Lond.

——— (David.) Remarks on the Improvement of Tidal Rivers. 8vo. plates, $1 00. Lond.

Stillie, (A.) Elements of General Pathology. 12mo. sheep, $1 50. Phila.

Stillingfleet, (Bishop.) Origines Sacræ; or, a Rational Account of the Grounds of Natural and Revealed Religion. 2 vols. 8vo. cloth, $4 50. Oxford, 1836.

——— Vindication of Archbishop Laud. 2 vols. 8vo. cloth, $4 50.

Stirling, (John.) Essays and Tales. Edited by J. C. Hare. 2 vols. cr. 8vo. cloth, $6 00. London, 1847.

——— (W.) Annals of the Artists of Spain. 3 vols. 8vo. cloth, illustrated with steel engravings, $17 00. London, 1849.

St. John, (B.) Adventures in the Lybian Desert, and the Oasis of Jupiter Ammon. 12mo. cloth, 75 cents. New York, 1849.

St. John, (Chas.) Wild Sports of the Highlands. Post 8vo. cloth, $1 75. London.

——— A Tour in Sutherlandshire, with Extracts from the Field Books of a Sportsman and Naturalist. 2 vols. 8vo. cloth, plates, $4 50. Lond.

——— (J. A.) The History of the Manners and Customs of Ancient Greece. 3 vols. 8vo. bds. $8 00. London, 1842.

——— (P. B.) French Revolution in 1848. 18mo. cloth, 63 cents. New York.

Stewart, (Dugald.) Elements of the Philosophy of the Human Mind, with References, Sectional Heads, Synoptical Tables of Contents, &c. By Rev. G. N. Wright. 8vo. cloth, $2 50. London, 1843.

——— 8vo. sheep, $2 50. Boston, 1847.

——— Works. 7 vols. 8vo. Cambridge.

——— (Rev. C. S.) Residence in the Sandwich Islands in 1822–25. 12mo. cloth, $1 00. N. Y.

——— (John.) Stable Economy; or, Management of Horses. 12mo. cloth, $2 00. Edin.

——— American edition. 12mo. cloth, $1 00.

St. Ligouri. The Way of Salvation. 12mo. cloth, 63 cents. Dublin, 1844.

Stocqueler, (J. H.) The Oriental Interpreter, and Treasury of East India Knowledge. Post 8vo. cloth, $3 25. London, 1848.

Stockhardt. Der Schule des Chimie. 12mo. paper, $2 50. Brunswick, 1849.

Stone, (E. M.) History of Beverly, Massachusetts, from its earliest Settlement. 12mo. cloth, $1 00. Boston.

——— (W. L.) Border Wars of the Revolution. 2 vols. 18mo. cloth, 90 cents. New York.

——— Life of Joseph Brandt. 2 vols. 8vo. $5 00.

——— Life of Red Jacket. 8vo. cloth, $3 00. New York.

——— (Mrs.) Chronicles of Fashion; or, English Society from the Time of Queen Elizabeth to the Present Day. 2 vols. 8vo. calf, gilt, portraits, $8 50. London, 1846.

——— (S.) Dictionnaire Classique Francais-Anglais et Anglais-Francais precede d'une Introduction, etc., etc., par Shrubsole et Thiebaut. 8vo. paper, $1 50. Paris, 1844.

Stoddart, (T. T.) Angler's Companion to the Rivers and Lochs of Scotland. Post 8vo. cloth, plate, $3 00. Edinburgh, 1847.

——— (Col. W. L.) Life and Times of Red Jacket; or, Sayo-ye-wat-ha; being the Sequel to the History of the Six Nations. 8vo. cloth, $3 00. New York.

Storer's Cathedral Antiquities of England and Wales. 4 vols. 8vo. cloth, 256 plates, $16 00. London.

Storrow on Water Works. 12mo. cloth, $1 25. Boston.

Story, (Jos.) Miscellaneous Writings. 8vo. cloth, $1 75. Cambridge.

Story of the Peninsular War, by Gen. C. W. Vane. 12mo. cloth, $1 00; paper, 75 cents. New York.

Stothard's Monumental Effigies of Great Britain. Folio, half mor. 147 engravings, $50 00. London.

Stowe, (The,) Catalogue, Priced and Annotated, with a History of the Family of Buckingham and Chandois, Historical Notice of Stowe, &c. Illustrated. 4to. half mor. $4 25. London, 1849.

Stow, (John.) Survey of London. Edited by W. J. Thoms. Medium 8vo. $1 75. Lond.

St. Pierre, (Bernardin de.) Etudes de la Nature. 12mo. $1 00. Paris, 1845.

——— Œuvres Choises. 12mo. $1 00; half mor. $1 75. Paris, 1846.

——— Works; including Studies of Nature, by Rev. E. Clark. 2 vols. 12mo. cloth, $2 25. London, 1846.

——— Studies of Nature. 8vo. sheep, $1 75. Philadelphia.

St. Paul. The Life of St. Paul, the Apostle of the Gentiles, for Young Persons, by Rev. G. E. Biber. 12mo. cloth, $1 38. Lond. 1849.

Strachey on Hamlet. An Attempt to find the Key to a Great Moral Problem by a Methodical Analysis of the Play. 8vo. $1 50.

Strauss, (Dr. F.) The Life of Jesus Critically Examined. Translated from the German. 3 vols. 8vo. cloth, $6 00. London, 1846.

Street, (A. B.) Frontenac; or, the Atotarho of the Iroquois, a Metrical Romance. 12mo. cloth, portrait, $1 25. New York, 1848.

Strickland, (W.) Public Works of the United States of America. 2 parts, folio, 40 plates, with Reports, Specifications, and Estimates of the Public Works, &c. 1 vol. 8vo. explanatory of the plates, $14 00. London.

——— (Agnes.) Lives of the Queens of England. 12 vols. cr. 8vo. cloth, $38 00. Lond.

——— The Same. 12 vols. in 6, 8vo. cloth, $10 00. Philadelphia.

Strong's Illustrated Natural History. 8vo. cloth, $1 75. New York.

Strutt's Dresses, from the Establishment of the Saxons in Britain till the present time, with an Historical Inquiry into every Branch of Costume. 2 vols. 4to. cloth, 153 plates, $25 00. London.

——— The Regal and Ecclesiastical Antiquities of England. 4to. half mor. in Roxburghe Style, 72 plates, beautifully colored, $25 00. London, 1842.

——— Sports and Pastimes of the People of England. 8vo. cloth, $3 00. Lond. 1834.

Stuart, (J. and S.) Costume of the Scottish Highland Clans. Folio, colored plates, $38 00.

——— Vestiarium Scoticum; or, Book of Tartans. Imp. 4to. $63 00. Edin.

——— (Sir H.) The Planter's Guide; a Practical Essay on the best Method of giving immediate Effect to Wood by the Transplanting of large Trees and Underwood. Third edition, with Memoir of the Author. 8vo. cloth, $6 50. London, 1848.

——— (R.) A Dictionary of Architecture, Historical, Descriptive, Topographical, Decorative, Theoretical, and Mechanical. Illustrated by 1000 drawings of Subjects referred to in the Work. 3 vols. 8vo. cloth, $9 00. Lond.

——— (Moses.) Hints on the Interpretation of Prophecy. 12mo. cloth, 63 cents. Andover, 1842.

——— A Critical History and Defence of the Old Testament Canon. 12mo. cloth, $1 25. Andover.

Stuart, (M.) Grammar of the New Testament Dialect. 8vo. cloth, $2 00. Andover

——— Hebrew Chrestomathy. 8vo. cloth, $1 75. New York.

——— On the Apocalypse. 2 vols. 8vo. cloth, $6 00. Andover.

——— et **Revett,** et **J.-J. Hittoff,** architectes. Antiquites d'Athenes et Antiquites de l'Attique, en 5 volumes, classees comme suit:—

Antiquites de Athenes, mesurees et dessinees par J. Stuart et N. Revett, peintre et architecte. Ouvrage traduit de l'Anglais, par L. Feuillet, bibliothecaire de l'Institut de France, et publiee par C. P. Landon, peintre, et Clemence, architecte. Cette edition contient des sculptures du Parthenon, inconnues aux editeurs anglais, lesquelles ont ete gravees, d'apres les dessins recueilles sur les lieux avant leur destruction, par M. de Nointel.

Quatre volumes in-folio de 191 planches gravees au trait et a l'eau-forte, par Ch. Normant et Beaujean-Ouvrare, termine et cartonne, $55 00.

Le cinquieme volume se compose des Antiquites inedites de l'Attique, contenant les restes d'architecture d'Eleusis, de Rhamnus, de Sunium et de Thuricus, par la Societe des Dilettanti. 1 vol. in-folio de 60 planches avec texte, $15 00.

——— and **Revett's** Antiquities of Athens, measured and delineated. Abridged edition. 12mo. cloth, $3 50. London.

Sturm's Morning Communings with God; or, Devotional Meditations for every Day in the Year. Translated from the German. New edition, post 8vo. cloth, $1 50. 1847.

——— (C.) Solution of Numerical Equations. Translated by W. H. Spiller. 4to. paper, $2 12. London, 1835.

Sturtevant, (S. T.) The Preacher's Manual. 8vo. cloth, $2 50. New York.

Suddard, (Rev. W.) The British Pulpit, Discourses by Eminent Divines of Great Britain. 2 vols. 8vo. cloth, $3 00. New York.

Suckling, (Rev. A.) Memorials of the Antiquities of the County of Suffolk; or, Historical, Genealogical, and Architectural Notices of the several Towns and Villages in that County. 4to. plates and wood-cuts, $12 50. London.

——— Antiquities, Architecture, Heraldry, and Family History of the County of Essex. 4to. cloth, plates, $8 50. London.

Sue, (E.) The Wandering Jew. Illustrated. 8vo. cloth, $5 00. New York.

——— Histoire de la Marine Francaise. 4 vols. 12mo. paper, $3 00. Paris, 1845.

Suetonii Opera omnia ex editione Baumgarten-crusii cum notis et interpretatione in usum Delphini, &c. 3 vols. 8vo. bds. $7 00. Valpy, London, 1826.

Sullivan's Revolutionary Campaigns in Western New York. 12mo. cloth, 50 cents. Rochester.

——— Public Men of the Revolution from 1783 to 1815, with a Biographical Sketch of the Author, with additional Notes, by his Son, J. T. Sullivan. 8vo. cloth, $2 00. Phila. 1847.

Summer, (Thos. H.) Method of Finding a Ship's Position at Sea. $1 25. Boston.

Summerfeldt, (H. A.) The Naval Architect's Portfolio, and the Student's Practical Instructor in the Constructing and Draughting Ships of War, Mercantile and Steam Packet Service, Iron and Timber. 8vo. cloth, with folio atlas, $3 75. London.

Sumner, (J. B.) Practical Exposition of the General Epistles of James, Peter, John, and Jude, in the Form of Lectures. 8vo. cloth, $2 75. London, 1840.

Supplement to the London Catalogue of Books, 1846–49, to the edition date, 1841, with a Classified Index. 8vo. cloth, $2 75. Lond.

Surenne, (Prof.) Standard Pronouncing Dictionary of the French and English Languages. 12mo. sheep, $1 50. New York.

Surrey and Wyatt's Poems, with Memoir, by Sir Harris Nicolas. 2 vols. 12mo. cloth, $2 75. Pickering.

——— (Henry Howard, Earl of.) Poems. 12mo. mor. gilt, portrait, $2 25. Lond. 1831.

Sutton, (C.) Disce Mori; Learn to Die. 18mo. cloth, $1 00. Oxford, 1840.

——— Do. do. Another edition. 18mo. cloth, 37 cents. New York, 1845.

——— Disce Vivere; Learn to Live. 18mo. cloth, $1 00. Oxford, 1839.

Swain, (C.) English Melodies. 12mo. cloth, $1 75. London, 1849.

Swainson, (W.) Treatise on Taxidermy, including a Bibliography of Natural History. 12mo. cloth, $1 75. London, 1840.

——— and **Shuckard's** History and Classification of Insects. 12mo. cloth, $1 75. London, 1840.

——— History and Classification of Fish, Reptiles, &c. 2 vols. 12mo. cloth, wood engravings, $3 50. London, 1838–39.

——— Natural History and Classification of Quadrupeds. 12mo. cloth, wood-cuts, $1 75.

——— Animals in Menageries. 12mo. cloth, $1 75. London.

——— Malacology; or, Classification of Shells and Shell-Fish. 12mo. cloth, $1 75. Lond.

——— Discourse on the Study of Natural History. 12mo. cloth, $1 75. Lond. 1834.

——— Habits and Instincts of Animals. 12mo. cloth, $1 75. London.

——— History and Classification of Animals. 12mo. cloth, $1 75. London.

——— History and Classification of Birds. 2 vols. 12mo. cloth, $3 50. Lond. 1836–37.

——— Exotic Conchology; or, Figures and Descriptions of Rare, Beautiful, or Undescribed Shells, with new letter-press descriptions. 4to. half mor. 94 beautifully colored Shells, $15 00. London, 1841.

Sweet, (R.) Cistineæ; the Natural Order of Cistus, or Rock Rose. Illustrated by colored figures and descriptions of all the Species that could be procured in Great Britain. Roy. 8vo. cloth, $9 00. Lond. 1830.

——— Flora Australasica; or, a Selection of Handsome and Curious Plants, Natives of New Holland and the South Sea Islands. Royal 8vo. 56 beautifully colored plates, cloth, $10 00. London, 1828.

Swedenborg, (E.) The Animal Kingdom considered. 2 vols. 8vo. cloth, $11 00. London.

——— Principia; or, Principles of Natural Things. 2 vols. 8vo. cloth, $9 00. Lond.

——— Heavenly Arcana. 13 vols. 8vo. cloth, $16 50. Boston.

Swedenborg, (E.) The Apocalypse Explained. 5 vols. 8vo. cloth, $12 50. Boston.

——— Treatise on Conjugal Love. 8vo. cloth, $1 75. Boston.

——— On Heaven and Hell. 12mo. cloth, 75 cents. Boston.

——— True Christian Religion. 8vo. cloth, $2 00. Boston.

Swedish and English Dictionary. 18mo. bds. $1 50. London.

Swift, (D.) The Closing Years of Dean Swift's Life, containing several of his Poems, hitherto unpublished, by W. R. Wilde. 8vo. cloth, $1 75. Dublin, 1847.

——— (Dr. J.) Works; containing additional Letters, Tracts, and Poems, not hitherto published, with Notes, and a Life of the Author, by Thos. Roscoe. 2 vols. royal 8vo. cloth, portrait, $7 50. London, 1843.

——— Poetical Works. (Aldine edition.) 3 vols. 12mo. cloth, $3 75; mor. neat, gilt leaves, $9 00; another copy, $7 00. London, 1833.

Syme, (J.) Principles of Surgery. 8vo. sheep, $1 75. Phila. 1832.

Symm, (W.) Elements of Perspective Drawing. New edition, by R. Couch. Long 4to. cloth, $1 00. London.

Symons, (J. C.) Tactics for the Times as regards the Condition and Treatment of the Dangerous Classes. 8vo. cloth, plates, $2 00. London, 1849.

Syria, the Holy Land, and Asia Minor. Illustrated in 120 Views, by Bartlett, Purser, and Allom, with descriptive letter-press, by John Carne. 3 vols. 4to. cloth, plates, $16 00. London, 1837.

Tables of Logarithms, Common and Trigonometrical. 12mo. paper, $1 00. Lond.

Tacitus Opera, edidit F. Ritter. 4 vols. 8vo. cloth, $8 50. London.

——— The Works of Cornelius Tacitus, with an Essay, his Life, and Genius, Notes and Supplement, by Arthur Murphy. 8vo. cloth, $2 00. London, 1849.

Taillandier, (Saint-Rene.) Histoire de la Jeune Allemagne etudes Litteraires. 8vo. paper, $2 00. Paris, 1848.

Talbot, (H. F.) Pencil of Nature, being the Actual Sketches taken from Nature, by the Process known as the Talbotype. Royal 4to. part 1, $3 50; part 2, $6 50; parts 3 to 5, each $2 25. London.

Tales explanatory of the Sacraments. 2 vols. 12mo cloth, $2 50. London, 1846.

Talfourd, (Thos. N.) Tragedies and Poems. 12mo. cloth, 63 cents. Boston.

——— and **Stephens'** Miscellanies. 8vo. cloth, $1 25. Philadelphia.

Talleyrand, (Prince.) Reminiscences of, with Extracts from his Manuscripts, Speeches, and Political Writings. 2 vols. post 8vo. cloth, $6 00. London, 1848.

Tannahill's Poems and Songs. Edited by Ramsay. 12mo. cloth, $1 50. Lond.

Tanquerel on Lead Diseases, with Notes and Additions on the Use of Lead Pipe and its Substitutes. Translated by Dr. S. L. Dana. 8vo. cloth, $2 25. Lowell, 1848.

Tappan, (Prof. H. P.) Elements of Logic, together with an Introductory View of Philosophy in general, and a Preliminary View of the Reason. 12mo. cloth, $1 00. New York.

—— The Doctrine of the Will applied to Moral Agency and Responsibility. 12mo. cloth, $1 00. New York.

—— Review of Edwards' Inquiry into the Freedom of the Will. 12mo. cloth, $1 00. New York.

—— Appeal to Consciousness to Determine the Doctrine of the Will. 12mo. cloth, $1 00. New York.

Tardieu. Manuel de Pathologie et de Clinique Medicales. 12mo. paper, $1 50. Paris, 1849.

—— Treatise on Epidemic Cholera. Translated by S. L. Bigelow. 12mo. cloth, $1 00. Boston, 1849.

Tarver, (J. C.) Royal Phraseological Dictionary. Vol. 1, English and French. Royal 8vo. $7 50. London.

Taschereau, (M. J.) Histoire de la vie et des ouvrages de Moliere. 12mo. paper, 50 cents. Paris, 1844.

Tasistro's Travels in the Southern States; or, Random Shots and Southern Breezes. 2 vols. 12mo. cloth, $1 50. New York.

Tasso. Godfrey of Bulloigne; or, the Recovery of Jerusalem. Done into English Historical Verse, from the Italian of Tasso, by Edward Fairfax. Introductory Essay, by Leigh Hunt, and the Lives of Tasso and Fairfax, by Charles Knight. 1 vol. 12mo. $1 25; cloth gilt, $1 75. London.

"The completest translation, and nearest like its original of any we have seen."—LEIGH HUNT.

"The Jerusalem Delivered is full, to the last stanza, of the most delightful inventions, of the most charming pictures of chivalric and heroic sentiment, of portraits of brave men and beautiful women—in fine, a prodigal mine of the choicest resources and effects of poetry. So it has been always known to the world, so Fairfax brings it to us."—MIRROR.

—— Jerusalem Delivered. Translated in the Spenserian Stanza, by J. H. Wiffen. 12mo. cloth, plates, $1 50; mor. $3 00. New York.

Tate, (W.) Modern Cambist; forming a Manual of Foreign Exchanges in the different Operations of Bills of Exchange and Bullion, with Tables of Foreign Weights and Measures. Sixth edition, edited by his Son, William Tate. 8vo. cloth, $3 75. London, 1847.

—— (T.) A Treatise on Factorial Analysis, with the Summation of Series; containing new Developments of Functions. 8vo. cloth, $1 25.

—— Principles of the Differential and Integral Calculus simplified. $1 38. Lond.

—— (J. R.) Naval Book-Keeping. Royal 8vo. cloth, $4 25. London

—— Theory and Practice of Gauging. 8vo. cloth, $3 50. London.

Tatham, (C. H.) Architectural Works Royal folio, half bound, $45 00. Lond.

—— Grecian and Roman Ornaments. Folio, cloth, $15 75. London.

—— Lexicon Egyptiaco-Latinum. 8vo. bds. $9 50. London.

Tayler, (Rev. C. B.) Margaret; or, the Pearl. 12mo. cloth, 75 cents. New York.

—— Lady Mary; or, Not of this World. 12mo. cloth, 75 cents.

Tayler, (Rev. C. B.) Mark Wilton; a Tale. 12mo. cloth, 75 cents.

—— Facts in a Clergyman's Life. 12mo. 75 cents. New York.

—— Thankfulness; a Narrative, comprising Passages from the Diary of the Rev. A. Temple. 12mo. cloth, 75 cents.

—— (J. J.) Retrospect of the Religious Life in England. Post 8vo. cloth, $1 75. London, 1845.

—— (J. N.) Plans for the Foundations of Harbors. 4to. cloth, $2 25. London.

—— (Thos.) Law Glossary of Foreign Languages. 8vo. bds. $2 75. London.

Taylor, (A. S.) Poisons in Relation to Medical Jurisprudence. 12mo. cloth, $3 75. London.

—— Medical Jurisprudence. 8vo. sheep, $2 50. Philadelphia.

—— (B.) Principles of Linear Perspective, by Jopling. 8vo. bds. $3 25. Lond.

—— (J. Bayard.) Poems and Ballads, with portrait. 12mo. cloth, 75 cents; cloth gilt, extra, $1 25. New York.

"A spirit of boldness and vigor pervades the volume."

"The Picturesque Ballads of California have a dash of boldness and adventure in them which contrasts pleasantly with the more purely sentimental poems."

—— Views A-Foot: or, Europe seen with Knapsack and Staff. New edition, with an additional Chapter of Practical Information for Pedestrians in Europe, and a Sketch of the Author in Pedestrian Costume; from a Drawing by T. Buchanan Read. 12mo. cloth, $1 25; fancy cloth, gilt extra, $1 75. N. Y.

"There is a freshness and force in the book altogether unusual in a Book of Travels. As a text-book for travellers the work is essentially valuable; it tells how much can be accomplished with very limited means, when energy, curiosity, and a love of adventure are the prompters; sympathy in his success likewise, is another source of interest to the book. The result of all this is, a wide-spread popularity as a writer, a very handsomely printed book, with a very handsome portrait of the Author, and we congratulate him upon the attainment of this and future honors."—UNION MAGAZINE.

—— Letters from California. 12mo. cloth. New York.

—— (Chas.) Treatise on Perspective. Roy 8vo. cloth, $4 50. London.

—— Treatise on Drawing. Royal 8vo. cloth, $3 25. London.

—— (Emily,) England and its People. 18mo. roan, $1 25. London.

—— Sabbath Recreations. 18mo. cloth, $1 50. London.

—— (H.) Bee-Keeper's Manual. 12mo. cloth, $1 25. London.

—— Edwin the Fair. 18mo. cloth, gilt, 87 cents. London, 1847.

—— Philip Van Artevelde. 18mo. cloth, 87 cents. London, 1847.

—— Notes from Life, in Six Essays. New edition, post 8vo. cloth, $2 00. Lond. 1848.

—— Notes from Books, in Four Essays. 12mo. cloth, $2 75. Lond. 1849.

—— (Isaac.) Ancient Christianity. 2 vols. 8vo. cloth, $5 50. London, 1844.

—— Elements of Thought. 12mo. cloth, $1 25. London, 1845.

—— Fanaticism. 12mo. cloth, $1 75. London, 1848

Taylor, (I.) Loyola and Jesuitism in its Rudiments. Cr. 8vo. cloth, $3 25. London, 1849.

——— 12mo. cloth, $1 00. New York, 1849.

——— Physical Theory of another Life. 12mo. cloth, $1 50. Pickering, 1847.

——— Home Education. 12mo. cloth, $1 50. London, 1842.

——— Lectures on Spiritual Christianity. 12mo. cloth, 87 cents. London, 1841.

——— Saturday Evening. 12mo. cloth, $1 50. London, 1844.

——— (Jane.) Contributions of Q. Q., with some Pieces not before published. 2 vols. 18mo. 87 cents. New York.

——— Memoirs and Correspondence, by her Brother, Isaac Taylor. 18mo. cloth, 50 cents. New York.

——— (Jeremy.) Works, with Life, by Heber. 15 vols. 8vo. cloth, $47 00. London.

——— Do. do. By Eden and Heber. Vols. 2 to 6. 8vo. cloth, each $3 00. Lond. 1847.

——— Holy Living and Dying. 2 vols. 8vo. black mor. unique, $12 00. Pickering, Lond.

——— The Same. 2 vols. 12mo. cloth, $3 00; mor. extra, by Hayday, $8 00. Pickering, Lond.

——— Rule and Exercise of Holy Living and Dying. 12mo. $1 25. Pickering, Lond. 1840.

——— American edition. 12mo. cloth, $1 00. New York.

——— (J.) Designs for Household Furniture. Imp. 8vo. half bound, $19 00. London.

——— Upholsterer and Cabinet-Maker's Assistant. 2 vols. 8vo. cloth, $12 50. London.

——— Diurnal Register, Remarks on the Barometer, &c. Oblong, $1 75. Lond.

——— (J. E.) The Fairy Ring; a new Collection of Popular Tales. Translated from the German of S. and W. Grimm, with 12 illustrations, by Doyle. Square 12mo. bds. $1 50; cloth, $1 00. London, 1847.

——— American edition, cloth gilt, $1 25.

——— (R.) Scientific Memoirs selected from the Transactions of Foreign Academies of Science, and from Foreign Journals. Parts 1 to 14. 8vo. paper, each $1 75. London.

——— (Thos.) Memoir of Mrs. Hannah More, with Notices of her Works, and Sketches of her Contemporaries. 12mo. cloth, $1 00. London, 1838.

——— (R. C.) Statistics of Coal. The Geographical and Geological Distribution of Fossil Fuel or Mineral Combustibles, &c., with colored maps and diagrams. 8vo. cloth, $5 00. Philadelphia.

——— (W.) Historic Survey of German Poetry, interspersed with various Translations. 3 vols. 8vo. cloth, $6 00. London, 1830.

——— Memoirs of, by J. W. Robberds. 2 vols. 8vo. cloth, $9 00. London.

——— (W. B.) History of the University of Dublin, its Origin, Progress, and Present Condition, with Biographical Notices, &c. 8vo. cloth, plates, $5 50. London, 1845.

——— History of Mohammedanism. 12mo. cloth, $1 63. London.

——— Natural History of Society. 2 vols. post 8vo. cloth, $6 50. London.

Taylor, (W. B.) Romantic Biography of the Age of Elizabeth. 2 vols. 8vo. cloth, $8 50. London.

——— History of Christianity. 12mo. cloth, $1 50. London, 1844.

——— (Jos.) Hindostanee and English Dictionary, by Smyth. 8vo. cloth, $19 00. Lond.

——— (W. C.) A Manual of Ancient and Modern History. 8vo. cloth, $2 50. New York.

——— (W. S.) A Manual of Fresco and Encaustic Painting, containing ample Instructions for executing Works of these descriptions. 8vo. cloth, $2 00. London.

——— Origin, Progress, and Present State of the Fine Arts in Great Britain. 2 vols. 8vo. cloth, wood-cuts, $2 75. London.

——— Life of William Cowper. 12mo. cloth, 50 cents.

——— History of the Revolutions of Europe. 2 vols. 8vo. cloth, $2 50. London.

——— and **Cresey's** Architectural Antiquities of Rome Measured and Delineated. Uniform with Stuart and Revett's Athens. 2 vols. folio, half Russia, $50 00.

Tegner, (Esaias.) Frithiof's Saga; a Legend of Norway. Translated from the Swedish into English Verse, with an Introduction, copious Notes, and a Mythological and Antiquarian Glossary, by George Stephens. 8vo. cloth, $3 00. London.

Telemachus. Translated by Hawksworth. 2 vols. 12mo. cloth, $1 25. New York.

Temple Church, (Architecture of.) By Essex and Smirke. 4to. plates, $12 50. Lond.

Temple, (E.) Travels in Peru. 2 vols. 8vo. cloth, $9 50. London.

——— (W.) Memoirs of, by T. P. Courtenay. 2 vols. 8vo. cloth, $4 50. London.

——— (Sir W.) Works. 4 vols. 8vo. cloth, $12 00. London.

Templeton, (W.) Operative Mechanic's Workshop Companion, and the Scientific Gentleman's Practical Assistant, &c. 18mo. $1 50. London, 1845.

——— The Millwright's and Engineer's Pocket Companion. 12mo. wood-cuts, $1 50. Lond.

——— Engineer's Pocket-Book. 12mo. $1 75. London.

——— The Engineer's Common Place Book of Practical Reference. 12mo. $1 75. Lond.

——— Mathematical Tables for Practical Men. 12mo. $1 25. London.

——— Incitements to the Studies of Steam and the Steam Engine. 18mo. cloth, 63 cents. London.

——— The Engineer's Common Place Book of Practical Reference. Third edition, improved, 12mo. cloth, $1 50. London, 1848.

——— The Locomotive Steam Engine popularly explained. Second edition, with lithographic illustrations. 12mo. cloth, $1 25. Lond. 1848.

Tennant, (W.) Anster Fair and other Poems. 12mo. cloth, $2 25. Lond.

Tenneman's Manual of the History of Philosophy. Translated from the German, by Rev. A. Johnson. 8vo. cloth, $3 00. Oxford, 1838.

Tennent, (J. E.) Copyright of Designs for Printed Fabrics. Post 8vo. cloth, $1 50. London

—— Pecchio and Humphrey's Picture of Greece. 2 vols. post 8vo. cloth, $5 50. Lond.

Tennyson, (Alfred.) Poems complete. 2 vols. 12mo. bds. $1 50; cloth, $1 75. Boston.

—— The Princess; a Medley. Bds. 50 cents; cloth, 63 cents. Boston.

Terry, (C.) New Zealand, its Advantages, &c. as a Colony. 8vo. cloth, $5 50. Lond.

—— Scenes and Thoughts in Foreign Lands. Post 8vo. $1 75. London.

Terentius cum Notis et Scholiis variorum ex editione Zeunii cura Giles; acced. Index copiosissimus. 8vo. cloth, $3 00. Lond. 1837.

Terence, with English Notes, by Dillaway. 18mo. cloth, 63 cents. Philadelphia.

—— Translated by Colman. 12mo. cloth, $2 25. London.

—— Translated by Phillips. 8vo. cloth, $1 00. London.

—— Translated by Cotter. 8vo. cloth, $3 50. London.

Testament, (New,) as Translated by Wycliffe. 4to. half bound in black letter, $12 50. London, 1848.

—— The Greek Text of Griesbach. 12mo. cloth, $2 25. London.

—— Translated by Edgar Taylor. 12mo. cloth, $2 25. London.

—— With English Notes, by Bloomfield. 2 vols. 8vo. cloth, $12 00. London.

Teste, (A.) Practical Manual of Animal Magnetism. 12mo. cloth, $1 75. Lond. 1843.

Texan, (The.) A Description of the Climate, &c. of Texas. 12mo. cloth, $1 00. Cincinnati.

Texas, (History of.) By Rev. C. Newell. 12mo. cloth, 75 cents. New York, 1838.

—— and the Texans. By Gen. Foot. 2 vols. 12mo. cloth, $1 25. Philadelphia.

Thackeray, (W. M.) History of Samuel Titmarsh and the Great Hoggarty Diamond. Square 12mo. bds. engravings, $2 00. London, 1849.

—— American edition, 25 cents.

—— Dr. Birch and his Young Friends. 12mo. bds. colored plates, $2 25. London.

—— Mrs. Perkins' Ball. Square 12mo. bds. colored plates, $3 25. London.

—— Irish Sketch Book. 2 vols. 12mo. engravings, cloth, $5 00. Lond. 1845.

—— Journey from Cornhill to Cairo. 12mo. cloth, 50 cents. New York, 1848.

—— Vanity Fair. 8vo. cloth, engravings, $1 25. New York, 1848.

—— History of Pendennis. 8vo. cloth, plates, New York.

—— Our Street. Square 12mo. bds. colored plates, $2 25. London.

—— (Rev. F.) Researches into the Ecclesiastical and Political State of Ancient Britain under the Roman Emperors. 2 vols. 8vo. cloth, $6 50. London, 1843.

Thackrah, (C. T.) Effects of Trades on Health and Longevity. 8vo. cloth, $2 25. London.

Thaer, (A. D.) Principles of Agriculture. Translated by W. Shaw and C. W. Johnson. 2 vols. 8vo. cloth, $8 00. London, 1844.

Thane, (J.) British Autography; a Collection of fac-similes of the Handwriting of Royal and Illustrious Personages. 3 vols. 4to. half mor. plates, $40 00. (Very scarce.) Lond.

Thatcher's Biography of Distinguished Indians; or, an Historical Account of those Individuals who have been Distinguished among the North American Indians, as Orators, Warriors, Statesmen, and other Remarkable Characters. 2 vols. 12mo. cloth, $1 00. N. York.

—— Tales of the American Revolution; being Rare and Remarkable Passages of the History of the War of 1776. 18mo. cloth, 37 cents. New York.

—— Indian Traits; being Sketches of the Manners, Customs, and Character of the North American Natives. 2 vols. 18mo. cloth, 75 cents. New York.

The Drawing-Room Scrap-Book for 1850. Edited by Charles Mackay, with 36 splendid engravings, elegantly bound in 4to. cloth gilt, $6 00. London, 1850.

The Game of Natural History; being a Series of Animals pictured on cards and colored, in case, with Robinson Crusoe's Farm-Yard. Square 18mo. half bound, designed to accompany the Game, $1 00; colored, $1 25. New York, 1849.

Theime's English and German—German and English Dictionary. 32mo. bds. $1 00.

The King of the Hurons; a Romance of the Last Century. 12mo. cloth, $1 00; paper, 75 cents. New York.

Theocritus, Bion et Moschus. Square 12mo. paper, 25 cents. (Tauchnitz edition.) Leips.

—— Recens. et edente Wordsworth, 8vo. cloth, $4 00. London.

—— Bion and Moschus. Translated by Chapman. Cr. 8vo. cloth, $3 00. London.

Theodoret's Ecclesiastical History. 8vo. cloth, $3 25. London.

Theological Essays. Reprinted from the "Princeton Review." First and Second Series. 2 vols. thick 8vo. cloth, $5 00. New York.

Theophilus. Essays upon various Arts in three Books, forming an Encyclopædia of Art of the Eleventh Century. Translated with Notes, by Hendric. 8vo. cloth, $6 00. Lond.

The Shakespeare Calendar; or, Wit and Wisdom for every Day in the Year. Edited by W. C. Richards. 32mo. cloth, 37 cents; cloth gilt, 63 cents. New York.

Thierry, (Augustin.) Histoire de la conquete de l'Angleterre par les Normands, avec Atlas et gravures. Lettres sur l'histoire de France. Dix ans d'etudes historiques. Recits des temps Merovingiens. 3 vol. in 8, et atlas, demi veau, $20 00. Paris, 1836–42.

—— Lettres sur l'Histoire de France, pour servir d'Introduction a l'etude de cette Histoire. 8vo. paper, $1 50. Brux. 1839

Thierry, (M. A.) Historical Essays and Narratives. 8vo. cloth, $1 25. Phila. 1845.

——— Architecte. Arc de triomph de l'Etoile. Plans, coupes, elevations, details de construction et sculptures d'apres les dessins de MM. Chalgrin, Raimond, et Goust. 1 vol. grand in-fol. atlas de 26 pl. gravees avec le plus grand soin et texte historique et descriptif, bnd. $22 50. Paris.

Thiers. Histoire de la Revolution Francaise. 9e edition, ornee de 50 nouvelles vignettes, gravees sur acier par Burdet, d'apres les dessins de Raffet. 10 vol. in 8, demi veau, $16 00. Paris, 1839.

——— Histoire de la Revolution Francaise. 5 vols. 12mo. paper, $3 75. Brux. 1845.

——— History of the French Revolution. Translated, with Notes and Illustrations from the most authentic sources, by Frederick Shoberl. 5 vols. 8vo. cloth, illustrated by many engravings, $6 50. London, 1846.

——— History of the French Revolution. 4 vols. 8vo. cloth, $5 00. Phila.

——— Consulate and Empire of Napoleon. Vol. 1, 8vo. cloth, $1 50. Philadelphia.

——— Etudes historiques sur sa vie Privee, Politique, et Litteraire de par A. Laya. 2 vols. 8vo. paper, $3 75. Paris, 1846.

——— De la Propriete. 8vo. paper, $1 25. Paris, 1848.

Thimm's (F.) Literature of Germany Historically Developed. 12mo. cloth, $2 00.

Thirlwall, (Rev. C.) History of Greece. A new edition. 8 vols. 8vo. cloth, with maps, $26 00. London, 1845–8.

——— History of Greece. 2 vols. 8vo. sheep, extra, $4 00. New York.

Thom, (A.) Nature and Course of Storms in the Indian Ocean. 8vo. cloth, $3 50. Lond.

——— (W. J.) Collection of Early Prose Romances. 3 vols. post 8vo. cloth, $9 00. London, 1828.

——— Book of the Court, exhibiting the History, Duties, and Privileges of the several Ranks of the Nobility and Gentry. 8vo. cloth, $6 00; por. $2 00. London, 1844.

Thomas, (B.) Shooter's Guide. 12mo. cloth, $2 00. London.

——— (R.) Observations on Railways. 8vo. cloth, $1 00. London.

——— (Capt.) Views in Simla, in India. Folio, cloth, $25 00. London.

——— (Ed.) On the Coins of the Patau Sultans of Hindostan. 8vo. cloth, $3 00. Lond.

——— (E.) The Workingman's Cottage Architecture; containing Plans, Elevations, and Details for the Erection of Cheap, Comfortable, and Neat Cottages. 12mo. cloth, $1 00. New York.

——— (F. S.) Ancient Exchequers of England and Ireland. 8vo. cloth, $3 00. Lond.

——— History of the State Paper Office. 8vo. cloth, $1 25. London.

——— (G.) Historical and Geographical Account of the Province, &c. of Pennsylvania and of West New Jersey in America. (Reprint,) in fac-simile, 12mo. cloth, map, $1 50. London, 1698.

Thomas, (J. J.) The American Fruit Culturist; containing Directions for the Propagation and Culture of Fruit Trees in the Nursery, Orchard, and Garden, with Descriptions of the Principal American and Foreign Varieties cultivated in the United States. 12mo. cloth, 300 engravings, $1 00. Auburn, 1849.

——— (W.) Designs for Monuments and Chimney Pieces. Imp. 8vo. bds. 24 plates, $5 00. London, 1843.

——— **De Aquino,** (St.) Summa Theologiæ; opera et studio J. Carroli Renati Billuart; editio nova, accurate emandata. 10 vols. 8vo. $12 00. Lugduni, Guyot & Sons, 1847.

Thompson, (B. F.) History of Long Island. 2 vols. 8vo. cloth, map and plates, $5 00. New York, 1848.

——— (D.) Lunar and Horary Tables. Royal 8vo. $3 00. London.

——— (D. P.) Introduction to Meteorology. 8vo. cloth, $3 75. London, 1849.

——— (E. P.) History of the Austrian Empire. Post 8vo. cloth, $3 50. London.

——— Life in Russia; or, Discipline of Despotism. Post 8vo. cloth, $3 50. Lond.

——— (E. P.) Note-Book of a Naturalist. Post 8vo. cloth, $2 75. London.

——— (G. A.) Geographical Dictionary of America. 5 vols. 4to. cloth, $63 00. Lond.

——— (J.) Retreats; a Series of Designs, consisting of Plans and Elevations for Cottages, Villas, and Ornamental Buildings. 4to. cloth, $12 00. London.

——— (J. W.) Treatise on Heat for Hot Houses. 8vo. paper, 75 cents. London.

——— (T.) First Principles of Chemistry. 2 vols. 8vo. cloth, $3 50. London.

——— History of Mexico, from Documents made while Resident in that Country as American Minister. 12mo. cloth, $1 63. New York.

——— (Wm.) The Natural History of Ireland. Vol. 1, Birds, comprising the Orders Raptores and Insessores. 8vo. cloth, $4 50. Lond. 1849.

Thomson, (Lieut. Col.) Failure of the Masonry of the Defensive Building of Fort Neuf. (Papers, R. E. vol. 8, 4to.) London.

——— Experiments on the Condensation of Gravel and Sand. (Papers, R. E. vol. 7, 4to.) London.

——— Account of the Failure of a Floor in Edinburgh in 1823. (Papers, R. E. vol. 7, 4to.) London.

——— On the Subject of Furnaces for Heating Shot. (Papers, R. E. vol. 1, 4to.) London.

——— Collection of the Songs of Burns, Scott, and other eminent Lyric Poets, &c., with Symphonies and Accompaniments for the Piano Forte, by Pleyel, Haydn, Beethoven, &c. Composed for and Collected by George Thomson, F. A. S. 6 vols. royal 8vo. half mor. gilt leaves, with 12 engravings, Music to each Song engraved on separate page, $22 00; por. $16 00. London, 1822.

——— (Mrs.) Memoirs of the Court of Henry VIII. 2 vols. 8vo. $8 50. London.

——— Memoirs of the Duchess of Marlborough. 2 vols. 8vo. cloth, $8 50. Lond.

——— Memoirs of the Jacobites of 1715–45. 3 vols. 8vo. cloth, $10 50. London.

Thomson, (A. T.) Domestic Management of the Sick Room. Post 8vo. cloth, $3 25. London.

——— Elements of Materia Medica. 8vo. cloth, $9 50. London.

——— Lectures on Botany. 8vo. cloth, $8 50. London.

——— London Dispensatory. 8vo. cloth, $6 50. London.

——— Conspectus of the Pharmacopœias. 12mo. cloth, $1 63. London.

——— American edition. 12mo. cloth, $1 00. New York.

——— (Jas.) Differential and Integral Calculus. 8vo. cloth, $3 75.

——— Elementary Treatise on Algebra. 12mo. cloth, $1 50. London.

——— Elements of Plane and Spherical Trigonometry. 8vo. cloth, $1 25. Lond.

——— (J.) Account of the Varioloid Epidemic in Scotland. 8vo. cloth, $3 25. Lond.

——— Edinburgh Dispensatory. 8vo. $3 50.

——— Sketches of the Varieties of the Small Pox. 8vo. cloth, $3 50. Lond.

——— (J. P.) Memoir of David Hale, (late Editor of the Journal of Commerce,) with Selections from his Miscellaneous Writings. 12mo. cloth, portrait, and interior view of the Tabernacle, $1 25. New York, 1850.

——— (James.) The Poetical Works, comprising all his Pastoral, Dramatic, Lyrical, and Didactic Poems, and a few of his Juvenile Productions, with Life of the Author, by Rev. P. Murdoch, and Notes, by Nicholls. Portrait, 12mo. cloth, $2 00. London, 1849.

——— Poetical Works. (Aldine edition.) 2 vols. 12mo. cloth, $2 50; mor. gilt edges, $6 00. Pickering, 1847.

——— The Seasons. Beautifully printed and illustrated with exquisite wood engravings, with Life, by Patrick Murdoch, and edited by Bolton Corney. Square 8vo. mor. gilt edges, $4 00; cloth gilt, $2 75. New York, 1842.

——— (R. D.) School Chemistry; or, Practical Rudiments of the Science. 12mo. cloth, $2 00. London.

——— (R.) Experimental Researches on the Food of Animals, and the Fattening of Cattle, with Remarks on the Food of Man, founded on Experiments, &c. 12mo. cloth, 50 cents. New York.

——— Essay on Magna Charta. 8vo. cloth, $5 00. London.

——— (Thos.) Elements of Chemistry. 8vo. cloth, $3 25.

——— Sciences of Heat of Electricity. Second edition, 8vo. cloth, $4 50.

——— System of Chemistry. 4 vols. 8vo. cloth. London.

——— Inorganic Chemistry. 2 vols. 8vo. cloth.

——— Brewing and Distillation, with Practical Instructions for Brewing Porter and Ales according to the English and Scotch Methods, by William Stewart. Post 8vo. cloth, $2 25. Edinburgh, 1849.

——— Chemistry of Animal Bodies. 8vo. cloth. $4 75. London.

Thomson, (Thos.) Chemistry of Organic Bodies. 8vo. cloth, $7 25. London.

——— (W.) An Outline of the Necessary Laws of Thought; a Treatise on Pure and Applied Logic. 12mo. cloth, $2 25. Lond. 1849.

——— and **Twining** on Diseases of the Liver. 8vo. sheep, $2 00. Phila.

Thoresby, (Ralph.) Diary and Correspondence from 1677 to 1724. Edited by Rev. J. Hunter. 4 vols. 8vo. cloth, $6 00. London, 1830.

Thorman, (R.) The Taunus Railway; a concise Account, Historical, Statistical, and Mechanical, of the Railway from Frankfort to Wiesbaden. 4to. cloth, 25 plates, $3 75. London.

Thorn, (Major.) Memoirs of the Conquest of Java. Royal 4to. cloth, $19 00. Lond.

——— Memoirs of the War in India, in 1803–6. 4to. cloth, $16 50. London.

Thornthwaite, (W. H.) Guide to Photography. 8vo. cloth, $1 00. London.

Thornton. Oregon and California in 1848, with an Appendix. 2 vols. 12mo. cloth, $1 75. New York, 1849.

——— (W. T.) Over Population and its Remedy. 8vo. cloth, $3 25. London.

——— Plea for Peasant Proprietors. Post 8vo. cloth, $2 25. London, 1848.

——— (Thos.) History of the Punjab. 2 vols. post 8vo. $6 50. London.

——— (Capt.) History of the East India Company. 8vo. cloth, $2 25. London.

——— (Ed.) Chapters on Modern History of British India. 8vo. cloth, $6 50. Lond.

——— Gazetteer of Scinde. 2 vols. 8vo. cloth, $7 50. London

——— History of British India. 6 vols. 8vo. cloth, $29 00. London.

Thorpe, (C.) British Marine Conchology. 12mo. cloth, $3 00. London.

——— Our Army in the Rio Grande. 12mo. cloth, $1 00. Philadelphia.

——— Our Army at Monterey. 12mo. cloth, 75 cents. Philadelphia.

Thorpe and Klipstein's Anglo-Saxon Gospels. 12mo. cloth, $1 25. New York, 1849.

Three Courses and a Dessert. Crown 8vo. half mor. with some of Cruikshank's best illustrations, $1 75. London, 1830.

Thrilling Incidents of the American Revolutionary War. Royal 8vo. cloth, 300 engravings, $3 50.

Thucydides. Greece. 2 vols. square 18mo. paper, (Tauchnitz edition,) $1 00. Leipsic.

——— De bello peloponnesiaco Libri VIII. cum indice Historico, curavit ant. Richter. 8vo. paper, $2 25. Leipsic, 1828.

——— Greek, with English Notes, by J. J. Owen. 12mo. bds. $2 00. New York, 1848.

——— Translated by Dale. 12mo. cloth, 88 cents. London, 1848.

——— Translated by Bloomfield. 3 vols. 8vo. cloth, $13 50. London.

——— Maps and Plans, Illustrative of. 8vo. cloth, $3 50. London.

Thucydides. History of the Peloponnesian War. Translated by William Smith. 8vo. cloth, $2 00. New York, 1849.

——— Traduit par Amb. Firmin Didot avec le texte en regard et notes. 4 vols. 8vo. paper, $5 00. Paris, 1833.

——— With English Notes, by Bloomfield. 2 vols. 8vo. cloth, $10 50. London.

Thurman, (J.) Observations and Essays on Statistics of Insanity. 8vo. cloth, $4 25. London.

Thynne, (Rev. W.) The History of Algebraic Equations; a Chapter of Elementary Algebra. 8vo. cloth, $1 75. Cambridge, 1849.

Ticknor, (G.) History of Spanish Literature. 3 vols. 8vo. cloth, $6 00; sheep, $6 75; half calf, $7 50. New York, 1849.

——— (C.) Popular Treatise on Medical Philosophy, &c. 12mo. cloth, 75 cents. New York, 1838.

Tieck. Der Blaubert ein Marchen, with Translation, by Apel. 12mo. cloth, $1 63. London.

——— (L.) Tales from the Phantasus. 12mo. paper, $1 50. London.

Tiedemann, (F.) Anatomy of the Fœtal Brain, by Bennett. 8vo. cloth, $3 50. Lond.

——— Comparative Physiology, by Gully and Lane. 8vo. cloth, $3 50. London.

Tiffany, (Osmond.) The Canton Chinese; or, the American's Sojourn in the Celestial Empire. 12mo. cloth, 87 cents. Boston, 1849.

Tilke, (S.) Nature and Treatment of Disease. 8vo. cloth, $3 00. London.

Till, (W.) Description of the Coronation Medals from Edward VI. to Victoria. 12mo. cloth, $1 50. London.

——— Essay on the Roman Denarius, &c. 12mo. cloth, $2 25. London.

Tillotson, (Archbishop.) Works, with Life, by Birch. 10 vols. 8vo. cloth, $31 50. London.

Tilly, (B.) Tailor's Tutor and Cutting-Room Companion. Post 8vo. cloth, $1 50. London.

Timbs, (John.) Year-Book of Facts in Science and Art; exhibiting the most important Discoveries and Improvements of the past Year. Illustrated with engravings. 12mo. cloth, $1 50. (Published annually.) London, 1845–50.

Timkowski, (G.) Travels through Mongolia to China. 2 vols. 8vo. cloth, $9 00. London.

Timperley's Account of the Harbor and Docks at Kingston-upon-Hull. (Paper in Trans. of I. C. Engineers, vol. 1, 4to.) Lond.

——— (C. H.) Encyclopædia of Literary and Typographical Anecdote, &c. Royal 8vo. cloth, $4 50. London, 1842.

——— Songs of the Press and other Poems, relative to the Art of Printers and Printing, with Notes, Biographical and Literary. 18mo. cloth, $1 25. London, 1845.

Timpson, (Rev. Thos.) British Female Biography; being select Memoirs of Pious Ladies in various Ranks of Public and Private Life. 12mo. cloth, 75 cents. London, 1846.

——— British Ecclesiastical History. 12mo. cloth, $2 75. London.

Timpson, (Rev. Thos.) Church History through all Ages. 12mo. cloth, $2 25.

——— A Key to the Bible; containing a Summary of Biblical Knowledge, &c. 8vo. cloth, maps and 124 engravings, $3 00. Lond. 1845.

——— Memoirs of Mrs. Elizabeth Fry. 12mo. cloth, portrait, 75 cents. London, 1847.

Tingry, (P. F.) House Painter and Colorman's Guide. 12mo. cloth, $2 25. Lond.

——— The Varnisher's Guide; a Practical Treatise on the Art of Making and Applying Varnishes. Third edition, 12mo. cloth, $1 50. London, 1849.

Tinmouth, (N.) Inquiry relative to various important points of Seamanship, considered as a Branch of Practical Science. 8vo. cloth, plates, $2 25. London, 1845.

Titford, (W. T.) Hortus Americanus. 4to. cloth, $10 50. London.

Titian, (Life of.) By Northcote, with Anecdotes. 2 vols. 8vo. cloth, portrait, $2 75. London, 1830.

Titsingh, (M.) Illustrations of Japan. Royal 4to. plates, $17 50. London.

Tizard, (W. L.) Theory and Practice of Brewing. 8vo. cloth, $7 50. Lond.

Tocqueville, (Alexis de.) Democracy in America. Translated by Henry Reeve, Esq. with Preface, by J. C. Spencer. 8vo. cloth, $2 00. New York, 1848.

Tod, (J.) Travels in Western India. Royal 4to. cloth, $22 00. London.

——— (G.) Plans for Hot Houses, Greenhouses, &c. Folio, 12 60. London.

Todd, (Rev.) Student's Manual. 12mo. cloth, 50 cents. Philadelphia.

——— Index Rerum; or, Common Place Book for the Student, with a Specimen Page. 4to. half roan, $2 00. Philadelphia.

——— and **Bowman.** The Physiological Anatomy and Physiology of Man. Cuts, 2 vols. 8vo. $9 00. London, 1849.

——— (H. J.) Lives of Gower and Chaucer. 8vo. cloth, $2 50. London.

Tolfrey, (F.) Sportsman in Canada. 2 vols. post 8vo. cloth, $6 50. London.

Toland, (John.) History of the Druids, by Huddleston. 8vo. cloth, $3 50. Lond.

Tombleson's Views on the Thames. 4to. cloth, plates, $6 00. London.

——— Views on the Rhine. 2 vols. royal 8vo. cloth, plates, $9 00. London.

Tomes, (J.) Lectures on Dental Physiology and Surgery. 8vo. cloth, $3 75. Lond.

Tomkins, (T.) Beauties of Penmanship. 4to. cloth, $9 50. London.

Tomline, (Bishop.) Elements of Christian Theology; containing Proofs of the Authenticity and Inspiration of the Holy Scriptures. 8vo. cloth, $2 50. London, 1837.

Tomlins, (F. G.) Brief View of the English Drama. 12mo. cloth, $1 25. Lond.

——— A History of England; combining the various Histories of Rapin, Henry, Hume, Smollett, and Belsham. Corrected by reference to Turner, Lingard, Mackintosh, Hallam, Brodie, Godwin, and other sources. 3 vols. bound in 6 vols. 8vo. half calf, gilt backs, marbled leaves, portraits, $14 00. Lond. 1842.

Tomlinson, (C.) Pneumatics for the use of Beginners. 12mo. cloth, 25 cents. (Weale's Rudimentary Series.) London, 1843.

——— (L.) Recreations in Astronomy. Third edition, 12mo. cloth, $1 25. London.

——— (C.) Rudimentary Mechanics for the use of Beginners. Illustrations. 12mo. 25 cents. London, 1849.

——— Introduction to the Study of Natural Philosophy for the use of Beginners. 12mo. cloth, 25 cents. London, 1849.

——— Amusements in Chess. 12mo. cloth, $1 50. London.

Tooke, (J. H.) Diversions of Purley. New edition, revised and corrected, with additional Notes, by Richard Taylor. 8vo. cloth, $3 75. London, 1840.

——— (T.) History of Prices in 1838, '39, with Remarks on the Corn Laws, and on some of the Alterations proposed in the Banking System. 8vo. cloth, $3 50. London, 1840.

——— Considerations on the State of the Currency. 8vo. cloth, $2 00. London.

——— History of Prices from 1792 to 1839. 3 vols. 8vo. cloth, $14 50. London.

——— Thoughts on High and Low Prices. 8vo. cloth, $4 50. London.

Topffer. Nouvelles Genevoises. 12mo. paper, $1 00.

Toplady, (A. M.) Works, with Memoir. 6 vols. 8vo. cloth, $16 25. London.

——— Works, with Memoir. 8vo. cloth, $4 50. London.

Toplis, (John.) Observations on the Weather. 12mo. cloth, $1 00. Lond. 1849.

——— A Treatise on Analytical Mechanics; being the First Book of Mecanique Celeste of M. Le Comte Laplace Translated, with Notes. 8vo. cloth, $3 25. London.

Torrens, (R.) Essay on Wages and Combination. 8vo. cloth, $1 50. Lond.

——— Colonization in South Australia. 8vo. $3 50. Lond.

——— Commercial and Colonial Policy. 8vo. cloth, $3 25. Lond.

——— Essay on the Production of Wealth. 8vo. cloth, $3 50. London.

Torrey and Gray's Flora of North America; containing descriptions of all the known Indigenous and Naturalized Plants growing north of Mexico, according to the Natural System. Vol. 1, 8vo. cloth, $6 00.

——— The Same. Vol. 2, parts 1 and 2, $1 50 each; part 3, $1 00.

Torrington, (Visct.) Farm Buildings, &c. 8vo. paper, $1 50. Lond.

Totten, (Col. J. G.) Essay on Hydraulic and Common Mortars, and Lime Burning. 8vo. cloth, $1 50. New York.

——— (Lieut.) The Naval Text-Book; containing a Series of Letters on Rigging, Equipping, and Managing Vessels; a Set of Tables for Stationing in Watches, at Quarters, and for all Evolutions, the Officers and Crews of all Vessels of War, &c., &c. 8vo. sheep, $3 00. Boston, 1841.

Tottie, (C.) Designs for Sepulchral Monuments. Folio, cloth, $10 75. Lond.

Towne's Farmer's and Grazier's Guide. Post 8vo. $3 00. London.

Tower, (J.) Domestic Gardener's Manual. 8vo. cloth, $4 00. London.

——— (J. B.) History, Description, and Illustrations of the Croton Aqueduct. Royal 4to. cloth, with 25 engravings, $3 50. New York.

Townley, (Jas.) Illustrations of Biblical Literature. 3 vols. 8vo. cloth, $12 50. Lond.

——— American edition. 2 vols. 8vo. cloth, $4 00. New York.

——— Literary History of the Bible. 12mo. cloth, $1 75. London.

——— Reasons of the Laws of Moses. 8vo. cloth, $3 25. London.

——— On Diseases of the Potato. 8vo. cloth, 75 cents. London.

Townsend, (G.) Life and Defence of Bishop Bonner. 8vo. cloth, $3 25. Lond.

——— Arrangement of the Old and New Testament. 2 vols. 8vo. bds. $5 00. Boston.

——— (G. F.) Ecclesiastical and Civil History considered. 2 vols. 8vo. cloth, $9 50. Lond.

——— (Jos.) Journey through Spain. 2 vols. 4to. $12 50. London.

——— Memoirs of. 8vo. cloth, $2 75. Lond.

——— Character of Moses as an Historian. 2 vols. 4to. cloth, $30 00. Lond.

——— Etymological Researches. 4to. cloth, $6 50. London.

——— Geological and Mineralogical Researches. 4to. cloth, $6 50. London.

——— (J. K.) Excursions in the Rocky Mountains. 2 vols. 8vo. cloth, $5 50. Lond.

Townshend, (W. C.) Lives of Twelve Eminent Judges. 2 vols. 8vo. cloth, $5 50. London.

——— History of the House of Commons. 2 vols. 8vo. cloth, $8 50. London.

——— Facts in Mesmerism, with a Dispassionate Inquiry into it. 12mo. cloth, 75 cents. New York.

Tracts for the Christian Seasons. 4 parts, i. e. 1, Advent; 2, Christmas; 3, Epiphany; 4, Lent. 12mo. paper, $1 00. Oxford.

——— For the People, designed to Vindicate Religious and Christian Liberty. 12mo. cloth, $1 75. London, 1840.

——— For the Times. 3 vols. 8vo. cloth, $5 00. New York.

Tracy, (J.) History of the Great Awakening in the Time of Whitfield. 8vo. cloth, $2 00. New York.

Traill, (T. S.) Physical Geography. 12mo. cloth, $1 25. Edinburgh.

Traite des Arbres Fruitiers: contenant leur figure, leur description, leur culture, &c., par M. Duhamel du Monceau. 2 vols. 4to. calf, gilt, plates, $12 00. Paris, 1768.

Transactions of the American Ethnological Society. 2 vols. 8vo. paper, $5 00. New York, 1845–48.

Trap, (A,) to Catch a Sunbeam. 12mo. cloth, 25 cents. Boston, 1849.

Travels of Ali Bey in Morocco, &c. 2 vols. 4to. cloth, $38 00. London.

——— Of Marco Polo in the Thirteenth Century. 4to. cloth, $16 00. London.

Traveller's Guide from Pittsburg to the Gulf of Mexico. $1 00. Cincinnati.

Travers, (B.) Inflammation and the Healing Process. 8vo. cloth, $3 25. Lond.

——— Inquiry on Injuries of the Intestines. 8vo. cloth, $4 50. London.

——— Inquiry on Constitutional Irritation. 2 vols. 8vo. cloth, $8 50. London.

——— Synopsis of Diseases of the Eye. 8vo. cloth, $7 50. London.

Treatise on Breeding, Rearing, and Fattening Poultry. 8vo. $1 50. London.

——— On Dyeing and Calico Printing. Royal 8vo. cloth, $3 50. New York.

——— On Perspective. (Thenot's System.) 8vo. cloth, $3 25. London.

——— On the Steam Engine, by the Artizan Club. 4to. cloth, plates, $8 00. London

Treasury of Knowledge and Library of Reference. 3 vols. 12mo. sheep, $4 00. New York, 1848.

Tredgold, (Thos.) An Account of some Experiments on the Expansion of Water by Heat. (Trans. I. C. E. vol. 1, 4to.) Lond.

——— On the Steam Engine. New edition, publishing in monthly 4to. parts, with Additions, &c. Edited by J. Hann, in 7 divisions; 1. Locomotives, to be completed in 12 parts. 2. Marine Engines. 3. Stationary Engines. 4. Engines for Raising Water. 5. Cornish Pumping Engine. 6. Engines for Mill Work. 7. High-Pressure and Non-Condensing Engines. 75 cents per part.

——— Practical Essay on the Strength of Cast Iron and other Metals. Fourth edition, improved and enlarged. 2 vols. 8vo. $7 50. London.

——— Practical Examples of Modern Tools and Machines. Plates in folio, text in 8vo. $5 00. London.

——— An Elementary Illustration of the Principles of Tension and of the Resistance of Bodies to being torn Asunder in the direction of their Length. (Trans. I. C. E. vol. 1, 4to.) London.

——— Elementary Principles of Carpentry, with Practical Rules and Examples; to which is added, an Essay on the Nature and Properties of Timber; also numerous Tables, &c. Third edition, with an Appendix, by P. Barlow. Plates, 4to. half mor. $12 50. Lond. 1840.

——— Tracts on Hydraulics. 8vo. cloth, $3 50. London.

Tree Rose, (The,) its Formation and Culture. 12mo. cloth, $1 25. London.

Trego, (C. B.) Pennsylvania; its Geography, History, &c., with an Account of its Climate, Soil, Agriculture, Resources, &c. 12mo. cloth, map, $1 00. Philadelphia.

Trench, (Sir F.) Papers relating to the Thames Quay. 4to. cloth, $16 00. Lond.

Trendall, (E. W.) Examples for Interior Finishings in Grecian and Italian Architecture. Folio, cloth, $5 50. London.

——— Designs for Roofs of Iron, Stone, and Wood. 4to. cloth, $2 50. London.

Tress, (R.) Modern Churches; Designs, Estimates, Working Drawings, and Specifications, of Modern Churches already Erected. Imp. 4to. cloth, $5 00. London, 1841.

Tressan, (Le Comte de.) Œuvres completes precedees d'une notice sur sa vie et ses ouvrages par M. Campenon, edition revue et corrigee, et accompagnee de notes, 16 gravures. 10 vol. in 8, veau, $15 00. Paris, 1822–23.

Triglott Evangelists, in Greek, Latin, and English Interlinear. 8vo. cloth, $8 50. London.

——— The Same, with Grammar. 8vo. cloth, $9 50. London.

——— or separately, St. Matthew, $2 75; St. Mark, $1 50; St. Luke, $2 75; St. John, $1 75.

Trimen, (A.) Church and Chapel Architecture, from the earliest period, &c., to which are added 1000 authenticated Mouldings, selected from the best examples. Post 8vo. cloth, plates, $3 25. London, 1849.

Trimmer, (J.) Practical Geology and Mineralogy, with Instructions for the Qualitative Analysis of Minerals. 8vo. cloth, $3 50. London.

Triper, (Louis.) Les Constitutions Francaises Depuis 1789–1848. 12mo. paper, $1 00. Paris, 1848.

Trollope, (Rev. W.) Belgium since the Revolution of 1830, comprising a Topographical and Antiquarian Description of the Country, &c. 12mo. cloth, map, $1 50. Lond. 1842.

——— History of Christ's Hospital. 4to. cloth. $12 50. London.

——— Analecta Theologica. 2 vols. 8vo. cloth, $3 25. London, 1842.

——— (Mrs.) A Visit to Italy. 2 vols. 8vo. cloth, $1 75. London, 1842.

——— Paris and the Parisians in 1835. 8vo. cloth, $1 50.

——— (T. Augustus.) A Summer in Brittany. Edited by Frances Trollope. Colored plates, 2 vols. 8vo. cloth, $1 75. Lond. 1840.

Trosseau, (A.) and **Beloc,** (H.) On Diseases of the Voice. 8vo. sheep, $2 50. Philadelphia.

Trotter, (A.) Method of Farm Book-Keeping. Royal 8vo. half bound, $2 25. Lond.

——— Manual of Logarithms. 12mo. cloth, $1 25. London.

——— (J.) A Key to Ingram's Concise System of Mathematics, containing Solutions of all the Questions prescribed in that Work. 12mo. bds. $2 00. London.

True and Faithful Relation of a Worthye Discourse between ye late Colonell Hampden and Colonell Oliver Cromwell. Foolscap 4to. in appropriate Binding. Cloth, $1 50. London, 1847.

Truefitt, (G.) Architectural Sketches on the Continent. 8vo. cloth, $3 00. London.

Trumbull, (J.) Autobiography, Letters, and Reminiscences, from 1776 to 1841. 8vo. cloth, $2 00. New York, 1841.

——— (B.) History of Connecticut. 2 vols. 8vo. cloth, $6 00. New Haven.

Tschudi, (Dr. J. J. Von.) Travels in Peru. 1 vol. 12mo. cloth, $1 00. New York.

"Braving the dangers of a land where throat-cutting is a popular pastime, and earthquakes and fevers more or less yellow, and vermin more or less venomous are amongst the indigenous comforts of the soil, a German, of high reputation as a naturalist and man of letters, has devoted four years of a life valuable to science to a residence and travels in the most interesting districts of South America, the ancient empire of the Incas, the scene of the conquests and cruelties of Francisco Pizarro."

Tuck, (J.) Brewer's Guide. 8vo. cloth, $1 50. London.

Tucker, (Col. J. M.) The Life and Naval Memoirs of Lord Nelson, compiled from original Documents. 8vo. cloth, wood-cuts, portrait, &c. $1 25. London.

——— (A.) Light of Nature pursued with Life, by Mildmay. 2 vols. 8vo. cloth, $4 50. London, 1848.

——— American edition. 4 vols. 8vo. cloth, $6 00. Boston.

——— (G.) Progress of the United States in Population and Wealth in Fifty Years, as exhibited by the Decennial Census. 8vo. cloth, $1 25. New York.

——— Elements of the Principles and Practice of Midwifery, with numerous illustrations. 12mo. cloth, $1 50. Philadelphia.

Tuckerman, (E.) Enumeration of North American Lichens. 12mo. cloth, 38 cents. Cambridge.

——— Synopsis of North American Lichens. 8vo. cloth, 75 cents. Cambridge.

——— (Henry.) Thoughts on the Poets. 12mo. cloth, 75 cents. New York.

——— Artist's Life. 12mo. cloth, 75 cents. New York.

——— Italian Sketch-Book. 12mo. cloth, $1 00. New York.

——— Characteristics of Literature. 12mo. cloth, 75 cents. Philadelphia.

Tudor, (H.) Narrative of a Tour in North America. 2 vols. 12mo. cloth, $2 00. London, 1834.

——— (W.) Life of James Otis. 8vo. cloth, $2 50. Boston, 1823.

Tulk, (A.) and **Henfrey's** Anatomical Manipulation; or, the Methods of Pursuing Practical Investigations in Comparative Anatomy and Physiology. 18mo. cloth, $2 25. London, 1844

Tuomey, (M.) Report on the Geology of South Carolina. 4to. cloth, map, plate, and numerous wood-cuts, $2 50. Columbia, S. C. 1848.

Tupper, (M. F.) The Crock of Gold, a Rural Novel. 12mo. cloth, 50 cents. New York.

——— The Twins, a Domestic Novel; and Heart, a Social Novel. 1 vol. 12mo. cloth, 50 cents. New York.

——— Proverbial Philosophy. 12mo. paper, 50 cents; cloth, 75 cents; cloth gilt, 87 cents; mor. $2 00.

——— (J. M.) Proverbial Philosophy. Small 4to. plates, cloth, $3 50; mor. gilt, gilt leaves, $4 00. Philadelphia, 1850.

——— Proverbial Philosophy. Small 4to. cloth gilt, gilt edges, $2 50; mor. $3 50. New York, 1849.

——— Miniature edition. 18mo. cloth, 50 cents; cloth gilt, 75 cents; mor. $1 50. New York.

——— Poetical Works, including Proverbial Philosophy, Hactenus, and a Thousand Lines, &c. 1 vol. 12mo. cloth, $1 25. New York.

Turcan's Practical Baker and Confectioner. 12mo. cloth, $1 50. London.

Turnbull, (Capt.) Description of the Coffer Dam used in the Construction of the Piers of the Alexandria Aqueduct. (Papers, R. E. vol. 3, 4to.) London.

Turnbull, (D.) Cuba, with Notices of Porto Rico and the Slave Trade. 8vo. cloth, map, $2 00. London, 1840.

——— (Rev. Robert.) The Genius of Italy; being Sketches of Italian Life, Literature, and Religion. 1 vol. 12mo. new edition, $1 00; 6 illustrations, extra, gilt edges, $2 00.

"Mr. Turnbull gives us the orange groves, and the fountains, and the gondolas, and the frescoes, and the ruins, with touches of personal adventure and sketches of biography, and glimpses of the life, literature, and religion of modern Italy, seen with the quick comprehensive glances of an American traveller, impulsive, inquisitive, and enthusiastic. His book is a pleasant record of a tourist's impressions, without the infliction of the tiresome minutiæ of his everyday experience."—LITERARY WORLD.

——— (A.) Use of Aconitine, &c. 8vo. cloth, $1 00.

——— (P.) Travels in Austria. 2 vols. 8vo. cloth, $7 25. London.

——— (R.) Dredge's Suspension Bridge explained upon the Principles of the Lever, &c. Royal 8vo. cloth, plate and wood-cuts, $1 50. London.

——— (William.) A Treatise on the Strength, Flexure, and Stiffness of Cast Iron Beams and Columns, showing their fitness to Resist Transverse Strains, Torsion, Compression, Tension, and Impulsion, with Tables of Constants. 8vo. cloth, $3 00. London, 1832.

——— A Practical Treatise on the Strength and Stiffness of Timber, intended as a Guide for Engineers, Architects, &c. 8vo. cloth, $3 50. London.

——— An Essay on the Construction of the Five Architectural Systems of Cast Iron Beams. 8vo. paper, 75 cents. London.

——— Essay on the Air-Pump and Atmospheric Railway. 12mo. cloth, $1 25. Lond.

——— Sections of Cast Iron Beams. 8vo. paper, $1 25. London.

Turner, (D.) Account of a Tour in Normandy, for the purpose of Investigating the Architectural Antiquities. 2 vols. 8vo. cloth, plates, $8 00. London.

——— (Edward.) Elements of Chemistry; including the actual State and prevalent Doctrines of the Science. Edited by Baron Liebig and William Gregory. Eighth edition, thick 8vo. cloth, $9 00. London, 1847.

——— American edition. Edited by Rogers. 8vo. sheep, $3 50. Phila. 1846.

——— Chemistry, by Johnstone. 12mo. sheep, $1 25. Philadelphia.

——— Introduction to Chemical Combinations. 18mo. cloth, 75 cents. London.

——— (J. M. W.) Views on the Southern Coast of England. 2 vols. 4to. plates, half bound, $63 00. London.

——— Views on the Southeast Coast of England. 4to. half bound, plates, $16 00. London, 1849.

——— Views in Richmondshire. Folio, cloth, plates, $19 00. London.

——— The Rivers of France. Royal 8vo. cloth, plates, $7 25. London.

——— Views in England and Wales. 2 vols. 4to. plates, $126 00. London.

——— (Jas.) Treatise on the Horse's Foot. Royal 8vo. cloth, $2 25. London.

——— (John.) Tables of Longitude. Royal 8vo. cloth, $3 25. London.

Turner, (O.) History of the Holland Purchase of Western New York. 8vo. cloth, $2 50. Buffalo, N. Y.

——— (S.) History of England from the time of the Anglo-Saxons to the Death of Elizabeth. 12 vols. 8vo. cloth, $48 00. Lond. 1828-36.

——— History of the Anglo-Saxons from the earliest period to the Norman Conquest. 3 vols. 8vo. paper, $2 25. Paris, 1840.

——— American edition. 2 vols. 8vo. $4 50. Philadelphia

——— Sacred History of the World attempted to be Philosophically considered. 3 vols. 18mo. cloth, $1 50. New York.

——— (S. H.) Companion to the Book of Genesis. 8vo. cloth, $1 00. New York.

Turretini Institutio Theologiæ Elenticæ. 4 vols. 8vo. cloth, $10 00. New York, 1846.

Turton, (William.) Conchylia Dithyra Insularum Britannicarum. The Bivalve Shells of the British Isles systematically arranged. 20 colored plates, 4to. $15 00. Lond.

——— (John.) Angler's Manual; or, Fly-Fisher's Oracles. 12mo. cloth, $1 00. Lond.

——— Conchological Dictionary. 12mo. cloth, plates, $2 75; colored, $4 25. London.

——— Manual of British Shells, by Gray. Post 8vo. cloth, $4 50. London.

Tuson, (E. W.) Anatomy, &c. of Inguinal and Femoral Hernia. Folio, $12 50. Lond.

——— System of Myology, with Supplement. 2 vols. folio, cloth, colored plates, $50 00. London, 1828.

——— Treatment in Curvature of the Spine. 8vo. cloth, $3 25. London, 1841.

Tuthill, (Mrs. L. C.) History of Architecture from the earliest times, with numerous llustrations. 8vo. cloth, plates, $3 50. Philadelphia, 1848.

——— The Nursery Book for Young Mothers. 18mo. 50 cents. New York, 1849.

"This volume will be a welcome present to young mothers. It comprises familiar letters on all topics connected with the medical and educational departments of the Nursery, and is just such a book as every mother will find practically useful, and all the more so as it is written by a competent and experienced person of their own sex."

——— Success in Life—the Merchant. A Biography, with Anecdotes and Practical Application for new beginners. 12mo. cloth gilt, half bound, 63 cents. New York, 1849.

——— Success in Life—the Mechanic. A Biographical Example. 18mo. (To be followed by "The Artist," "The Lawyer," &c.)

"The aim of this Series is to develop the talent and energy of boys just merging into manhood, and to assist them in choosing their pursuits for life."

"Success! How the heart bounds at the exulting word. Success! Man's aim from the moment he places his tiny foot upon the floor till he lays his weary gray head in the grave. Success, the exciting motive to all endeavor and its crowning glory."—Extract from Preface.

Twamley, (L. A.) Romance of Nature. 8vo. mor. gilt, colored plates, $9 00. London, 1839.

——— Our Wild Flowers. Post 8vo. mor. gilt edges, beautifully colored plates, $6 00. London.

Twining, (H.) On the Philosophy of Painting; a Theoretical and Practical Treatise. Imp. 8vo. cloth, $6 50. London, 1849.

Twiss, (T.) The Oregon Question examined in respect to Facts and the Laws of Nations. 8vo. maps, cloth, $3 50. Lond. 1846.

——— History and Discovery of the Oregon Territory, &c. 8vo. cloth, 75 cents. N. York.

——— (H.) Life of the Lord Chancellor Eldon. 2 vols. 8vo. cloth, $3 50. Phila.

——— View of the Progress of Political Economy in Europe. 8vo. cloth, $3 25. Lond.

Tyas, (Rob.) Favorite Field Flowers; or, Wild Flowers of England popularly described. 12 colored groups of flowers. 12mo. cloth gilt, $2 25. London, 1848.

Tyerman and Bennet's Voyage round the World. Post 8vo. cloth, $2 25. London.

——— American edition, 3 vols. $1 87. Boston.

Tyler, (John.) Life and Speeches. 8vo. paper, 50 cents. New York.

——— (Sam.) Baconian Philosophy. 12mo. cloth, $1 00. Baltimore.

——— Robert Burns as Poet and as Man. 12mo. cloth, 75 cents. New York, 1848.

Tyndale, (W.) The New Testament. The original edition of 1526, to which is added the essential Variations of Coverdale's, Cranmer's, the Genevan, &c., as Marginal Readings, by J. P. Dabney. 12mo. cloth, $1 75. Andover, 1837.

Tyrrell, (F.) On the Diseases of the Eye. 2 vols. 8vo. $10 75. London.

Tytler, (A. F.) Essay on the Principles of Translation. 8vo. cloth, $3 50. London.

——— Universal History. 2 vols. 8vo. cloth, $3 25. Boston

——— Elements of General History, by Nares. 12mo. cloth, $4 25. London.

——— History of Scotland. Third edition, 7 vols 8vo. cloth, $22 00. Edin. 1845.

——— Historical View of the Progress of Discovery on the more Northern Coasts of America. 18mo. cloth, 50 cents. New York.

Ude, (Louis.) French Cook. Post 8vo. cloth, $3 50. London.

Uhland, (L.) Poems and Memoirs. Translated by A. Platt. 12mo. cloth, $2 50. London, 1847.

Ullman, (C.) Worship of Genius and Character of Christianity. 12mo. cloth, $1 00. London.

Ulloa and Juan's Reports on South America, by Barry. Royal 4to. cloth, $19 00. London.

Ulrici. Shakespeare's Dramatic Art and his Relation to Calderon and Goethe. 8vo. cloth, $2 50. London, 1847.

Un Heros histoire contemporaine. 12mo. broche, $1 00. Paris, 1840.

United States Gazetteer. By Haskell and Smith. 8vo. sheep, $3 00. New York, 1846.

Universal History, Ancient and Modern, from the earliest accounts of Mankind to the Peace of 1815; forming the third division of the Encyclopædia Metropolitana. Edited by Revs. E. Smedley, Hugh James Rose, Henry John Rose. Maps and charts. 5 vols. 4to. cloth, $30 00. London, 1848.

Universal Songster; or, Museum of Mirth; forming the most complete, extensive, and valuable collection of Modern Songs in the English Language. Illustrated by G. and R. Cruikshank. 3 vols. 8vo. cloth, $4 50. Lond.

Universal Picture Gallery; comprising engravings from the Works of the best Masters, Ancient and Modern. 4to. cloth, plates, $2 50. London.

Upham's Life of Faith; embracing some of the Scriptural Principles or Doctrines of Faith, &c. 12mo. cloth, $1 00. New York.

——— Life of Madame C. Adorna; including some leading Facts and Traits in her Religious Experience. 12mo. cloth, 50 cents. New York.

——— Principles of the Interior; or, Hidden Life. 12mo. cloth, $1 00. New York.

——— Life, Religious Opinions, and Experience of Madame Guyon. 2 vols. 12mo. cloth, $2 00.

——— Treatise on the Will. 12mo. sheep, $1 25. New York.

——— Imperfect and Disordered Mental Action. 18mo. cloth, 50 cents. New York.

——— Elements of Mental Philosophy; embracing the Two Departments of the Intellect and the Sensibilities. 2 vols. 12mo. sheep, $2 50. New York.

——— (E.) History of Buddhism. Imp. 4to. cloth, $19 00. London, 1829.

——— Sacred and Historical Books of Ceylon. 3 vols. 8vo. cloth, $12 50. London.

Ure, (A.) Cotton Manufacture of Great Britain. 2 vols. post 8vo. $6 50. Lond. 1836.

——— Philosophy of Manufactures. Post 8vo. cloth, $3 25. London.

——— Dictionary of Arts, Manufactures, and Mines, to which is appended a Supplement of recent improvements to the present time. 8vo. sheep, with 1500 engravings, $5 00. New York, 1848.

——— A new System of Geology, in which the great Revolutions of the Earth and Animated Nature are Reconciled at once to Modern Science and Sacred History. 8vo. cloth, $2 00. London.

Urquhart, (D.) Turkey and its Resources. 8vo. cloth, $3 00. London.

Useful Arts, (Encyclopædia of.) Illustrated with engravings. 4to. cloth, $6 00. London.

——— Employed in the Construction of Dwelling Houses. 12mo. cloth, wood-cuts, 75 cents. London, 1845.

——— Employed in the Production of Clothing. 12mo. cloth, wood-cuts, 75 cents. Lond. 1845.

——— Employed in the Production of Food. 12mo. cloth, wood-cuts, 75 cents. Lond. 1844.

Usher, (Archbishop.) A Body of Divinity; or, the Sum and Substance of Christian Religion. New edition, by Dr. Robinson. 8vo. cloth, $3 50. London, 1841.

——— Life of, by C. R. Elrington. 8vo. cloth, $3 75. London.

Vail, (A.) Magnetic Telegraph. 8vo. half bound, $1 00. Philadelphia.

——— Notice sur les Indiens de l'Amerique du Nord. 8vo. map and plates, $1 50. Paris, 1840.

Valcour, (P. L. De.) Memoires sur l'Agriculture et les Instruments aratoires et d'economy rurale. 8vo. avec atlas, $3 00. Paris, 1841.

Valentine, (John.) Elements of Practical Harmony. 8vo. cloth, $1 00. London.

——— (J. S.) The Assistant Engineer; embodying Ten Sets of Experiments on the Strength of Materials, by G. Rennie, with Working Drawings and Specifications, &c. 120 illustrations, 8vo. cloth, $6 50. London, 1848.

Valentine Vox. 8vo. cloth, plates, 75 cents. Philadelphia.

Vallery, (M.) Correspondence inedite de Mabillon et de Montfaucon avec l'Italie, suivie des lettres inedites du P. Quesnel. 3 vols. 8vo. paper, $4 50. Paris, 1847.

Valmore, (Mme. de.) Poesies, avec notice par S. Beuve. 12mo. paper, $1 00.

Valpy's Greek Grammar. Edited by Anthon. 12mo. bds. 50 cents. New York.

Van Buren, (M.) Life of, by Crockett. 12mo. cloth, 63 cents. New York.

Vandenhoff, (G.) Elocution. 12mo. roan, cloth sides, $1 13. New York.

Vanderstracten's Improved Agriculture. 8vo. cloth, $3 25. London.

Vane, (B.) Treatise on the Nail Trade. Oblong 4to. cloth, $6 50. London.

Vanherman. Every Man his own House Painter and Colorman. 8vo. cloth, $1 50. London.

Van Schaack, (P.) Life of, by his Son, H. C. Van Schaack. 8vo. cloth, $2 50. New York.

Van Worrell's Dutch and Flemish Painters of the Old School. Square 18mo. $3 25. London.

Varley, (O.) Rudimentary Mineralogy. 2 parts. 12mo. cloth, 50 cents. Lond. 1849.

——— (I.) Precepts of Landscape Drawing. 4to. cloth, $1 50. London.

——— Principles of Landscape Design. Folio, half bound, $12 00. London.

——— Studies for Drawing Trees. 4to. cloth, $1 50. London.

——— Treatise on Drawing in Perspective. 4to. cloth, $2 75. London.

——— (Mrs.) Engineer's Manual of Mineralogy and Geology. 12mo. cloth, $1 00. Lond.

Vasari, (G.) Vies des Peintres Sculpteurs et Architectes, traduit par L. Leclanche. 10 vols. 8vo. and atlas of plates, $15 00. Paris, 1841.

Vattel, (M. de.) Law of Nations, by Chitty. Royal 8vo. bds. $6 50. London.

Vaughan, (R.) The Age and Christianity. 12mo. cloth, $1 75. London, 1849.

——— Age of Great Cities; or, Modern Civilization. Post 8vo. $2 25. London.

——— Protectorate of Oliver Cromwell. 2 vols. 8vo. cloth, $9 50.

——— Essays on History, Philosophy, and Theology. 2 vols. 12mo. cloth, $2 50. London, 1849.

Vaughan, (Dr.) History of England from 1603 to 1688. 2 vols. 8vo. cloth, $3 75. London, 1840.

——— (W.) Essay on Headaches. 8vo. cloth, $3 25. London.

——— Tracts on Docks and Commerce. 8vo. cloth, $1 75. London.

Vauthier et Lacour. Monuments de sculpture anciens et modernes, recueillis, dessines et graves par Vauthier et Lacour. Nouvelle edition, augmentee de 16 planches, representant entre autres le fronton du Pantheon, celui de la Madeleine, les huit statues qui decorent la place de la Concorde, et des trophees sur la valeur militaire, les arts, les sciences, la marine, etc. 1 vol. in folio de 84 planches avec texte, $14 00. Paris.

Vaux, (Thos.) System of Tilling and Fertilizing Land. 8vo. cloth, $2 00. Lond.

Velpeau, (A.) Midwifery, by Meigs. 8vo. sheep, $3 50. Philadelphia.

——— Operative Surgery, with Notes, by Valentine Mott. 3 vols. 8vo. sheep, with atlas in 4to. $20 00. New York, 1847.

Venables, (R.) Aphorisms on Chemistry and Toxicology. 12mo. cloth, $2 25. Lond.

——— Clinical Report on Dropsies. 8vo. cloth, $2 50. London.

——— Treatise on Diabetes. 8vo. cloth, $3 25. London.

——— (R. L.) Domestic Manners of the Russians. Post 8vo. cloth, $2 75. London.

——— Experienced Angler. 12mo. cloth, $2 25. London, 1828.

Venturoli, (G.) Practical Mechanics, by Cresswell. 8vo. cloth, $2 50.

——— Theory of Mechanics, by Cresswell. 8vo. cloth, $2 25. London.

Vericour's Modern French Literature. 12mo. cloth, $1 25. Boston.

Vermont, (History of.) By Rev. H. Beckley. 12mo. cloth, $1 00. Burlington, Vt.

——— Drawing-Book of Landscapes, by Bishop Hopkins. 6 numbers, $2 50. Burlington, Vt.

——— Geological Report on, in 1845, '46. 2 parts, 12mo. paper, 75 cents. Burlington, Vt.

——— History of, by Thompson. 8vo. cloth, $3 50. Burlington, Vt.

Vernon, (E. J.) Guide to the Anglo-Saxon Tongue. 12mo. cloth, $1 63. London.

Verplanck, (G. C.) Addresses on American History, &c. 12mo. cloth, 63 cents. New York.

——— Influence of Moral Causes. 12mo. 19 cents. New York.

——— Right Moral Influence. 12mo. cloth, 25 cents. New York.

Vertot, (Abbe de.) Histoire des Chevalier de Malte. 12mo. paper, 50 cents. Tours, 1847.

Vestiges of the Natural History of the Creation, with Sequel. 12mo. cloth, $1 00. New York.

——— Another edition. 18mo. cloth, 38 cents. New York, 1849.

Vethake, (H.) Political Economy. 8vo. cloth, $2 00. Philadelphia.

Vetus Testamentum Græcum juxta Septuaginta Interpretes, cum Latina Translatione, ed. J. N. Jager. 2 vols. royal 8vo. paper, $7 00. Paris, 1839.

Veuillot. Les pelerinages de Suisse, gravures. 1 vol. in 8, maroquin, $1 75. Tours, 1845.

Vicars, (John.) England's Worthies under whom all the Civil and Bloody Warres since Anno 1642 to Anno 1647 are related. 12mo. half mor. portrait, $1 50. (Reprint of 1647.) London, 1845.

Vicat's Treatise on Mortars and Cements. Translated by Smith, 8vo. cloth, $3 25. London, 1837.

Vico. La Science Nouvelle. 12mo. paper, $1 00. Paris, 1845.

Victor Hugo. Notre Dame de Paris. 2 vols. 12mo. paper, $2 00. Paris.

——— Hans d'Islande. 12mo. paper, $1 00. Paris.

——— Dernier Jour d'un condamme, et Bug-Jargal. 12mo. paper, $1 00. Paris.

——— Voix interieurs, et les Rayons et les ombres. 12mo. paper, $1 00. Paris.

——— Theatre, Nouvelle edition. 2 vols. 12mo. paper, $2 00. Paris.

——— Cromwell, drame. 12mo. paper, $1 00. Paris.

——— Litterature et Philosophie. 12mo. paper, $1 00. Paris.

——— Odes et Ballades. 12mo. paper, $1 00.

——— Orientales. 12mo. paper, $1 00. Paris.

——— Feuilles d'automne et chants du Crepuscule. 12mo. paper, $1 00. Paris.

——— Œuvres. 16 vols. 12mo. half mor. $24 00. Paris.

Vidocq. Memoirs of, as a Convict Spy and Agent of the French Police. 12mo. cloth, plates, $1 50. London.

Vieusseux, (A.) The History of Switzerland from the first Irruption of the Northern Tribes to the present time. 8vo. cloth, map, $1 25 London, 1846.

Views on the Nile, from Cairo to the Second Cataract, drawn on stone, by G. Moore, from Sketches taken in 1832 and 1833, by Owen Jones and the late Jules Goury, with Historical Notices of the Monuments, by Samuel Birch. Imp. folio, half mor. $16 00. Lond. 1843.

Vieyra's Portuguese Dictionary. 2 vols. 8vo. cloth, $10 75. London.

——— Portuguese Grammar. 8vo. bds. $2 25.

Vigny, (A. de.) Cinq-Mars. 12mo. paper, $1 00 Paris.

——— Stello. 12mo. paper, $1 00. Paris.

——— Nouvelles. 12mo. paper, $1 00. Paris.

——— Theatre. 12mo. paper, $1 00. Paris.

——— Poesies completes. 12mo. paper, $1 00. Paris.

——— Servitude et Grandeur Militaires. 12mo. broche, $1 00. Paris, 1845.

——— Cinq Mars; a Romance. Translated by Hazlitt, 88 cents. London.

Vigors, (N.) Inquiry into the Nature of Poetic License. 8vo. cloth, $3 50. London.

Villehardouin, (G. de.) Chronicles. Translated by Smith. 8vo. cloth, $3 25. London.

Villemain. Cours de Litterature Francaise. Tableau de la Litterature au XVIIIe siecle, 4 vols. Tableau de la Litterature du Moyen Age, 2 vols. Etude de Litterature ancienne et etrangere, 1 vol. Etudes d'Histoire Moderne, 1 vol. Discours et Melanges Litteraire, 1 vol. Tableau de l'Eloquence Chretienne au IXe siecle, 10 vols. 12mo. broche, $10 00. Paris, 1849.

——— Cours de Litterature Francaise. Tableau de la litterature au XVIII siecles. Litterature au moyen age. Etudes d'Histoire Moderne. Etudes de litterature. Discours et Melanges. 8 vol. in 8, demi maroquin, $20 00. Paris, 1846.

Vince, (S.) The Principles of Hydrostatics. 8vo. bds. $1 25. London.

——— System of Astronomy. 3 vols. 4to. bds. plates, $31 50. (Scarce.) London.

——— The Elements of Astronomy, designed for the use of Students in the University. 8vo. $1 25. London.

Vine, (Rd.) Treatise on Diseases of the Horse. 8vo. cloth, $3 75. London.

Vinet, (A.) Etudes sur la Litterature Francaise au dix-neuvieme siecle, tome premier, Mad. De Stael et Chateaubriand. 8vo. $2 00. Paris, 1849.

——— Vital Christianity. Translated by Rev. R. Turnbull. 12mo. cloth, $1 13. Boston.

Virgilii Opera omnia, ed. Forbiger. 3 vols. 8vo. paper. Leipsic, 1845–6.

——— Opera, in usum scholarum ad novissiman Heynii, editionem exacta. 8vo. bds. $3 00. London, 1819.

——— Opera Latina. Square 12mo. paper, (Tauchnitz edition,) 63 cents. Leipsic.

——— Edited by Drs. Schmitz and Zumpt. 12mo. cloth, $1 38. Edin. 1848.

——— Delphini. 8vo. sheep, $1 75. Phila.

Virgil. The Works of, literally translated into English Prose, by Davidson. 12mo. cloth, $1 00. London, 1847.

Virginia. Historical Collections of, by H. Howe. 8vo. cloth, $3 50. Charleston.

——— The Mineral Springs of Western Virginia and their Use and Application to various Diseases, by W. Burke. 12mo. cloth, map, 75 cents. New York, 1846.

——— History of, by Howison. 2 vols. 8vo. cloth, $4 00. Richmond.

——— History of Smith. 2 vols. 8vo. cloth, $6 00. Richmond.

Visconti on the Elgin Marbles. 8vo. cloth, $3 75. London.

Vishnu Purana; a System of Hindoo Mythology and Tradition. Translated from the Sanscrit, by H. H. Wilson. 4to. cloth, $12 50. London.

Vivian, (G.) Views from the Gardens of Rome and Albano. Folio, cloth, $31 50. London.

——— Scenery in Portugal and Spain. Folio, $25 00. London.

Vitet, (M. L.) Etudes sur les Beaux Arts et sur la Litterature. 2 vols. 12mo. broche, $2 00. Paris, 1846.

Vocalist, (The.) Short and Easy Glees, by Mason and Webb, $1 00. Boston.

Vodges, (W.) Mensuration, with Key. 2 vols. 12mo. sheep, $1 50. Philadelphia.

Vogel, (J.) Pathological Anatomy. 8vo. sheep, $3 00. Philadelphia.

——— (Dr. T.) Niger Flora; or, an Enumeration of the Plants of Western Tropical Africa, collected by the late Dr. Vogel in 1841. Edited by Sir W. J. Hooker. 8vo. cloth, 2 views, a map, and 50 plates, $5 75. Lond. 1849.

Vogt, (C. F.) Letters on Chess; containing an Account of some of the Principal Works on that celebrated Game. 12mo. cloth, $1 25. London, 1848.

Voices of the Church in Reply to Strauss; comprising Essays in Defence of Christianity, by Divines of various Communions, collected by Rev. J. R. Beard. 8vo. cloth, $3 50. London.

Volney. Œuvres completes precedes d'une notice sur sa vie et ses ecrits. 1 fort vol. grand in 8, orne d'un portrait de gravures et de plusieurs cartes, $3 50. Paris.

——— Œuvres completes, precedees d'une notice sur sa vie et ses ecrits par Adolphus Bossange. 8 vol. in 8, half veau, avec portrait, gravures et cartes, $12 00. Paris, 1825.

Voltaire. Theatre. 12mo. broche, $1 00; half mor. $1 50. Paris, 1845.

——— Contes, Satires, Epitres, &c. 12mo. broche, $1 00; half mor. $1 50. Paris, 1844.

——— Romans. 12mo. broche, $1 00; half mor. $1 50. Paris, 1845.

——— Siecle de Louis XIV. 12mo. broche, $1 00; half mor. $1 50. Paris, 1845.

——— Histoire de Charles XII. 12mo. $1 00; half mor. $1 50. Paris, 1845.

——— Œuvres completes. 66 vols. in 8vo. avec 160 gravures, $75 00. Paris, Renouard, 1819–23.

——— Dictionnaire Philosophique. 8 vols. 12mo. broche, $4 00. Paris.

——— La Henriade, poeme. 1 vol. in 8vo. paper, $1 50. Paris.

——— La Pucelle d'Orleans, poeme. 2 vols. 12mo. une figure a chaque chant, $1 25. Paris.

——— Romans et Contes. 2 vols. in 8, broche, $2 50. Paris.

——— Theatre complet. 7 forts vols. in 8, ornes de 45 gravures de Moreau, $5 00. Paris.

——— History of Charles XII. 12mo. cloth, $1 00. Hartford.

Von Behr's Hand-Book of Anatomy. 8vo. sheep, $2 25. Philadelphia.

Von Bonninghausen, (C.) Therapeutic Pocket Book. 8vo. half roan, $1 50. New York.

Von Kobel, (F.) Instructions for the Discrimination of Minerals by simple Chemical Experiments. 8vo. paper, 63 cents. Glasgow, 1841.

Von Raumer, (F.) America and the American People. 8vo. cloth, $2 00. New York, 1846.

Voyage ou il vous Plaira. Livre ecrit a la plume et au crayon, avec vignettes, notes, legendes, commentaires, episodes, incidents et poesies, par MM. Tony Johannot, Alfred de Musset et P. J. Stahl. 1 vol. grand in 8, $4 00. Paris.

Vulliamy. Ornamental Sculpture. Imp. folio, $18 00. London.

Vyse, (Col. Howard.) Operations carried on in the Pyramids of Gizeh in 1837, with an Account of a Voyage into Upper Egypt. 3 vols. 8vo. cloth, $12 00. London

——— (R.) Treatise on Fox-Hunting. Royal 8vo. cloth, $12 50. London.

Wace, (Master.) His Chronicle of the Norman Conquest. From the Roman de Rou. Translated, with Notes and Illustrations, by Edgar Taylor. 8vo. cloth, with numerous wood-cuts. London, 1840.

Wade, (John.) Unreformed Abuses in Church and State, with a Preliminary Treatise on the Continental Revolutions. 12mo. 75 cents. London, 1849.

——— (J.) British History Chronologically arranged, comprehending a Classified Analysis of Events and Occurrences in Church and State, from the First Invasion by the Romans to the Accession of Queen Victoria. Fifth edition, with Supplement. 8vo. cloth, $5 00. London, 1847.

——— (Thos.) Treatise on Dry Rot in Timber. 8vo. cloth, $1 50. London.

Waddington, (Major Chas.) Account of the Battle of Meanee, with a Plan. (Papers, R. E. Vol. 9, 4to.) London.

——— (Dean.) History of the Church from the Earliest Ages to the Reformation. Enlarged edition, 3 vols. 8vo. cloth, $6 00. Lond. 1841.

——— American Edition. 8vo. cloth, $1 75. New York.

——— History of the Church during the Reformation. 3 vols. 8vo. cloth, $6 00. London, 1841.

Wagner, (R.) Comparative Anatomy of Vertebrate Animals, by Tulk. 8vo. cloth, $2 75. London.

Wagstaff, (W. R.) History of the Society of Friends, compiled from its Standard Records and older authentic Sources. 8vo. cloth, $2 00. New York.

Wainwright, (J. M.) Women of the Bible. Illustrated with finely executed engravings. Royal 8vo. $7 00; mor. extra, $10 00. New York.

Waistell's Designs for Architectural Buildings, by Jopling. 4to. $6 50. Lond.

Wake, (Archbishop.) The Genuine Epistles of the Apostolical Fathers, St. Clement, St. Polycarp, St. Ignatius, St. Barnabas, and the Martyrdom of St. Polycarp and St. Ignatius. 12mo. cloth, $1 00. Oxford, 1841.

Wakefield, (E. J.) New Zealand in 1839 to 1844. 2 vols. 8vo. cloth, $8 50. London, 1845.

——— Illustrations to Do. Folio, cloth, $19 00; colored, $28 00. Lond. 1845.

——— England and America; a Comparison of the Social and Political State of both Nations. 8vo. cloth, $1 25. New York.

Walbran, (C. J.) Dictionary of Shakespeare Quotations arranged in Alphabetical order. 12mo. cloth, $1 50. Lond. 1849.

Walker's Analysis of Beauty in Woman; preceded by a Critical View of the general Hypotheses respecting Beauty, by Leonardo da Vinci, Mengs, Winckelmann, Hume, Hogarth, Burke, Knight, Alison, and others. New edition, royal 8vo. illustrated by 22 beautiful plates, after drawings from life, by H. Howard, by Gauci and Lane; elegantly bound in gilt cloth, $6 50. 1846.

——— (Mrs. A.) Female Beauty. Post 8vo. bds. colored plates, $9 00. Lond.

——— (B. J.) Code of Signals for the Mercantile Navy. Royal 8vo. cloth, 2 parts, $5 50. London, 1841.

——— (C. V.) Electrotype Manipulation; being the Theory and Plain Instructions in the Art of Working in Metals. 2 parts, 75 cents. Philadelphia.

——— (Don.) Manly Exercises. 12mo. cloth, wood-cuts, $1 50. Philadelphia.

——— Defensive Exercises. 12mo. cloth, $1 25. London.

——— Exercises for Young Ladies. 12mo. bds. plates, $2 75. London.

——— (G.) Chess Studies; comprising 1000 Games of Chess as really played by the first Chess-Players, &c. 8vo. cloth, $3 50. London, 1844.

——— New Treatise on Chess. Fourth edition, 12mo. cloth, $3 00. Lond. 1847.

——— Jaenisch's Chess Preceptor; a new Analysis of the Openings of Games. Translated from the French, with Notes. 8vo. cloth, $4 00. London.

——— (G. A.) Gatherings from Graveyards. 8vo. cloth, $2 50. London, 1844.

——— (J.) On Ventilating and Lighting Tunnels, particularly in reference to the one on the Leeds and Selby Railway. (Trans. I. C. E. vol. 1, 4to.) London.

——— (J.) Critical and Pronouncing Dictionary and Expositor of the English Language. 8vo. sheep, $1 25. Philadelphia.

——— (Thos.) The Original, Essays, &c. Cr. 8vo. cloth, $2 50. London.

——— (W. C.) Tailor's Philosophy; or, Science of Cutting. 8vo. cloth, $8 25. Lond.

——— Corpus Poetarum Latinorum. New edition, royal 8vo. cloth, $5 00. Lond. 1848.

Wall, (C. W.) Ancient Orthography of the Jews. 3 vols. royal 8vo. $13 50. Lond.

——— (Wm.) The History of Infant Baptism; together with Gale's Reflections and Dr. Wall's Defence. New edition, by Dr. H. Cotton. 4 vols. 8vo. cloth, $11 00. Oxford, 1846.

Wallace, (R.) Practical Mechanic's Pocket Guide. 32mo. cloth, 50 cents. Glasgow.

——— Universal Calculator's Pocket Guide. 32mo. cloth, 50 cents. Glasgow.

——— Mathematician's Pocket Guide. 32mo. cloth, 50 cents. Glasgow.

——— Practical Engineer's Pocket Guide. 32mo. cloth, 50 cents. Glasgow.

——— Dissertation on the True Age of the World. 8vo. cloth, $3 75. Lond.

Wallace, (W. C.) Wonders of Vision; a Treatise on the Eye. 12mo. cloth, 50 cents. New York, 1841.

Wallbridge, (Arthur.) Bizarre Fables. 12mo. cloth, $1 38. London.

Wallich, (N.) Planta Asiaticæ Rariores; or, Descriptions and Figures of a select number of Unpublished East Indian Plants, in 12 parts, forming 3 vols. imp. folio, containing 300 beautifully colored plates, $144 00. Lond. 1830–32.

Waller, (J. A.) British Domestic Herbal. 8vo. cloth, plates, $5 50; colored, $9 00. London.

Wallis, (S. T.) Glimpses of Spain; or, Notes of an Unfinished Tour in 1847. 12mo. cloth, $1 00. New York, 1849.

Walpole, (Capt.) A Description, with Memoranda, of the Bridge across the Kat River, at Fort Beaufort, Cape of Good Hope. (Papers, R. E. vol. 7, 4to.) London.

——— (Horace.) Anecdotes of Painting in England, with some Account of the Principal Artists, and Incidental Notes on the Arts. Also, a Catalogue of Engravers who have been born or resided in England. Corrected by the late George Virtue, digested and published from his original MSS. with additions, by Rev. J. Delancey. New edition, revised, &c., by R. N. Wornum. 3 vols. 8vo. cloth, plates, $11 00. London, 1849.

——— Letters addressed to the Countess of Ossory from 1769 to 1797, now first printed from original MSS. Edited, with Notes, by Rt. Hon. Vernon Smith. Portraits, 2 vols. 8vo. cloth, $9 00. London, 1848.

——— Letters; including numerous Letters now first published from the original MSS. 4 vols. 8vo. cloth, portrait, $8 00. Phila. 1842.

——— New Letters to Sir Horace Mann. 2 vols. 8vo. cloth, $2 50. Phila. 1844.

——— Memoirs of the Reign of King George III. Edited, with Notes, by Sir Deniss Marchant. 2 vols 8vo. cloth, $2 50. Phila. 1845.

Walsh, (Le V.) St. Louis et son siecle. Imp. 8vo. paper, illustrated with portraits, engravings, and wood-cuts, $5 50. Tours, 1847.

——— (Robt.) Essay on Ancient Coins, Medals, and Gems. 12mo. cloth, $1 75. Lond.

——— Notices of Brazil in 1828 and '29. 2 vols. 8vo. cloth, $10 00. London, 1836.

——— (W. H.) Nature and Treatment of Cancer. 8vo. cloth, $4 50. London, 1846.

Waller and Smith's Designs for Cottage and Villa Architecture. 4 parts, 4to. $10 00. London.

Walton, (Bishop.) Memoirs of the Life and Writings of; with Notices of his Coadjutors on his Polyglot Bible, and his Vindication of it, by Rev. H. J. Todd. Portrait, 2 vols. 8vo. cloth, $2 50. London, 1821.

——— The Lives of Donne, Walton, Hooker, Herbert, and Sanderson. By Izaak Walton. New edition, 12mo. green cloth, $1 00.

"The Lives are the most delightful kind of reading. Walton possesses an inimitable simplicity and vivacity of style."—Mrs. Kirkland.

——— (I.) Angler, by Sir H. Nicholas. 2 vols. imp. 8vo. cloth, plates, $38 00; L. P. $63 00. London, 1836.

Walton and Cotton's Complete Angler; or, the Contemplative Man's Recreation, with copious Notes, and a Bibliographical Preface, giving an Account of Fishing and Fishing-Books, from the earliest Antiquity, by Rev. Dr. Bethune. 12mo. cloth, wood-cuts, $1 25; with portraits and engravings, $1 50; large paper, $10 00. New York, 1848.

——— (W.) The Alpaca, its Naturalization in the British Isles considered as a National Benefit and as an Object of Immediate Utility to the Farmer and Manufacturer. 12mo. cloth, $1 37. Edin.

——— Account of the Peruvian Sheep. 8vo. cloth, $2 50. London.

——— Account of the Philippine Islands. 8vo. cloth, $3 63. London.

——— (W. L.) Amateur's Drawing-Book. Oblong folio, cloth, $3 63. London.

Wandering Jew, (The.) Illustrated edition. 8vo. cloth, $5 00. New York.

Wanderings and Fortunes of some German Emigrants. 12mo. cloth, 75 cents. New York, 1848.

Warburton, (Bp.) The Divine Legation of Moses demonstrated, with an Account of the Life of the Author, by Bishop Hurd. New edition, plates, 3 vols. 8vo. $7 50. Lond. 1846.

——— (Eliott.) Memoirs of Prince Rupert and the Cavaliers, including their Private Correspondence. Portraits, 3 vols. 8vo. cloth, $12 00. London, 1849.

——— The Crescent and the Cross; or, the Romance and Reality of Eastern Travel. 12mo. cloth, $1 25. New York, 1848.

——— Hochelaga; or, England in the New World. 12mo. cloth, $1 00. New York.

——— Conquest of Canada. 3 vols. 8vo. $8 50. London, 1849.

——— The Same. 12mo. New York.

Ward, (F. O.) Outlines of Human Osteology. 18mo. cloth, $1 75. London, 1838.

——— (J. H.) On Ordnance and Steam. 8vo. cloth, $2 50. Philadelphia.

——— (N. B.) Treatise on the Growth of Plants in Glazed Cases. 8vo. cloth, $1 50. London.

——— (Rev. W. G.) Ideal of a Christian Church considered in Comparison with existing Practice. 8vo. cloth, $2 25. Lond. 1844.

——— (W.) View of the History, Literature, and Religion of the Hindoos. 3 vols. 8vo. cloth. London, 1817.

Ware, (H., Jr.) Complete Works. 4 vols. 12mo. cloth, $3 50. Boston, 1846.

——— (John.) Treatise on the Proportion of Arches. Royal 8vo. cloth, $5 50. London.

——— (Sam.) Tracts on Vaults and Bridges. Royal 8vo. $6 50. London.

——— Remarks on Theatres. 8vo. cloth, $1 75. London.

——— (W.) Zenobia; or, the Fall of Palmyra; a Historical Romance. 2 vols. 12mo. $1 25. New York.

——— Julian; or, Scenes in Judea. 2 vols. 12mo. $1 25. New York.

——— Aurelian; or, Rome in the Third Century. 2 vols. 12mo. $1 25. New York.

Warner, (Jas. F.) Universal Dictionary of Musical Terms. 8vo. paper, 25 cents. Boston.

——— The Primary Note Reader; or, First Steps in Singing at Sight. 12mo. paper, 25 cents. New York.

——— Rudimental Lessons in Music, containing the Primary Instruction requisite for all beginners in the Art. 18mo. bds. 50 cents. New York.

——— (John.) On the Cultivation of Flax, &c. 8vo. cloth, $2 25. London.

Warren, (Jos.) Hints to Young Composers in Music. 12mo. cloth, $1 00. London.

——— (Rev. J.) A Treatise on the Geometric Representation of the Square Roots of Negative Quantities. 8vo. cloth, $1 50. Lond.

——— (S.) Ten Thousand a Year; a Novel. 8vo. cloth, 75 cents. Phila.

——— Diary of a Late Physician. 3 vols. 18mo. muslin, $1 38. New York.

——— Introduction to Law Studies. 8vo. $3 50. New York.

——— Moral, Social, and Professional Duties of Attorneys and Solicitors. 12mo. cloth, 75 cents. New York.

——— Now and Then. 12mo. cloth, 63 cents. New York.

Warrington, (R.) Chemical Tables. Oblong 4to. $1 00. London.

——— (W.) History of Ancient Stained Glass. Folio, bds. plates, $38 00. London.

Warton, (Thos.) History of English Poetry. 3 vols. 8vo. cloth, $6 50. Lond. 1840.

Washburn, (E.) Sketches of the Judicial History of Massachusetts from 1630 to the Revolution in 1775. 8vo. cloth, $1 50. Boston, 1840.

Washington, (G.) Works and Life, by Jared Sparks. 12 vols. 8vo. cloth, portrait and plates, $18 00. New York.

——— Life. By John Marshall. 5 vols. 8vo. sheep, first edition, with atlas of plates, $10 00. Philadelphia, 1804.

——— The Same. Second edition, revised. 2 vols. 8vo. sheep, atlas, $5 00. Phila.

——— Life of George Washington, by Washington Irving. 12mo. cloth. (In press.)

——— Life. By Jared Sparks, with maps, &c. 8vo. cloth, $3 00. Boston.

——— Agricultural Correspondence. 4to. cloth, $3 50. New York.

Water Cure in America; an Account of 220 Cases of various Diseases treated with Water, by American Water Cure Physicians. 12mo. cloth, 75 cents. New York.

Waterhouse, (G. R.) A Natural History of the Mammalia. 2 vols. 8vo. cloth, plates, $14 50; colored, $20 75. Lond. 1846–48.

Waterland, (Rev. D.) Works, to which is prefixed a Review of the Author's Life and Writings, by W. Van Mildert. 6 vols. 8vo. cloth, $18 00. Oxford, 1843.

Waterston, (William.) Cyclopædia of Commerce, Mercantile Law, Finance, Commercial Geography, and Navigation. New edition, with a Treatise on the Principles, Practice, and History of Commerce, by J. R. M'Culloch. 1 very thick, closely printed vol. 8vo. (900 pages) with 4 maps, extra cloth, $3 00. Lond. 1847.

Waterston, (R. C.) On Moral and Spiritual Culture. 12mo. cloth, 67 cents. Boston.

——— (J. J.) A Method of Representing by Diagram and Estimating the Earth Work in Excavations and Embankments. (Trans. I. C. E. vol. 1, 4to.) London.

Waterton's Essays on Natural History. First and Second Series. 12mo. cloth, $4 25. London, 1844.

Watherston, (J. H.) Art of Assaying Gold and Silver. Post 8vo. cloth, $1 00. London.

Watkins, (T. C.) Treatise on Cucumbers and Melons. 8vo. cloth, $1 00. London.

Watson, (B. L.) Code of Signals for Vessels at Sea. 8vo. cloth, $3 25. London.

——— (H. C.) Cybele Britannica; or, British Plants and their Geographical Relations. 2 vols. 8vo. cloth, $6 50. Lond. 1847–49.

——— (J. F.) Annals of New York City and State. 8vo. cloth, $2 00. New York.

——— Annals of Philadelphia. 2 vols. 8vo. cloth, $4 00. Philadelphia.

——— (J. T.) Poetical Quotations; consisting of Elegant Extracts on every Subject, compiled from various Authors, and arranged under appropriate heads. 8vo. cloth, plates, $3 50; small edition, 12mo. cloth, without plates, $1 50. Philadelphia, 1849.

——— (Thos.) Practice of Physic, by Condie. 8vo. sheep, $3 25. Phila. 1849.

——— (W.) The Forester's Manual. 12mo. cloth, $1 25. London.

Watt, (Jas.) Life of, by M. Arago, with Memoir of Machinery. 8vo. cloth, $1 00. Lond.

——— (P.) Progress and Science of Life Insurance. 8vo. cloth, $1 75. London.

Watts, (I.) Horæ Lyricæ; Poems Sacred to Devotion and Piety, to Virtue, Honor, and Friendship, and to the Memory of the Dead, with Memoir of the Author, by Robert Southey. 18mo. cloth, 50 cents. London, 1837.

Waverley, (The,) Gallery. A Series of 36 Portraits of Females, beautifully engraved. 8vo. mor. $9 00. London.

——— Gems; being Illustrations of the Scenes and Scenery of the Novels, &c. 8vo. cloth, $4 00; mor. $6 00. London, 1848.

Wayland, (Prof.) Principles of Political Economy. 12mo. $1 25. Boston.

——— (F.) Elements of Moral Science. 12mo. cloth, $1 25. Boston.

——— Elements of Political Economy, abridged. Half roan, 50 cents. Boston.

——— Sermons delivered at the Chapel of Brown University. 12mo. cloth, $1 25. Boston.

Waylen's Ecclesiastical Tour in the United States. 8vo. cloth, $2 00. New York.

Weale. Quarterly Papers on Architecture. Illustrated with above 500 wood, steel, and copper engravings, many of which are highly and expensively colored. 4 vols. 4to. cloth, $37 50. London.

——— Rudimentary Work for Beginners. 12mo. cloth, 25 cents per vol.

First Series.

Rudimentary Chemistry, by Professor Fownes, F. R. S. &c. Third edition, and on Agricultural Chemistry for the use of Farmers.

——— Natural Philosophy, by Charles Tomlinson.

Rudimentary Geology, by Lieut. Col. Portlock, R. E., F. R. S., F. G. S. &c.
—— Mineralogy, by D. Varley, Author of "Conversations on Mineralogy." Second edition, vol 1.
—— Do. vol. 2.
—— Mechanics, by Charles Tomlinson.
—— Electricity, by Sir Wm. Snow Harris, F. R. S. &c.
—— Pneumatics, by Chas. Tomlinson.
—— Civil Engineering, by Henry Law C. E. vol. 1.
—— Do. vol. 2.
—— Architecture (Orders), by W. H. Leeds, Esq.
—— Do. (Styles—their several examples), by Talbot Bury, Archt., F. I. B. A.
—— Principles of Design in Architecture, by E. Lacy Garbett, Archt.
—— Perspective, by George Pyne, Artist, Author of "Practical Rules in Drawing for the Operative Builder and Young Student in Architecture," vol. 1, second edition.
—— Do. vol. 2, second edition.

Second Series.

Rudimentary Art of Building, by E. Dobson, C. E., Assoc. Inst. C. E., Author of Railways of Belgium.
—— Brick-Making, Tile-Making, by the same.
—— Masonry and Stone-Cutting, by the same.
—— Illustrations of the preceding, in 4to. atlas size, 13 plates.
—— House Painting and Mixing Colors, by George Field, Esq.
—— Draining Districts and Lands, by G. Drysdale Dempsey, C. E.
—— Draining and Sewerage of Towns and Buildings, by G. Drysdale Dempsey, C. E.
—— Well-Sinking and Boring, by John George Swindell, Architect.
—— Use of Instruments generally, by I. F. Heather, M. A. of the Royal Military Academy, Woolwich.
—— Constructing Cranes for the Erection of Buildings and for Hoisting Goods, by Joseph Glynn, F. R. S., C. E.
—— Treatise on the Steam Engine, by Dr. Lardner, LL.D. (Written specially for these Rudimentary volumes.)
—— Art of Blasting Rocks and Quarrying, and on Stone, by Maj. Gen. Sir John Burgoyne, K. C. B., R. E., &c. &c.
—— Dictionary of Terms used by Architects, Builders, Civil Engineers, Artists, Ship-Builders, and the several connecting Arts, vol. 1.
—— Do. vol. 2.
—— Do. vol. 3.

Third Series.

To carry out this new Series successfully and methodically, the most eminent men in scholastic erudition and elementary instruction have been selected, under the able management and editing of Mr. James Hann, Mathematical Master of King's College, London, who, with the co-operation of the following gentlemen, will produce a set of books that shall be efficient both for public and self-instruction :—

W. S. B. Woolhouse, F. R. A. S., Actuary of the National Loan Fund. Author of several Scientific Works.
Henry Law. Civil Engineer, Editor and Author of several Professional Works.
James Haddon, Arithmetical and Second Mathematical Master, King's College, London.

Elementary Treatise on Arithmetic, with numerous Mathematical and Commercial Examples for Practice and Self-Examination.
A Practical System of Book-Keeping, with Concise Modes of Calculation, Forms of Commercial Documents in English, French, German, and Italian, Mercantile Phraseology, &c., forming a complete Introduction to the Counting-House.
Elementary Treatise on Algebra.
—— Principles of Geometry.
—— Principles of Analytical Geometry.
Elementary Treatise on Plane Trigonometry.
—— Treatise on Spherical Trigonometry.
Elements and Practice of Mensuration and Geodesy.
The whole System of Logarithmic Tables, for Reference and Practice
Elementary Treatise on Popular Astronomy.
Principles and Practice of Statics and Dynamics.
Theory and Practice of Nautical Astronomy and Navigation.
Differential Calculus, in which the Principles will be clearly elucidated.
Integral Calculus, in which the Principles will also be clearly elucidated.
Collection of Examples of the Differential and Integral Calculus.

Fourth Series.

Rudimentary Treatise on Cottage Building, or Hints for Improving the Dwellings of the Laboring Poor, by Charles Bruce Allen, Architect.
—— Treatise on Tubular Bridges, Girder Bridges, &c., more particularly the Conway and Britannia Bridges, describing the Experiments made to determine their form, strength, and efficiency, together with the construction of the same, the floating and raising the tubes, &c.
Rudimentary Art of Making Foundations, Concrete Works, &c. by E. Dobson, C. E
—— Treatise on Limes, Calcareous Cements, Mortars, Stuccos, and Concrete, by George R. Burnell, C. E.
—— Art of Laying out and Making of Roads for New and Old Countries, by H. Law, C. E.
—— Treatise on the Construction of Light-Houses, more particularly those of Britain, by Alan Stevenson, LL. B., F. R. S. E., M. Inst. C. E.
—— Do. the Continuation of the same subject.
—— Law of Contracts for all kinds of Buildings, for Employers, Contractors, and Workmen, by David Gibbons, Esq., Author of Treatises on the "Law of Dilapidations," and on the "Law of Fixtures," &c.
—— Treatise on Hydraulic Engineering and on Tunnelling through various kinds of Strata, with Plates, forming a third volume of the Engineering (and completing that subject), published in the First Series.
—— Treatise on Locomotive Engines, describing them on the various Railways for their several purposes, and their duty and efficiency, by J. Sewell, C. E.
—— Treatise on Marine Engines and Steamboats, for Sailors and Engineers.
—— Art of Ship-Building. The Elementary Principles, with plates, by J. Peake, H. M. Naval Architect.
—— Do. The Practice, with plates, by J. Peake, H. M. Naval Architect.
—— Do. Masting, Mast-Making, and Rigging of Ships.
—— Do. Sailor's Sea-Books, Directions for Signals, Flags of all Maritime Nations.

Fifth Series.

Rudimentary Treatise on Magnetism, by Sir W. Snow Harris, F. R. S &c.
—— Treatise on Conchology, &c. (Fossils and Shells,) vol 1.
—— Continuation of the same subjects, vol. 2.
—— Elements of Music, with plates of Examples, vol. 1.
—— Practice of Music, with plates of Examples, vol. 2.
—— Instruction on the Piano Forte.
—— Descriptive Geometry, applied to Shipbuilding. (text.) By J F. Heather, M. A.
—— Do Atlas of Plates illustrative (drawing-book.) Oblong 4to. By J. Peake, H. M. Naval Architect.
—— Do. Applied to Architecture (text.) By I. F. Heather, M. A.
—— Atlas of plates illustrative (drawing-book.) Oblong 4to. by I. F. Heather, M. A.
—— Do. Applied to Civil Engineering (text.) By I. F. Heather, M. A.
—— Atlas of plates illustrative (drawing-book.) Oblong 4to. by I. F. Heather, M. A.
—— Do. Applied to Mechanical Engineering (text.) By I. F. Heather, M. A.
—— Atlas of plates illustrative (drawing-book.) Oblong 4to. By I. F. Heather, M. A.
—— Dictionary of the Holy Bible, adapted for instructive popular use, with explanatory and easy reference, by Rev. J. H. Page, M. A., &c., &c.

The whole, forming a most useful and instructive Library of general instruction, in 75 volumes, illustrated by numerous engravings, $22 50. London.

Weaver's Hints on Cottage Architecture; being a Selection of Designs for Cottages, with Plans, Elevations, and Estimates. Folio, cloth, $7 50. London.

Webb, (Rev. B.) Sketches of Continental Ecclesiology; or, Church Notes in Belgium, Germany, and Italy. 8vo. cloth, $5 00. London, 1848.

—— (G. J.) American Glee-Book, $1 13. Boston.

—— Vocal Class-Book for Schools, $1 00. Boston.

Weber, (G.) Theory of Musical Composition. 2 vols. 8vo. cloth, $5 00. Boston.

Webber. Old Hicks, the Guide; or, Adventures in the Camanche Country in Search of a Gold Mine. 12mo. cloth, $1 00. New York.

Webster, (D.) Diplomatic and Official Papers. 8vo. cloth, $1 75. New York, 1847.

—— Speeches and Forensic Arguments. 3 vols. 8vo. cloth, $5 50. Boston.

—— (J. W.) Manual of Chemistry. 8vo. cloth, $3 00. Boston.

Webster, (N.) American Dictionary, without Abridgment. 4to. sheep, containing the whole Vocabulary of the quarto, with Corrections, Improvements, and several thousand Additional Words, $6 00. Springfield, 1848.

—— Dictionary, abridged. Royal 8vo. sheep, $3 50. New York.

—— (Thos.) Principles of Hydrostatics. Post 8vo. cloth, $2 25. London.

—— On the Changes of Temperature consequent on any Change in the Density of Elastic Fluids, considered especially with Reference to Steam. (Trans. I. C. E. vol. 1, 4to.) London.

—— (T.) An Encyclopædia of Domestic Economy; comprising such Subjects as are most immediately connected with House-Keeping. 8vo. sheep, $4 00. New York.

—— Elements of Physics. 12mo. cloth, $2 00. London, 1837.

—— (W. H.) Voyage to the South Atlantic Ocean. 2 vols. 8vo. cloth, $8 50. London.

Weddell, (Jas.) Voyage to the South Pole. 8vo. cloth, $5 50. London.

—— (T.) On Solving Numerical Equations. 4to. $1 50. London.

Weeden, (John.) Treatise on the Growth of Cucumbers. 8vo. cloth, $3 25. London.

Weeks on the Management of Bees. 12mo. 38 cents. Boston.

Weil, (Dr. G.) The Bible, Koran, and Talmud; or, Biblical Legends compiled from Arabic Sources, and compared with Jewish Tradition. 12mo. cloth, $1 00. London.

—— American edition, 50 cents. N. Y. 1848.

Weisbach, (J.) Principles of the Mechanics of Machinery and Engineering. 1000 wood engravings. 2 vols. 8vo. cloth, $7 50. Philadelphia, 1849.

Weiss, (Dr.) Inventions and Improvements in Surgical Instruments. 8vo. cloth, $4 50. London.

—— (J.) Hand-Book of Hydropathy; for Professional and Domestic Use, with an Appendix on the best Mode of Forming Hydropathic Establishments. From the second London edition. 12mo. cloth, $1 00. Philadelphia, 1848.

Weld, (C. R.) A History of the Royal Society, with Memoirs of the Presidents. Compiled from Authentic Documents. 2 vols. cr. 8vo. cloth, $5 75. London.

—— (Rev. H.) Women of the Scriptures. 8vo. cloth, plates, $3 50; mor. $4 50. Phila.

—— (J.) Scenery of Killarney. Royal 8vo. cloth, $7 50. London.

Wellbeloved, (Rev. Chas.) Translation of the Bible. (A portion only.) 2 vols. 4to. cloth, $21 00. London.

Wellington, (Duke of.) Life of, by Maxwell. 3 vols. 8vo. cloth, plates and maps, $10 00. London, 1841.

—— Dispatches. Edited by Gurwood. 12 vols. 8vo. bds. $72 00. London.

—— Dispatches of, during his various Campaigns in India, Denmark, Portugal, Spain, the Low Countries, and France, from 1799 to 1818, compiled from Official and Authentic Documents. By Lieut. Col. Gurwood. The compressed edition, 1 thick vol. medium 8vo. gilt cloth, $4 50. London, 1842.

Wellington's Maxims and Opinions. Selected from his Writings and Speeches, with a Biographical Memoir, by G. H. Francis. 8vo. post, $4 00. London, 1845.

Wells, (J.) Epitome of Perspective. Folio, cloth, $3 25. London.

—— (W. C.) Essay on Vision, Dew, &c. with Life. 8vo. cloth, $3 50. London.

—— (N. A.) The Picturesque Antiquities of Spain, described in a Series of Letters, with illustrations, representing Moorish Palaces, Cathedrals, &c. Royal 8vo. $4 50. Lond.

Welsford, (H.) On the Origin of the English Language. 8vo. cloth, $3 25. Lond.

Wellsted's City of the Caliphs, and Travels along the Shores of the Persian Gulf and the Mediterranean, including a Voyage to the Coast of Arabia, and a Tour on the Island of Socotra, Adventures among the Bedouin Arabs, &c. 2 vols. 8vo. map and plates, cloth, $3 50. 1840.

Wemyss, (Thos.) Job and his Times; or, a Picture of the Patriarchal Age, between Noah and Abraham, with a new Version of Job. 8vo. cloth, $1 50. London, 1839.

Werner's Nomenclature of Colors, by Syme. 8vo. cloth, $4 25. London.

—— Practical Instructions for Flower Drawing Royal 4to. $7 50. London.

Wernick's Dutch and English Dictionary. Square 12mo. bds. $3 75. London.

Wesley, (J.) Works. 7 vols. 8vo. sheep, $12 00. New York.

—— Sermons. 3 vols. 8vo. $7 50. Lond.

—— Journal from 1735 to 1790, being a Record of his Travels and Labors. 2 vols. 8vo. sheep, $4 50. New York.

—— Life of, by Robert Southey. 2 vols. 8vo. cloth, $8 50. London.

Wesleyan Preacher, (The.) 4 vols. 8vo. cloth, $10 00. London.

West, (Benj.) Life and Studies of, by John Galt. 8vo. cloth, $4 25. London.

—— (J.) Remarks on Management of Woods and Plantations. 8vo. cloth, $1 75. Lond.

Westgarth, (W.) Australia Felix; or, Account of Port Phillip. Post 8vo. $3 25. London.

Westmacott, (R.) British Galleries of Painting. Royal 8vo. cloth, $3 50. Lond.

Westminster Review. From its Commencement in January, 1824, to June, 1847. 47 vols. 8vo. half calf, neat, $75 00.

Westwood's Illuminated Illustrations of the Bible. Imp. 8vo. cloth, $9 50. Lond.

—— (J. O.) Modern Classification of Insects. 2 vols. 8vo. cloth, $13 00. London.

—— Entomologist's Text-Book; an Introduction to the Natural History, Structure, Physiology, and Classification of Insects. 12mo. colored plates, $1 50. London, 1838.

—— British Butterflies and their Transformations, with Characters and Descriptions, arranged and illustrated in a series of plates, by H. N. Humphreys. 4to. $8 00. London.

Westwood, (J. O.) Cabinet of Oriental Entomology; being a Selection of some of the Rarer and more Beautiful Species of Insects, Natives of India and the adjacent Islands, the greater portion of which are now for the first time described and figured. 4to. colored plates, $12 00. London, 1848.

Wetten, (Robert.) Designs for Villas in the Italian Style of Architecture. 4to. cloth, $9 50. London, 1848.

Wharton, (F.) State Trials of the United States during the Administrations of Washington and Adams. 8vo. sheep, $4 50. Philadelphia, 1849.

Whately, (Archbishop.) Christianity, Independent of Civil Government. 12mo. cloth, $1 00. New York.

——— Kingdom of Christ and Errors of Romanism. 8vo. cloth, 75 cents. New York.

——— Logic, with Questions. 12mo. cloth, 81 cents. Boston.

——— Rhetoric, with Questions 12mo. cloth, 81 cents. Boston.

——— Lessons on Reasoning. 12mo. cloth, 63 cents. Boston.

——— (Thos.) Remarks on some Characters of Shakespeare. 12mo. cloth, $1 25. Lond.

Wheatley, (C.) Rational Illustration of the Book of Common Prayer. Imp. 8vo. cloth, 87 cents. (Bohn's St. Lib.) Lond. 1848.

——— (H.) The Rod and the Line; or, Practical Hints and Dainty Devices for the Taking of Trout, Grayling, &c. Foolscap 8vo. cloth, 9 colored plates, $3 25. Lond. 1849.

Wheaton, (H.) History of the Law of Nations in Europe and America, from the earliest Times to the Treaty of Washington, 1842. 8vo. sheep, $6 50. New York, 1845.

——— Elements of International Law. 8vo. cloth, $4 50. Philadelphia, 1846.

Wheeler, (H. G.) Biographical and Political History of Congress. 2 vols. 8vo. cloth, portraits, $6 00. New York.

Whewell, (Prof.) History of the Inductive Sciences, 3 vols. Philosophy of the Inductive Sciences, 2 vols. Elements of Morality, 2 vols. Together, 7 vols. 8vo. calf gilt, gilt backs and marbled leaves, $32 50. Lond. 1837–45.

——— History of the Inductive Sciences from the earliest to the present time. 3 vols. 8vo. cloth, $12 00. London.

——— Philosophy of the Inductive Sciences. 2 vols. 8vo. cloth, $9 00. London.

——— (W.) The Mechanical Euclid; containing the Elements of Mechanics and Hydrostatics, with Supplement. Fifth edition, 12mo. $1 50. London, 1849.

——— Treatise on Dynamics. 2 vols. 8vo. cloth, $6 50.

——— On the Motion of Points Constrained and Resisted, and on the Motion of a Rigid Body. 8vo. cloth, $3 75.

——— Mechanics of Engineering. 8vo. cloth, $8 25. London.

——— Elements of Morality and Polity. 2 vols. 12mo. cloth, $1 00. New York.

——— 2 vols. 8vo. calf, gilt, $7 00. Lond. 1845.

Whewell, (W.) Astronomy and General Physics considered with reference to Natural Theology. 12mo. cloth, $1 50. Lond. 1847.

——— Astronomy and General Physics. 12mo. cloth, 50 cents. New York.

Whichelo, (H.) Student's Guide to Drawing in Perspective. Oblong 4to. $2 25. London.

Whipple, (E.) Lectures on Subjects connected with Literature and Life. 12mo. cloth, 63 cents. Boston, 1850.

——— Essays and Reviews. 2 vols. 12mo. cloth, $2 00. Boston, 1848.

Whist, its History and Practice. Illustrations by Meadows. 12mo. cloth, $1 25. London.

Whistlebinkie. A Collection of Songs. Thick 18mo. cloth, $1 00. Glasgow.

Whiston's Josephus. Illustrated edition of, complete; containing both the Antiquities and the Wars of the Jews. 2 vols. 8vo. handsomely printed, embellished with 52 beautiful wood engravings, by various artists, cloth, $4 25. London, 1845.

Whitby, (Mrs.) Manual for Rearing Silk Worms. 12mo. cloth, 50 cents. Lond.

White, (C.) Belgic Revolution of 1830. 2 vols. post 8vo. $4 25. London.

——— (E.) Treatise on Billiards. Post 8vo. cloth, $3 25. London.

——— (F. S.) History of Inventions and Discoveries. 8vo. cloth, $4 25. London.

——— (G.) Treatise on Weaving by Hand and Power Loom. 8vo. cloth, $4 25. Lond.

——— (Gilbert.) Natural History of Selborne, with Observations on various parts of Nature, and the Naturalist's Calendar. New edition, with Additions, by Sir W. Jardine. 18mo. many pretty wood-cuts of Birds, by Branston. extra cloth bds. 75 cents; plates beautifully colored, $1 50. London, 1836.

——— Natural History of Selborne, with Notes, by Rev. L. Jenyns. 12mo. wood-cuts, $2 25. London, 1843.

——— (H. Kirke.) Poetical Works, with Memoir, by Sir H. Nicolas. 12mo. cloth, $1 50; mor. gilt edges, $3 00. Pickering.

——— (J. B.) Memoirs of, by himself. Edited by Rev. J. H. Thom. 3 vols. post 8vo. cloth, $7 25.

——— (J.) Rural Architecture illustrated in a new Series of Designs for Ornamental Cottages and Villas. Folio, 98 plates, $15 00. Lond.

——— Dictionary of the Veterinary Art; containing Concise Explanations of the various Terms used in Veterinary Medicine and Surgery. 12mo. cloth, $2 00. London.

——— Improved Art of Farriery, with Additions by Rosser. 8vo. cloth, plates, $2 50. London, 1847.

——— (Thos.) Theory and Practice of Ship Building. 8vo. plates, folio, $5 00. Lond.

Whitehead. East Jersey under the Proprietary Government. 8vo. cloth, $2 50. New Jersey Historical Society, 1846.

Whiteside, (J.) Italy in the Nineteenth Century. 3 vols. post 8vo. $9 50. Lond

Whiting, (Thos.) Astronomy. 4to. cloth, $14 50. London.

Whitley, (N.) The Application of Geology to Agriculture and to the Improvement and Valuation of Land, with the Nature and Properties of Soils, &c. $2 25. London, 1843.

Whitlock, (N.) Miniature Painter's Manual. 12mo. cloth, $1 25. London.

——— On the Construction of Shop Fronts. 4to. cloth, $3 50. London.

——— The Decorative Painter's and Glazier's Guide; containing the most approved Method of Imitating Oak, Mahogany, Maple, Rose, and every other kind of Fancy Wood, Marbles, &c. Also, Designs for Decorating Apartments. 4to. cloth, 90 plates, mostly colored, $7 50. London, 1841.

Whitling, (H. J.) Original Designs for Shop Fronts, forming a Collection suitable to Persons connected with the Practical part of Building. 4to. paper, $3 25. Lond. 1834.

Whittaker, (Henry.) The Practical Cabinet-Maker and Upholsterer's Treasury of Designs, House Furnishing and Decorating Assistant, interspersed with Designs. 4to. cloth, $8 50. London, 1849.

——— (T. H.) Diagrams of Chemical Decompositions. 8vo. cloth, $1 38. London.

Whittier's Supernaturalism in New England. 12mo. cloth, 38 cents. New York.

——— (J. G.) Poems. Illustrated with engravings, by H. Billings. 8vo. cloth gilt, $4 00. Boston.

——— Old Portraits and Modern Sketches. 12mo. cloth, 75 cents. Boston, 1850.

Whitmarsh on the Mulberry Tree and Silk Worm. 12mo. cloth, 38 cents. Phila.

Whittock, (N.) New Manual of Perspective for all Classes. Foolscap 8vo. $1 00. London, 1849.

Whole, (The,) Duty of Man laid down in a Plain and Familiar Way for the Use of all, but especially the Meanest Reader, with Private Devotions. 12mo. cloth, $2 00. Pickering, 1842.

Wicksted, (Thos.) Experimental Inquiry concerning the relative Power and Useful Effect produced by the Cornish, Boulton and Watt Pumping Engines, and Cylindrical and Wagon-Head Boilers. 4to. $2 00. Lond.

——— Atlas to the above, containing 8 large elaborate illustrations of these Engines, $12 00.

——— On the Evaporative Power of Coal. (Paper in Engineer's and Contractor's Pocket-Book.)

——— Description of the Balance-Gates at the Compensation Reservoir of the E. L. Water Works at Old Ford. (Paper in Reports of the Royal Engineers, vol. 7, 4to.)

——— On the Effective Power of the High-Pressure Expansive Condensing Engines in use at some of the Cornish Mines. (Trans. I. C. E. vol. 2, 4to.) London.

Wiffen, (J. H.) Garcilaso de la Vega. Post 8vo. cloth, $3 75. London.

——— Tasso's Jerusalem Delivered. 12mo. cloth, plates, beautifully printed, $1 50; mor. gilt edges, $3 00. New York.

Wiffen, (J. H.) Historical Memoirs of the House of Russell, from the time of the Norman Conquest. 2 vols. 8vo. cloth, $12 00. London, 1833.

Wigan, (Dr. A. L.) Duality of the Mind, proved by the Structure, &c. &c. 8vo. cloth, $4 00. London, 1844.

Wigger's, (Dr. G.) Life of Socrates. Translated from the German, with Notes. 12mo. cloth, $1 00. London, 1840.

Wight, (R.) Figures of Indian Plants. 4 vols. 4to. cloth, 1270 colored plates, $100 00. Madras, 1838–48.

——— Illustrations of Indian Botany. 2 vols. 4to. 134 colored plates, $37 00. Madras, 1838–41.

——— Selection of Neilgherry Plants. Drawn and colored from Nature. 4to. bds. 100 colored plates, $22 50. Madras, 1846.

Wightwick's Modern English Gothic Architecture. 8vo. paper, 5 plates, $2 25. London, 1845.

——— Palace of Architecture; a Romance of Art and History. Imp. 8vo. cloth, 211 plates, $7 00. London, 1840.

——— Hints to Young Architects, together with a Model Specification. 8vo. cloth, $2 25. London.

——— American edition. Edited by Downing. 8vo. cloth, $1 50. New York.

Wikoff, (H.) Biographical and Personal Sketches of Napoleon Louis Bonaparte. 12mo. cloth, 63 cents. New York, 1849.

Wilberforce, (W.) Memoirs of, by his Sons. 5 vols. post 8vo. cloth, portrait, $13 50. London.

——— (R. J.) The Doctrine of the Incarnation of our Lord Jesus Christ in its relation to Mankind and the Church. Second edition, 8vo. cloth, $3 75. London, 1849.

——— (Bp.) Six Sermons, Preached before the University of Oxford, in St. Mary's Church, 1837, '38, '39. Second edition, foolscap 8vo. cloth, $1 50. London, 1848.

Wilcocks, (T.) History of Russia. 12mo. cloth, $1 75. London.

Wild, (C.) Architectural Grandeur in Belgium, Germany, and France. 4to. cloth, 24 plates, $5 00. London.

——— (W.) Elementary and Practical Instructions on the Art of Building Cottages and Houses for the Humbler Classes. 8vo. cloth, plates, $2 50. London, 1835.

Wild Flowers and their Associations. Illustrated with Natural Plants, tastefully arranged, elegantly bound, cloth extra, $6 00. London, 1847.

Wilde, (W. R.) Austria, its Literary and Scientific Institutions. Post 8vo. cloth, $2 75. London.

Wilkes, (C.) Narrative of the United States Exploring Expedition, during the Years 1838 to 1842. 5 vols. 8vo. maps and plates, cloth, $10 00. Philadelphia, 1848.

——— The Same. 5 vols. imp. 8vo. fine edition, with large maps and steel engravings, cloth, $25 00. Philadelphia, 1845.

Wilkes, (C.) Narrative of the United States Exploring Expedition, during the Years 1838 to 1842. 5 vols. 4to. cloth, maps and plates, $60 00. (Government edition.) Phila. 1845.

——— The Same. Vol. 6, containing Ethnology and Philology, by Horatio Hale. 4to. cloth, $10 00. Philadelphia, 1846.

——— The Same. Vol. 7. Dana on Zoophytes. 4to. cloth, with an atlas of plates beautifully colored in folio, cloth, $45 00. Phila. 1848–49.

——— Vol. 8. Dana's Geology of the United States Expedition. 4to. with an atlas of plates in folio, cloth, $15 00. Phila. 1849.

——— Vol. 9. Pickering's Races of Men and their Distribution. 4to. cloth, colored plates and map, $10 00. Boston, 1848.

——— Western America; including California and Oregon, with maps of those Regions and of the Sacramento Valley. 8vo. paper, 75 cents. Philadelphia, 1849.

Wilkie, (Sir D.) Sketches in Turkey, Syria, and Egypt, taken during the Years 1840 and 1841. Imp. folio, half mor. 26 plates, $21 00. London, 1843.

——— Spanish and Oriental Sketches, drawn on stone, by Joseph Nash. Imp. folio, half mor. 26 plates, with portrait of Washington Irving consulting the Archives at Cordova, $25 00. London, 1847.

——— Life of, by Allan Cunningham. 3 vols. 8vo. cloth, portrait, $12 50. London.

——— Modern Egypt and Thebes; being a Description of Egypt, with Information for Travellers in that Country. 2 vols. 8vo. cloth, $10 00. London, 1843.

Wilkins, (W.) Prolusiones Architectonicæ; or, Essays on Subjects connected with Grecian and Roman Architecture. Royal 4to. cloth, 40 fine engravings, $6 50. London.

——— (Chas.) Sanskrit Grammar. 4to. cloth, $25 00. London.

Wilkinson, (W.) Account of Wallachia and Moldavia. 8vo. $2 75. Lond. 1820.

——— Two Important Diseases of the Horse. 8vo. cloth, $3 75. London.

——— (H.) History of Engines of War. 8vo. cloth, $2 75. London.

——— Londina Illustrata; or, Graphic and Historical Illustrations of Interesting and Curious Monuments in the City of London, &c. 2 vols. imp. 4to. half bound, 207 copperplate engravings, $31 50. London, 1819–25.

——— (Sir G.) Modern Egypt and Thebes. 2 vols. 8vo. $12 50.

——— Manners and Customs of the Ancient Egyptians, derived from Hieroglyphics, Sculpture, &c. still existing, compared with Ancient Authors. 5 vols. 8vo. cloth gilt, 600 illustrations, $21 00; or whole bound in calf, neat, marbled leaves, $35 00. Lond. 1847.

——— Dalmatia and Montenegro, with a Journey to Mostar, in Herzegovina, and Remarks on the Sclavonic Nations; the History of Dalmatia and Ragusa; the Uscocs, &c. &c. 2 vols. 8vo. cloth, $12 00. London, 1848.

——— (G.) Practical Geology and Architecture of Ireland. 8vo. cloth, $8 50. London.

Wilkinson, (G.) South Australia, its Advantages and its Resources; being a Description of that Colony and a Manual of Information for Emigrants. 8vo. cloth, $3 00. London.

Will's Outlines of the Course of Qualitative Analysis followed in the Giessen Laboratory, with a Preface, by Baron Liebig. 8vo. $1 75. London.

——— American edition. 12mo. cloth, 75 cents. Boston, 1847.

Willard, (Mrs. E.) A Treatise on the Motive Powers which produce the Circulation of the Blood. 12mo. cloth, 50 cents. New York.

——— Last Leaves of American History; comprising Histories of the Mexican War and California. 12mo. cloth, map, $1 00. New York, 1849.

——— Republic of America. 8vo. sheep, $1 50. New York, 1845.

Williams, (B.) Manual for Teaching Model Drawing from Solid Forms, the Models founded on those of M. Dupuis, combined with a Popular View of Perspective. 8vo. cloth, $5 00. London, 1843.

——— Practical Geodesy; comprising Chain Surveying and the Use of Surveying Instruments, together with Trigonometrical, Colonial, Mining, and Maritime Surveying, also Levelling and Hill Drawing, &c. 8vo. cloth, plates, $3 75. London, 1842.

——— (Capt.) Description of Wrought Iron Roofs erected over two Building Slips in the Royal Dockyard at Pembroke. (Papers, R. E. vol. 9, 4to.) London.

——— (C. J.) Principles of Medicine and Pathology, by Clymer. 8vo. sheep, $2 00. Philadelphia.

——— On Respiratory Organs, by Clymer. 8vo. sheep, $2 50. Philadelphia.

——— (C. W.) Treatise on the Combustion of Coal. 4to. cloth, part 1, $3 25. London.

——— (D. E.) Life and Correspondence of Sir Thomas Lawrence, with Portrait. 2 vols. 8vo. cloth, $3 25. London, 1831.

——— (E.) The Statesman's Manual; Presidents' Messages, Inaugural, Annual, and Special, from 1789 to 1846. 2 vols. 8vo. cloth, $5 00. New York, 1848.

——— (G.) Historical and Descriptive Memoir of the Town and Environs of Jerusalem, accompanied by a map printed on Canvas, being a copy of the Ordnance Map. 8vo. cloth, $2 50. London, 1849.

——— The Holy City; Historical and Topographical Notices of Jerusalem. Second edition, with considerable additions, including the Architectural History of the Holy Sepulchre, by Prof. Willis, Plan of the Town and Environs of Jerusalem. 2 vols. 8vo. cloth, $13 50. London, 1849.

——— (J.) History of the Native Bengal Infantry. 8vo. cloth, $3 75. London.

——— Natural History of Minerals. 2 vols. 8vo. cloth, $4 25. London.

——— (J. F.) Account of Inventions and Discoveries. 2 vols. 8vo. cloth, $7 25. Lond.

Williams, (J. M.) The Elements of Euclid, containing the First Six Books. 12mo. cloth, $1 75. London.

—— (M.) An Elementary Grammar of the Sanskrit Language. 8vo. cloth, $4 00. Lond.

—— (R. F.) Sketch of the Art of Sculpture in Wood. 8vo. cloth, $1 50. London.

—— (S. W.) A Survey of the Geography, Government, Education, Social Life, Arts, Religion, &c. of the Chinese Empire and its Inhabitants, with a new Map of the Empire, and numerous illustrations. 2 vols. 12mo. half bound, gilt top, $3 00. New York, 1848.

—— (W. D.) History of Maine. 2 vols. 8vo. sheep, $5 00. Hallowell, Me.

—— (W. J.) Steam Manual for the British Navy. 12mo. cloth, 75 cents. London.

—— Biography of American Physicians. 8vo. cloth, $3 00. Philadelphia.

Willis, (N. P.) Complete Works. 1 vol. royal 8vo. cloth, $5 00. New York.

—— Prose Works. 8vo. cloth, $3 00. Phila.

—— Poems 1 vol. 8vo. $2 00. New York.

—— Poems, illustrated with engravings. 8vo. cloth gilt, $5 00; mor. $7 00. Phila.

—— Dashes at Life with a Free Pencil. 3 vols. 12mo. cloth, $2 25. London.

—— Rural Letters and other Records of Thought at Leisure. 12mo. cloth, $1 25. New York, 1849.

—— People I have Met. 12mo. cloth, $1 25. New York, 1850.

—— (R.) Urinary Diseases and their Treatment. 8vo. sheep, $1 50. Phila. 1839.

—— (Rev. R.) Architectural History of the Church of the Holy Sepulchre at Jerusalem. 8vo. cloth, plates, $2 50. Lond. 1849.

—— (R.) Principles of Mechanism. 8vo. cloth, $4 50. London.

Willmott, (R. A.) Lives of the English Sacred Poets. 2 vols. 12mo. cloth, $3 00. London.

—— Gems of Epistolary Correspondence, with Introductory and Biographical Notes. Cr. 8vo. cloth, $1 25. London, 1846.

—— Pictures of Christian Life. 12mo. cloth, 75 cents. London, 1841.

—— Life of Bishop Jeremy Taylor, his Predecessors, Contemporaries, and Successors. 12mo. half calf, neat, $1 37. London, 1848.

Willson, (M.) American History, comprising Historical Sketches of the Indian Tribes, American Antiquities, History of the United States, History of the British Provinces, History of Mexico, and History of Texas. 8vo. cloth, wood-cuts, $2 00. New York, 1847.

—— (H.) Use of a Box of Colors. Imp. 8vo. $7 25. London.

Wilme, (B. P.) Hand-Book for Mapping, Engineering, and Architectural Drawing. Plates, 4to. half bound, $7 50. London.

—— (B.) Manual of Writing and Printing Characters, Ancient and Modern. 4to. cloth, $3 75. London.

Wilmot, (T. E.) View of the Losses, &c. of American Loyalists. 8vo. cloth, $2 75. London.

Wilson, (A.) Natural History of Birds. 4to. bds. with 135 figures, $3 00. Edinburgh, 1839.

—— American Ornithology. 3 vols. 8vo. colored plates, $25 00. London.

—— and **Bonaparte's** American Ornithology. Edited by Robert Jameson. 4 vols. 12mo. cloth, $3 00. Edin. 1838.

—— (E.) Human Anatomy. 8vo. sheep, $3 25. Philadelphia.

—— Practical Treatise on Diseases of the Skin, &c. 12mo. cloth, $1 00. New York.

—— (H.) Sanskrit and English Dictionary. 4to. cloth, $34 00. London.

—— An Introduction to the Grammar of the Sanskrit Language. 8vo. bds. $4 75. Lond.

—— (Jas.) Natural History of Birds. 4to. cloth, $3 75. London.

—— Natural History of Fishes. 4to. cloth, $2 75. London.

—— Quadrupeds and Whales. 4to. $3 75. London.

—— Treatise on Insects. 4to. cloth, $4 50. London.

—— (J.) Treatise on Grammatical Punctuation. 12mo. cloth, 75 cents. Lond. 1846.

—— (J. M.) Historical and Traditional Tales of the Scottish Border. 2 vols. 8vo. $5 00. New York, 1848.

—— (Josh.) French and English Dictionary. Imp. 8vo. cloth, $7 00. London, 1846.

—— (Prof.) The Foresters; a Tale. 12mo. cloth, 75 cents. New York.

—— Critical and Miscellaneous Essays. 3 vols. 12mo. cloth, $3 00. Phila. 1842.

—— Another edition. 8vo. cloth, portrait, $1 00. Phila. 1848.

—— Rereations of Christopher North. 3 vols. post 8vo. $9 50. Edinburgh.

—— (R.) A System of Plane and Spherical Trigonometry, to which is added a Treatise on Logarithms. 8vo. cloth, $3 00. Lond.

Wilton, (Countess of.) Art of Needle-Work from the earliest Ages, including some Notices of the Ancient Historical Tapestries. 12mo. cloth, $1 50. London, 1844.

Wincklemann, (John.) The History of Ancient Art. Translated by G. H. Lodge. Vol. 2. imp. 8vo. cloth, (Greek Art.) Illustrated with 18 fine engravings, chiefly in outline, $3 50. Boston, 1849.

Windham and Huskisson's Speeches. 8vo. sheep, $2 00. Phila.

Windus, (T.) On the Portland Vase. Roy. 4to. cloth, $12 00. London.

Winer, (W. C.) Idioms of the New Testament. 8vo. cloth, $3 00. New York.

—— (G. B.) Lexicon Manuale Hebraicum et Chaldaicum in veteris testamenti libros ordine etymologico descriptive. 8vo. cloth, $6 00. New York.

Winkle's Architectural and Picturesque Illustrations of the Cathedral Churches of England and Wales. 3 vols. royal 8vo. cloth, 150 steel engravings, $13 50. Lond.

Winslow, (Rev. B. W.) Sermons and Poetical Remains. Edited by Bishop Doane. 8vo. cloth, $1 50. New York.

Wirt, (W.) Life of Patrick Henry. 8vo. sheep, $1 75. Philadelphia.

Wise, (H.) Analysis of One Hundred Voyages to and from India, &c. Royal 8vo. cloth, $4 25. London.

Wishaw, (Francis.) The Railways of Great Britain and Ireland practically described and illustrated. Second edition, with additions. Plates, 4to. cloth, $10 00. Lond.

Wistar, (C.) Anatomy, with Notes, by Horner. 2 vols. 8vo. sheep, $6 00. Philadelphia, 1842.

Witham, (H.) Observations on Fossil Vegetables. 4to. cloth, $6 50. London.

Withers, (W.) The Acacia Tree, Robinia Pseudo Acacia; its Growth, Qualities, and Uses, with Observations on Planting, Manuring, and Pruning. 8vo. cloth, $6 00. Lond. 1842.

Wittich, (W.) Curiosities of Physical Geography. 2 vols. 8vo. cloth, $1 00. Lond.

Wodarch, (Chas.) Introduction to Conchology. Post 8vo. cloth, colored plates, $4 25. London.

Wolff's, (Dr.) Narrative of a Mission to Bokhara in 1843–45, to ascertain the Fate of Colonel Stoddart and Captain Connolly. 8vo. cloth, wood-cuts, $2 00. New York.

Wolsey, (Cardinal.) Life of, by John Galt. 12mo. cloth, portrait, 87 cents. Lond.

Women of the Bible; delineated in a Series of Sketches of Remarkable Females mentioned in the Holy Scriptures. Edited by J. M. Wainwright, D. D. Imp. 8vo. with 18 steel engravings, $7 00; mor. elegant, $10 00; with colored plates, mor. elegant, $15 00. New York.

Women of the Old and New Testament; a Series of Portraits, with Characteristic Descriptions. Edited by W. B. Sprague, D. D. Imp. 8vo. bds. illustrated with 18 fine engravings, $7 00; mor. elegant, $10 00; colored, $15 00. New York, 1850.

Wonderful Inventions. A History of, illustrated with numerous engravings on wood. 12mo. cloth, $1 50. Lond. 1849.

——— American edition. 12mo. paper, 75 cents; cloth, $1 00. New York, 1849.

Wood, (G. B.) Practice of Medicine. 2 vols. 8vo. sheep, $7 00. Phila. 1849.

——— (H.) Designs for Furniture and Decoration. Oblong 4to. $18 00; colored, $36 00. London, 1845.

——— Designs for Chairs. Oblong folio, colored plates, $7 50. London.

——— Designs for Mounting Berlin Needle-Work. Folio, $6 00. London.

——— (Jas.) Elements of Optics. 8vo. cloth, $1 75. London.

——— Elements of Algebra. 8vo. bds. $1 50.

——— Personal Narrative of a Journey to the Sources of the River Oxus. 8vo. map, $1 00. London, 1841.

——— (J. G.) Footsteps to Drawing. Royal 4to. cloth, $6 50. London.

Wood, (M. A.) Letters of Royal and Illustrious Ladies of Great Britain. 3 vols. post 8vo. cloth, $5 50. London, 1848.

——— (N.) A Practical Treatise on Railroads. 8vo. cloth, wood-cuts, $2 50. Lond. 1838.

——— (W.) Catalogue of Insects. 8vo. cloth, $19 00; colored, $50 00. London, 1839.

——— Catalogue of Shells. 2 vols. 8vo. cloth, $13 00; colored, $42 00. Lond. 1828.

——— (W.) General Conchology. Royal 8vo. cloth, $21 00. London.

——— Zoography; or, the Beauties of Nature Displayed, &c. 3 vols. 8vo. cloth, $22 00. London, 1807–11.

——— General Conchology; or, a Description of Shells arranged according to the Linnæan System, and illustrated with 60 plates. 8vo. $8 00. London.

——— (W. M.) Wandering Sketches of People and Things in South America, Polynesia, California, and other places visited during a Cruise on board of the U. S. Ships Levant, Portsmouth, and Savannah. 12mo. cloth, $1 00. Philadelphia, 1849.

——— Architectural Antiquities and Ruins of Palmyra and Balbec. 2 vols. in 1, imp. 8vo. containing 110 fine copperplate engravings, some very large and folding, half mor. uncut, $18 00. London, 1827.

——— and **Bache's** Dispensatory of the United States. 8vo. sheep, $6 00. Philadelphia, 1849.

——— Suppressed History of Adams' Administration. Edited by J. H. Sherburne. 12mo. cloth, $1 25. Philadelphia.

Woodbridge and Willard's Geography and Atlas of colored maps, $2 25. Hartford.

Woodcroft, (B.) A Sketch of the Origin and Progress of Steam Navigation from Authentic Documents. 4to. half bound, plates, $3 50. London.

Woodfall's Letters of Junius. 8vo. cloth, $2 00. Middleboro', 1848.

Woodhouse, (R.) Treatise on Astronomy. 2 vols 8vo. cloth, $9 00. Lond.

——— Physical Astronomy. 8vo. cloth, $5 50. London.

Woodville, (W.) Medical Botany enlarged, by Sir W. J. Hooker. 5 vols. small 4to. half bound, 310 plates, carefully colored after Nature, $31 50. London, 1832.

Woodward, (Charles.) Familiar Introduction to the Study of Polarized Light, with a Description of and Instructions for using the Table and Hydro-Oxygen Polariscope and Microscope. Engravings, 8vo. cloth, $1 00. London, 1848.

Woolhouse, (W. S.) Essay on Musical Intervals and Harmonies. 12mo. cloth, $1 50. London.

Woolsey, (T. D.) Alcestis of Euripides. 12mo. cloth, 56 cents. Boston.

——— Antigone of Sophocles. 12mo. cloth, 56 cents. Boston.

——— Electra of Sophocles. 12mo. cloth, 56 cents. Boston.

——— Prometheus of Æschylus. 12mo. cloth, 56 cents. Boston.

Worcester, (J. E.) An Historical Atlas, containing a Series of Charts on History, Mythology, Chronology, and Biography. Folio, half bound, $1 50. Boston, 1833.

—— (Marquis of.) Century of Inventions, by Partington. 12mo. cloth, $2 25. London.

—— On Cutaneous Diseases. 8vo. sheep, $3 50. New York.

—— (J. E.) Dictionary of the English Language. 8vo. sheep, $3 50; or Library edition, sheep, $5 00. Boston, 1846.

Words of Wisdom and Truth. Illuminated in colors and gold. Small 4to. bds. $1 25. London.

Wordsworth, (Christopher.) On the Canon of the Scriptures of the Old and New Testaments, and on the Apocrypha; being the Hulsean Lectures for 1847. 8vo. cloth, $3 25. London, 1848.

—— Ancient Writings on Walls, &c. of Pompeii. 8vo. cloth, $1 50. London.

—— Elements of Instruction concerning the Church and the Anglican Branch of it. 12mo. cloth, $1 00. London, 1849.

—— Greece, Pictorial, Descriptive, and Historical, with 350 engravings on wood and 28 on steel. Royal 8vo. cloth, $8 00. London, 1844.

—— (W.) Poetical Works, complete in one vol. royal 8vo. cloth, portrait and vignette, $6 00; mor. extra, $10 00. Lond. 1847.

—— Poetical Works. 7 vols. 12mo. cloth, $8 75; mor. gilt edges, $20 00. Lond. 1846.

—— Poetical Works. Edited by Professor Reed. 1 vol. royal 8vo. $4 00. Phila.

Wornum, (Ralph.) A Sketch of the History of Painting, Ancient and Modern, showing its gradual and various Development, from the earliest ages to the present time. 18mo. cloth, $1 00. London, 1847.

Wotton, (Sir H.) and **Raleigh,** (Sir W.) Poems. Edited by J. Hannah. 12mo. cloth, $1 50. London.

Wrangell, (Von.) Narrative of an Expedition to the Polar Seas in 1820 to 1823. New edition, by Sabine. Post 8vo. cloth, map, $1 75. London, 1844.

Wraxall, (Sir N. W.) Historical Memoirs of my own Time. 8vo. cloth, $1 25. Philadelphia, 1845.

—— Posthumous Memoirs of his own Time. 8vo. cloth, $1 25. Phila. 1845.

Wray's Practical Sugar Planter; a complete Account of the Manufacture of the Sugar Cane according to the latest and most improved Processes. 8vo. cloth, with numerous engravings, $6 00. London, 1848.

Wreck of the Glide, with Recollections of the Feejees, and of Wallis Island, from the MSS. of Mr. James Oliver. 12mo. 63 cents. New York.

Wright, (Lieut. H.) A Brief Practical Treatise on Mortars, with an Account of the Processes employed at the Public Works in Boston Harbor. 12mo. cloth, $1 00. Boston, 1845.

—— and **Halliwell's** Reliquæ Antiquæ. Scraps from Ancient Manuscripts, illustrating chiefly Early English Literature and the English Language. 2 vols. 8vo. $6 50. London, 1841.

Wright, (Thos.) Early Mysteries, and other Latin Poems of the Twelfth and Thirteenth Centuries. 8vo. cloth, $3 25. Lond. 1838.

—— Early English Poetry. Printed in black Letter. 4 vols. square 16mo. half mor. $6 00. London, 1836.

—— Literature, Popular Superstitions, and History of England, in the Middle Ages. 2 vols. 8vo. cloth, $2 00. London, 1846.

—— England under the House of Hanover, its History and Condition during the Reigns of the three Georges. Illustrated from the Caricatures and Satires of the day, with numerous illustrations executed by F. W. Fairholt. Second edition, 2 vols. 8vo. cloth, $9 00. London, 1848.

—— St. Patrick's Purgatory; an Essay on the Legends of Purgatory, Hell, and Paradise. 12mo. cloth, $1 50. London, 1844.

—— (J. M. F.) The Principia of Newton, with Notes, Examples, and Deductions, containing all that is Read at the University of Cambridge. 8vo. bds. $2 50. Cambridge, 1830.

Wyatt, (M. D.) Specimens of the Geometrical Mosaic of the Middle Ages, with a brief Historical Notice of the Art, founded on Papers read before the Royal Institute of British Architects, Royal Society of Arts, &c. 21 magnificently illuminated plates, folio, $15 00. London, 1849.

—— (Thos.) Natural History. 8vo. 49 colored plates, $7 00. Philadelphia.

—— Manual of Conchology, according to the System laid down by Lamarck. 8vo. cloth, 36 plates, $2 75; colored, $8 00. New York.

—— Memoirs of the Generals, Commodores, and other Commanders who distinguished themselves in the American Army and Navy during the Wars of the Revolution and 1812. Royal 8vo. cloth, 82 engravings on steel, $2 50. Philadelphia, 1848.

Wycherly, Congreve, Vanburgh, and Farquhar's Dramatic Works, with Biographical Notice, by Leigh Hunt, with portrait and vignette. Royal 8vo. cloth, $4 00; calf, m. e. $6 00. London, 1840.

Wycliffe, (John.) Translation of the New Testament, by Baber. 4to. cloth, $6 50. London, 1810.

Wyld's Popular Atlas of the World. Illustrated by Geographical and Statistical Descriptions. 48 maps, $12 00; colored, $18 00. London, 1847–48.

Xenophon. Opera Gr. et Lat. 10 vols. 12mo. bds. $27 00; L. P. $40 00. London

—— Opera omnia Græce. 6 vols. square 12mo. paper, $2 00. Leipsic.

—— Translated by various Authors. 1 thick vol. 8vo. cloth, $3 00. New York, 1849.

—— Anabasis. Edited by Owen. 12mo. half bound, $1 25. New York.

—— Cyropœdia. Edited by Owen. 12mo. half bound, $1 50. New York.

—— Memorabilia of Socrates. 12mo. cloth, $1 00. Philadelphia.

—— Works complete. Translated by various hands. 8vo. cloth, $2 50. New York, 1849.

Ximenes, (Cardinal.) Life of, by Barrett. 8vo. cloth, $2 75. London.

Yarrell, (W.) History of British Birds. Illustrated with wood-cuts of each Species. 3 vols. 8vo. cloth, $18 00. Lond. 1840.

—— History of British Fishes. Illustrated by 400 beautiful wood-cuts. 2 vols. 8vo. $18 00. London, 1840.

—— Growth of Salmon in Fresh Water. Folio, cloth, $3 75. London.

Yates, (Jas.) The Art of Weaving among the Ancients. 8vo. cloth, 16 plates, $7 50. London, 1843.

—— Modern History and Condition of Egypt, exhibited in a Personal Narrative of a Residence and Travels in that Country, with a History of Mohammed Ali, from 1801 to 1843; interspersed with Illustrations of Scripture History. 2 vols. 8vo. 15 plates, cloth, $3 75. (Pub. at $8 00.) London, 1843.

—— Account of New Zealand. Post 8vo. $3 25. London.

—— Essays on the Currency and Circulation. 8vo. cloth, $1 50. London.

Year-Book of Facts in Science and Art for 1848, exhibiting the most important Discoveries during the Year. Published annually, with portrait and engravings. 12mo. cloth, $1 50. London.

Yolland, (Capt.) Extract of a Paper on a Reflecting Level invented by Lieut. Col. Burel. Translated from the "Memorial du Genie." (Papers, R. E. vol. 2, 4to.) London.

York, (J. O.) Tables on the Weight of Wrought Iron. 12mo. $1 50. London.

Yosy's Costume of Switzerland. 50 plates, beautifully colored, 2 vols. super-royal 8vo. gilt cloth, $8 50. 1815.

Youatt, (W.) Stock Raiser's Manual. 8vo. cloth, $2 50. Philadelphia.

—— On the Horse. Edited by Skinner, $1 75. Philadelphia.

—— On the Dog, by Lewis. 8vo. $1 50. Philadelphia.

—— and **Clater's** Cattle Doctor. 8vo. paper, 50 cents. Philadelphia.

—— The Complete Grazier; or, Farmer's and Cattle-Breeder's and Dealer's Assistant. 8vo. cloth, illustrated with 123 engravings, $5 00. London.

—— The Pig; a Treatise on the Breed, Management, Feeding, and Medical Treatment of Swine. 12mo. cloth, wood-cuts, 75 cents. Philadelphia, 1847.

Young American's Primer. Illustrated with some hundreds of wood-cuts. 12mo. half cloth, 25 cents. New York, 1849.

Young Brewer's Monitor. 8vo. cloth, $1 75. London.

Young, (A.) Natural History and Habits of the Salmon. 12mo. cloth, 50 cents. Lond.

—— and **Brisbane**, (J.) Nautical Dictionary. Post 8vo. cloth, $3 25. Lond.

—— (A. W.) First Lessons in Civil Government. 12mo. cloth, 67 cents. New York.

—— Science of Government. 12mo. sheep, 75 cents. Buffalo.

Young, (E.) The Complaint; or, Night Thoughts on Life, Death, and Immortality. Royal 18mo. mor. gilt, gilt leaves, $1 75. London, 1848.

—— Poems, with Memoir, by Mitford. 2 vols. 12mo. cloth, $3 00. Pickering.

—— Night Thoughts. 18mo. cloth, 38 cents. New York.

—— (J.) Designs for Shop Fronts, Porticoes, &c. 4to. cloth, $3 75. London.

—— Lectures on Intellectual Philosophy. 8vo. $2 50. London.

—— (J. R.) Cubic and Biquadratic Equations. 12mo. cloth, $1 75. London.

—— Algebra. 8vo. sheep, $1 50. Phila.

—— Analytical Geometry. 8vo. sheep, $1 50.

—— Geometry. 8vo. sheep, $1 50. Phila.

—— Mathematical Tables. 12mo. sheep, $1 13. Phila.

—— Mechanics. 8vo. sheep, $1 50. Phila.

—— Plane and Spherical Trigonometry. 8vo. sheep, $1 50. Philadelphia.

—— On the Differential Calculus. 8vo. cloth, $3 75. London.

—— On the Integral Calculus. 12mo. cloth, $2 75. London.

—— Mathematical Dissertations. 8vo. cloth, $3 00. London.

—— Theory and Solution of Algebraic Equations. 8vo. cloth, $4 50. London.

—— (S.) Cotton Spinner's and Mechanic's Arithmetic. 12mo. $1 38. London.

—— (Thos.) Discoveries in Hieroglyphical Literature. 8vo. cloth, $2 25. Lond.

—— Residence on the Mosquito Shore, 1839–41. 12mo. cloth, $1 38. Lond.

—— (Alex.) Chronicles of the First Planters of the Colony of the Massachusetts Bay in New England, from 1623 to 1635. 8vo. cloth, portrait, $2 50. Boston, 1846.

—— Chronicles of the Pilgrim Fathers of the Colony of New Plymouth in New England, from 1602 to 1623, &c. 8vo. cloth, portrait, $2 50. Boston, 1844.

—— (T.) Lectures on Natural Philosophy. 2 vols. 8vo. cloth, $5 00. London.

—— History of Mexico. 8vo. cloth, $2 50. New York.

Youth's Hand-Book of Entertaining Knowledge; in a Series of Familiar Conversations on the most Interesting Productions of Nature and Art, &c. By a Lady. 2 vols. post 8vo. cloth, $1 50. London, 1844.

Yriarte's Literary Fables. Translated by Andrews. 8vo. cloth, $1 75. London.

—— Fabulas Literarias a Josse. Post 8vo. paper, $2 25. London.

—— Compendio de la Historia de Espana. 12mo. $1 75. London.

Yule, (Major.) Mode of Constructing a Breakwater and of Stopping the Movement of Shingle on the Sea-Coast. (Papers, R. E. vol. 8, 4to.) London.

Zach, (Le Baron de.) Correspondance Astronomique et Geographique. 14 vol. in-8, broche, $63 00. Paris.

Zastrow, (A. V.) Histoire de la Fortification Permanente, traduite par Neuens. 8vo. paper, with atlas, $6 00. Liege, 1846.

Zeni et Deshays. Renseignements sur le material de l'artillerie navale de la Grande-Bretagne et les fabrications qui s'y rattachent, recueillis en 1835. 4to. avec atlas en folio, paper, $7 50. Paris, 1840.

Ziegler's Royal Lodges of Windsor Park. Folio, $9 50; colored plates, $19 00. Lond.

Zimmerman, (J. G.) On Solitude. 12mo. cloth, 75 cents. New York.

——— Countries about the Caspian and Aral Seas. 8vo. cloth, $2 25. London.

Zornlin, (R. M.) Recreations in Geology. 12mo. cloth, $1 50. London, 1841.

——— Recreations in Hydrology. 12mo. cloth, $1 75. London.

——— What is a Voltaic Battery? 18mo. cloth, gilt, 75 cents. London.

Zornlin, (R. M.) Physical Geography. 12mo. cloth, $1 75. London, 1849.

Zschokke, (Heinriche.) The Gold-Makers' Village. 38 cents. New York.

——— Tales. Translated by Park Godwin. 12mo. $1 00. New York, 1845.

——— Incidents of Social Life amid the European Alps. Translated. 12mo. cloth, $1 00. New York.

——— (H.) Hours of Meditation and Devotional Reflection. Translated by J. D. Haas. 12mo. cloth, $1 50. London, 1847.

——— Autobiography of. 8vo. cloth, $1 50. London.

Zumpt, (Prof.) Grammar of the Latin Language. Translated by Leonhard Schmitz, with numerous additions, by the Author. 8vo. cloth, $2 50. London, 1845.

——— American edition. 12mo. cloth, 88 cents. New York.

ADDENDA.

Account of the Demolition of the Glaciere Bastion at Quebec in 1828. (Papers, R. E. vol. 2, 4to.) London.

Adalbert, (Prince of Prussia.) Travels of, in the South of Europe and in Brazil, with a Voyage up the Amazon and the Xingu. Translated by Sir R. H. Schomburgh and J. G. Taylor. Plates, 2 vols. 8vo. cloth, $7 50. London, 1849.

Adams' Illustrated Descriptive Guide to the Watering Places of England and Companion to the Coast. By E. L. Blanchard. 12mo. cloth, map and cuts, 50 cents. Lond. 1848.

Adamson, (Rev. J. L.) Scripture Metaphors. 8vo. cloth. Edinburgh, 1849.

Æschylus. The Prometheus and Agamemnon of. Translated into English Verse, by H. H. Herbert. 12mo. cloth, 75 cents. Cambridge, 1849.

Æsthetic Papers. Edited by E. P. Peabody. 8vo. paper, $1 25. (To be published occasionally.) Boston, 1849.

Aguilar, (G.) Home Influence; a Tale for Mothers and Daughters, with Memoir of the Author. 12mo. paper, 75 cents; cloth, $1 00. New York, 1849.

Airy, (G. B.) Six Lectures on Astronomy, delivered at Ipswich. 8vo. cloth, illustrated with steel engravings, $3 25. Lond. 1849.

Akenside, (M.) The Pleasures of Imagination. 12mo. bds. 75 cents. Lond. 1825.

Alderson, (Capt.) Memorandum on Paving Stables. (Papers, R. E. Vol. 2, 4to.) London.

Alderson, (Col.) Report on the Manchester, Cheshire, Staffordshire, and the South Union Lines of Railway. (Papers, R. E. vol. 2, 4to.) London.

——— (Lieut. Col.) Notes on Acre and some of the Coast Defences of Syria. (Papers, R. E. vol. 6, 4to.) London.

——— Additional Notes on Acre. (Papers, R. E. vol. 7, 4to.) London.

——— On Horizontal Loopholes. (Papers, R. E. vol. 8, 4to.) London.

——— On Siege Gun and Mortar Platforms. (Papers, R. E. vol. 8, 4to.) London.

Alexander, (Capt.) Description of a Bomb-Proof erected at Woolwich, with detailed Experiments as to the Effects produced on it by the Fire of Artillery. (Papers, R. E. vol. 1, 4to.) London.

——— (Sir Jas. E.) L'Acadie; or, Seven Years' Explorations in British America. 2 vols. post 8vo. cloth, $6 50. London, 1849.

Allen, (J.) An Inquiry into the Rise and Growth of the Royal Prerogative, &c. New edition, 8vo. cloth, $3 50. London, 1849.

American Historical and Literary Curiosities; consisting of fac-similes of Original Documents relating to the events of the Revolution, &c., &c., with a variety of Relics, Antiquities, and Modern Autographs, collected and edited by J. J. Smith and J. F. Watson. Fourth edition, 4to. half mor. gilt edges. $6. N. York, 1850.

"A never failing source of amusement to the drawing-room circle."—HOME JOURNAL.

"A volume of curiosities, not of Literature only, but of American History."—COMMERCIAL ADVERTISER.

American Railroads formed on a Foundation of Piles. (Papers, R. E. vol. 6, 4to.) Lond.

Americus Vespucius. Life and Voyages of, by C. E. Lester and A. Foster. 8vo. cloth, $2 00. New York.

Ampere, (M. J. J.) La Grece, Rome, et Dante, etudes Litteraires d'apres nature. 12mo. paper, $1 00. Paris.

Andersen, (H. C.) Contes pour les enfans Traduits du Danois, par V. Caralp. Cr. 8vo. cloth gilt, and gilt edges, plates, $2 75. Paris.

Andre, (L'Abbe.) Cours alphabetique et Methodique de droit canon mis en rapport avec le droit civil, ecclesiastique, ancien et moderne. 2 vols. royal 8vo. $4 50. Migne, 1845.

Animal Biography; consisting of Narratives and Anecdotes illustrative of the Habits, Dispositions, Instinct, and Sagacity of the various Tribes of Animals. 8vo. bds. $1 50. London, 1840.

Anthon, (Chas.) A System of Ancient and Mediæval Geography for Schools and Colleges. 8vo. cloth, $1 50. New York, 1850.

Antoine. Hotel des Monnaies de Paris. Plans des divers etages et coupe de l'Hotel des Monnaies a Paris. Un cahier grand in folio, de 12 planches grand in folio, with texte, $3 50.

Arago's Scientific Notices of Comets in general, and in particular of the Comet of 1832, whose Revolution is of Six Years and Three Quarters Duration. 12mo. cloth, $1 00. London, 1833

——— Popular Lectures on Astronomy. Translated, with Notes, by W. K. Kelly. Royal 8vo. paper, illustrated with numerous woodcuts, 63 cents. London.

Architecture of the Middle Ages in Italy, by E. Cresey and G. L. Taylor. 4to. $8 00. London.

Aristarchus; or, the Principles of Composition, containing a Methodical Arrangement of the Improprieties frequent in Writing and Conversation, &c. 8vo. cloth, $1 25. London, 1822.

Art, (The,) of Sailmaking as Practiced in the Royal Navy, and according to the most approved Methods in the Merchant Service. 8vo. cloth, $2 75. London, 1843.

Arminius, (James.) Memoirs of, by Rev. N. Bangs. 12mo. cloth, 50 cents. New York, 1844.

Armstrong, (John.) Lectures on the Morbid Anatomy, Nature, &c. of Acute and Chronic Diseases. 8vo. sheep, $2 75. Philadelphia, 1837.

Arnold, (Thos.) Life and Correspondence, by A. P. Stanley. 8vo. cloth, $2 00. New York.

Ashley, (A.) The Art of Etching on Copper and Steel. Illustrated with 14 etchings by the Author, elegantly bound in a cover designed by Owen Jones, $3 25. Lond. 1849.

Astronomy, (Encyclopædia of,) being the Treatises from the Encyclopædia Metropolitana. 4to. $6 00. London.

Atlas of Physical Geography, constructed by Augustus Petermann, with descriptive letterpress, embracing a general view of the Physical Phenomena of the Globe, by Rev. Thomas Milner. 4to. cloth, $5 00. Lond. 1849.

Avant-Postes de cavalerie legere par de Brack; suivi du Manual du service de la Cavalerie, par le Compte de la Roche-Amyon. 12mo. cartonne, $1 50. 1844.

Avedichian Origines et Raison de la Liturgie Catholique en forme de Dictionnaire ou Nations Historiques et Descriptives, suivies de la Liturgie Armenienne; traduite en Francaise sur le texte Italien par J. B. E. Pascal. $2 50. Migne, 1844.

Aytown, (W. F.) Lays of the Scottish Cavaliers. Cr. 8vo. cloth gilt, $4 50. London, 1849.

Babbage, (C.) Tables of Logarithms of the Natural Numbers from 1 to 108,000. Fourth edition, 8vo. $1 75. London.

Babcock, (J. S.) Visions and Voices, with a Biographical Sketch of the Author. 12mo. cloth, portrait, $1 00. Hartford, 1849.

Bacon. Œuvres, edition Francis Riaux. 2 vols. 12mo. paper, $2 00. Paris.

Bailey, (P. J.) The Angel World and other Poems. 12mo. cloth. Boston, 1850.

——— (F.) Catalogue of Nine Thousand Fixed Stars. New edition, 4to. $20 00. Lond.

——— and **Lund's** Treatise on the Differential Calculus, designed for the Use of Students in the University. 8vo. $3 00. Lond.

Bainbrigge, (Capt.) Project of Defence. (Papers, R. E. vol. 9, 4to.) London.

Baird, (R.) History of the Albigenses, Vaudois, and Waldenses. 8vo. cloth, $2 00. Philadelphia.

Balfour, (J. H.) A Manual of Botany; being an Introduction to the Study of the Structure, Physiology, and Classification of Plants. Illustrated with wood-cuts. 12mo. cloth, $3 75. London, 1849.

Balmaine, (W. H.) Lessons on Chemistry for the Use of Schools, &c. $1 75.

Baltard. Vues des Monuments antiques et principales fabriques de Rome, dessinees d'apres nature par Baltard, gravees a l'aquatinte par Piringer. 1 vol. in 4 de 48 planches, $5 00. Paris.

Balzac, (H. de.) Œuvres. 8 vols. imp. 8vo. paper, $24 00. Bruxelles, 1837.

——— Louis Lambert, Seraphita. 12mo. paper, $1 00. Paris.

——— La Recherche de l'Absolu. 12mo. paper, $1 00. Paris.

——— Le Lis dans le Vallee. 12mo. paper, $1 00. Paris.

——— Histoire des Freize. 12mo. paper, $1 00.

——— Cesar Birotteau. 12mo. paper, $1 00.

——— Le Medecin de Campagne. 12mo. paper, $1 00. Paris.

——— La Peau de Chagrin. 12mo. paper, $1 00.

——— Le Pere Goriot. 12mo. paper, $1 00.

——— Physiologie du Mariage. 12mo. paper, $1 00. Paris.

Balzac, (H. de.) Eugenie Grandet. 12mo. paper, $1 00.

——— Scenes de la vie privee. 2 vols. 12mo. paper, $2 00.

——— Scenes de la vie de Province. 2 vols. 12mo. paper, $2 00.

——— Scenes de la vie Parisienne. 2 vols. 12mo. paper, $2 00.

——— Le Depute d'Arcis Scenes de la vie Politique. 2 vols. 12mo. paper, 63 cents. Bruxelles, 1848.

——— Le Vicaire des Ardennes. 2 vols. 12mo. paper, $1 00. Bruxelles, 1837.

Barante, (M. de.) Tableau de la Litterature Francaise au Dix-Huitieme siecle. 12mo. paper, $1 00. Paris, 1847.

Baretti. Dictionairio portatil Espanol-Ingles. 2 vols. 16mo. $1 25. Paris, 1848.

Barlow, (P. W.) On the Strain to which Lock Gates are subjected. (Trans. I. C. E. vol. 1, 4to.) London.

——— On the Force excited by Hydraulic Pressure in a Bramah Press, the Resisting Power of the Cylinder, and Rules for computing the Thickness of Metal for Presses of various Powers and Dimensions. (Trans. I. C. E. vol. 1, 4to.) London.

——— (P.) and **Herschel,** (Sir J. W.) Encyclopædia of Natural Philosophy, being a portion of the Encyclopædia Metropolitana. Illustrated with numerous engravings, 4to. $12 00. London.

——— (W. H.) Description to Diagrams for Facilitating the Construction of Oblique Arches. Large plate, 4to. $1 00. London.

——— (W.) Magnetical Advertisements; or, Diverse Pertinent Observations and approved Experiments concerning the Nature and Property of the Loadstone. A new edition, with Notes, by W. Sturgeon. 12mo. cloth, wood-cuts, $1 00. London, 1843.

Barrett, (A. C.) The Propositions in Mechanics and Hydrostatics which are required of Questionists not Candidates for Honors, with Illustrations and Examples. Cr. 8vo. cloth, $1 87. Cambridge, 1847.

Bartholomew, (A.) Specifications for Practical Architecture, $6 00. Lond.

Bartlett, (W. H.) The Nile Boat; or, Glimpses of the Land of Egypt. Royal 8vo. cloth, illustrated with 52 engravings drawn upon steel, with maps and wood-cuts, $3 50. London, 1849.

Barton, (Miss.) Selections from the Poems and Letters of Barnard Barton. 12mo. cloth, $3 00. London, 1849.

Bayard, (Chevalier.) Life of, by W. G. Simms. 12mo. cloth, $1 00. New York.

Beattie, (Dr. W.) Life and Times of Thos. Campbell, with an Introductory Letter, by Washington Irving, Esq. 2 vols. 12mo. cloth. New York, 1850.

Beatson, (Lieut.) Memoranda relative to the Reconstruction of certain portions of the Admiralty Sea-Wall at Haslar Beach, Portsmouth. (Papers, R. E. vol. 6, 4to.) Lond.

Beaudoux, (Mme. Cl.) La Science Maternelle ou Education morale et Intellectuelle des Junes Filles. 12mo. paper, $1 00. Paris, 1844.

Beaumarchais. Theatre precede d'une notice sur sa vie et ses ouvrages par M. Auger. 12mo. $1 00. Paris, 1846.

Beauties of the Court of Queen Victoria; comprising 14 portraits beautifully engraved. 4to. cloth, extra gilt, $6 00. Lond. 1850.

Beauvalet et Ch. **Normand.** Fragments d'Architecture, Sculpture, Peinture, Arabesques, etc. dans le style antique. 2 vol. in-folio, contenant 144 pl. representant plus de 700 sujets differents, $25 00. Paris.

Belcher, (Capt. Sir E.) Narrative of a Voyage round the World during the Years 1836–42; including Details of the Naval Operations in China. Map, &c. 2 vols. 8vo. cloth, $5 00. London, 1843.

Bell's Mechanism of the Hand and its Vital Endowments as evincing Design. 12mo. cloth, wood-cuts, 63 cents. New York.

Benjamin, (A.) The Architect; or, Practical House Carpenter. 4to. $4 00. Boston.

Bennett, (J.) Arcanum; comprising a concise Theory of Practicable Elementary and Definitive Geometry. 8vo. $1 50. Lond.

Beranger, (P. J. de.) Œuvres de mises dans un nouvel ordre et ornees de 40 gravures. 5 vols. 12mo. paper, $3 00. Brux. 1828.

Bernard, (Chas. de.) La Peau du Lion. 12mo. paper, 63 cents. Bruxelles.

Bethune, (Rev. G. W.) Essays, Orations, and Occasional Discourses. 12mo. cloth, $1 25. New York, 1849.

Beveridge, (Dr. W.) On the Thirty-Nine Articles. 8vo. cloth, $3 37. Oxford, 1846.

Biblical Reading-Book for Schools and Families, containing, with Illustrative Sketches in Sacred Biography, History, and Antiquities, a Life of Christ, &c. by the Author of the People's Dictionary of the Bible. 12mo. cloth, $1 25. London, 1849.

Bielfield, (C. F.) Gothic Ornaments drawn from examples executed in the Improved Papier Mache. 4to. $3 00. Lond.

Bigelow's Useful Arts considered in connection with the Applications of Science. 2 vols. 12mo. cloth, numerous wood-cuts, $1 50. New York.

Biley, (E.) Supplement to the Horæ Paulinæ of Archdeacon Paley. 8vo. cloth, $2 25. London, 1845.

Billings, (W.) Architectural Illustrations of the Temple Church. 31 plates, 4to. $8 00. London.

——— Illustrations of the Architectural Antiquities of the County of Durham, Ecclesiastical, Castellated, and Domestic. $8 00. Lond.

Billington, (J.) Architectural Director; being a Guide to Builders, Draughtsmen, Students, and Workmen. 8vo. cloth, plates, $3 00. London, 1834.

Biographie Impartiale des Representants du Peuple a l'Assemblee Nationale. 12mo. paper, $1 50. Paris, 1848.

Bird, (Golding.) Lectures on Electricity and Galvanism in their Physiological and Therapeutical Relations. 12mo. cloth, wood-cuts, $1 75. London, 1849

Blackburne, (E. L.) Sketches, Graphic and Descriptive, for a History of the Decorative Painting of the Middle Ages as applied to English Architecture. Illustrated by 24 plates, highly illuminated. Imp. 4to. cloth, $16 00. London.

Blacker, (W.) Catechism of Fly- aking, Angling, and Dyeing, comprising most essential information. 12mo. bound, gilt edges, with many engravings on steel, $3 75. Lond. 1843.

Blakey, (R.) Temporal Benefits of Christianity exemplified in its Influence on the Social, Intellectual, Civil, and Political Condition of Mankind. 8vo. cloth, $3 50. Lond. 1849.

Blaze, (Henri.) Poesies completes. 12mo. paper, $1 00.

Blunt, (E. M.) American Coast Pilot; containing Directions for the Principal Harbors, Capes, and Headlands on the Coasts of North and South America. 8vo. $4 00. New York.

Bloch, (M. E.) Plates to Bloch's Ichthyology. 2 vols. folio, 216 beautifully colored plates, $30 00. Paris, 1793–95.

Blondel et Lusson, Architectes. Marche Saint-Germain. Plans, coupes, elevations et details de construction du nouveau marche Saint-Germain, le plus vaste et le plus magnifique des marches de Paris, dessines et mesures par Blondel et Lusson, architectes. 1 cahier grand in-folio de 11 planches avec texte explicatif, $2 50. Paris.

Blyth, (J.) Outlines of Qualitative Chemical Analysis for the Use of Agricultural Students. $1 38.

Bobee, (A.) De la Royaute et de la Democratie ou coup d'œil. 8vo. 75 cents. Paris, 1849.

Bobierre, (A.) Traite de Manipulations Chimiques Description Raisonnee de Toutes les operations Chimiques et des appareils dont elles necessitent l'emploi avec planches gravees et figures intercalees dans le texte. 8vo. paper, $1 50. Paris, 1844.

Boccace. Le Decameron ou les dix Journees galantes, translatees par S. de Castres, nouvelle edition, par P. Christian. 12mo. broche, $1 00. Paris, 1846.

Boccaccio's Decameron; or, Ten Days' Entertainment. Translated from the Italian, with Remarks on the Life and Writings of the Author. 8vo. cloth, $1 50. London, 1845.

Boileau-Despreaux. Œuvres Poetiques de avec les notes de tous les commentateurs par M. Aime-Martin. 12mo paper, $1 00. Paris, 1845.

Boker, (G. H.) Anne Boleyn; a Tragedy, in Five Acts. 12mo. cloth, 75 cents. Philadelphia, 1850.

Bolton, (Major.) Account of the Dam constructed across the Waste Channel at Long Island, on the Rideau Canal, in 1836. (Papers, R. E. vol. 4, 4to.) London.

——— (R.) History of Westchester County, New York. 2 vols. 8vo. cloth, $4 00. New York, 1848.

Bomhoff, (D.) English and Dutch Dictionary. 2 vols. 12mo. paper, $4 50. Nimmegen, 1832.

Bonaparte, (Charles L.) American Ornithology; or, Natural History of Birds inhabiting the United States not given by Wilson, with figures drawn, engraved, and colored from Nature. 4 vols. folio, half mor. $25 00. Philadelphia, 1825.

——— (N.) Life of, by Sir Walter Scott. 8vo. cloth, $1 50. New York.

——— Life of, by William Hazlitt. 3 vols. 12mo. cloth, $3 00. Philadelphia.

——— Life of. Translated from the French of L'Ardeck. 2 vols. 8vo. cloth, $4 00. New York.

Bond, (J. B.) The Master Mariner's Guide in the Management of his Ship's Company, with respect to their Health, being designed to accompany a Ship's Medicine Chest 12mo. paper, 25 cents. Boston, 1847.

Bonnefoux, (Baron de.) Dictionnaire de Marine a voiles et a vapeur, publie vous le auspices de Ministre de la Marine Royal. 8vo. $3 00. Paris.

Book of Ruth, from the Holy Scriptures, with colored borders from illuminated MSS. by H. Noel Humphreys. Square 12mo. embossed, $6 00.

Bordwine, (J.) Memoirs of a Proposed New System of Permanent Fortification, $2 50. London.

Borguis, (M. J. A.) Traite elementaire de la composition des Machines. 10 vols. small 4to. calf, neat, numerous plates, $75 00. Paris, 1818–23.

Borrow, (George.) Lavengro; an Autobiography. 12mo. cloth. New York.

Borthwick, (M. A.) Memoir of the Use of Cast Iron in Piling, particularly at Brunswick Wharf, Blackwall. (Trans. I. C. E. vol. 1, 4to.) London.

Bossuet. Œuvres philosoph. ed. J. Simon. 12mo. paper, $1 00. Paris.

——— Discours sur l'histoire universelle. 12mo. paper, $1 00. Paris, 1846.

——— Oraisons Funebres precedes de l'essai sur l'oraisson funebre par M. Villemain, &c. 12mo. $1 00. Paris, 1845.

Bouchardat, (M. A.) Formulaire Veterinaire; contenant le mode d'action, l'emploi et les doses des medicaments simples et composes. 16mo. broche, $1 00. Paris, 1849.

Boucharlat's Elementary Treatise on Mechanics. Translated from the French, with additions and emendations, by Prof. E. H. Courtenay. 8vo. sheep, plates, $2 25. New York.

Bouchut, (E.) Traite des signes de la mort et des moyens de prevenir les enterrements prematures. 12mo. paper, $1 00. Paris, 1849.

Boudin, (J. Ch. M.) Statistique de l'etat sanitaire et de la mortalite des armees de terre et de mer. 8vo. broche, $1 00. Paris, 1846.

——— Etudes de Geologie Medicale sur la Phthisie Pulmonaire et la Fievre Typhoide. 8vo. broche, 75 cents. Paris, 1845.

——— Essai de Geographie Medicale, ou etudes sur les lois President a la distribution geographique des Maladies, &c. 8vo. broche, 75 cents. Paris, 1843.

Bouille, (R. de.) Histoire des ducs de Guise. Vols. 1 and 2, 8vo. paper, each $1 75. Paris, 1849.

Bouillet, (M. N.) Dictionnaire Universelle et de Geographie. Thick 8vo. paper, $6 00. pp. 1968. Paris, 1849.

Bowditch, (N.) New American Practical Navigator. 8vo. $4 00. New York.

Bowdler, (J.) Practical Christianity, in a Series of Essays. 18mo. cloth, 50 cents. Boston, 1845.

Bowen, (F.) Lowell Lectures on the Application of Metaphysical and Ethical Science to the Evidences of Religion. 8vo. cloth, $2 50. Boston, 1849.

Bowman's Introduction to Practical Chemistry, including Analysis. 12mo. $1 25. Philadelphia.

Brack, (F. de.) Avant-postes de cavalerie legere suivi du Manuel du Service de la cavalerie legere en campagne par le Comte de la Roche-Aymon. 12mo. broche, $1 50. Breda, 1834.

Bradford, (D.) The Wonders of the Heavens; being a Popular View of Astronomy, including a full illustration of the Mechanism of the Heavens. 4to. half bound, illustrated with engravings, $6 00. Boston, 1845.

Brainard, (J. G. C.) The Poems of, a new and Authentic Collection, with an original Memoir of his Life. 12mo. cloth, portrait and vignette, 63 cents. Hartford, 1842.

Bramah and Sons' Experiments on the Force required to Fracture and Crush Stones. (Trans. I. C. E. vol. 1, 4to.) London.

——— (F.) A Series of Experiments on the Strength of Cast Iron. (Trans. I. C. E. vol. 2, 4to.) London.

——— and **Woods**, (E.) On Certain Forms of Locomotive Engines. (Trans. I. C. E. vol. 2, 4to.) London.

——— Proof of an Earthenware Pipe for Lieut. Denison. (Papers, R. E. vol. 3, 4to.) Lond.

Brandon, (R. and J. A.) Analysis of Gothic Architecture. Illustrated by a Series of upwards of 700 examples of Doorways, Windows, &c. 2 vols. 4to. $28 00. London.

Brandreth, (Capt. H. R.) Notes on the Island of Ascension. (Papers, R. E. vol. 4, 4to.) London.

——— Memorandum relative to a System of Barracks for the West Indies. (Papers, R. E. vol. 2, 4to.) London.

Bremer, (Miss F.) Works. 12mo. cloth, each $1 Uniform with Irving's, Cooper's, and Miss Sedgwick's Works.

——— The Neighbors; a Tale of Everyday Life, illustrated with a Portrait, and Preface written expressly for this edition.

——— Home. 12mo. cloth, $1 New York.

Breviarum Romanum. 4 thick vols. 12mo. mor. gilt edges, $6 00. Dublin, 1844.

Brewster's Letters on Natural Magic, addressed to Sir W. Scott. 12mo. cloth, 50 cents. New York.

Bridgeman's Young Gardener's Assistant. 8vo. cloth, $2 00. New York.

Briffault, (E.) Paris dans l'Eau. Illustre par Bertall. 12mo. paper, $1 00. Paris, 1844.

Brigham, (A.) Observations on the Influence of Religion upon the Health and Physical Welfare of Mankind. 12mo. cloth, 75 cents. Boston, 1835.

Brillat-Savarin. Physiologie du Goût. 12mo. paper, $1 00.

Brinkley's Elements of Plane Astronomy. Edited by Luby. 8vo. $3 50. London.

British Association. Report of the Eighteenth Meeting of the British Association for the Advancement of Science. 8vo. bds. $2 75. London, 1849.

Bronson, (Prof.) Elocution; or, Mental and Vocal Philosophy, involving the Principles of Reading and Speaking. 8vo. half sheep, $1 00. Louisville, 1845.

Brown, (Capt. Thos.) The Taxidermist's Manual; or, the Art of Collecting, Preparing, and Preserving Objects of Natural History. 12mo. cloth, plates, $1 00. Lond. 1849.

——— (J. P.) The Turkish Evening Entertainments. The Wonders of Memorials, and the Rarities of Anecdotes. By Ahmed Ben Hemden, the Kiyaya. Translated from the Turkish, by J. P. Brown. 12mo. cloth, $1 00; cloth gilt, $1 75. New York.

——— (R.) Carpenter's Assistant; containing an Account of the various Orders of Architecture. 60 plates, $4 00. Worcester.

Browning, (Robert.) Poems. 2 vols. 12mo. cloth, $2 00. Boston, 1850.

Bruyere, (L.) Etudes relatives a l'Art des constructions, par L. Bruyere, ingenieur, inspecteur general des ponts et chaussees, directeur des travaux publics de Paris. Deux volumes grand in-folio renfermant 184 planches gravees au trait avec texte explicatif, $30 00. Paris.

——— Les Caracteres suivis de son discours a l'Academie Francaise. 12mo. paper, $1 00. Paris, 1846.

Bryan, (Michael.) Biographical and Critical Dictionary of Painters and Engravers, from the Revival of the Art under Cimabue, the alleged Discovery of Engraving by Finiguerra, to the present time, with the Ciphers, Monograms, and Marks used by each Engraver. New edition, revised, enlarged, and continued; comprising above 1000 additional Memoirs, and large accessories to the Lists of Pictures and Engravings. Also new plates of Ciphers and Monograms. By George Stanley. Imp. 8vo. cloth, $11 00. London, 1849.

Buck, (Rev. Chas.) A Theological Dictionary; containing Definitions of all Religious Terms, &c. New American edition, by Rev. G. Bush. 8vo. sheep, $1 00. Phila. 1847.

——— (G. W.) Practical and Theoretical Essay on Oblique Bridges. 12 large folding plates, 4to. cloth, $4 50. London.

Buckingham, (J. S.) America, Historical, Statistic, and Descriptive. 2 vols. 8vo. cloth, portrait and cuts, $3 50. New York, 1841.

——— France, Piedmont, Italy, Lombardy, the Tyrol, and Bavaria; an Autumnal Tour. Plates, 2 vols. 8vo. cloth, $4 00. Lond. 1849.

Buisson, (Eugene.) La Famille son influence sur le developpement et le progres de l'etre moral. 12mo. broche, 75 cents. Paris, 1849.

Bull, (W.) Account of the Wooden Bridge over the Calder at Mirfield, Yorkshire. (Trans. I. C. E. vol. 2, 4to.) London.

Bunyan, (John.) The Pilgrim's Progress. Illustrated with 300 engravings on Wood. 8vo. cloth. New York.

Burchell, (W. F.) Memoir of Thomas Burchell, Twenty-two Years a Missionary in Jamaica. 12mo. cloth, portrait, $1 31. London, 1849.

Burder, (Rev. G.) Memoirs of, by Rev. H. F. Burder. 12mo. cloth, 75 cents. Boston.

Burghman, (Capt.) Coffer Dam constructed in Devonport Dockyard. (Papers, R. E. vol. 8, 4to.) London.

Burne, (Peter.) The Teetotaler's Companion; or, a Plea for Temperance, &c. Royal 8vo. cloth, colored plates, $2 50. Lond. 1847.

Burnet, (Bishop.) History of his own Times, from the Restoration of Charles II. to the Treaty of Peace at Utrecht. New edition, with Historical and Biographical Notes. Portrait, imp. 8vo. cloth, $4 50. Lond.

Burr, (A.) Memoirs of, by M. L. Davis. 2 vols. 8vo. cloth, $3 75. New York.

Burton, (John Hill.) Political and Social Economy, its Practical Applications. Post 8vo. cloth, 75 cents. Edin. 1849.

Bury et Ribault. Modeles de marbrerie choisis en France et en Italie pour tout ce qui concerne l'interieur des habitations et des monuments civils et religieux. 12 livraisons, formant un vol. in-folio de 72 pl. dessinees par Bury, architecte, et gravees par Ribault; cartonne avec son texte, $12 50.

Bushnell, (Rev. H.) The Fathers of New England; an Oration before the New England Society. 12mo. paper, 13 cents; limp cloth, 25 cents. New York, 1850.

Butler, (Rev. R. A.) Lives of the Fathers, Martyrs, and Saints. 12 vols. 32mo. cloth, $5 00. New York.

Caffin, (Lieut.) A Description of a New Steam Apparatus for Drying Gunpowder. (Papers, R. E. vol. 4, 4to.) London.

Calhoun, (J. C.) Life and Speeches of. 8vo. cloth, $1 13. New York.

Callaway, (Thos.) A Dissertation upon Dislocations and Fractures of the Clavicle and Shoulder Joint. 8vo. cloth, plates, $2 00. London, 1849.

Campbell, (Thos.) Frederick the Great, his Court and Times, with an Introduction. 3 vols. 12mo. cloth, $2 00. Phila. 1843.

——— (John Lord.) The Lives of the Chief Justices of England from the Norman Conquest to Lord Mansfield. 2 vols. 8vo. cloth, $6 00. London, 1849.

Canova, (A.) Works of, engraved in outline, by H. Moses, with descriptions, by the Countess Albrizzi, and Memoir, by Count Cicognara. 3 vols. royal 8vo. half bound, 155 plates, $13 50. London.

Carpenter, (W. H.) Pictorial Notices; consisting of a Memoir of Sir A. Van Dyck, with a Descriptive Catalogue of the Etchings executed by him, and a variety of interesting particulars, &c. 4to. cloth, plates, $8 25. London, 1844.

Carter, (Mrs.) Letters to Mrs. Montague between the Years 1755 and 1800, chiefly upon Literary and Moral Subjects 3 vols. in 1, 8vo. bds. $3 50. London, 1817.

Catlow, (A.) Popular Conchology; or, Shell Cabinet arranged, being an Introduction to the Modern System of Conchology. 12mo. cloth, numerous wood-cuts, $3 25. London, 1843.

Cattermole, (G.) Portfolio of Drawings; containing 12 original Drawings, printed in lithrotinte, and colored after the originals, mounted on thick imperial boards, $60 00. London.

Ceeley, (R.) Observations on the Variolæ Vaccinæ. 8vo. bds. colored plates, $6 00. Worcester, 1840.

Chalmers, (Dr. Thos.) Congregational Sermons. 3 vols. 12mo. cloth, $3 50. Glasgow.

Chapman, (F. H.) Naval Architecture, by Inman. 4to. cloth, $12 50. London.

Chaptal's Chemistry applied to Agriculture, with an extra Chapter by Davy, Essay by Puvis, and Observations by Prof. Renwick. Translated and edited by Rev. W. P. Page. 18mo. half sheep, 50 cents.

Chase, (H.) Treatise on the Radical Cure of Hernia by Instruments. 8vo. bds. $2 00. Philadelphia, 1836.

Chaudet, (M.) L'Art de L'Essayeur. 8vo. broche, $2 50. Paris, 1835.

Chasles, (P.) Etudes sur l'Espagne et sur les influences de la Litterature Espagnole en France et en Italie. 12mo. broche, $1 00. Paris.

——— Etudes sur les premiers temps du Christianisme et sur le moyen age. 12mo. broche, $1 00. Paris.

——— Le Dix-Huitieme Siecle en Angleterre. 12mo. broche, $1 00. Paris.

——— Etudes sur l'Antiquite precedees d'un Essai sur les phases de l'histoire Litteraire et sur les influences Intellectuelles des Races. 12mo. broche, $1 00. Paris, 1847.

——— Etudes sur le Seizieme Siecle en France precedees d'une histoire de la Litterature et de la Langue Francaise de 1470 a 1610. 12mo. broche, $1 00. Paris.

Chateaubriand. Memoirs of, from his Birth in 1768, till his return to France in 1800. 12mo. cloth, portrait, $1 25. Lond. 1849.

Cheever, (Rev. H. T.) The Whale and his Captors; or, the Whalemen's Adventures and the Whale's Biography. 18mo. cloth, 60 cents. New York, 1849.

Chefs-Œuvre des Auteurs Comiques. 8vo. broche, $7 00. Paris, 1845.

——— Des Auteurs Tragiques. 12mo. broche, $1 75. Paris, 1845.

Chevereul. De la loi du contrast simultane des coleurs et de l'assortiment des objets colores considere d'apres cette loi, dans les rapports avec la peinture, les tapissieres des gobelins, les tapissieres de Beauvais pour meubles, les tapis de la Savonnerie, la mosaique, les vitraux colores, etc. 1 vol. in 8, avec atlas in 4 de 40 planches colorees, $7 50. Paris, 1839.

Chevreul, (M. G.) Cours de Chimie Appliquee a la teinture. 2 vols. 8vo. $6 00. Paris.

Child, (Mrs.) Memoirs of Madame de Stael and Madame Roland. 12mo. cloth, 63 cents. New York.

Christian Doctrines, from the Words of our Lord, of the Apostles, and the Prophets. 12mo. illuminated in colors and gold, and bound in embossed calf, gilt edges, $3 50. London, 1849.

Christmas Tyde; a Series of Sacred Songs and Poetical Pieces suited to the Season. 12mo. cloth, $1 50. Pickering, 1849.

Churchill, (F.) On the Diseases of Infants and Children. 8vo. sheep, $3 00. Philadelphia, 1850.

Clark, (J. B.) Life of Dr. Adam Clarke. 12mo. cloth, $1 25. New York.

——— (John.) A Treatise on the Mulberry Tree and Silk Worm, and on the Production and Manufacture of Silk. 12mo. cloth, woodcuts, 50 cents. Philadelphia, 1839

Clay, (H.) Life and Speeches. 2 vols. 8vo. cloth, $1 50. New York.

Cleaveland, (M.) Greenwood; a Directory for Visitors. 12mo. cloth, 124 wood-cuts, $1 25; cloth gilt, $1 50. New York, 1849.

Coad, (J.) A Memorandum of the Wonderful Providences of God to a Poor Unworthy Creature during the time of the Duke of Monmouth's Rebellion, and to the Revolution in 1688. Square foolscap 8vo. $1 38. London, 1849.

Coghlan, (Rev. J) A Popular Companion to the Study of the Holy Scriptures. 8vo. cloth, wood-cuts, $3 50. Lond. 1843

Coit, (Thos. W.) Puritanism; or, a Churchman's Defence against its Aspersions. 12mo. cloth, $1 00. New York, 1845.

Coleridge, (Sam. Taylor) Preliminary Treatise on Method. 12mo. cloth, 75 cents. London, 1849.

Colton, (C.) The Life and Times of Henry Clay. 2 vols. royal 8vo. cloth, portrait, $5 00. New York, 1846.

Combe, (A.) Principles of Physiology applied to the Preservation of Health, &c. 18mo. cloth, 50 cents. New York.

——— (G.) Elements of Phrenology. 12mo. bds. 63 cents. Boston, 1835.

Conder, (Jos.) A Dictionary of Geography, Ancient and Modern. 12mo. cloth, $2 75. London, 1834.

Cooper, (James.) Description of the Plan of Restoring the Arch Stones of Black Friar's Bridge. (Trans. I. C. E. vol. 1, 4to) Lond.

——— (W. W.) Practical Remarks on Near Sight, Aged Sight, and Improved Vision, with Observations upon the Use of Glasses and an Artificial Light. 12mo. cloth, wood-cuts, $2 00. London, 1847.

Corkran, (J. F.) History of the National Constituent Assembly from May, 1848. 12mo. cloth, 75 cents. New York, 1840.

Cormack, (J. R.) Natural History, Pathology, and Treatment of the Epidemic Fever at present prevailing in Edinburgh and other Towns. 8vo. cloth, $1 75. Lond. 1843.

Cowper, (W.) Homer's Iliad, with Notes for Colleges and Schools, by M. A. Dwight. 12mo. cloth, $1 25. New York.

——— A Library edition. 8vo. cloth, illustrated by Flaxman's designs, $3 00; cloth gilt, $3 50. New York, 1850.

Crockett, (D.) Life of, written by himself. 12mo. cloth, 63 cents. New York.

Crosse, (J. G.) A Treatise on the Formation, Constituents, and Extraction of the Urinary Calculus. 4to. cloth, plates, $11 00. London, 1841.

Crawley, (Capt.) Method of reclaiming the Tantamar and adjoining Marshes from the Sea. (Papers, R. E. vol. 8, 4to.) London.

——— Survey of a Line for a Canal to unite the Bay of Fundy with the Gulf of St. Lawrence. (Papers, R. E. vol. 8, 4to.) London.

——— Description of a Watercourse, Wharf, and Water-Wheel erected at Waltham Abbey, Essex, in 1845, with some Account of the Mode of Construction. (Papers, R. E. vol. 9, 4to.) London.

Cubitt, (W.) An Abstract Account of Coals used in Coke Ovens and Retorts, and Coke produced from one Year's Work at the Ipswich Gas Works. (Trans. I. C. E. vol. 1, 4to.) London.

Cuming's Memorandum with reference to the accompanying Sketches of the Officers' Barracks erected at George Town, Demerara. Description of Barracks at Lucca in Jamaica. (Papers, R. E. vol. 2, 4to.) London

Cumming, (Rev. A.) A Memoir of the Rev. E. Payson, late of Portland, Maine. Thick 18mo. cloth, portrait, 63 cents. N York, 1830.

Cunningham, (Peter.) Thoughts on the Causes of Compass Variation and the Motions of Planets, Comets, Whirlwinds, Hurricanes, and Earthquakes. 12mo. sewed, 38 cents. London, 1843.

Curiosities of Modern Travel; a Year-Book of Adventure. 5 vols. 12mo. cloth gilt, plates, $4 00. London, 1844.

Damer, (Hon. Mrs. G. L. D.) Diary of a Tour in Greece, Turkey, Egypt, and the Holy Land. 2 vols. post 8vo. cloth, plates, $3 00. London, 1842.

Darlington, (W.) Memorials of John Bartram and Humphry Marshall, with Notices of their Botanical Contemporaries. 8vo. cloth, plates, $2 75. Philadelphia, 1849.

Dana, (R. H.) Poems and Prose Writings. 2 vols. 12mo. cloth, $2 50. New York, 1850.

Daniell's Illustrations of Natural Philosophy, prepared by James Renwick, LL.D. 12mo. cloth, 69 cents. New York.

Davies, (J.) An Estimate of the Human Mind; a Philosophical Inquiry, &c. 8vo. cloth, $4 25. London, 1849.

Debay, (A.) Medecine du Visage et Hygiene de la Peau, &c. 12mo. broche, 75 cents. Paris, 1850.

Dechastelus, (J. P. Maurice.) Soixante ans de l'Histoire de France ou les oscillations de l'Esprit Humain. 12mo. broche, 50 cents. Paris, 1849.

De la Rive, (A.) Treatise on Electricity 2 vols. 8vo. illustrated with wood-cuts. London, 1849.

Dempsey, (G. D.) On Railways. Description of the Mode adopted for Repairing and Supporting the Western Retaining Wall of the London and Birmingham Railway. (Papers, R. E. vol. 7, 4to.) London.

—— Description of the Saw Mills and Machinery for Raising Timber in Chatham Dockyard. (Papers, R. E. vol. 6, 4to.) Lond.

Denison, (Lieut.) Description of a new Weigh Bridge lately erected in Woolwich Dockyard. Description of a Single Coffer Dam across the entrance of the New Dock in Woolwich Dockyard. Notes on Injecting Cement or Hydraulic Lime into Leaky Joints of Masonry. Description of the Roof of the Chapel of the Royal Artillery Barracks at Woolwich, showing the Failure of the Principals and the Mode of Restoring them. (Papers, R. E. vol. 4, 4to.) London.

—— (Capt.) Description of the Machinery in Operation at the Royal Arsenal for the Manufacture of Leaden Bullets by Compression. Description of a Dock lately constructed in Woolwich Dockyard. (Papers, R. E. vol. 5, 4to.) London.

—— Description of some Iron Roofs erected at different Places within the last few Years. (Papers, R. E. vol. 6, 4to.) London.

—— Description of a Swing Bridge erected over the Canal in the Regent's Park. (Papers, R. E. vol. 7, 4to.) London.

—— Description of the Balance Gates at the Compensation Reservoir of the East London Water Works at Old Ford, designed and erected by Thos. Wicksteed, C. E. (Papers, R. E. vol. 7, 4to.) London.

—— Notes on Concrete; also, a Description of the Method adopted by Mr. Taylor for Underpinning with Concrete the Store-Houses in Chatham Dockyard. (Papers, R. E. vol. 1, 4to.)

—— Notes on the Charges of Military Mines. Notes on the Formation of Breaches by Artillery, containing an Abstract of the Experiments at Metz, and an Account of the Practice against Carnot's Wall at Woolwich. Rideau Dams Notes on Concrete. (Papers, R. E. vol. 2, 4to.)

—— A Series of Experiments on different kinds of American Timber. (Trans. I. C. E. vol. 2, 4to.) London.

—— Detailed Description of some of the Works on the Rideau Canal, and of the Alterations and Improvements made therein since the Opening of the Navigation. Description of a Series of Bridges erected across the River Ottawa, connecting Upper and Lower Canada, and especially of a Wooden Arch of 212 Feet Span crossing the main branch of the River. (Papers, R. E. vol. 3, 4to.) London.

Dent, (E. J.) Treatise on the Aneroid; a newly invented Portable Barometer, with a short Historical Notice of Barometers in general. 8vo. paper, 50 cents. Lond. 1849.

De Quincey, (Thos.) Miscellaneous Writings of the English Opium Eater. 12mo. cloth. Boston, 1850.

—— The Logic of Political Economy. 8vo. cloth, $1 50. Edinburgh, 1844.

Description of the Large Chimney for Conveying the Smoke from the various Buildings connected with the Steam Machinery Factory in Woolwich Dockyard. (Papers, R. E. vol. 9, 4to.) London.

Description of the Rolling Bridge at Fort Regent, Jersey. Letter from Capt. G. Thomson, E. I. C. Engineers, to Col. Pasley, R. E. (Papers, R. E. vol. 4, 4to.) London.

—— Of the Cast Iron Bridge erected over the River Trent, near the confluence of the Trent and Soar, on the line of the Midland Counties Railway, and near the Village of Sawley, in the County of Derby. (Papers, R. E. vol. 4, 4to.) London.

—— Of a Wooden Swing Bridge erected over the Grenville Canal, Canada. (Papers, R. E. vol. 6, 4to.) London.

—— Of a Saw Mill used in America. (Papers, R. E. vol. 6, 4to.) London.

Desmarest, (A. G.) Considérations générales sur la Classe des Crustaces des Espèces de ces Animaux, qui vivent dans la mer, sur les Côtes, ou dans les eaux douces de la France. 8vo. bds. 56 plates, $7 50. Paris, 1825.

Detail of some Experiments for the purpose of ascertaining the Resistance of Brickwork under various Conditions. (Papers, R. E. vol. 6, 4to.) London.

Discussion, (The,) on the Character, Education, Prerogatives, and Moral Influence of Woman. 12mo. cloth, 50 cents. Boston, 1837.

Ditson, (G.) Circassia; or, a Tour to the Caucasus. 8vo. cloth, $1 50. N. York, 1850.

Dixon, (H.) The London Prisons, their Past and Present Condition, with some Account of the more distinguished Persons who have been confined in them. Foolscap 8vo. cloth, $1 75. London, 1849.

—— (R. V.) A Treatise on Heat. Part 1. 8vo. cloth, $3 75. Dublin, 1849.

Donkin, (B.) An Account of some Experiments made in 1823, '24, for determining the Quantity of Water flowing through different shaped orifices. (Trans. I. C. E. vol. 1, 4to.) London.

—— Description of Mrs. H. Guy's Method of giving a True Spherical Figure to Balls of Metal, Glass, Agate, or Hard Substances. (Trans. I. C. E. vol. 2, 4to.) London.

—— (John.) Some Account of Borings for Water in London and its Vicinity. (Trans. I. C. E. vol. 1, 4to.) London.

Dover, (Lord.) Lives of the Sovereigns of Modern Europe. 12mo. cloth, 50 cents. New York.

Doubourg, (J. H.) Life of Cheverus, Archbishop of Doubourg, $1 00. Phila.

Dowling, (John.) The History of Romanism from the earliest Corruptions of Christianity to the present time. 8vo. cloth, $3 00. New York, 1849.

Doyle, (R.) Manners and Customs of ye Englyshe in 1849. Small 4to. cloth, $1 75. London, 1849.

Drake, (S. G.) Indian Captives; or, Life in the Wigwam, being true Narratives of Captives who have been carried away by the Indians from the Frontier Settlements of the United States from the earliest period. 12mo. cloth, $1 25. Auburn, 1850.

Drawbridges of Bermuda. (Papers, R. E. vol. 9, 4to.) London.

Duggan, (George.) Specimens of the Stone, Iron, and Wooden Bridges, Viaducts, Tunnels, Culverts, &c. of the United States Railroads, illustrated by drawings from Actual Measurement of the Works, with Appendix on the Art of Bridge Building as practiced in Europe, &c. &c. To be completed in 12 parts, illustrated with 48 folio plates, each part 75 cents. New York, 1850.

Durand, (Lieut. H. M.) Notes on the Field Equipment of the Engineer Department, with the Bengal Portion of the Army of the Indus. (Papers, R. E. vol. 6, 4to.) Lond.

——— Passage of the Indus by the Bengal Portion of the Army of the Indus. (Papers, R. E. vol. 4, 4to.) London.

East, (R.) The Two Dangerous Diseases of England, Consumption and Apoplexy, their Nature, Causes, and Cure. 12mo. cloth, $1 50. London, 1842.

East India Sketch-Book, (The.) By a Lady. 2 vols. post 8vo. bds. $2 50. London, 1833.

Eastman, (Mrs. M.) Dahcotah; or, Life and Legends of the Sioux around Fort Snelling. 12mo. cloth, plates, $1 00. New York, 1849.

Eaton, (Amos.) Geological Text-Book prepared for Popular Lectures on North American Geology. 8vo. cloth. Albany, 1830.

Ehrenberg, (C. G.) Die Infusions thierchen als vollkomme Organismen, with an atlas of plates, colored, in folio, $41 00. Leipsig, 1838.

Ellet, (Mrs.) Evenings at Woodlawn. 12mo. cloth, $1 25. New York, 1849.

Elwin, (F. H.) Mens Corporis; a Treatise on the Operations of the Mind in Sleep. 12mo. cloth, $2 00. London, 1843.

Emerson, (R. W.) Nature, Lectures, Addresses, and Orations. 12mo. cloth, $1 00. Boston, 1849.

——— Representative Men. Seven Lectures. 12mo. cloth, $1 00. Boston, 1850.

Encyclopædia of the Fine Arts. 4to. cloth, $9 00. London.

——— Of the Useful Arts. 4to. cloth, $6 00.

——— Of Universal History, Ancient and Modern, from the Creation of the World to the present time. 5 vols. 4to. cloth, $28 00.

——— Of Pure Mathematics. 4to. cloth, $9 50.

——— Of Mechanical Philosophy. By Profs. Barlow and Sir J. Herschel. 4to. cloth, $12 00.

——— Of Natural History. 4to. cloth, $16 50.

——— Of Medical Sciences. 4to. cloth, $6 00.

——— Of Astronomy. 4to cloth, $6 00.

——— Of Experimental Philosophy. 4to cloth, $9 00.

Engineer's and Mechanic's Pocket-Book. 12mo. roan tuck, wood engravings, $1 25. New York, 1848.

Englemann, (W.) Bibliotheca Medico-Chirurgica et Anatomico-Physiologica. 8vo. paper, $3 75. Leipsic, 1848.

Englemann, (W.) Bibliotheca Zoologica et Palæontologica; or, a Systematic Catalogue of the Works on those Sciences, published to the end of 1845 in England, France, Germany, Italy, Holland, and other Countries. 8vo. paper, $3 75. Leipsig, 1846.

——— Bibliotheca Scriptorum classicorum et Græcorum et Latinorum; an Alphabetical Catalogue of the Greek and Latin Authors that have appeared in Germany, &c. up to 1846. 8vo. paper, $2 50. Leipsig, 1847.

Episodes of Insect Life. Second Series. Cr. 8vo. cloth, beautifully illustrated, $4 75; colored, $6 50. London, 1849.

Erskine, (Lord.) Speeches. Royal 8vo. cloth, $1 50. London, 1846.

Euler's Letters on Natural Philosophy, with Notes and Life, by Sir David Brewster, and additional Notes, by Griscom. 2 vols. 12mo. cloth, $1 00. New York.

Eustace, (J. C.) A Classical Tour through Italy. 3 vols. post 8vo. cloth, map and plans, $4 50. London, 1841.

Everest, (Rev. C. W.) The Poets of Connecticut, with Biographical Sketches. 8vo. cloth, with a vignette View of Connecticut River, $2 00. New York, 1849.

Experiments carried on in Chatham by the late Lieut. Hope on the Pressure of Earth against Revetments and the best form of Retaining Walls. (Papers, R. E. vol. 7, 4to.) London.

Fairbairn's Account of the Construction of the Britannia and Conway Tubular Bridges. Plates, large 8vo. half mor.

Fairfield, (J.) Life of Sumner Lincoln Fairfield. 12mo. cloth, portrait, 50 cents. New York, 1817.

Fanshawe, (Maj. Gen.) A Short Account of the Demolition of the Piers of the Entrance Chamber of the Large Basin at Flushing in 1809. (Papers, R. E. vol. 2, 4to.) Lond.

——— (Col.) Report on the Effect of Climate on Yorkshire Paving. (Papers, R. E. vol. 3, 4to.) London.

Faris, (Capt.) Loopholed Barrack intended as a Keep for a Square Fort. (Papers, R. E. vol. 8, 4to.) London.

Farrar's First Principles of the Differential and Integral Calculus; or, the Doctrine of Fluxions. 8vo. bds. $1 00. Boston, 1836.

Farey, (J.) On the Relation between the Temperature and Elastic Force of Steam, when confined in a Boiler containing Water. (Trans. I. C. E. vol. 1, 4to.) London.

——— An Approximate Rule for Calculating the Velocity with which a Steam Vessel will be impelled through Still Water by the exertion of a given amount of Mechanical Power or Forcible Motion by Marine Steam Engines. (Trans. I. C. E. vol. 1, 4to.) London.

Fau, (Dr. J.) The Anatomy of the External Forms of Man, intended for the Use of Artists, Painters, and Sculptors. Edited, with additions, by Robert Knox, M. D. 8vo. cloth, with an atlas of 28 plates in 4to. $7 50; colored, $11 00. London, 1849.

Federalist, (The,) on the New Constitution written in the Year 1788, by A. Hamilton, J. Madison, and John Jay, with an Appendix and Index. 8vo. cloth, $2 00. Phila. 1847

Felton, (J. B.) The Horse Shoe; a Poem spoken before the Phi Beta Kappa Society in Cambridge, July 19, 1849. 12mo. 25 cents. Cambridge, 1849.

——— (Prof.) A History of the Acadians. 12mo. cloth. Boston, 1850.

Ferguson. History of the Roman Republic. New edition. 8vo. cloth, $1 75.

Field, (J. A.) Experiments on the Power of Men. (Trans. I. C. E. vol. 2, 4to.) Lond.

——— On an Improved Canal Lock. (Trans. I. C. E. vol. 1, 4to.) London.

Findlay, (A. G.) A Classical Atlas to illustrate Ancient Geography, comprised in 25 maps, with an Index of Ancient and Modern Names. 8vo. half bound, $3 75. N. Y. 1849.

Fisher, (E.) Marrow of Divinity. 12mo. cloth, $1 00. London, 1837.

Fitzgerald, (Capt. W. R.) Memorandum of the Operations for Removing the Wreck of the Equitable Barque in the Fultah Reach of the River Hooghly. (Papers, R. E. vol. 5, 4to.) London.

Fleury, (M. l'Abbe.) Ecclesiastical History, from the Year 381 to 456. Translated, with Notes and an Essay on the Miracles of the Period. 3 vols. 8vo. cloth, $9 75. 1842–44.

Follen, (E. L.) Life of Charles Follen. 12mo. cloth, $1 00. Boston.

Foote, (Rev. W. H.) Sketches of Virginia, Historical and Biographical. 8vo. cloth, $2 25. Philadelphia, 1850.

Form, (The,) of Solemnization of Matrimony. Illuminated in the Missal Style, by Owen Jones. Square 18mo. white calf, $6 00. Lond. 1850.

Forman, (Capt.) Treatises on several very important Subjects in Natural Philosophy. 8vo. bds. 75 cents. (Scarce.) Shepton Mallet, 1832.

Forsyth, (R.) Observations on Genesis and Exodus. 12mo. cloth, $1 50. Edin. 1846.

Foster, (Mrs.) Hand-Book of European Literature. Foolscap 8vo. cloth, $2 50. London, 1849.

Fountain, (The,) of Living Waters, by a Layman. 12mo. cloth, 50 cents; cloth gilt, gilt edges, 75 cents. New York, 1849.

Fox, (W.) Plans and Elevations for Baths and Wash-Houses. Oblong folio, paper, plates, $6 50. Liverpool, 1848.

——— (W. J.) On the Religious Ideas. 8vo. cloth, $3 25. London, 1849.

Foy, (Dr. F.) Manuel d'Hygiene. 12mo. broche, $1 25. Paris, 1845.

Francatelli, (C. E.) The Modern French Cook; a Practical Guide to the Culinary Art in all its branches. Royal 8vo. cloth, $2 50. Philadelphia, 1846.

Francis, (John.) Chronicles and Characters of the Stock Exchange. 8vo. cloth, $5 75. London, 1849.

Friendship, Love, and Truth; containing Articles illustrative of the Principles of Odd Fellowship, contributed chiefly by Members of the Order. 12mo. cloth, 75 cents. New York, 1849.

Frothingham, (R.) History of the Siege of Boston and of Battles of Lexington, Concord, and Bunker Hill. 8vo. cloth, maps and plates, $2 25. Boston, 1849.

Frome, (Capt.) Account of the Causes which led to the Construction of the Rideau Canal, connecting the Waters of Lake Ontario and the Ottawa, the Nature of the Communication prior to 1827, and a Description of the Works by means of which it is converted into a Steamboat Navigation. (Papers, R. E. vol. 1, 4to.) London.

Fry, (Rev. J.) New Translation and Exposition of the very Ancient Book of Job. 8vo. cloth, $2 00. London, 1827.

Fleetwood's Life of Christ and History of the Jews. 8vo. cloth, $2 50. Phila.

Fuster, (Dr.) Des Changements dans le climat de la France Histoire de ses Revolutions Météorologiques. 8vo. paper, $1 38. Paris, 1845.

Furniss, (W.) The Old World; or, Scenes and Cities in Foreign Lands, with map and plates. 12mo. cloth, $1 25. New York, 1849.

——— Waraga; or, the Charms of the Nile. 12mo. cloth, colored plates, $1 50. New York, 1850.

Galton, (D.) On Drawbridges, chiefly from the French of M. de Poncelet. (Papers, R. E. vol. 5, 4to.) London.

Garrod and Ballard's Elements of Materia Medica and Therapeutics. 8vo. cloth, $3 37. London, 1845.

Gaudry, (L.) Cours pratique d'Arboriculture, &c. 12mo. broche, 75 cents. Paris, 1848.

Genlis, (Mme. de.) Le Siege de La Rochelle. 12mo. broche, $1 00. Paris, 1847.

Gesner, (A.) New Brunswick; comprehending the Early History, an Account of the Indians, Settlement, Topography, Statistics, Commerce, Timber, Manufactures, Agriculture, Fisheries, Geology, Natural History, Social and Political State, Immigrants, and Contemplated Railways of that Province, with Notes for Emigrants. 8vo. cloth, plates, $2 00. London, 1847.

——— Industrial Resources of Nova Scotia, comprehending the Physical Geography, Topography, Geology, Agriculture, Fisheries, Mines, Forests, Wild Lands, Lumbering, Manufactories, Navigation, Commerce, Emigration, Improvements, Industry, Contemplated Railways, Natural History, and Resources of the Province. 8vo. cloth, with a map of the Province and lithographed view of West Bay, near Partridge Island, $1 50. Halifax, N. S. 1847.

Gibbs, (Prof. W.) A Chemical Text-Book. 12mo. cloth. New York.

Gibbes, (R. W.) Memoir of the Fossil Genus Basilosaurus, from the Eocene Green Sand of South Carolina. 4to. paper, plates, $1 00. Philadelphia, 1847.

Gilbert, (Jas.) Summary of the Occupations of the People of England, Wales, and Scotland. 4to. bds. 3 colored maps, $1 25. London, 1844.

Giles, (Henry.) Lectures, Essays, and Miscellaneous Writings. 12mo. cloth. Boston, 1850.

Gilfillan, (G.) A Second Gallery of Literary Portraits. Cr. 8vo. cloth, $3 25. Edinburgh, 1849.

——— The Same. 12mo. New York, 1850.

Gillespie, (W. M.) Rome as seen by a New Yorker in 1843. 12mo. cloth, 75 cents. New York.

Girardin, (E. de.) Les 52. 8 vol. 12mo. broche. Contenant—1. Apostasie. 2. Le Gouvernement le plus simple. 3. L'Equilibre Financier par la Réforme Administrative. 4. La note du 15 Décembre. 5. Respect de la Constitution. 6. La Constituante et la Legislative. 7, 8. La Politique de la Paix. $2 00. Paris, 1849.

——— Questions Administratives et Financères. 12mo. broche, 75 cents. Paris, 1849.

——— Le Pour et le Contre. 12mo. broche, 75 cents. Paris, 1849.

Gladstone, (W. E.) The State in its Relations with the Church. 2 vols. 8vo cloth, $3 00. London, 1841.

Gleig, (G. R.) True Story of the Battle of Waterloo. 12mo. cloth, 88 cents. New York.

Glossary of Provincial Words used in Teesdale, in the County of Durham. 12mo. cloth, with map, $1 75. London, 1849.

Glover, (R. M.) On the Pathology and Treatment of Scrofula. 8vo. cloth, $2 87. London, 1846.

Glynn, (J) Description of Wharf Cranes made by the Butterley Company. (Papers, R. E vol. 4, 4to.) London.

——— Description of a Traversing Crane used by the Butterley Company in erecting Cast Iron Bridges and other Public Works. (Papers, R. E. vol. 5, 4to.) London.

Goldsmith, (O.) Miscellaneous Works. Edited by James Prior, comprising several Pieces now first published in this Country. 4 vols. 12mo. cloth, $5 00. New York, 1849.

——— Letters from a Citizen of the World to his Friends in the East. Square 12mo. cloth, $1 00. London, 1840.

Gore, (Mrs.) The Rose Fancier's Manual. Post 8vo. cloth, $1 50. Lond. 1838.

Goodrich, (S. G.) Memoirs of Celebrated Women. 18mo. cloth, 63 cents. Boston.

Goodwyn, (Capt.) The Taper Chain Tension Bridge at Balbec Khal, Calcutta, in its renewed form, after the Failure in June, 1845. (Papers, R. E. vol. 9, 4to.) London.

Gorham, (G. C.) Examination before Admission to a Benefice, by the Bishop of Exeter, followed by Refusal to Institute on the Allegation of Unsound Doctrine respecting the Efficacy of Baptism, $1 75. London, 1848.

Gosse, (P. H.) Popular British Ornithology. Square 12mo. cloth, colored plates, $2 75. London, 1849.

Gostick, (J.) German Literature 12mo. cloth, 75 cents. Edinburgh, 1849.

Graham, (Lieut. Gen.) Memoranda relating to the Defence of Cadiz, and Explanatory Details of the Position Intrenched by the British Troops under him in 1810. (Papers, R. E. vol. 3, 4to.) London

Grant, (Capt.) On the Fact of Small Fish Falling during Rain in India. (Papers, R. E. vol. 2, 4to.) London.

Gravatt, (W.) Some Account of the several Sections through the Plastic Clay Formation in the Vicinity of London. (Trans. I. C. E. vol. 1, 4to.) London.

Gray, (Thos.) The Works of, collated from the various editions, with Memoirs of his Life and Writings, by William Mason. 8vo. cloth, $1 50. London, 1827.

——— (J. T.) Exercises in Logic for Students. 12mo. cloth, 75 cents. London, 1845

——— (G. R,) The Genera of Birds; comprising their Generic Characters, a Notice of the Habits of each Genus, and an extensive List of Species, referred to their Genera. 3 vols. imp 8vo. half mor. gilt tops, 186 plain and 185 colored plates, $189 00. Lond. 1845–49.

Green, (J.) Description of the Perpendicular Lifts for Passing Boats from one Level of Canal to another, as erected on the Great Western Canal. (Trans. I. C. E. vol. 2, 4to.) London.

——— (M. A. E.) Lives of the Princesses of England. 2 vols. post 8vo. cloth, portrait, $6 00. London, 1849.

Greene, (G. W.) Historical Studies. 12mo. cloth, $1 25. Putnam, New York, 1850.

Greener, (W.) The Gun; or, a Treatise on the various Descriptions of Small Firearms. 8vo bds. illustrated with plates and wood-cuts, $4 50. London, 1835.

Greenwood, (Grace.) Greenwood Leaves; a Collection of Sketches and Letters. 12mo. cloth, $1 25. Boston, 1850.

Gregg, (Rev T. D.) Free Thoughts on Protestant Matters. 8vo. cloth, $1 75. Dublin, 1847.

Gresset, (P.) Le Dentiste des Familles ou Manuel d'Hygiène de la Bouche. 12mo. broche, 75 cents. Paris, 1845.

Griffith, (H. W.) A Lift for the Lazy Second edition, revised, corrected, and enlarged. 12mo. cloth, 75 cents. New York, 1850.

——— (J. W.) Practical Manual, &c. on the Characters of the Blood and Secretions of the Human Body. 12mo. cloth, $1 37. London, 1846.

Griffin, (J. J.) Chemical Recreations; a Popular Compendium of Experimental Chemistry. Ninth edition, 18mo. roan, $2 25.

——— System of Crystallography, with its Application to Mineralogy. 8vo. cloth, $4 25.

——— Scientific Miscellany. 160 engravings. Thick 8vo. cloth, $4 00.

Griscom's Animal Mechanism and Physiology. 12mo. cloth, wood-cuts, 50 cents. New York.

Griswold, (Dr. R. W.) An Encyclopædia of Biography, Ancient and Modern, embracing more than 2000 Articles relating to Americans. Edited from various sources. 3 vols. royal 8vo. cloth. New York, 1850.

Grouvelle et Jaunez, (MM.) Guide du Chauffeur et du Proprietaire de Machines a Vapeur. 8vo. paper, with atlas of plates, $3 00. Paris, 1840.

Guthrie, (G. J.) Treatise on Gun-Shot Wounds. 8vo. bds. $4 50. Lond. 1827.

Hackley, (C. W.) Elementary Course of Geometry. 12mo. sheep, 75 cents. New York, 1847.

Haillot, (C. A.) Statistique Militaire et recherches sur l'Organization et les Institutions des Armeés etrangers. 3 vols. 12mo. $2 50. Bruxelles, 1846.

Hair, (T. H.) Sketches of the Coal Mines in Northumberland and Durham. 4to. plates, $12 50. London, 1839.

Hale, (Mrs. S. J.) Flora's Interpreter and Fortuna Flora. 12mo. cloth gilt, colored plates, $2 00. Boston, 1849.

——— (Mrs. C. V. R. M.) Saturday Evenings; a Series of Moral and Religious Essays. 12mo. cloth, 75 cents. New York, 1845.

Halliwell, (J. O.) An Introduction to Shakespeare's Midsummer Night's Dream. 8vo. half mor. $1 50. Pickering, 1840.

——— The Life of William Shakespeare; including many particulars respecting the Poet and his Family never before published. 8vo. half calf, gilt, illustrated with numerous woodcuts, $5 50. London, 1848.

Hamilton, (Count A.) Fairy Tales and Romances. 12mo. cloth, portrait, 88 cents. London, 1849.

——— (Joseph.) Treatise on the Cultivation of the Pine Apple, &c. 12mo. cloth, $1 75. London, 1844.

Hampden, (R. D.) Sermons preached before the University of Oxford, in the Cathedral of Christ Church. 8vo. bds. $3 50. London, 1848.

Happy Ignorance; or, the Church and State; a Religious Adventure, with Notes, by the Editors. 12mo. cloth, 75 cents. London, 1847.

Harding's Baronial Halls, Picturesque Edifices, and Ancient Churches of England. Drawn in lithotint, by W. Harding, with text, by S. C. Hall. 3 vols. folio, half bound, $34 50. London, 1845.

Harness, (Capt.) On Contoured Plans and Defilade. (Papers, R. E. vol. 2, 4to.) Lond.

——— Description of a small Observatory erected at Chatham for the Use of the Officers of the Corps of R. E. (Papers, R. E. vol. 7, 4to.) London.

——— On Suspension Bridges. (Papers, R. E. vol. 9, 4to.) London.

Harris, (Sergt.) An Account of the Mode in which a Stranded Ship was Blown to Pieces, in a Letter to Col. Pasley. (Papers, R. E. vol. 2, 4to.) London.

——— Dental Dictionary. 8vo. sheep, $5 00. Philadelphia.

Harrison, (Thos. E.) Description of the Drops used by the Stanhope and Tyne Railroad Company for the Shipment of Coals at South Shields. (Trans. I. C. E. vol. 2, 4to.) London.

Haswell's Engineer's and Mechanic's Pocket-Book. 12mo. roan-tuck, $1 25. New York, 1849.

Hautefeuille, (L. B.) Des Droits et des Devoirs des Nations neutres en Temps de Guerre Maritime. 4 vols. 8vo. broche, $7 50. Paris, 1849.

Hawker, (R.) A Concordance and Dictionary to the Sacred Scriptures, both of the Old and New Testament, &c. 12mo. cloth, $1 50. London, 1846.

Hawkins, (E.) Historical Notices of the Missions of the Church of England, &c. 8vo. cloth, $2 75. London, 1845.

Hawks, (Rev. F. L.) Auricular Confession in the Protestant Episcopal Church considered in a Series of Letters. 12mo. paper, 25 cents; cloth, 38 cents. New York, 1850.

Hays, (W. B.) Account of a Machine for Cleansing and Deepening Small Rivers, in Use on the Little Stour River, Kent. (Trans. I. C. E. vol. 2, 4to.) London.

Heber, (Reginald.) The Poetical Works of. 12mo. cloth, 75 cents. Phila. 1841.

Henderson, (E.) The Vaudois; comprising Observations made during a Tour to the Valleys of Piedmont, &c. 12mo. cloth, map, $1 75. London, 1845.

Henshaw, (J. S.) Manual for United States Consuls; embracing their Rights, Duties, Liabilities, and Emoluments. 12mo. cloth, $1 25. New York, 1849.

Henwood, (W. J.) On the Expansive Action of Steam in some of the Pumping Engines at the Cornish Mines. (Trans. I. C. E. vol. 2, 4to.) London.

Hering, (G. E.) The Mountains and the Lakes; or, Sketches in Switzerland, the Tyrol, and Italy. Small folio, beautiful plates in lithotint, $8 00. London, 1845.

——— (Dr. C.) Medecine Homœopathique Domestique traduit par Dr. L. Marchant. 8vo. broche, $1 50. Paris, 1849.

Heroine of a Week, (The.) Conversations for the Teacher and the Taught. 18mo. cloth, 75 cents. London, 1845.

Herschell, (Sir John.) Outlines of Astronomy. Cr. 8vo. cloth, plates, $1 75. Philadelphia, 1849.

——— Instructions for Making and Registering Meteorological Observations at various Stations in Southern Africa and other Countries in the South Seas, as also at Sea. (Papers, R. E. vol. 2, 4to.) London.

——— On the Study of Philosophy; a Preliminary Discourse. 12mo. cloth, 63 cents. New York.

Hervey, (James.) Meditations and Contemplations. 12mo. half mor. portrait, $1 25. London, 1840.

——— (Lord.) Court and Times of George II. 2 vols. 12mo. cloth, $2 50. Phila.

Higgins, (W. M.) The Entertaining Philosopher; an Exposition of the most interesting Phenomena of Natural and Experimental Philosophy, &c. 12mo. cloth, 100 wood-cuts, $1 00. London.

Hindostan, its Landscapes, Palaces, Temples, Tombs, the Shores of the Dead Sea, and the Sublime and Romantic Scenery of the Himalaya Mountains. Illustrated in a Series of Views drawn by Turner, Stanfield, Prout, Cattermole, Roberts, Allom, &c., with Descriptions, by Emma Roberts. 2 vols. 4to. cloth, gilt, $15 00. London, 1845.

Histoire de Genevieve de Brabant, representee en Douze dessins au trait avec un frontispiece graves, par Charles Johannot. 4to. paper, $2 00. Paris, 1813.

Hitchcock, (E.) Report on the Geology, Mineralogy, Botany, and Zoology of Massachusetts. 8vo. cloth, $5 00. Amherst, 1833.

——— Final Report on the Geology of Massachusetts. 2 vols. 4to. cloth, colored maps, $8 00. Northampton, 1841.

Hodge, (Paul R.) Analytical Principles and Practical Application of the Expansive Steam Engine. Plates, 4to. half mor. $18 00. London, 1849.

Hodgson, (Rev. C.) Family Prayers for One Month. Post 8vo. cloth, $1 00. London, 1843.

Hoffman, (C. F.) Winter in the West. 2 vols. 12mo. cloth, $1 50. New York.

Holdich's Life of Prof. W. Fisk. 8vo. cloth, $2 00. New York.

Holly Grange: a Tale, by Me. de K.—— 12mo. cloth, plates, $1 00. Lond. 1844.

Homer's Iliad. Translated into English Blank Verse, by William Cowper. Edited by Robert Southey, with Notes, by M. A. Dwight. Royal 8vo. cloth gilt, illustrated with Flaxman's designs, $3 50; cloth, $3 00; small paper, without plates, $1 25. N. York, 1850.

Hone, (W.) Everyday Book, 2 vols. Year Book, 1 vol. Table Book, 1 vol. In all, 4 vols. 8vo. profusely illustrated with wood engravings, $8 00. London.

Home, (The,) Treasury; comprising new Versions of Cinderella, Beauty and the Beast, Grumble and Cheery, the Eagle's Verdict, the Sleeping Beauty. Revised and illustrated. Small 4to. cloth gilt, 50 cents. New York, 1849.

Hope, (Rev. F. W.) The Coleropterist's Manual, part 2, containing the Predaceous Land and Water Beetles of Linnæus and Fabricius. 8vo. cloth, colored plates, $2 00. London, 1838.

Horæ Biblicæ; being a connected Series of Notes on the Text and Literary History of Bibles or Sacred Books of the Jews and Christians, and the Books accounted Sacred by the Mahometans, Hindoos, Parsees, Chinese, and Scandinavians. 12mo. cloth, 50 cents. Boston, 1845.

Howard, (Frank.) Imitative Art. Illustrations, foolscap 8vo. cloth, $1 25. Lond.

——— Lectures on Painting, with Memoir. Post 8vo. cloth, $2 25. Lond.

——— Sketcher's Manual. Plates, foolscap 8vo. cloth, $1 25. Lond.

——— (J. E.) Eight Lectures on Truths most opposed to Puseyism. 18mo. cloth, 75 cents London, 1845.

Howe, (J.) Outpouring of the Holy Spirit and the Redeemer's Dominion over the Invisible World. 18mo. cloth, 75 cents. Lond

Howlett, (S. B.) Table for determining Altitudes with the Mountain Barometer. A new Method of Making Perspective Drawings from Plans and Dimensions. A new Field Protractor and Sketch-Book. A new Method of Plotting a Survey. A new Station Pointer, and a new Line Divider and Universal Scale. (Papers, R. E. vol. 1, 4to.) London.

——— Description of an Engraved Protractor. (Papers, R. E. vol. 8, 4to.) London.

——— On Copying Maps and Plans. (Papers, R. E. vol. 5, 4to.) London.

——— Safety Box for connecting a Locomotive Engine and Tender to the Train. (Papers, R. E. vol. 4, 4to.) London.

——— Description of a Barometer that requires no Corrections either for Zero or for Temperature. (Papers, R. E. vol. 3, 4to.) Lond.

——— A Method of taking Perspective Outlines from Nature. (Papers, R. E. vol. 2, 4to.) London.

Hounslow, (T.) Description to accompany the Plans of the Method of Raising Buildings by Screws in Canada and the United States. (Papers, R. E. vol. 6. 4to.) Lond.

Hughes, (G. W.) Report on the System of Drainage of Low Lands of Holland. (Papers, R. E. vol. 7, 4to.) London.

Hull, (R.) Essays on Determination of Blood to the Head. 12mo. cloth, $1 75. London, 1842.

Humble, (W.) Dictionary of Geology and Mineralogy; comprising such Terms in Botany, Chemistry, Comparative Anatomy, Conchology, Etymology, Palæontology, Zoology, and other Branches of Natural History as are connected with the Study of Geology. 8vo. cloth, $1 50. London, 1843.

Humboldt, (W. V.) Letters to a Female Friend. Translated from the Second German Edition, by C. M. A. Cowper. 2 vols. post 8vo. cloth, $3 25. London, 1849.

——— (Baron Von.) Aspects of Nature in different Lands and different Climates, with Scientific Elucidations. Translated by Mrs. Sabine. 12mo. cloth, $1 25. Phila. 1849.

——— English edition. 2 vols. 12mo. paper, $1 25; cloth, $1 50. London, 1849.

——— Personal Narrative of Travels in South America in 1799–1804, $22 50. London, 1822–26.

——— Voyages aux regions equinoxiales du nouveau continent, faits en 1799–1804 et vues des Cordilleres et Monuments Mexicains indigenes de l'Amerique. 16 vol. in-8 figures $31 00. Paris, 1815–30.

Humphrey, (H. N.) Ancient Coins and Medals; an Historical Sketch of the Origin and Progress of Coining Money in Greece and her Colonies, &c. Illustrated by numerous fac-simile examples in actual Relief, and in the Metals of the respective Coins. 8vo. bds. $7 50. London, 1850.

Hunt, (Robert.) Panthea; the Spirit of Nature. 8vo. cloth, $3 25. Lond. 1849

Hunter, (Rev. J.) The Hallamshire Glossary. 12mo. cloth, $1 00. Lond. 1829.

Hutchinson, (Lieut.) Account of the Demolition and Removal by Blasting of a Portion of the Round Down Cliff, near Dover, in 1843. (Papers, R. E. vol. 6, 4to.) Lond.

——— On the Conducting Power of Water as applied to Submarine Explosions, by Voltaic Electricity, with Details of Apparatus. (Papers, R. E. vol. 7, 4to.) London.

——— (Thos.) The History and Province of Massachusetts Bay, from 1749 to 1774, comprising a detailed Narrative of the Origin and Early Stages of the American Revolution. 8vo. bds. $3 00. London, 1828.

Hydraulic Press for Proving Girders. (Papers, R. E. vol. 6, 4to.) London.

Imaginations and Imitations, by Hope. Cr. 8vo. cloth, $2 00. Lond. 1846.

Ingleby, (J. T.) Facts and Cases in Obstetric Medicine, with Observations on some of the most important Diseases incidental to Females. 8vo. bds. $3 00. Lond. N. D.

Introduction, (An,) to the Study of Gothic Architecture. Square 18mo. numerous wood-cuts, cloth, $1 25. Oxford, 1849.

Ireland, (John.) Paganism and Christianity compared in a Course of Lectures. 8vo. cloth, $1 50. London, 1825.

Iron Roofs erected over Building Slips. (Papers, R. E. vol. 9, 4to.) London.

Irving, (T.) The Fountain of Living Waters. 18mo. cloth, 50 cents; cloth gilt, 75 cents. New York, 1849.

James, (G. P. R.) Dark Scenes of History. 12mo. paper, 75 cents; cloth, $1 00. New York, 1850.

——— (Rev. J. B.) Thoughts on Passages selected from the Fathers. 12mo. cloth, $1 00. London, 1848.

Jameson, (Mrs.) Studies and Summer Rambles in Canada. 2 vols. 12mo. cloth, $1 50. New York.

Jamieson, (A.) Mechanics of Fluids for Practical Men. 8vo. cloth, wood-cuts, $1 87. London, 1837.

Jane Eyre; an Autobiography. 8vo. paper, 25 cents; a Library edition. 12mo. cloth, $1 00. New York, 1850.

Jarrin, (G. A.) The Italian Confectioner; or, Complete Economy of Desserts. 12mo. cloth, portrait, $2 50. London, 1829.

Jeans, (H. W.) Rules and Examples in Navigation. 12mo. paper, 63 cents. London, 1849.

——— Problems in Astronomy, Surveying, and Navigation, with their Solutions. 12mo. cloth, $1 75. London, 1849.

Jebb, (Major.) On the Construction and Ventilation of Prisons. (Papers, R. E. vol. 7, 4to.) London.

——— Notes on the Theory and Practice of Sinking Artesian Wells. (Papers, R. E. vol. 5, 4to.) London

——— (Capt.) Description of a Drawbridge on the London and Birmingham Railway, at Weedon. (Papers, R. E. vol. 3, 4to) Lond.

Jennings, (Lieut. E.) Hints on Sea Risks, addressed to Merchants, Ship-Owners, and Mariners. 8vo. cloth, $1 00. Lond. 1843.

Johnes, (A. J.) Philological Proofs of the Original Unity and Recent Origin of the Human Race, derived from a Comparison of the Languages of Asia, Europe, Africa, and America. 8vo. cloth, $1 25. Lond. 1846.

Johnstone, (Mrs.) The Edinburgh Tales, by various Authors, and edited by Mrs. Johnstone. 3 vols. in 1, 8vo. cloth, $4 00. London, 1850.

Johnston, (J. F. W.) Experimental Agriculture; being the Results of Past and Suggestions for Future Experiments in Scientific and Practical Agriculture. 8vo. cloth, $2 50. London.

Jones, (G.) Recollections of the Life, Practice, and Opinions of Sir Francis Chantrey. Post 8vo. cloth, $2 50. Lond. 1849.

——— (Rev. J.) The Book of the Young; an Invitation to Early Christian Piety. 12mo. cloth, $1 00. Oxford, 1837.

——— (J. H.) Life of Ashbel Green, V. D. M. begun to be written by himself in his 82d Year, and continued to his 84th. 8vo. cloth, portrait, $2 00. New York, 1849.

——— (J. E.) Account and Description of Youghal Bridge, designed by Alexander Nimmo. (Trans. I. C. E. vol. 2, 4to.) Lond.

Jones, (Lieut. Col.) Account of the Destruction of the Bridge at Carrack, with Gunpowder, in 1845. (Papers, R. E. vol. 9, 4to.) Lond.

——— Destruction of Banagher and Rooksey Bridges on the Shannon. (Papers, R. E. vol. 8, 4to.) London.

——— (Col. J. T.) Memoranda relative to the Lines thrown up to cover Lisbon in 1810. (Papers, R. E. vol. 3, 4to.) London.

——— (Major H. D.) Memoranda relating to the Well in Fort Regent, Jersey. (Papers, R. E. vol. 4, 4to.) London.

——— Table on the Description and Weight of the Packages of various Articles of Traffic. Notes on Lintz. Report on Paving Stables at Brighton. (Papers, R. E. vol. 3, 4to.) Lond.

——— Memoranda and Details of the Mode of Building Houses, &c. in the Island of Malta. (Papers, R. E. vol. 5, 4to.) Lond.

——— (Thos. R.) A General Outline of the Animal Kingdom and Manual of Comparative Anatomy. 8vo. cloth, illustrated with 336 wood engravings in the best style, $11 50. London, 1841.

Jongh, (L. J. de.) Three Kinds of Cod Liver Oil comparatively considered with reference to their Chemical and Therapeutic Properties. Translated by E. Carey, with Appendix, by Dr. Dunglison. 12mo. cloth, 90 cents. Philadelphia, 1849.

Kaemtz, (L. F.) Course of Meteorology, by C. V. Walker. Thick 12mo. cloth, $3 75. London, 1846.

Kames, (Lord.) History of Man; or, the Wonders of Human Nature. 2 vols. 8vo. cloth, $3 00. London, 1790.

Keating, (E. H.) Historical Centuries from the Christian Era to the present time. 4to. cloth, $3 75. London, 1846.

Keith, (A.) The Land of Israel according to the Covenant with Abraham, &c. 12mo. cloth, map and plates, $1 25. N. York, 1844.

Kelly, (W. K.) Syria and the Holy Land, their Scenery and their People. 8vo. cloth, illustrated with wood-cuts, $2 00. Lond. 1844.

Kennedy, (J. P.) Memoirs of the Life of William Wirt. A new and revised edition. 2 vols. 12mo. cloth, portrait, $2 25. Philadelphia, 1850.

Kenrick, (W.) The new American Orchardist; or, an Account of the most valuable Varieties of Fruit of all Climates adapted to Cultivation in the United States, with an Appendix on Silk, &c. &c. 12mo. cloth, $1 00. Boston, 1841.

——— (J.) Essay on Primeval History. 12mo. cloth, $1 50. London.

King of the Hurons, (The.) 12mo. cloth, $1 00. New York, 1850.

King, (R.) On the Preservation of Infants in Delivery. 12mo. cloth, $1 25. Lond. 1847.

Kinsey, (Rev. W. M.) Portugal. Illustrated in a Series of Letters. Imp. 8vo. plates and cuts, $5 00. London, 1823.

Klopstock's Sammtliche Werke. 12 vols. in 6, half bound, $6 00. Leipzig, 1823.

Knight, (Chas.) Studies of Shakespeare. 8vo. cloth, $2 25. London, 1849.

Knight's Guides to Service and Trade. 12mo. paper. Lond.
—— Baker, (The,) 31 cents.
—— Banker's Clerk, (The,) 75 cents.
—— Carver and Gilder, (The,) 31 cents.
—— Chemist and Druggist, (The,) 31 cents.
—— Clerk, (The,) 45 cents.
—— Cook, (The,) 700 Receipts, 90 cents.
—— Cook with Confectioner, (The,) $1 50.
—— Confectioner, (The,) 45 cents.
—— Cooper, (The,) 31 cents.
—— Cowherd, (The.) 31 cents.
—— Dairy-Maid, (The,) 25 cents.
—— Farm-Bailiff, (The,) 45 cents.
—— Farmer, (The,) 60 cents.
—— Gardener, (The,) 45 cents.
—— Governess, (The,) $1 00.
—— Groom and Coachman, (The,) 60 cents.
—— Housemaid, (The,) 25 cents.
—— Joiner and Cabinet-Maker, (The,) 31 cents.
—— Lady's Maid, (The,) 25 cents.
—— Laundry Maid, (The,) 25 cents.
—— Maid of all Work, (The,) 25 cents.
—— Miller, (The,) 31 cents.
—— Milliner and Dress-Maker, (The,) 31 cents.
—— Nurse, (The,) 31 cents.
—— Nursery-Maid, (The,) 31 cents.
—— Ploughman, Carter, &c. (The,) 31 cents.
—— Plumber, Glazier, &c. (The,) 31 cents.
—— Poultry-Maid, (The,) 31 cents.
—— Printer, (The,) 31 cents.
—— Shepherd, (The,) 31 cents.
—— Shoemaker, (The,) 75 cents.
—— Tailor, (The,) 31 cents.

Knight's Weekly and Monthly Volumes Paper, 31 cents; cloth, 45 cents. Lond.
—— Backwoods of Canada, by a Lady. 1 vol.
—— Bacon, his Writings and Philosophy, by Craik. 3 vols.
—— Banfield's Industry of the Rhine, Agriculture, &c. 2 vols.
—— Book of Table-Talk, by various Contributors. 2 vols.
—— Brougham's Dialogues on Instinct. 1 vol.
—— Brougham's Discourses on Objects, &c. of Science. 1 vol.
—— Brougham's Sketches of Statesmen, George III. 6 vols.
—— Butler, his Hudibras and other Works, by Ramsay. 1 vol.
—— Cabinet Portrait Gallery of British Worthies. 12 vols. portraits.
—— Chaucer's Canterbury Tales, &c. by Saunders. 3 vols.
—— Craik's History of British Commerce. 3 vols.
—— Craik's History of Literature, &c. in England. 6 vols.
—— Craik's Pursuit of Knowledge. 3 vols.
—— Craik's Spencer and his Poetry. 3 vols.
—— Davis's Description of China and the Chinese. 3 vols.
—— Davis's Sketches of China. 1 vol.
—— Dennis' Cid, Chronicle of the Poetry of Spain. 1 vol.
—— Dodd's Account of the Manufactures of Great Britain. 6 vols.
—— Elephant, Horse, and Dog, by Knight and Martin. 3 vols.
—— History of Monkeys. 1 vol.
—— History of Mammalia. 6 vols.
—— Jameson's Lives of Italian Painters. 2 vols.
—— Kitto's Lost Senses, Deafness and Blindness. 2 vols.
—— Kitto's Physical Geography of the Holy Land. 2 vols.
—— Knight's Capital and Labor, and Results of Machinery. 1 vol.
—— Knight's Life of Caxton. 1 vol.
—— Knight's Volume of Varieties. 1 vol.
—— Lamb's Tales from Shakespeare. 2 vols.
—— Lane's Arabian Tales and Anecdotes. 1 vol.
—— Lankester's Food of Man. 2 vols.
—— Lewes' Biographical History of Philosophy. 4 vols.

Knight's Weekly and Monthly Volumes. Paper, 31 cents; cloth, 45 cents. Lond.
—— Lewes' Spanish Drama. 1 vol.
—— McFarlane's Cabinet History of England. 26 vols.
—— McFarlane's Customs, Sports, &c. of South Italy. 1 vol.
—— McFarlane's Life of Sir T. Gresham. 1 vol.
—— McFarlane's Old English Novelties. 4 vols.
—— McFarlane's Romance of Travel—East. 2 vols.
—— Malkin's Historical Parallels. 3 vols.
—— Martineau's Billow and the Rock; a Tale. 1 vol.
—— Martineau's Feats on the Fiord. 1 vol.
—— Memoirs of a Working Man. 1 vol.
—— Mind among the Spindles. 1 vol.
—— Nicolay's History of the Oregon Territory. 1 vol.
—— Nugent's Sacred and Classic Lands. 2 vols.
—— Paley's Natural Theology, by Lord Brougham and Sir C. Bell. 4 vols.
—— Planche's History of British Costume. 2 vols.
—— Plutarch's Lives, Selection by Prof. Long. 5 vols.
—— Pompeii, its Destruction and Re-discovery. 2 vols.
—— Poole's Englishman in Egypt. 3 vols.
—— Popular Tumults, illustrative of Social Ignorance. 1 vol.
—— Pratt's Field, Garden, and Woodland. 1 vol.
—— Pratt's Flowers and their Associations. 1 vol.
—— Racine, Moliere, Corneille, and the French Classic Drama. 3 vols.
—— Rennie's Bird Architecture and Bird Miscellanies. 3 vols.
—— Rennie's Insect Architecture. 2 vols.
—— Secret Societies of the Middle Ages. 2 vols.
—— Settlers and Convicts; or, the Australian Backwoods. 2 vols.
—— Smith's Philosophy of Health. 4 vols.
—— Tasso's Recovery of Jerusalem, by Fairfax 2 vols.
—— Thorn's Rambles by Rivers. 4 vols.
—— Vieusseux, Buildings and Revolutions of Paris. 3 vols.
—— Vieusseux, Life of Napoleon Bonaparte. 2 vols.
—— Wittich's Curiosities of Physical Geography. 2 vols.
—— Wittich's Visit to the West Coast of Norway 1 vol.
—— Wornum's History of Painting, Ancient and Modern. 2 vols.

Kyan's Process for the Preservation of Timber from Dry Rot, with a Description of the Tank erected for that purpose in the Royal Arsenal, Woolwich, by Col. Alderson. (Papers, R. E. vol. 1, 4to.) London.

Laborde, (M. La de.) Journey through Arabia Petrea to Mount Sinai and the Excavated City of Petra, the Edom of the Prophecies. 8vo. cloth, map and engravings, $3 00. London, 1838.

Laird of Logan's Jest-Book. 18mo. cloth, 75 cents. Glasgow.

Lamb, (E. B.) Studies of Ancient Domestic Architecture, principally selected from original Drawings in the Collection of the late Sir R. Burrell, with Observations on the Application of Ancient Architecture to the Pictorial Composition of Modern Edifices. 20 fine plates. Imp. 4to. $7 50. London.

Lander, (W.) Observations on Painting Timber when exposed to Damp. (Papers, R. E. vol. 5, 4to.) London.

Landsborough, (Rev. D.) Popular History of British Sea Weeds. Royal 16mo. cloth, 22 plates, colored, $3 25. Lond. 1849.

Larcom, (Capt.) Memoir of the Professional Life of the late Captain Drummond. (Papers, R. E. vol. 4, 4to.) London.

Lardner, (N.) The Works of, with a Life, by Dr. Kippis. 10 vols. 8vo. cloth, $20 00. London, 1838.

Latham, (P. M.) Lectures on Clinical Medicine, comprising Diseases of the Heart. 2 vols. 12mo. cloth, $2 25. Lond. 1846.

Laurel, (The.) Fugitive Poetry of the Nineteenth Century. 18mo. mor. gilt edges, $1 50. London, 1838.

Lawrence, (W.) A Treatise on the Diseases of the Eye. 8vo. cloth, $4 50. London, 1811.

——— Lectures on Comparative Anatomy, Physiology, Zoology, and the Natural History of Man. 12mo. cloth, with 12 new engravings, 88 cents. London, 1848.

Layard, (A. H.) New Researches at Nineveh, &c. 8vo. cloth, uniform with "Nineveh and its Remains." (In preparation.) N York

Lea, (J.) Observations on the Genus Unio, with Descriptions of New Genera and Species in the Families Naides, Conchæ Colimacea, Lymnæana, Melaniana, and Peristomania, with colored plates, $5 00. Philadelphia.

Le Bas's Life of Archbishop Cranmer. 2 vols. 18mo. cloth, $1 00. New York.

Lebert, (H.) Physiologie Pathologique ou recherches Cliniques, experimentales et Microscopiques sur l'Inflammation, etc. 2 vols. 8vo. paper, with atlas of plates, $5 50. Paris, 1845.

——— Traite Pratique des Maladies Scrofuleuses et Tuberculeuses. 8vo. broche, $2 75. Paris, 1849.

Lee, (E.) Treatise on some Nervous Disorders. 8vo. cloth, $2 25. Lond. 1838.

——— The Baths and Watering Places of England considered with reference to their Curative Efficacy, &c. 12mo. cloth, 50 cents. London, 1848.

——— Continental Travel, with an Appendix on the Influence of Climate, the Remedial Advantages of Travelling, &c. 8vo. cloth, plates, $1 00. London, 1848.

——— Elements of Geology; containing a Description of the Geological Formations and Mineral Resources of the United States. 12mo. cloth, wood-cuts, 50 cents. New York.

——— (Mrs. R.) Life of Baron Cuvier. 12mo. cloth, 50 cents. New York.

——— (Mrs.) Life and Times of Thomas Cranmer. 12mo. cloth, 50 cents. Boston, 1841.

Leech, (J.) Young Troublesome; or, Master Jacky's Holidays. A Series of Etchings on steel, $1 63; colored, $2 25. Lond. 1849.

Le Gai, (H.) Almanach Facetieux Recreatif, Comique et Proverbial pour 1850. 18mo. broche, 25 cents. Paris, 1850.

——— Almanach des Jeux, &c. 18mo. broche, 25 cents. Paris, 1850.

Leithead, (W.) Electricity, its Nature, Operation, and Importance in the Phenomena of the Universe. 12mo. cloth, $2 50. London, 1837.

Leslie, (Chas.) Theological Works. 7 vols. 8vo. cloth, portrait, $16 00. Oxford, 1832.

Lever, (Chas.) Roland Cashel. 8vo. cloth, with illustrations by Phiz, $1 00. New York, 1850.

Lewis, (Mrs. S. A.) Records of the Heart. 12mo. bds. $1 00. New York, 1844.

——— (G. C.) Babrii Fabulæ Æsopeæ. 12mo. cloth, $1 50. Oxonii, 1846.

——— (Col.) On the Use of Fascines in Forming Foundations to Buildings. (Papers, R. E. vol. 6, 4to.) London.

——— Observations on the Value of Fortresses, Intrenched Camps, and Field Fortresses, their Application to the present System of Railroads for the Protection of the Metropolis South of the Thames. (Papers, R. E. vol. 9, 4to.) London.

——— Report on the Applications of Forts, Towers, and Batteries to Coast Defences and Harbors. (Papers, R. E. vol. 7. 4to.) Lond.

——— (W.) A Treatise on the Game of Chess, containing several new Modes of Attack and Defence, particularly the Gambits, to which are added 25 new Problems on Diagrams. Thick 8vo. cloth, $5 50. Lond. 1849.

Library of Anecdote, (The,) containing the Remarkable Sayings, Efforts of Genius, Wit, and Humor, &c. &c. 12mo. cloth, 75 cents. London, 1839.

Lillie, (Charles.) The British Perfumer; being a Collection of choice Receipts and Observations made during an extensive Practice of Thirty Years. 12mo. cloth, $1 00. London, 1822.

Lindley, (G.) A Guide to the Orchard and Fruit Garden; or, an Account of the most valuable Fruits cultivated in Great Britain, with additions of all the most valuable Fruits Cultivated in America, by Michael Floy. 12mo. cloth, colored plates, $1 50. New York, 1846.

Lindsay, (Lord.) Sketches of the History of Christian Art. 3 vols. 8vo. cloth, $8 50. London, 1847.

List, (W. B.) Panama, Nicaragua, and Tehuantepec; or, Considerations upon the Question of Communication between the Atlantic and Pacific Oceans. Map, 8vo. cloth, $1 25. London, 18 9.

Little, (W. J.) On Ankylosis, or Stiff Joint. 8vo. cloth, $2 75. London, 1848.

Livermore, (A. A.) Review of the Mexican War. 12mo. cloth, $1 00. Boston, 1850.

London, (The,) Dissector; or, Guide to Anatomy. Revised and corrected by J. Chaisty, $1 00. Philadelphia, 1842.

Lopham, (J. A.) Wisconsin, its Geography, History, &c. 12mo. cloth, $1 00. Milwaukie.

Lowell, (J. R.) The Nooning and other Poems. 12mo. cloth. Boston, 1850.

——— Poems. 2 vols. 12mo. bds. $1 50; cloth, $1 75. Boston, 1850.

Lowrie's Memoirs of the Rev. W. M. Lowrie, Missionary to China. 8vo. cloth, portrait, $1 50. New York, 1849.

Lloyd, (W. W.) Xanthian Marbles; the Nereid Monument; an Historical Mythological Essay. 8vo. cloth, $2 25. Lond. 1845

Luke, (F. C.) Remarks on Herm Granite, with some Experiments on the Wear of different Granites. (Trans. I. C. E. vol. 1, 4to.) London.

Luxmore, (Lieut.) Description of the Groins used on the Coast of Sussex for Preventing the Encroachments of the Sea. (Papers, R. E. vol. 1, 4to.) London.

Lympsfield and its Environs; being a Series of Views, with Descriptions of that Village and Objects of interest in its vicinity, and the Old Oak Chair, a Ballad, with illustrations, by George Cruikshank. 8vo. cloth, plates, $1 00. Westerham, 1838.

Lyre, (The.) Fugitive Poetry of the Nineteenth Century. 18mo. mor. gilt edges, beautifully printed, $1 50. Lond. 1838.

Macculloch's Researches in the Aboriginal History of America. 8vo. cloth, $2 00. Baltimore.

McLean, (John.) Notes of a Twenty-Five Years' Service in the Hudson Bay Territory. 2 vols. post 8vo. cloth, $6 25. Lond. 1849.

M'Culloch, (J. R.) On Commerce. 8vo. bds. 75 cents. London, 1833.

McFarlane, (Charles.) The French Revolution. Portraits and engravings, 2 vols. square 12mo. cloth, $4 50. London.

Mackay, (A.) The Western World; or, Travels in the United States in 1846 and '47, exhibiting them in their latest Development, Social, Political, and Industrial. 2 vols. 12mo. cloth, $2 00. Phila. 1849.

Mackenzie, (W.) Account of the Bridge over the Severn, near the Town of Tewkesbury, in the County of Gloucester, designed by T. Telford, and erected by him. (Trans. I. C. E. vol. 2, 4to.) London.

Machinery used in the Manufactory of Cannon. (Papers, R. E. vol. 8, 4to.) Lond.

Mackie, (W.) Castles, Palaces, and Prisons of Mary, Queen of Scots. Royal 8vo. cloth gilt, plates, $7 50. Lond. 1849.

Macneil, (Sir J.) New Canal Boat Experiments. (Trans. I. C. E. vol. 1, 4to.) Lond.

Madden, (R. R.) The Island of Cuba, its Resources, Progress, and Prospects, considered in relation especially to the Influence of its Prosperity on the Interests of the British West India Colonies. 12mo. cloth, $1 25. London, 1849.

Maginn, (W.) Homeric Ballads; the Greek Text, with a Metrical Translation and Notes, collected from Fraser's Magazine and revised. Foolscap 8vo. cloth, $1 75. Lond. 1849.

Maire, (Dr.) Nouveau Guide des Meres de Famille. 8vo. broche, $1 25. Paris, 1843.

Manesca, (J.) A Philological Recorder adapted to the Oral System of Teaching Living Languages. Oblong paper, 63 cents. New York, 1843.

Mann, (H.) A Few Thoughts to Young Men, being the Substance of a Lecture. 8vo. paper, 25 cents. Boston, 1850.

Manning, (H. E.) The Unity of the Church. 8vo. cloth, $3 00. Lond. 1845.

Manual of Commercial Correspondence, English and French; or, a Selection of Commercial Phrases, taken from a number of Letters, &c., by a Merchant. 12mo. cloth. N. York, 1850.

Mant, (Rev. R.) Primitive Christianity exemplified and illustrated by the Acts of Primitive Christians. 8vo. cloth, $2 00. London, 1842.

Maran-Atha in Connection with the Future History of the Jewish Nation. 12mo. cloth, 50 cents. Dublin, 1839.

Marryatt, (Capt.) The Little Savage; being the History of a Boy left alone on an Uninhabited Island. 12mo. paper, 38 cents; cloth, 50 cents. New York, 1849.

—— (J.) A History of Pottery and Porcelain, with a Description of the Manufacture from the earliest period in various Countries. 8vo. cloth, plates and wood-cuts. Lond.

Marsden, (W.) History of Sumatra. 4to. half bound, maps and plates, $6 50. London, 1811.

Marshall, (Major.) Memoranda on the Demolition of the South Face of Fort Schulemburg, Corfu. (Papers, R. E. vol. 2, 4to.) London.

Marivaux. Marianne. 12mo. paper, $1 00. Paris.

Marvel, (M.) The Battle Summer—Reign of Blouse. 12mo. cloth, $1 25. New York, 1850.

Maximilian. Prince of Wied's Travels in the Interior of North America. Translated by H. E. Lloyd. 4to. half mor. gilt leaves, 84 elaborately colored plates, $150 00. London, 1843.

Maxwell, (W. H.) Rambling Recollections of a Soldier of Fortune. Cr. 8vo. cloth, portrait, $1 25. Dublin, 1842.

Melville, (H.) Redburn, his First Voyage; being the Confessions of a Sailor Boy and Reminiscences of the Son of a Gentleman in the Merchant Service. 12mo. paper, 75 cents; cloth, $1 00. New York, 1849.

Memoirs of Mrs. W. Veitch, Mr. Thomas Hog, of Killearn, Mr. H. Erskine, and Mr. John Carstairs. 12mo. cloth, 50 cents. Edin. 1847.

Memes, (J. S.) History of Sculpture, Painting, &c. 18mo. cloth, $1 00. London.

Meredith, (Mrs. C.) Romance of Nature; or, the Flower Seasons Illustrated. Cr. 8vo. green mor. gilt, with 28 beautifully colored plates, $10 00. London, 1839.

Merriman, (S.) Synopsis of the various kinds of Difficult Parturition, with Practical Remarks. 8vo. cloth, $2 00. Lond. 1820.

Metcalf, (Dr. S. L.) A New Theory of Terrestrial Magnetism. 8vo. cloth, $1 00. New York, 1833.

Miall, (E.) Views of the Voluntary Principle. 12mo. cloth, $1 12. Lond. 1845.

Micali, (G.) Monumenti Inediti a Illustrazione della storia degli antichi Popopli Italiani. 8vo. bds. with atlas of plates, some colored, in folio, $10 75. Firenze, 1844.

Middleton, (C.) On the Primitive Fathers. 12mo. paper, 25 cents. Lond. 1844.

—— (H.) The Government and the Curreney. 12mo. cloth. New York, 1850.

Miers, (John.) Description of the Machinery employed in Deptford Dockyard for Spinning Hemp and Manufacturing Ropes and Cables. (Papers, R. E. vol. 5, 4to.) London.

Mill, (W. H.) Sermons on several occasions before the University of Cambridge. 8vo. cloth, $3 00. Cambridge, 1845.

Miller, (W. H.) Elements of Hydrostatics and Hydronamics. 8vo. bds. plates, $1 75. Cambridge, 1831.

Milman, (Rev. R.) The Life of Tasso. 2 vols. post 8vo. cloth, $6 50. Lond. 1850.

Milner, (T.) A Descriptive Atlas of Astronomy and of Physical and Political Geography. 4to. cloth, illustrated with 80 maps, $10 50; half bound in Russia, $12 50. London, 1849.

Mimpriss, (R.) The Gospel History of our Lord's Life and Ministry, &c. 12mo. cloth, 75 cents. London, 1842.

——— A Harmony of the Four Gospels. 12mo. cloth, colored map, 75 cents. Lond. 1845.

Mitchell, (Lieut. T. H.) System of Light Drill, &c. 12mo. cloth, plates, $1 25. London, 1843.

Montalba, (A. R.) Fairy Tales from all Nations, with illustrations, by Doyle. Paper, 70 cents; cloth, 88 cents; cloth, gilt edges, $1 00. New York, 1849.

Moore, (Thos.) Life of Lord Edward Fitzgerald. 2 vols. 12mo. cloth, $1 00. New York.

——— Songs, Ballads, and Sacred Songs. 12mo. cloth, $1 50. London, 1849.

——— Irish Melodies. Folio, beautifully illustrated with Finden's Beauties, cloth, $6 00; mor. gilt, $12 00. Phila. 1850.

——— Lalla Rookh, with the Autobiographical Preface from the Collective edition of the Author's Poetical Works. 16mo. cloth, vignette, by Maclise, $1 50. Lond. 1849.

——— Irish Melodies. 16mo. cloth, with vignette, by Maclise, $1 50. Lond. 1849.

Moorsom, (Capt. C. R.) On the Principles of Naval Tactics, with Exemplifications of the Practice, &c. 8vo. cloth, plates, $1 50. Birmingham, 1846.

Moreau-Boutard, (L. M. A.) Precis de Chirurgie Elementaire. 12mo. broche, 75 cents. Paris, 1845.

Morgan, (Lady.) Woman and her Master. 2 vols. 12mo. cloth, $1 00. Phila.

Morning, (The,) Exercises at Cripplegate, St. Giles in the Fields, and in Southwark; being divers Sermons, preached A. D. 1659–1689. Edited, with Notes and Translations, by James Nichols. 6 vols. 8vo. cloth, $16 50. London, 1844.

Mosca, (Chevalier.) Details of the Construction of a Stone Bridge erected over the Dora Riparia, near Turin. (Trans. I. C. E. vol. 1, 4to.) London.

Moseley's Illustrations of Mechanics. Edited by James Renwick. 12mo cloth, 50 cents. New York.

——— Treatise on Hydrostatics and Hydronamics. 8vo. $3 75. Cambridge, 1830.

Motte, (P. H. de la.) On the various Applications of Anastatic Printing and Papyrography, with illustrative Examples. Cr. 8vo. bds. 17 plates, $1 25. London, 1849.

Mudie, (R.) Gleanings of Nature; containing Fifty-seven Groups of Animals and Plants, with Popular Descriptions of their Habits. Imp. 8vo. cloth, colored plates, $2 75. London, 1838.

——— Guide to the Observation of Nature; or, Hints of Inducement to the Study of Natural Productions, &c. 12mo. cloth, 50 cents. New York.

Muehry, (Dr. A.) Comparative State of Medicine in France, England, and Germany. Translated by E. G. Davis. 8vo. bds. $1 87. Philadelphia, 1839.

Mullen, (Sam.) The Pilgrim of Beauty; the Cottager's Sabbath and other Poems, now first collected. 8vo. cloth, 23 steel engravings, $3 00. London, 1845.

Muller, (K. D.) Handbuch des Archæologie der Kunst. 8vo. half calf, neat, $3 50. Breslau, 1835.

Murray, (Lindley.) The Power of Religion on the Mind, &c. 18mo. cloth, 38 cents. London, 1845.

——— (J.) System of Materia Medica. 2 vols. 8vo. sheep, $1 50. New York, 1821.

Nasmyth's Patent Steam Hammer—Patent Steam Pile Driving Machine. (Papers, R. E. vol. 8, 4to.) London.

Natural Philosophy for Beginners. 12mo. cloth, wood-cuts, 75 cents. Lond. 1845.

Neale, (Rev. J. M.) Hierologus; or, the Church Tourists. 12mo. cloth, $1 75. London, 1843.

Neander, (Dr. A.) History of the Planting and Training of the Christian Church by the Apostles. Translated by J. E. Ryland. 8vo. cloth, $1 25. Phila. 1844.

Neilson, (J. B.) On the Hot Air Blast. (Trans. I. C. E. vol. 1, 4to.) London.

——— (P.) Life and Adventures of Zamba, an African Negro King, and his Experience of Slavery in South Carolina. Post 8vo. cloth, portrait, $2 00. London, 1847.

Nelson, (Lieut.) On Shot Furnaces; Engineering Details; Notices on the New Victualling Establishment at Devonport, with drawings of its Cast Iron Roofs. (Papers, R. E. vol. 4, 4to.) London.

——— Part of a Report on the last 150 Miles of the Great Fish River, South Africa. (Papers, R. E. vol. 5, 4to. cloth.) Lond.

——— (R.) Companion for the Festivals and Fasts of the Church of England, with Collects and Prayers for each Solemnity. 8vo. cloth, $2 25. Oxford, 1843.

——— (Capt.) Notes on Swing or Flying Bridges. Memoranda on Transition Lime and Limestone as obtained from different Quarries at Plymouth. (Papers, R. E. vol. 7, 4to.) London.

——— (R. J.) Report on Beaufort Bridge. On the Mode of Bending Timber adopted in Prussia. Rough Sketch of the Suspension Bridge over the Lahn at Nassau. (Papers, R. E. vol. 3, 4to.) London.

Newcome, (W.) An English Harmony of the Four Evangelists disposed after the Manner of the Greek. 8vo. cloth, map, $2 00. London, 1827.

Newman, (S. P.) Elements of Political Economy. 12mo. half bound, 75 cents, New York, 1841

Newton, (Rev. John.) The Works of, wit a Life of the Author, by the Rev. Richar Cecil, and an Introduction, by Rev. F. Cunning ham. Royal 8vo. cloth, portrait, $6 00. London, 1839.

Nicholas, (Sir H.) The Chronology of History, containing Tables, Calculations, and Statements indispensable for Ascertaining the Dates of Historical events and of Public and Private Documents from the earliest period to the present time. 12mo. cloth, $1 75. London, 1840.

Nicol, (W.) The Villa Garden Directory; or, Monthly Index of Work to be done in Town and Villa Gardens, &c. 12mo. cloth, $1 00. Edinburgh, 1823.

Nicolls, (Col.) Experiments tried at Quebec as to the Properties and Adhesive Qualities of Cements. (Papers, R. E. vol. 3, 4to.) London.

Noel, (Rev. B. W.) Essay on Christian Baptism. 18mo. cloth, 63 cents. New York.

Notes on the Employment of Sand for Foundations in Marshy or Soft Soil, compiled from an article in the Annales des Ponts et Chaussees for 1835. Memorandum of the Engineer operating at the Taking of Ghuznee in July, 1839. (Papers, R. E. vol. 4, 4to.) Lond.

——— On the Ministry of Cardinal B. Pacca, Secretary of State to Pope Pius VII. 8vo. cloth, $2 50. Dublin, 1843.

Nouet's Life of Jesus Christ in Glory, adapted for the Use of Members of the Church of England. 12mo. cloth, $2 25. Lond. 1847.

Nuns of Minsk, (The.) Narrative of Makren Mieczyslawska, Abbess of the Basilian Convent of Minsk; or, the History of a Seven Years' Persecution suffered for the Faith, by her and her Nuns, &c. 12mo. cloth, 31 cents. London, 1846.

O'Brien, (E.) The Lawyer, his Character and Rule of Holy Life. 12mo. mor. gilt, $3 25. London, 1842.

Ogle, (N.) Mariame, the last of the Asmonean Princesses; an Historical Novel of Palestine, $1 25. London, 1843.

Œttinger, (E. M.) Bibliographie Biographique; ou, Dictionnaire de 2600 ouvrages, tant Anciens que Modernes, relatifs a l'Histoire de la vie Publique et Privee des Hommes celebres de tous les Tems et toutes les Nations. Royal 8vo. paper, $13 50. Lond. 1849.

Oldershaw, (Capt.) Description of the One Arch Wooden Bridge of 205 feet span at Paradenia, with an Account of the Execution of the Work and the Means employed in throwing it across the River Mahavillaganga, in Ceylon. (Papers, R. E. vol. 3, 4to.) London.

Oliffe, (C.) Waverley Sketch-Book. 8vo. calf, neat, $2 50. Paris, 1840.

On the Means of Preventing Damp in Walls. Experiments on an Open Cast Iron Girder. Notes and Experiments on Iron Girders. Experiments on the Strength of the Principals of a Wrought Iron Roof. Memorandum on the Use of Asphalte in Covering Casements. (Papers, R. E. vol. 7, 4to.) London.

Opie, (Mrs.) Adeline Mowbray; or, the Mother and Daughter; a Tale. 12mo. cloth, $1 00. London, 1844.

Ord, (Lieut. Col.) Horizontal Loophole and Loopholed Window. (Papers, R. E. vol. 8, 4to.) Lond.

——— (Major.) Notes to Aid in Correcting the Operations of Ascertaining the Heights of Mountains by Means of Boiling Water. (Papers, R. E. vol. 3, 4to.) London.

Osmond, (William.) Christian Memorials. 23 plates, 4to. cloth, $4 50. Lond. 1848.

Osler, (E.) Life of Admiral Viscount Exmouth. 12mo. mor. gilt edges, $1 63. London, 1841.

Overman, (F.) The Manufacture of Iron in all its Branches, &c., to which is added an Essay on the Manufacture of Steel. 8vo. cloth, 150 wood-cuts, $5 00. Phila. 1850.

Outram, (Lieut. F.) Description of the Method of Roofing in Use in the Southern Concan in the East Indies. (Trans. I. C. E. vol. 1, 4to.) London.

Paley, (W.) Works, with Illustrative Notes, and Life of the Author. Royal 8vo. Russia, gilt, portrait, $5 75. Lond. 1842.

Palmer, (H. R.) Experiments on the Resistance of Barges moving on Canals. (Trans. I. C. E. vol. 1, 4to.) London.

——— (G. H.) On the Application of Steam as a moving Power, considered especially with reference to the Economy of Atmospheric and High-Pressure Steam. (Trans. I. C. E. vol. 2, 4to.) London.

Parkes, (Jos.) On the Evaporation of Water from Steam Boilers. (Trans. I. C. E. vol. 2, 4to.) London.

Parnell, (E. A.) Dyeing and Calico Printing. 8vo. cloth, wood cuts, $2 25. London, 1849.

Pasley, (Sir C. W.) Extracts from a Report on the Copper Pontoons used in the Neapolitan Service in 1805, with Remarks on the Inefficiency of all Open Pontoons of the common Rectangular Form for the Passage of Rapid Rivers. (Papers, R. E. vol. 1, 4to.) London.

Paterculus, (M. V.) Abridgment of the History of Rome. 8vo. cloth, $1 25. London, 1814.

Paulding, (J. K.) The Puritan and his Daughter. 12mo. cloth, $1 25. New York, 1849.

Peacock, (G.) Treatise on Algebra. 2 vols. 8vo. bds. $7 75. Cambridge, 1842–45.

Peers, (Rev. B. O.) American Education; or, Strictures on the Nature, Necessity, and Practicability of a System of National Education suited to the United States. 12mo. cloth, 75 cents. New York, 183 .

Penrice, (Lieut.) Journal of Practical Operations in Mining at Chatham in 1845, with Appendix. (Papers, R. E. vol. 8, 4to.) Lond.

——— On Embrasures. (Papers, R. E. vol. 9, 4to.) London.

People's and Howitt's Journal. New Series. Vol. 1, royal 8vo. cloth, illustrated with engravings, $1 50. Lond. 1850.

Pettigrew, (Thos. J.) Bibliotheca Sussexiana; a Descriptive Catalogue, accompanied by Historical and Biographical Notices of the Manuscripts and Printed Books contained in the Library of his Royal Highness, the Duke of Sussex, in Kensington Palace. 3 parts, in 2 vols. royal 8vo. half mor. $20 00. Lond. 1827.

Phelps, (R.) Elementary Treatise on Optics; intended chiefly to Elucidate the Principles of the Construction of Telescopes and some other Optical Instruments, with three other Tracts on Optics, &c. 8vo. half mor. neat, $3 00. Cambridge, 1838.

Phillpotts, (Lieut. Col.) Report on the Canal Navigation of the Canadas. (Papers, R. E. vol. 5, 4to.) London.

Pinelli's Etchings, illustrative of Italian Manners and Costumes, comprising Picturesque Costumes of Rome. The Carnival, and the Adventures of Massaroni, the Brigand. Folio, half mor. 27 plates, $5 00. Rome, 1844.

Piper, (Major.) Memorandum of the Manner in which the several Repairs of the Chain Pier at Brighton have been executed, together with some Reflections on its Construction and Durability. (Papers, R. E. vol. 2, 4to.) London.

Pocket Anatomist, (The.) 32mo. roan, 50 cents. Geneva, N. Y. 1843.

Poe, (E. A.) The Works of, with Notices of his Life and Genius, by N. P. Willis, J. R. Lowell, and R. W. Griswold. 2 vols. 12mo. cloth, portrait, $2 50. New York, 1850.

Politics for the People. 8vo. bds. 75 cents. London, 1848.

Poor Artist, (The;) or, Seven Eyesights and but One Object. 12mo. cloth, $1 50. London, 1850.

Poo e, (G. A.) Life and Times of St. Cyprian. 8vo. cloth, $2 25. Oxford, 1840.

Pope, (Chas.) The Merchant, Ship-Owner, and Ship-Master's Import and Export Guide. 8vo. bds. $1 50. London, 1831.

——— The Poetical Works of Alexander Pope. Edited by the Rev. H. F. Carey. Royal 8vo. cloth, vignette, $2 75. Lond. 1850.

Portlock, (Capt.) On the Superior Slopes of Parapets. (Papers, R. E. vol. 8, 4to.) London.

——— Notes on Platforms. (Papers, R. E. vol. 8, 4to.) London.

Portwine, (E.) The Steam Engine from the earliest period to the present time. Atmospheric Railways. The Electric Printing Telegraph, and Screw Propeller. 18mo. cloth, 25 cents. London, 1847.

Posthumous Records of a London Clergyman. Edited by Rev. Hobart Caunter. 12mo. cloth, $1 00. London, 1835.

Powell, (Thos.) Living Authors of America. 12mo. cloth, $1 00. New York, 1850.

Powers' Sketches in New Zealand with Pen and Pencil. Post 8vo. plates, $3 75. London, 1849.

Pratt, (A.) The Pictorial Catechism of Botany. Square 12mo. cloth, wood-cuts, $1 00. London, 1842.

Precept and Examples. Instructive Letters and Lives of Eminent Men. 12mo. cloth. London, 1825.

Prichard, (W. B.) Treatise on Bar Harbors. 4to. cloth, with colored plates, $5 75. London.

Pridham, (Rev. J.) Church of England, her Excellencies and Defects. 8vo. cloth, $1 75. London, 1842.

Proudhon, (P. J.) Les Confessions d'un Revolutionnaire pour servir a l'histoire de la Revolution de Fevrier. 12mo. broche, 75 cents. Paris, 1850.

Puckle, (James.) The Club; or, a Gray Cap for a Green Head; a Dialogue between a Father and Son. 12mo. cloth, gilt edges, portraits and wood-cuts, $1 00. Lond. 1839.

Puritan Discipline Tracts.

——— Hay any Worke for Cooper, by Martin Mar-Prelate. 12mo. cloth, 75 cents. London, 1845.

——— An Epistle to the Terrible Priests of the Convocation House, by Martin Mar-Prelate. 12mo. cloth, 75 cents. Lond. 1843.

——— An Epitome of Dr. John Bridges' Defence, by Martin Mar-Prelate. 12mo. cloth, 75 cents. London, 1843.

——— An Almond for a Parrot; a Reply to Martin Mar-Prelate. 12mo. cloth, 75 cents. London, 1846.

Pursh, (F.) Flora Americæ Septentrionalis; or, a Systematic Arrangement and Classification of the Plants of North America. 2 vols. 8vo. cloth, 24 colored plates, $6 00. London, 1844.

Putnam, (G. P.) The World's Progress; or, Dictionary of Dates; being a Record of Remarkable Occurrences, Political, Literary, and Scientific, in the Annals of all Nations. Alphabetically and Synchronistically arranged. 8vo. New York, 1850.

Ram Raz, Essay on the Architecture of the Hindoos. 4to. half bound, illustrated with 48 plates, $12 00. London, 1834.

Ramsay, (Thos.) Life and Literary Remains of Barbara Hofland. 12mo. cloth, portrait, $1 75. London, 1849.

——— (A. C.) The Other Side; or, Notes for the History of the War between Mexico and the United States, written in Mexico, and translated from the Spanish. Thick 12mo. cloth, portraits, $1 50. New York, 1850.

Readings in Natural Theology; or, the Testimony of Nature to the Existence of God. 12mo. calf, neat, $2 00. London, 1838.

Remedies Suggested for the Perils of the Nation. 12mo. cloth, $1 75. Lond. 1844.

Richards, (W. C.) The Shakespeare Calendar; or, Wit and Wisdom for every Day in the Year. 18mo. cloth, 38 cents; cloth, gilt, 63 cents. New York, 1849.

Rioffrey, (Dr.) Physical Education specially adapted to Young Ladies. 12mo. cloth.

Robinson, (Rev. P.) Immortality; a Poem, in Ten Cantos. 12mo. cloth, $1 50. New York, 1846.

Romance of Modern Travel; a Year-Book of Literature. 12mo. cloth, colored plates, $1 50. London, 1850.

Romer, (F.) Physiology of the Human Voice. 12mo. cloth, $1 00. Lond. 1845.

Ross, (W. A.) A Yacht Voyage to Norway, Denmark, and Sweden. Cr. 8vo. cloth, plates, $4 00. Lond. 1849.

Ryland, (J. E.) Life and Correspondence of John Foster. Thick 12mo. cloth, $1 50. New York, 1849.

Saint Leger; or, the Threads of Life. 12mo. cloth, $1 00. New York, 1850.

Saravia, (H.) Treatise on the Different Degrees of Christian Priesthood. 12mo. cloth, 75 cents. Oxford, 1840.

Scandret, (J.) Sacrifice the Divine Service. 18mo. cloth, 63 cents. Oxford, 1840.

Scharling, (E. A.) On the Chemical Discrimination of Vesical Calculi. Translated from the Latin by S. E. Hoskins, M. D. Post 8vo. cloth, plates, $1 87. Lond. 1842.

Schmid, (Ch.) Contes. Traduction de la Cerfberr de Medelsheim, illustrations par Gavarni. Royal 8vo. half mor. gilt edges, $8 50. Paris, 1843.

Scoutetten, (Dr. H.) Rapport sur l'Hydrotherapie. 8vo. broche, 50 cents. Paris, 1844.

Scott, (W.) Plane Trigonometry and Mensuration. 8vo. roan, $2 63. Lond. 1845.

Sculpture and the Plastic Art, compiled by the Author of the History of the Art of Painting. 12mo. cloth, $1 00. Boston, 1850.

Sewell, (E. M.) The Child's First History of Rome. 12mo. cloth, 50 cents. New York, 1849.

Seymour, (E. S.) Sketches of Minnesota, the New England of the West, with Incidents of Travel in that Territory. 12mo. Yew York, 1850.

Sharpe, (E.) Decorated Windows; a Series of Illustrations of the Window Tracery, or the Decorated Style of Ecclesiastical Architecture. 8vo. cloth, plates, $6 00. London, 1849.

Shirley, by the Author of Jane Eyre. 8vo. paper, 38 cents; a Library edition, 12mo. cloth, $1 00. New York, 1849.

Shelley, (P. B.) Poetical Works, with Life. 2 vols. 12mo. half mor. $4 50. Lond. 1834.

Sidonia, the Sorceress, by the Author of the Amber Witch. 8vo. paper, 50 cents. New York, 1849.

Simon, (John.) A Physiological Essay on the Thymus Gland. 4to. cloth, wood-cuts, $6 50. London, 1845.

Simson, (R.) Opera Quædam Reliqua. 4to. old calf, $4 00. Glasgow, 1776.

Sinclair, (Catharine.) Sir E. Graham; or, Railway Speculators. 8vo. paper. New York, 1850.

Smith, (H.) The Heart in its State by Nature, and as Renewed by Grace. 18mo. cloth, 50 cents. New York, 1844.

——— (Dr. A.) Illustrations of the Zoology of South Africa. 5 vols. 4to. cloth, 277 plates, beautifully colored from Nature, $108 00. London.

Smith, (J. T.) The Streets of London. Cr. 8vo. cloth, $1 00. London, 1849.

——— (Dr. S.) Philosophy of Health. 2 vols. 18mo. cloth, wood-cuts, $1 75. Lond. 1848.

——— (G.) The Hebrew People from the origin of the Nation to the time of Christ. Cr. 8vo. cloth, $3 75. Lond. 1849.

——— (Thos.) On the Nature, Causes, Prevention, and Treatment of Acute Hydrocephalus, or Water Brain Fever. Cr. 8vo. cloth, $1 75. London, 1845.

Smyth, (J. R.) Miscellaneous Contributions to Pathology and Therapeutics. 8vo. cloth, $3 00. London, 1844.

Sobieski and Stewart's Tales of the Century; or, Sketches of the Romance of History, from 1746 to 1846. Post 8vo. cloth, $1 75. Edinburgh, 1847.

South, (J. F.) Description of the Bones, for Students in Anatomy. 12mo. cloth, $2 25. London, 1837.

Soler, (M. C. J.) Traductor Ingles. 12mo. cloth, $2 50. Cambridge, 1840.

Songs of the Prophets, with Prose Remarks and Metrical Versions. 18mo. cloth, 50 cents. London, 1835.

Southey, (R.) Common-Place Book. Second Series. (Special Collections.) Edited by J. W. Warter. 8vo. cloth, $5 25. Lond. 1849.

Spurzheim, (J. G.) Examination of Objections to the Doctrines of Gall and Spurzheim. 12mo. cloth, 50 cents. Boston, 1833.

——— (G.) Phrenology; or, the Doctrine of Mental Phenomena. 2 vols. 8vo. half calf, $3 00. Boston, 1832.

Steinbrenner, (C. C.) Traite sur la Vaccine. 8vo. paper, $1 37. Paris, 1846.

Steinetz, (Francis.) The Moderate Monarchy; or, Principles of the British Constitution described in a Narrative of the Life and Maxims of Alfred the Great and his Counsellors, from the German of A. V. Haller, with Notes and Commentaries on the present State of the British Constitution. Plates, post 8vo. calf, $3 25. London, 1849.

Stevenson, (W. F.) The Composition of Hydrogen and Non-decomposition of Water demonstrated, &c. Second edition, 12mo. cloth, $1 00. London, 1849.

Stocqueler, (J. H.) The Hand-Book of India; a Guide to the Stranger and the Traveller, and a Companion to the Resident. Cr. 8vo. cloth, maps, $4 00. Lond. 1844

Stoddart, (Sir John.) Universal Grammar; or, the Pure Science of Language and Glossology, or the Historical relations of Language. 12mo. cloth, $1 75. Lond. 1849.

Stonehouse, (Sir J.) Life of, with Extracts from his Tracts and Correspondence. 12mo. cloth, 75 cents. Oxford, 1844.

Sumner, (Chas.) Orations and Public Addresses. 12mo. cloth. Boston, 1850.

Taylor, (C. B.) Legends and Records, chiefly Historical. 12mo. half mor. gilt edges, plates, $3 00. London, 1845.

——— (W. C.) Modern British Plutarch. Post 8vo. cloth, $1 75. London, 1846.

Taylor, (W. C.) Illustrations of the Bible from the Monuments of Egypt. Cuts, &c. 12mo. cloth, $1 75. London, 1838.

Temple, (E.) Christian's Daily Treasury; a Religious Exercise for every Day in the Year. 12mo. cloth, $1 00. Boston, 1847.

Teste, (A.) Le Magnetisme Animal explique, &c. 8vo. broche, $2 25. Paris, 1845.

Thackeray, (W. M.) Rebecca and Rowena; or, a Romance upon Romance. 12mo. cloth, plates, $1 50; colored, $2 75. London, 1849.

Thomson, (J.) First Six, Eleventh, and Twelfth Books of Euclid's Elements, &c. 12mo. cloth, $1 50. Lond. 1845.

Thore, (A. M.) Etudes sur les Maladies incidentes des Alienes. 8vo. broche, $1 25. Paris, 1847.

Traill, (T. S.) Outlines of a Course of Lectures on Medical Jurisprudence. Post 8vo. cloth, $1 25. Edin. 1840.

Treasury of Pleasure Books, (A,) for Young Children, with 100 illustrations, by Absolom and Weir, $1 25; colored, $2 25. London, 1849.

Trebuchet, (A.) Jurisprudence de la Medicine de la Chirurgie et de la Pharmacie en France. 8vo. broche, $2 50. Paris, 1834.

Truman, (M.) Food and its Influence on Health and Disease. 12mo. cloth, $2 00. London, 1842.

Tuckerman, (H. T.) The Optimist. 12mo. cloth. New York, 1850.

Tytler, (M. F.) Tales of the Great and Brave. 2 vols. 12mo. cloth, $3 00. Edinburgh, 18 2.

Van Mons, (J. B.) Arbres Frutiers leur Culture en Belgique et leur propagation par la graine. 2 vols. 12mo. paper, $2 00. Louvain, 1835.

Virgilli Opera notis ex Editione Heyniana excerptis Illustrata. 8vo. cloth, $3 00. London, 1839.

Walker, (Rev. S. A.) Church Missions in Western Africa. 8vo. cloth, map, $3 50. Dublin, 1845.

——— (Rev. W.) Church Discipline. 18mo. cloth, 31 cents. Boston, 1844.

Walsingham, (F.) A Search made into Matters of Religion. Post 8vo. cloth, $2 50; reduced to $1 50. London, 1843.

Wardlaw, (R.) National Church Establishments examined in a Course of Lectures. 8vo. cloth, $2 25; reduced to $1 50. Lond.

Warter, (J. W.) The Teaching of the Prayer-Book, &c. 8vo. cloth, $2 00; reduced o $1 50. London, 1845.

Wells, (E.) An Historical Geography of the Old and New Testament. 8vo. cloth, maps, 1 63. Oxford, 1840.

Whewell, (W.) Of Induction, with especial reference to J. S. Mill's System of Logic. 8vo. paper, 63 cents. London, 1849.

——— Indications of the Creator. Second edition, with additional Preface. 8vo. cloth, $1 63 London, 1849.

White and Gould's Tyrolian Lyre; a Glee-Book. Oblong 4to. $1 00. Boston, 1847.

White, (G. S.) Memoirs of S. Slater, with a History of the Rise and Progress of the Cotton Manufacture in England and America, &c. 8vo. cloth, portrait and plates, $3 50. Philadelphia, 1836.

——— (G.) Statistics of the State of Georgia, including an Account of its Natural, Civil, and Ecclesiastical History, together with a particular Description of each County, Notices of the Manners and Customs of its Aboriginal Tribes, and a correct Map of the State. 8vo. cloth, colored map, $2 50. Savannah, 1849.

——— (Rev. H.) Practical Reflections on the econd Advent. 12mo. cloth, 50 cents. New York, 1847.

Whittier, (J. G.) Songs of Labor and other Poems. 12mo. cloth. Boston, 1850.

Williams, (W. R.) Miscellanies. 8vo. cloth, $1 25. New York, 1850.

Wightwick, (G.) Selection from the Museum of the Vatican of Vases, Altars, Chairs, &c. Folio, bds. $2 25. Lond. 1837.

Willis, (W.) Journals of Rev. Thos. Smith and the Rev. Samuel Deane, Pastors of the First Church in Portland, with Notes and Biographical Notices, and a Summary History of Portland, Maine. 8vo. cloth, portraits and map, $2 00. Portland, 1850.

Woodhouse, (Rev. G. W.) Parochial Sermons. 8vo. bds. $4 25. Lond. 1844.

Woolley, (John.) Sermons preached in the Chapel of Rossal College, Fleetwood, $2 87; reduced to $1 75. London, 1847.

Worgan, (T. H.) Speculum Ecclesiæ Anglicanæ; or, some Account of the Principles and Results of the Reformation of the Church of England. 8vo. cloth, $2 50. Lond. 1843.

Worsley, (Thos.) Province of the Intellect in Religion. 2 vols. 8vo. cloth, $4 00. London, 1846.

Wyatt, (Rev. G) Lachryma Ecclesia. 12mo. cloth, $1 75. Lond. 1844.

Young, (J. R.) Euclid's Elements. 12mo. cloth, $1 50. London, 1842.

Mennechet, (E.) Le Plutarque Francaise vies des Hommes, et Femmes, Illustres de la France. 8 vols. imp. 8vo. half mor. gilt leaves, portraits, $25 00. Paris, 1838.

Moreau, (A. L.) Icones Obstetricæ; a Series of Sixty Plates. Folio, cloth, colored plates, $35 00. Lond. 1842.

Winkle's French Cathedrals, from Drawings on the Spot, by R. Garland, with Historical and Descriptive Account. 4to. cloth, plates, $11 50. London, 1837

Cross, (M.) Selections from the Edinburgh Review. 6 vols. 8vo. calf neat, $12 50. Paris, 1835

INDEX.

Anatomy.

Antiquities.

Angling.

Armor.

Archæology.

Architecture.

Archery.

Arithmetic, (not including A. S. Books.)

Art, (See also *Painting, Sculpture, &c.*)

Artificial Flowers.

Assaying.

Astronomy.

Atlases.

Baking.

Banking

Bees.

Bells.

Belles Lettres.

Bibliography.

Biography, (Letters, Collected Works, &c.)

Bleaching.

Book-Binding.

Book-Keeping.

Boot and Shoe Making.

Botany.

Brewing.

Brick-Making.

Bridges. (See *Engineering*.)

Building.

Calico-Printing.

Carriages.

Carpentry, Joinery, &c.

Chemistry.

Chess.

Chronology.

Classics.

Coal.

Coins. (See *Numismatics.*)

Color.

Commerce.

Comparative Anatomy.

Conchology. (See *Natural History.*)

Cookery.

Cooperage.

Page.

Costume.

Cotton Spinning.

Cyclopædia. (See also *Encyclopædias.*)

Differential and Int. Calculus.

Distillation.

Domesticated Animals.

Domestic Economy.

Draining.

Dramatic Literature.

Engraving.

Encyclopædias. (See *Cyclopædias.*)

Flax.

Food.

Furniture. (See *Upholstery.*)

Gardening.

Heraldry, Genealogies, Peerages, &c.

Herpetology. (See *Natural History.*)

Hieroglyphics.

History.

Horology.

Horse. (See *Domesticated Animals.*)

Horticulture. (See *Gardening.*)

House Painting, Glazing, &c.

House Servants.

Hydraulics.

Mapping

Masonry. (See *Building.*)

Mathematics.

Mechanics.

Medicine.

BIBLIOGRAPHY AND TERMS

BLOOD.

BRAIN, (Diseases of.)

CALCULI.

CANCER.

CHEMISTRY.

CHEST, (Diseases of.)

CHILDREN, (Diseases of.)

CHOLERA.

CLIMATE.

COUNTER-IRRITATION.

CUTANEOUS DISEASES.

Mesmerism.

Metallurgy.

Metaphysics.

Meteorology.

Mints.

Monuments, (Mural.)

Monumental Brasses.

Moral Philosophy.

Mosaic. (See *Art.*)

Music.

Mythology.

Natural History.

COLLECTIONS AND TREATISES.

PALÆONTOLOGY.

INFUSORIA, ANIMALCULÆ AND ENTOZOA.

ZOOPHYTES.

Natural Philosophy.

Nautical Routine, Rigging, &c.

Needlework. (See *Millinery*.)

Numismatics.

Painted Glass.

Paper Making.

Perfumery.

Philosophical Instruments.

Phonography.

Photography.

Phrenology.

Physiognomy.

Pneumatics.

Poetry.

Political Economy.

Population.

Poultry.

Precious Stones.

Ship-Building.

Silk. (Growth and Manufacture.)

Soap.

Social Economy.

Speeches.

Sports and Pastimes.

Statistics and Dynamics.

Page.

Statistics.

Steam.

Steam Engine.

Steam Navigation.

Sugar, (Growth and Manufacture of.)

Surveying.

Tobacco, (Growth and Manufacture.)

Trigonometry.

Topography.

Trades, Callings, &c.

Trials.

Page.

Turning.

Typography. (See *Printing.*)

Upholstery.

Useful Arts, &c.

Veterinary Art.

Voyages and Travels.

Warming and Ventilating.

Weaving.

Well Sinking and Boring.

Woods.

Wool.

Writing.

Zoology. (See *Natural History.*)

Zoophytes. (See *Natural History.*)

THE END.

www.ingramcontent.com/pod-product-compliance
Lightning Source LLC
LaVergne TN
LVHW050524100826
845148LV00002B/433

9781425520151